# CHAPTERS FROM
# THE AGRARIAN HISTORY OF
# ENGLAND AND WALES
## 1500–1750

2

ral Society

# CHAPTERS FROM THE AGRARIAN HISTORY OF ENGLAND AND WALES, 1500–1750

EDITED BY

JOAN THIRSK

*Sometime Reader in Economic History,
University of Oxford*

---

VOLUME 2

Rural Society: Landowners, Peasants and Labourers, 1500–1750

With new Introductory material by
CHRISTOPHER CLAY, JOYCE YOUINGS, BRIAN HOWELLS,
GLANMOR WILLIAMS, JOAN THIRSK AND DAVID HOWELL

EDITED BY

CHRISTOPHER CLAY

*Professor of Economic History, University of Bristol*

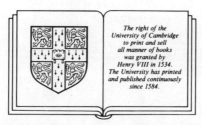

CAMBRIDGE UNIVERSITY PRESS

CAMBRIDGE

NEW YORK   PORT CHESTER   MELBOURNE   SYDNEY

Published by the Press Syndicate of the University of Cambridge
The Pitt Building, Trumpington Street, Cambridge CB2 IRP
40 West 20th Street, New York, NY 10011, USA
10 Stamford Road, Oakleigh, Melbourne 3166, Australia

© Cambridge University Press 1990

First published 1990

Printed in Great Britain by the
University Press, Cambridge

*British Library cataloguing in publication data*
Chapters from the Agrarian History of
England and Wales, 1500–1750.
1. England. Agricultural industries,
ca. 1350–1870
I. Thirsk, Joan II. The Agrarian
History of England and Wales
338.1'0942

*Library of Congress cataloguing in publication data*
Chapters from the agrarian history of England and Wales. 1500–1750/
edited by Joan Thirsk.
p. cm.
Rev. ed. of: Vols. 4 and 5 of the Agrarian history of England and
Wales. 1967–
Bibliography.
Includes index.
Contents: v. 1. Economic change/edited by Peter J. Bowden – v.
2. Rural society/edited by Christopher Clay – v. 3. Agricultural
change/edited by Joan Thirsk – v. 4 Agricultural markets and
trade. 1500–1750/edited by John Chartres – v. 5. The buildings of
the countryside. 1500–1750/edited by M. W. Barley.
ISBN 0 521 36884 7 (v. 1)
1. Agricultural – Economic aspects – England – History.
2. Agricultural – Economic aspects – Wales – History. 3. England – Rural
conditions. 4. Wales – Rural conditions. I. Thirsk, Joan.
II. Agrarian history of England and Wales.
HD1930.E5C47 1989
338.1'0942 – dc19 88-38786 CIP
ISBN 0 521 36883 9

UP

# CONTENTS

List of tables and text-figures / page ix

Editor's Preface / xi

List of abbreviations / xiii

Introduction / 1

## 1 Landlords in England, 1500–1640

- A The Crown / 21
  BY GORDON BATHO, M.A., F.R.HIST.S., Professor of Education, University of Sheffield
  1. The golden age of the Crown estate, 1461–1509 / 21
  2. The decline of the chamber system, 1509–54 / 25
  3. The weaknesses of Crown land administration, 1554–1603 / 30
  4. The failure of efforts at reform in the reign of James I / 33
  5. The exploitation of wardships under the early Stuarts / 39
- B Noblemen, gentlemen and yeomen / 41
  BY GORDON BATHO
  1. The historian's sources / 41
  2. The peerage: a declining class? / 45
  3. The profits of office, profession, and trade / 50
  4. The gentry and the enduring qualities of land / 55
  5. The yeomanry and the opportunities for the capable / 66
- C The Church / 71
  BY JOYCE YOUINGS, B.A., PH.D., F.R.HIST.S., Emeritus Professor of History, University of Exeter
  1. The monasteries / 71
     (a) Introduction / 71
     (b) The monastic estate / 72
     (c) Monastic estate management / 76
         (i) The early decades of the sixteenth century / 76
         (ii) The last decade, 1529–39 / 89
     (d) The Crown takes over / 97
     (e) The disposal of monastic lands / 103
         (i) The break-up of the monastic estates / 103

|     |     | (ii) The terms of Crown disposal | 106 |
|     |     | (iii) Profits | 110 |
|     |     | (iv) The grantees | 117 |
|     | 2   | The secular clergy | 120 |

## 2  Landlords in Wales, 1500–1640 — 122

A  The nobility and gentry — 122
BY THE LATE T. JONES PIERCE
1  The settlement pattern — 123
2  Peasant proprietors — 125
3  The ancient clanlands — 128
4  Tenurial law and custom — 131
5  Social change — 135
6  Types of freehold estate — 137
   (a) Estates of adventitious origin — 138
   (b) Privileged estates — 139
   (c) The clanland estate of hereditary origin — 140
   (d) The clanland estate of non-hereditary origin — 140
7  The growth of estates and enclosure — 141

B  The Church — 146
BY GLANMOR WILLIAMS, C.B.E., M.A., D.LITT., F.B.A., F.S.A., F.R.HIST.S.,
Emeritus Professor of History, University of Wales
1  Introduction: before the Reformation — 146
2  The dissolution of the monasteries — 148
3  Lay pressure on the secular clergy, 1536–58 — 152
4  Economic tensions, 1558–1640 — 154
5  The reaction of the clergy — 157

## 3  Farm Labourers, 1500–1640 — 161
BY ALAN EVERITT, M.A., PH.D., F.S.A., F.R. HIST.S.,
Emeritus Professor, University of Leicester

A  The labouring population — 161
B  Holdings and common-rights — 165
C  Enclosure and encroachment — 171
D  Cottage husbandry and peasant wealth — 177
E  By-employments — 190
F  Work, wages and employers — 195
G  Domestic life — 207
H  The changing pattern of labouring life — 219

## 4  Select bibliography, 1500–1640 — 231

## 5  Landlords and estate management in England, 1640–1750 — 246
BY CHRISTOPHER CLAY, M.A., PH.D., Professor of Economic History, University of Bristol

| | | | |
|---|---|---|---|
| A | | The Civil War and Interregnum | 246 |
| | 1 | Private landowners | 246 |
| | | (a) War and sequestration | 246 |
| | | (b) Composition fines and confiscations | 262 |
| | | (c) The long-term consequences | 272 |
| | 2 | Institutional landowners | 281 |
| | | (a) The Crown | 281 |
| | | (b) The Church | 283 |
| B | | The evolution of landed society after the Restoration | 289 |
| | 1 | Introduction | 289 |
| | 2 | Demographic factors | 292 |
| | 3 | The land market | 297 |
| | | (a) Yeoman farmers and petty gentry | 304 |
| | | (b) Piecemeal purchases by substantial owners and moneyed newcomers | 313 |
| | | (c) Major purchases by substantial owners | 325 |
| C | | The management of estates | 325 |
| | 1 | Types of tenancy | 325 |
| | | (a) Customary tenure and life leasehold | 325 |
| | | (b) Tenancies-at-will | 335 |
| | | (c) Tenancies from year to year and by lease for years | 339 |
| | | (d) The conditions of rack-rent leases | 341 |
| | | (e) Rents and the terms of tenancy | 351 |
| | | (f) The importance of leases | 355 |
| | 2 | Beyond the formal agreement | 357 |
| | | (a) Financial forbearance in time of trouble | 357 |
| | | (b) Positive action to support the rental | 359 |
| | | (c) Landlords, cottagers, and the provision of employment | 363 |
| | | (d) Different landlords, different approaches | 368 |
| | 3 | Landlords' investment in their estates | 372 |

**6 Landlords and estate management in Wales, 1640–1750** — 379

By DAVID W. HOWELL, M.A., PH.D, Senior Lecturer in History, University College of Swansea, University of Wales

**7 Select bibliography, 1640–1750** — 425

*Index* — 444

# TABLES

**1500–1640**

| | |
|---|---|
| 1 The size of labourers' holdings | 167 |
| 2 Distribution of population in rural Kent: analysis of the Compton Census, 1676 | 175 |
| 3 Peasant labourers' cattle | 178 |
| 4 Peasant labourers' livestock | 180 |
| 5 The pattern of peasant labourers' wealth | 186 |
| 6 Labourers' by-employments | 193 |
| 7 Labourers' houses—1 | 208 |
| 8 Labourers' houses—2 | 209 |

**1640–1750**

| | |
|---|---|
| 9 Movement of land prices | 300 |

# TEXT-FIGURES

| | |
|---|---|
| 1 Wales: distribution of various gentry seats, 1640–1750 | *page* 380 |

# EDITOR'S PREFACE

Since a survey of English agriculture is a large part of the economic history of England in the sixteenth to eighteenth centuries, it has seemed desirable to make the volumes of *The Agrarian History of England and Wales* available in a cheaper format to a wider readership. With this purpose in mind, each of the general chapters published in volume IV of *The Agrarian History*, and spanning the years 1500–1640, has been combined with its partner in volume V, 1640–1750, to give a survey covering two hundred and fifty years.[1] Here then is a view of a long chain of development. And while the individual authors fix a piercing gaze upon single themes in the sequence, the amalgamation of their studies reveals a larger pattern unfolding. Particularly striking are the differences in the economic circumstances ruling between the two periods, from 1500 to 1650 on the one hand, and from 1650 to 1750 on the other. Whereas rising food prices boosted the production of mainstream crops in the first period, stable or falling prices encouraged diversification, and the commercial production of a more varied range of plants and animals in the second. These differing circumstances also obliged landowners and all other classes living off the land to devise different strategies for survival. Changes in consequence did not follow one linear path. Human ingenuity turned in two different directions in the two periods, and, in fact, some of the subsidiary, not to say frivolous, activities in the first period (such as the production of luxury fruit and vegetables for the rich) proved to be among the most rewarding of the strategies for survival in the second.

The authors of all chapters in these two volumes have been given the chance to bring their surveys up-to-date by drawing attention to new work published since they first wrote. As volume IV was published in 1967, this means that they have more to say about their earlier writing than the later (published in 1985–6). These introductions should guide the reader to the most recent research. But it is also hoped that the juxtaposition of chapters from both volumes will offer a new perspective on the period as a whole, and so promote further discussion and

---

[1] The only chapters omitted from this paperback series, which appeared in the hardback version, are those describing regional farming systems, namely chapters I and II in volume IV, and all the chapters in part I of volume V.

understanding of the significance of the two phases within it. For while some of the solutions to problems in the second half of the period plainly sprang from developments in the first half, we must also bear in mind that within this whole web of human activity lay certain notable successes with new crops, new farming systems, and new ways of getting a living, which launched another phase of boisterous agricultural, and industrial, expansion in the later eighteenth century. To see agricultural development in a long view across two-and-a-half centuries is a particularly salutary experience for us who live in another changing agricultural world.

# ABBREVIATIONS

| | |
|---|---|
| *Agric. Hist.* | *Agricultural History* |
| AHEW | *Agrarian History of England and Wales*, Cambridge, 1967– |
| AHR | *Agricultural History Review* |
| *Amer. Hist. Rev.* | *American Historical Review* |
| AO | Archives Office |
| APC | *Acts of the Privy Council*, London, 1890– |
| *Arch. Aeliana* | *Archaeologia Aeliana* |
| *Arch. Camb.* | *Archaeologia Cambrensis* |
| *Arch. Cant.* | *Archaeologia Cantiana* |
| *Arch. J.* | *Archaeological Journal* |
| B. Acad. | British Academy |
| BE | N. Pevsner, *The Buildings of England*, London, 1951–74 |
| BL | British Library |
| BM | British Museum |
| Borthwick IHR | Borthwick Institute of Historical Research |
| BPP | British Parliamentary Papers |
| *Bull. BCS* | *Bulletin of the Board of Celtic Studies* |
| *Bull. IHR* | *Bulletin of the Institute of Historical Research* |
| *Bull. JRL* | *Bulletin of the John Rylands Library* |
| CCC | M. A. E. Green, *Calendar of the Proceedings of the Committee for Compounding. etc., 1643–1660*, 5 vols. London, 1889–92 |
| C,Ch. | Proceedings in the Court of Chancery |
| CJ | Commons Journals |
| CP 40 | Court of Common Pleas, Plea Rolls, PRO |
| CPR | Calendar of Patent Rolls |
| CRO | Cumbria Record Office, Carlisle |
| *CSPD* | *Calendar of State Papers Domestic* |
| *CW2* | *Cumb. and Westmor. Antiq. and Arch. Soc.*, 2nd series |
| E | Exchequer Records, PRO |
| E 134 | Exchequer, Depositions |
| E 159 | Exchequer, King's Remembrancer, Memoranda Rolls |

## ABBREVIATIONS

| | |
|---|---|
| E 164 | Exchequer, King's Remembrancer, Miscellaneous Books |
| E 178 | Exchequer, Special Commissions |
| E 315 | Exchequer, Augmentations Office, Miscellaneous Books |
| E 318 | Exchequer, Augmentations Office, Particulars for Grants |
| E 321 | Exchequer, Augmentations Office, Proceedings |
| EcHR | *Economic History Review* |
| EFC | M. W. Barley, *The English Farmhouse and Cottage*, London, 1961 |
| EHR | *English Historical Review* |
| EPNS | English Place-Name Society |
| EVH | Eric Mercer, *English Vernacular Houses: A Study of Traditional Farmhouses and Cottages*, RCHM (England), London, 1975 |
| GLCRO | Greater London Council Record Office |
| GMR | Guildford Muniment Room |
| Hist. Mon. C. | Historical Monuments Commission |
| HMC | Historical Manuscripts Commission |
| J. | Journal |
| JCH | *Journal of Comparative History* |
| JFHS | *Journal of the Friends' Historical Society* |
| JMH | *Journal of Modern History* |
| KRO | Cumbria Record Office, Kendal |
| LAO | Lincolnshire Archives Office |
| LJ | Lords Journals |
| LJRO | Lichfield Joint Record Office |
| LP | *Letters and Papers of Henry VIII* |
| LPL | Lambeth Palace Library |
| LR | Exchequer Office of the Auditors of Land Revenue, PRO |
| LUS | Land Utilization Survey |
| Mont. Coll. | Montgomeryshire Collections |
| NLW | National Library of Wales |
| NQ | *Notes and Queries* |
| PP | Parliamentary Papers |
| PP | *Past and Present* |
| PRO | Public Record Office, Chancery Lane and Kew, London |
| PS | *Population Studies* |
| RASE | Royal Agricultural Society of England |
| RCAM | Royal Commission on Ancient Monuments |

## ABBREVIATIONS

| | |
|---|---|
| RCHM | Royal Commission on Historical Monuments |
| Req., Req. 2 | Proceedings in the Court of Requests |
| RHS | Royal Historical Society |
| RO | Record Office |
| Roy. Inst. Cornwall | *Royal Institution of Cornwall* |
| SC | Special Collections, PRO |
| SP | State Papers |
| T & C | *Seventeenth-Century Economic Documents*, ed. J. Thirsk and J. P. Cooper, Oxford, 1972 |
| TED | *Tudor Economic Documents*, ed. R. H. Tawney and Eileen Power, 3 vols., London, 1924 |
| UCNWL | University College of North Wales Library, Bangor |
| *VCH* (name of county in italics) | *Victoria County History* |
| *Yorks. Bull.* | *Yorkshire Bulletin of Economic and Social Research* |

# INTRODUCTION

The chapters from the *Agrarian History of England and Wales*, volumes IV and V, gathered together in this book represent a series of essays, each one substantial enough to stand in its own right but nevertheless complementing the others in either a chronological, social or geographical sense. All are at once syntheses of historical understanding at the time of their writing, and at the same time in varying degrees original contributions to that understanding, drawing directly on archival research undertaken by the authors. It would, of course, be invidious for an introduction to lay stress on the value of certain chapters, and in so doing by implication to disparage the value of others. Nevertheless, readers new to the study of landed society in this period may be glad of a few signposts.

The opportunity to consider the structure of society in Wales and the changes it underwent both for its own sake and for the sake of comparisons with neighbouring England, is one which is not commonly offered to readers and must be accounted a particular virtue of the book. Within the chapters devoted specifically to English landownership, Professor Batho's treatment of the crown estate provides a survey which is not simply useful, but indispensable in the absence of any comparable treatment elsewhere in the literature. His treatment of Noblemen, Gentlemen and Yeomen has become dated in parts, as is made clear below, but the judicious approach adopted towards what was, at the time of writing, still a highly controversial subject has ensured that it may still be read as a whole with great profit. Dr Youings's chapter on the Church from vol. IV may still be regarded as essential reading on the economic aspects of the Dissolution of the Monasteries, while Professor Clay's is likewise essential on the impact of the Civil War upon landowners. Finally, special mention must be made of Professor Everitt's chapter on Farm Labourers which has justly become renowned as a classic, and should be taken as a starting point by anyone seriously interested in the lower echelons of rural society in the Tudor and Stuart periods.

Some aspects of rural society, however, are conspicuous by their absence from this book, not because they were considered unimportant when the *Agrarian History* volumes were being planned, but because insufficient research had been done to make a satisfactory treatment possible. The great landowners and the middling gentry are well treated, but few references will be found to the parochial gentry in either the period 1500–1640 or 1640–1750, and they represent a group about which even today very little indeed is known. As a subject they are therefore still crying out for investigation: historical sources that will throw light upon them certainly exist, but ingenuity will have to be used to elicit what is required. Yeomen, husbandmen and the labourers are dealt with for the period covered by vol. IV of the *Agrarian History*, but not for that covered by vol. V. However, the contents and arrangement of vol. V, in two parts, have left open the possibility of a third part being written at some future time which will deal with these elements in society. At present our knowledge of changes in the whole social structure of the countryside is lamentably deficient. Yet the subject deserves the same careful analysis, region by region, as that given to farming regimes.

The remaining part of this introduction consists of a series of brief bibliographical essays, drawing attention to the literature which has been published in the fields covered by the various *Agrarian History* chapters since they were written. Most were compiled by the authors of the chapters in question, but for a variety of reasons those relating to the chapters by Professor Batho, Professor Jones Pierce and Professor Everitt, were respectively undertaken by Professor Clay, Dr Brian Howells and Dr Joan Thirsk.

### LANDLORDS IN ENGLAND: THE CROWN (1540–1640)

The lands of the Crown have not been a subject which has attracted a great deal of research since chapter v of volume IV (chapter 1 of the present volume) was written in the early 1960s. However, the work of B. P. Wolffe on the royal demesne in the later Middle Ages has thrown additional light on their administration at the very beginning of the period. Furthermore Professor Wolffe's calculations on the size of Henry VII's landed income in his later years (about £40,000 p.a.) serves to underscore the great fiscal and political importance of the crown estate in the early sixteenth century and by implication, therefore, of its dissipation under Elizabeth and the early Stuarts.[1] Some short but interesting articles have been published on the use made by the Tudors of their lands to reward courtiers and others by outright grants or leases

---

[1] B. P. Wolffe, *The Royal Demesne in English History*, London, 1971, esp. pp. 217–19; and *idem*, *The Crown Lands, 1461–1536*, London, 1970.

on favourable terms, a use which inevitably conflicted with any policy of extracting the maximum possible revenue from them.² On the question of management, and its undoubted shortcomings, at least by the later sixteenth century, the particular case of the royal forests in Northamptonshire has been investigated in detail by Dr P. A. J. Pettit.³ Finally, some particular aspects of the sales of Crown lands in the late sixteenth and early seventeenth centuries have received detailed consideration,⁴ but the full story of the sales, then and later, still remains to be properly expounded. Meanwhile, however, some relevant general information to add to what may be derived from the sources available to the author of this chapter may be found scattered through Mrs Menna Prestwich's definitive study of the career of Lionel Cranfield, Earl of Middlesex, businessman and ultimately Lord Treasurer in 1621–4.⁵

## LANDLORDS IN ENGLAND: NOBLEMEN, GENTLEMEN, AND YEOMEN (1540–1640)

The sections dealing with lay landlords in the period 1500–1640 were written at a time when the famous controversy over 'the rise of the gentry' was still very much in the forefront of historians' minds. In the intervening period this has been well and truly laid to rest,⁶ an interment which perhaps owed more to the publication of Lawrence Stone's *The Crisis of the Aristocracy* than to anything else.⁷ This massive work, incorporating an enormous volume of original research into the archives of the major landowning families of the later sixteenth and early seventeenth centuries, lifted historical discussion of both

---

² D. Thomas, 'Leases in Reversion on the Crown's Lands, 1558–1603', EcHR, 2nd ser., xxx, No. 1, 1977; K. S. Wyndham, 'Crown Land and Royal Patronage in Mid-Sixteenth Century England', *Journal of British Studies*, xix, No. 2, 1980.

³ P. A. J. Pettit, *The Royal Forests of Northamptonshire. A Study in Their Economy 1558–1714*, Northants. Record Society, xxiii, 1968.

⁴ R. Ashton, *The Crown and the Money Market 1603–1640*, Oxford, 1960, esp. ch. 6; R. B. Outhwaite, 'The Price of Crown Land at the Turn of the Sixteenth Century', EcHR, 2nd ser., xx, No. 2, 1967, and idem, 'Who Bought Crown Lands? The Pattern of Purchases, 1589–1603', *Bull. IHR*, xliv, 1971.

⁵ M. Prestwich, *Cranfield. Politics and Profit under the Early Stuarts*, Oxford, 1966, esp. pp. 78–9, 112–13, 339–40, 373, 462–5.

⁶ The issue did, however, receive attention from Sir John Habakkuk in 'The Rise and Fall of English Landed Families, 1600–1800. III. Did the Gentry Rise?', *Trans. RHS*, 5th ser., 31, 1981. See also the useful work of synthesis, covering the whole period from the Middle Ages to modern times by G. E. Mingay, *The Gentry. The Rise and Fall of a Ruling Class*, London, 1976.

⁷ L. Stone, *The Crisis of the Aristocracy 1558–1641*, Oxford, 1965.

landowners and landownership on to quite a new plane and, although it is now more than twenty years old, it remains both essential and enjoyable reading for anyone interested in these aspects of English history. Breaking away from the insubstantially documented generalizations of the other protagonists in the gentry controversy, Stone based his conclusions on the economic, social, and cultural experience of the aristocracy partly on a great battery of statistics that he had himself compiled, and partly on a rich tapestry of descriptive evidence which has continued to dazzle readers ever since it was first revealed. The land market, aristocratic incomes, estate management, involvement in other forms of economic activity, the profits of office, credit, conspicuous expenditure, and both the economics and the psychology of marriage at this high level of society, were all discussed in fascinating detail and with innumerable fresh insights. So ambitious a work inevitably attracted much critical attention, and both Stone's statistics and certain of his conclusions aroused controversy, but of its lasting historical importance there has never been any doubt.[8]

In general, however, over the last two decades the interests of historians have moved away from the history of the elite to that of other social groups, especially those at the base rather than the apex of the social pyramid. As a result relatively few other works of substance about the aristocracy and gentry of this period have been published during the last twenty-five years.[9] Certainly, given the great deluge of archives which has been pouring forth from country mansions into the County Record Offices ever since the Second World War, surprisingly few new detailed case studies, either of individual families or of the landowners of particular areas, have been undertaken to add to those already in print in the early 1960s. Of the family studies, some of the most substantial were again from the pen of Lawrence Stone in his *Family and Fortune*, in which, among others, the Cecils, Earls of Salisbury, and the Manners, Earls of Rutland, received detailed treatment.[10] The land purchases of one of the great *nouveaux riches*, Lionel Cranfield, have been analysed as part of a full scale biography, and more recently the Stanleys, Earls of Derby, have been the subject of a book by Dr Barry Coward. There has been a scattering of articles,

---

[8] For discussions of Stone's work, see particularly G. E. Aylmer, review article, 'The Crisis of the Aristocracy, 1558–1641', *PP*, 32, 1965; D. C. Coleman, 'The Gentry Controversy and the Aristocracy in Crisis, 1558–1641', *History*, LI, 1966; J. Hexter, 'The English Aristocracy. Its Crises and the English Revolution, 1558–1660', *Journal of British Studies*, VIII, No. 1, 1968; R. Ashton, 'The Aristocracy in Transition', *EcHR*, 2nd ser., XXII, no. 2, 1969.

[9] A major exception to this generalization is Stone's more recent work referred to in note 52 below, which is mentioned in the context of the period covered by vol. V.

[10] L. Stone, *Family and Fortune. Studies in Aristocratic Finance in the Sixteenth and Seventeenth Centuries*, Oxford, 1973.

including some about less prominent families, but that is all.[11] Some more or less detailed studies of the gentry of Dorset, Lancashire and the North-West, may now be set alongside the older work on the gentry of Yorkshire by J. T. Cliffe, but no other region has yet received such detailed treatment as the latter county.[12] However, several of the books investigating the 'county community' in the period before the Civil War provide a good deal of relevant information, Kent, East Anglia, and Sussex having been particularly well treated in this respect.[13] Comparable studies on the country landowners of the early *sixteenth* century have, on the other hand, been fewer, but Julian Cornwall's article on the early Tudor gentry may be consulted, and there is a regional study of the West Riding of Yorkshire in the 1530s and 1540s by Dr R. B. Smith.[14]

A variety of writers have treated particular aspects of the social and economic life of the landowners by means of general surveys rather than detailed case studies. Estate management policies have not received much attention, but marriage settlements and the economics of aristocratic and gentry marriage have received a good deal,[15]

---

[11] Prestwich, *op. cit.*, ch. 9; B. Coward, *The Stanleys, Lords Stanley and Earls of Derby 1385–1672*, Manchester, Chetham Soc., 3rd ser., xxx, 1983; C. Cross, 'Supervising the Finances of the Third Earl of Huntingdon, 1580–1595', *Bull. IHR*, XL, 1970; A. Cameron, 'Sir Henry Willoughby of Wollaton', *Thoroton Society*, LXXIV, 1970; M. D. G. Wanklyn, 'John Weld of Willey, 1585–1665', *West Midland Studies*, III, 1970; M. K. McKintosh, 'The Fall of a Tudor Gentle Family: the Cookes of Gidea Hall, 1579–1629', *Huntington Library Quarterly*, XLI, No. 4, 1978; R. Virgoe, 'The Recovery of the Howards in East Anglia, 1485 to 1529', in E. W. Ives, R. J. Knecht and J. J. Scarisbrick (eds.), *Wealth and Power in Tudor England*, London, 1978.

[12] J. P. Ferris, 'The Gentry of Dorset on the Eve of the Civil War', *Genealogists' Magazine*, xv, No. 3, 1965; B. G. Blackwood, 'The Economic State of the Lancashire Gentry on the Eve of the Civil War', *Northern History*, XII, 1976; see also *idem*, *The Lancashire Gentry and the Great Rebellion 1640–60*, Manchester, Chetham Society, 3rd ser., xxv, 1978; C. B. Phillips, 'The Gentry in Cumberland and Westmorland 1600–1665', unpublished Ph.D. thesis, University of Lancaster, 1973. The work of J. T. Cliffe, available only as an unpublished thesis when Vol. IV was written, has since been published as *The Yorkshire Gentry from the Reformation to the Civil War*, London, 1969.

[13] A. Everitt, *The Community of Kent and the Great Rebellion*, Leicester, 1966; C. Holmes, *The Eastern Association and the Civil War*, Cambridge, 1974; A. Fletcher, *A County Community in Peace and War. Sussex 1600–1660*, London, 1975.

[14] J. Cornwall, 'The Early Tudor Gentry', EcHR, 2nd ser., XVII, No. 3, 1965; R. B. Smith, *Land and Politics in the Reign of Henry VIII*, Oxford, 1970.

[15] J. P. Cooper, 'Patterns of Inheritance and Settlement by Great Landowners from the Fifteenth to the Eighteenth Centuries', in J. Goody, J. Thirsk and E. P. Thompson, *Family and Inheritance*, Cambridge, 1976; L. Bonfield, *Marriage Settlements 1601–1740*, Cambridge 1983; R. B. Outhwaite, 'Marriage as Business: Opinions on the Rise in Aristocratic Bridal Portions in Early Modern England', in N. McKendrick and R. B. Outhwaite (eds.), *Business Life and Public Policy*, Cambridge, 1986. See also the other items listed in note 53 below, although these relate mainly to the later seventeenth and eighteenth centuries.

whilst on a related issue there has been an important article on younger sons by Joan Thirsk.[16] Finally, two brave attempts have been made to trace long-run changes in the social distribution of landed property, by Professor F. M. L. Thompson and Mr John Cooper respectively, neither of which arrive at very startling or very secure conclusions, but which seem to confirm that there was a gradual and more or less continuous tendency for ownership to become concentrated into fewer hands, a process considered explicitly by Sir John Habakkuk in his important article, 'La disparition du paysan anglais'.[17]

These investigations into the social distribution of landed property are, of course, also relevant to any consideration of the economic experience of the yeomanry. Historians have, however, found the imprecise and partly subjective descriptions of socio-economic status used by contemporaries difficult to apply to their purposes, and different authors have tended to use terms such as 'yeoman', 'freeholder' and 'peasant' in different ways.[18] But whatever the terminology preferred, some interesting studies have appeared since the publication of vol. IV, based on detailed research into village communities in several quite different parts of the country. Inevitably these deal not only with the wealthy commercial farmers, but also with the poor husbandmen and even the labourers too, and the approach has varied according to the outlook of the author and the nature of the sources available. The studies by Dr Margaret Spufford of three very different villages in Cambridgeshire, and by Dr Cicely Howell of Kibworth Harcourt in Leicestershire, are particularly important,[19] but valuable investigations have also been undertaken into the villages of Sherington in Buckinghamshire and Myddle in Shropshire, while for the early part of the period, down to 1540, Dr Christopher Dyer's work on the properties of the See of Worcester in Worcestershire and adjacent counties should be

---

[16] J. Thirsk, 'Younger Sons in the Seventeenth Century', *History*, LIV, 1969.

[17] F. M. L. Thompson, 'The Social Distribution of Landed Property in England since the Sixteenth Century', EcHR, 2nd ser., XIX, No. 3, 1966; J. P. Cooper, 'The Social Distribution of Land and Men in England, 1436–1700', EcHR, 2nd ser., XX, No. 3, 1967; H. J. Habakkuk, 'La disparition du paysan anglais', *Annales. E.S.C.*, XX, No. 4, 1965.

[18] D. M. Hirst, 'The Seventeenth Century Freeholder and the Statistician: a Case of Terminological Confusion', and F. M. L. Thompson, 'A Terminological Confusion Confounded', both in EcHR, 2nd ser., XXIX, No. 2, 1976; J. V. Beckett, 'The Peasant in England: a Case of Terminological Confusion?', AHR, XXXII, Part II, 1984. See also A. McFarlane, *The Origins of English Individualism*, Oxford, 1978, and his 'The Myth of the Peasantry' in R. B. Smith (ed.), *Land, Kinship and Life-Cycle*, Cambridge, 1974.

[19] M. Spufford, *Contrasting Communities*, Cambridge, 1974; C. Howell, *Land, Family and Inheritance in Transition: Kibworth Harcourt, 1280–1700*, Cambridge, 1983.

mentioned.[20] Over the years the focus of research on the groups below the gentry has tended to shift increasingly towards social issues, and Dr Wrightson's *English Society 1580–1680* summarizes much recent research in this direction and may be usefully consulted about the yeomen as about other groups in society.[21] One social issue which has received particular attention and which has obvious economic implications is that of inheritance customs.[22]

C. CLAY

### LANDLORDS IN ENGLAND: THE CHURCH (1500–1640)

Twenty years ago knowledge of this field was so meagre that little could be said with confidence except about the monasteries. This imbalance can now to a great extent be rectified, especially with regard to the bishops. Dr Phyllis Hembry's work on the See of Bath and Wells is in print and the Tudor archbishops of York are now receiving attention.[23] On a much broader front Dr Felicity Heal has moved on from her early work on the bishopric of Ely to range widely over the whole episcopate. In particular, she has investigated the extent of the bishops' economic losses, and concludes that taken altogether their income of nearly £30,000 in 1535 had been reduced to about £27,000 in 1603, during a period in which there had been inflation of some 300 per cent. In terms of temporalities some 650 manors in 1500 had been reduced a century later to about 450, from which it must be concluded that the bishops had lost a good many particularly large properties.[24] A factor contributing to the loss of income was, of course, the granting of long leases. Dr Christopher Dyer's work on the estates of the bishopric of Worcester has revealed many leases for ninety-nine years, and at very low rents, in existence even before the Reformation, the recipients being largely gentlemen, with some graziers and even merchants among

[20] A. C. Chibnall, *Sherington. Fiefs and Fields of a Buckinghamshire Village*, Cambridge, 1965; D. Hey, *An English Rural Community. Myddle under the Tudors and Stuarts*, Leicester, 1974; C. Dyer, *Lords and Peasants in a Changing Society*, Cambridge, 1980. Another study of conditions on an ecclesiastical estate at the end of the Middle Ages which is useful for the yeomanry of the early sixteenth century is F. R. H. Du Boulay, 'Who were Farming the English Demesnes at the End of the Middle Ages', EcHR, 2nd ser., XVII, No. 3, 1965.

[21] K. Wrightson, *English Society 1580–1680*, London, 1982.

[22] A number of contributions, by several different authors, will be found in Goody, Thirsk and Thompson (eds.), *Family and Inheritance*. See also the various essays on this and other aspects of the history of the yeomen and other categories of villager in R. M. Smith (ed.), *Land, Kinship and Life-Cycle*, also cited in note 18 above.

[23] Phyllis M. Hembry, *The Bishops of Bath and Wells, 1540–1640*, London, 1967; Claire Cross, 'The Economic Problems of the See of York: Decline and Recovery in the Sixteenth Century', AHR, Supp., XVIII, 1970.

[24] Felicity Heal, *Of Prelates and Princes: a Study of the Economic and Social Position of the Tudor Episcopate*, Cambridge, 1980, especially pp. 328–9.

the principal beneficiaries.[25] Dr Heal concludes that such had been their mulcting that the Elizabethan bishops were reduced to making do with incomes barely equivalent to those enjoyed by the wealthier of the country gentry.

Dr Peter Heath's penetrating study of the pre-Reformation parochial clergy underlines their problems, even before inflation stiffened the resistance of the parishioners from whom they attempted to exact their tithes. Indeed, Dr Rosemary O'Day's summary of their income in 1535 does not suggest that laymen had much cause for envy.[26] Nor did Protestantism add to the number of testamentary provisions in respect of 'tithes forgot', althogether John Hooker of Exeter, himself one of the 'hotter sort', wrote of Devon about 1600 that "there be few parishes whose tithe wools be not worth 20 nobles by the year ... and in some places worth £100 or better, which I could name were it not for offending the owners". Dr Ralph Houlbrooke's excellent book on the mid-Tudor church courts, in particular those of the diocese of Norwich, points the way for historians less inhibited than Hooker.[27] The parson who occupied his own glebe and received his tithes in kind, or let them out on short terms, could clearly survive the impact of inflation, though even he could only pray for good harvests. Of no other members of the farming community could it be said that calculations about how to use their land were based not so much on what it would best yield, but what would best complement the farming specialities of their neighbours, and there are interesting questions about their contribution to practical agriculture and to changing farming systems that need to be answered. How far were parsons driven to experiment? To what extent did they contrive to furnish the market? Were Puritan parsons better farmers than their more conventional brother priests?

The original section in vol. IV also totally ignored the chantry priests and the secular colleges, although they too drew their support largely from the land, albeit almost entirely in fixed rent charges and small scattered parcels. Dr Christopher Kitching has begun to unravel a story about their property every bit as interesting as that of the dispersal of the lands of the dissolved monasteries. He finds that it was a buyers'

[25] Christopher Dyer, *Lords and Peasants in a Changing Society*, Cambridge, 1980, pp. 209–17.

[26] Peter Heath, *English Parish Clergy on the Eve of the Reformation*, 1969, especially ch. 8; Rosemary O'Day, *English Clergy: the Emergence and Consolidation of a Profession, 1558–1642*, Leicester, 1979, p. 173. Also relevant is Michael Zell, 'Economic Problems of the Parochial Clergy in the Sixteenth Century', in R. O'Day and F. Heal (eds.), *Princes and Paupers in the English Church, 1500–1800*, Leicester, 1981.

[27] John Hooker, 'Synopsis Chorographical of the County of Devon', British Library, Harl. MS 5827, fo. 47; Ralph Houlbrooke, *Church Courts and the People during the English Reformation, 1520–1570*, Oxford, 1979, chapter v.

## INTRODUCTION

market and that much of the property found its way, through agents, into the hands of the sitting tenants.[28] By such means many quite humble people must have obtained their first freeholding, a step as important in its own way as the purchase directly from the Crown of a large monastic manor by an already established country gentleman. For the historian of small farmers there is much scope here in local records.

Neither the administration of their estates by the monks and nuns, nor the disposal of their property by the Crown have, by themselves, been the subjects of much inquiry since 1967. The trickle of local studies came to an end with the publication of Dr R. B. Smith's book on the East Riding of Yorkshire.[29] Of medieval specialists only Dr Barbara Harvey has carried her work on the estates of Westminster Abbey into the sixteenth century. She finds the monks' administration "ineffectual" rather than "benevolent", and the many long leases at low rents certainly cast their shadow before.[30]

The most notable advance, and it is one which rather vitiates the plan of this book, is the appearance of studies in which the disposal of monastic lands is subsumed into a more broadly based consideration of the Tudor land market. Dr John Kew's work on Devon goes a long way towards explaining how prospective purchasers raised the necessary capital, and shows how the availability of monastic land unlocked a further supply so that demand was rarely, if ever, greatly frustrated.[31] In the counties of Somerset and Kent the dispersal of Crown lands *in toto* has been vigorously pursued by Dr Katherine Wyndham and Dr Michael Zell respectively, but in neither case do they go far beyond the initial grants.[32] Clearly, in future, efforts must be made to encompass all possible dimensions. But anyone contemplating a computer-assisted inquiry will need to consider carefully what data-base to select. For all its limitations the *Valor Ecclesiasticus* of 1535 has much to commend it, all later valuations being chronologically incompatible. Even the Crown had to tailor its marketing formulae to a variety of contempor-

---

[28] Christopher Kitching, 'The Disposal of Monastic and Chantry Lands', in F. Heal and R. O'Day (eds.), *Church and Society in England: Henry VIII to James I*, London, 1977, especially pp. 128–36. See also G. H. Woodward (ed.), *Calendar of Somerset Chantry Grants, 1548–1603*, Somerset Record Society, 77, 1982.

[29] Smith, *op. cit*. The present author (J. Youings) has little to add to her *Dissolution of the Monasteries*, London, 1971.

[30] Barbara Harvey, *Westminster Abbey and its Estates in the Middle Ages*, Oxford, 1977. For an even more extended abbey history, see S. F. Hockey, *Quarr Abbey and its Lands, 1132–1631*, Leicester, 1969.

[31] John Kew, 'The Disposal of Crown Lands: the Devon Land Market, 1536–58', AHR, XVIII, part 2, 1970.

[32] K. Wyndham, 'The Royal Estate in Sixteenth-Century Somerset', *Bull. IHR*, LII, 1979; M. Zell, 'The Mid-Tudor Market in Crown Land in Kent', *Archaeologia Cantiana*, XCVII, 1981.

ary considerations.³³ It may well be that, if the scale is sufficiently large to iron out the enormous variety in its size and constituent components, the manor will regain the importance it had for Professor R. H. Tawney when he first invited historians to ponder the effects of the Dissolution.

JOYCE YOUINGS

LANDLORDS IN WALES: THE NOBILITY AND GENTRY (1540–1640)

Although more than twenty years have passed since Professor T. Jones Pierce wrote the essay printed below, some aspects of his subject have in the meantime received little further attention. The number of researchers working on Welsh agrarian history is small, and most work on pre-nineteenth-century Wales has been done within a local or regional context. Inevitably, therefore, knowledge of Welsh agrarian development in the early modern period remains patchy: some areas, notably Gwynedd, Glamorgan and Pembrokeshire have received close attention, whilst others, like Cardiganshire, Radnorshire and Monmouthshire, remain largely unexplored. Jones Pierce's most impressive researches in agrarian history related to Gwynedd (north-west Wales), and it was mainly on the basis of his work on that region that he generalized about developments in other parts of *Pura Wallia*, the heartland of Wales which remained Welsh in speech and custom and subject to native rulers until the Edwardian conquest. Whether his views on such matters as settlement patterns and tenemental change may be applied wholesale to all parts of *Pura Wallia* outside Gwynedd is doubtful, especially in view of the fact that localism was as marked in medieval and early modern Wales as it was in England. Further research is needed to resolve this matter.³⁴

In the first paragraph of his essay, Jones Pierce observed that he was not concerned with those "Normanized parts of the March which were situated in the coastal lowlands and eastward-facing valleys of the

---

³³ See, besides Youings, *op. cit.*, pp. 124–31, Outhwaite, 'The Price of Crown Land', and his 'Who Bought Crown Lands?', both cited in note 4 on p. 3 above.

³⁴ The writings of T. Jones Pierce are most conveniently studied in J. B. Smith (ed.), *Medieval Welsh Society. Selected Essays of T. Jones Pierce*, Cardiff, 1972. For other work on Gwynedd, see J. B. Smith, 'Crown and Community in the Principality of North Wales in the Reign of Henry Tudor', *Welsh Hist. Rev.*, III, 1966; Ll. B. Smith, 'The Gage and the Land Market in Late Medieval Wales', EcHR, 2nd ser., XXIX, no. 4, 1976; *idem*, '*Tir Prid*: Gages of Land in Late Medieval Wales', *Bull. BCS*, XXVII, 1977; G. R. J. Jones, 'Early Customary Tenures in Wales and Open-Field Agriculture', in T. Rowley (ed.), *The Origins of Open Field Agriculture*, London, 1980; A. D. Carr, *Medieval Anglesey*, Langefni, 1982; C. Gresham, *Eifionydd: A Study of Land Ownership from the Medieval Period to the Present Day*, Cardiff, 1973; W. O. Williams, *Tudor Gwynedd*, Caernarfon, 1958; C. Thomas, 'Enclosure and the Rural Landscape of Merioneth in the Sixteenth Century', *Transactions, Institute of British Geographers*, XLII, 1967.

south". These areas were occupied by a peasantry of mixed Welsh, English, and, in some cases, Flemish origins, embraced much of the best farmland in Wales, and were, in the Tudor period, heavily dotted with gentry houses.³⁵ This omission needs to be redressed. By the early sixteenth century the gentry of these lowland manors were no longer mainly of English descent: most, indeed, were of mixed blood, and some were Welsh in speech. The majority of mansions held there by the leading gentry occupied the sites of the *capita* of medieval honorial baronies and knights' fees, a fact which partly explains why a considerable number of medieval stone castles and fortified houses remained in use as gentry seats until the Civil Wars and, in some instances, even later. Most of the large estates were composite in structure, consisting of one or more manors with their demesne lands and embracing a scattering of freehold farms, usually held by military tenures, leaseholds, and even customary tenements within manors belonging to other landlords. Small tenements held outside their own manors were usually exploited by rack-renting them to small peasant farmers.³⁶

There is little reliable evidence from any part of Wales about the rentals of the gentry in this period, but it is evident that they were generally small. Pembrokeshire and Glamorgan were two of the richest counties in Wales, yet in 1592 the annual rent-roll of Sir John Perrot, the greatest magnate in the former county, came to little more than £850, whilst in 1595–6 the Glamorgan rents of the earl of Pembroke totalled just over £646. As elsewhere within the realm, rents in Wales rose with increased pressure of people upon land, the rents derived by the earls of Pembroke from their Glamorgan estates rising by 160% between 1570 and 1631. Even less evidence is available about the global incomes of the Welsh gentry in this period than about their rentals, but it is clear that, from about 1540 onwards, fines paid by their tenants became an increasingly important element in estate profits, and that, apart from supplying their own households, many of the gentry produced corn and livestock for the open market. In particular, the reduction in the level of lawlessness following the Union settlement of 1536–43, and the growth of the London food market, made possible a

---

[35] W. Rees, *South Wales and the March, 1284–1415: a Social and Agrarian Study*, Oxford, 1924, remains the most far-reaching and authoritative discussion of this subject. For Glamorgan, which alone has received adequate treatment in recent years, see G. Williams (ed.), *Glamorgan County History*, III, Cardiff, 1971. See also P. Smith, *Houses in the Welsh Countryside*, London, 1975.

[36] See W. R. B. Robinson, 'The Marcher Lords of Wales 1525–1531', *Bull. BCS*, XXVI, 1974–6, and 'The Landowners of the Englishry of Gower in the Early Sixteenth Century', *Bull. BCS*, XXIX, 1981; G. Williams (ed.), *Glamorgan County History*, IV, Cardiff, 1974; B. G. Charles, *George Owen of Heallys. A Welsh Elizabethan*, Aberystwyth, 1973; B. E. Howells, 'Pembrokeshire Farming *circa* 1580–1620', NLWJ, IX, 1955–6 and 'The Elizabethan Squirearchy in Pembrokeshire', *The Pembrokeshire Historian*, I, 1959.

massive expansion of the livestock trade, sheep and cattle being sent to England in the charge of licensed drovers. Like their English counterparts, the Welsh gentry participated in trade and industry, scrambled for paid office under the Crown, and followed the law and the profession of arms, sometimes with spectacular results.[37]

Inflation, social competition and opportunities to enrich themselves through the more rigorous development of their estates led many of the Welsh gentry to put heavy pressure on their tenantry as Elizabeth's reign wore on, this finding expression in marked rises in rents and fines, the more stringent exploitation of manorial dues and services, challenges to peasants' security of tenure and the appropriation of wastes. In some instances, more land was taken in hand and the scale of farming activities increased.[38] Possibly the gentry were more aggressive towards their tenantry in the agriculturally advanced lowlands than in upland areas, but this, like so many other matters, remains open to discussion.

BRIAN HOWELLS

### LANDLORDS IN WALES: THE CHURCH (1540–1640)

Very little new work has been undertaken on this subject in recent years, and much the most important addition to our knowledge has come from Dr Madeleine Gray.[39] Dr Gray found that, although some monastic houses entered into a number of leases during the years 1535 and 1536, in Monmouthshire later leases tended to be shorter than the earlier ones. The remaining demesne at Monmouth Priory was, in 1534, leased for as short a period as six years, while efficient estate administration at Usk is further reflected in the comparatively short lease terms, the commonest being for thirty years. Leasing by some of the small houses tended to collapse after September 1535, suggesting that imminent dissolution may have acted as a deterrent to tenants.

Dr Gray has also established that, in Monmouthshire, land was sold at a slower rate than might have been expected, and sales there did not reach their peak until the mid-1550s. Generally, it was the large manors and whole estates which went first, whereas scraps of urban and chantry land were not disposed of until late in the sixteenth century or early in the seventeenth, when they were frequently sold to minor figures among the lesser gentry, to yeomen, and to townspeople, with

---

[37] H. A. Lloyd, *The Gentry of South-West Wales*, Cardiff, 1968.

[38] For some examples, see B. Howells, *Early Modern Pembrokeshire, 1536–1815*, Haverfordwest, 1987. Numerous studies of gentry families are to be found in Welsh local history journals, NLWJ, *Welsh History Rev.*, and *Trans. Hon. Soc. Cymmrodorion*.

[39] Madeleine Gray, 'The Dispersal of Crown Property in Monmouthshire, 1500–1603', Ph.D. Thesis, University College, Cardiff, 1985.

the assistance of agents like Richard Budd. The fact that monastic land was often sold to lesser families may account for the slowness of the market; the purchasers had insufficient capital or connexions to be able to buy quickly. Few totally new families were founded in Monmouthshire but the pattern of landholding and influence within the county was considerably changed. This was particularly true of the towns, where there emerged a number of new families of urban gentry, like the Gunters of Abergavenny, the Joneses of Usk, the Williamses of Monmouth and the Joneses of the Friary, Newport. There was surprisingly little dealing in ecclesiastical land after it left the Crown's hands, though the market in small properties was more active. This slowness to respond to opportunity, and the reluctance to part with land once acquired, suggest a highly conservative landed society which was still partly isolated from economic developments taking place elsewhere.
GLANMOR WILLIAMS

### FARM LABOURERS (1500–1640)

The condition of farm labourers, described in chapter VII of volume IV (chapter 3 of the present volume), was a notable pioneering survey on a topic for which documentary evidence is not readily forthcoming.[40] It presented a framework which was appropriate not only to the period 1500–1640 but to the succeeding period, 1640–1750, treated in volume V, and should be read as such, since no comparable chapter appeared in volume V.

Many years elapsed after its publication in 1967 before this general survey of labourers' conditions was carried further. In the last six years, however, two important studies have appeared, which, while not approaching the breadth of Professor Everitt's work, tackle chosen aspects in depth. The first (in 1981) by Professor Anne Kussmaul examined living-in farm servants, paying attention to regional and gender differences.[41] The second, by Dr K. D. M. Snell (1985), studied the changing conditions of life of the labouring poor in southern England, both male and female, between 1600 and 1900.[42] Despite the dates given in the title of Snell's book, the main weight of his evidence

---

[40] Ill health prevented the author from writing this section, and so it has been prepared by Joan Thirsk, and approved by the author.

[41] A. Kussmaul, *Servants in Husbandry in Early Modern England*, Cambridge, 1981. But for Professor Everitt's critical review of Professor Kussmaul's oversimplified regional generalizations, see EHR, XCIX, 1984, pp. 383–6. See also B. Short, 'The Decline of Living-In Servants in the Transition to Capitalist Farming: a Critique of the Sussex Evidence', *Sussex Archaeolog. Collections*, CXXII, 1984.

[42] K. D. M. Snell, *Annals of the Labouring Poor. Social Change and Agrarian England, 1660–1900*, Cambridge 1985.

falls on the period after 1750; nevertheless, it stimulates reflection on the previous two centuries as it ranges widely over family structure and poor relief as well as the economic consequences of enclosure and the decline of apprenticeship. Both books have greatly illuminated our understanding of the seasonality of labour demands, as well as underlining further the emphasis, already placed by Professor Everitt, on the different opportunities available in champion (or fielden) and in woodland country. Since William Cobbett in the nineteenth century was also struck by this fact, it must remain a continuing theme in all future investigations of rural classes between the sixteenth and nineteenth centuries. However, it is capable of further refinement. Pastoral landscapes need to be divided between forests, fens, marshes, moorlands and vales, and forests may even need to be divided between those on clay soils and those on sands and gravels. Different arable regimes need to be distinguished also, for some were especially successful in the cultivation of industrial or horticultural crops that offered unusual opportunities for intensive labour.[43]

Many local studies have incidentally illuminated the changing fortunes of labourers, as crops and farm systems were diversified, enclosure proceeded in one region rather than another, and changes occurred in the numbers of middling and large farms. But these afford fleeting glimpses only, since local studies at present favour a broad account of changing social structures and economic organization, and focus on landholders rather than on labourers.[44]

Some further glimpses of changing economic opportunities for labourers can be obtained from another growing corpus of historical work — that concerning the rural industries that were by-employments alongside agriculture. Most of this literature focusses on the textile industry in its early progress towards a factory system, but all of it impinges on the history of labourers, since industries in their early phases of development offered many agricultural families an additional occupation to farming. In the end, of course, they drew multitudes of labourers into the towns.[45]

Relations between masters and men under different agricultural regimes is a further aspect of the labourers' history, hardly broached so

---

[43] For a summary of regional differences, see Joan Thirsk, *England's Agricultural Regions and Agrarian History, 1500–1700*, London, 1987, pp. 37 ff., and for clay *versus* sandy forests, p. 49.

[44] For example, M. Spufford, *Contrasting Communities: English Villagers in the Sixteenth and Seventeenth Centuries*, Cambridge, 1974; C. Howell, *Land, Family and Inheritance in Transition*, Cambridge, 1973; K. Wrightson and D. C. Levine, *Poverty and Piety in an English Village – Terling, 1525–1700*, London, 1979.

[45] For a generous bibliography of this subject, see Maxine Berg, *The Age of Manufactures, 1700–1820*, London, 1985.

far, but the best portrayal yet is expected from the study under way at present by Professor Hassell Smith of Nicholas Bacon's household at Stiffkey, Norfolk.[46] Many accounts survive for this gentleman's domestic management covering the years between 1570 and 1630. When completed it should inspire a similar scrutiny of estates in pastoral country, such, for example, as that of the Howard family at Naworth Castle in Cumberland, whose detailed household accounts between 1612 and 1640 were printed, but not analysed, more than a century ago.[47]

The increasing importance of migrant labour in the course of the seventeenth century drew comment from Professor Everitt in 1967, and fragmentary information about this continues to emerge. Seasonal hop-pickers in Canterbury's hop gardens, for example, included silk-weavers, while elsewhere in the county itinerant Irish and Welsh workers worked alongside local families.[48] At Milcote in Warwickshire, casual gang labour from villages near at hand was employed for weeding and picking woad in 1626.[49] At the same time Midland parish registers also record the deaths of woadmen of unknown name, pointing to the practice of migrant workers coming from further afield. A courageous historian, however, is needed to explore this subject more deliberately. Writing the history of the labourer in the early modern period will always call for arduous toil in scattered places.

JOAN THIRSK

LANDLORDS AND ESTATE MANAGEMENT IN ENGLAND (1640–1750)

The picture painted in the first section of chapter 14 in volume V (chapter 5 of the present volume), of the impact of the Civil War on the agrarian economy in general, and on the incomes of landowners in particular, has been amplified and reinforced by a number of studies published since it was written in the early 1970s.[50] Similarly, new research by Ian Gentles and W. J. Sheils into the confiscation and sale of estates by the victorious parliamentarians, has added to the body

[46] For an account of the Stiffkey project, see A. Hassell Smith, 'A Squire and his Community: the Stiffkey Project', *Bulletin of Local History: East Midland Region*, XVI, 1981, pp. 13–18.

[47] 'Selections from the Household Books of the Lord William Howard of Naworth Castle', ed. Rev. George Ornsby, *Surtees Soc.*, LXVIII, 1877.

[48] Dennis Baker, *Agricultural Prices, Production, and Marketing, with Special Reference to the Hop Industry: North-East Kent, 1680–1760*, New York and London, 1985, pp. 485, 502, 548–9.

[49] Joan Thirsk, *Economic Policy and Projects*, Oxford, 1978, p. 5.

[50] I. Roy, 'England turned Germany', *Trans. RHS*, 5th ser., XXVIII, 1978; D. Pennington, 'The War and the People', in J. Morrill (ed.), *Reactions to the English Civil War*, London, 1982; M. Bennett, 'Contribution and Assessment: Financial Exactions in the English Civil War, 1642–1646', *War and Society*, IV, No. 1, 1986.

of knowledge synthesized there, but it does not demand any reinterpretation.[51]

Discussion of the evolution of landed society in the seventeenth and eighteenth centuries as a whole has been profoundly influenced by the recent publication of Lawrence and Jeanne C. Fawtier Stone's *An Open Elite? England 1540–1880*.[52] This book, like *The Crisis of the Aristocracy*, at once presents a huge volume of new factual information about the greater landowners and their ways of life, and advances an interpretation about developments in landowning society of which all future writing on the subject will have to take notice. Its aim was to try to establish how much the composition of the landed elite altered over time, in order to ascertain whether its ranks were as open to invasion by the newly wealthy as has often been alleged. By the ingenious device of equating possession of a country house above a certain size with membership of the county elite, the Stones were able to provide a quantitative index upon which to base their conclusion that landed society was much *more* stable than historians have tended to believe. No frontal assaults have yet appeared, but many reviewers expressed their reservations about this finding and the process whereby it was arrived at, and a continuing historical debate about it may be expected. The other main development in historical writing about the English landowners in this period over the last few years – and it is a development which is also relevant to the periods before 1640 and after 1750 as well – concerns the nature, purpose and effects of family settlements. The issues under debate are sometimes technical but they are nevertheless important, and they spread beyond the socio-economic to the nature of emotional relationships within the upper-class family.[53]

On the broad subject of how English landlords managed their estates in the period between 1640 and 1750 nothing has yet appeared in print which calls for any significant revision of the account given in the last part of chapter 14 in volume V (chapter 5 below). In his recently

[51] I. J. Gentles and W. J. Sheils, *Confiscation and Restoration: the Archbishopric Estates and the Civil War*, Borthwick Papers, No. 59, Borthwick Institute of Historical Research, York, 1981.

[52] L. Stone and J. C. Fawtier Stone, *An Open Elite? England 1540–1880*, Oxford, 1984. This, as the title indicates, also pertains, although in lesser measure, to the period covered by ch. 1 below.

[53] See particularly L. Bonfield, 'Marriage Settlements and the Rise of the Great Estates: the Demographic Aspects', EcHR, 2nd ser., XXXII, No. 4, 1979; idem, 'Marriage Settlements, 1660–1740: the Adoption of the Strict Settlement in Kent and Northamptonshire', in R. B. Outhwaite (ed.), *Marriage and Society*, London, 1981; idem, *Marriage Settlements 1601–1740*, Cambridge, 1983; idem, 'Marriage, Property and the "Affective Family"', in *Law and History Review*, I, No. 2, 1983; B. English and J. Saville, *Strict Settlement. A Guide for Historians*, University of Hull, Occasional Papers in Economic and Social History, No. 12, Hull, 1983; E. Spring, 'The Family, Strict Settlement, and Historians', *Canadian Journal of History*, XVIII, 1983; idem, 'Law and the Theory of the Affective Family', *Albion*, 16, 1984; R. B. Outhwaite, 'Marriage as Business', in McKendrick and Outhwaite, *op. cit.*

published book on *The Aristocracy in England 1660–1914*,[54] J. V. Beckett provides additional illustrative material, but much of his discussion relates to the later eighteenth and nineteenth centuries,[55] and no new detailed case studies of the management of particular estates have appeared to add to those listed in n.246 on p. 345.[56]   C. CLAY

LANDLORDS AND ESTATE MANAGEMENT IN WALES (1640–1750)

Recent work dealing with the fortunes of Welsh landed families has emphasised the significance of numerous failures of male heirs between 1690 and 1760, and the consequently heightened importance of the marriage factor in influencing changes in landed property. While J. G. Parry (for Caernarvonshire) agrees with the author of this chapter in seeing a relatively faster growth of large estates between the 1680s and the 1750s, T. M. Humphreys (for Montgomeryshire) and Mrs J. O. Martin (for Glamorgan) do not see evidence for the rise of great estates, and P. Jenkins (for Glamorgan) stresses that the concentration of landed estates derived less from any inherent advantages possessed by the largest properties than from failures in the male line.[57] No work has been done for Wales to test L. Bonfield's assertion that strict settlements did not exert a crucial influence on estate building, though some doubt is cast upon its validity by Dr Humphreys's claim that in Montgomeryshire the will was as important a vehicle of strict settlement as was the marriage settlement.[58]

Recent research has emphasized that the lesser Welsh gentry had perforce to farm their demesnes for the market in order to maintain a comfortable life-style.[59] As elsewhere in Britain, the more lucrative

[54] J. V. Beckett, *The Aristocracy in England 1660–1914*, Oxford, 1986, chs. 4 and 5.

[55] Dr Beckett has also produced a number of important articles on English landownership which likewise refer to a longer period than the one covered by ch. 5 below. Of these 'The Pattern of Landownership in England and Wales, 1660–1880', EcHR, 2nd ser., XXXVII, No. 1, 1984, provides a useful guide to the state of the literature at the time of its writing.

[56] However, it may be noted that J. R. Wordie's account of the Leveson-Gower estates, in 1979 still available only as a typescript thesis, has since been published as *Estate Management in Eighteenth-Century England. The Building of the Leveson-Gower Fortune*, RHS, London 1982.

[57] J. G. Parry, 'Stability and Change in Mid-Eighteenth-Century Caernarvonshire', unpublished M. A. thesis, University of Wales, 1978, pp. 8–25; D. W. Howell, *Patriarchs and Parasites: The Gentry of South-West Wales in the Eighteenth Century*, Cardiff, 1986, pp. 17–18, 212–13; T. M. Humphreys, 'Rural Society in Montgomeryshire in the Eighteenth Century', unpublished Ph.D. thesis, University of Wales, 1982, pp. 56–7, 76, 537; J. O. Martin, 'The Landed Estate in Glamorgan, circa 1660–1760', unpublished Ph.D. thesis, University of Cambridge, 1978, p. 299; P. Jenkins, *The Making of the Ruling Class: The Glamorgan Gentry 1640–1790*, Cambridge, 1983, p. 50.

[58] Private correspondence with Dr Humphreys. For Bonfield's work, see Fn. 53 above.

[59] G. H. Williams, 'Estate Management in Dyffryn Conwy c. 1685', *Trans. Hon. Soc. Cymmrodorion*, 1979, pp. 32–46, 74; Martin, *op. cit.*, p. 122; Humphreys *op. cit.*, p. 98.

returns to be had from farming for the market, as compared with those to be had from land let to tenants, were a necessary means of boosting their limited incomes from rents.[60]

Chapter 15 of vol. V (chapter 6 below) shows that some landowners, great and small, experimented on their home farms. But Humphreys demonstrates that in Montgomeryshire it was the lesser gentry, the small freeholders, and the large tenant farmers who were the important innovators. In a similar vein, Mrs Martin argues that in Glamorgan it was the lesser estate-owners, themselves practical farmers in direct contact with their tenants, who were the more likely to have influenced neighbouring farmers towards adopting improvements.[61]

Humphreys and Martin support the claim advanced in chapter 6 that attempts at the rationalisation of landholding patterns, and consolidation of holdings, made only limited progress in this period. Humphreys contends that smaller, resident landowners were more active than larger, non-resident ones in this respect. Although landlords dealt harshly with squatters who interfered with their tenants' grazing rights on common land, both Humphreys and Martin show that encroachments onto common land were sometimes tacitly approved by landowners, for they offered an opportunity of extending their property if the encroachers could be made to accept formal tenancies.[62]

Recent findings on the subject of leases indicate that while three-life leases became increasingly common on certain estates in south-west Wales by the mid-eighteenth century, in Montgomeryshire shorter leases at rack were the most common form of tenure by the early eighteenth century, and if in Glamorgan the three-life system was the most common tenure before 1750, tenancies-at-will were on the increase there from the 1680s.[63] Shorter leases gave landlords greater control, enabling them to exert a greater influence over their tenants' farming practices, although in Glamorgan this power was but little exercised before the 1770s. Absence of strict husbandry clauses was a feature of both the old three-life leases and twenty-one year leases on Glamorgan estates before 1760, and no strict husbandry clauses existed in Montgomeryshire either.[64] The assertion of Chapter 15 that 'very few leases before 1750 aimed at encouraging improved husbandry' thus stands confirmed.

[60] Mingay, *The Gentry*, pp. 82–3.
[61] Humphreys, *op. cit.*, p. 144; Martin, *op. cit.*, p. 102.
[62] Humphreys, *op. cit.*, pp. 155, 136; Martin, *op. cit.*, pp. 91, 84.
[63] Humphreys, *op. cit.*, pp. 119–22; Martin, *op. cit.*, pp. 63, 71; A. H. John, 'The Old Order', in G. Williams and A. H. John (eds.), *Glamorgan County History*, Vol. v, Cardiff, 1980, p. 10.
[64] Martin, *op. cit.*, pp. 69–70, 119; Humphreys, *op. cit.*, p. 123.

Humphreys and Martin corroborate the author's statement that generally landowners adventured only small amounts of capital on their properties but, in contrast to his claim that allowances were made to tenants for building or repairs in difficult years, they show that they did not increase their capital outlays in depressed years to placate tenants.[65] Notwithstanding the greater financial resources of the large estates, which the author believed allowed their owners to invest more liberally, Martin argues that in the period 1660–1760 the greater owners seem to have been reluctant to spend money on their tenanted farms, while Humphreys contends that large owners were inhibited from investing because of debt.[66]

Indeed, both writers argue that small estates were better administered than were large ones because tenants on small properties were kept up to scratch by the landowner who was resident and 'closer' to his estate. There is also the question of whether the prevalence of absentee landownership in parts of Wales, to which Sir John Habakkuk has recently drawn attention, was a handicap to efficient agriculture.[67] Habakkuk indicates that absenteeism could have meant *improved* management by the very fact of association with a distant, more substantial landed estate. Nor is there any doubt that absentee-owners and their agents corresponded at length, that accounting methods were better on large properties, and that large owners were less likely to be short of capital.

DAVID HOWELL

[65] *Ibid.*, pp. 113–14, 118; Martin. *op. cit.*, p. 51.

[66] J. O. Martin, 'Estate Stewards and their Work in Glamorgan, 1660–1760', *Morgannwg*, XXIII, 1979, p. 26; Humphreys, *op. cit.*, pp. 67–8.

[67] Martin, 'Estate Stewards', p. 26; *idem*, 'The Landed Estate in Glamorgan', p. 102; Humphreys, *op. cit.*, pp. 67–8, 145; Parry, *op. cit.*, p. 185; Sir John Habakkuk, 'Marriage and the Ownership of Land', in R. R. Davies, R. A. Griffiths, J. G. Jones and K. O. Morgan (eds.), *Welsh Society and Nationhood*, Cardiff, 1984, pp. 178–98.

# 1

# LANDLORDS IN ENGLAND, 1500–1640

## A. THE CROWN

### 1. *The golden age of the crown estate, 1461–1509*

The nature of early Tudor kingship is now recognized to have been not a 'new monarchy' but fundamentally medieval. The strength of the government lay in feudal power and in the possession in the king's hands, as Sir John Fortescue pointed out, of as much land as possible. Edward IV made a famous statement on the royal finances to his Commons in 1467: "I purpose to live upon my own, and not to charge my subjects but in great and urgent causes, concerning more the weal of themselves, and also the defence of them and of this my realm, rather than my own pleasure."[1] The phrase, 'to live of his own', meant strictly that the king should live on what was lawfully his, or in other words that he should live within his income. It was found expedient, by sovereigns who sought independence of action and by parliaments which were loath to grant taxes alike, to interpret this as meaning that, apart from the revenues from the customs, the king should ordinarily live on the rents from his Crown lands and on the income from his rights, especially escheat and wardship, as a feudal suzerain.[2]

There was no considerable landed estate in the country which did not include land held directly from the Crown, and the extent of the Crown land was greatly increased in the reign of Henry VII. Besides his own estates as earl of Richmond, Henry confirmed the addition to the Crown lands of those of the duchy of York and the earldom of March by his politic marriage to Elizabeth of York. Parliament assured him of the ancient inheritances of the Crown, including the duchy of Lancaster, as well as restoring all lands alienated from the Crown during the Wars of the Roses, by acts of resumption passed within two years of the victory at Bosworth, and a further act of 1495 gave him the authority to resume certain alienations made by Edward III and Richard II and all lands which Henry VI had possessed on the 2nd of October 1455.[3] Not all these resumptions were effected, but the

---

[1] *Rotuli Parliamentorum*, 1783, v, p. 572, quoted by B. P. Wolffe, 'The Management of English Royal Estates under the Yorkist Kings', EHR, LXXI, 1956, p. 1.

[2] On the phrase, 'to live of his own', see B. P. Wolffe, 'Acts of Resumption in the Lancastrian Parliaments 1399–1456', EHR, LXXIII, 1958, p. 584.

[3] *Rotuli Parliamentorum*, VI, pp. 270, 336, 403, 459.

legislation provided the Crown with an additional formidable hold over the nobility. Moreover, parliamentary attainders, of which there were 122 in the period 1485 to 1503 alone, led to further and often large accretions to the Crown lands; for example, the lands of Sir William Stanley, the lord chamberlain who so dramatically fell from power in 1495, added more than a thousand pounds a year to the royal income.[1] Precisely what the extent of the Crown lands were at this time, we do not know, but we do know that Chief Justice Fortescue estimated that one-fifth of England was in the hands of the Crown at one time or another in the course of the reign of Edward IV and that the duchy of Lancaster, admittedly the largest single entity of the royal demesne, included not only the county palatine but also estates in Wales, London, Calais, and thirty-three English counties. It has been estimated that, whereas the income from the Crown lands in the last year of Edward IV was £6,471, Henry VII received some £13,633 in the first year of his reign.[2]

The degree to which the Crown benefited from its advantageous position clearly depended upon the efficiency of the administration of this vast collection of lands scattered through the length and breadth of the kingdom. Royal finances were normally controlled in the later Middle Ages by the Exchequer, a department of state with an established 'course' or process of passing accounts. The Exchequer was divided into the Lower Exchequer or Exchequer of Receipt, for the receipt and disbursement of revenue, and the Upper Exchequer or Exchequer of Account, for the auditing and recording of accounts. By the later fifteenth century the Exchequer had experienced personnel with a reputation for probity but suffered from a number of defects which made it a less flexible organization than the situation demanded. It had come to deal not so much in cash as in instruments of credit, the famous 'tallies'. Its processes were slow—audits commonly took two years—and its system of accounting was designed rather to provide a record of the responsibilities of individual officers than to reveal the overall position of the royal income. The estate management of the Crown lands was cumbersome and its divisions dictated by political rather than by geographical factors. The larger palatine estates were administered separately, each with its own staff of officials; large estates which accrued to the Crown demesne were arbitrarily grouped together; and many particular properties were administered directly or leased to tenants. In the face of these rigidities, Henry VII, like his Yorkist predecessors, found it convenient to develop the Chamber as a

[1] W. C. Richardson, *Tudor Chamber Administration, 1485–1547*, 1952, p. 12.
[2] F. C. Dietz, *English Government Finance, 1485–1558*, 1921, p. 21. The figures given by Dietz are less than reliable and must be used with caution.

financial department and not to attempt any major reform of the Exchequer. For the creation of a new system of royal estate management to provide the king with an income independent of the Exchequer and of an organization capable of assigning money to different departments of state independently of Exchequer control began not, as was at one time supposed, in 1485 but in 1461.[1] As Professor Richardson has written: "the 'newness' of the Tudor rule lay not in any novelty of the governmental system, but in the thoroughness with which it was administered."[2]

The organization of the Chamber was not designed to replace the Exchequer in its fundamental functions as a treasury for the receipt of such revenues as the customs and as a court of record, but to supplement the Exchequer where it failed to meet the vital Crown requirements of the provision of ready cash and of that close and personal supervision of the localities without which there could be no adequate augmentation of the Crown revenues at a time of rapid change. The new system which the Crown adopted for its estate administration was essentially that which had been developed on the larger lay estates. The Crown lands came to be grouped into territorial divisions, each with professionally trained officers as surveyors, receivers, and auditors, men such as were beginning to appear on the larger noble estates in the middle of the fifteenth century. These men, often trained in the law, were eminently qualified to make a survey of the lands, to compile a *valor*, to search out feudal rights, and to advise on the problems of estate management at a time when demesne farming was declining and when money rents were showing "a universal, though uneven, tendency to fall."[3] The duties of the royal officers were well expressed in a signet office docket book of 1484: "to ride, survey, receive and remember on every behalf that might be most for the king's profit and thereof yearly to make report."[4] Many of these men were drawn from the service of the nobility, like John Touke, in the royal service after 1478, who had been auditor to the duke of Clarence and to Margaret, Lady Hungerford. Many of them, again, were drawn from the personnel of the Household or Exchequer, like Richard Harper, the first receiver-general of the duchy of Lancaster in Henry VII's time, who had been in the Exchequer of Receipt.[5] Such men were equally at home in central and local appointments and indeed the lesser administrative posts of the Crown estate provided a useful training for men who later progressed to high offices of state.

[1] Wolffe, EHR, LXXI, 1956, pp. 1–27.
[2] Richardson, *op. cit.*, p. 1.
[3] *Ministers' Accounts of the Warwickshire Estates of the Duke of Clarence, 1479–80*, ed. R. H. Hilton, Dugdale Soc., 1952, p. xx.    [4] Wolffe, *op. cit.*, p. 9.
[5] *Ibid.*, p. 4; R. Somerville, *History of the Duchy of Lancaster*, I, 1953, p. 263.

It was a system which depended for its success upon no elaboration of process but upon constant, informal, personal control from above and upon simple checks and balances. The treasurer of the Chamber received and paid on direct commands from the king and only rarely by warrants under the signet, the chancellor of the duchy of Lancaster learnt the king's mind upon details of administration by conversation and not by any more formal direction, and the responsibility for the tightening of the entire revenue administration fell upon a small group of personal servants of the king. Chief of these in Henry VII's reign was Sir Reginald Bray, who had been receiver-general and steward to Sir Henry Stafford, the second husband of Henry's mother, Lady Margaret Beaufort, and who remained in Lady Margaret's service after he had become *de facto* chief financial minister. It was Bray who became chancellor of the duchy of Lancaster upon Henry's accession, who revitalized the administration of that institution which had enjoyed a separate organization ever since it came under the royal control by the accession of Henry IV. Arrears were the perennial thorn in the flesh of all land administrators in the period; under Bray, letters were sent under the duchy seal every year in February and March, after the audit, to tenants or lessees, demanding the payment of arrears. As in the reign of Edward IV, many special commissions of enquiry were appointed to investigate neglect or decay—the derelict state of the demesne lands at Willingdon in 1491, or the defects of the town wall of Leicester and the occupation of Crown land without payment of rent in 1497, or the inefficiency of the duchy officers at Tutbury in 1498. Sometimes commissioners were appointed with wide powers, as were those who were charged with the improvement of all the royal lands in Gloucestershire in 1466 and as were Andrew Dymock and John Cutte who were sent on a progress of the duchy lands in the north in 1497. These latter have left us a record of their recommendations for improvements in administration and of their success in adding £120 annually to the revenue, by new or increased rents or by the restoration of rents which had decayed or been withheld. The sale of wardships was often dealt with by the king in person, or by Bray on his behalf, and, from the first year of the reign, receivers-general were appointed for the lands of royal wards and for the investigation of concealments in groups of counties at a time. So energetic was the pursuit of the Crown's feudal rights that the Chancery issued a writ for the holding of an *inquisition post mortem* wherever there was the least chance of finding that the land was held *in capite*.[1]

---

[1] Ibid., pp. 265–6, 267; *Cal. Pat. Rolls, 1461–7*, p. 553; H. E. Bell, *An Introduction to the History and Records of the Court of Wards & Liveries*, 1953, pp. 3–5. For a biographical sketch of Bray, see Richardson, *op. cit.*, pp. 451–8.

The success of these policies was such that the period from 1461 to 1509 has been termed "the golden age of the Crown estate."[1] After the assignments for the maintenance of the Wardrobe and Household have been deducted, the net annual yield of the Crown lands was approximately £2,500 in the early years of Henry VII. It rose from £3,765 to £24,145 between 1491 and 1504. The extent to which the Chamber was responsible for this remarkable increase may be judged from the surviving accounts. By the end of the reign the Chamber was receiving five times the Exchequer's income from the landed revenues, and where the total receipts of the Exchequer, apart from subsidies, benevolences, and loans, varied between £32,000 a year in 1485 and £48,000 in 1509, the Chamber's receipts multiplied ten times at least.[2] Yet the estates increased in size more than in yield, for they were encumbered with such charges as pensions and annuities and burdened with arrears which defied collection, and they were utilized to reward the services of government officials of every description. The surplus which Henry VII accumulated was not appreciable until 1497 and most of the wealth which he left at his death was not fluid; his income from ordinary revenues had not sufficed to save him from borrowing, from benevolences, or from occasional resort to parliamentary grants.

Even before Henry VII's death, a degree of more formal organization of the Crown revenues was necessary. Immediately after the death of Bray in 1503, the office of master of the wards was established to oversee, manage, and at any rate initiate the sales of wardships, though even now the income from sales and from fines for liveries continued to be collected by less formal methods. In August 1508 Sir Edward Belknap was appointed 'surveyor of the king's prerogative', with the task of supervising the exploitation of the king's rights independently of Exchequer control. Meanwhile, Richard Empson and Edmund Dudley, the king's servants, were pursuing through the 'king's council learned in the law', again outside Exchequer control, that active collection of fines on penal statutes which earned them such notoriety.[3]

## 2. *The decline of the Chamber system, 1509–1554*

The death of Henry VII, "the most uniformly successful of English kings,"[4] and pressure from vested interests in the Exchequer threatened the continuance of the 'Chamber system'. The office of surveyor of

[1] R. B. Pugh, *The Crown Estate*, 1960, p. 9.
[2] Dietz, *op. cit.*, pp. 28–30, 80–4.
[3] Bell, *op. cit.*, pp. 6–7; Richardson, *op. cit.*, pp. 153–6, 198–214; G. R. Elton, *The Tudor Revolution in Government*, 1953, pp. 29–30.
[4] S. T. Bindoff, *Tudor England*, 1950, p. 66.

the prerogative quickly fell into abeyance and the learned council met only spasmodically from this time. The use of the Chamber as the leading revenue department, however, was too well established to be abandoned as yet; instead, it was gradually placed upon a more formal, and therefore more bureaucratic, basis. First by letters patent from 1511, then by statutes renewed and frequently revised from parliament to parliament between 1515 and 1535, when the offices were made permanent, two general surveyors of the Crown lands were appointed, one at least of whom was always a baron of the Exchequer, and these offices came to constitute "the first distinct organ of government permanently concerned with the profitable management of Crown lands."[1] The Chamber auditing system begun by Henry VII was perfected and the management of all the lands, woods, and revenues, other than those of the duchy of Lancaster, was centralized and made more efficient, while legal and judicial business continued to be the concern of the Exchequer. The restoration of some lands to their former owners by act of parliament at the start of the reign, grants to royal favourites, and increased assignments for the Household, meant that the treasurer of the Chamber was receiving £24,719 less from the annual land revenues within his province in 1515 than in 1508 and that the total income from revenues in the survey of the general surveyors and of the duchy of Lancaster was only £16,367. By 1531, however, the importance of the office of the surveyors had exceeded that of the Exchequer, for it was yielding more than £40,000 annually against £30,000 to £40,000, and the net revenue of the duchy of Lancaster was averaging £13,000.[2]

A radical change in Crown land administration was to take place between 1536 and 1554, which was to establish a pattern of organization which survived with only minor modifications until the middle of the eighteenth century. The occasion of this change was the vast extension of the lands in the possession of the Crown. The attainders which followed the Pilgrimage of Grace, Lady Jane Grey's abortive attempt for the succession to the throne, and Wyatt's rebellion, added markedly to the steady accretion of attainted lands which had taken place since the accession of the Tudors and before. From 1531 to 1545, too, the royal honorial units were consolidated by the judicious purchase or exchange of lands. Most important of all, of course, the dissolution of the monasteries made the king incomparably the largest landowner in the country; by 1539 over eight hundred religious institutions, many of them richly endowed, had passed to the Crown.

[1] Elton, *op. cit.*, pp. 45-51, 167; *The Tudor Constitution*, ed. G. R. Elton, 1960, pp. 134-6; Pugh, *op. cit.*, p. 9.
[2] Dietz, *op. cit.*, pp. 89-90; Richardson, *op. cit.*, p. 278.

From 1536 Thomas Cromwell initiated a policy which, whether deliberately conceived (as Dr G. R. Elton has argued convincingly) or not, was effectively to reduce the importance of the Chamber and ultimately to re-establish the position of the Exchequer in the administration of the land revenues. The very act which made their office permanent restricted the general surveyors to the supervision of the Crown lands which were already within their purview; they were reduced to the fixity of a court by an act of 1542 which, though passed after Cromwell's fall from power, was the logical conclusion of his reforms. Another act of 1536 had established the court of Augmentations to administer not only the lands of the dissolved monasteries but also all lands purchased by the king—a responsibility which until this time had belonged to the general surveyors. The court of Augmentations modelled its procedure on that of the duchy of Lancaster and had identical fees and allowances, but subsequently broke new ground by abandoning the honorial structure of the lands, so largely preserved by the general surveyors, and adopting a new system by which all its lands, regardless of their previous tenure, were included in the accounts for the county in which they were situated. In 1540 two further courts were given statutory basis—the court of First Fruits and Tenths, and the court of Wards and Liveries.[1]

By 1542, then, six departments of state had been created, each with its own curial establishment and each with specific responsibilities for the collection of the royal revenues. The fall of Cromwell removed the unifying factor which was needed to promote efficiency and to prevent corruption, but the reforms which were subsequently introduced to simplify the administration and which resulted in the final elimination of the Chamber from control of the Crown lands were the work of experts who had been trained under Cromwell, and especially of Sir William Paulet. A patent of January 1547, adopting the recommendation of a commission of enquiry into the state of the revenue, amalgamated the court of Survey with the court of Augmentations to form the second court of Augmentations. It was the dissolution of this second court of Augmentations, again as the result of a commission of enquiry, which in 1554 established the control of all the land revenues, except those from wardships and the duchy of Lancaster, in the Exchequer.[2]

These experiments and measures of reorganization occurred when an unprecedented expansion of the Crown lands was taking place, largely as the outcome of the dissolution of the monasteries, and it was

[1] Elton, *Tudor Constitution*, pp. 139–42; Elton, *Tudor Revolution*, pp. 177 sqq., 203–19; W. C. Richardson, *History of the Court of Augmentations, 1536–1554*, 1961, pp. 38–9; *Statutes of the Realm*, III, pp. 798 sqq.; 802 sqq.; 860 sqq.
[2] *Ibid.*, IV, pp. 208–9; LP, XXI, ii, no. 770 (1).

the court of Augmentations which proved the most important of the Crown's treasuries in the period. The average annual net receipts of the court between 1536 and 1547 were £120,000; in the peak year, 1543-4, it collected over £253,292. None of the other departments approached Augmentations in importance—the court of First Fruits never collected more than £78,000 a year, the court of Survey seldom more than £38,000, while the duchy of Lancaster was yielding for the king's use at the most £11,000 and the court of Wards produced a mere £4,466 in 1542. Precise figures for the profits of the Dissolution properties are difficult to calculate, but the average annual income of the Augmentations from the rents of the former monastic lands was over £36,000 in the first decade, and it has been estimated that the sale of Crown estates between the time of the first important commissions for sale of December 1539 and March 1540 and the dissolution of the court in 1554 exceeded one million pounds.[1] Cromwell's wish to reserve the monastic properties as a means of enabling the Crown to live of its own, a policy which might have had far-reaching effects upon the development of English constitutional history, was doomed to frustration by the incessant demands of the government to meet its increasing expenses and, in particular, those of a series of costly wars—the fighting with Scotland and France in the early 1540's cost nearly £2,200,000 in itself.[2] It is difficult to believe that large-scale land sales could have produced the best possible capital gains; moreover, the rents which were reserved to the Crown upon lands conveyed in fee farm were fixed and, therefore, liable to be rendered less valuable by inflation. Yet it is clear from the studies which have been undertaken of alienations in particular counties that the monastic lands were not given away at bargain prices as used to be thought; grants were usually made at twenty years' purchase at this time and subsequent increases in the rates were adopted to allow for the rise in annual values as the century progressed. Equally, it is clear that not all the monastic lands were disposed of by 1547; Dr Youings has estimated that only three fifths of the monastic property in Devon had been sold or given in reward for services by the time of Henry VIII's death, for example, and a few vestiges of monastic land, indeed, are in Crown hands today, like Burwell manor in Cambridgeshire.[3] The amalgamation of the court of

---

[1] Richardson, *Tudor Chamber Administration*, pp. 322-3, 368; Somerville, *op. cit.*, p. 304; Bell, *op. cit.*, p. 47; J. Hurstfield, 'The Profits of Fiscal Feudalism', EcHR, 2nd Ser., VIII, 1955, p. 55; Richardson, *Court of Augmentations*, pp. 24, 77, 235.

[2] Dietz, *op. cit.*, p. 147.

[3] H. J. Habakkuk, 'The Market for Monastic Property, 1539-1603', EcHR, 2nd Ser., X, 1958, especially pp. 363-70; J. A. Youings, *Devon Monastic Lands*, Devon and Cornwall Rec. Soc., NS 1, 1955, *passim*, and 'The Terms of the Disposal of the Devon Monastic Lands, 1536-1558', EHR, LXIX, 1954, pp. 18-38.

Survey and the first court of Augmentations is not, therefore, to be interpreted as "a measure of the speed of alienation." Although lands worth about £8,250 a year and £3,500 respectively were alienated in 1545 and 1546, the receipts in Augmentations were £59,255 in 1545–6 and £48,303 in 1546–7, sufficiently useful sums in any context. Moreover, the court of Augmentations left one legacy which was to be of lasting benefit to the administrators of the Crown estate—surveys of all lands and property assigned to it, usually the work of its local officials but upon occasion compiled by its central staff sent out upon special commissions. These surveys were neither as well organized nor as uniform as those made for Parliament in the next century, though some were nearly as complete, and with the acquisition of the records of the court of Survey in 1547 the court of Augmentations had full descriptions of the vast majority of Crown lands.[1]

There is no doubt, however, that the opportunities for peculation, for graft, and for the oppression of the weak by officers of the courts of revenue were many, or that the succession of a boy king in 1547 increased those opportunities. Much of the property which accrued to the Crown by the dissolution of the chantries under Edward VI, which had been planned in the reign of his father, was disposed of before 1553 and lands of an annual value of £27,000 were given away, more in fact than were sold in the reign. The wasteful overstaffing of offices in the various departments was a source of considerable expense to the Crown, just as the excessive fees charged by court officials were to the public. The court of Augmentations, for instance, was paying its principal officers, according to one contemporary estimate, £7,085 a year in 1551 as against £4,749 in 1536, and to salaries must be added expense accounts. The absence of a strong minister led to laxity in administration which seems to have gone virtually unchecked in Edward VI's reign until the report of the commission of investigations in 1552, which in effect documents the charges made against the revenue courts some years earlier by Henry Brinkelow, when he declared that "for their own advantage they make many times the king to rob his subjects, and they rob the king again." The act of 1552–3 for improving the revenues required all receivers to be bonded, and noted that they had been keeping in their own hands revenues which they had collected on behalf of the Crown.[2] The two outstanding examples of this practice

---

[1] Pugh, *op. cit.*, p. 10; Elton, *Tudor Revolution*, p. 225; Richardson, *Court of Augmentations*, pp. 300–3.

[2] Dietz, *op. cit.*, p. 180; 'The Certificate of Thomas Lord Darcy', BM Add. MS 30198, ff. 40–52; Richardson, *Chamber Administration*, pp. 425–32; H. Brinkelow, *Complaynt of Roderyck Mors*, ed. J. M. Cowper, Early Eng. Text Soc., Extra Ser., XXII, 1874, p. 24; *Statutes of the Realm*, IV, pp. 161–4.

were provided by Richard Whalley, receiver of the Crown revenues in Yorkshire from 1546 to 1552, who confessed to a series of misdemeanours which involved an embezzlement of over £2,000, part of of it accomplished by the disguising of revenues received as 'arrearages', and Sir John Beaumont, receiver-general in the court of Wards, who concealed in his arrearages various sums which totalled over £21,000.[1]

## 3. *The weaknesses of Crown land administration, 1554–1603*

The value of the attainted lands which came to the Crown under Mary was in great part off-set by her surrender of the first-fruits and tenths, by her restorations to the church of spiritualities received at the dissolution of the monasteries, and by the re-establishment of half a dozen monasteries. The gross value of the lands and properties surrendered or given away by Mary was given in a contemporary document as £49,000; of this, Elizabeth quickly recovered by resumptions £24,429, and, with the approval of Parliament, exchanged the spiritualities for most of the temporalities of the bishops. This measure was to prove a valuable addition to the Crown revenue. The lands lately the bishop of Ely's, for instance, yielded £638 in 1559–60 against an income from the rest of the Crown lands in Norfolk and Suffolk of £3,049, while in 1573 the lands of the bishops of Winchester and of Bath and Wells contributed £625 and £113 respectively to a total income from the Crown estate in Somerset of £4,920. Accretions by attainder, escheat, and inheritance continued to occur from time to time, of course; the confiscations which followed the Rising in the North of 1569 were the largest of the reign and added lands of an annual value of £2,502. Major sales, on the other hand, were carefully restricted in Elizabeth's time to periods of extreme national crisis— to meet the debts of the Scottish campaign of 1560, to pay for the defences against the Spanish Armada of 1588, and to finance the Irish expeditions at the turn of the century; the capital realization of Crown lands on these three occasions amounted to £263,000, £126,000, and £213,000.[2] Elizabeth had, in the words of her able lord treasurer, Burghley, "as great care to preserve the revenues of the Crown as a mother could have for her children;" she had energetic and competent ministers; and this was an age of rising rents. Yet the Crown estates in the last year of her long reign produced only £88,767, merely £22,319 above the yield in 1558. Where the duchy of Lancaster estates had

---

[1] Richardson, *Court of Augmentations*, pp. 232–3; J. Hurstfield, 'Corruption and Reform under Edward VI and Mary', EHR, LXVIII, 1953, pp. 24–7.

[2] F. C. Dietz, *English Public Finance, 1558–1641*, 1932, pp. 19, 64, 87, 294–5; BM Lansdowne MS. 4, ff. 182 *sqq.*; SP 12: 1, 64; 12, 50; 228, 3, 30; 274, 146.

provided Henry VII with £8,040 in 1508–9, the revenues received from the ancient duchy lands in 1579–80 were £8,038. The net revenue of the court of Wards was £7,638 in the first year of Edward VI, including £1,117 from the sale of wardships; by 1559 the income had risen to £20,290, with sales contributing £5,003; but there followed, under the mastership of Burghley himself, a period of static or even declining income—the net revenue from the court in 1607 was no more than £17,810.[1]

Corruption and moderation have been put forward as the two most likely explanations of this failure to secure a substantial improvement in the royal revenues in Elizabeth's time, and both certainly existed. The sheer size of the administrative problem presented by the Crown estate, coupled with the strength of the resistance in the period to the feudal exactions of the Crown, are likely to prove the more important factors when further research has been undertaken. Professor Hurstfield has drawn attention to the increasing use of socage tenure 'as of the manor of East Greenwich' in grants for sales from the reign of Edward VI onwards, which was one significant expression of the resistance to feudal charges, and the administrative history of the court of Wards in Elizabeth's reign provides a striking illustration of the problems which the Crown faced in its relationship with its tenants.[2]

As Professor Plucknett has pointed out, the Crown had had increasing difficulty in keeping track of its tenants-in-chief from the time of Edward I at least. Under Burghley's mastership, the court of Wards made consistent but not altogether successful efforts to discover tenants-in-chief. Commissioners were appointed in 1556–7 to compile a list of lands held by knight service in the county palatine from the Exchequer records at Chester, feodaries—the officers responsible for maintaining this information—were provided with notes from the court's own records in 1570 and were required to keep their own books in 1600, but the task was, in Plucknett's words, "wellnigh hopeless." For all who held the smallest item of land, or even a reversion, by knight service in chief were affected. Even though from early in Elizabeth's reign the Crown began to reward informers, not all tenants were as unfortunate as John Sheparde who suffered the full exactions of wardship in Mary's reign because out of lands of an annual value of £18 2s., two shillings' worth was held *in capite*. It was only in the second half of Burghley's mastership that the Crown appreciated

---

[1] Dietz, *op. cit.*, p. 296; Somerville, *op. cit.*, p. 305; Bell, *op. cit.*, pp. 47, 48, 57; Hurstfield, EcHR, 2nd Ser., VIII, p. 55; SP 12: 255, 84; 282, 75.

[2] J. Hurstfield, 'Lord Burghley as Master of the Court of Wards, 1561–98', *Trans. RHS*, 4th Ser., XXXI, 1949, pp. 95–114; and 'The Greenwich Tenures of the Reign of Edward VI', *Law Qtrly Rev.*, LXV, 1949, pp. 72–81.

that the feodaries' surveys could not only act as records of lands held but also provide a more realistic valuation of the lands than the *inquisitions post mortem* and so make a positive contribution to the increase in revenue which was so necessary.[1]

What the Crown lost by its inability to make a maximum profit out of its possessions, the lessee and the grantee gained. "The significance of the feudal revenues in the Tudor period," Professor Hurstfield has stated, "lies not in their direct yield to the state but as a method of payment, albeit indirectly and capriciously, to ministers and civil servants," and a contemporary recorded that Elizabeth had granted more leases in reversion "to her servants and captains and such like in her time than has been granted since the Conquest."[2] There was no general increase in duchy of Lancaster rents in leases granted under its seal from early in the reign of Henry VIII to the end of the sixteenth century, and even the fines were increased only moderately. In Elizabeth's time twice the annual rent was normally exacted for a lease lasting thirty-one years, and thrice for a twenty-one years' lease. There is every reason to believe that what was true of the duchy estates was generally true of all Crown lands.[3] Three examples will serve to show how the grantee could benefit. When Writtle in Essex escheated to the Crown in 1521 by the attainder of the duke of Buckingham, it had an income which was valued at £140 a year. By 1547 the rents had fallen to £109, about a quarter of the customary tenements were in abeyance, and the lord's profits of courts were being plundered. Sir William Petre, secretary of state, had receipts of £200 a year from the manor within two years of his being granted it at a valuation of £76 13s. 4d. in 1554, and this was achieved by recoveries alone without rent increases or fines.[4] Two patents under Chancery and duchy of Lancaster seals in 1575 empowered Sir Henry Lee to search out bondmen and agree with them on terms for their manumission on any of the Crown lands, including those alienated since Elizabeth's accession. Just how much Lee profited is not known, but the duchy records contain numerous mentions of such manumissions between 1575 and 1599, and many bondmen were well-to-do men who were able to pay anything from twenty to sixty pounds.[5] In 1587, again, the third

---

[1] T. F. T. Plucknett, *The Legislation of Edward I*, 1949, p. 105; Bell, *op. cit.*, pp. 50–7.
[2] Hurstfield, EcHR, 2nd Ser., VIII, p. 59; BM Lansdowne MS. 105, no. 31, f. 141.
[3] Somerville, *op. cit.*, p. 306; Habakkuk, *op. cit.*, pp. 370–2; E. Kerridge, 'The Movement of Rent, 1540–1640', EcHR, 2nd Ser., VI, 1953, pp. 30–3.
[4] W. R. Emerson, *The Economic Development of the Estates of the Petre Family in Essex in the Sixteenth and Seventeenth Centuries*, Oxford D.Phil. thesis, 1951, pp. 101–2.
[5] S. Peyton, 'An Elizabethan Inquisition concerning Bondmen', *Beds. Hist. Rec. Soc.*, IX, 1925, p. 62; E. K. Chambers, *Sir Henry Lee*, 1936, pp. 45–6; TED I, p. 71.

earl of Huntingdon, lord president of the council in the North, successfully petitioned for the exchange of a compact holding of land in fee simple, the manors of Bradbury and Hilton in Durham, worth £400 a year, for 101 scattered parcels of Crown lands of a nominally equivalent value which he could resell, through agents, in smaller lots. Huntingdon had no difficulty in disposing of the lands and had completed the resales by July 1591; again, no total is available for the profit made, but he recovered the value of Bradbury and Hilton when he sold the manor of Framfield for £8,400.[1] These grants did not represent total loss to the Crown, for its servants were rewarded and they were often of items from which a private individual could more readily profit than an institution, because of more energetic management and of local knowledge, but they do illustrate the weaknesses of Crown land administration.

## 4. The failure of efforts at reform in the reign of James I

Elizabeth, it has been calculated, sold Crown lands in her reign of an annual value of £24,808 at a cash yield of £813,332, but many of her sales were advowsons or small quillets of land, so that the real reduction in income must have been much smaller than is indicated by the nominal rental value of the properties. James I did not even attempt seriously to keep the landed inheritance of the Crown intact. He quickly embarked upon a lavish distribution of grants to favourites and had sold Crown lands for £426,151 by 1609; the net receipts of the general receivers of Crown lands fell in the first five years of his reign by £13,000 compared with the last five years of Elizabeth's.[2] The interest of the period for the historian, however, lies in the information left in the state papers on the problems of the Crown estate, revealed by the unprecedented series of commissions for selling, leasing, or farming the king's possessions which were appointed at the rate of one or two a year for the first part of James's reign. Many of these problems clearly were not peculiar to James and much of the history of Crown land administration in the later sixteenth and early seventeenth centuries is illuminated by the reports of these commissions. In the face of a demanding sovereign and of the refusal of intransigent parliaments to give the king an adequate income from other sources, James's treasurers in these early years, Dorset and Salisbury, achieved more than Burghley had done in improving the management of the lands which remained, but the years from 1603 to 1613 may be said to constitute the moment

[1] M. Claire Cross, 'An Exchange of Lands with the Crown, 1587-8', *Bull*. IHR, XXXIV, 1961, pp. 178-83.
[2] Dietz, *op. cit*., pp. 114, 125; SP 14: 44, 61; 47, 61, 99-102; 48, 35; 52, 6.

of truth for the Crown lands when the formidable nature of the obstacles to any dramatic increase in their yield was revealed.

At the beginning of the reign a proposal was made for the enfranchisement of the royal copyhold and customary lands. In return for the remission of their labour services and other incidents, customary tenants were to pay in two instalments a cash equivalent of one hundred years' purchase of their rents, which were to be reserved to the Crown with such heriots, reliefs, and suits of court as the commissioners should think expedient. But enfranchisement, as the king was to be told by his commissioners, was "rather to be wished than hopeful suddenly to be effected." The enfranchisement was not likely to be general, "for as it is not to be expected that it will be desired in all manors, so it is also improbable that all the tenants in any one manor will agree in that desire"—many would be either unwilling or unable to be purchasers. The days of payment would have to be set at least at two six-monthly intervals after the date of composition, to allow for the preparation of the assurance and because "many a tenant, not expecting he should have been a purchaser, must sell part to pay for the rest." Nor would the price be as high as the king wished, for there were many precedents of cheaper compositions. The whole undertaking would demand a great many commissioners who would be hard to find and the fees of the bailiffs would have to be increased to ensure efficiency of collection, for "the copyhold doth and must pay his rent, or else he forfeits his estate; but a fee farmer not often payeth till he be, or be afraid to be, distrained." Even when the Crown reduced its demands, copyhold tenants did not prove keen for enfranchisement, as is witnessed by the "careless" response of the tenants of Spaldwick manor in Huntingdonshire to Salisbury's offer of enfranchisement at seven years' purchase in 1611. They were afraid that they would lose their rights of common, that their freedom would not be secure, and that they would be subjected to such fresh burdens as jury service, while they suspected that the reliefs alone might amount to as much as their fines had done.[1]

Other attempts were made to convert uncertain fines into certain on the Crown lands. Some of these were more successful; the instructions sent in the summer of 1609 to all stewards of Crown manors where there were customary tenants led to a number of compositions which raised "good sums of money" and broke "the ice for the stream to run more currently after," it was reported in February 1610. The directions for these conversions make it clear that the Crown's attitude in the matter of fines had compared favourably with that of private landlords. Heriotable estates had previously been subject to a fine of one and a half year's rent at an improved value, and unheriotable to a

[1] SP 14: 59, 44; 71, 91.

fine of two years' rent; these rates were now reduced to one year's rent. "For every 20s. the king had formerly, he shall have £10 for ever, and £10 fine, in some places £20. And so if his copyholds yielded him £1,000, they shall yield him £10,000 besides the present fine." Even where the rack-rent was ten or twenty times the copyhold rent, the terms were reasonable, and there was little opposition evidently to these proposals, except where the copyhold tenants believed that their fines had been certain, as at Pontefract in Yorkshire where the officers found the people "the most headstrong...in that country."[1]

Leases which had been granted on Crown lands were either compounded for or renewed at improved rents; a note made in 1609 shows that rents on demises of the king's lands had been increased by nearly a quarter within the reign, and the Crown was constantly being advised to convert its copyhold tenements to leases. "By this means," Sir Lawrence Tanfield, the chief justice, told George Calvert in December 1609, "the abuses of stewards will be prevented, his Majesty's charge of many stewards and bailiffs eased, and his yearly revenue much increased, for if the lands be let at half the improved value, every 20s. rent of assize would yield twenty marks per annum." Several commissions were issued to enquire into 'concealed lands' and individuals also undertook, in the best Elizabethan manner, to search out such estates on condition of being granted the whole or part of the lands discovered. Six commissions were issued in five years from 1605 for compositions for assarts, wastes, and purprestures, and by the end of 1609 £26,013 had been received from this source.[2] But the fundamental need then, as it had surely been very much earlier, was for a thorough survey of all the Crown lands. A report which appears to have been prepared for Salisbury early in 1608 lists some fifteen advantages which would accrue to the Crown from such a survey and marks the following six points as of especial importance—the true understanding of the quality, quantity, rent, and value of the lands; the general controlment of the accounts of all officers; the discovery and maintenance of all manner of tenures, "which now are so generally omitted as scarce there is the remembrance of them, except of known tenures *in capite*;" the prevention of suits arising from uncertainties; the hindrance to the erection of cottages on the waste; and the avoiding of confusion in the custom of manors. "By the untruth and uncertainty thereof," the report remarks about the last point, "infinite loss doth daily grow unto his Majesty." With that one could not quarrel, but when the report goes on to suggest that it is "as much disadvantage to the tenants," one is rather

[1] SP 14: 37, 107; 43, 113.
[2] SP 14: 38, 25; 50, 30. See also CSPD 1603-10, pp. 163, 196, 331, 335, 379, 432.

dubious. It was a cogently argued report, however, and Salisbury proceeded to act upon it.[1]

Another suggestion which was made at this time was that income could be raised from an improved administration of the Crown forests and woods, set as they were in the rigour of tradition with a large staff of permanent officials paid both in cash and kind. A surveyorship of Crown woods, outside the ancient forest organization, had been established as early as 1521, and the office had been enlarged and become better organized in response to the acquisition of the woodlands of the monastic estates. But the office never became important in the way that other accounting offices did, and it is clear from the fragmentary and scattered records of woodsales in the 1540's and 1550's that woods never yielded any considerable income. In 1546, for example, only two counties showed a profit of more than £100 each, while twenty counties produced less than £300 between them; in 1558-9 the total receipts were only £2,845 or an average of £89 a county. So desultory was the exploitation of the Crown woods and forests under Elizabeth that in 1598 John Manwood was able to declare that the forest laws "are gone clean out of knowledge"—doubtless an overstatement of the case, but a clear indication of the trend of events. By the early seventeenth century there appears to have been a growing shortage of timber for building and wood for fuel. Whereas in the sixteenth century timber prices had lagged behind agricultural prices, now they rose more rapidly. In much of the east Midlands and of the eastern counties of England the shortage of fuel was so great that men were burning dried dung and furze for lack of it. Yet, though most Crown woods were specially surveyed between 1604 and 1612, and a conscious effort made to produce coppices for quick sales and ready returns of profit, no great success was had. For want of buyers, no more than sixteen of the forty or fifty thousand acres of coppice surveyed had been let by August 1612. Some 9,301 acres of the portion which was let produced an income of only £3,157. The shortages of which contemporaries complained and of which historians have made so much were probably highly localized, as Mr Hammersley has suggested. Although the iron works and shipbuilding took so much wood and timber in Kent and Sussex, for example, there was no general shortage in those counties. Even labourers were almost invariably burning wood there till 1640, few areas show more timber building of this period at the present time, and these counties remain among the best wooded in the country. Administration costs of scattered woods in local fees and the expenses of sales were at all times heavy, and for the Crown inevitably so. The woodward of Yorkshire who was left in 1545 with only

[1] SP 14: 37, 102.

£56 in ready money, after his costs of £10 were allowed, had many successors in the course of the next century; local commissioners reported in 1617 that the profit to the Crown of the wood in the Forest of Dean, with its advantageous access to lines of communication, was only £21 a year before 1610, and the total income from all royal woods in a good year probably did not exceed £10,000 in the early seventeenth century, of which perhaps as much as a quarter was taken by the costs of administration. It was even more true of Crown woods than of Crown lands that they "had their value for men who did not legally own them." Fraudulent officials like the keeper of Needwood forest who sold over eight hundred loads of wood in a single year in 1540 before being discovered, and those who lawfully possessed rights of common in the forests and Crown woods, profited more than the monarchy. It is no wonder that from 1607 till after the death of Charles I revenue commission after revenue commission advocated the sale of forest land, with its consequent reduction in staffing costs, rather than the exploitation of the Crown's resources of timber for building and wood for fuel, of which there was no general shortage except in the immediate vicinity of London and for which there was consequently no ready market.[1]

While Salisbury lived, he made every effort to preserve the Crown estate and to improve the royal income from it. By entails of July 1604 and May 1609, the most valuable of the Crown lands were assured against alienation; the entail of 1609 provided for the assurance of manors and lands in the Exchequer and duchy of Lancaster of the value of £50,089 and of £16,782 worth of fee farms and rents reserved. The surveys of 1608 were never completed, though those which were carried out showed clearly enough that by raising ancient rents to their true level the Crown could have increased its income, as Sir Julius Caesar, the chancellor of the Exchequer, calculated at the time, in the proportion of five to two. In the North and East Ridings of Yorkshire the surveyor reported improved valuations of £11,449 against ancient rents of £3,291; in Cumberland, Westmorland, and the West Riding, Crown tenants were found to be paying £2,206 for lands worth £9,294; and in the west country lands worth £7,500 were producing as little as £506. Under alert administration, fees and expenses on the Crown lands were reduced from £18,448 in 1606 to £9,329 in 1619. The size of the Crown debts in the 1600's and the extravagance of the Court rendered some sales unavoidable; hence the need for the second entail of 1609. But Dorset and Salisbury were able to restrict them very

[1] Richardson, *Chamber Administration*, pp. 261–74, and *Augmentations*, pp. 302–15; G. Hammersley, 'The Crown Woods and their Exploitation in the Sixteenth and Seventeenth Centuries', *Bull.* IHR, xxx, 1957, pp. 136–61.

largely to items which were relatively uneconomic from the Crown's point of view, to parsonages and tithes scattered in small parcels throughout the land and to mills removed from any large Crown holding.[1]

In 1610 a strenuous effort was made to exchange the king's feudal rights for an annual allowance from Parliament which would permit him to put his finances upon a sound basis—the 'Great Contract'. It was defeated by disagreement over the manner of levying the allowance and by Sir Julius Caesar's belief, which may well have been shared by Salisbury, that the sum of £200,000 which was offered was an insufficient recompense for the surrender of royal incomes of £115,000 —£44,000 from the court of Wards, £50,000 from the royal prerogative of purveyance, and £21,000 from assarts, defective titles, and information upon penal statutes.[2] Had abatements in expenditure taken place, had the policy of improving Crown rents systematically continued, and had sales of Crown land been halted, Caesar's argument would have been justified. In fact, the failure of the negotiations for the Great Contract and the death of Salisbury were the prelude to a disastrous period in which precisely the reverse occurred. The expenses of administration and the assignments for Household purposes from the Crown lands were alike increased, the improvement in Crown rents was not pursued, and sales on a large scale were resumed. In 1619 James I was receiving only £72,664 net from the Crown lands, excluding the revenues of the duchy of Cornwall, which were assigned to the prince of Wales, and those of the duchy of Lancaster, which did not normally exceed the £11,000 to £13,000 a year which they had yielded at the start of Elizabeth's reign. Lands of the value of £216,310 were conveyed to the city of London in 1625 in satisfaction of loans and by 1635 some £642,742 had been raised in ten years from Crown land sales. The average yield of the Crown lands, including the duchy of Cornwall, was only £86,000 between 1630 and 1635. Assignments had reduced the net income to the Crown from lands accountable in the Exchequer to as little as £22,980 in 1619; after 1628, it fell to less than £10,000.[3] In short, the Crown lands had ceased to be an important part of the royal income, where a century before the Crown had been the principal landowner in the country and might have been rendered independent of parliamentary sources of supply.

---

[1] Dietz, *op. cit.*, pp. 106, 116–18, 298, 299; BM Lansdowne MS 169, ff. 83, 85, 87, 91.

[2] BM Lansdowne MS 151, ff. 23 *sqq.*, 126 *sqq.*

[3] Dietz, *op. cit.*, pp. 223, 271, 296, 297, 300, 301; BM Harleian MS 3,796, ff. 35–6; BM Add. MS 11598.

## 5. The exploitation of wardships under the early Stuarts

The consequence was that the Crown extracted from the court of Wards what it could no longer hope to obtain from the Crown lands. Assignments from the revenues of the court of Wards multiplied in the 1620's and 1630's especially. In 1624 pensions were granted from its income to the duke of Buckingham, Sir Thomas Edmondes, and Sir Edward Villiers of £1,000, £750, and £500 respectively. In 1625 the dowager duchess of Lennox was given an annuity for three lives of £2,100, besides a cash payment of £3,350 that same year, and another of £1,000 in 1628. As much as £27,051 might be spent on pensions and gifts in a single year. A series of instructions to the masters of the court in the 1610's and 1620's produced a dramatic increase in the court's yield. This could not have taken place without the preparatory work of Burghley and Salisbury in the encouragement of private informers of concealments, in the production of the feodaries' surveys and other checks on the validity of the *inquisitions post mortem*, and in the raising of the rates for sales of wardships from the one or one and a half times the yearly value of the lands which had been customary in Elizabeth's time to three times the yearly value which prevailed by 1610. Where between 1617 and 1622 the net revenues of the court averaged just under £30,000 a year, in the last four normal working years of the court between 1638 and 1641 inclusive they were little short of £69,500. When these figures are examined more closely and an analysis made of the way in which the increase came about, a fascinating and significant fact emerges—namely, that the various elements of the increase are directly related to the sort of difficulties of administration and collection which beset the Crown in its land revenues. The largest increase was achieved in the simplest transaction, sales of wardships; here a thirty-one fold increase occurred between 1540 and 1640. Where the average sales in 1547-9 were £1,271 a year, in 1639-41 they were £39,819. The next largest increase was achieved from the relatively straightforward leasing of wards' properties, though, as with lands, profits were reduced by the allowances demanded by the collecting officials, in this case the feodaries, and by the problem of arrearages, which was partly solved by granting them as rewards under James and Charles. Here the increase over the century was seven-fold; 'issues', as the profits of leasing were termed, rose from an average of £5,420 in 1547-9 to £36,968 in 1639-41. By contrast, fines for liveries never attained a steady level and yielded surprisingly little more in 1639-41 than in 1547-9—£3,798 a year against £2,363.[1] Feodaries'

[1] HMC Cowper, I, p. 291; Bell, *op. cit.*, pp. 46-7, 51, 54, 57-62, Table A opposite p. 192; SP 14, 61.

surveys of liveries of full age tended to return lower values than those of liveries within age, and abuses arose from the over-continuances of liveries and from the high fees charged by the court's officers of those who sued livery. The subject could hope to share with the Crown in the spoils of a sale or lease of a wardship, but in a suit for livery the subject stood to lose and there were opportunities for the officers of the court to benefit themselves rather than the Crown.

The financial consequences of the exploitation of wardships were satisfactory enough under the early Stuarts, but the political price which was paid was too high. The court of Wards was increasingly unpopular; as early as Burghley's death in 1598 propositions had been made for its abolition, and the ruthless exactions of the court under Charles I helped to undermine the Crown's standing in the country. Feudalism was felt to be an anachronism and it would have been better if the Crown had accepted the Great Contract, for "bearing in mind how many of the Parliament party held lands in chief of the Crown, it is not unfair to include the court as an important subsidiary cause of the Civil War."[1]

Some at least of the sins which have been attributed in the past to the policies of sales and grants carried out in the reigns of Henry VIII and Edward VI must now be seen as the evils of administrative problems connected with the Crown lands which proved too great for the Crown to remedy sufficiently. It was not so much sales which rendered the Crown revenues from land so inadequate by 1603 as the failure of the Crown to secure its feudal dues and generally to adapt the administration of its lands to the changed circumstances brought about by a new demand for land and by a price revolution. No matter what aspect of revenue from land, whether direct or indirect, one examines closely, the same recurring themes arise—a conservatism of management, a rigidity of procedure, a baffling complexity of circumstance varying from one area to another, and a veritable army of officials to be paid. If Cromwell's policy of keeping the acquisitions from the dissolution of the monasteries as an endowment had been pursued, it seems likely that the Crown would never have extracted a proper return from its lands within the sixteenth century by reason of these overwhelming administrative difficulties. If, on the other hand, the composition for the feudal dues had been accepted by James I, if the improvements envisaged by Salisbury had been carried through on a Crown estate rationally consolidated into compact areas and shorn of uneconomic isolated holdings, then the Crown lands might have

[1] Bell, *op. cit.*, p. 149.

become, as Caesar called them in 1610, "the surest and best livelihood of the Crown,"[1] and the possibility of an English Civil War would have been decidedly reduced.

### B. NOBLEMEN, GENTLEMEN, AND YEOMEN

#### 1. *The historian's sources*

The basic difficulty which besets any discussion of lay landownership in the Tudor and early Stuart periods is the absence of any considerable body of systematic and objective evidence. This is true even of such prosaic records as accounts. The accounts of the largest of landowners were not designed to yield a balance of income and expenditure. Proceeds from entry fines and from the sales of lands and woods were commonly included with rents, for the good reason that clear distinctions between capital and income, and between recurring and non-recurring income, did not exist in the contemporary mind. The system of accountancy which was used in both estate and household accounts, 'charge and discharge', differed in no material respect from the methods employed in medieval times and was, as the earl of Northumberland's auditor reminded his master in 1606, "more material for matter of records, posterities, and royalties than for any present profit."[2] The 'charge' of an account, for instance, would include for years in succession 'arrearages' which had not been collected, merely to provide a record of them. On a large estate a number of receivers would be employed at any one time, just as in a large household perhaps as many as ten officers might account in any audit-period. Since there was never any sharp or rigid distinction between the responsibilities of either estate or household officers, and any one type of receipt or expense might be entered under three or four different heads, neither income nor expenditure may be calculated with any degree of accuracy without the examination of a long series of accounts. Recurring items, like 'rents resolute' on the leases of particular properties and formal fees accruing to the landlord for a position of state or to the estate officer for his duties, may fairly readily be traced from *valors* or accounts. Yields from estates which came in kind instead of cash, and perquisites of office and 'casualties' of all descriptions which were incidental or spasmodic (but nonetheless substantial), on the other hand, are likely to be concealed from the historian's view. Household accounts of all kinds, whether preliminary, diurnal records, or formal declarations made at the annual audit, which may be very useful in assessing a

[1] Dietz, *op. cit.*, p. 138.
[2] Syon House MS at Alnwick Castle, Q. I. 31.

landlord's pattern of expenditure, have proved especially ephemeral records; few families still possess, as the Percies do, virtually complete records of their ancestors' domestic expenses for the century before the Restoration.

The estate papers of many families, especially the lesser landowners, have been lost altogether, and, indeed, in some instances the accounts were never set down formally. Thomas Buttes of Riborough, Norfolk, for example, who had a part interest in a group of small manors on the borders of Essex and Suffolk, took the deliveries of cash from his bailiffs in person and kept such records as he needed in his notebook.[1] Among the manuscripts of larger landowners, some have been steadily dispersed over the centuries and others have lain for years, ill-sorted and little used, in repositories to which access has been difficult. One must look for the Cliffords' Westmorland estate documents at Appleby, for their Craven records at Leeds, for their Bolton Priory and Londesborough muniments at Chatsworth, and for other cognate papers at Althorp. The bulk of the Talbot estate papers for the sixteenth and early seventeenth centuries were taken from the duke of Norfolk's Arundel Castle collection and from his Sheffield estate office to the Sheffield City Library only as recently as 1959; other manuscripts likely to supplement our knowledge of the Talbot estates are still to be found scattered between the collections at the College of Arms, the British Museum, Lambeth Palace Library, Chatsworth, Longleat, and Leeds.

The records of land transactions and of the borrowing of 'ready money' are equally dispersed and incomplete, and demand equally cautious interpretation. The patent rolls, feet of fines, and close rolls, which together form a record of conveyances of land, are collectively incomplete and separately very inadequate. The variety of form of obligation for debt in the period is confusing and makes it exceedingly difficult to trace any man's borrowings completely. Bonds and bills obligatory, which were used extensively for small loans and current debts in the later sixteenth and early seventeenth centuries, were unrecorded in any court of law and consequently rarely survive. Recognizances and statutes, which were recorded obligations, were sometimes entered into for legal and not financial reasons, and present particular difficulties of interpretation. Many transactions, again, were done in the names of servants and not directly by the landowner.

Documents arising at death are no more satisfactory; in any case many have disappeared. Wills, which Gervase Holles held to be "the noblest sort of records,"[2] were proved in a great variety of courts in

[1] Alan Simpson, *The Wealth of the Gentry, 1540–1640*, 1961, p. 9.
[2] Gervase Holles, *Memorials of the Holles Family* ed. A. C. Wood, Camden Soc., 3rd Ser., LV, 1937, p. 20.

the period—prerogative courts, archdeacons' courts, peculiar courts, manorial courts, and local courts like London's court of Hustings—and even now are dispersed among a great variety of repositories, public and private, national and local. The inventories of all the deceased's "goods, chattels, wares, merchandizes, as well moveable as not moveable" which were required by the statute of 21 Henry VIII c. 5 were appraised by friends, neighbours, or dependants and related only to personal estate; they did not, for instance, include lands in entail, but they did include leases, though often the mention of deeds was laconic. The court of Wards was constantly seeking to avoid frauds in the *inquisitions post mortem* required when lands were held *in capite*, but never approached success and this type of record notoriously undervalued lands, besides presenting the difficulty of being made separately for holdings in each county. The feodaries' surveys, which frequently set down the true or 'improved' value of the properties, have not survived in all instances and did not become generally reliable in their valuations until towards the end of Burghley's long mastership of the court of Wards. Taxation records are no more reliable or better preserved. At first sight, the papers of the Committee for Compounding, established to deal with the royalist delinquents in the Civil War, offer extensive and reliable data on the estates of one section of the landed class in the late 1640's, for the committee was not likely to be biased in favour of the landowners and any significant concealment was subject to heavy penalties. But many prominent royalists were not allowed to compound and the papers are incomplete. Again, from 1523 peers were assessed as a class for their subsidies by special commissioners, where the rest of the nation was assessed regionally. Quite apart from the fact that not all the assessments have survived, their evidence of peers' incomes, though reasonably accurate for the reign of Henry VIII, is for most of the reign of Elizabeth very unsatisfactory. Sir Walter Raleigh commented in 1601 on subsidy assessments in general: "our estates, that be thirty or forty pound in the Queen's books, are not the hundred part of our wealth."[1]

It is little wonder that, in the face of these and similar obstacles, historians have turned to the literary evidence of the age in attempts to gain an understanding of the general trends in landowning. These sources are, if anything, more misleading still, for they are essentially

[1] H. E. Bell, *An Introduction to the History and Records of the Court of Wards*, 1953, pp. 53–5; W. G. Hoskins, 'The Estates of the Caroline Gentry', in W. G. Hoskins and H. P. R. Finberg, *Devonshire Studies*, 1952, pp. 334–6; E. L. Klotz and G. Davies, 'The Wealth of Royalist Peers and Baronets during the Puritan Revolution', EHR, LVIII, 1943, p. 217; H. Miller, 'Subsidy Assessments of the Peerage in the Sixteenth Century', *Bull.* IHR, XXVIII, 1955, pp. 16, 23, 30–1.

subjective accounts. The lack of objectivity in Philip Stubbes's *Anatomy of the Abuses in England, A.D. 1583* is obvious enough in such a passage as this:

"...when a gentleman or other has a farm or a lease to let, first he causes a surveyor to make strict enquiry what may be made of it, and how much it is worth by year, which being found out and signified to the owner, he racks it, strains it, and as it were sets it on the tenterhooks, stretching every vein and joint thereof, as no poor man can live of it... though he pay never so great an annual rent, yet must he pay at his entrance a fine, or (as they call it) an income of ten pound, twenty pound, forty pound, threescore pound, a hundred pound, whereas in truth the purchase thereof is hardly worth so much...The devil himself, I think, will not be so strait-laced nor yet so niggardly to his servants, as they are to their poor tenants."[1]

But both Professors Tawney and Trevor-Roper, as Professor Hexter has pointed out, have quoted Sir Edward Montague's claim of penury in Northamptonshire in the time of James I—"most of the ancientest gentlemen's houses in the county are either divided, diminished, or decayed" and "there has been within these three or four years many good lordships sold within the county, and not a gentleman of the county has bought any, but strangers, and they no inhabitants"— without apparently realizing that this was but one of the many examples of special pleading to be found in the official correspondence of the age. For Sir Edward had a considerable estate in the county and was writing to the lord lieutenant in 1614, when the government was pressing the landed proprietors throughout the country for a benevolence.[2] When Thomas Wilson made his famous estimates of the incomes of the various social classes in his *The State of England Anno Domini 1600*, he was able to claim unusually good sources for his material:

"I have seen divers books which have been collected by secretaries and counsellors of estate which did exactly show the several revenues of every nobleman, knights and gentlemen through the realm, and curiously collected by an uncle of mine which not long since was principal secretary to the Queen."[3]

Wilson was the nephew of Dr Thomas Wilson, secretary of state 1577 to 1581. A statistical approach, however, was basically alien to the

[1] *Phillip Stubbes's Anatomy of the Abuses in England, A.D. 1583*, ed. F. J. Furnivall, 1882, part II, p. 29.
[2] J. H. Hexter, 'Storm over the Gentry', *Encounter*, X, 1958, p. 23.
[3] 'The State of England Anno Domini 1600 by Thomas Wilson', ed. F. J. Fisher, *Camden Soc. Miscellany*, XVI, 1936, p. 21.

thinking of the era, even at governmental level, and Wilson's estimates must be used with as much caution as Stubbes's polemics.

It is true, then, of lay landownership, as Professor Simpson has written, that "our present state of knowledge is one of mitigated ignorance."[1] It is also true, as Klotz and Davies commented of the parliamentary compositions made by royalists between 1643 and 1660, that "in historical studies the absence of full data is no reason why what survives should not be used."[2] The dust has settled sufficiently on the controversy over the 'rise of the gentry', and the interest which that controversy aroused has stimulated the production of such a number of detailed studies of the fortunes of individual landowners and of the state of landowning in particular areas at this time, for it to be possible to essay an analysis of the principal factors affecting lay landownership in Tudor and early Stuart times.

## 2. *The peerage: A declining class?*

Professor Tawney attempted to draw a clear distinction between the trends in the fortunes of the peerage and in those of the gentry in this period.[3] He argued that the peerage differed from the gentry both quantitatively and qualitatively in that, first, the proportion of land held by the peers was tending to decline where the landholding of the gentry was tending to increase and, secondly, the peers were failing as a class to extract adequate incomes from their estates. A conservatism of management kept peers' incomes down, Tawney held, at a time when prices were rising and the expenditure associated with their status, such as hospitality and the building of great houses, was notably increasing. The evidence upon which he based his thesis—a combination of literary references and statistical analysis based upon the counting of manors held by various types of landowner at particular dates—has been subjected to several reappraisals. While it now seems clear that the total amount of land held by the peers did not rise in proportion to their increased numbers when new creations doubled the size of the class in the early seventeenth century, the consensus of recent opinion has placed less emphasis than did Tawney upon the division between the old and the new families among the peers, and between the peerage and the gentry, and more emphasis upon the factors which affected all landowners alike.

For the peerage did not constitute a sharply defined class clearly

---

[1] Simpson, *op. cit.*, p. 21.
[2] Klotz and Davies, *op. cit.*, p. 217.
[3] R. H. Tawney, 'The Rise of the Gentry', EcHR, XI, 1941, pp. 1–38, and 'The Rise of the Gentry: a Postscript', EcHR, 2nd Ser., VII, 1954, pp. 91–7.

separable from the gentry under the Tudors and early Stuarts. The English peerage is not, in the strictest sense, a nobility; an English peer's position, though admittedly normally hereditary, is personal and is not shared with the cadets of his family. The composition of the English peerage in 1640 was radically different from its composition in 1485 and, with a few exceptions, the new creations came from the gentry families. One half of the medieval noble families of England had been extinguished in the male line by the end of Henry VIII's reign, partly by attainders which removed in Pollard's phrase, "the tallest heads," but natural failure of new as well as old families was numerically the more important cause.[1] Elizabeth was sparing in her creations, but so was Charles I after 1629 and the Elizabethan peerage was scarcely less new than the Stuart; of the sixty-two peers in 1560, thirty-seven held titles which had been conferred since 1509. James I raised forty-six commoners to the peerage and Charles I as many as twenty-six in the first four years of his reign, but the majority of the newly ennobled came from the same sort of families as had been given titles under Henry VIII. It is, therefore, wrong to think of the early Stuart peerage as different in kind from the Tudor peerage.

Mr Lawrence Stone has analysed the evidence of land transfers in twelve and a half counties recorded by the Victoria County Histories for the period 1558–1642. The area covered happens to be predominantly the Home Counties and therefore normally (with the exception of the old-enclosed county of Kent) most subject to the pressure of the London land market; properties which remained in continuous ownership throughout the period may in some instances have been omitted; and some transfers from the Crown, which tend to be recorded as gifts, may in point of fact have been purchases. Allowing for all these factors, each of which would weight the figures against the peerage, Mr Stone's analysis supports other calculations, such as those made by Professor Tawney, which lead to the conclusion that the landholding of peers was tending to decline at this time. Between 1558 and 1602, the net sales of manors by peers created before 1602 amounted to 28 per cent of the manors owned, inherited, and granted in the area within the reign of Elizabeth. Between 1603 and 1642, the net sales by the Elizabethan peerage amounted to 16 per cent of those owned, inherited, and granted within the reigns of James I and Charles I. Though the peerage had doubled in numbers, the class as a whole held slightly fewer manors in the area in 1642 than it had in 1558. Nor is there much evidence to support the hypothesis that many of these sales may

---

[1] A. F. Pollard, *The Reign of Henry VII from Contemporary Sources*, 3 vols., 1913–14, III, p. 319; H. Miller, 'The Early Tudor Peerage' (thesis summary), *Bull.* IHR, XXIV, 1951, pp. 88–91.

have been the result of a deliberate policy to consolidate estates in compact, easily-managed holdings.[1]

Some individual case-studies of the fortunes of peers in the period have been made which rest upon a sufficient corpus of documentary material to remove the conclusions drawn from the realm of speculation or debate. The third earl of Cumberland could be said to epitomize the decadent peer of the Elizabethan age who drew his income from inherited lands and spent it on the conspicuous waste which has been held to be characteristic of the class. He was the heir to one of the richest land inheritances of the reign. The Cliffords had acquired their considerable northern estates, centred round their principal houses at Appleby, Brougham, Brough, and Pendragon in Westmorland, Skipton in Craven, and Londesborough in the East Riding of Yorkshire, partly by exchange and purchase, but chiefly by Crown grants and by a series of well-chosen marriages with heiresses. Henry the tenth Lord Clifford, the 'Shepherd Lord', had been restored in blood and lands by Henry VII after the family troubles in the Wars of the Roses, and by careful management had grown rich in "money, chattles, and goods, and great stocks of ground."[2] His son was created earl of Cumberland in 1525. Both the first and second earls had periods of extravagant living at Court, but followed them by periods of prudence and prosperity from royal favour. Two particularly valuable acquisitions made in Henry VIII's reign were the Percy fee in Craven, which the first earl's second wife brought to the family, and the grant of Bolton and other monastic properties in 1542. The third earl's net income from land was returned to the Crown (and therefore probably underestimated) as £1,821 a year; the death of a childless uncle in 1578 added further to his estate.

At first, Cumberland continued the policy of his father and grandfather of selling minor and widely dispersed parts of the estate and consolidating the lands in compact groups. From the early 1580's, however, he attended Court regularly and lived extravagantly, with the result that he began to sell land for quick returns and by 1585 was in debt for £5,000. His famous privateering ventures seem to have been motivated in the first instance by this indebtedness, but the profits of some of his early voyages did no more than pay the debts of others and a more general lack of success with voyages after 1594 meant that his debts rose to over £20,000. He was obliged to look to his lands to

---

[1] L. Stone, 'The Elizabethan Aristocracy—a Restatement', EcHR, 2nd Ser., IV, 1952, pp. 309–11. For the wealth of the gentry in Kent, see Alan Everitt, *Kent and its Gentry 1640–60*, London Ph.D. thesis, 1957, pp. 494–8.

[2] 'A Summary of the Lives of the Cliffords' by Lady Anne Clifford, in *Clifford Letters of the Sixteenth Century*, ed. A. G. Dickens, Surtees Soc., CLXXII, 1962, p. 135.

overcome his financial embarrassment, first mortgaging some to his tenants but subsequently embarking upon more desperate measures. Individual manors, capital messuages, demesnes, and woods, especially on his Craven estates, were exploited by a variety of methods—outright sales, fee farm grants, long leases with nominal or full rents reserved—and the income of his successors imperilled. He died in 1605 in debt for £80,000. Even so, his heirs might have survived successfully, for the third earl left, as well as debts and lands impoverished of their full rents, the legacy of a cloth licence which for a quarter of a century after 1601 made a substantial contribution to the family income, and the Clifford estates were producing as much as £4,500 a year in 1646. However, a disputed inheritance, the weak estate policy of the fourth earl, an inability to compete for office under Charles I because of the reduced income, and a failure in the male line, added to the depredations of the third earl, ultimately made recovery impossible, and a great estate disintegrated.[1]

The older peerage families did not as a class show any lack of energetic management of their lands. The sixth earl of Shrewsbury, the guardian to Mary, Queen of Scots, for instance, pursued an active, if not very profitable, exploitation of the mineral resources of his vast midland estates, working coalmines, establishing smelting works, founding ironworks, promoting the nascent steel industry, and making glass, as well as engaging in shipping ventures, farming many of his demesnes, and taking an active interest in the collection of his general estate revenues. During the widowhood of his equally business-like second wife, 'Bess of Hardwick', his son enjoyed a net revenue from land of £5,396 in 1592, which by a particularly ruthless approach he was able to improve in the course of the next few years.[2]

The story of the Percies' estate management in the Tudor and early Stuart periods is as fully documented as that of any family and shows the ability of a large medieval collection of lands, scattered from Sussex in the south to Northumberland in the north, to survive economic, political, and personal adversities. The heads of the family in the first four decades of the sixteenth century, the 'Magnificent' fifth earl and the 'Unthrifty' sixth earl, were not improving landlords, but there is no evidence of lax estate administration. The rise in the receipts from rents and farms on the Percy lands between 1471 and 1537 was slight over the estates as a whole. Yet individual properties

---

[1] R. T. Spence, *The Cliffords, earls of Cumberland, 1579–1646*, London Ph.D. thesis, 1959, *passim*.

[2] L. Stone, 'The Nobility in Business, 1540–1640', in *The Entrepreneur*, 1957, pp. 14–16; 'A Breviary of the Rents of the Earl of Shrewsbury, 1592', Sheffield Corn Exchange MSS of the duke of Norfolk, A.P./C, now in Sheffield City Library.

showed marked increases, and the appointment of commissioners to travel the estates from 1474, to supervise their management and grant leases, is a clear indication of an active policy. The fifth earl paid attention to entry fines and extended to the estates in Northumberland and Yorkshire the custom of Cumberland, which stressed their significance, but the rates were no more than one or one and a half year's rents, so that there was no dramatic addition to the family revenues. The net annual value of rents and farms on the Percy estates was approximately £3,600 in the early 1520's, to which should be added perhaps £300 as the average receipt from entry fines. Contrary to popular tradition, the sixth earl inherited in 1527 an estate which was free of serious encumbrance. For psychological reasons, and not from any necessity, he elected in the course of the next decade to alienate his inheritance, first large portions of lands to favourites and then the remainder to the Crown, which received it the more willingly because it was hostile to the power of great feudal nobles, especially in the north.[1]

The effect of this drastic, eccentric step was, in the event, mitigated by the attainder of the sixth earl's heir for his part in the Pilgrimage of Grace, since the family titles and most of the lands were restored after an interval of twenty years. The seventh earl was himself executed for rebellion in 1572, but the letters patent of 1557 had provided for a remainder to his brother. The lands were consequently unimpaired by this attainder and, more than that, the entail of the vast majority of the Percy estates by the 1557 restoration successfully prevented their dispersal in the later 1580's. At that time, the *abandon* of the young ninth earl incurred heavy debts which, as he has himself attested, might have been met by ill-considered land-sales, had it not been for the entail. As it was, heavy wood-sales, the raising of some fines on the renewal of leases for twenty-one years at low rents, a failure to pay some debts promptly, and the raising of a little borrowed money sufficed. In the mid-1590's the earl turned to a remarkably sound administration of his estates which so improved the income from them in the course of the next fifty years that, aided by the fact that his mother was co-heiress of the last Lord Latimer and by his own marriage to a widow, he became one of the wealthiest landowners in England. The adoption of scientific surveying of his estates, the judicious purchase of lands and leases to consolidate his inherited holdings in some eight counties of England and Wales, the granting of leases on carefully calculated principles, large-scale enclosure on his northern lands, and, above all, unremitting personal supervision based on serious study, all these measures allowed

[1] J. M. W. Bean, *The Estates of the Percy Family 1416–1537*, 1958, pp. 43–68, 135–57.

the ninth earl to leave his son a vastly improved estate. This was achieved without his holding for any length of time any significant office of state, and despite a period of personal disgrace which involved his imprisonment for sixteen years, as well as payment to the Crown of some eleven thousand pounds. It was not achieved without heavy borrowing, but heavy borrowing, we have come to understand, may be an indication of economic health rather than of impending bankruptcy.[1] It certainly was a case of economic health with the ninth earl of Northumberland, for his debts never exceeded twice his landed income and for every period when his borrowing increased markedly it is possible to find an extraordinary expense—a military expedition, house-building, the payment of his fine in Star Chamber, exceptional purchases of land, or the provision of a dowry for a daughter. The earl told Salisbury in 1612 that "my wife, children and myself must starve," as a result of his fine, but whereas in 1582 the net annual income from Percy lands had been £3,602, it was as much as £12,978 by 1636, after the second renewal of the leases which he had misguidedly granted in the early 1590's had taken effect. A policy of modernization and reorganization under an alert landowner had overcome political adversity, the peculations of officers, the resistance of tenants to feudal claims and to rationalized rents, reductions in the income from large parts of the estates in years of bad harvest such as the early 1620's, and increases in household expenditure in years when the earl was sowing wild oats or indulging the taste of his class for glorifying its residences.[2]

## 3. *The profits of office, profession, and trade*

If we can no longer accept unreservedly Professor Tawney's thesis that the gentry rose at the expense of the peerage between 1540 and 1640, or that the Jacobean peerage differed markedly in its estate management from the Elizabethan, there is no gainsaying the rise within the landed class of certain families, or that many of these families, especially in the early Stuart period, owed their improved status to the profits of office, profession, or trade rather than to the yields of their lands. Professor Trevor-Roper found that only one of seventy Elizabethan and Jacobean great houses was founded on a largely landed fortune; all

---

[1] H. R. Trevor-Roper, 'The Elizabethan Aristocracy: an Anatomy Anatomized', EcHR, 2nd Ser., III, 1951, p. 297.

[2] G. R. Batho, 'The Finances of an Elizabethan Nobleman', EcHR, 2nd Ser., IX, 1957, pp. 433–50, and *The Household Papers of Henry Percy, ninth Earl of Northumberland*, Camden Soc., 3rd Ser., XCIII, 1962, pp. xlvii–lvi; M. E. James, *Estate Accounts of the Earls of Northumberland 1562–1637*, Surtees Soc., CLXIII, 1955, pp. xxxv–lv; E. B. DeFonblanque, *Annals of the House of Percy*, 2 vols., 1887, II, p. 314.

the rest were built with fortunes derived mostly from important offices of state, professional careers, or success in business. Again, the evidence of *inquisitions post mortem*, of building, of the subsidy assessments of 1546, 1560, 1572, and 1626, and of contributions to the Armada loans has been analysed for seventy-eight gentry families in Elizabethan Sussex. Among the twenty-five families which on this evidence appear to have been flourishing, four were supported chiefly by land, but the majority had heads who were ironmasters, managers of forges and furnaces, merchants, or lawyers.[1]

Sir William Petre, one of the commissioners for the surrender of monasteries, a master in chancery, and principal secretary of state from 1544 to 1557, is an interesting example of a man who rose to wealth in the middle of the sixteenth century largely on the profits, direct and indirect, of his profession and of office. He came of a family which ranked between the yeomanry and gentry. He had, therefore, no considerable inheritance. His first wife was the youngest daughter of an Essex squire, his second a widow whose father was a London alderman and merchant; this second marriage in 1542 brought him lands which were worth £284 a year at the time. He made no extensive gains from the dissolution of the monasteries, for he paid in cash to the Crown or to lay vendors market prices totalling £2,946 for the church lands of an annual value of £180 which he bought, and his single gift from the Crown was the manor of South Brent, Devon. His salaries and fees, even when swollen for two years by a pension from King Philip, never exceeded £871 a year, and there is no evidence of his receiving any substantial gifts or bribes. Yet he was able to spend some £22,000 on land purchases between 1537 and 1571 without incurring debt, and at the end of his life he owned over twenty thousand acres in his native west country and nearly as much again in the county of his adoption, Essex. What Petre did, he did slowly and methodically, not by any dramatic strokes of fortune. Office had furnished him with a satisfactory, if relatively small, income, and he had used the knowledge of the property market which office had given him to invest that income to advantage in acquiring, almost manor by manor, two compact estates. His estate policy was conservative; his sole important innovation was the introduction on his Essex estates of rents in kind to be paid by leaseholders above their money rents, thus facilitating the provisioning of his London and Ingatestone households. A lawyer, he kept administrative costs to the minimum and used the "court roll, the custumal, and the estreat roll rather than the rack-rent" to improve

[1] H. R. Trevor-Roper, *The Gentry 1540–1640*, 1953, pp. 16, 17; J. E. Mousley, 'The Fortunes of Some Gentry Families of Elizabethan Sussex', EcHR, 2nd Ser., XI, 1959, pp. 476–7, 481.

his income. He granted no beneficial leases and made no attempt to obtain from his tenants rents which represented the market values of his properties but in 1570 he was receiving a net income from his estates of £2,274.[1]

There are remarkable parallels to Petre's career in that of Sir Nicholas Bacon, solicitor to the court of Augmentations from 1536, attorney in the court of Wards from 1545, and lord keeper to Queen Elizabeth from 1558. Like Petre, he came of a yeoman family. He married the daughter of a mercer first and the sister-in-law of Burghley second. He invested heavily in former monastic lands, mostly in Suffolk, but also in London, Norfolk, Hertfordshire, and Dorset, and bought at market prices. His salaries and fees were larger than Petre's naturally, as were the expenses of his position, but even as lord keeper they amounted to only £960 a year, besides an annuity from the Queen of £100. He acquired twenty-one wardships but seems to have made no appreciable profit from them and some may have been taken out of friendship to the families involved. Yet he was able to invest about £500 a year in land in the two decades after his appointment to the court of Augmentations, and about £1,150 a year during his lord keepership, without incurring debt. His estate policy, like Petre's, was conservative; its main features were thorough surveys of his estates, the consolidation of his properties by purchase as the occasion offered, the provision of a stock of sheep or cattle where appropriate, an interest in rents in kind, and a restrained pressure for higher entry fines and for improved yields from woods. In these ways his income from land rose from under £1,000 in 1559 to nearly £2,500 in 1575—and the increase was due more to purchase than to improvement.[2]

The survival of the receiver-general's accounts for Robert Cecil, first earl of Salisbury, between 1608 and 1612 has enabled Mr Stone to calculate with some degree of precision the profits from office of a great Jacobean statesman. It is clear that these were of great proportions, even if one singles out only the three main sources of profit from his offices. The fees of his most important office, the lord treasurership, were no more than £400 a year, but the sales of offices in his gift and other more dubious receipts added perhaps as much as £4,000 a year to his income. The fees of the mastership of the court of Wards were of the order of £480 a year, but private sales of wardships yielded about £2,100 a year more. The farm of the silk customs, for which he

---

[1] F. G. Emmison, *Tudor Secretary*, 1961, especially pp. 185–6, 271–6; W. R. Emerson, *The Economic Development of the Estates of the Petre Family in Essex in the Sixteenth and Seventeenth Centuries*, Oxford D.Phil. thesis, 1951, pp. 53, 98, 108–9, 149, 160.

[2] Simpson, *op. cit.*, pp. 28–89.

secured leases from Elizabeth in 1601 and from James in 1604 and 1610, were sublet to farmers, producing £1,333 a year in the later 1600's and as much as £7,000 after 1610. His father had settled on Salisbury his estate at Theobalds and most of his lands in Hertfordshire and the Home Counties, properties which produced an annual income of £1,700. From his political rewards and from his successful ventures in privateering and in the acquisition of a monopoly for the manufacture of starch, he was able in the course of fourteen years from his father's death to acquire one of the largest estates in England; his average receipts from land in the last four years of his life were about £7,000 a year. Salisbury's expenses were high—the maintenance of his large household cost an average of £8,500 a year at this time and he was spending as much as £13,500 a year on building—and by July 1611 his debts were no less than £53,000, but these were shortly reduced by land-sales and his successors inherited estates which have formed the nucleus of a great family's fortune.[1]

Salisbury profited from office, sometimes by means which were less than scrupulous, but he served the country well and retained some principles of conduct. Sir Arthur Ingram, by contrast, founded a landed family in the early Stuart period by ruthless exploitation of opportunities which came his way through the patronage of a succession of James I's ministers, and his outlook has been compared by his biographer with that of the dustman in Shaw's *Pygmalion*. He inherited his father's London business as a tallowchandler, but he would never have made a fortune with the limited capital placed at his disposal by that business. In Salisbury's time he established a position for himself in the customs service. He was a controller of the port of London from 1603 to 1613 at a salary of £200 a year, he was collector of the new impositions paid by alien merchants from 1608 on a commission and expenses basis, and he assisted Salisbury with his negotiations for the leasing and subletting of the silk farm in 1604, for which he was rewarded with annuities of £217 out of the Exchequer. His major profits, however, came from the holding of large cash balances for considerable periods from his customs positions, and from his activities as a middleman who brought together the courtiers who had grants and the businessmen who had the capital which was needed to exploit them. He organized syndicate after syndicate, to dispose of the cargo of captured ships, to sell Crown lands, to develop a monopoly of starch-making, and to establish the alum industry in England. After Salisbury's death he found new patrons, first in the Howard family whose right to license taverns and wine shops he helped to exploit,

[1] L. Stone, 'The Fruits of Office', in *Essays in the Economic and Social History of Tudor and Stuart England*, ed. F. J. Fisher, 1961, pp. 89–116.

then in Lionel Cranfield, earl of Middlesex, under whom he formed a syndicate to raise the rates over the renewal of the great customs farm in 1621, and finally, until they had a bitter quarrel, in Thomas Wentworth, earl of Strafford, for whom he secured the farm of recusancy fines in the north of England. Exactly what his profits were, it is impossible to assess in most instances. But they were sufficient for him to be able to purchase the secretaryship of the council of the North in 1613 and for him to found a landed family. At first he bought lands from the Crown or from private individuals which he improved and then sold again. After 1622 he deliberately consolidated his estates in Yorkshire. He already had one large house in the city of York and another at Sheriff Hutton in the forest of Galtres, ten miles away, as well as some lands in the county. In 1622 he acquired the estate of Temple Newsam, outside Leeds, for £12,000 and exchanged large estates in Warwickshire with Cranfield for even larger in Yorkshire. With other acquisitions, these purchases and exchanges meant that in the 1630's Ingram had a landed income of eight or nine thousand pounds. The parvenu had arrived among the landed class.[1]

The importance of office-holding and of political influence in raising some families in the social hierarchy must not, however, be exaggerated. While large incomes were enjoyed by the fortunate few, the majority of household and central government posts were poorly paid and did not permit of large gains apart from the official fees, even in Stuart times. Of 240 office-holders in the period 1625-42 whose finances have been examined, only forty acquired landed property worth more than £1,000 a year or increased their landed income by that amount. If the rise of some families can be directly related to office-holding, as was the case with the Egertons, earls of Bridgwater, and with the Fanshawes and the Osbornes of the upper Exchequer, the rise of other families is to be attributed at least as much to the good management of lands acquired as to the fruits of office, as was the case with the Brownlows of Belton and the Henleys of Hampshire and Somerset. Among both big men and small, office could involve debts which spelt disaster to their families. Sir Thomas Shirley, treasurer at war to the earl of Leicester's expedition to the Netherlands, left debts which the sale of old family property did not suffice to meet and ruined his family. George Goring, receiver-general in the court of Wards, died in debt to the Crown for nearly twenty thousand pounds and much of the family income was appropriated to the Crown throughout his son's lifetime. Sir Christopher Hatton, receiver of tenths and first fruits and lord chancellor to Queen Elizabeth, left debts to the Crown of approximately £42,000; his heirs were obliged to dispose of his personal

[1] A. F. Upton, *Sir Arthur Ingram*, 1961, especially pp. 1-22, 43-52, 148-71, 192.

property and to convey to the Crown his hereditary manor of Holdenby.[1]

Strafford provides a fascinating instance of the perils of office. He had a personal fortune; his grandfather had married the heiress of the Gascoignes, his father left him a landed income of £4,000 a year, and he married the daughter of the earl of Clare, one of the newly-risen gentry. He held high office which brought him opportunities for corresponding gain. He was president of the council of the North from 1629; he was able to use large cash balances in his hands from the collection of the knighthood fines in 1630-1 and from his receivership of recusants' rents in the north from 1629; he enjoyed the lease of the alum farm from 1638 with a probable income of £2,500 a year; and he was lord deputy of Ireland from 1632 until his fall from power, a position which brought him incidentally the farm of the Irish customs. Both in England and in Ireland he was able to invest heavily in lands. By 1639, apart from his salaries and the farm of Irish tobacco which he had acquired for himself in 1637, his income amounted to £22,800 a year. He was also heavily in debt. Had political trouble not intervened, he would have been able to eliminate his debt easily, but as it was he died owing £107,000. His son sold nearly half of the English lands and the family might have been ruined for ever if they had not retained the Irish lands which, though worthless in the 1640's and 1650's, came to be the salvation of the family fortunes.[2]

## 4. *The gentry and the enduring qualities of land*

That land could be a successful basis for the rise of a family in the sixteenth century is proved by the remarkable story of the Spencers of Althorp. Sir John Spencer the first came from a family of Warwickshire graziers. At first he rented his pastures, but from 1506 he was sufficiently affluent to buy carefully selected sheepwalks in compact groups on the borders of Warwickshire and Northamptonshire, which he stocked with animals largely of his own breeding. His successors added to both lands and flock. From at least the 1570's to the late 1620's the Spencers had a flock of 14,000 head or so; moreover, they dealt direct with the powerful London market and so were assured of ready sales. Their prosperity allowed them to make advantageous

---

[1] G. E. Aylmer, *The King's Servants*, 1961, pp. 264, 314, 331-3; E. Hopkins, *The Bridgewater Estates in North Shropshire in the first half of the Seventeenth Century*, London M.A. thesis, 1956, pp. 1-10, 221-2; Mousley, *op. cit.*, p. 478; E. St J. Brooks, *Sir Christopher Hatton*, 1946, pp. 360-1.

[2] J. P. Cooper, 'The Fortune of Thomas Wentworth, Earl of Strafford', EcHR, 2nd Ser., XI, 1958, pp. 227-48.

marriages from the first. Sir John's son, Sir William, allied the family with one of the oldest and wealthiest Northamptonshire gentry families, the Knightleys; Sir John the second married the daughter of the city of London merchant, Sir Thomas Kitson; Sir John the third, the heiress of the prosperous lawyer, Sir Robert Catlin; William, the second Baron Spencer, the eldest daughter of the earl of Southampton. Though they came to match with some of the great families in the land, the Spencers did not adopt aristocratic expenses. They built no large house in this period, they lived simply but well, and they refused the earldom which was offered them in 1618 for £10,000. By the early seventeenth century they came to have an annual income of between £6,500 and £8,000, of which perhaps £4,000 was derived from their flock and the rest from their investments in lands which they were leasing out.[1]

The Spencers have been held to be a great exception, and it must be said that they enjoyed great advantages in the siting of their lands, in the size of their transactions, and in the consistent efficiency of their management over several generations. Sheep-farming did not constitute a short cut to wealth in the period, but it is clear that it was usually profitable in the long run for any landowner who had some capital available to counteract the temporary depressions in returns which disease and variations of demand were liable to bring in the conditions of the age. The labour costs were particularly light and profits rose, at first steeply and then slightly. It has been calculated for East Anglia that the owner of a thousand sheep (in long hundreds) could confidently expect a profit of forty pounds a year by the late 1540's, perhaps twice as much as he would have received in the 1520's. This figure must be trebled for the late 1580's; by the 1630's it would have been of the order of £140.[2]

There is no reason to believe that it was only sheep-farmers who prospered among those landowners of the period whose income was derived primarily from land. All landowners from the 1540's on had relatively fixed expenses and increasing selling prices. Wages, especially of unskilled labour, rose less than prices from the second decade of the sixteenth century; this remained true despite the gradual, though irregular, rise of wages which occurred from the 1620's on. Food prices rose almost continuously, and in some decades dramatically, from 1500 to 1640. By 1550 they were at least double the level in 1500, by 1590 they were almost quadrupled, the 'great dearth' of 1594–7

---

[1] M. E. Finch, *The Wealth of Five Northamptonshire Families 1540–1640*, Northants. Rec. Soc., XIX, 1956, pp. 38–65.

[2] J. H. Round, *Studies in Peerage and Family History*, 1901, p. 281; Trevor-Roper, *op. cit.*, p. 16; Simpson, *op. cit.*, p. 194.

brought a sharp increase which was not quite maintained in the 1600's, but by 1640 food prices were almost six times what they had been in 1500. Nor is it true that rents lagged behind prices and as a consequence impoverished the landlords of Tudor and early Stuart England. In general terms, rents rose considerably, especially on new takings, before and especially around the middle of the sixteenth century; in the sixties, seventies, and eighties rents tended not to rise appreciably in most areas, though on the Bures estate in East Anglia they doubled in the period; from 1590 to the early 1620's rents rose considerably, while the bad harvests of the 1620's led to a general decline. A building labourer's daily wage rate in 1650 was less than twice what it had been a century before; food prices were more than double; rents were on many holdings at least twice what they had been in 1550.[1]

There were, of course, variations between areas and between different tenures. The rent of some meadowland in Derbyshire rose fourfold between 1543 and 1584, that of some arable even more. In East Anglia the rent of arable land rose six times between 1590 and 1650, but the rent of pasture and meadow rose only two or three times. The rent yield of some manors in Wiltshire increased as much as ten times between 1510 and 1650. The prosperity of the Kentish gentry was legendary, because of the proximity of their lands to the London food market; as Lambarde commented in the early 1570's, this was "not so much by the quantity of their possessions, or by the fertility of their soil, as by the benefit of the situation of the country itself." The poverty of Northumberland was readily exaggerated by its inhabitants when the occasion served, but it was nonetheless real. Dean James of Durham held in 1597 that five hundred ploughs had decayed in the previous half century within the bishopric and "want and waste have crept into Northumberland, Westmorland, and Cumberland." The ninth earl of Northumberland, again, wrote to his receiver in 1623, "I am made the more sensible of the general poverty of those parts by the poor reckonings which I in my particular have received of those demesnes which rest in my hands, and the ill proof of the stock upon them."[2]

In Northumberland, as in the other counties in the far north, such as Cumberland and Westmorland, tenants could offer an especially strong resistance to the attempts of the landlord in this period to raise

[1] Y. S. Brenner, 'The Inflation of Prices in Early Sixteenth Century England', EcHR, 2nd Ser., XIV, 1961, pp. 227, 231, 237, and 'The Inflation of Prices in England, 1551–1650', EcHR, 2nd Ser., XV, 1962, pp. 266–8, 270–3, 279–84; E. Kerridge, 'The Movement of Rent, 1540–1640', EcHR, 2nd Ser., VI, 1953, pp. 16–34; Simpson, op. cit., pp. 197–202.

[2] Kerridge, op. cit., p. 17; P. Laslett, 'The Gentry of Kent in 1640', Camb. Hist. J., IX, 1948, p. 153; SP 12, 362, 10 and 11; Syon House MS at Alnwick Castle, P. I. 3 n.

his income. For many held their lands by a customary tenant-right which varied from manor to manor but which was, in effect, "tantamount to freehold." The security which was given to customary tenants by the growth of copyhold tenure throughout the country was such that Coke declared in the reign of James I that, provided the copyholder had performed the duties and services required of him, "then let the lord frown, the copyholder cares not, knowing himself safe." Few landowners anywhere, indeed, could escape the presence on their manors of a bewildering complexity of tenures. John Rowe had been the steward of the manors of Lord Abergavenny in Sussex for a quarter of a century when in 1622 he was asked to compile a survey of them. Yet he wrote of one manor: "Its customs I find so variable as that I cannot certainly resolve myself thereof, much less satisfy others." Of another manor he reported: "I find their estates to be entangled with the like difficulties, fitter for the reverend judges of this kingdom upon mature deliberation than for mine insufficiency to determine."[1]

New families like the Spencers benefited by being able to select their lands with these and other landlord difficulties in mind, but old families with scattered properties like the Percies could off-set stable or declining incomes from some lands by increased yields from others. Even in the far north, the landlord wishing to improve his rent from lands which were largely in the hands of copyholders could treat with them for the substitution of leases for copyholds, as did Sir Thomas Chaloner at St Bees in 1560; or he could deny the customary nature of the tenure, as Anthony Knipe denied in 1561 that Myles Briggs of Crosthwaite held by tenant-right; or he could claim high entry fines, as Sir Thomas Wharton did from his Cumberland tenants in 1537; or, what amounted to the same thing, he could exact entry fines with great frequency, as the Percies did in Cumberland between 1527 and 1537. Where entry fines were uncertain, and many either were or could be made to appear so by a steward who knew his business, they could be raised to the limits which tenants would pay; many tenants in the period would have echoed the statement of the Methwold jury in 1606: "For our fines, they were certain; but now, by what means we know not, our custom is so broken that they are arbitrable." In any case, few landlords had manors which were composed solely of copyholds, and leases yielded markedly increased profits in many areas not merely after the 1580's, when the process became general, but also before. The manor of Ilketshall Hall, part of the Mettingham College estate which Sir Nicholas Bacon bought of Henry Denny in

[1] C. M. L. Bouch and G. P. Jones, *A Short Economic and Social History of the Lake Counties 1500–1830*, 1961, p. 65; Sir Edward Coke, *The Compleat Copyholder*, 1719, p. 31; W. H. Godfrey, ed., *The Book of John Rowe*, Suss. Rec. Soc., XXXIV, 1928, p. 93.

1562, was leased for £10 a year in the 1530's; Denny granted a lease for 21 years at £13 6s. 8d. in 1561, but when this expired in 1581, Bacon was able to lease it for £60, and by 1646 it was being leased at £160. The leasehold income of the whole estate showed an increase of nine hundred per cent between 1530 and 1656. William Harrison commented in 1587: "whereas in my time, although peradventure four pounds of old rent be improved to forty, fifty, or a hundred pounds, yet will the farmer think his gains very small toward the end of his term, if he have not six or seven years' rent lying by him, therewith to purchase a new lease," and he went on to speak of entry fines being doubled, trebled, and even increased seven times. On the other hand, even on manors where entry fines were uncertain, it was by no means always the case that tenants were squeezed; on many holdings rents remained virtually unchanged between 1500 and 1640.[1]

Sir Thomas Cornwallis, treasurer of Calais and comptroller of the household to Queen Mary, held no office under Elizabeth and acquired little land after his retirement from a mere five years at Court. His papers, therefore, give some indication of how far land could provide a satisfactory income when other sources were lacking. His patrimony had amounted to perhaps £300 a year, to which he added by his marriage and from the fruits of his office. Just what his profits were from office we do not know, but contemporary gossip held that he built his house at Brome in Suffolk from the proceeds of his treasurership and his household accounts show that his income of approximately £2,500 was more than halved when he left office. Twelve years after his father's death in 1544 he had a landed income of £650–700; in 1558 he received grants of leases of two manors from the Crown, Walsham in Suffolk which he sold to Sir Nicholas Bacon, and Wilton in Cleveland, Yorkshire, for which he paid a yearly rent of £50 but which yielded a net income of £180 a year without casualties. After the accession of Elizabeth, Cornwallis added little to his lands, apart from the purchase of a thousand pounds' worth of land in Brome and Oakley, the centre of his main estate, between 1565 and 1570, and the purchase of a town house in Norwich in 1571 for £400. His net income averaged £1,200 between 1575 and 1595. Some rents did not expand at all; these were from manors with little leasehold income. Entry fines and wood-sales on some of the larger of the manors, however, could inflate the income in certain years appreciably; thus Wilton, which normally produced £240 a year, yielded over £850 in 1573–5 and £1,500 in 1593–4, when entry fines were levied, and contributed £245 in wood-sales in 1595. Fines were rarely charged in

[1] Bouch and Jones, *op. cit.*, p. 72; Bean, *op. cit.*, p. 66; Simpson, *op. cit.*, pp. 80, 202–8; TED III, p. 71.

East Anglia on leasehold, but rents were raised as elsewhere; the income from the manor of Tivetshall was trebled between 1565 and 1579 and that from the manor of Basildon in Essex doubled between 1558 and 1595 in this way. Cornwallis's retirement from Court meant that he could reduce his living expenses from about £1,800 a year to a thousand a year, but, without selling any land, he built two houses afterwards, he lived as a county gentleman, and he was buried in an impressive tomb. A recusant, he was commanded by the queen to reside in London in 1587-9, but his estate income shows no signs of the economic decline which Miss Mousley has suggested for the catholic gentry of Sussex. His land did not make him a rich man, certainly; with the expenditure of no more than £1,500 capital, however, it was yielding an income in 1595 which was about 80 per cent better than that of 1560.[1]

The Yorkshire gentry, it is generally agreed, were relatively poor and the vast majority of them were entirely dependent upon their lands. They enjoyed none of the advantages of easy marketing which the proximity to London gave the Kentish gentry, and more than half of them had an annual income in 1642 of less than £250. The average Yorkshire knight probably disposed of less wealth than a Buckinghamshire or Worcestershire squire, and a yeoman in Norfolk or Kent was sometimes as well off as a lesser gentleman in Yorkshire. Yet there is every indication that as a class the Yorkshire gentry were prospering in the early Stuart period. They built in that time over eighty manor houses. The gentry who owed their position to office, business, or the law, like the Ingrams at Temple Newsam and the Wandesfords at Kirklington Hall, built the larger houses and carried out the bigger improvements to existing houses, but older gentry were also building and reconstructing, like the Kayes at Denby Grange and at Woodsome. The Yorkshire gentry were indulging in hunting and hawking on some scale. William Vavasour of Hazlewood declared on the eve of the Civil War that within eight miles of his family seat there were no fewer than thirty-two parks and two chases of deer, and a number of families obtained grants of free warren on their property to allow them to keep rabbits, hares, and game. In 1611 seven Yorkshire gentlemen bought baronetcies, and several purchased peerages from the early Stuarts, as Sir Thomas Fairfax of Denton bought the Scottish barony of Cameron in 1628. It was becoming increasingly common for the gentry to educate their sons expensively, to send one or more to the university or to one of the inns of court, and for the upper gentry families like the Wentworths to send their eldest sons on foreign tours. Nor was it only the wealthiest families who had a surplus in this

---

[1] Simpson, *op. cit.*, pp. 142-69; Mousley, *op. cit.*, pp. 478-9.

period. Sir Marmaduke Langdale of North Dalton had a patrimony which was one-eighth of Thomas Wentworth's—he was receiving a mere £500 a year on his succession to his estates in 1617. A good marriage and particularly shrewd estate management sufficed to allow him to expend over twelve thousand pounds in land purchases between 1627 and 1635. Steady acquisition over a long period was naturally more common among the country gentry. The Kayes afford a Yorkshire parallel to the Furses of Devon whose story has been told by Dr Hoskins; John Kaye (1578–1641) improved his estate by careful husbandry and, like his father and grandfather before him, added to the family property, buying land of the value of £279 a year in his time. Even a recusant family could prosper in the period, as the Gascoignes of Barnbow demonstrated. The head of the family was a convicted recusant throughout the period 1603–42 and the family was paying sixty pounds a year rent for its properties in consequence. By prudent management, including enclosure, mining ventures, and improved rents, and by purchases with the profits of land management, they raised their income from about a thousand a year in 1603 to about £1,700 a year in 1642, and in 1635 John Gascoigne was able to afford to be the first Englishman to purchase a baronetcy of Nova Scotia.[1]

What Sir John Oglander of the Isle of Wight wrote with his own blood in 1632 may have been true for the lesser country gentleman—"by only following the plough he may keep his word and be upright, but will never increase his fortune." But many families did succeed in living comfortably off quite small estates. Westcote records of the Brembridges of Devon, for example, that they had lived on an estate of seventy-five acres "with such a temperate moderation in every succession, that greedy desire of riches hath neither much increased, nor prodigality decreased it." Good estate management could bring rewards to noble and gentry families as well as to yeoman families like the Loders, as the advices to heirs which were so fashionable in the early seventeenth century were concerned to stress. "Understand your estate generally better than any one of your officers," the ninth earl of Northumberland exhorted his son; "before your lordship can direct your estate," John Guevara told Robert Bertie, Lord Willoughby of Eresby, soon after his father's death, "you ought necessarily understand what it is: for more have been undone by blindfold expense than by youthful courses." Sir Thomas Tresham suffered penalties for recusancy of nearly eight thousand pounds, had to provide for a large family of three sons and six daughters, and indulged in expensive hospitality,

[1] J. T. Cliffe, *The Yorkshire Gentry on the Eve of the Civil War*, London Ph.D. thesis, 1960, pp. 86, 90, 92, 96, 98, 99; W. T. Jordan, *Philanthropy in England 1480–1660*, 1959, pp. 332–4; Hoskins, *op. cit.*, pp. 356–65.

extensive litigation, and some building. But the application of business methods to his estates and his employment of an outstanding surveyor, George Levens, allowed him to survive all, to leave debts of under £11,500 which amounted to no more than four years' income. Without his handicaps, and if he had not been succeeded by irresponsible sons, he would by sheer acumen have developed the family fortunes beyond fear of damage.[1]

Disaster was obviously more common among the smaller gentry families than among the larger landowners. The smaller landowners had none of the resources of the larger, either to overcome temporary financial embarrassments or to apply professional expertise to estate management. The estate officials on the smaller manors were, Smyth of Nibley, steward to the Lords Berkeley, tells us, often ill-educated, and Clay testifies in 1619 to the losses sustained by the smaller landowners by trying to administer their own estates. Many a family like the Elands of Carlinghow, who had been landowners in Batley for three hundred years, were forced to sell their estates and sank unheralded into oblivion. Above the level of landowning where contemporaries might have been left in doubt whether to call the head of the family yeoman or gentleman, however, it required an exceptional combination of circumstances to destroy a landed family. The earls of Oxford had been declining for some time when in Elizabeth's reign Edward de Vere, the seventeenth earl, was reduced by quite extraordinary extravagance to "the mentality of a failed gambler" and to living on a royal pension. The main line of the Markhams of Nottinghamshire, whose ancestry can be traced to pre-Conquest times and who had served the Crown from the twelfth century onwards, was severely impoverished in the early seventeenth century. But Robert Markham, the heir to Sir John, had been left a reduced inheritance, for the greater part of Sir John's lands were willed away to the sons of a second marriage, and his manor house at Cotham had been virtually stripped of furniture and heirlooms. Robert's resources were drained by service at Court and by his having to provide for eight children; his heir, Sir Robert, not only had eight children himself but was also, according to Thoroton, "a great unthrift and destroyer of this eminent family."[2]

[1] *A Royalist's Notebook*, ed. F. Bamford, 1936, p. 75; T. Westcote, *A View of Devonshire in 1630*, 1845, p. 119; *Advice to his Son by Henry Percy, ninth Earl of Northumberland*, ed. G. B. Harrison, 1930, p. 75; Lincs. AO, 2 Ancaster MSS 14/17; Finch, *op. cit.*, pp. 72–92.

[2] J. Smyth of Nibley, *The Lives of the Berkeleys*, ed. Sir J. Maclean, 3 vols., 1883–6, II, p. 416; T. Clay, *A Chorological Discourse of the Well Ordering of an Honorable Estate*, 1619, pp. 52–5; Cliffe, *op. cit.*, p. 21; A. L. Rowse, *The England of Elizabeth*, 1950, p. 257; F. N. L. Poynter, *A Bibliography of Gervase Markham*, Oxford Bibliog. Soc., 1962, pp. 5–8.

One common cause of decline among landed families was beyond their control—the vagaries of the demographic factor. No fewer than 102 of 859 gentry families in Yorkshire, for example, died out in the male line between 1603 and 1642. The Onleys of Pulborough in Sussex were a family which suffered particularly in this regard. Owen Onley died in October 1590 leaving an only son, William, a minor; William was later found to be a lunatic and the Onley inheritance passed to a married sister. Large families could imperil the maintenance of a landed estate as an entity and the continuance of the family as landowners, especially if there were no supplies of ready cash to meet such contingencies, and among the smaller families who were dependant upon land there rarely was any ready cash. Provision for younger sons had often enough to be made by carving estates out of the main inheritance, so reducing it seriously, and the size of marriage portions for daughters, which were always a major expense for a family, was tending to increase in the early seventeenth century. The Spencers of Althorp did not materially alter their provision for younger sons between the early sixteenth century and the middle of the seventeenth century, but they provided marriage portions for their daughters which were ten times as large in 1642 as they had been two generations earlier, and thirty times as large as in 1532. Where large families occurred in two successive generations it was often ruinous. Sir John Mallory of Studley in Yorkshire, for example, had to provide for his nineteen children; his father had had seventeen children and his grandfather nine.[1]

The personality of the landowner was even more material in making or marring a family's fortunes. The industry and care with which John Isham of Lamport and his blind son Thomas husbanded the resources of their estates were as important factors in founding that landed family as John's wealth acquired as a merchant. Sir Richard Gargrave of Nostell Priory inherited an estate which was so large that he could ride over his own land from Wakefield to Doncaster, but his penchant for gambling was such that he had lost most of it within twenty years and he was found dead in 1649 with his head resting on the saddle of one of the packhorses with which he had been travelling in his poverty. Ignorance could waste an inheritance; Dr Nathaniel Johnston has recorded of Sir Francis Foljambe of Aldwark, who succeeded to property worth £3,000 a year but left only £1,000 a year at his death, that he was "a man of no estate or fortune, and of small understanding by reason of his education to manage so great an estate."

[1] Cliffe, *op. cit.*, p. 20; Mousley, *op. cit.*, p. 478; Finch, *op. cit.*, pp. 59–60; *Memorials of the Abbey of St Mary of Fountains*, ed. J. R. Walbran and J. Raine, Surtees Soc., LXVII, 1878, pp. 325–6.

Extravagance combined with ignorance was even more catastrophic; witness the career of Henry, Lord Berkeley, which is recorded for us by his steward, John Smyth of Nibley. He knew nothing of business, was married above his station to the sister of the duke of Norfolk, and lived, until wiser counsels prevailed, far above his income. He was also unfortunate, for litigation about the will of the marquis of Berkeley, who had died in 1492, continued for more than a century, and his son inherited the youthful extravagance of his father. In sixty years Lord Henry had sold lands worth £41,400.[1]

The need to balance income and expenditure was imperative for landowners in the period. "Except you do this," Sir Nicholas Bacon warned his son-in-law, Sir Henry Woodhouse, in the 1570's, "surely that will follow that will bring great disquietness and grief to yourself and your friends." It was sound advice which John Guevara had to offer Lord Willoughby a generation later: "the surest course, for any man that will live, and better his estate, is by casting it up truly, and dividing it into three parts: whereof the one is to be bestowed in maintaining himself and family, in household charges; the second may be dispended in apparel, and extraordinary expenses; the third ought to be laid up, or disposed, for the good of posterity." There were no long-term credit facilities in the sixteenth and early seventeenth centuries and interest rates were high—the statute of 13 Elizabeth c. 8 fixed interest at 10 per cent and scriveners' charges were commonly another pound per cent. If the landowner was unable to repay a loan on the appointed day, he forfeited his bond or, worse, his mortgage, his personal credit was impaired, and he would find it difficult to renew his short-term loans, usually for six months only at a time, or to secure new loans. Land-sales would then be probably his only recourse.[2]

By the 1630's, the situation had altered considerably. Usury charges were reduced, the statute of 21 James I c. 17 fixing them at 8 per cent, and scriveners were now charging only five shillings per cent. The development of the equity of redemption, even more significantly, converted the mortgage into a long-term security and freed the landowner from fear of forfeiture, provided that he could meet the interest charges. Indebtedness could now be a method not merely of providing ready cash for a particularly large expenditure, but of gaining a long respite in which a family's fortunes which had been seriously impaired could be restored by careful management over a long period. Land-sales could thus be avoided and family estates retained intact. Christopher

---

[1] Finch, *op. cit.*, pp. 6–28; J. Hunter, *South Yorkshire*, 2 vols., 1828–31, II, pp. 213–14; N. Johnston, 'History of the Family of Foljambe', *Collectanea Topographica et Genealogica*, II, 1835, pp. 79–81; Rowse, *op. cit.*, pp. 257–8.

[2] Simpson, *op. cit.*, p. 15; Lincs. AO, 2 Ancaster MSS 14/17.

Wandesford, for example, has explained in his *Book of Instructions* how he paid off his father's debts: "by the credit of my friends and my own good and careful performance (I mean keeping time) with my creditors, I supplied my occasions with money at the usual rates; which I was forced to do continually, rather than by the sale of some part of my lands, by mortgages or some more disadvantageous bargains, to weaken my estate and lessen my revenue." Where Sir Thomas Tresham in the 1590's and 1600's had been forced to sell land and to undertake drastic schemes of improvement which affected his relationships with his tenants adversely, the Fitzwilliams half a century later were able to survive debts which consumed two-thirds of their annual income in interest alone. It was these changes in credit facilities which allowed many of the Caroline gentry to survive their high degree of indebtedness which has been observed in many areas, and which was brought about by such factors as the extravagance or incompetence of one generation, the religious penalties of a recusant head of family in the 1600's and 1610's, the economic difficulties of a decade like the 1620's, or the political adversity of a royalist in the 1640's.[1]

Where a family chanced to suffer a multiplicity of misfortunes, however, even a fair-sized estate could not readily prevent a decline, as the story of the Temples of Stowe demonstrates. Peter Temple founded the family in the middle of the sixteenth century by a combination of successful sheep-farming on leased lands and good management of purchased properties. The active policy of his son John, who had the reputation of being "a frugal and provident gentleman," assured the Temples' position among the county gentry of Buckinghamshire. John's purchase of lands in Burton Dassett in Warwickshire, to consolidate an important family holding there, for some £9,000 in 1593 and his expenditure of a further £3,200 to buy leases which had been granted by the previous owner meant, however, that he left the estates heavily encumbered with debt at a time when it was not easy to obtain long-term credit. He also left eleven children for whom provision had to be made. His eldest son, Sir Thomas, moreover, had fifteen children. Despite careful management, the reduction of interest charges after 1624, and the sale of some lands, Sir Thomas was unable to remove the burden of debt from the family. For the family debts were increased in his time not only by provision for cadets of the family but also by the agricultural depression of the 1620's, by prolonged litigation between him, his brothers, and eldest son, and between his sons, and by the extravagance of his heir, Sir Peter. By 1653 Sir

[1] Finch, *op. cit.*, pp. 167–9; T. Comber, ed., *Christopher Wandesford's Book of Instructions*, 2 vols., 1777–8, 1, p. 92; on indebtedness of the Caroline gentry see e.g. Hoskins, *op. cit.*, p. 353.

Peter was reduced to agreeing to a settlement by which trustees were to administer his estates for a term of years on behalf of his 105 creditors to whom some £24,000 was owed. Sir Peter's death that year resulted in a more favourable settlement which ultimately enabled his heir to straighten out the family finances, but it is clear that the debts of John Temple, the incidence of large families, and the unthrifty personality of Sir Peter had imperilled for more than fifty years the stability of what was otherwise a prospering landed family.[1]

## 5. *The yeomanry and the opportunities for the capable*

Thomas Fuller called the yeomanry "an estate of people almost peculiar to England, living in the temperate zone between greatness and want." But there was no sharp division between the lesser gentry and the richer yeomen. The position of men of both classes was determined, as Tawney has written of the lesser gentry, "not by legal distinctions, but by common estimation." Sir Edward Coke, following a century-old precedent, defined a yeoman in the early seventeenth century as "a freeholder that may dispend forty shillings per annum." In fact, the definition was virtually meaningless, for many a yeoman in Tudor and early Stuart times, like Latimer's father, had no land of his own, but was a copyholder or leaseholder. In innumerable wills and legal documents of the age a man is described in one place as a yeoman and in another as a gentleman, or a man describes himself as a gentleman but is described by others as a yeoman. For it was not gentility of birth nor degree of wealth which distinguished the classes. Many of the younger sons of the lesser gentry became yeomen; many gentry were newly risen from the yeomanry or, with the aid of business or professional profits, from humbler origins still. Few gentry could have traced back their ancestry for three centuries, as some yeomen families like the Reddaways of Devon could. Many yeomen, again, were far richer than some gentry, like Thomas Bradgate of Peatling Parva in Leicestershire, who was not merely the richest yeoman in the county in 1524 but had the second highest tax assessment there in any class. The principal characteristic of the yeoman was his contentment with a simple way of life, even when he could afford more comfort; he was, in Fuller's phrase, "a gentleman in ore," and he could live without the expenses of a gentleman. Even in the prosperous south-east, yeomen houses remained until late in the sixteenth century distinguished from lesser men's by the number of rooms rather than by the quality of their

[1] E. F. Gay, 'The Rise of an English Country Family', *Huntington Lib. Qtrly*, I, 1938, pp. 367–90, and 'The Temples of Stowe and Their Debts', *ibid.*, II, 1939, pp. 399–438.

furnishings, and the long house persisted in parts of the north until very much later.[1]

Although some yeomen combined agricultural and industrial activities, as did the yeomen clothiers of the Huddersfield district of Yorkshire and the Northumberland men who made some profit from the salt and coal on their lands, yeomen relied for their income primarily upon the land. As direct producers, they were among the first to benefit from the rise in prices of the age and were always assured of food and clothing, but they shared most of the perils as well as the opportunities of other landowners in the period. They were subject to the same natural misfortunes—a failure of heirs or the succession of a reckless spendthrift could ruin yeomen as well as gentry families. They were subject to the same fluctuations in prices—the sudden falls in the price of wheat in years such as 1582–4, 1591–2, 1603–4, and 1619–20 affected them as it affected others. They were subject to the same variation of conditions between different districts. In arable areas yeomen farmed anything from twenty-five to two hundred acres, and a Kentish yeoman with only twenty-five acres, like Alexander Paramore in the 1570's, could be sufficiently well off to make friendly loans to his neighbours; in pastoral areas no man could have made a good living from so small a farm, and the wealthy yeoman might have as many as five or six hundred acres. The chances to amass wealth were far greater within reach of London than in the more remote areas of the country, and the average wealth of a Norfolk yeoman, which has been calculated at £443 in the period 1480–1660, was perhaps four times as much as that of a Somerset yeoman.[2]

It was an age when, in the words of Gras, there was "opportunity for the capable, loss for the incapable." From the 1540's there was taking place what Hoskins has termed "the largest transference of land ownership since Domesday." Many yeomen became owners of the lands which their fathers and grandfathers had farmed before them as tenants, and rose into the gentry as a result of successful landownership. If contemporary opinion may be accepted, the land market was especially active about the turn of the century. Thomas Wilson wrote in 1600: "I find great alterations almost every year, so mutable are worldly things and worldly men's affairs," and John Norden, who surveyed so many noble estates and made topographical studies of so

[1] M. Campbell, *The English Yeoman under Elizabeth and the Early Stuarts*, 1942, pp. 23–4, 62; R. H. Tawney, 'The Rise of the Gentry', EcHR, XI, 1941, pp. 2–3; Jordan, *op. cit.*, p. 324; W. G. Hoskins, *Devon*, 1954, pp. 88–9, and *Essays in Leicestershire History*, 1950, pp. 153–4; M. W. Barley, *The English Farmhouse and Cottage*, 1961, pp. 41–3, 52–4, 121.
[2] Campbell, *op. cit.*, pp. 102, 162–4; Barley, *op. cit.*, pp. 41–3; Jordan, *op. cit.*, p. 334.

many counties, wrote in 1610: "lands pass from one to another more in these latter days than ever before." Yeomen as well as gentry were building up estates, in the north as well as in the favoured south. Adam Cooke, a yeoman of Kendale, for example, owned at his death in 1624 seven messuages and tenements in Killington and eighty-six acres of land, including thirty-six of arable. The extent to which yeomen were benefiting as a class from this transference of land may be illustrated from two counties, though it could be seen almost everywhere in England. The 1634 visitation of Lincolnshire contains the names of seventy-eight families who were not listed in 1562; two dozen of these families came from other counties, but of the remaining forty-four, half were risen yeomen. One hundred and fifty eight of the 679 gentry families in Yorkshire in 1642 were 'new' in the sense that they had entered the county or the class since the accession of Elizabeth. The families who were new to the county were mostly those of business or professional men who were settling in the country, or men who had married heiresses and had come to reside on their newly acquired estates. But of the fifty-seven Yorkshire families who were granted arms between 1603 and 1642, more than half were wealthy yeomen.[1]

Yeomen were not perhaps "worldly men" in some respects, but there was nothing unworldly about the attitude of many to the exploitation of their lands. The survival of his accounts has made Robert Loder of Berkshire immortal. He was not content with subsistence farming, but grew for commercial marketing the wheat and barley which he knew would sell readily at London and at the market towns within reach of his estate. He improved his land in the manner advocated by the plethora of books on good husbandry which appeared in Elizabethan and early Stuart times and bought lime, for example, every year to fertilize his ground. As the editor of his accounts has written of him: "He wanted as large a financial return for his expenditure of capital, managerial work, and manual work as he could get, and did his utmost to maintain it." It is hard to believe that Loder's approach was not typical of hundreds more, for whenever an individual farmer's records have survived, their predominant themes are experimentation and diversity of farming. At the other end of the scale, the decline of villeinage to the point of extinction by the early seventeenth century meant that others were rising from the husbandry to be yeomen and the distinctions between husbandmen and yeomen were being blurred. Hoskins has remarked of the division between the two groups in

[1] N. S. B. Gras, *The Economic and Social History of an English Village*, 1930, p. 99; W. G. Hoskins, *Essays in Leics. Hist.*, p. 155; Wilson, ed. F. J. Fisher, *op. cit.*, p. 22; J. Norden, *The Surveyor's Dialogue*, 1610, p. 10; Bouch and Jones, *op. cit.*, p. 94; Campbell, *op. cit.*, pp. 37–8; Cliffe, *op. cit.*, pp. 27 *sqq.*

Leicestershire, and it was evidently the case generally, that "in the main it seems to have been, by the sixteenth century, a matter of personal wealth and of a man's scale of activities and living."[1]

The interest of the landlord and of the tenant was often consistent. Thomas, Lord Brudenell of Deene, demonstrated this when he succeeded in doubling the yield of his estate in Northamptonshire between 1606 and 1642 by the creation of new demesne enclosures and by the adoption of improvements on his lands not in demesne which were designed to advance his more substantial tenants as well as to increase his own profits. "Be very kind and loving unto your tenants," James Bankes of Winstanley in Lancashire exhorted his children, "so shall you prosper." Robert Furse of Morshead, a yeoman, had much the same advice to offer his children on their dealings with their tenants in 1593: "Burden them not with more fines, rents, or services more than they be well able to pay you, displace not an honest, friendly tenant for a trifle or small sum of money." Constant enquiry into the customs of manors and into the evidences of tenants' titles was, however, one of the outstanding features of Elizabethan and early Stuart times, as literally thousands of surviving documents testify. "In these days there go more words to a bargain of ten-pound land a year than in former times were used in the grant of an earldom," Norden commented in *The Surveyor's Dialogue* in 1607. The rise in rents which occurred in the 1590's was coupled with the adoption of more scientific surveying of their estates by many landlords and was more marked than any previous general rise in rent level, but it was in most areas only one of many attempts by landlords to safeguard themselves against the inflation of prices of the age. The yeoman who failed to protect his title was lost, entry fines as well as rents rose markedly in the period, and the length of leases, which were increasingly substituted for other tenures, was generally reduced, especially in the south-eastern counties, where the pressure on land was greatest. Competition for land among yeomen was so marked by the early seventeenth century that Robert Churton was able to declare that tenants "by reason of this greediness and spleen one against another [are] more their own enemies than is either the surveyor or the landlord." John Taylor wrote of the smallholder in 1630:

> "...if a gentleman have land to let,
> He'll have it, at what price so 'ere 'tis set,
> And bids and overbids, and will give more
> Than any man could make of it before."

---

[1] G. E. Fussell, ed., *Robert Loder's Farm Accounts, 1610–1620*, Camden Soc., 3rd Ser., LIII, 1936, pp. xxiii–vi; Campbell, *op. cit.*, pp. 16, 178; Hoskins, *op. cit.*, p. 151.

Taylor's poetic licence must not deceive us; the landlord could not have raised rents or fines beyond the levels which tenants were both able and willing to pay, so that this movement was probably no more than a redistribution of profits from land. Some yeomen were landlords themselves and more were living like landlords by the early seventeenth century. As Hooker remarked of the Devonshire yeoman about 1599: "his fine being once paid he liveth as merrily as does his landlord and giveth himself for the most part to such virtue, conditions, and qualities as doth the gentleman."[1]

For there is every reason to believe that yeomen were advancing as a class both absolutely and relatively more than any other landed group of the time. Robert Reyce thought that the Suffolk yeomen were the one group who were doing well in 1618: "Continual underliving, saving, and the immunities from the costly charges of these unfaithful times, do make them so to grow with wealth of this world that whilst many of the better sort, as having passed their uttermost period, do suffer an utter declination, these only do arise, and do lay such strong, sure, and deep foundations, that from thence in time are derived many noble and worthy families." Where in the early sixteenth century the yeoman were in many counties no more than "an emerging class," according to one modern estimate based on records from areas covering one third of England, their average wealth doubled between the time of Elizabeth and the Civil War. The yeoman way of life with its emphasis on frugality buttressed the majority of families against the sudden demands for resources which a bad harvest or a rise in rents could make, and many rose slowly but surely over the period, perhaps like John Lyon, the founder of Harrow School, having no desire to be termed anything other than yeomen. An examination of more than three thousand deeds describing the land transactions of yeomen between 1570 and 1640 showed that 59 per cent were for purchases amounting to less than a hundred pounds, and 78 per cent were for purchases involving less than two hundred pounds. What Robert Furse recorded in 1593 of his ancestors, who a century before had been farming tenements of no more than ninety acres in Devon, must have been true of most yeomen families—they "always kept themselves within their own bounds that by these means we are come to much more possessions, credit and reputation than ever any of them had."[2]

---

[1] Finch, op. cit., pp. 154–63; *The Memoranda Book of James Bankes 1586–1617*, ed. Joyce Bankes, 1935, p. 6; H. J. Carpenter, 'Furse of Morshead', *Devon Assoc.*, XXVI, 1894, p. 172; Campbell, op. cit., pp. 58, 77–83, 106; cf. Simpson, op. cit., p. 202.

[2] Campbell, op. cit., pp. 53, 62, 78; Jordan, op. cit., p. 334; Hoskins, op. cit., p. 159; Rowse, op. cit., p. 233.

Professor Campbell has written of the Elizabethan yeomen that "their profits came by small rather than by large gains. And in their struggle for those gains, their own wit, industry, and initiative counted for much." So it was of all who owned land in the Tudor and early Stuart period. Some by recklessness, extravagance, over-large families, or a failure to adapt themselves to economic changes fell into "an utter declination." Some rose by royal favour, commercial success, or profits made in profession or office. Some by good marriages and good management were able to increase their landholdings. But most, like the Furses, progressed "by little and little" and constituted what Professor Simpson has called "the perdurable gentry." These were the families who in succeeding generations by their industry and initiative countered adverse circumstances and benefited from advantageous situations to remain stable within their class but in possession of their land, the soundest long-term investment of the age and the surest means of support for their descendants. Only a failure in the male line could remove these families, such were the enduring qualities of land.[1]

## C. THE CHURCH[2]

### 1. *The Monasteries*

(a) *Introduction*

There can have been few parishes in England in 1500 the products of whose fields and pastures were not contributing in some way towards the maintenance of one or more of over eight hundred religious communities. The nature of the contribution varied, from fixed rent-charges through the whole range of rents, customary, 'at will', and leasehold, both in cash and in kind; tithes, great and small; profits of manor courts; labour services and other customary obligations; to the crops and stock produced on land kept in hand by the monks and nuns themselves. It is impossible, therefore, to define the extent of the monastic landed estate in terms of acreage. The counting of manors and other types of property is equally inappropriate and offers only a very rough indication of the economic value of the monastic lands.

---

[1] Campbell, *op. cit.*, p. 220; Simpson, *op. cit.*, p. 216.

[2] Professor Dom David Knowles and Professor H. J. Habakkuk were kind enough to read an early draft of this section and to make some valuable suggestions. I am most grateful to them and also to the following who have allowed me to draw upon their unpublished dissertations: J. Kennedy (*The Dissolution of the Monasteries in Hampshire and the Isle of Wight*, London M.A., 1953); G. W. O. Woodward (*The Benedictines and Cistercians in Yorkshire in the Sixteenth Century*, Trin. Coll. Dublin, Ph.D., 1955); S. M. Thorpe (Mrs Jack) (*The Monastic Lands in Leicestershire on and after the Dissolution*, Oxford B.Litt., 1961); and R. J. Mason (*The Income, Administration, and Disposal of the Monastic Lands in Lancashire*, London M.A., 1962).—J.Y.

More realistic in this respect, and by far the most ambitious reckoning attempted by a modern scholar, is Professor Savine's calculation, based on the *Valor Ecclesiasticus*, that the gross annual value of the monastic lands of England in 1535 was in the region of £160,000.[1] The addition of several large estates, such as that of St Augustine's Abbey, Bristol, and the lands of the colleges and some of the hospitals, all of which, for various reasons, Savine excluded, together with some allowance for under-valuation of demesne, would bring the total much nearer £200,000. It is impossible to say exactly what relation this bore to the total landed wealth of the kingdom, but it was probably between one fifth and one quarter of the whole.[2]

To the majority of early Tudor countrymen the monastery was first and foremost a landlord, a powerful possessor of wealth. Monastic tenants would no doubt have regaled the stranger with talk of crippling rents, low prices, neglected repairs, and inescapable tithes. At the abbot's table the tale would have been a different one, of miserably low rents, quite unrelated to the profit being enjoyed by his tenant farmers, of the high cost of foodstuffs and of the other bare necessities of the convent, and of the profitless task of improving such parts of the estate as could from time to time be taken in hand. But all this in 1500 was mere neighbourly chaffing, the rubbing along together of members of the farming community, their relations little affected as yet by the busy world of politics. A whole generation of monks was to pass before rumours of the disendowment of the Church began to be spread abroad, and a third of a century before Henry VIII and Thomas Cromwell embarked upon the wholesale confiscation of monastic resources. Meanwhile the life of the countryside was relatively undisturbed, save by the challenge of an increasingly buoyant national economy.

(b) *The monastic estate*

Inextricably entwined as were the landed resources of the monks with those of their lay and ecclesiastical neighbours, the monastic lands nevertheless comprised a clearly identifiable estate. Continuity of ownership, and the care with which, as corporate bodies, the monasteries cherished their title deeds, went a long way to ensure this. Equally important was the persistence of the manor as a tenurial unit. Even for agrarian historians, impatient to get to grips with fields and pastures, this is important. Well over half of the monastic landed estate took the form of manors. In Devon in 1535 one hundred and

[1] A. Savine, *English Monasteries on the Eve of the Dissolution*, Oxford Studies in Social and Legal History, ed. P. Vinogradoff, I, 1909, pp. 76–100.

[2] This proportion has no statistical basis: it represents the consensus of the more reliable contemporary and modern impressions.

thirty monastic 'manors', using the term in its contemporary connotation, accounted for over 60 per cent of the total monastic landed resources in the county.[1] Disintegrating forces had long been at work. Not only had there been the retreat from demesne farming and the commutation of labour services, but also, on the estates of some of the larger houses, the fragmentation of manorial issues among monastic obedientiaries. But the administrative framework had held firm. The manors retained their identity, buttressed by the regular holding of their courts, and by an administrative system which, however it might change at the centre, in the countryside rested firmly on the duties and perquisites of an army of lay bailiffs.

Monastic manors were for the most part indistinguishable from their lay neighbours, comprising the lord's demesne, often described as the 'chief messuage' of the manor, the lands of the tenants, woods, commons, mills, fisheries, and the manor court. Like them, too, they varied enormously in size, in geography, and in tenurial composition. Most of the large, territorially compact, manors had a long history of uninterrupted administrative cohesion going back beyond the time when they had first been given "to God and the church of St... and to the abbot and monks there serving God." Such were the manors of Abbots Ripton, Upwood, Houghton, Holywell, and Warboys, to name only a few of the twenty-five in Huntingdonshire alone which had belonged to Ramsey Abbey since the tenth century. Each manor had its own peculiar combination of old demesne and free and customary holdings, overlaid to varying degrees by leasehold tenancies. To select at random, the manor of Alvington in Gloucestershire belonged to the priory of Llantony. In 1535 the priory was drawing 40s. in freehold rents, £24 16s. 9d. from customary tenements, 40s. for the 'farm' of the chief messuage, and 110s. 4d. from the rest of the demesne, all of which had been let. The mill was at farm for 46s. 8d. and court profits amounted to 13s. 7d. in an average year, making a gross revenue of £37 7s. 4d. The customary holdings characteristically provided the greater part, about two thirds, of the rent income, but it is more than likely that the lands of the customary tenants accounted for an even greater proportion of the total area of the priory estate in Alvington.[2]

Other 'manors', so-called, were more artificial creations, being

---

[1] This figure is based on the gross annual value, as set down in the *Valor Ecclesiasticus*, ed. J. Caley and Jos. Hunter, 1810–34, of all the monastic lands in the county, irrespective of the location of the monastery to which they belonged, allowing for regular deductions such as manorial bailiffs' fees and clerical stipends, but not for the fees of the higher administrative officers nor for charitable disbursements. For a discussion of the value of the *Valor*, see infra, pp. 89–90.

[2] J. A. Raftis, *The Estates of Ramsey Abbey*, 1957, pp. 20–1; *Valor Eccles.*, IV, pp. 271–5; II, p. 426.

composed of scattered tenements, accumulated piecemeal over the years by gift and purchase, and grouped together for convenience of administration. The 'manor' of Pilton in north Devon comprised most of the resources of the small priory there, and was made up of dozens of farms, parts of farms, and semi-urban tenements, scattered around at least eight local parishes. Rather more compact was the 'manor' of Canonbury, a collection of tenements belonging to St Augustine's Abbey, Bristol, mostly lying within the bounds of the large lay lordship of Berkeley and gathered piecemeal over the years. It included a portion of demesne, and the abbot held a court. Syon Abbey in Middlesex derived part of its income, a mere 68s., from a dozen freehold rents in the Devon parish of Washfield. Here was no demesne and the abbess did not hold a court, but she did claim the sole right of granting licences to fish that part of the river Exe which runs through the parish, and also profits arising from waifs, strays, felons' and fugitives' goods.[1]

Rather more organic in their composition than the agglomerations of odd rents were the numerous monastic estates which had originated with the gift of a parish church, with its glebe and its tithes and other parochial revenues, and which had been augmented over the years by gifts and purchases of nearby property. Such estates, which were of course at this time owned only by the Church, were to be found in all parts of the country. Their characteristic feature was that the income from tithes usually greatly exceeded that from land rents or demesne farming. In such cases while the monastery was far from being the principal landowner in the parish, as owner of the tithes it was deeply involved in local farming operations. No form of income could be closer to the actual yield of the soil. Out of every ten stooks of corn, every ten new lambs, every ten gallons of milk, every ten loads of hay, or apples, nine were a man's own. The tenth belonged to the Church, and, in a very large number of cases, this meant a monastic house, near at hand or at a distance.[2]

Equally characteristic of monastic estates up and down the country were the great tracts of land known as 'granges' and associated particularly with houses of the Cistercian order. Little attention has been paid to these outside Yorkshire, but hundreds of them can be identified up and down the country. Granges normally consisted of enclosed demesne land, arable or pasture, sometimes running into

---

[1] E 318, 946, 180, 945; A. Sabin, *Some Manorial Accounts of Saint Augustine's Abbey, Bristol*, Bristol Rec. Soc., XXII, 1960, pp. 147-54; PRO SC 11, 164.

[2] R. H Hilton, *The Economic Development of Some Leicestershire Estates*, 1947, pp. 36-7, and VCH *Leics.*, II, p. 171; J. S. Purvis, *Select Sixteenth Century Causes in Tithe*, Yorks. Arch. Soc., Rec. Ser., CXIV, 1949, *passim*.

hundreds of acres, and unencumbered by ancient customary tenures. Many of them lay adjacent to or within a few miles of the house to which they belonged. Sibton Abbey, a small Suffolk house, possessed at least half a dozen of these enclosed farms, containing nearly three thousand acres in all, the two largest, South Grange and North Grange, in the parish of Sibton itself, comprising 963 and 818 acres respectively. Fountains Abbey possessed at least a score of granges, some of them a considerable distance from the abbey. As one would expect these granges were particularly numerous in the old enclosed south-western counties, where they were known as 'bartons'. Hartland Abbey in Devon, for instance, situated in the parish of Stoke St Nectan, possessed not only the large manor of Stoke but also Stoke Barton. This large home farm, still identifiable today, consisted of over five hundred acres of land divided into about twenty-five 'closes', some of which, for instance Southdown Close, Langland Close, and Putshole Close, extended to over fifty acres each.[1] On these great farms the monks had enjoyed exclusive occupation at a very early date. Their character is best appreciated when one compares them with the demesne of many Midland monasteries, scattered abroad, or only partially consolidated, among the strips of open fields. Newnham Priory in Bedford, for example, according to a rental of 1506–7, possessed over three hundred acres of demesne, three and a half acres in Conduit Field, seventy-two acres in Middle Field, one hundred and thirty acres in Bury Field, and 114 acres in East Field. A further seventy-two acres purchased by the priory as recently as 1502–3 also lay in strips, subject probably to a rigid customary routine. The demesne of De La Pré Abbey, Northamptonshire, when surveyed by the royal commissioners in June 1539, was found to consist of forty-six acres of meadow, only eight of which were "severell all the yere," sixty-six acres of pasture, partly enclosed and partly open, and over one hundred and seventy acres of arable land, nearly all of which lay in the East Field and West Field of Hardingstone. At Canons Ashby in the same county the demesne pasture, 153 acres, lay in closes, but the whole of the demesne arable, 341 acres, lay in the open fields. The nuns at Catesby had over two hundred and fifty acres of enclosed pasture and shared a further 535 acres with their tenants. Of their one hundred and sixty acres of arable land, all but seven acres lay open.[2]

---

[1] T. A. M. Bishop, 'Monastic Granges in Yorkshire', EHR, LI, 1936; A. H. Denney, *The Sibton Abbey Estates. Select Documents*, Suffolk Rec. Soc., II, 1960, p. 148; *Valor Eccles.*, v, p. 253; E 315, 215, f. 4. For the derivation of the word 'barton', see H. P. R. Finberg, *Tavistock Abbey*, 1951, p. 49.

[2] B. Crook and W. N. Henman, *Rentals of Bedford Priory*, Beds. Rec. Soc., 1947, pp. 15–103; E 315, 399, ff. 118, 126, 120.

In spite of much judicious purchasing and exchange of lands, few monasteries possessed compact estates. A good deal of the dispersal was, or had once been, convenient for intermanorial husbandry, but in many cases possession of remote properties can have been convenient only for peripatetic abbots. A map plotting every part of the monastic estate would show some eight hundred overlapping networks, some reaching out across several counties. The nuns of Canonsleigh in Devon owned property in East Anglia. Studley Priory, Warwickshire, had to send for part of its revenues to Devon. Neighbouring estates, on the other hand, belonged to different houses. Sherborne Abbey, Dorset, owned the Devon manor of Littleham-and-Exmouth, while the adjoining manors of East Budleigh and Otterton belonged to Syon Abbey, Middlesex. So great was the dispersal, however, that of few localities anywhere in the kingdom can it be said that the interests of monastic landlords predominated over those of the laity.

(c) *Monastic estate management*

(i) *The early decades of the sixteenth century.* The pattern of late medieval estate management, monastic, episcopal, capitular, as well as lay, is familiar enough in its broad outlines. With whatever sizeable estate one is concerned, at some point, usually during the century 1350–1450, large-scale demesne farming operations ceased, land hitherto in hand was let, piecemeal or *en bloc*, to peasant farmers, labour services due from customary holdings were commuted, and the landlord became a *rentier*.[1] By 1500 the economic conditions which had been largely responsible for these almost universal developments were fast disappearing. The energetic landowner sought wherever possible to take land in hand, either to farm himself or to create new tenancies for shorter terms and with a higher cash yield. Monastic records for the reign of Henry VII are few, and fewer still have been intensively studied, so all conclusions about monastic reactions to the new possibilities must be very tentative. No religious house has yet been found pursuing a really aggressive policy of resumption. Canterbury Cathedral Priory probably enjoyed the rule of one of the most enlightened superiors of his age in Thomas Goldston II (1495–1517). But all the demesnes of the priory except one had been let out as early as 1411 and in the middle of the fifteenth century leases had been regularly made for terms of up to ninety years. From about 1470 the terms of new and renewed leases became much shorter but there was

---

[1] R. A. L. Smith, *Canterbury Cathedral Priory*, 1943, pp. 192–4, 200; E. M. Halcrow, 'The decline of demesne farming on the estates of Durham Cathedral Priory', EcHR, 2nd Ser., VII, 1955, pp. 345–56; R. H. Hilton, *The Economic Development of some Leicestershire Estates*, pp. 88–94.

no apparent revival of interest in active farming. In the west country, by contrast, the retreat from demesne had not gone quite so far by 1500. Lacock Abbey in Wiltshire had leased out very few of its manorial demesnes by 1476. Thereafter the process continued, slowly but steadily, with no noticeable change of policy in the early Tudor period. Some time before 1517 the great East Farm at Chittern was leased, with the abbey flock of fifteen hundred sheep. There followed a lull until 1527–33 when extensive leasing took place, and by 1535 all the demesnes were let except those in Lacock itself. At Tavistock Abbey as late as 1497 the demesnes of four manors were still in hand. One of these, at Werrington, was let for the first time in 1500, and another, at Morwell, in 1501. This time-lag was not due to sheer west-country inertia, for more than once during the preceding century the abbey had embarked on a policy of converting arable land to pasture on its large demesne farm at Hurdwick, arriving by the early Tudor period at a situation in which a stable balance between arable and pastoral farming had been achieved. The leases of Werrington and Morwell were made only for the comparatively short terms of forty and twenty years respectively. This was prudent but hardly energetic estate management.[1]

Signs are not lacking however that some monasteries in other parts of the country, not long after the turn of the century, were reclaiming part of their arrented demesnes. For example, accounts relating to the estates of Oseney Abbey, Oxford, for a number of years between 1507 and 1520, show that each year more land formerly leased was taken in hand. On the manor of Weston, in 1509–10, demesne lately farmed by John Cocks for £6 was reserved for the abbot's husbandry. This represented an estate of at least sixty acres and probably much more. At Turkdean, pasture for one hundred and sixty sheep, summer and winter, was let for 40s., but only for as long as it was not required by the abbot. At Hampton Gay, pasture for two hundred and forty sheep which the abbey had previously leased for 20s. was kept in hand this year. All this meant, of course, forgoing rents. At Walton this amounted to 40s. previously paid for cattle and sheep pasture, and the abbot put it on record that the herbage of a meadow called Kingsmead, now in hand, used to be sold for £13 13s. 4d., suggesting that even he was not sure how long this new policy was going to last. In 1520–1 the abbey thought better of it and sold the herbage, for only £5 18s.

It will be noticed that it was mostly pasture land that Oseney took in hand. The steward's accounts show that in 1507–8 twenty sacks of wool were sold to "Mr Audelet" of Abingdon, part at £6 13s. 4d. a sack and the rest at £7 6s. 8d., a total of £142 13s. 4d. Nearly half this

[1] Smith, *op. cit.*, pp. 192–200; VCH *Wilts.*, III, pp. 312–3; Finberg, *op. cit.*, pp. 256–7, 253, 258.

wool, however, had been purchased by the abbey, possibly from tenants. Two years later total sales fell to £91 15s. 8d. The price and the abbey production remained about the same but less had been bought. In 1520-1 only nine sacks were sold, but John Busby of Burford paid £9 2s. per sack. Here, unfortunately, the accounts end, but they are enough to suggest that the monks at Oseney were not altogether lacking in enterprise. In 1530 and 1532, according to a list among the state papers, wool for export to Calais was coming not only from Oseney but also from Bruern Abbey in the same county, from Cirencester, Gloucester, Winchcombe, Hailes, Pershore, Evesham, Llantony, and Bordesley further west, and from Canons Ashby in Northamptonshire. Not all of this was necessarily from the abbeys' own flocks: some will have been collected from tenants, either by purchase or in rent or tithe.[1] There are indications, however, that pastoral farming was being carried out on a considerable scale by a number of monasteries during the first two decades of the sixteenth century. On the estates of Norwich Cathedral Priory expansion was impressive, from one flock of about one thousand sheep in 1475 to eight flocks numbering nearly eight thousand five hundred sheep in 1515. In 1521 the abbess of Wilton paid to one Richard Thurston over £180's worth of wool, presumably from the abbey's own flocks, for vestments, and even at Tavistock the marketing of wool, although it was never on a large scale, never actually ceased during the early sixteenth century. During the first two decades of the century it varied between two hundred and fifty and four hundred fleeces and between fifty and one hundred lambs' fleeces a year. But at Tavistock conversion to pastoral farming was never carried to extremes, and receipts from the sales of corn, largely oats, usually equalled those from pastoral farming.[2]

Sibton Abbey in Suffolk, having leased out most of its demesne, retained half of North Grange, and established there, in or before 1507, a new dairy farm. Katherine Dowe was in charge, with four other women as her assistants, and the abbey kitchener travelled to Norwich and Stourbridge to purchase additions to the stock. There were sixty-six cows in 1507, rising to one hundred and forty by 1513. The main product was cheese, over half a wey per cow, as well as considerable quantities of butter, milk, and also cream. In their spare time the dairy-maids wove woollen and linen cloth and looked after pigs, geese,

---

[1] H. E. Salter, *Cartulary of Oseney Abbey*, vi, Oxford Hist. Soc., CI, 1936, pp. 208 sqq.; LP *Addenda*, I, pt. i, pp. 244, 320.

[2] K. J. Allison, 'Flock Management in the Sixteenth and Seventeenth Centuries', EcHR, 2nd Ser., XI, 1958, p. 100; VCH *Wilts.*, III, p. 237; Finberg, *op. cit.*, pp. 150, 145, 148-9, 157.

chickens, and ducks. In the accounts an attempt was made to show a profit, which rose from £29 in 1507 to £45 in 1513. In fact, the 'sales' were to the abbey guest house and the abbot's stables, but since trouble was taken to enter up market prices it suggests at least an attempt to discover whether the project could pay its way.[1] The interest in careful purchasing is noteworthy at a time when most of the smaller houses were less particular about the way in which they augmented their stock. There is, for instance, evidence from many houses of stock being accepted in payment for corrodies. These involved contracts between laymen and the monasteries whereby the latter undertook to provide the former with board and lodging for their lives. In 1518 John and Agnes Hudson surrendered to Esholt Priory, Yorkshire, thirteen cattle, three calves, forty sheep, six wethers, thirty-four lambs, and 20s. in cash, in return for their maintenance. This must have been a considerable addition to the stock of the small priory. John died shortly afterwards, but Agnes was still alive, aged 80, in 1536, enjoying the nuns' hospitality.[2]

One would very much like to know whether the produce of the Sibton dairy was at any time sent to market. The Tavistock Abbey accounts, which are more complete, show a modest but regular sale of from thirty to fifty stones of cheese and from a dozen to fifteen stones of butter each year, right down to the eve of the abbey's dissolution.[3] But the home farm, part arable, part pastoral, was a normal adjunct to the life of any religious community, and it was a far cry from marketing small surpluses to embarking on a deliberate policy of large-scale farming for the market. Only where there is a record of intensive sheep-farming can one safely assume that the monks had their eyes on the expanding market. An increased demesne production of crops and meat and dairy products may only point to an enlarged conventual household, and we know that the number of monks and nuns, and with them their household servants, reached a high level in the 1520's.[4] Moreover, too much must not be expected of the monasteries in an age when their lay neighbours were only just beginning to take the initiative. Demesne farming on any appreciable scale raised problems of the recruitment of lay labour and the developing of entrepreneurial talent within the community, as well as those of resuming fields and pastures. In fact, had the internal life of the monastic communities been of a higher standard during these years, the monks might have been commended for continuing to turn their backs on the outside world. There was also the administrative factor. The widespread

---

[1] Denney, *op. cit.*, pp. 37-9, 141-4.  [2] Woodward, *op. cit.*, pp. 78-9.
[3] Finberg, *op. cit.*, pp. 135-44.
[4] D. Knowles, *The Religious Orders in England*, III, 1959, pp. 256-7.

attachment to the obedientary system was hardly conducive to agrarian enterprise. Each official was allocated certain sources of revenue, or, in the case of those responsible for catering, of produce. If his sources were inadequate, he merely asked that they be augmented. Within his restricted sphere there was little room for enterprise. Only the abbot would be likely to show any initiative. Hence it was in those abbeys where a centralized financial system persisted, as at Oseney, that interest in marketing possibilities was more likely to emerge.

In 1529 a statute was passed curtailing monastic commercial activities, especially in the larger houses. The monks were in future to confine themselves to supplying the needs of their own households and of their guests. There must have been some excuse for parliamentary action, but the object of the legislation was probably merely to irritate.[1] It seems unlikely that laymen were either genuinely afraid of monastic competition or concerned about monks wasting time on worldly pursuits. There was, in fact, no apparent outcry by the victims, nothing comparable with the cries of woe which went up from abbots who, very soon after, were prohibited from leaving the precincts of their houses. By 1529, in fact, as far as most houses were concerned, the legislation was out of date. The evidence so far available points to the years 1505-25 as the period of monastic agrarian enterprise. Thereafter, with a few exceptions, the general picture is one of steady retreat.[2]

More important on a long-term view than commercial ventures was the energy being expended by the monks in improving their land, either by drainage or by reclaiming it from the marsh. The work of the priors of Canterbury in reclaiming Appledore marsh is already well known. Recently some details have come to light of the progress made by St Augustine's Abbey, Bristol, in extending its lands at Almondsbury in Gloucestershire by draining the marshy banks of the river Severn. Initial operations were complete by 1500, but in the following decades the new pastures demanded constant expert attention. Until the 1520's special *appruatores* were appointed for this work. The new lands fetched high rents but most of the increased income went on maintenance. Similar evidence may yet emerge from other parts of the country. Very probably, however, it will be found that most houses which were interested at all in improving their land preferred to let their tenants do it for them. At Haseley in Warwick-

---

[1] *Statutes of the Realm*, III, pp. 292-6. The statute of 1533-4 (*ibid.*, pp. 453-4) which prohibited individuals from keeping more than 2,400 sheep, exempted from its provisions not only all flocks kept for household purposes but also those of "spiritual persons," a clear contradiction of the act of 1529.
[2] Relying largely on the *Valor Ecclesiasticus*, Professor Knowles (*op. cit.*, p. 250) does not admit of any revival of monastic high farming in the early sixteenth century.

shire, for instance, in 1523, the prior of Wroxall leased a messuage, three crofts, and a grove to Richard Shakespeare and Richard Woodham for twenty-five years, on condition that they eradicated all briars, brambles, thorns, and underwood, and prepared the ground for arable or pasture farming, leaving it well-enclosed and fenced at the end of the term. The term was not a long one, but long enough to encourage the tenants to take trouble over effecting improvements and offering to the abbey the prospect of cashing in on the improved value at a not-too-distant date.[1]

Finally there must be included under the general heading of improvements some mention of enclosure. It is now generally agreed that the greater part of the most ruthless enclosure, involving the depopulation of whole villages, took place before 1485. And certainly all that is known of monastic activity in this direction bears this out, and underlines the point already made that the monks were not incapable of energetic action. A good deal of enclosure was no doubt effected quite peaceably by arrangement with tenants and neighbours. But there is also sufficient evidence of the kind of enclosure which led to depopulation of the countryside to justify Sir Thomas More's "yea and certain abbotts, holy men no doubt..." In Leicestershire, the county for which we have the most comprehensive information, the monastic houses appear to have played a part at least commensurate with their share of the county's landed wealth. Leicester Abbey itself, having first acquired the manor of Ingarsby in 1352, added gradually to its lands there and carried through the complete enclosure of some 1,152 acres in 1469. In 1500–1 the process was repeated at Baggrave, north of Ingarsby, where 216 acres of arable land were converted to pasture and a year later this new 'grange' was extended by the acquisition of adjoining lands by exchange. Leicester's example was followed by Launde Priory, which, partly by exchanges and partly by purchase, managed to extend its control over the village fields of Whatborough, which it then proceeded to enclose and depopulate. Other notorious enclosers were Garendon Abbey, Langley Priory, Croxton, and Kirby Bellars. Generally speaking, in their engrossing of tenements, their encroachment on commons, and their conversion of much land to pasture, there is little to distinguish the monasteries from their lay neighbours, except that they had done it all before, and that the monastic enclosures of the late fifteenth and early sixteenth centuries simply added to the granges and bartons with which the monks had long been familiar. There were, incidentally, the odd occasions when the monks, in this

[1] Smith, *op. cit.*, pp. 203–4; Sabin, *op. cit.*, pp. 133 *sqq.*; W. B. Bickley, *Bailiffs' Accounts of Monastic and other Estates in the County of Warwick*, Dugdale Soc., 1923, p. 20.

matter of enclosure, were on the side of the angels. In or about 1509 Thomas Walshe, prior of Bradenstoke, Wiltshire, accused one of his tenants, John Anne, lessee of the priory's manor of North Aston for a term of thirty-three years commencing in 1485, of enclosing some 142 acres out of a total arable of three hundred acres, resulting, he alleged, in the decay of twelve houses and seven ploughs.[1]

Contemporary opinion of the monks as *rentiers* was somewhat divided. In the late 1520's they were the objects of much popular denunciation, especially as raisers of rents:

> Wheare a farme for xx *li*. was sett
> Under xxx they wolde not it lett,
> Raysynge it vp on so hye a some
> That many a good husholder
> Constrayned to geve his farme over
> To extreme beggary did come.[2]

Charges of extortionate practices were regularly brought against them in the court of Star Chamber. For example, the abbot of Fountains was accused of refusing to accept rent from one of his leasehold tenants in order to effect his eviction.[3] But the evidence from their accounts, indentures of leases, etc., is quite overwhelming. The early Tudor monks were not increasing their regular rents to any appreciable extent. Irrespective of their relation to the real value of the land, the "old and accustomed" rents were normally reserved at the renewal of tenancies, including leaseholds. Occasionally rent increases were made in renewing leases of demesne land. For instance, the rent of Staunton Grange was twice raised by Garendon Abbey, Leicestershire, between 1500 and its dissolution, first from £4 13s. 4d. to £8, and then, in 1529, to £12. The same abbey raised its rents from three other granges during the same period by over 50 per cent. Far more often, however, even rents for demesne land remained unchanged over a long period. In 1489 St Augustine's Abbey, Bristol, leased the chief messuage of its manor of Roborough, comprising buildings, land, and woods, to William Harris and John Squire, and John's wife, Joan, for sixty years determinable on their lives, at a rent of 60s. Nearly forty years later, in 1527, the property was leased to John and Margaret Backewell and their son John for their lives at the same rent.[4]

---

[1] I. S. Leadam, *The Domesday of Inclosures, 1517–18, passim;* W. G. Hoskins, 'The Deserted Villages of Leicestershire', *Essays in Leicestershire History*, 1950, pp. 75, 80, 105; VCH *Wilts.*, III, pp.285–6.

[2] TED III, pp. 20–1.

[3] J. Lister, *Yorkshire Star Chamber Proceedings*, iv, Yorks. Arch. Soc., Rec. Ser., LXX, 1927, pp. 1–3.

[4] Thorpe, *op. cit.*, p. 47; Sabin, *op. cit.*, pp. 31–2, 194.

The increased value of land at this period, whether customary or leasehold, was reflected, if at all, not in rents but in entry fines. Information on this score for the very early decades of the sixteenth century is, however, very scrappy. The amount of the fine, and we can take it for granted that a fine was always paid at the commencement or renewal of a tenancy, was rarely recorded in rentals or in the indentures of leases. Tenants often claimed in the course of court actions that they had paid heavy fines. For example, John Clerke of Loddiswell, Devon, pleaded in Chancery that on the 1st of June 1523 he had paid to the prior of Studley, Warwickshire, £9 for the reversion of forty acres of land in Loddiswell, to himself, his wife, and their son, for their lives. But he had not been able to get his lease put into writing. If this was the same land which he subsequently held by a lease dated 1530 at a rent of 10s., then indeed he had paid considerably more than the fine of two years' rent which contemporaries apparently regarded as reasonable. Court rolls provide some details of fines for copyholdings. At the manor court of the abbess of Syon at Yarcombe, Devon, held in September 1527, fines totalling more than £40 were recorded. These were payable in instalments over a number of years, an indication that they were regarded as additions to the regular manorial income. Christopher and John Hellier agreed to pay £13 6s. 8d. for the reversion, for their lives, of two furlongs of land then in the tenure of their father, Thomas Hellier. The next entry concerns Alice Hellier, who was to pay £8 for a lease of half a virgate. By contrast John Gardiner paid only 40s. for the reversion of four closes of barton land, to hold for the lives of himself and his two sons after the death of the present tenant. The relatively low fine can probably be accounted for by the barton land being let at a more economic rent.[1] A great deal more information from many parts of the country is needed before any firm conclusion can be reached about the extent to which entry fines were being levied to offset low rents in the early decades of the sixteenth century. But the information so far available goes some way to counter the other contemporary belief, current after the Dissolution, that the monks were easy-going landlords. Professor Knowles, in dealing with the overall monastic budget, has drawn attention to the apparent ease with which abbots who wished to rebuild or to embellish conventual buildings were able to lay their hands on large sums of ready cash.[2] It would be interesting, if the necessary accounts and court rolls were available, to collate monastic building activity, of which there was a great deal in the early Tudor period, with the renewal of tenancies. It was the same type of masterful, energetic, abbot who embarked on

[1] C 1, 623, 23 and E 318, 1390, m. 5; Devon RO, 346M/M2.
[2] Knowles, *op. cit.*, pp. 22, 252–3, 259.

ambitious building schemes who would discover ways and means of applying pressure on his tenants.

Reference to court rolls raises the question of the difference between customary and leasehold tenure. In theory the lease was a form of grant entered into by two freely contracting parties, their agreement involving no customary obligations and recorded in indentures sealed by both parties. This remained the legal theory, but when the contents of some of the monastic indentures are examined it is very difficult to see how their conditions differed in practice from those of copyhold grants. Of the dozens of surviving indentures of leases made by the abbots of Buckland in Devon during the fifteenth and early sixteenth century, nearly all bind the lessee to pay suit of court twice a year, and mill-suit, and also to perform harvest work, and carry out repairs to weirs, fisheries, mills, etc. They were also all bound to pay 2d. a year "geld", and heriots. Similar conditions have been found in conventual leases from many other west country houses, and also in Warwickshire. Prof. Hilton found them in Gloucester Abbey leases for lives in the late thirteenth century and concluded that they resulted from conversions from old customary tenures. There was a case on the lands of Tilty Abbey, Essex, of an expressly double tenure. On Easter Saturday 1487 at a court at Tilty, in the abbot's presence, John Pampheton of Great Easton, husbandman, was granted some land by copy of court roll and for a rent of 40s., the term being unspecified; and at the same time, at John's request and without impairing his copyhold, he was given a lease of the property at the same rent, on condition that he paid suit at Tilty, kept his fences in repair, etc., and John had the right to alienate or sell or assign the property at death, provided that the lands were not divided.[1] In their conversion from customary to leasehold tenure the monks and their tenants clearly had a foot in what lawyers regarded as two completely different worlds.

Monastic policy with regard to the length of terms of leases varied to such an extent during this period that it is impracticable to write of "long" and "short" terms. Terms of forty years were "long", apparently, in Leicestershire and Huntingdonshire.[2] But monasteries in other parts of the country were regularly granting tenancies for terms as long as ninety years during the greater part of the fifteenth century and right down to the Dissolution. Buckland Abbey in Devon granted

---

[1] Plymouth RO, Roborough MSS., 126–52, 180–6, 206, 214–17, 247–59; Finberg, *op. cit.*, pp. 249–51; Bickley, *op. cit., passim;* R. H. Hilton, 'Gloucester Abbey Leases of the Late Thirteenth Century', *Univ. Birmingham Hist. J.*, III, ii, 1952, pp. 9–14; W. C. Wallen, 'Tilty Abbey', *Essex Arch. Soc.*, New Ser., IX, 1904–5, pp. 118–22.

[2] R. H. Hilton, VCH *Leics.*, II, p. 195; Raftis, *op. cit.*, p. 291, n. 19.

leases for sixty, seventy, and even ninety years, from the 1430's. In 1486 the abbot leased to Richard Talbot, his son Philip, and Philip's wife, Joan, a farm at Gnatham in Walkhampton for seventy years at a rent of 66s. 8d. The farm was still held by Joan, widow of Philip Talbot, at the same rent, in 1538, when a reversionary lease was granted to John and Agnes Servington on the same terms. At Dunkeswell Abbey, on the other side of the county, during the same period, leases for lives, those of two, three, and four members of a family, were the rule. But up at Hartland, in north Devon, when John Heard, tenant of a farm called South Chaladon, tried to persuade the abbot to add his son's life to those of his own and his wife's, the abbot said he would not do it, even for £20, for none of his tenants had terms of more than two lives.[1]

Leases for lives were frequently surrendered before the lessees had died, so that, for a consideration, a new life or lives might be added. Many of the longer leases for terms of years were also surrendered long before they expired, usually at the death of the lessee. A reversionary interest had usually already been created. For example, in 1531 the prior of Bridlington leased to Isabel Tunstall, widow, the rectory of Fraystrop for sixty years. In 1536 he granted a lease of the property in reversion to Brian Tunstall, also for sixty years, to date from Isabel's death.[2] It is possible that no term of years was regarded as secure, and, indeed, although the law decided in favour of the tenant for years in 1499, the lease for years remained a chattel interest only, unlike a lease for life, which was a form of real property.[3] Hence, it would appear that Buckland Abbey, in spite of the length of its terms, was being less generous than Dunkeswell, and that the changeover at Tavistock Abbey in 1517, from leases for forty years to leases for lives,[4] marked a victory for the tenants. A number of the long monastic leases for term of years were, in fact, expressly determinable on lives. This type of lease is usually thought to have made its appearance in the later sixteenth century, but examples are to be found over a century earlier among monastic leases. The lease by St Augustine's Abbey, Bristol, in 1489, of its demesne at Roborough even has the phrase so familiar later on, "si tam diu vixerint seu unus eorum vixerit," but at this period there was more often the rather clumsy provision that if all the named lives expired within the specified term of years, the tenement

---

[1] Plymouth RO, Roborough MSS, *passim* and 252, 261; Exeter City RO, DD. 22593-22734; E 321 12, 98.
[2] J. S. Purvis, *A Selection of Monastic Records and Dissolution Papers*, Yorks. Arch. Soc., Rec. Ser., LXXX, 1931, pp. 7-10.
[3] W. S. Holdsworth, *Historical Introduction to the Land Law*, 1927, pp. 71-3.
[4] Finberg, *op. cit.*, p. 250.

would revert to the grantor.¹ It was a type of lease which, carrying a life interest, had obvious attractions for the tenant. In 1530 Robert Howe, who already held a number of properties at Cullompton on leases from the abbot of Buckland for terms of seventy and eighty years, took yet another piece of land from the monastery, this time for eighty years determinable on five lives. All the life-tenants had to be living already, of course, but this sounds like a very good bargain on Howe's side and suggests a weakening on the part of the abbey.² The whole subject needs further study, but it seems likely that when later Tudor lay landlords, seeking to convert their copyholdings, turned to the lease for years determinable on lives, they were following an example already set on west-country monastic estates.³

Reference has already been made to the payment of monastic rents in kind. There is no sign of any tendency towards their commutation in the early sixteenth century: rather were they on the increase. They were, of course, a splendid cushion against inflation, every bit as effective as demesne farming, as well as being useful to abbots who liked to spend part of the year at their outlying manor houses. In 1504-5 the garnerer of Christ Church Priory, Canterbury, gathered in nearly seven hundred quarters of corn from food-farms, leaving less than one hundred quarters to be purchased that year. In 1521-2 the under-cellarer of Worcester Priory took delivery of over three hundred quarters of grain from leasehold and customary tenants. A lease made by Coventry Priory in 1533 provided that the rent, eight quarters of corn and twenty of barley, was to be drawn from the best grain grown by the tenant, or was to be bought at Coventry market.⁴ That rents in kind were to the monks' advantage is confirmed by the fact that indentures of leases usually provided for future commutation, at the lessor's option. It was a particularly convenient arrangement when demesne hitherto in hand was being leased, perpetuating the arrangement whereby the demesnes provided the main source of supply for the abbey household. It was also convenient that when the monks ceased to cultivate any part of their estate for themselves, demesne stock and implements should be handed over to the lessee as part of the contract, to be returned in kind at the termination of the lease. Bath Abbey leased its grange at Launcedon, part of the manor of Weston, with a stock of eighteen oxen, ten cows, five yearlings, five

¹ *Supra*, p. 82, n. 4; Bickley, *op. cit.*, pp. 59–61.
² Exeter RO, DD. 22505.
³ W. G. Hoskins, *Devon*, 1954, p. 91; R. B. Pugh, *Antrobus Deeds before 1625*, Wilts. Arch. & Nat. Hist. Soc., Records Branch, III, 1947, p. xl; I. P. Collis, 'Leases for Term of Years determinable with lives', *J. Soc. Archivists*, I, 1957, pp. 168–71.
⁴ Smith, *op. cit.*, p. 201; J. M. Wilson, *Account of Worcester Priory, 1521-2*, Worcs. Hist. Soc., 1907, p. 6; Bickley, *op. cit.*, p. 59.

calves, and other stock appertaining to husbandry, for an annual rent of fifty-two quarters of wheat, seventy quarters of barley, five quarters of oats, six loads of hay, four loads of straw, and the feeding of two fat oxen from St Martin's Day to Holy Cross. For a further rent of £20 2s. 6d. the farmer also leased the abbey flock of 440 wethers and 540 ewes. The actual amount of produce rent was usually fixed in the indentures, but when, in 1500, Tavistock Abbey leased its demesne and stock at Werrington to its bailiff for forty years at a rent of £3 and thirty-two quarters of wheat and all the cheese produced on the manor, there was also a proviso that if the price of wheat varied the rent should be adjusted accordingly. In 1529 a new agreement was made whereby the rent was raised to £8 and the wheat reduced to twenty quarters.[1] Not all 'stock and land' leases were accompanied by rents in kind, nor, of course, do rents in kind necessarily imply the initial provision of stock. But where both were present it seems fairly clear that here was a very convenient arrangement with the advantages equally balanced between both parties.

Another regular source of provisions for the monastic households was tithe. In fact, in the case of some houses whose resources included a good deal of 'spiritual' income, collection of all of it in kind would have embarrassed the abbey kitchens. In any case, transport from distant parishes was expensive. The most common practice seems to have been to sell the tithes from year to year, to local dealers. Leasing, too, was commonly resorted to, but usually for short terms, perhaps from five years to five years, rarely more than ten or twelve, and occasionally for one life. St Augustine's Abbey, Bristol, made new contracts each year, falling back on leases only in the later 1520's.[2]

By and large the early Tudor monks did not lease out their manors in their entirety and in fact this period probably saw the reversal of earlier tendencies in this direction. The usual pattern was to retain the seigneurial rights, including the manor-court, in hand, let out the demesne or chief messuage to a farmer, and retain a bailiff to collect the rents and deal with repairs. Bailiff and farmer were very often one and the same. Thereby the monks retained full control over the granting of tenancies and collected the fines. In a number of cases they also retained the manorial sheepwalks long after they had let out the demesne arable land, or at least made an arrangement with the farmer

---

[1] PRO SC 6, Henry VIII, 3144, m. 17 and E 321, 6, 97; Finberg, *op. cit.*, p. 99. Savine (*op. cit.*, pp. 164–5) associates food-rents, even from demesne, with "a certain lack of progress to be observed in the monastic economy," and is followed by Dr Finberg (*op. cit.*, p. 241). Their advantages were rediscovered, however, by many lay landowners during the period of inflation later in the sixteenth century.

[2] Sabin, *op. cit., passim.*

for the continued pasturing of the abbey flocks. Sometimes the farmer undertook to manage the stock as part of his 'rent', and in that case he accounted for sales of wool, etc., in his manorial account. Winchcombe Abbey leased its arable demesne at Sherborne in Gloucestershire as early as 1464, but must have reserved the pasture, for in 1485 nearly three thousand of its sheep were collected there for washing and shearing. As late as 1535 the demesnes of the abbey manor of Frampton were still in hand in their entirety, and at Snowshill, Hawling, and Charlton Abbots pastures were still in hand although the rest of the demesnes had been leased.[1]

Finally, even when the last of the pasture had been let, there were the woods, which were always reserved by the monastic landlords. A typical provision was that made in a lease by Wroxall Priory, Warwickshire, on the 1st of April 1529, whereby three acres of land were let for thirty-two years. The farmers were expressly forbidden to fell any timber growing on the premises but they were permitted to "lop and crop the same, according to the custom of the manor there, for repairs to the fence and hedge."[2] Monastic estates were well provided with timber, continuity of ownership having resulted in greater conservation than elsewhere. Wood sales brought in welcome supplies of ready cash and were always negotiated under the direct supervision of the abbots themselves. Bailiffs disposed only of fallen timber and underwood.

It is, of course, a well-known fact that laymen were employed in great numbers by the monasteries as stewards, auditors, receivers, and manorial bailiffs. But it would be a great mistake to assume that the monks thereby relieved themselves of worldly cares. Not even unpleasant tasks were delegated to laymen. It was the monk treasurer of Garendon Abbey in Leicestershire who informed the tenants at Dishley that they were no longer to enjoy common rights there on land which the priory had enclosed. At Merevale Abbey, too, a house which was still deeply involved in sheepfarming in the early sixteenth century, the movement of flocks from one grange to another was organized by the monk treasurer. In 1535 the abbot of Glastonbury, in a letter to Thomas Cromwell, explained that leases made "at a courte and letten by copie of the courte roll" were always arranged "by on(e) of the religion and ceculer men appoynted to hym." Incidentally he adds, in defence against the very common charge that leases were being made without the consent of the whole convent, "if they schuld made no leese but by assent of the more parte of the covent, it

[1] R. H. Hilton, 'Winchcombe Abbey and the Manor of Sherborne', *Gloucestershire Studies*, ed. H. P. R. Finberg, 1957, pp. 110 *sqq.; Valor Eccles.*, II, pp. 456-7.
[2] Bickley, *op. cit.*, p. 18.

schuld be verie tedyous bothe to them and to ther tenauntes."[1] In fact, lay officers were for the most part either servants, responsible to the monks and accountable to them for their day-to-day duties, or sinecurists, being men of some influence in lay society who were retained by the monks for what the monks called their 'counsel'. It seems unlikely that either group dictated monastic agricultural policy.

The regular fees to be earned as manorial bailiffs will have augmented many a peasant farmer's income, but it was as lessees of the abbey lands that laymen, during the early sixteenth century, were making their greatest inroads into monastic landed wealth. Until we know more about the capital outlay required by way of entrance fines the question of the actual extent of their advantage must remain unanswered. It is, however, among the ranks of those farmers who were both bailiffs and lessees of the monks that we should look for the ancestors of some of the more prosperous yeomen farmers of later Tudor England.

(ii) *The last decade: 1529–39.* The late 1520's saw the end of normal economic relationships between the monks and their tenants. Between about 1527 and 1534 external pressures, especially from government circles, increased steadily, and after 1535 the floodgates were wide open. Monastic lands, acquired over many centuries, sometimes mismanaged but never before wholly despoiled, were exploited with the full legal connivance of their owners, with little thought for the future, and with a great deal of overt encouragement by the Crown and its representatives, at times apparently indecently anxious to allow others to anticipate its own depredations. The actual story of the Dissolution need not be retold here: it has already been related with admirable clarity elsewhere.[2] One point only needs to be emphasized in this context, namely that the process of confiscation was a protracted one, beginning, for all practical purposes, in the summer of 1536, but not completed until well into 1540, with the dissolution of the colleges and chantries still to follow later. What must concern us is the effect of this situation, when some houses had already fallen and others were still fully operational, on the relations of the monks with their tenants, and, more particularly, on the extent of their own farming operations.

Descriptions of the state of the monastic lands on the eve of the Dissolution often rely entirely on the *Valor Ecclesiasticus* of 1535. This was, of course, a remarkable survey, and it is quite indispensable to the historian of monastic lands. No other record can rival its comprehensiveness, and its compilation made the subsequent confiscation

---

[1] Thorpe, *op. cit.*, pp. 31–3; T. Wright, *Three Chapters of Letters relating to the Suppression of the Monasteries*, Camden Soc., 1843, p. 64.
[2] Knowles, *op. cit.*, chaps. xxii–xxix.

of the monastic lands by the Crown administratively possible. But for all its considerable reliability it is only a survey of current regular gross income. As has so often been demonstrated, its valuations of demesne still in hand were, to say the least, conservative.[1] But this was as much due to underestimation of the extent of the demesne as to actual undervaluation. In dealing with Studley Priory, Oxfordshire, the commissioners put it on record that demesne pasture in hand had been valued at 1s. per acre and arable at 4d.[2] This was low but resulted in figures which were almost certainly nearer the real value of the land than the bare rents which represented the customary holdings. On the other hand, the commissioners must have exaggerated the actual net income from arrented land for no allowances were made for expenditure on repairs, or for rents in arrears, both of which figure prominently in most current bailiffs' accounts. Setting the one deficiency against the other, it seems probable that the gross values of the *Valor* were not far off the mark. Its most serious limitation as a record of what passed to the Crown is that it takes no account, naturally enough, of the tenurial developments of the years 1536–9. These, however, can be very largely reconstructed from post-Dissolution records, notably the surveys made at the moment of surrender, together with the enrolments of confirmations of conventual grants.[3]

The smaller houses which were dissolved in the summer of 1536 had never farmed on any scale and their preparations to avert the crisis had been negligible. Most of them had a small domestic home farm to provide for their daily needs and in most cases this was in working order right up to the last. At the dissolution of Thremhall Priory in Essex the commissioners found there a dairy stock of six milking cows, two bullocks, and a dozen pigs. In the stable were eight cart-horses, a cart, a dung-cart, and a plough with coulter and share. In store were six bushels of wheat and a load of hay, and in standing corn, thirty-six acres of barley and fourteen of wheat. There were also thirteen sheep. Here was a small mixed farm comparable with those of the more substantial yeomen farmers of the district. At Prittlewell Priory in the same county arable fields were not mentioned but the stock was much larger than at Thremhall. There were seventeen horses in all, various cattle, including a bull, 139 sheep, and seventy-six lambs. In store were one pack and seventy-one pounds of wool, on which the commis-

[1] Savine, *op. cit.*, pp. 73–4, followed by Knowles, *op. cit.*, pp. 245, 312. See also A. Evans, 'Battle Abbey at the Dissolution', *Huntingdon Lib Qtrly*, IV, July 1941, pp. 393–442 and Nov. 1942, i, pp. 53–105.
[2] *Valor Eccles.*, II, p. 186.
[3] For further details of post-Dissolution sources see J. A. Youings, *Devon Monastic Lands: Particulars for Grants, 1536–58*, Devon and Cornwall Rec. Soc., New Ser., I, 1955, pp. xxxiv–xxxvii.

sioners placed a value of £4 3s. 4d. Stock and dairy farming predominated on the rest of the smaller Essex houses for which inventories have survived. Plough and cart-horses were valued by the commissioners at prices varying between 6s. and 12s., sows at 1s. or 1s. 6d., and sheep about the same. In fact the variety in prices suggests that the king's officers took a great deal of trouble, and took careful note of the quality of the stock and of prevailing local market prices. Local men were no doubt only too ready to proffer advice, but town and country were not so far divorced in Tudor England that civil servants like Richard Pollard and Sir Thomas Moyle would not be perfectly capable, if time allowed, of distinguishing between good and poor stock. At Sawtry in Huntingdonshire in May 1536 the commissioners proceeded from the abbey church and domestic quarters to a forge, where they listed a vice, hammers, tongs, and bellows, and then to the "cart-ware," which included three shod carts, shares and coulters, seven pairs of cart gear, eight pairs of plough-traces, a dung-cart, roller and harrows, spades and dung-forks. Here, among the so-called 'paper surveys' of 1536, is much material for the historian of farming gear, and a great deal of information on current local prices.[1] The same surveys also provided in some cases lists of agricultural labourers. At Cockersand Abbey, Lancashire, in May 1536, the commissioners enumerated sixteen hands, including two women "winnowers of corn." Wages ranged from 33s. 4d. for the wright down to 8s. 2d. for the women. An odd "tasker" and a plough-driver received only food and clothing. This seems a more than adequate labour force for a farm whose stock amounted only to eighteen pigs, fifty-eight milking cows, thirty heifers, forty-two bullocks, twenty-four oxen, and a miscellaneous collection of horses. Only forty-seven acres of land was under crop. The abbey was, in fact, reprieved until 1539. However, according to figures given by Professor Knowles relating to seventy of the houses dissolved in 1536, the average number of agricultural labourers, male and female, on these smaller establishments, was twenty.[2]

Though no one in 1536, not even the king and Cromwell, knew if, and certainly not exactly when, the larger houses and those which had bought exemption would ultimately surrender or be forcibly dissolved, the acquisitive instincts of all parties, court, country, and the monasteries themselves, except a few quite exceptional communities, now came

[1] R. C. Fowler, 'Inventories of Essex Monasteries in 1536', *Essex Arch. Soc.*, New Ser., x, 1909, pp. 345, 390, and *passim;* E 315, 402, ff. 45v-48; Knowles, *op. cit.*, p. 313.
[2] W. Farrer, *Chartulary of Cockersand Abbey*, iii, pt. 3, Chetham Soc., New Ser., LXIV, 1909, pp. 1154 *sqq.*; Knowles, *op. cit.*, p. 262.

into full play. Outright conveyance of monastic lands, either by gift or sale, although suspected by the Crown, was not widely detected, if indeed it took place. In any case there was little need. The process of capitalization was effected so much more easily by the granting of long leases in return for heavy fines, or, when the prospect for the monks became really black, merely in the hope of lay favour. Conventual leases from all parts of the country point to 1538 as the peak year.[1] Buckfast Abbey in Devon may not be typical, but its operations illustrate very well what was happening. Few leases for long terms were granted by the house in the early 1530's, but from 1536 Abbot Gabriel Donne became very busy with the abbey seal. Out of thirty leases made in 1538 for which details survive, thirteen were for terms of ninety-nine years, and all but three were for three or more lives or for sixty years and over. What is more important is the much fuller information now available about entry fines. For one tenement paying an annual rent of 20s. a lessee paid £40 for a lease for one life. On the other hand, for a lease for four lives at a rent of £5 4s. another tenant paid only £5 13s. 4d. For leases each of ninety-nine years' duration at rents of 19s. 3½d. and 24s. 4d. two others paid £2 and £20 respectively. The abbess of Wilton, who in 1530 and 1531 had been content with fines of one or two years' rent, was exacting five or six times the annual rents for the renewal of copyholdings for life in 1534 and 1535. In 1537 and 1538 she obtained ten, and even fifteen, times the rent. For instance, on the 29th of April 1538 Richard Ellis paid her £7 13s. 4d. for a lease of a messuage on the manor of Fugglestone in Wiltshire. This comprised nineteen acres in the open fields, two small closes, and common pasture for six cattle and fifty sheep. The rent was low, only 11s. 11d. and a cock and a hen.[2] There is absolutely no pattern and no means of discovering how these terms were made. Personal and political considerations as well as purely economic ones no doubt played a part. But there can be no doubt that many houses, or more likely their abbots, were able during the last few years to put by very considerable sums of ready money which the Crown was never able to touch. It is perhaps ironic that the Crown later paid out large sums in settlement of monastic debts.[3]

The royal agents frequently reported to Cromwell that leases had been made "unthrifftelye," i.e. at reduced rents. But only one clear

[1] PRO SC 6, Henry VIII (Ministers' Accounts of Monastic Lands), *passim*.

[2] *Ibid.*, 597 and Exeter City RO, DD. 22786, 22867, 22809, 22810, 22808, 22843; C. R. Straton, *Surveys of the Lands of William, first earl of Pembroke*, Roxburghe Club, 1909, I, pp. 57 and *passim*.

[3] Professor Knowles's conclusion (*op. cit.*, pp. 253–5) that the monastic houses were not, generally speaking, heavily in debt, does not alter the fact that large numbers of monastic creditors obtained repayment from the court of Augmentations.

instance has been found of an old rent being lowered by the monks and balanced by a large fine. This was at Holme Cultram in Cumberland, where in 1537 for a fine of £13 13s. 4d., the abbot leased some land to Steven Skelton for twenty-one years at a rent of 10s. instead of at the old rent of 20s. Over the full term, had he remained to enjoy the rent, the abbot would have made £3 3s. 4d. on the deal. As it was, he had a substantial part of the total in hand.[1] If such practices were indeed more widespread, the Crown was well and truly forestalled.

After 1535 a much larger proportion of the conventual leases, especially those of demesne hitherto in hand, was taken up by knights and gentlemen. In 1538 Sir Philip Champernon obtained from the abbot of Buckfast a lease for sixty years of the chief messuage of the manor of Englebourne, to date from the death of the tenant in occupation, Robert Screech, a local farmer, who with his son had leased the property in 1528. The same thing was happening in the Midlands, too, especially on the coveted granges. Edward Villiers succeeded the Pickering family who had farmed Costock, Nottinghamshire since the late fifteenth century. Of the Leicestershire houses, only Croxton, for reasons unknown, resisted offers from gentlemen as long as possible, even inserting in indentures a prohibition against subletting to gentlemen or even to gentlemen's servants. Finally, it gave in and leased its demesne at Waltham to Sir John Uvedale, one of its stewards.[2] Many of the lessees of the later 1530's were friends, potential supporters, and relations of the monks. For example, in 1536 Sir Thomas Dennis, very prominent among the Devon gentry and steward of Newenham Abbey (among others), obtained from the abbot a ninety-nine year lease of some abbey land. The last abbess of Lacock in Wiltshire, Joan Temmse, made sure of keeping a good deal of the abbey resources in her own family. In 1529 her brother Thomas, who was also her auditor and steward of her courts, took her manor of Shorwell for eighty years; in 1533 another brother, Christopher, steward of her household, took Hatherop for sixty years; and at the same time her brother-in-law, Robert Bath, clothier, leased Bishopstrow for ninety-nine years. Christopher also leased a tenement in Lacock with pastures and part of the tithes. This was in 1537, and the following year Thomas bought the abbey flock at Chittern for £150.[3] But there was also a market for leases among the gentry, for they are to be found paying reasonable, if not heavy, fines. Examples have been found in all parts of the country. In 1538 William Westby, esquire, paid the

---

[1] E 315, 399, fo. 26v.
[2] Exeter City RO, DD. 22838, 22823; Thorpe, *op. cit.*, pp. 20–7.
[3] Exeter City RO, DD. 6800; VCH *Wilts.*, III, pp. 313–4. See also A. L. Rowse, *Tudor Cornwall*, 1941, pp. 178–80.

abbot of Cockersand, Lancashire, a fine of £10 for a ninety-nine year lease of some lands in Medlar in Amounderness, at the accustomed rent of £4. Sir Robert Hesketh paid twenty marks to the same prior for a similar lease of lands in Tarleton, Lancashire, at the old rent of £4 19s. 8½d. William Standish paid a fine of £50 on the 30th of August 1537 for a lease of the Ulverscroft Priory grange of Chorley, and in 1536 Simon Catesby, a Nottinghamshire gentleman, paid Lenton Priory £40 for a forty-five year lease of Wigston rectory, the rent being £22 7s. 4d.[1]

But the gentry had by no means entirely ousted the yeomen farmers from the best of the abbey lands by 1538–9. Many thousands of yeomen were securely entrenched with long leases, all over the country. In Leicestershire they held more than half of the monastic leaseholdings.[2] Many manorial bailiffs now obtained, or renewed, leases of the demesne which they already administered. In 1535 John Collins, bailiff of the St Augustine's Abbey manor of Leigh, obtained from the abbot a lease for three lives of the manor house and demesne, at a rent of £10. Two years later he added a lease for sixty years of the sheephouse, Sheephouse Close, and common pasture for five hundred sheep, at a rent of £1; and finally, in 1538, the office of bailiff was assured to him for life, by indenture, with a fee of £1 6s. 8d. Collins was one of thousands of manorial bailiffs, mostly small local farmers, who, following the lead given by the gentlemen who held the higher monastic administrative offices, had their contracts put in writing in the 1530's.[3]

It would be a mistake to conclude that during the last year or so before the Dissolution conventual seals were being used carelessly. Very few of the leases and other grants were ever called in question. Occasionally the omission of a clause of distress or failure to reserve woods came to light in the course of subsequent litigation. But such cases were rare: the monks knew their business in this respect. Most of the legendary roguery took place after the Dissolution, usually through the convent seals getting into the wrong hands.

Enough has perhaps been said to indicate that even during the last year or so before the Dissolution the monks were still able to strike a hard bargain, and that they were not nearly so pliable as Thomas Cromwell and his circle would have liked them to be. It would be unwise, in fact, to assume that in every case the Dissolution was casting

---

[1] Farrer, *op. cit.*, pp. 1189–1200; E 303, 292; W. G. Hoskins, *The Midland Peasant*, 1957, p. 131.     [2] Thorpe, *op. cit.*, p. 28.

[3] Sabin, *op. cit.*, p. 16; PRO, SC 6 (Ministers' Accounts) *passim*. Dr R. H. Hilton (VCH *Leics.*, II, p. 195) places greater emphasis on the advantageous position gained by the gentry. See also A. G. Dickens, *Register of Butleigh Priory, Suffolk*, 1951, *passim*.

its shadow before. A great many of the leases of the 1530's, even those made almost on the eve of surrender, merely represent the culmination of a long process of retreat from demesne farming and not a frantic attempt to prepare for the end. One house, at least, prepared for any eventuality. St Werburgh's Abbey, Chester, on the 10th of October 1538 leased the parsonage of Sutton in Wirral to William Goodman and Hugh Aldersey, "uppon condycon yf the seyd monastery be nott dissoluyd that then the seyd William and Hugh to redelyver the seyd indenture."[1]

The royal officials who were engaged in effecting the 'surrender' of the monasteries adopted an air of great concern about these last-minute leases of demesne hitherto in hand. In 1538 John Freeman reported from Lincolnshire that all the houses remaining in the county were "in readiness to surrender," which, he went on, "doth appear by their acts, for they are in a customed sort of spoil and bribery... for they leave neither demesnes unlet nor honest stuff in their houses, but also minisheth the greater part of their stock and store."[2] What Cromwell's informants did not mention, even if they were aware of the fact, was that the leasing of demesne on distant manors had been almost complete by 1535. In Hampshire, according to the *Valor Ecclesiasticus*, less than one fifth of the monastic manors had at that time any demesne in hand.[3] By 1538-9 the withdrawal had gone a good deal further, and portions of nearby demesne had been leased. But in nearly every case, as the commissioners' own surveys show, the core of the estate, the adjacent home farm, was being worked by the monks right up to the end. Selby Abbey in Yorkshire was one of the last to be dissolved and had plenty of time to prepare for suppression. In March 1540 its demesnes were listed. Within the precincts were the usual gardens and orchards and beyond them some 190 acres of arable, which the commissioners valued at rates varying from 6d. an acre for the coarser ground to 1s. 8d. an acre for meadow. All of this was still in hand, as also were a further two hundred acres, mostly woodland, known as Stayner Grange. But Haysteads meadow in Wystowe Inges, extending to five acres and formerly kept for the abbey mill horses, had been let in August 1538 to Robert Good for 10s. a year. The fishery of the Ouse, previously reserved by the monks for their own use, had been let very recently to Richard Kirk for 13s. 4d., and four corn mills to Robert Beverley of Selby for 40s. Thorpe Grange had been let as recently as January 1539.[4] Clearly the final retreat had

---

[1] E 315, 397, f. 42.     [2] LP XIII, ii, p. 207.
[3] Kennedy, *op. cit.*, p. 57. See also Savine, *op. cit.*, pp. 153-4.
[4] J. T. Fowler, *Coucher Book of Selby Abbey*, Yorks Arch. Soc., Rec. Ser., 1893, pp. 349 *sqq*.

begun, but in very few cases had there been sufficient time for it to be complete.

For the county of Leicester it has been calculated that 20–25 per cent of the total monastic land (in terms of the gross values set down in the *Valor Ecclesiasticus*) was still in hand at the Dissolution. Broken down, this proportion ranged from 9 per cent at Kirby Bellars, of which five sixths was arable land, to 51 per cent at the small priory of Bradley, which was still pasturing considerable flocks on its 130 acres of pasture.[1] These figures illustrate something which is probably true for the whole country, namely that the houses which had retained the greater proportion of land in hand were those most interested in pastoral farming. This is particularly true of the granges. Pastoral farming, of course, involved greater acreages, so that the actual amount of land still in hand in some counties was quite considerable. In Devon, where the monastic economy had been less weighted on the side of pastoral farming, the proportion of demesne still in hand at the Dissolution, whether in terms of value or acreage, was much less than in Leicestershire. In Hampshire there was great variety between the houses, but here also, pasture predominated on the land acquired by the Crown with vacant possession.[2]

Few communities, or at least their superiors, can have lacked warning of impending dispersal, and even if tenants had not actually been installed, it was hardly to be expected that the commissioners would find farming operations in full swing. In many there will have been divided counsels. The Carthusian brothers at Axholme, in Lincolnshire, for example, less anxious than their prior to prepare for the end, complained bitterly of his negligence. Not only, they asserted in 1538, had he been selling off their goods and stock and let part of the demesne to his kinsmen, but, worst of all, he had dismissed their labourers, so that,

"...our husbandry is not lokyd upon, our lond is not tylde, muke is not led, our corne lyth in the barn, sum is threshte, and sum is husbondyd, and mych is yit to threshe, and taketh hurt with vermyn... and shortly hay tyme shall cum, and when it shuld be sped, other thynges shalbe to do."[3]

Many indeed were the reports reaching London of the wholesale selling-off of stock by the abbots and priors, and these are very difficult to check. The most that can be said is that, here again, the commissioners' own reports belie some of the hair-raising tales which they were sending to Cromwell. At Fountains Abbey, in 1539, for instance, they listed a 'store' of over two thousand horned cattle, over one thousand

[1] Thorpe, *op. cit.*, pp. 38–9, 291, 296.
[2] Kennedy, *op. cit.*, pp. 47–9, 54.
[3] Wright, *op. cit.*, pp. 175–6.

sheep, eighty-six horses, and nearly as many pigs. There cannot have been much excess marketing of stock here. There is, moreover, evidence of the purchase of stock by some houses not long before the Dissolution. Oxen were being purchased for the farm at Hurdwick by the bailiff of Tavistock Abbey in 1538, and at Glastonbury, during 1538-9, at a time when most of the other Somerset houses had already fallen, money was being laid out on the restocking of Shapwick moor.[1]

The retreat from active farming had undoubtedly accelerated considerably in the 1530's, and especially during the years 1538-9, but there was still a good deal of land left to be handed over to the Crown with full possession, and in good shape, land fit for the immediate occupation of the king himself or of one of the more fortunate of his subjects. Richard Pollard, having sent the abbot to his tragic fate on the tor just outside the town, wrote from Glastonbury in November 1539:

"The house is greate, goodly, and so pryncely as we have not sene the lyke, with iiii parkes adjoynynge, the furthermoste of them but iiii myles distaunte from the house; a great mere, which ys v miles cumpas... well replenished with greate pykis, bremes, perche, and roche; iiii faire manour placis, belonginge to the late abbott... beynge goodly mansions."[2]

*(d) The Crown takes over*

The statute of 1539, unlike that of 1536 which actually authorized dissolution, was merely intended to set aside all doubts about the legality of the royal title to monastic lands, especially, no doubt, the misgivings of those who had already purchased portions or were contemplating doing so.[3] There was assured to the king the "very actual and real seisin and possession" of the property of all dissolved monasteries, whether suppressed by the act of 1536, voluntarily surrendered, or to be surrendered in the future, or whose superiors had been attainted. The king was to be regarded as absolute owner of the property, "in as large and ample manner and form" as the monasteries. Henry and Cromwell could, presumably, have gone one stage further, either in 1536 or 1539, and obtained a statutory declaration that all contracts entered into by the monks were null and void. This they did not do. It was most important that the interests of laymen should not be disturbed. The statute only invalidated leases made within a year of surrender, and then only of lands not usually let to farm, or leases in reversion or not reserving the old rent, or leases of growing wood, and even these provisions the Crown chose very

[1] Dugdale, *Monasticon*, v, p. 291; Finberg, *op. cit.*, p. 135; Dom Aelred Watkin, 'Glastonbury, 1538-9', *Downside Review*, LXVII, 1949, p. 448.
[2] Wright, *op. cit.*, p. 258.   [3] *Statutes of the Realm*, III, pp. 575-8, 733-9.

largely to ignore. Many hundreds of long leases which could statutorily have been called in were allowed to run their full term. For example, only a few months before the dissolution of Kenilworth Priory, Warwickshire, the priory manor of Salford Priors had been let for ninety-nine years. The manor was still in Crown hands in 1547, its conventual lease still running. The same priory had, as long ago as 1521, leased its wool tithes at Bidford for forty-six years to commence on 20 April 1540. This lease also was still operating in 1547.[1] Only very occasionally was the term of a long lease reduced or a rent 'restored', i.e. raised, by the Crown to what was regarded as the customary figure. Moreover, there is no substance in the records of the court of Augmentations for the suggestion often made that the tenants of the former monastic lands were in a state of "anxious suspense," eager to exchange their titles for new ones and only too willing to pay a heavy fine to the Crown to ensure security.[2]

The ease, the speed, and the comparative lack of local disturbance with which the great confiscation was carried through was largely due to the establishment, at the very commencement of the operation in 1536, of the court of Augmentations, with its central and local officers. The same local, i.e. regional, officers who carried out the dissolution of the smaller houses in 1536, remained to administer the property, and, as the larger houses fell, in their case to bodies of special commissioners, to deal with their property too. Apart from the estates which were handed over to the duchy of Lancaster, only the lands of the attainted abbots were dealt with separately, by the General Surveyors of Crown lands. Once the Augmentations men arrived the 'take-over' was swift and remarkably simple. The *rentier* character of so much of the monastic estate facilitated this. The monastic bailiffs and farmers accounted to the Augmentations receivers instead of to monastic treasurers. Where they had formerly been accountable to more than one monastic obedientiary this must have been a welcome relief, or at any rate a simplification. For the great mass of monastic tenantry the changeover can have made very little difference.[3]

---

[1] Bickley, *op. cit.*, pp. 34–6. These conclusions are confirmed by a recent study of Lancashire monastic lands (Mason, *op. cit.*, pp. 137–9). It must be stressed that the Augmentations officers had no statutory authority to 'meddle' with leases made, on whatever terms, more than a year before the dissolution of the house concerned.

[2] Savine, *op. cit.*, p. 54. The confirmations of conventual leases are in E 315, 90–105. The act of 1540 requiring the observance of all covenants in conventual leases (32 Henry VIII, c. 34), applied to both landlords and tenants.

[3] *Statutes of the Realm*, III, pp. 574, 734. For the parallel administration of the court of Augmentations, the General Surveyors, and the duchy of Lancaster, in the county of Lancashire, see Mason, *op. cit., passim*. The workings of the court of Augmentations in the county of Devon are dealt with in Youings, *op. cit.*, pp. viii–xiv.

At the earliest opportunity, however, the administration of the new Crown estate was rationalized. No longer were there monastic households to feed. All resources in kind were converted into ready cash or into a regular cash income. Stock, live and dead, stores of all kinds, and standing corn were sold. Many people, including the monks, no doubt made the most of any period of confusion, or of delay in the arrival of the king's officers, to spirit away stock, goods, and even parts of the fabric. But great quantities were sold by the royal officers. The prices which are recorded seem reasonable and there are few reports of difficulty in finding purchasers. At Netley Abbey, Hants., in 1536, Michael Lister and William Sharland paid over £100 for all the cattle and other stock. At Wintney, Richard Paulet, receiver of the court of Augmentations, bought half the grain crop himself.[1] Sales of stock invariably realized far more than sales of standing crops or grain. It seems likely, as Savine suggests, that such a wholesale dispersal must have depressed local prices for a time, although it is reported that in 1537 people came from all parts of the south to buy the Furness Abbey cattle.[2] In a very large number of cases, stock, and even household equipment, was sold to those who took over the demesnes. Lord Scrope bought a good deal of the stock in hand of Easby Priory, Yorkshire, and also obtained possession of the site and demesnes. John Herbert did the same at Ellerton Priory. In some cases part of the stock and grain was distributed among the departing monks. At the surrender of Roche Abbey, Yorkshire, in 1538, the abbot, in addition to a pension of £33 6s. 8d., was sent on his way with £30 in cash and a quarter of the abbey stock, including sixty oxen, 120 sheep, and forty swine.[3] Rents in kind were an embarrassment to the Crown and were speedily commuted. For example, in 1539 the leasehold rent due to Bath Abbey from Weston in Somerset was converted into £24 8s. by pricing the wheat at 5s. 4d. per quarter, barley at 2s. 8d., and oats at 1s. 4d. The cartloads of hay were valued at 1s. each, and those of straw at 4d., and the feeding of the oxen at 4s. a head.[4] Cash equivalents had sometimes already been provided for in the indentures of leases. In a number of cases the rent in kind, instead of being commuted, was farmed out by the Crown to a third party. For example, in December 1542 Sir George Throckmorton of Coughton, Warwickshire, took from

[1] Kennedy, op. cit., p. 149.
[2] Savine, op. cit., p. 196; LP XII, ii, p. 88. Savine bases his conclusions on the valuations of stock set down in the commissioners' surveys. The actual sale prices are to be found in some of the accounts of the Receivers of the court of Augmentations (PRO SC 6, Henry VIII, Monastic Lands).
[3] J. M. Clay, *Yorkshire Monasteries: Suppression Papers*, Yorks. Arch. Soc., Rec. Ser., XLVIII, 1912, pp. 99, 105; Woodward, op. cit., p. 362.
[4] PRO SC 6, Henry VIII, 3144, m. 17.

the Crown for twenty-one years a lease of thirty-seven quarters of wheat, eighty-two quarters of barley, besides a small quantity of rye, payable by various tenants of the lands late of Worcester Cathedral Priory. He paid a total rent of £24 4s. 10d. One of these rents in kind was payable by John and Thomas Charlett and John Harborne, lessees of the former priory's tithes at Cleeve, who, unfortunately for Throckmorton, "off theyr malycyous froward synyster myndes and intentes," did not pay up promptly, and Robert Throckmorton and William Sheldon, assigns of Sir George, complained to the court of Augmentations.[1] As prices rose many of these lessees of grain rents must have made handsome profits.

Most important of all, such monastic property as came into the king's hands with vacant possession was very promptly rented on a temporary basis. Richard Pollard wrote from Glastonbury, "Cattell we intende to sell for redy money, and to let owte the pastures and demeynes now from Mighelmas for the quarterly, untill the kingis pleasure therin be further knowyne to thentente his grace shall lease (lose) no rent, for thabbott had muche pasture grounde in his hande."[2] In 1536 the rent of vacant demesne was usually fixed by reference to the *Valor Ecclesiasticus*, or by some hasty estimation, and was for the most part below its market value. Robert Southwell reported from Yorkshire in 1537 that monastic demesnes were being sublet by Crown lessees at a profit. Sir Thomas Wharton had the demesnes of Healaugh Park Priory for £23 and was subletting at £26 13s. 4d. Leases were being sold even more profitably. According to Southwell, that of Rosedale Priory had changed hands for £200 although the rent due to the Crown was only £7. He knew, he said, of local men who would give a great deal for these 'farms', and he begged Cromwell to hold his hand until the property could be surveyed "by eye and measure, and not by credit, as the commissioners for the suppression did."[3] But to have leased these lands on the open market would have put an almost impossible strain on the newly-established administrative machinery. Moreover, the possibility must not be ruled out that the government was deliberately enabling numbers of laymen to share in the proceeds of the Dissolution. In 1538–9, however, demesne in hand was more carefully surveyed. At De la Pré Abbey, Northamptonshire, meadow subject to common grazing for part of the year was valued at 3s. per acre, meadow lying 'several' all the year at 3s. 4d. Pasture was valued at 1s. 6d. per acre, and arable land in the open fields at 6d. At St Andrew's Priory in the same county, arable land described as

[1] E 321, 16, 73.
[2] Wright, *op. cit.*, p. 258.
[3] LP XII, i, p. 255; ii, pp. 88, 206.

'lying in furlongs was valued at 8d. per acre, and meadow at 5s. At Pipewell Abbey commonable meadow was set at 2s. 4d. and open field arable at 8d., and at Welbeck closes of pasture were valued at 8d., closes of arable at 4d., and of meadow at 1s. 4d.[1] These initial lettings of demesne were most important, for the rents fixed then were usually adhered to in subsequent more formal leases, and also formed the basis of later valuations for outright grants. Formal leases followed at a later date, sometimes within months, and in a few cases only after some years had passed. As laid down in the statute of 1536, Crown leases were normally for twenty-one years. Woods were always carefully reserved.[2]

As a landlord the Crown was always conservative. Rents remained fixed, although land values more than doubled between 1540 and 1590. In the 1530's and 1540's fines for leases were low, rarely more than one year's rent. In the 1550's some attempt was made to take account of the rise in the value of land, in the 1560's fines for new leases reached four and five times the annual rent. If this came anywhere near to closing the gap early in Elizabeth's reign, it failed to keep up with subsequent inflation, so that by the end of the century, according to Professor Habakkuk's calculations, "fines were probably only some five years' purchase of the excess of annual value over annual rent."[3] Winchcombe manor in Gloucestershire had been in Crown hands during the greater part of the sixteenth century. In the early seventeenth century it was sold to the Whitmores, one of whom went down to inspect the property in 1612 and tried to hold a court. He reported as follows:

"...and for herriots wee might have had naked children, and for distresses for rent, patched petticoats, the Common pasture for all the quicke Cattle, and when we spake of fines and raysinge of rentes, we had a Chain of Scoulds, raysinge their voyces to 'God save the Kinge and the lawes; and they and their ancestours had lived there And they would live there,' and without the danger of hotte spittes and scaldinge water and fiery tongues, there is no gaineinge of possession."

---

[1] E 315, 399, f. 118; ff. 131–8; f. 148; ff. 216–7. For a longer Crown lease in Mary's reign, see M. E. Finch, *The Wealth of Five Northamptonshire Families, 1540–1640*, Northants Rec. Soc., 1956, p. 70.

[2] Attention is often drawn to the fact that the revenues recorded in the early post-Dissolution ministers' accounts considerably exceed those set down in the *Valor Ecclesiasticus*, implying that the Crown was effecting 'improvements' in its income. But in most cases detailed examination of the figures will show that the increases are due to the inclusion in the Crown accounts, or the more realistic valuation of, demesne which had been in hand in 1535.

[3] E 323, 1–8, *passim*; H. J. Habakkuk, 'The Market for Monastic Property, 1539–1603', EcHR, 2nd Ser., x, 1958, pp. 370–72.

He went on to report that in the end the poorer tenants, who could not afford to pay fines, agreed to their rents being raised.[1]

The court of Augmentations, besides administering the former monastic lands, was charged, through its chancellor, with "minister(ing) equal justice to rich and poor to the best of (his) cunning, wit and power," and was soon very busy dealing with a multitude of complaints. Many were of the kind regularly being dealt with by the king's other courts, cases of disputed tenure, claims to leases for which no written evidence could be shown, and so on. Many, however, arose from the peculiarities of the lands concerned. Liability to pay tithe was a frequent subject of litigation. Quite apart from the reputed freedom from tithe of certain monastic land, a good deal of it had not paid tithe before the Dissolution simply because the monasteries concerned were themselves owners of the tithe. The Dissolution inevitably altered the situation when tithes and demesnes were leased or sold separately. The lessee of the site and demesnes of Tywardreath Priory, Cornwall, when charged with non-payment of tithe by the lessee of the parsonage, cited the statute of 1539 which assured the lands to the king exactly as they had been enjoyed by the monks.[2] Many disputes arose over boundaries between adjacent manors now in separate occupation. A great many people were no doubt hoping to take advantage of the confusion brought about by the change in ownership to lay false claims. The settlement of the ensuing disputes led to many former abbots and monks being called on for their testimony. On the whole the proceedings of the court make dull reading for the historian of agriculture. Only occasionally did a refreshing whiff of country air blow through the courts at Westminister, as when one of the tenants of the manor of Lenthall Stark, late of Wigmore Abbey, Herefordshire, told the court about five parcels of meadow, part of the lord's demesne, called Lady Plocks, where, immediately after midsummer and the gathering of the first "math" and crop, until Candlemas, the tenants had been accustomed to enjoy with their beasts "the later math, crop, vesture, edgrowe, or depasturacon." One is reminded, too, of the benevolent abbots of the legends when one reads the plea of the parishioners of Longney in Gloucestershire. The prior of Great Malvern, the court was told, owner of fifty messuages in their village, had always contributed half the cost of repairing their sea defences, giving them two "crybbes" and certain "throughes" and gates. Since the Dissolution no help had been forthcoming and they had had to sell

---

[1] D. Royce, *Landboc sive Registrum Monasterii de Winchelcumba*, II, 1903, p. lxx. The conservatism of Crown management is amply demonstrated in Lancashire by Mr Mason (*op. cit.*, pp. 157–63, 224–6).

[2] E 321, 9, 69. See also Savine, *op. cit.*, pp. 108 *sqq.*

jewels from their church to raise the necessary money.¹ But by and large the proceedings of the court of Augmentations, together with those of the courts of Star Chamber and Requests, which also dealt with cases concerning monastic lands, do not give one the impression that the Dissolution had inflicted great hardships on the peasants. In fact, the plaintiffs were very often the new landlords, endeavouring to establish their right to enjoy their grants. With only the depositions extant it is usually very difficult, at this distance, to judge which of the parties was at fault. But we can sympathize with Isabel Best who in 1544 bought, at second hand, a tenement in Hawksworth, Yorkshire, late of Esholt Priory. She complained that Thomas Wood of Hawksworth, "having neither right nor title" to the property, refused to give her possession. In this case, reference to the particulars prepared for the initial sale by the Crown establishes that he was a tenant-at-will.²

(e) *The disposal of monastic lands*

(i) *The break-up of the monastic estates.* Whatever the king and Cromwell may or may not have intended, outright alienation of the monastic lands began almost at once and rapidly rose to a peak in the early 1540's. The first grant according to the date of the letters patent was that on the 1st of April 1536, to Sir Henry Parker, of the site of Latton Priory, Essex, with property belonging to the priory in Essex, Hampshire, and Middlesex.³ Over the country as a whole well over half of the total monastic estate had been alienated by the Crown before the end of Henry VIII's reign. Large portions of the remainder were disposed of during the reign of Edward VI, and a smaller amount during that of Mary. By 1558 about three quarters had left Crown ownership. Elizabeth continued the distribution, along with other church lands, but a not inconsiderable estate still remained to be drawn on by her early Stuart successors. These are conclusions based on the only national estimates available, those of Professor Dietz, modified by the more detailed figures now available for several counties.⁴ If the figures for the counties so far

¹ E 321, 9, 2; 11, 49.
² E 321, 20, 71, and E 318, 755.  ³ LP x, p. 325, g. 6.
⁴ F. C. Dietz, *English Government Finance, 1485–1558*, 1920, p. 149. Here Dietz speaks of two-thirds of the monastic lands having been "alienated" by 1547. One can only assume that he is including grants by exchange, gift, and sale. In a later work (*English Public Finance, 1558–1641*, 1932, p. 291) he puts the proportion of the monastic lands "sold" during the same period at seven-eighths. The county of Lancashire, where, owing to the large proportion of the former monastic lands which had been annexed to the duchy of Lancaster, less than half the total had been alienated by the Crown by 1558 (Mason, *op. cit.*, p. 146), may be regarded as an extreme case, probably unparalleled elsewhere.

studied are representative, Professor Dietz's figures are rather high. The discrepancy is probably to be explained by the fact that at county level it is possible to be more precise on details, to allow, for instance, for the restoration of part of the land to the Crown by sale, exchange, or escheat. The figures for the counties agree remarkably well for the separate reigns, but they differ a little when compared over the years. Whereas in Leicestershire the peak came early, some 36 per cent of all the monastic land in the county having been alienated by 1542, in Hampshire the climax came in 1544-6.[1]

On whatever terms the grant was to be made, the initiative was taken by the prospective grantee in deciding what particular estates he wanted. Even from 1539 onwards, when the lands were put on the open market, although the total amount which the commissioners were empowered to sell was limited, the officers of the Crown did not attempt to sell specific properties. From time to time attempts were made to dispose of certain types of property. In the case of odd tenements of small value which were expensive to administer, this was done by making tenurial or financial concessions.[2] A certain brake was always applied to the disposal of properties which, usually on account of their size or because they were near other royal estates, it was not advisable for the Crown to part with. But, broadly speaking, all the monastic land was potentially on the market.

Given the initiative to this extent, it was obvious that prospective grantees would pounce first on the most desirable properties. The sites of monastic houses figure very largely in early grants. These included the remains of extensive buildings, gardens, fishponds, orchards, and in fact the makings of desirable country residences, whether for letting or occupation. A good deal of the fabric, especially of the conventual churches, had been dismantled and sold by the royal commissioners. The greater part, however, especially of the domestic quarters and agricultural buildings such as barns, was left intact. Equally sought-after were the monastic home-farms and the bartons or granges which so often lay conveniently adjacent to the conventual buildings. But most grantees had to be satisfied with the monastic manors. These were sought not so much on account of their size, though available capital must often have been a limiting factor, as of their location, and the opportunity this offered of adding to an already existing estate, or, especially where monastic manors lay adjacent, of accumulating a new one.

[1] Thorpe, *op. cit.*, pp. 119-21, 191; Kennedy, *op. cit.*, p. 167; J. A. Youings, 'The Terms of the Disposal of the Devon Monastic Lands, 1536-58', EHR, LXIX, 1954, pp. 34, 37.
[2] Youings, *ibid.*, pp. 31-3; J. Hurstfield, 'The Greenwich Tenures of the reign of Edward VI', *Law Qtrly. Rev.*, LXV, 1949, pp. 72-81.

The size of grants varied greatly, from the enormous grants, mostly confined to the very early years and to the reign of Edward VI, to men like John Lord Russell, Thomas earl of Rutland and others, through hundreds of grants of land worth £20 or thereabouts, to numbers of grants of small properties or groups of tenements worth less than £5 in all.[1] While subsequent grants and also resales did on occasion re-unite parts of the total monastic estate, the general effect of disposal was to split the whole into thousands of portions, most of it to be loosely joined to lay estates of infinite variety as regards both size and geographical distribution.

Some of the early grants, especially those made on favourable terms to the king's closest associates, included the site, demesnes, and practically the whole of the former monastic estate appertaining thereto. Thus, in July 1537, Sir Edward Grey, Lord Powis, was granted the site and demesnes of Buildwas Abbey, Shropshire, ten of the abbey's granges in Shropshire, Staffordshire, and Derbyshire, and three of its rectories.[2] But for the most part, and especially when sale of the property was in full swing after 1539, purchasers were more selective and the estates of individual houses went into the melting pot. The *rentier* character of most of the monastic lands meant that the break-up of the estate did not materially affect the agricultural management of constituent parts or leave them in novel isolation. Indeed the dispersal of the property among lay owners made for more compactness in the geographical pattern of landownership. For whereas monasteries had been largely dependent on benefactors, the new lay owners had more freedom to select their acquisitions. In the long run this must have led to improvements in local agrarian efficiency.

Monastic manors, however, were invariably disposed of intact. Such fragmentation as did take place was confined to the more loosely knit and territorially scattered 'manors' of more recent origin. But, whether of ancient or recent origin, the monastic manor came, in lay hands, to assume more than an administrative significance, the manor being the key unit of landholding in the feudal tenurial structure which the Tudor monarchy was energetically striving to perpetuate. In this respect, as far as most of the monastic tenants were concerned, the effect of the transference of ownership was of little consequence. The great majority of them, free, customary, and leasehold, merely became tenants of the king, instead of tenants of the monasteries. Most of the free tenants held by 'socage' tenure which was free from feudal incidents. A handful of landowners in each county, however, who had held part of their land by military tenure of the monasteries, became, as a result of the Dissolution, military tenants of the Crown, and later of

[1] LP, CPR, and E 318, *passim*.    [2] LP XII, ii, p. 166, g. 13.

other landowners, with all the accompanying disadvantages.¹ Far more important, however, when the monastic lands were alienated in fee by the Crown to its subjects, care was taken to secure, and potentially to expand, the Crown's feudal interests. It was laid down, in the statute of 1536 which established the court of Augmentations, that on all conveyances of monastic property in fee there should be reserved tenures by knight service in chief of the Crown, and, with minor concessions later on, this provision was carried out. As a result, the amount of land which was of interest to the Office (from 1540, the Court) of Wards was considerably increased. The combined outcome, therefore, of the Dissolution and the disposal of monastic lands was to perpetuate the existing tenurial structure of the countryside, the only difference being that almost the whole of the former monastic estate was now held either by, or immediately of, the Crown itself.²

Finally, as the result of the Dissolution and of the subsequent alienation of the monastic property by the Crown, in thousands of parishes throughout the kingdom, some or all of the tithes, which had often been leased by laymen, now came, for the first time, into the outright ownership of laymen.

(ii) *The terms of Crown disposal.* In December 1539 Sir Richard Rich, chancellor of the court of Augmentations, and Thomas Cromwell, were empowered by letters patent to sell the former monastic and other Crown lands to the total annual value of £6,000, at twenty years' purchase. Urban property could be sold at a lower rate.³ A good deal of the monastic property had already been alienated by the Crown during the three preceding years, some as free gifts, some by exchange for other land, some at fee-farm rents, and some by sale. It can be shown that the standard rate of twenty years' purchase had already been adopted, though there is no record of its having been officially authorized.⁴ The procedure for obtaining a grant had also

---

¹ The abbess of Wilton had a considerable number of tenants by knight service, and, as the surveyor of the earl of Pembroke, who acquired most of the Wilton Abbey lands, wrote of them in 1567-8, "... and so Homage, Fealtie, and Escuage draweth unto them Warde, Maryage, and Reliefe" (Straton, *op. cit.*, 1, pp. 3-6, and *passim*).

² J. Hurstfield, *The Queen's Wards*, 1958, Part 1, 'The Revival of Royal Wardship', pp. 3-29.     ³ LP XIV, ii, p. 301, g. 36.

⁴ For example, in March 1537 there was granted to Sir Edmund Bedingfield and his wife, Grace, the site and estates of Redlingfield Priory, Suffolk. No purchase price appears in the letters patent (LP XII, i, p. 353, g. 39), but the annual value of the property is given as £31 4s. 5d. and an annual rent of 63s. 6d., i.e. one tenth, is mentioned. The accounts of the Treasurer of the court of Augmentations, however, record the payment by Sir Edmund of £400, part of £561 19s. due for the purchase of Redlingfield (E 323, 1, 1, m. 5). This works out at almost exactly twenty years' purchase of the net annual value. See also TED I, p. 18. Dietz states, quite unaccountably, that sales commenced in March 1539 (*English Government Finance*, p. 148).

already been established. The suitor had first to seek out the appropriate auditor of the court of Augmentations and obtain a certificate of the current annual value of the property he wished to acquire. This valuation was then placed before the appropriate royal officials, either the chancellor of the court of Augmentations if any royal bounty or any exchange of land was involved, or, in the case of a straightforward sale, the commissioners. In either case a 'rate' was appended. From the net annual value as certified by the auditors was deducted the statutory reserved rent of one tenth, and any allowance by way of royal gift, or for lands surrendered to the king in exchange. Additions were made for woods. Finally the balance was made payable, either as a perpetual fixed 'fee-farm' rent or as a capital sum calculated at a number of years' purchase. For example, in 1545 William Sneyd desired to purchase the manor of Keele in Staffordshire, lately belonging to the Order of St John of Jerusalem. The auditor certified that the current annual value was confined to the rent of £18 reserved on a lease of the manor in 1528 for forty years to Sir Henry Dewes. The commissioners noted this, deducted the normal reserved rent of one tenth, i.e. 36s., and rated the balance at twenty years' purchase. To this they added £10 for the woods and required the total, £334, to be paid in hand.[1]

The auditors' basic valuations were obviously very important. Except where, as at Keele, manors had been farmed out as a whole, individual totals were given for free and customary rents. Leasehold rents were usually given in detail and the date and term cited if the information was to hand. Like the *Valor* of 1535, from which, in fact the auditors would seem often to have copied, the particulars for grants contain accurate summaries of strictly current regular annual income. It is likely that the figures given for an average year's casual revenue, court profits, fines, etc., were low. On the other hand, as in the *Valor*, no allowances were made for arrears of rent, 'decayed' or vacant holdings, or for expenditure on repairs. Full allowance was made for inescapable charges such as outgoing rents, bailiffs' fees granted for life, and stipends, synodals, etc., payable out of 'spiritual' revenues. Very rarely, however, were grantees burdened with the 'fees', annuities, and other general expenses with which the monks had charged their revenues. Responsibility for these, together with the pensions granted to the monks, was usually retained by the Crown. Only in the case of some of the 'gifts' of land were these burdens passed on, thereby limiting considerably the grantees' immediate enjoyment of the royal bounty. Woods were separately valued, at a capital sum based on acreage or on the number of growing trees. In Devon the normal value put on timber by the Surveyor of Woods was 6d. per acre per year's

[1] E 318, 1021.

growth, i.e. ten acres of eight years' growth were set at 40s. Odd trees were priced at from 4d. to 1s., according to age, and a further sum was added in respect of the natural increase and the herbage, usually 4d. or 6d. per acre, *per annum*. By comparison the treatment of such conventual and farm buildings as had survived the stripping of their lead was casual, and these rarely figured in the valuation. In most cases, however, they were already occupied by the farmers or their assigns, whereas woods had always been carefully reserved by the owners.[1]

Using the gross figures of the *Valor* of 1535 as a rough guide, together with the details in the particulars for grants, it is possible to ascertain, very approximately, how much monastic land was actually given away by the Crown, how much went by exchange, etc., and how much was sold. Calculations of this kind have so far been made only on a county basis, and they are complicated by the grants which included land from more than one county. However, for Devon, it has been calculated that during the period 1536–58, rather less than 25 per cent of the total monastic landed wealth in the county was given away by the Crown. For Leicestershire the proportion seems to have been considerably less, under 15 per cent of the whole.[2] Calculation of the proportion alienated in exchange for other lands is even more difficult. For Leicestershire a figure of $7\frac{1}{2}$ per cent of the whole monastic estate has been suggested.[3] Apart from the small amount which was accounted for by the reservation of a fee-farm rent, the rest was sold, and in this category one can safely include by far the greater part of the former monastic lands throughout the country. Savine calculated that nearly three quarters of the grants made by Henry VIII were by sale, and recent local studies have amply confirmed what H. A. L. Fisher wrote as long ago as 1906, that the greater part of the monastic lands throughout the kingdom was sold at or above the "good market price" of twenty years' purchase.[4]

During the very early years, when there was rather more likelihood, and certainly greater hope, of royal generosity, there was something of a scramble for grants. Everyone in Court circles, and many who were hardly known at Court, hoped for a share of the confiscated lands on favourable terms, and few hesitated to press their suit in what they hoped was the right quarter, usually with Thomas Cromwell. Some even offered to pay whatever the king might regard as a fair

[1] The form of the particulars for grants is more fully described in Youings, *Devon Monastic Lands, loc. cit.*, pp. xiv–xx.
[2] Youings, EHR, LXIX, 1954, p. 30; Thorpe, *op. cit.*, p. 133.
[3] Thorpe, *ibid.*, where the figures are given as proportions of the total monastic estate alienated before 1558. They have been corrected by reference to the estimate (*ibid.*) of a total alienation of the Leicestershire property by 1558 of 75 per cent.
[4] H. A. L. Fisher, *Political History of England, 1485–1547*, 1906, pp. 482, 499.

price. After 1539, when sales began in earnest, supply and demand, at the Crown's price, seem to have been about equally balanced. There is no reflection in the terms of the grants either of competition for individual properties, or of any greater demand for estates in the home counties as opposed to those in the more distant parts of the kingdom. Whatever the location, the commissioners calculated the price in accordance with current routine instructions. In fact the Crown seems to have found little difficulty at any time in disposing of as much of the monastic property as it wished to sell, and those of its subjects who possessed the necessary capital had little difficulty in acquiring the lands they wanted.

During the 1540's, when the volume of sales was at its height, the standard rate of twenty years' purchase was adhered to with great regularity, and this was the case whatever the length of time which remained before the grantee might, by the falling-in of leases, enjoy the advantages of full possession of his property. Thus, in 1544, John Maynard bought a number of properties scattered over several counties. These included a mill and some land in Chaddesley, Worcestershire, leased to a tenant by Bordesley Abbey in 1479 for eighty years, and a farm in Sherrington, Buckinghamshire, let in 1534 by the Northamptonshire abbey of De La Pré for ninety-nine years. Of the former, and of several similar properties, the auditor noted, "I thinke ther wold be good fynes given for the same if they were nowe to be letten," but the commissioners rated all together at twenty years' purchase.[1] The commissioners alone were responsible for arranging the terms of sale, and they were busy ministers of the Crown. It would have been impossible for them to have gauged the value of each piece of property on the open market: there had to be a simple formula. The practice of rating the property at twenty years' purchase of the net annual value worked very well in the early years, and, bearing in mind existing leases, it probably ensured a reasonable bargain to both sides until about the end of Henry VIII's reign. Occasionally, even in these early years, when the auditors indicated that a property was considerably under-rented, the rate was slightly increased. By the mid and later 1540's the rise in prices was making nonsense of most existing rents, and twenty years' purchase of current annual values was clearly realizing much less than the real value of the land. Gradually, therefore, the rate of sale of all but fixed or 'improved' rents was increased, first to twenty-five and thirty years' purchase, and, by the 1590's, to as much as forty times the current annual value.[2] This was the rough-and-ready

[1] E 318, 755.
[2] Habakkuk, *op. cit.*, pp. 372–6. The whole of this paragraph owes a great deal to Professor Habakkuk's article.

method adopted of obtaining something approaching twenty years' purchase of the real value of the land, which nobody doubted was a fair price, and it was not, as has sometimes been suggested, a response to a greater demand for monastic land, although the fact that it apparently did not depress sales suggests that the demand was always a resilient one. The rise in the rating from the 1550's probably never quite caught up with the general rise in land values during the following century. Whether this was due to administrative inertia or to deliberate Crown policy, it probably helped to sustain interest in the purchase of monastic lands. Far more important in this respect, however, was the appearance in the land market during the half century following the Dissolution of a steady stream of men on the look-out for land with which either to form the nucleus of a new estate or to augment a patrimony. Such men were not easily persuaded to pay greatly inflated prices, but neither were they speculators, needing to buy cheaply. Location was more important to them and they were quite prepared to suffer a low yield for a generation or more.

(iii) *Profits*. What was monastic land worth to the grantee, were he a recipient of royal bounty or one of the majority who had paid ready money for his estate? By and large such a question must form part of a general inquiry into land values and profits during the century between the Dissolution and the Civil War.[1] There were, however, certain features which characterized, even if they were not peculiar to, monastic estates. It is quite obvious from what we have seen of the activities of the monks during the decade preceding the Dissolution that the majority of monastic tenants enjoyed considerable security of tenure. Moreover, as we have seen, the Crown did nothing to undermine or lessen this security. The amount of revenue which the Crown, and after the Crown, the lay grantees, could hope to enjoy, immediately and in many cases for decades, was limited almost entirely to the regular current rents being paid in the 1530's. This is easily illustrated from estate accounts and surveys of former monastic lands in private hands up and down the country. A survey made in 1590 of the manor of Brilley in Herefordshire, once belonging to Abbey Cwmhir, shows tenant after tenant still in possession of lands granted to their predecessors for ninety-nine years in the early years of the century. Richard ap Thomas paid 4s. a year for thirty-five acres leased to his forebears by the abbot for ninety-nine years on the 28th January 1495; David ap Richard, 7s. for forty-three acres on a ninety-nine year lease made in 1527.[2] The disadvantage to the landlord of such long terms lay not so much in the persistence of old and accustomed rents as in the length of time that must elaspe before he could levy fines for the renewal of

[1] See vol. I of this paperback series, pp. 13 *sqq.*    [2] Hereford RO, LC Deeds, 6581.

tenancies. In so far as the monks had gathered in large sums on the eve of the Dissolution, by that much were the lay owners precluded from repeating the process for some considerable time.

Tenancies-at-will, of course, offered the greatest scope to the new owners. But, on the whole, the proportion of monastic land held on such terms was small. Few abbots had been able to resist the offers made by their tenants for some security of tenure, on the eve of their departure if not before. A few tenancies fell in, in the normal course of events, within a short time, but the number of reversions granted shortly before the Dissolution kept these at a minimum. Life tenancies offered to landlords at least a sporting chance of profitable resumption. Many of the customary holdings of Wilton Abbey, most of which were for one life only, fell in in the 1540's, but, whether debarred by the custom of the manors, or by a glut of available holdings, or by inclination, the new owner, the earl of Pembroke, exacted entry fines which were appreciably lower than those which the abbess had levied a decade earlier.[1] Of the leases for years with which the monastic lands were encumbered, the comparatively short Crown leases for twenty-one years probably offered the earliest hope of surrender. When John lord Russell acquired the site and demesnes of Woburn Abbey in 1547, at a partial fee-farm rent, any immediate profit or possession was barred by two Crown leases held by Sir Francis Bryan and Sir John Williams or their assigns and not due to expire until 1565–6.[2] But this, by current standards, was but a short interval. Customary tenures were, in the long run, less profitable to the landowner, and some of the latter found ways of persuading their customary tenants to exchange copies for indentures of leases. At Tavistock, in the 1540's, Russell had done this with some success. Even so, the increase in his income was probably far from commensurate with the real value of his estate. On his large manor of Werrington, for example, valued at £125 for the grant of 1539, conversion from copyhold to leasehold tenure had little effect on rents. By the death of Francis Russell, second earl of Bedford, in 1585, regular annual income had risen to only £128. Fines levied at the granting of tenancies during the preceding two decades amounted to approximately £3,000, but, spread over the years, this barely doubled the annual income.[3] Sir Nicholas Bacon built up an estate in East Anglia and the neighbouring counties during the period 1540–79, much of it former monastic property. By 1646 some of this was producing an annual rent income ten, and even fourteen, times that of

[1] Straton, *op. cit.*, pp. 7–11 and *passim*.
[2] G. Scott Thomson, 'Woburn Abbey and the Dissolution of the Monasteries', RHS, 4th Ser., XVI, 1933, pp. 129 *sqq*.
[3] Finberg, *op. cit.*, p. 271, and PRO SP 1, Elizabeth, case 9, no. 2.

a century earlier. To a certain extent Bacon was fortunate, and also showed himself to be a shrewd judge of property, in that his purchases were not encumbered with unduly long leases. But he, or rather his descendants, had to wait until at least the turn of the century before their income rose appreciably. At Redgrave in Suffolk, where Bacon wanted immediate possession, he had to buy out existing interests. At Rickinghall, too, he had to buy out Crown leases which still had seventeen years to run. In 1558 Sir Robert Molyneux, having purchased the manor of Altcar in Lancashire from the Crown for £1000, then paid 500 marks to the tenant in occupation for the remaining sixty years of a conventual lease of 1537.[1] Thus, in order to obtain immediate possession, both Bacon and Molyneux had had to find two lots of capital.

There were, no doubt, many landowners who resorted to oppressive and illegal means of evicting tenants and of increasing rents. But the history of landlord-tenant relations cannot fairly be reconstructed from the records of law-suits, especially from those cases for which we have only the plaintiffs' depositions and not the decrees of the courts concerned. Moreover, it has yet to be proved that the grantees of monastic lands were more successful than the Crown in upsetting conventual grants, or even any more intent on doing so.[2] Not all Tudor landowners valued financial gain more than a well-chosen complex of properties and a good name. Sir John Gostwick was a typical servant of Henry VIII's new regime. He was also busy in the 1540's augmenting his estate. His purchases of monastic lands were made with great deliberation, beginning with properties late of Warden Abbey near his home at Willington in Bedfordshire. Later he added to his estate, mostly in the same county, but with outlying portions in Northamptonshire and Staffordshire. For all of this he paid the full standard price. But he seems to have had no desire for quick returns, even if these were possible. He advised his son neither to levy large fines nor to raise his rents unless this could be justified by the fact that his tenants were subletting at a considerable profit.[3]

[1] A. Simpson, *The Wealth of the Gentry, 1540–1660*, 1961, pp. 66–84, 202–9, 214; Mason, *op. cit.*, p. 215. See also J. H. Hexter, *Reappraisals in History*, 1961, pp. 132–3.

[2] It is possible (I owe the suggestion to Professor Habakkuk) that those who, in the latter part of the century, purchased at more than twenty years' purchase property still encumbered by long leases, did so in the hope that they would be able to upset conventual grants. Further study of the judicial records of the courts of Augmentations and Exchequer and of private estate records is needed before we can be sure how far such hopes were either experienced or fulfilled. Meanwhile, this at least is certain: at no time was there any discernible relation between the number of years' purchase and the unexpired terms of existing leases.

[3] A. G. Dickens, 'Estate and Household Management in Bedfordshire, c. 1540', *Beds. Hist. Rec. Soc.*, XXXVI, 1956, pp. 44–5, and H. P. R. Finberg, 'The Gostwicks of Willington', *ibid.*, pp. 57–75.

For the majority of laymen, whether gentlemen or yeomen farmers, quicker profits were to be made by leasing than by buying monastic lands. A jury in 1549 found that Simon Catesby's rectory of Wigston was worth £60 a year more to him than the £22 7s. 4d. which he was paying to the king. The fine of £40 which he had paid to Lenton Priory in 1536 had been money well spent, and his lease still had over thirty years to run. In 1531–2 the earl of Cumberland obtained from the abbot of Furness a lease for eighty years of Winterburn Grange. The rent was £40. In 1537 the property was valued by the king's officers at £51 6s. 8d., but the earl had no difficulty in obtaining confirmation of his lease and his assigns were still paying the same rent to the duchy of Lancaster in the early part of Elizabeth's reign.[1] Finally, when Sir Thomas Dennis died in 1561 he was still enjoying the lease of sixty acres of marsh and moorland which his old employer, the abbot of Newenham, had granted to him in 1536. His son and heir later assigned the remainder of the term to his brother, who sold the residue of thirty-five years to a Henry Parson in 1600 for £220. Not until 1631 did Parson surrender the lease to the owner, Sir William Petre, who had brought the property, along with a great deal more, from the Howards in 1605.[2] It seems possible that it was the gentlemen lease-holders, most of them well versed in the law, who led the way in showing that the long lease for term of years could be made to run its full term.

Without any doubt the laymen who were in the best position of all to profit from monastic lands were those who were able to buy land of which they themselves were already conventual or Crown lessees. This applied particularly to those who bought monastic sites, with home farms which had been kept in hand to the very end by the monks, provided they were able to complete the purchase before the Crown granted a lease to a third party. The site of Marrick Priory, Yorkshire, was first leased by the Crown and then sold to John Uvedale. That of Nun Appleton fell in similar fashion to Robert Darkenall.[3] Both were active and energetic royal servants, alert to the speed with which their fellow Crown officers installed tenants into vacant properties. Others were not quick enough. Arthur Plantagenet, Lord Lisle, was at a disadvantage in that he carried on his negotiations from Calais through his agent, John Hussey. He actually began his bid for Frithelstock Priory in north Devon before the house was dissolved on the 27th of August 1536. The royal commissioners installed a local farmer, John Winslade, as temporary tenant. On the 6th of September Hussey informed Lisle that the site and barton had been let by the Crown to

[1] W. G. Hoskins, *The Midland Peasant*, 1957, p. 131; Mason, *op. cit.*, p. 138.
[2] Exeter City RO, DD. 6800.    [3] Clay, *op. cit.*, pp. 134–5, 140–1.

George Carew, and that unless Lisle could compound with Carew he would have to be content with the bare rent for twenty-one years. As Lisle later remarked in a letter to Ralph Sadler, he did not expect to live that long. Meanwhile, Carew sold his interest to John Winslade. Hussey advised Lisle to content himself with the reversion of the property, for the woods would be worth at least £100. The grant, in part a gift from the Crown and part at fee-farm, was completed on the 4th of September 1537.[1] Here and there one comes across individuals who purchased manors, direct or at second hand, whose demesne they already held by conventual lease. For example, the Horners, Thomas and John, who bought the manor of Mells and Leigh in Somerset from the Crown in 1543, already enjoyed possession of a farm called Melcombe which Thomas had leased from the abbot of Glastonbury at a rent of £6 6s. 8d. But this formed only a small part of the total property, for which, at a net valuation of £56 3s. 2½d., they paid twenty-four years' purchase. Unless Horner had Melcombe at a very low rent, this was not a very good bargain, for the greater part consisted of customary holdings, not easily 'improved'.[2]

Woods, which were extensive on monastic lands in many parts of the country, having been carefully reserved in leases, offered to the new owners some of the best opportunities of immediate profit. For instance, when Sir Philip Champernon bought the manor of Maristow, near Plymouth, in 1544, he obtained seventy-three acres of woodland, of which nineteen had already been felled, and eight appertained to the chief messuage for repairs, etc., leaving forty-six acres of timber varying from six to sixty years' growth. At 6d. per acre per year's growth, and £12 10s. for the "spring of the wood," Champernon paid the Crown £41 19s. Five years later his son Arthur sold the wood and underwood, but not the land, to four local farmers for £109.[3]

A great deal of the monastic land was resold by the original grantees, some of it changing hands many times, but the market was not so brisk, nor the speculation so rife, as many writers have suggested. In the county of Leicestershire out of about 64 per cent of the total monastic property, i.e. excluding the land still in Crown hands, which can be accounted for in 1558, nearly 40 per cent of the total was still in the hands of the original grantees or their heirs. These comprised only thirty-two out of the 105 original private grantees, excepting corporate bodies, but they were, on the whole, the recipients of the best estates. In Hampshire, in 1558, out of a total of 124 monastic manors, sixteen were still in Crown hands, seventy-seven in the

---

[1] Youings, *Devon Monastic Lands*, pp. 1–2; LP XI, pp. 111, 168, 513; LP *Addenda*, I, pt. 1, pp. 391–2; LP XII, ii, p. 281.
[2] E 318, 619.   [3] E 318, 257; Plymouth RO, Roborough MSS, 197.

possession of the original grantees, and only thirty-five had changed hands. Of the 130 manors in Devon which accounted for 60 per cent of the monastic property, seventeen were still in Crown hands in 1558, eighty-two were held by the original grantees or their descendants, twenty-two had changed hands once more, six twice more, two three times more, and one, the manor of Sherford, five times more, including two restorations to the Crown. Not all these changes of ownership were clear sales. Releases of parts of property between partners to a grant have been ignored, but some of the early 'resales' may have been simply releases by agents to their principals.[1]

Attention has often been drawn to the small band of grantees who would seem, from the patent rolls, to have hunted in pairs all over the country, buying up an extraordinary collection of scattered, and, on the whole, smaller, properties, most of which they disposed of at once. Richard Andrews, a native of Hailes, Gloucestershire, and Leonard Chamberlain of Woodstock, Oxford; the same Andrews in partnership with one Nicholas Temple; John Bellow of Grimsby and John Broxholme of London; Richard Brokylsbye of Glentworth, Lincolnshire, and John Dyon; and others, they are all familiar names to those who pursue monastic lands in any county. Apart from their activities in the monastic land market they were quite unknown in contemporary society. However, as Professor Habakkuk has pointed out, they were not necessarily speculators, buying to sell at a profit. Their purchases were too diverse and deliberate for that. They were agents, engaged in negotiating grants for clients all over the country, many of whom were unfamiliar with the procedure for acquiring monastic lands from the Crown.[2] This interpretation of their activities is strengthened by the fact that, where prices are recorded they were apparently disposing of the property for the same money as they gave for it. They were most active in the middle 1540's when, over the country as a whole, the disposal of monastic property was at its peak.

For something nearer pure speculation one has to look for purchases of accumulations of small properties confined to one or more localities. George Rolle and George Haydon certainly made a relatively large profit by buying most of the scattered north Devon properties of Pilton Priory in 1544 at twenty years' purchase and selling them to the occupiers or to other local men. To John Downe of Pilton, husbandman, they sold three messuages for £80, which was more than twice what they had paid for them. A farm called Lilly in the parish of Goodleigh, which they had bought for £18, they sold within six weeks to

[1] Thorpe, *op. cit.*, pp. 195–6; Kennedy, *op. cit.*, p. 202; Youings, *Devon Monastic Lands*, p. xxiii.
[2] Habakkuk, *op. cit.*, pp. 377–80.

William Downe of Pilton, for £28.[1] Both Rolle and Haydon were lawyers, sprung from minor local freeholding families, and their descendants, by the early seventeenth century, were among the greatest landowners in the county. But the scale of their dealings in monastic lands was not such as to bring them great wealth. It was just one of many ways in which modest fortunes were founded. They had their counterparts in other counties, but perhaps not many.

It is by no means easy to find out at what price monastic lands were resold. Only very occasionally was the 'consideration' recorded, either in the actual conveyances or in their enrolments in the various courts of record. It is never mentioned in the royal licences to alienate land held by military tenure. Profits made after the lapse of a decade or more are of little significance: it was to be expected that the value of land would appreciate in an age of fairly rapid inflation. Thus it is hardly surprising that the earl of Bedford sold his Devon manor of Burrington in 1577 for £700, a profit of 100 per cent on what it would have cost him at the standard rate in 1539.[2] Evidence of considerable short-term gains on large manorial properties does emerge here and there, but careful enquiry usually reveals that this had been made possible by some peculiarity in the terms of sale by the Crown, such as a valuation based on the nominal or low rent reserved on a life grant, as opposed to a lease, to a favourite subject. The officers of the court of Augmentations, especially in the early years, could usually be relied upon to 'work to rule' in such cases and the shrewd purchaser was able to buy the reversion to the property very cheaply. For example, in 1549 the earl of Warwick bought the site, demesne, and manor of Polsloe, near Exeter, by exchange and fee-farm rent, the whole being valued at just under £30 a year. Two days later he sold the property to Sir Richard Sackville, who sold it less than a year later to Sir Arthur Champernon for £1,048, a capital appreciation, assuming the standard rate of twenty years' purchase had been charged to Warwick, of 75 per cent. Either Warwick or Sackville had made a handsome profit, but at the expense of the Crown, not of Champernon, for the real value of the estate was about £70. It had been granted in 1541, for their lives, to Sir George Carew and Mary, his wife, at the low rent set in Warwick's particulars. Sir George had died in 1545 and his widow had married Sir Arthur Champernon.[3] He, presumably, was very happy to pay just under

---

[1] Youings, *Devon Monastic Lands*, pp. 44, 71. These were not all urban properties as suggested by Professor Habakkuk (*op. cit.*, p. 377, n. 2).

[2] Woburn Abbey, G 1, 54, for details of which I am indebted to Miss Gladys Scott Thomson.

[3] Youings, *op. cit.*, p. 102. See also G. W. O. Woodward, EHR, LXXIX, 1964, pp. 778–83.

fifteen years' purchase for the freehold rather than merely to occupy the estate in the right of his wife's life interest.

Generally speaking, however, the evidence, though limited, suggests that short-term capital gains were very rare in the monastic land market. Moreover, not even the use of agents will account for the number of people, courtiers, lawyers, and country gentry, who were content to buy at second hand. Had there been a larger profit on resales, more purchasers would surely have bought direct from the Crown, and this, in its turn, might have led to competitive offers. In fact, however, it is open to doubt whether contemporaries thought of land as a source of quick returns, least of all monastic lands, whose value could not rapidly be improved. At any rate, the comparative absence of short-term gains on resales confirms the impression that the Crown, having decided, rightly or wrongly, to alienate the monastic lands, normally obtained a fair capital return.

In the final analysis it will probably be found that the balance of economic advantage from the Dissolution lay neither with the Crown nor with any particular section of society, aristocratic, old or new gentry, or peasant. In the short run it undoubtedly lay with the tenants, whether peasants or gentlemen, and in the long run with the owners of the freehold. It was the latter, however, who were the real successors of the religious communities, and it is they who must now be considered.

(iv) *The grantees.* The task of discovering who were the new owners was begun over fifty years ago by Professor Savine, who established from the patent rolls the names of all the original grantees during the reign of Henry VIII. His method of classifying them, partly by class, and partly by occupation, has not been generally acceptable, but it is still the only attempt to achieve results on a national scale. In very round figures Savine's analysis indicates that, of that portion of the monastic land which was alienated by the Crown before 1547, 14 per cent went to peers, 18 per cent to courtiers and royal officials, and 21 per cent to country gentry.[1]

The main drawback of Savine's table is that it deals only with original Crown grantees, and in printing it H. A. L. Fisher drew attention to the need to consider the effect of subsequent resales. Over thirty years later this point was taken up by Professor Tawney, and he himself gave a lead by considering the history of some two hundred and fifty former monastic manors in Gloucestershire, Northamptonshire, and Warwickshire. He found that initially rather more than one sixth was acquired by seventeen peers. Crown officials and business men also had a share but the greater part went immediately to members of already well-established local landowning families.

[1] Fisher, *op. cit.*, p. 499.

Pursuing his manors through almost to the eve of the Civil War, Professor Tawney found that, as time went on, more and more came into the possession of local gentry, but their names included those of Thynne, Spencer, and Cecil. In fact, in these particular counties the long-term effect of the Dissolution was "not so much (to) endow an existing nobility, as (to) lay the foundation of a new nobility to arise in the next century."[1]

Some progress has been made in recent years in pursuing the ownership of former monastic lands on a strictly county basis, but the study has in no case been carried systematically beyond the end of Mary's reign. In three widely separated counties, Leicestershire, Hampshire and the Isle of Wight, and Devonshire, results so far obtained suggest certain local peculiarities, but the general pattern is remarkably uniform, and, on the whole, Professor Tawney's conclusions have been considerably reinforced. In each of the three counties large initial grants were made to men very close to the king, and, in each case, the lands were retained almost intact by their descendants for several generations. In Leicestershire the earls of Rutland acquired and retained lands worth, on the eve of the Dissolution, some £300 a year, and by 1558 about 30 per cent of the total monastic estate in the county had gone to peers of the realm. This included over half the demesne and land held 'at will', and it had been granted mostly as royal gifts or in exchange for other lands. In Hampshire, by 1558, the Wriothesleys, earls of Southampton, owned just over 20 per cent of the former monastic manors in the county, about half of which they had paid for in cash. The Lords Sandys and Paulet had acquired a further 18 per cent between them, so that nearly 40 per cent of the monastic estate in the county, in terms of manors, if not in value, had gone to three owners. In Devon one very large estate was carved out of monastic lands, that of the Russells, later earls of Bedford, worth in 1535 over £800 a year. This comprised about 12 per cent of the monastic land in the county. Altogether, by 1558 just over 27 per cent of the Devon monastic lands were held in large portions by seven owners, including, besides the earl of Bedford, the dean and canons of Windsor.[2]

The next largest share in Devon, nearly 20 per cent, went in parcels of land worth between £50 and £100 a year, mostly to men bearing the names of established local families but who were also themselves well known in London political and administrative circles. Such men

---

[1] R. H. Tawney, 'The Rise of the Gentry', EcHR, XI, 1941, pp. 23–8.

[2] Thorpe, *op. cit.*, pp. 184–7 (figures relate to original grants only); Kennedy, *op. cit.*, pp. 190, 195 (figures relate to lands alienated by 1558 and have been adjusted to indicate proportion of total monastic estate); Youings, *Devon Monastic Lands*, pp. xxv–xxvi (do.).

almost without exception had paid in full for their monastic property. By comparison the share of the lands acquired by purely local interests was rather less. Some sixty persons in this category in Devon had, by 1558, purchased a bare 15 per cent of the whole.[1] In none of the counties so far investigated do yeomen figure appreciably. Occasionally they bought small farms or parts of farms already in their own occupation, but rarely did they buy manors or lordships. Such men stood to gain far more by using what capital they had either to buy leases or to improve land they already held on long monastic leases.

With the notable exception of the rising aristocracy such as the earls of Bedford and Southampton, very few new or appreciably enlarged estates were built up by 1558 entirely or even principally of monastic lands. In Devon it is possible to identify only nine of these. In Leicestershire some fourteen had appeared by 1558, but of these only five lasted very much longer.[2] There is no particular significance in the fact that so few men put all their capital into monastic lands. Sir Arthur Champernon showed quite exceptional caution among his contemporaries when, in 1550, he had inserted in the deed of bargain and sale to him of the Polsloe Priory estate near Exeter, a covenant whereby the vendor, Sir Richard Sackville, was to repay the purchase money should the property ever be seized by the Crown.[3] The attitude of most men of his time amounted to a firm resolution that capital expended on the purchase of monastic lands would not lightly be surrendered. Politics hardly entered into it, and, it must be remembered, even Mary Tudor sold portions of the monastic estate. As always, men bought, when they were able to afford to, with discrimination, building up in the process either a compact or a dispersed estate, whichever suited their purpose. They kept an eye on the land market as a whole, and monastic lands were not by any means all that were available, nor were they necessarily the best bargains. John Arscott, of the Middle Temple and surveyor of woods beyond Trent for the court of Augmentations, the younger son of an old-established family of minor gentry in north-west Devon, was in a very fair position to purchase when and what he wanted directly from the Crown. But in fact he confined his monastic acquisitions to the two manors of Bradford, late of Launceston Priory, and Hatherleigh, late of Tavistock Abbey, which he bought in 1552 at second-hand, though within a matter of days after the original grant, from Lord Clinton and Saye. Both manors lay near his old home, but when he retired it was to the non-monastic manor of Tetcott, also on the Cornish border, which he bought, also in 1552, from Sir John Neville. Richard Duke, another

---

[1] Youings, *ibid*.  [2] Youings, *ibid*., p. xxvii; Thorpe, *op. cit*., pp. 286–7.
[3] Exeter RO, DD. 41941.

Devon lawyer and clerk of the court of Augmentations, was earlier in the field. He was, in fact, the first purchaser of monastic land in Devon. He made a number of further purchases, building up a compact estate in the vicinity of his small patrimony in east Devon where his descendants flourished for at least two centuries.[1] Men like Arscott and Duke, most of them younger sons of already established landowning families, were building up new patterns of landownership all over the country during the century following the Dissolution. Only in so far as the capital with which they acquired their new estates had been accumulated in the service of the Crown did they owe their landed wealth to the dissolution of the monasteries.

## 2. *The secular clergy*

The administration of the non-monastic ecclesiastical estates, from those of the archbishops to those of the parish clergy, has attracted very little attention from agricultural historians of the period 1500–1640. There is insufficient scholarly work available upon which to base a long account of the subject. In part this is due to the scanty nature of the ecclesiastical estate records of the period and, until quite recently, these have not all been easily accessible. But no one has yet analysed that part of the *Valor Ecclesiasticus* of 1535 which deals with non-monastic lands, so that it is not yet known what was the extent of the Church's landed resources at a time when complete disendowment was being seriously envisaged.[2]

During the century 1540–1640 episcopal and capitular estates were extensively plundered, both by the Crown, and by the laity aided and abetted by the Crown. But although examples abound, neither the rate nor the short and long-term effects of the process are yet at all clear. It appears, on the evidence so far available, that the Church's regular income was depleted more by the granting of long leases at old rents than by the outright alienation of large properties, although the latter was certainly taking place.[3] The only large estate so far thoroughly investigated is that of the bishop of Bath and Wells. The results

---

[1] CPR Edward VI, IV, pp. 224, 231; PRO, CP 40, 1151, m. 6d.; LP xv, p. 105, xviii, i, p. 539, xxi, i, p. 250; PRO C 142, 163, 13. For further examples of families who built up considerable estates during the period 1540–1640, partly but not exclusively from former monastic lands, see M. E. Finch, *op. cit.*, pp. 50–1 (Sir Robert Catlin), p. 69 (Thomas Tresham), p. 141 (the Brudenells), and p. 176 (the Spencers).

[2] LP vii, pp. 551–2 for Chapuys' well-known despatch; L. Stone, 'The Political Programme of Thomas Cromwell', *Bull.* IHR, xxiv, 1951, pp. 1–18.

[3] C. Hill, *The Economic Problems of the Church*, 1956, *passim* and especially chap. ii, 'The Plunder of the Church'; F. R. H. du Boulay, 'Archbishop Cranmer and the Canterbury Temporalities', EHR, lxvii, 1962, pp. 19–36.

suggest that the most disastrous inroads were made before the accession of Queen Elizabeth, who has traditionally been held to blame for the impoverishment of the secular clergy. Between 1539 and 1559 the gross annual revenue of the see fell by 55 per cent, from over £2,000 to under £1,000, largely as the result of the surrender of lands to Henry VIII and the Protector Somerset. In 1560 the first Elizabethan bishop, Berkeley, complained to the queen about the improvident leases granted by bishop Bourne, his Marian predecessor. Like the departing monks, Bourne had obliged not only neighbouring gentry but also his own family, some of whom were still in possession of the house and demesnes at Wiveliscombe in 1623. In spite of the statutory prohibitions of 1559 and 1571, Berkeley was able to raise large sums by way of fines for long leases. However, both he and Bourne exerted pressure on their smaller tenants, and Berkeley succeeded in stabilizing the revenues of his see. Although these never reached pre-Reformation levels, they did rise to over £1,300 by the turn of the century.[1]

Rather more attention has been given to the parochial clergy of the period. For the most part theirs was an ever-increasing struggle to extract the tithes upon which they very largely depended. But most of them kept a few animals and tilled their glebe acres.[2]

Conflicting solutions for the economic problems of the Church— Puritan disendowment *versus* Laudian resumption and conservation— these certainly loomed large in the public controversies of the early Stuart period. But we are still far from knowing how great those problems really were. It is even possible that the archbishop himself had little cause for concern over his own revenues.[3] To the agricultural historian the more important question is whether the dead hand of the Church over so considerable a part of the landed wealth of the country had a stifling effect on agricultural experiment. Certainly the day had long since gone when bishops had produced crops and stock for the market. At the same time there is no reason why some of those long leases should not have acted as a spur to improvement by others.

---

[1] P. Hembry, *The Bishops of Bath and Wells, 1535–1647: a Social and Economic Study*, unpublished London Ph.D. thesis, 1956, *passim*, and especially pp. 97, 111, 126–48, 181, 164, 184, 191–8, 200–1, 286–9, 304.

[2] Hill, *op. cit.*, chaps. v and vi; A. Tindall Hart, *The Country Clergy in Elizabethan and Stuart Times, 1558–1660*, 1958, pp. 28, 51; W. G. Hoskins, 'The Leicestershire Country Parson in the Sixteenth Century', in *Essays in Leicestershire History*, 1950, pp. 1–23.

[3] Du Boulay, *op. cit.*, p. 36.

# 2

# LANDLORDS IN WALES, 1500–1640

## A. THE NOBILITY AND GENTRY[1]

Although there are many familiar features in the agrarian history of the period under review which are common to both sides of the border, there is every reason why Wales should in some measure be the subject of separate treatment in this volume. It is true that on a purely physical level there are very few elements in the Welsh settlement pattern which are not found elsewhere in the highland zone of Britain. Wales, moreover, had experienced most of the tensions which had been at work in England during the later Middle Ages—tensions which had exposed traditional methods of landholding to much the same kind of influence which concurrently was beginning to reshape the manor in England. On the other hand, a fundamental distinction emerges from the fact that manorial institutions never took natural root in Wales outside certain Normanized parts of the March which were situated in the coastal lowlands and eastward-facing valleys of the south—areas which account for only a fraction of the total land surface of the country, and with which for the time being we have no concern. As for the rest of Wales, including some districts lying to the east of the present Anglo-Welsh border, landownership in 1500 rested on a basis of intrinsically native institutions. Those institutions were admittedly already passing through a process of internal modification at that date, but the essential framework of the so-called 'tribal system' had survived virtually intact.

In the chaos which followed the failure of the Glyndŵr rising at the opening of the fifteenth century, alienation of small clan holdings, though not unknown before the outbreak of the rebellion, began for the first time to be a critical factor in the fate of the older hereditary tenures; and in the course of the century the process continued at so phenomenal a pace that by 1500 several freehold estates of considerable size had appeared, as well as a great many nuclei of smaller estates on which the economic and social power of an emergent squirearchy

---

[1] This section was received from the late Professor Jones Pierce a few days before his untimely death. The text was complete but it lacked footnotes. The editor is deeply indebted to Mr Beverley Smith, Mr Glanville Jones, Dr Colin Thomas, and Mr Ogwen Williams for supplying, from their own knowledge, the majority of the footnotes. All papers by Prof. Jones Pierce, cited below, have since been published in *Medieval Welsh Society: Selected Essays*, ed. J. B. Smith, Cardiff, 1972.

would rest in the ensuing century. Notable though these inroads into the crumbling organization of the clan were, the essential features of the medieval landscape were nevertheless clearly visible at the beginning of the sixteenth century; and small peasant proprietors whose rights in the soil derived from clan status were still the most prominent element in Welsh rural society. Moreover, the fact that a new type of proprietor, having as often as not no personal association with the clan in occupation, was replacing some of the hereditary owners, had not disrupted the unity of clan territories as a whole since knowledge of the precise nature of a constituent holding and its appurtenances, whether alienated or not, continued to be necessary both for safeguarding the fiscal interests of the Crown or marcher lord, and for ensuring the landed title of old and new owners alike. For it must be realized that even under these conditions of mixed proprietorship, all title to rights appurtenant to arable holdings—particularly to those relating to common pasture—were regarded as being derived from a common juridical source and therefore continued to be linked to the clan territory in its entirety. This is reflected in the fact that the increasing tempo observed in transfers of land during the fifteenth century was not much facilitated by the intrusion of English legal practice, except perhaps along the borderlands, where, despite the survival of the clan-land and many of the native customs associated with it, English methods of conveyancing would appear to have entirely replaced the sanctions of native custom. But over the greater part of Wales, and in particular within the area of the two principalities of north and west Wales, the majority of ordinary Welshmen in 1500, and, as will be seen, for a considerable time afterwards, thought in terms of their own legal concepts where landownership, including the processes of alienation, was concerned. Such changes as had appeared in 'tribal' society by 1500, and indeed all the developments which will occur during the next century or so, must therefore be viewed against a continuing institutional background of early medieval origin, with stress on four major surviving factors, namely (1) a long-established settlement pattern; (2) a widespread peasant proprietorship; (3) a network of rights anchored to ancient clanlands; (4) a body of innate tenurial law and custom. Each of these factors will be treated in turn.

## 1. *The settlement pattern*

The mould in which settlement had been shaped in Wales during the central period of the Middle Ages was the township (*tref*) which functioned both as a sphere of influence for a number of interrelated kindreds and as a unit of fiscal and agrarian administration. In places like

Anglesey and the promontories of Llŷn and Pembroke, and indeed all along the narrow coastal lowlands and the broader estuarine valleys of the north and west, townships normally occupied a relatively small superficial area, although even in these low-lying territories there were townships of considerable size, some virtually co-extensive with entire commotes (the commote being the local government division later identified with the English hundred), and others broken up into two or more members including pastoral detachments in the hills. The townships of the interior, on the other hand, were in general very extensive, and included a large acreage of mountain land which merged valleywards with lower-lying pastures (*ffridd*) and the scattered homesteads (*tyddyn*) which were characteristic of the settlement pattern in these upland districts. It was in these narrow valleys of the interior, where the balance of activity was heavily slanted on the pastoral side, that the isolated homestead, traditionally associated with the 'celtic' countryside, dominated the landscape. Under suitable physical conditions, however, stretches of arable and meadow, shared among several proprietors, occurred—a feature which on a more extensive scale was normal in lowland settlement where there was greater stress on field husbandry. Here on the periphery of the mountain zone, the unit of settlement was the hamlet (*rhandir*) which basically consisted of open field made up of irregular-shaped parcels of varying size and engirdled with a cluster of homesteads set in small enclosures. Modifications of landscape in the lowlands, and to some extent in parts of the uplands, during the fifteenth century were produced by alienation and concentration of holdings in these open sharelands—a term which conveys the literal meaning of *rhandir* rather better than the word hamlet. This was a continuing process which was accelerated in the course of the sixteenth century, when further modifications appeared through complete or partial hedging in the open fields, and, though purely in a secondary sense, through enclosure of common appurtenant to arable holdings. The most prominent factor, however, in reshaping the rural scene in the uplands was undoubtedly the practice of assimilating portions of waste to the land already appropriated round an isolated homestead, a practice which, as will be seen,[1] assumed no small proportions as the sixteenth century advanced, and which in fact was then considerably extended by large, independent intakes from the waste on the part of the more powerful landowners who had emerged from, and had profited by, the breakdown of the medieval social system.

[1] See *infra*, pp. 142 *sqq*.

## 2. *Peasant proprietors*

Control of the soil in the average free township (a minority class of bond township will be examined in a separate context), at the beginning of the sixteenth century was shared among a mixture of small, medium, and, in varying degrees, fairly substantial proprietors—the small proprietor still predominating and the larger proprietor representing both resident and non-resident interests. While the records reflect a greater concentration of ownership than had existed a century earlier, small survivors of an older social system continued to be very numerous. Outside one or two areas where escheat for example had facilitated the premature creation of rather larger estates in land, free townships had remained almost to the end of the fourteenth century in the hands of exclusive groups of resident kindred, among whom there would appear to have been few glaring disparities of wealth or social status. It has been calculated that the average lowland holding of arable land in the fourteenth century consisted of some six to ten acres which were usually dispersed in scattered parcels over the fields of several hamlets; and that this was also the average size of enclosures associated with homesteads in areas where the detached farmstead predominated. Even if the exercise were feasible, however, no useful purpose could be served by attempting to strike an average in the circumstances which had supervened by the beginning of the sixteenth century, because in broad general terms, although the position varied widely from district to district and township to township, the gulf between smaller and larger proprietors is one of the more striking features of the agrarian situation in Wales at this time—the large proprietor, as well as many of the medium-sized owners, having evidently benefited meanwhile from the morcellation of the average fourteenth-century holding.

What would appear on a superficial acquaintance with the agrarian problem in Wales at the close of the Middle Ages to have been a relatively sudden internal collapse of the medieval system of tenure—itself the product of a movement going back no further than the twelfth century—occurred largely as a logical consequence of the operation within a system which, in at least a juridical sense, had become fully extended before 1350, of the traditional practice of partible succession—known in the vernacular as *cyfran*, and better known to English readers as *gavelkind*. This fragmentation of holdings, which in some parts had clearly begun on the eve of the Glyndŵr rising, and which was reaching its climax during the period of the early Tudors, was naturally felt more acutely in lowland vills with their more tightly-woven agrarian structure, and in so far as the interior was affected, in those areas where joint appropriation of land had led to the creation of sharelands. Commentators writing at the close of the period covered by this volume were very much aware of this as a major factor in producing the agrarian changes of the preceding two centuries. George Owen, writing of conditions in south-west Wales, observed that "the use of gavelkind among most of these Welshmen to part all of the father's patrimony" had led in process of time to the whole country being "brought into small pieces of ground and intermingled up and down one with another, so as in every five or six acres you shall have ten or twelve owners."[1] Sir John Wynn, commenting on a similar situation in the north, refers to descendants of certain well-known tribal stocks who had been brought "by the division and subdivision of gavelkind (the destruction of Wales)...to the estate of mean freeholders, and so having forgotten their descents and pedigree have become as if they never had been."[2] Both writers were of course concerned in retrospect with the results of a process to which Welsh rural society had been sharply exposed between say 1425 and 1535, but which in some degree was halted by the Union legislation of 1536-42. It is therefore of interest to observe that the writer of a fifteenth-century legal tract can assume quite incidentally in dealing with an entirely different matter that an inheritance of land could descend "in small shares among forty or sixty co-inheritors."[3] The witness of contemporary record, moreover, bears out the observations of the writers who have been quoted, since the average size of holdings subject to alienation or falling in by way of escheat during the period in question is shown to have been much lower than the fourteenth-century average. Apart from the fact that an aggregate of one or two acres is far more common than in the preceding century, a significant feature of the late fifteenth-century accounts is the appearance within these aggregates of items which fall below one acre. So striking indeed is this feature in contrast with earlier conditions that one tends to conclude that extreme morcellation had been formerly avoided by assarting from individual assets in waste; and that this procedure was becoming increasingly difficult for many proprietors in lowland vills because of the contraction of their stakes in the waste, and in some cases perhaps because of growing physical limitation on expansion.

George Owen realized that it was this proliferation of uneconomic units which, more than any other single factor, had encouraged those developments, still proceeding at the time when he was writing,

[1] George Owen, *The Description of Pembrokeshire*, ed. H. Owen, I, 1892, p. 61.
[2] Sir John Wynn, *The History of the Gwydir Family*, 1927, p. 14.
[3] *Ancient Laws and Institutes of Wales*, ed. A. Owen, II, 1841, pp. 430-3.

whereby fragmented holdings had been "brought together by purchase and exchange."[1] These were of course conditions which had appeared in the type of country with which Owen was familiar in west Wales, where shareland farming had long been customary and where dwindling resources placed a limit on the extension of holdings. But in hill country, where the possibilities of expansion were far less restricted, the effects of partible inheritance could not have been felt in quite the same way. Under mainly pastoral conditions of living, holdings in mountain districts could remain undivided for several generations on a quasi-patriarchal basis, a method of circumventing the acuter consequences of gavelkind not uncommon in the lowlands. Since the evidence points to the fact that there was not much hiving-off of families into new settlement during the later Middle Ages, and since the population of inland regions does not appear to have been much, if at all, thinner than along the coastlands, increasing needs must have been met by appropriations from joint common or *cytir* in the immediate neighbourhood of farmsteads, thus foreshadowing in the years before 1500 those massive invasions of the waste which went on steadily as the sixteenth century advanced.[2] At the same time, at the beginning of the century estates had also emerged in the Welsh heartland, although they were growing at a slower pace, in response to the same influences as were at work elsewhere in Wales, including the factor of partible inheritance. While at least one of these upland estates can be shown to have had its origin in a single farmstead enlarged by absorption of surrounding waste (there are many others which have all the appearances of having been launched in this way), most of them began as concentrations of small holdings in valley sharelands, and were subsequently extended by the acquisition of more isolated hill farms—a salutary warning against drawing too rigid a distinction between highland and lowland.

Owen, however, seems to have been under the impression that the consolidation of holdings to which he refers was a process which began only with the statutory abolition of gavelkind some threescore years before his time. But we have already indicated, and the point will be illustrated in rather greater detail at a later stage, that within the limitations already stated, the growth of the modern freehold estate was already reasonably advanced when the parliamentary provisions which finally brought Wales within the complete orbit of English administration between 1536 and 1542 gave a new *legal* direction to the business of estate building without impinging, at least directly and in the short-term, on the continuity in organic growth of these estates.

[1] George Owen, *op. cit.*, p. 61.
[2] See *infra*, pp. 142 *sqq*.

Whatever the impact of 1536 and the years which immediately followed on Welsh society (and this too is a matter which will have to be considered in due course), this is a date which in the study of the rise of modern freeholds in Wales can no more be regarded as crucial than the year 1500, since the sixteenth and early seventeenth centuries merely witnessed the continued operation of agencies which had their effective origin in the crises which followed the political cataclysm of the early fifteenth century. The problem here is to discover in broad terms (detailed calculations are not at the moment practicable) the extent to which the structural growth of these estates from 1500 onwards altered the overall pattern of small peasant proprietorship which, in spite of the preludial changes which have been noted, was still, when our period opens, the most prominent surviving phenomenon of an older agrarian order.

### 3. *The ancient clanlands*

The student of English agrarian history will not be altogether unfamiliar with some of the features which have been hitherto unfolded. But at this point the picture becomes complicated by the intrusion of those other factors mentioned at the outset which centre round the survival of certain institutions traditionally associated with the former working of the kindred system. The fact is that the influences which had brought about the slow erosion and, with the Edwardian conquest, the collapse of most aspects of kindred organization, did not begin seriously to impinge on the function of kindred in relation to the native law on 'land and soil' until the fifteenth century. It is true that here and there an association of kindred had lost control of some individual holdings which had passed to the lord by way of escheat, holdings which thereby ceased to be held by Welsh tenure, but rarely had this happened on a scale large enough to effect serious breaches in the unity of clan territories. Of much greater significance is the fact that commutation, where not already completed, became more or less universal at the time of the Edwardian settlement, thus making the discharge of communal dues and services, which had been one of the more important collective functions of kindred, no longer necessary.[1] With cash rents henceforth anchored to recognizable units of land, and with the personal bonds of kindred in consequence loosened and undermined, the substitution of alienees for hereditary proprietors was

---

[1] T. Jones Pierce, 'The Growth of Commutation in Gwynedd during the Thirteenth Century', *Bull. BCS*, x, 1941, pp. 309–30; *Idem*, 'Some Tendencies in the Agrarian History of Caernarvonshire in the later Middle Ages', *Trans. Caernarvonshire Hist. Soc.*, 1939, pp. 18–36.

facilitated when in due course other factors, such as the onset of morcellation, gave rise to the kind of situation earlier described as existing during the initial decades of the sixteenth century. But the steady dissolution of established groupings of agnatic kindred which that situation reveals had not resulted in much corresponding loss in local knowledge of where and how alienated as well as surviving hereditary holdings fitted into an aggregate of rights once enjoyed by an undisrupted kindred. In other words, the growing divorce which had been taking place between personal and tenurial elements in the structure of kindred—or in vernacular terms between the *gwelygordd* (clan) and its territorial basis in *gwely* or *gafael* (clanland)—did not, until the repercussions of the Act of Union began to be felt, eliminate the need to know how the clanland was related *inter alia* to shareland and farmstead, so vital did this knowledge continue to be if proprietary interests, whether official, innate, or acquired, were to be safeguarded.

Originating far back in the twelfth century in a primary settlement set in a township over which a single occupying family normally had sole control, the nuclei of the multipartite and often sprawling clanlands (*gwelyau*) which are described in some Tudor and Stuart rentals,[1] arose out of the partition of a primary settlement among a first generation of co-heirs whose names became permanently associated with these clanlands throughout all subsequent stages of growth and subdivision. The peculiar shape which the clanland eventually assumed grew out of the need for simultaneous appropriations from the waste as families with heritable interests, derived from the original stocks, increased in number and spilled over into secondary sharelands, thus producing an intermingling of clanland offshoots and a pattern of landholding in which every quillet and plot could be identified as a member of one of the clanlands represented in a township's fields. It should be added, however, that in the hillier parts of the interior the differences already observed in the matter of settlement are also reflected in the institutional overlay. Whereas in townships where the *gwely* type of clanland flourished (usually in lower-lying districts) unappropriated waste continued to be undivided, larger upland townships were parcelled out into separate pastoral divisions known as

[1] T. Jones Pierce, 'An Anglesey Crown Rental of the Sixteenth Century', *Bull. BCS*, x, 1940, pp. 156–76; Idem, 'Medieval Settlement in Anglesey', *Trans. Anglesey Antiq. Soc.*, 1951, pp. 1–33; Idem, 'Agrarian Aspects of the Tribal System in Wales', *Géographie et Histoire Agraires, Annales de L'Est*, Mémoire no. 21, Nancy, 1959, pp. 329–37; G. R. J. Jones, 'Medieval Rural Settlements in North Wales', *Trans. Inst. British Geographers*, XIX, 1953, pp. 51–72; Idem, 'The Distribution of Medieval Settlement in Anglesey', *Trans. Anglesey Antiq. Soc.*, 1955, pp. 27–96; Idem, 'Medieval Open Fields and Associated Settlement Patterns in North-west Wales', *Géographie et Histoire, op. cit.*, 1959, pp. 313–26.

*gafaels* in each of which a particular stock (*gwelygordd*) had exercised exclusive rights. Nevertheless, sharelands developed the same features here as elsewhere, except that the number of stocks participating in the formation of sharelands had normally been larger in *gafael* than in *gwely* settlement, a factor which tended to impose somewhat greater complexity on the ultimate form of sharelands falling within the former category. Otherwise the similarities were so close that an expert English observer when recording his impressions of shareland conditions in the fourteenth century failed to understand why there should have been a distinction of nomenclature at all.[1]

Now the actual outlines of some of these medieval clanlands continue as late as the time of Elizabeth and James I[2] to figure in official rentals where internal arrangements are described in such expansive detail that problematical factors in the purely medieval evidence can often be resolved in the light of data which they contain. These rare documents, moreover, are invaluable as standards whereby one can interpret very similar detail in other contemporary rentals from which known *gwely* and *gafael* affiliations are nominally omitted.[3] The primary purpose, of course, which all these rentals served, apart from the few extant examples compiled for private use, was to pinpoint sites on which ancient quit-rents were leviable; and certainly by the end of our period this was virtually the only practical value which can be ascribed to them. But the kind of information which such rentals preserve, whether actually recorded or verbally transmitted, had more than merely fiscal implications for those who paid chief-rents, until, during the half century or so which followed the union with England, circumstances on the periphery of ancient holdings became, both from the legal and physical angles, progressively more confused. After all, the very fact that a holding formed part of a clanland imposed certain restrictions on the individual freedom of proprietors, if for no other reason than the need for mutual protection of rights appurtenant to arable holdings, and for the preservation of the intrinsically hereditary nature of clanland or *gwely* tenure—both matters which now call for brief consideration.

---

[1] *Survey of the Honour of Denbigh, 1334*, ed. P. Vinogradoff and F. Morgan, 1914, p. 211. See also T. Jones Pierce, 'Pastoral and Agricultural Settlements in Early Wales', *Geographiska Annaler*, XLIII, 1961, pp. 182–9.

[2] T. Jones Pierce, *Bull. BCS*, x, loc. cit.; *The Lordship of Oswestry, 1393–1607*, ed. W. J. Slack, 1951, pp. 38–141. See also PRO SC 12, 21, 13; E 178, 7213.

[3] PRO LR 2, 205; LR 2, 236; SC 12, 23, 42; SC 12, 24, 1. See G. R. J. Jones, 'The Llanynys Quillets', *Denbighshire Hist. Soc. Trans.*, XIII, 1964, pp. 133–58.

## 4. Tenurial law and custom

Although at higher levels English administrative procedure had tended from the start to regard Welsh proprietors (*priodorion*) as *liberi tenentes*, in practice the underlying realities of the native system of tenure were observed in accordance with official policy, thus ensuring the survival into the sixteenth century of traditional tenurial concepts and of the technicalities of language in which these were expressed—a survival which was made all the easier by the fact that the business of administration at commote level was continuously in the hands of local officials drawn from the ranks of native proprietors themselves. The weightiest claim which a hereditary proprietor (*priodawr*, pl. *priodorion*, a term which would appear to have been still current in the sixteenth century) had in the general assets of the community was to a share in the pasture, wood, and waste which the community controlled, and which constituted what was known as *cytir* or joint-land. Limited to the *gafael*, rather than to the township as a whole, in districts where that class of clanland flourished, a *priodawr's* share in *cytir* formed an integral part of his patrimony (*treftadaeth*), the extent of which share was determined by the past operation of partible succession (*cyfran*), and calculated in comparable acreages of land already appropriated (*tir priod*), such as homesteads (*tyddynod*) and scattered arable holdings (*tir gwasgar*). Concentration of holdings therefore involved a corresponding accumulation of hereditary rights in *cytir*, or for that matter in other appurtenances such as shares in collective mills, which were sometimes bought in infinitesimal fractions over a period of several generations. By 1536 large engrossers on the fringes of hill country are known to have acquired considerable tracts of unenclosed wood and pasture in which their claims had to be assessed in relation to those arable units of clanland to which such claims were tied, and to a variety of similar interests likewise based on *gwely* tenure.

The chances of disengagement for acquired interests were still further restricted by another cardinal feature of native custom which enshrined hereditary proprietorship in a kind of fiction of indestructibility. A measure of flexibility had, however, been attained quite early by permitting, in exceptional circumstances, and with the combined consent of the lord and coheirs, the substitution of a guardian (*gwarcheidwad*) who, in return for an agreed consideration (*pridwerth*), would have possession of the whole or part of a patrimony for a defined period without prejudice to the innate title of the hereditary proprietor. The most advantageous of the permissible arrangements, and the most far-reaching in its long-term consequences, allowed for a kind of lease or mortgage (*prid*) covering in the first instance a four-year term, which could be renewed for additional quadrennial periods in the event of the *prid* continuing to be unredeemed. Although resort to this principle was unusual before 1400, in the exigencies of the period which followed *prid* provided the one loophole through which large-scale, permanent alienation of land could be brought about without trespassing unduly on native custom. This trend seems to have been facilitated by the rule (possibly evolved late in the day by the action of native jurists themselves) which gave absolute title to the mortgagor (*pridwr*) if *prid* was unredeemed after sixteen years, a contingency which it is on record was sometimes followed by the execution of a deed of quitclaim on the English model.[1] Records are extant which show how several small estates in the fifteenth century were built up along these lines; and in the case of the largest landowner in north Wales at the end of the century, his estate is said to have consisted entirely of either hereditary land or *terre pridate*. Though the growth of the vast majority of small estates in Wales is undocumented, particularly during the earliest phases, the models we have and the numerous cross-sections which emerge from collections of early deeds suffice to show, in the light of our knowledge of native custom, how the revolutionary extension of a principle which was originally intended to alleviate the rigours of native tenure proved, while still continuing for a long time ahead to impede the process of complete extrication, the most effective bridge in easing the transition from medieval to modern conditions of tenure over a large part of Wales.

In the long run, the more substantial estate builders naturally preferred to allow *prid* lands, on ceasing of the time bar, to pass into estates in fee simple rather than revert, as would have been the case if they had adhered to native custom, to the condition of a new hereditary tenure. With clefts already in being through the withdrawal of escheat holdings, this imposed new pressures on the overall cohesion of the traditional system of tenure; and with the voluntary rejection of gavelkind and the open adoption of English methods of conveyancing, including entail, by certain landowners, among whom there were some who lived in more remote western districts, the resultant picture during the first half of the sixteenth century was in some ways strikingly different from what it had been a century earlier. But the average countryman still turned in a familiar *milieu*, seeking to have his interests protected by Welsh law which, as interpretations recorded in current law-books make clear, had been trying to keep pace with the agrarian trends of the age. On the eve of the Union, litigants in west Wales persisted in submitting claims in the Welsh manner to the judgement

[1] T. Jones Pierce, 'The Law of Wales—The Last Phase', *Trans. Hon. Soc. Cymmrodorion*, 1963, pp. 17–19; *Idem, Trans. Caern. Hist. Soc.*, 1939, pp. 31–3.

of native suitors in established commote courts, or as elsewhere, were resorting to quasi-judicial arbitration by local landowners, versed in the intricacies of Welsh tenures, who, in this twilight phase of the older jurisprudence, must have been called upon to unravel many a knotty problem arising from the interlocking claims which had been fostered by the transitional nature of the times.[1] With forward-looking agencies thus working relentlessly against the grain of a conservatively oriented agrarian structure, the legislation of 1536–42, at least in so far as it was directed towards the assimilation of Welsh tenures, must have been received with profound relief by those aggressive elements in Welsh society who were bent on increasing and consolidating their stake in the soil.

In addition to introducing new and streamlining existing judicial machinery, the cumulative force of the legal provisions incorporated in the statutes of 1536 and 1542[2] was to give English legal processes, including the exclusive use of the English language, an all-embracing warrant throughout the recently completed Welsh shire system. In relation to most sectors of legal practice this decisive step amounted to virtual recognition of a *fait accompli*, as, indeed, it also was to some extent in its bearing on dealings in real property, a fact which the statute of 1542 seems to imply in certain references to current procedures in the principality courts of north Wales. The proscription of what the redactors of the statutes regarded as "sinister customs and usages" could only have been seriously motivated therefore by a desire to eradicate methods of landholding which were still tied to ancient clanlands, and to bring Welsh tenure (*terra Wallensica* or *tir Cymraeg*) into line with those holdings of English land (*terra Anglicana* or *tir Saesneg*) with which, although they were as a rule a minority element, the average Welsh township was by this time inlaid. This is borne out by the fact that specific statements about such "usages" mention only tenurial customs which, after having been the subject of some hesitation and uncertainty when the statute of 1536 was enacted, were dealt with, in concise but no uncertain terms, in *three* key clauses towards the end of the later statute of 1542.[3] All real property due to descend by inheritance after 24 June 1541, it was enacted, was to be held by English tenure according to the common law of England, and was to devolve henceforth without division among male heirs "according to the custom of gavelkind." All impediments on freedom to part with land, moreover, were swept away by the clauses which provided that after the same 24th June transfers of property in fee-simple, fee-

---

[1] T. Jones Pierce, *Trans. Hon. Soc. Cymmrodorion*, 1963, pp. 2–4, 20–6.
[2] I. Bowen, *The Statutes of Wales*, 1908, pp. 75–93, 101–33.
[3] *Ibid.*, pp. 122–3.

tail, or for terms of life or years could proceed without restriction; and that mortgages not executed in compliance with the common and statute law of England would no longer be legally valid, "Welsh law and custom heretofore used in the said country or Dominion of Wales to the contrary thereof notwithstanding."

It will no doubt have been observed that the provision governing future modes of inheritance allowed an ample margin of time for lands held under Welsh tenure to become gradually merged into an integrated system; and if events had followed a logical course, the desired adjustments could have been completed in a generation or so. But in actual fact the transition was prolonged far beyond the preconceived span, although it has to be admitted that we are here confronted with one of the most tantalizingly blurred phases in Welsh social history, for the simple reason that from the time of the Union onwards, matters calling for the attention of courts and lawyers were interpreted in terms of an alien law and recorded in a foreign tongue, so that record evidence rarely more than hints at continued conflict between law and custom, as a rule concealing the reactions of that creature of ingrained habit, the inarticulate smaller man. There are however clear indications that Welsh custom persisted until well into the seventeenth century in colouring the attitudes of the humbler freeholder—the kind of man who managed to avoid involvement in litigation, or if the law did catch up with him, succumbed to the threats or blandishments of his betters who had become expert at manipulating the new legal position in their own interests; and who did not scruple about encouraging false witness, securing custody of title deeds, or extracting a full measure of advantage from the inability of their victims to prove an interest in customary freehold in the language of the newer jurisprudence. Among other social customs, such as *cynnwys* (this had allowed natural sons to share inheritances, and although banned by an Edwardian ordinance as far back as 1284, the prohibition had been consistently evaded by direct personal conveyance),[1] the usages surrounding partible inheritance and native forms of mortgage lingered on in the folk life of parts of Wales into the nineteenth century; and until at least the second half of the seventeenth century, it would appear that such matters were the subject of extracurial arbitration in unofficial assemblies which are described in a contemporary diary as *dadlau*,[2] the term used in medieval law books for the old moots in which legal issues had been determined.

[1] *The Extent of Chirkland, 1391-93*, ed. G. P. Jones, 1933, pp. 61-2.
[2] T. Jones Pierce, *op. cit.*, p. 19.

## 5. Social change

Meanwhile, released finally from the limitations of the old order, families who had already risen above their neighbours, together with others who had similar aspirations, pressed forward, in fierce competition with each other, in the business of extending existing estates or fashioning new ones, a process which would have accelerated at a far quicker rate after 1542 if the cash resources of the average Welsh landowner of this class had not been so restricted. The opportunities afforded before 1536 for acquiring modest emoluments and exercising a degree of local pressure through the enjoyment of office at commote level (and sometimes through service in quite humble capacities at court or in great English households)—opportunities which had given certain families an initial advantage in the contest which lay ahead—were after that date vastly increased for the enterprising with the admission of Welshmen into the full civic and social privilege of the Englishman. When the fruits of office fell short of expectation or were unattainable, entry on a professional career in the Church or in legal practice could prove a profitable additional source of income—forms of livelihood into which, with trade, younger sons were now freely launched; and there were also the possibilities afforded by expanding English markets which as time went on were increasingly exploited from the resources of those unshared 'dairy farms' which were now appearing in hill country, not to mention the splendid openings for illicit commerce available in coastal regions. When it could be asserted, not without some degree of truth, that in 1536 there were very few landowners above Brecknock with lands worth ten pounds a year,[1] and again about a century later, that it was then easier to find fifty gentlemen of a hundred pounds per annum in Wales than five of five hundred pounds,[2] it will be appreciated how great was the need for seeking out all avenues for supplementing income. Considering the handicaps from which most Welshmen suffered before the Union, some of the results were indeed astounding. A notably impressive feature of the period is the swiftness with which so many families of sparse means, with no other backing than an intense pride of lineage, rose to positions of no mean eminence in Church and State both at home and across the border, ploughing back their financial gains into estates which soon brought them power and influence in their shires, rivalling that of established families who had started off with rather more fortunate inheritances from the tribal past.

But viewed in terms of English social stratification, the average

[1] PRO SP 1, 102, f. 199, calendared in LP x, p. 182.
[2] A. H. Dodd, *Studies in Stuart Wales*, 1952, p. 2.

member of the so-called 'squire' class attained a position which was little more than that of a reasonably substantial, home-keeping yeoman —an ascription which is found substituted for "gentleman" in certain items included in the same run of family deeds, so unsure were English notaries of how to equate Welsh social attitudes with English usage. Living mainly on the produce of a consolidated demesne situated on the site, and bearing the name, of a former *rhandir* or *tyddyn* (or possibly still farming partially consolidated tenements in different parts of a township), and with an undertenant or two holding leases on land acquired in marginal areas, the squireen was distinguished from lesser neighbours by the subtlest of social nuances. Conscious of distant ties of kinship with smaller surviving freeholders, and even with some of the emergent tenantry (more solidly based families, such as the Wynns of Gwydir or the Vaughans of Nannau, continued to be very much aware of blood relationships with humbler folk),[1] they rarely, until well into the seventeenth century, copied the growing fashion among the more substantial squires of adopting territorial or personal surnames in place of the traditional triple patronymic. The common social denominator among all gradations of the squirearchy was their tenacity in continuing to endow personal pedigree with a social significance which in concrete terms it no longer possessed since the protection of tenurial interests was fast ceasing to depend on expert interpretation of genealogical affiliations. The sense of belonging to a "gentle" (*bonheddig*) society which was so widely diffused among the agnatic clan groupings of medieval Wales, together with the egalitarianism which such a feeling engendered, endured at lower levels of rural society[2] until, with the approach of the Restoration, the ranks of the dispossessed having become increasingly enlarged with freeholders diminishing in number and middling families shedding their numerous offspring into a growing mass of unlineaged peasantry (*gwerin didras*), social cleavages gradually broadened, and under the stress of subsequent agrarian and cultural pressures there emerged the peculiar sociological pattern which characterized rural Wales in Victorian times.

While cultural pressures from without were naturally intensified after 1536, at no level of society did anglicization before 1640 prove to be more than superficial in its effects, manifesting itself mainly in material standards and modes of living, and, among the upper crust, in close identification with English methods of administration which in

[1] John Wynn, *op. cit.*, pp. 35–6; Univ. College North Wales, Bangor, Nannau MS 1178.
[2] W. Ogwen Williams, *Calendar of the Caernarvonshire Quarter Sessions Records*, I, pp. lxviii–lxix.

itself called for increasing acquaintance with the English language. But even the wealthiest and most sophisticated of the squire class, who had every reason to welcome the legal provisions of the Union legislation, had no hesitation in clinging to ancient customs when such customs, *cymortha* and *arddel*[1] for example, continued to serve their interests. On one issue in particular the largest landowner, when it suited him, could appeal on the same footing as the smallest freeholder to former custom, and that was when it was thought desirable to defend his real or reputed claims to *cytir*. Welsh tenures in the class of township which we have been considering, having been reduced in law to the common category of free socage, the township itself had in turn to be fitted into the manorial framework of English real property law. The official tendency after the Edwardian conquest in the principalities of north and west Wales, and in the newly created marcher lordships of the north-east, to identify the commote for fiscal purposes with the manor, on the lines of the manorialized hundreds of northern England, took on a definite and permanent shape after the Union.[2] Thus over a large part of Wales, except for townships which as former bond vills were regarded as manors in themselves or as church lands were members of dispersed ecclesiastical manors, the tacitly assumed interests of the Crown as manorial lord came at once into conflict with traditional attitudes on ownership and control of the waste. In older established manors of the March, moreover, where Welsh tenure had persisted until late in the day, the same issue of principle led to much tension between lord and freeholder at a time when all over Wales, in Crown and private manor alike, more and more holdings were being carved out of the waste, and when it was becoming increasingly difficult to distinguish even in terms of Welsh custom between legitimate appropriation and illegal encroachment, or indeed to determine, in view of the stress on the force of custom in English manorial theory, the exact position of Welsh manorial lords under the legislation of 1536–42. This is one of the major problems surrounding the development of landownership in our period, and will call for rather closer attention at a later stage.

## 6. *Types of freehold estate*

Up to this point we have been concerned in general terms with the broad background, and with the principles which alone can explain the character of the early freehold estate in Wales. The growth and structure of these estates now calls for slightly more detailed considera-

---

[1] For *commorth* see G. Dyfnallt Owen, *Elizabethan Wales, the Social Scene*, 1962, pp. 26–8.
[2] W. Ogwen Williams, *op. cit.*, pp. li–lii, lxv.

tion, and for convenience of exposition they can be divided into four categories:

(a) the estate of adventitious origin created by foreign settlers in Wales;
(b) the privileged estate established by members of a native official class;
(c) the clanland estate of hereditary origin;
(d) the clanland estate of non-hereditary origin.

(a) *Estates of adventitious origin*

Estates of adventitious origin were those established outside areas of Norman settlement by non-Welsh families, which, allowing for some inevitable cross-fertilization in an indeterminate borderland, were almost wholly confined to the hinterlands of English urban foundations in north Wales. The earliest large concentration of this kind, which appeared among clanlands near Conway between 1420 and 1453,[1] was inherited by the Bulkeleys who, with a modest cluster of seven burgages of their own in Beaumaris, were at this time poised for a similar drive into the clanlands of Anglesey.[2] By 1630 the estimated annual value of the Anglesey estate alone had reached the phenomenally high figure of £4,000. Compared with the Salusburys, who were next in importance among landowners of English origin, and who emerged with a rent-roll of some £1,400, having started off, in 1334, with thirty acres of escheat land outside Denbigh,[3] the Bulkeleys, it will be seen, are the outstanding example of a class of landowner, bearing English surnames, who in this period launched out, with varying degrees of success, as estate builders from bases in burgage and escheat holdings. Most of them in time retired from the fray, either sinking into the ranks of the small freeholder, or becoming grafted on to native stocks; and certainly not many succeeded in attaining genuine county status, still less in acquiring the means to enable cadet branches to secure estates of their own, which was a conspicuous feature in the annals of the more notable families. Furthermore, in the course of the sixteenth century these descendants of former garrison elements in the population of north Wales became less and less distinguishable

---

[1] T. Jones Pierce, 'The Gafael in Bangor MS 1939', *Trans. Hon. Soc. Cymmrodorion*, 1942, pp. 158 *sqq*.
[2] D. C. Jones, 'The Bulkeleys of Beaumaris, 1440–1547', *Trans. Anglesey Antiq. Soc.*, 1961, pp. 1–17; C. M. Evans, *The Borough of Beaumaris and the Commote of Dindaethwy, 1200–1600*, unpublished M.A. thesis, University of Wales, 1949, pp. 147 *sqq*. and pp. 328–34.
[3] Vinogradoff and Morgan, *op. cit.*, pp. 63, 66, 69; W. J. Smith, *Calendar of Salusbury Correspondence*, 1954, pp. 1–17.

from the rest of society, so closely were they identifying themselves with Welsh speech and culture. They were, nevertheless, a minority force in comparison with those native operators who were equally diligent in playing havoc with clanlands on the purlieus of urban settlement. Among Welsh estate builders there was also a resistive instinct at work which was seemingly opposed to settler penetration much beyond urban hinterlands, so thinly distributed were English pickings in the hills and valleys situated at no great distance from the towns themselves. Indeed, west of Caernarvon almost every trace of English settlement had disappeared by the end of the sixteenth century from boroughs facing the Cardigan Bay; and the phenomenon of mixed racial participation in the dissolution of medieval agrarian institutions in Wales ceases to have much relevance until it appears in rather different guise in and around the lowland manors of south Wales.

*(b) Privileged estates*

Estates in the second category, namely those derived from official status antedating the Edwardian conquest, were far less numerous, although it is in this class that the true prototypes of the modern estate, one in north Wales and the other in the south, occur. In both cases the bases of attack on circumjacent clanlands were certain bond vills (constituents of a widely scattered feudal complex granted to a highly favoured official of the thirteenth-century princes) which had devolved on the founders of the Penrhyn and Dinefwr estates under the rule of partible inheritance. A striking feature in the rise of Penrhyn is the scale on which the clanlands of neighbouring free townships had been penetrated from these quasi-manorial units even *before* 1400. By 1500 the estate (including incidentally almost the entire inheritance of the Tudor branch of the house of Ednyfed) had expanded so rapidly along both banks of the Menai Straits that successive members of the Griffith family (among the first families in Wales to adopt the English fashion in surnames) succeeded in attaining high office in principality administration, not altogether unaided by a calculating choice of brides from distinguished settler stock. When the estate in its original form began to disintegrate towards the middle of the sixteenth century, it must have been worth at a rough estimate at least £400 a year. Although not so firmly delineated, the Dinefwr estate arose from a nucleus of Ednyfed manors in Carmarthenshire and Cardiganshire, to which much Welsh freehold (*uchelwrdir*) had been added quite early in the fourteenth century. When under Sir Rhys ap Thomas, the leading supporter of Henry VII in south Wales, this estate was amalgamated through maternal inheritance with lands recently accumulated by himself and his immediate forbears, the annual value of the entire estate at the time of Sir Rhys's death in 1525 has been estimated at about £600, a figure which belies the exaggerated notions about his wealth which arose from the power and influence which had been his in south-west Wales. Though for personal reasons both estates suffered premature contraction before mid-century, their history illustrates the advantages which could accrue from an early application of entail, in contrast with lands in the upper valley of the Dee, also based on old Welsh barony (*tir pennaeth*) lands which by the sixteenth century had become so highly morcellated from the operation of gavelkind that descendants of princes had been reduced to 'yeoman' status, or which at best had become indistinguishable from the estates of the mass of Welsh squires,[1] the vast majority of which can be placed in one or other of our final categories.

## (c) The clanland estate of hereditary origin

Estates in the third category had evolved along lines already indicated from hereditary nuclei in clanlands in which the owners' ancestors had in unbroken succession enjoyed an interest since the central period of the Middle Ages. A considerable proportion of the squirearchy living in the northern coastal shires (including at least half the leading landowners of Anglesey)[2] could trace their original title back in this way, and that in regions where English settlement had left so deep an impress; and the proportion could be shown to have been even higher south of Snowdonia and throughout central Wales.

## (d) The clanland estate of non-hereditary origin

Barely distinguishable from these estates of hereditary origin were those in the equally numerous category of estate built up from a base in clan holdings which had been alienated to an interloper, not infrequently a scion of an ancient clan, bent on matching parental enterprise or urged by a desire to avoid the consequences of gavelkind. Although, irrespective of type, the growth of only a select number can at present be traced in reasonable detail, the general indications are that in every shire literally dozens of these estates had rapidly crystallized during the fifteen and early sixteenth centuries, thereafter increasing at a slower, though on the whole a progressively steady, pace. Certainly there were very few districts where, by 1536, at least one complex of small estates,

---

[1] A. D. Carr, *The Barons of Edeyrnion, 1282–1485*, unpublished M.A. thesis, University of Wales, 1963, pp. 226–8.

[2] Emyr Gwynne Jones, 'Some Notes on the Principal County Families of Anglesey in the Sixteenth and Seventeenth Centuries', *Trans. Anglesey Antiq. Soc.*, 1939, pp. 61–75, and 1940, pp. 46–61.

united by close family and heraldic ties, had not appeared as the result of a break-away by junior branches from a parent estate of hereditary origin, thus renewing in a different setting the impulsions which had given shape to the clanland several centuries earlier. As the sixteenth century advanced, this outward drive led to the spread of some of these family alliances over a wider field, when younger sons acquired whole estates at a single bid through marriage, purchase, or investment in Crown lands, a tendency which gave a sharper edge to a form of bastard 'tribalism' which preceding developments had encouraged, and which was not without a strong impact on the local politics of the Welsh shires in the post-Union period.[1]

## 7. *The growth of estates and enclosure*

On the evidence at present available it is impossible to suggest an overall range of rentals in areas of Welsh tenure much before 1580. With the exception already noted, the largest estate to have emerged before that date (an estate which was unique in that it already had ramifications in four counties) was Gwydir; and yet between 1569 and 1571 Gwydir rents produced less than £150 a year. It will therefore be seen that, allowing for a measure of increase meanwhile in the size of estates, a decidedly upward trend in rents between 1580 and 1640 is revealed in the fact that the norm in this period for reasonably substantial estates, such as Nannau or Mathafarn, Cochwillan or Brynkinallt, which were much smaller than Gwydir, was about £300 to £400. Rentals above £1,000 (those exceeding £2,000 are rare) are as a rule found to have been inflated, as in the case of Trawsgoed or Gelli Aur, by the profits of leasehold or monastic land, or as with Llewenni and Clenennau, by early coalescence of estates through intermarriage, thus bringing the freehold content nearer to the £500 bracket which, as we have already observed, was regarded as a rather exceptional thing in Wales. There remained the profusion of petty 'gentlemen', including the proverbial 'mountain squire', with estates under £100, who merged almost imperceptibly with the legion of smaller freeholders who had survived into the seventeenth century.

Records in which chief-rents are listed show much local variation during these forty years in the number of small owner-occupiers, a variation which was no doubt dictated by differences in the pressures exerted by the land-hungry; and when comparison is possible, a decline, though by no means dramatic, can be detected in the number of tenants responsible for chief-rents. At one extreme we have Anglesey

[1] For an account of the growth of a typical estate within this category, see Professor Jones Pierce's introduction to *Clenennau Letters and Papers*, 1947.

and some of the lower-lying sectors of south-west Wales where the number of minor freeholders had dwindled considerably in comparison with large areas of central Wales and even parts of the borderland. An analysis of a substantial cross-section, covering forty-nine townships in Merionethshire, has shown that there were only eleven townships in which more than half the land had ceased to be held by owner-occupiers, and in only one of these had the proportion of owner-occupied land fallen to as low as a quarter; there were three vills in which there were no tenanted farms at all, and fourteen in which the proportion of tenant farmers was never higher than 25 per cent.[1] In a rather similar sample embracing an entire commote in Montgomeryshire, which can well be regarded as typical of this region, 50 per cent of landowners possessed less than thirty acres; whereas, with the exception of the leading squire who had over two thousand acres, there were only four landowners in the 500–1000 acres class.[2] Indeed, in districts as far apart as Llŷn and Oswestry, there were entire townships which had scarcely felt the hand of the large exploiter, and so still retained a landscape which preserved much of its medieval character. There was therefore still plenty of room for upcoming families to expand their properties when near home opportunities became circumscribed because of the initiative of competitors or the resistance of smaller men. Thus the Vaughans of Nannau, whose ancestors had been *priodorion* of a single *tyddyn* in Nannau, had by 1600 acquired only a third of the holdings in that vill, the rest of the estate lying characteristically scattered over a dozen other townships within a ten-mile radius of the mansion house, and intermingled with offshoots of sundry other estates of various shapes and sizes.[3]

One of the most striking changes in landscape, however, was produced by the enlargement of holdings to which quit-rents were tied through permanent enclosure of portions of adjoining waste, and further afield by taking into severalty larger blocks of upland pasture. The extent to which this erosion of common had proceeded is vividly illustrated in Leicester's dealings with the freeholders of five counties in north Wales where between 1561 and 1588 he controlled the greater part of the Crown's manorial interests. When Leicester's agents raised the equivocal issue of the commons, they were met with such explosive and tenacious opposition that one is left with a firm impression that by

[1] This analysis, based on PRO LR 2, 236, is made by Colin Thomas in *The Evolution of Rural Settlement and Land Tenure in Merioneth*, Ph.D. thesis, University of Wales, 1965..
[2] Elwyn Evans, *Arwystli and Cyfeiliog in the Sixteenth Century*, unpublished M.A. thesis, University of Wales, 1939, p. 133.
[3] Colin Thomas, *op. cit.*

1560 encroachment had become widespread, and that the legal questions involved had become matters of crucial importance to every grade of freeholder. This impression is confirmed when, an uneasy accommodation having been eventually reached whereby freeholders undertook to pay *new* in addition to established rents, fresh surveys were prepared—surveys in which these new rents appear so consistently alongside the old as to indicate that the habit of encroachment had become well-nigh universal.[1] An inventory of encroachments covering four commotes in which Leicester's agents were active, gives some idea of the extent to which intakes along the edges of ancient freehold had taken place, as well as the degree to which the hill commons had been invaded. Of 631 recorded plots, as many as 322 (51 per cent) were below ten acres; 257 (30·8 per cent) were under sixty acres; 16 (2·5 per cent) varied between sixty and one hundred acres; and 36 (5·7 per cent) exceeded one hundred acres. But it is of the utmost significance that the landowners represented in the last bracket claimed between them to control 5,080 acres, or 40·2 per cent of the total area surveyed, namely 12,729 acres, in contrast with 1,405 acres possessed by smallholders in the lowest bracket. Almost without exception, the really large encroachments of several hundred acres consisted of high pasture and sheepwalk which had been enclosed, usually within convenient distance of demesne and mansion house, by local figures of county standing. On the other hand, the mass of small and medium encroachers (the inventory[2] which is by no means exhaustive contains about five hundred names) had advanced in the main into moorland fringes (*ffriddoedd*) from established bases in *tyddyn* and *rhandir*, reproducing in this new phase of colonization the irregular field pattern of medieval settlement.

Now this remarkably microscopic view of a considerable cross-section of the Welsh countryside mirrors tendencies which, through the medium of much patchy and uneven documentation, can be discerned at work in every Welsh shire, as well as in those cymricized regions along the border which had been incorporated into English shires at the time of the Union.[3] That pressures on the waste would appear to have been heavier in smaller, lower-lying, coastal townships (where minor freeholders were tending to be squeezed out by actual physical restrictions on their capacity to enlarge their stakes in the soil) is suggested by endeavours to improve marshy ground, a process which is seen to stem as a rule from the individual enterprise of smaller men bent on wresting a few additional acres from the poorer margins of

[1] Colin Thomas, *op. cit.*
[2] Colin Thomas, 'Encroachment onto the Common Lands in Merioneth in the Sixteenth Century', *Northern Universities' Geogr. J.*, v. 1964, pp. 33–8.
[3] W. J. Slack, *op. cit.*

attenuated *cytiroedd*.[1] But even in the larger townships on the edges of the mountain zone and along the valley basins of the interior, where there were fewer quantitative limitations on expansion (after all two fifths of the entire land surface of the country still consisted of moor and mountain at the end of the eighteenth century), large sectors of mountain land were being withdrawn from communal use and the rims of our moorlands were being increasingly absorbed into private ownership, thus blurring the contours of the medieval landscape, bringing a new threat, despite some small temporary gains, to the traditional livelihood of the smallholder, and confining future settlement to barren squatter holdings high up in the hills.[2] Moreover, when shacks for temporary use under customs of seasonal transhumance (*hafodtai* and *lluestai*) are sometimes found converted into permanent settlements, one can also detect the beginnings of that breach between lowland and upland farmstead which in time produced the modern social dichotomy between valley and mountain communities. Finally, slight though the evidence is, there is no reason to suppose that dubious invasions of the commons unsanctioned by communal custom had assumed serious proportions until the sixteenth century was reasonably well advanced, nor that encroachments had amounted to much more than cautious movement into waste in the immediate vicinity of existing holdings. Actual enclosure of upland pasture on the scale indicated could not have been set in motion until time-worn procedures for controlling the waste began falling to pieces, and this did not occur until near mid-century when separable interests became so discordant as to encourage irresponsible elements to overstock the commons to the hurt and detriment of fellow proprietors, who then, from motives of sheer self-preservation, proceeded to seize and enclose pasture on a scale commensurable with personal status or influence.[3] As for lowland enclosure, although much cultivated land still lay open, particularly in areas where estate building had been slight, even in central Wales there were men at the beginning of the seventeenth century, who, while recalling a time when fences and enclosures were little known except for "a dead hedge round an acre of wheat," could assert that unenclosed arable was an unusual phenomenon in their day, that enclosure was still proceeding consequent upon partition among coheirs of legitimately heritable waste, and that land which was once "waste and wilderness" had been brought into "present fertility" through the diligence and foresight of freeholders.[4]

[1] *Ibid.*, p. 71.   [2] This statement is based upon the work of Colin Thomas.
[3] T. I. Jeffreys-Jones, *The Enclosure Movement in South Wales in the Tudor and Early Stuart Periods*, unpublished M.A. thesis, University of Wales, 1936, pp. 395–7.
[4] Elwyn Evans, *op. cit.*

It will be seen that England and Wales faced different problems in relation to 'enclosure', although in Wales there are aspects of the movement which without doubt did set the stage for the peasant discontents of a later age. In Wales enclosure was accompanied by an actual extension of tillage which was encouraged among the more enlightened by the abandonment of old predatory techniques in favour of improved agricultural methods; and displacements of population resulting from lowland consolidation and enclosure were to all appearances cushioned by local need for labour and migration to England. Exploitation of pasture, stimulated, it is true, by the need to meet the requirements of steadily increasing numbers of livestock reared for commercial purposes, went on almost fortuitously and in piecemeal fashion within the familiar context of the native pastoral tradition. The tensions which enclosure of waste did engender in Wales arose from the competitive scramble which followed a rather sudden collapse of the physical and legal controls which had governed the management of the commons for centuries past. Hence the frequent difficulty in determining, in face of local reticence or resentment, and after generations of official neglect, the exact boundaries between the various intercommoning divisions of a commote; or within townships themselves the infinitely more troublesome question of distinguishing between enclosure which on the one hand represented improper invasion of the waste and quasi-legitimate intake sanctioned by ancient custom on the other.[1] Disorders, even the rather more serious outbreaks of violence caused by 'enclosure', were wholly sporadic and impetuous protests motivated by particular local circumstances, and, as one would expect from the nature of Welsh society at that time, free of any flavour of class struggle; and if there was a common factor in all these commotions, it is usually found to have been discord between rival groups of freeholders. On the other hand, unless manorial lords or their assignees happened also to be members of the local squirearchy, or unless, as for example in the Leicester affair, there were freeholders who were prepared to side with the enemy, the outsider who ventured to oppose the claim of freeholders to control their own common lands with foreign notions of what was due to the lord of the manor met with a united front. To the very end of our period it was insistently asserted in face of repeated threats from manorial lords that the wastes were not "commons" but *cyd-tir* (joint land) the ownership of which was vested in *cyd-tirogion* (co-parceners) who, as tenants of adjoining freeholds, were entitled to enclose and improve them without licence and at their will and pleasure. Chief-rents, it was claimed, were paid for waste and severed land "as well for the one as for the other";

[1] T. I. Jeffreys Jones, *op. cit.*, p. 394.

and as late as 1637 objections were being raised to the claim that certain unenclosed wastes in central Wales were commonable on the ground that the land in question was in fact made up of "distinct and several holdings" owned by "co-parceners in gavelkind."[1] These successors of the medieval *bonheddig* were, however, engaged in a rearguard action against official insistence on treating the term *cytir* as no more than the Welsh equivalent of *common*, and on regarding the claim for which it stood as no more than an "ancient dream." Nevertheless, the confusion surrounding this "vain conceit" remained for several centuries ahead to benight manorial theory and to bewilder those who were concerned with what emerged as the problem of Crown lands.[2]

### B. THE CHURCH

#### 1. *Introduction: before the Reformation*

The Welsh Church before the Reformation was not wealthy.[3] Three of the four Welsh bishoprics—Bangor (£131), Llandaff (£144), and St Asaph (£187)—had a total net annual value, according to the *Valor Ecclesiasticus*, of not much more than the poorest English bishopric, Rochester (£411). The remaining one, St David's (£457), came below every other English bishopric but Rochester. Gross temporal income (i.e. income from landed estates and their perquisites) of the dioceses ranged from £311 19s. 3d. (63 per cent) in St David's through £131 14s. 1d. (76 per cent) for Llandaff and £85 13s. 7d. (56 per cent) for Bangor, to £25 10s. 0d. (12 per cent) for St Asaph. Gross spiritual income (i.e. income from tithes and other comparable offerings) showed corresponding disparities: £179 18s. 11½d. (37 per cent) for St David's, £38 (24 per cent) for Llandaff, £65 9s. 5½d. (44 per cent) for Bangor, and £177 1s. 6d. (88 per cent) for St Asaph. Both temporalities and spiritualities were leased out on a considerable scale, in many instances to the same families who were active in leasing monastic possessions. The endowments of the cathedral clergy, all of whom belonged to chapters of secular clergy in Wales, were correspondingly as modest as those of the bishops. Some of the best, for example the archdeaconry of St Asaph or the archdeaconry of St David's, were worth only £74 and £56 respectively, while most of the Welsh prebends were far less valuable than many of the richer

[1] Elwyn Evans, *op. cit.*
[2] Professor Jones Pierce approached the problem of the Crown lands in his paper 'Notes on the History of Caernarvonshire in the Reign of Elizabeth', *Trans. Caernarvonshire Hist. Soc.*, 1940, pp. 35–57.
[3] Details in Glanmor Williams, *The Welsh Church from Conquest to Reformation*, 1962, chs. VIII and X.

rectories and vicarages in England. Apart from the cathedrals there were only six collegiate churches, namely, Holyhead, Clynnog, Ruthin, Llanddewibrefi, Abergwili, and the College of B.V.M. at St David's, in the whole of Wales, and they were worth on the average between £40 and £50 a year. Among the parochial clergy poverty was widespread: an analysis of the livings listed in *Valor Ecclesiasticus* shows that only 6 per cent of them were valued at more than £20 a year, 23·5 per cent at between £10 and £20, 46 per cent at between £5 and £10, and the rest at less than £5. Examination of the sources of incumbents' income in a typical rural deanery like that of Abergavenny reveals that on the average glebe accounted for 16 per cent, the tithes of corn and hay for 39 per cent, and the tithes of natural increase (i.e. livestock) for about 30 per cent, while the remainder was made up from miscellaneous minor sources. In addition to the beneficed clergy there were about as many unbeneficed stipendiary clergy whose average income was about £4 a year. Chantries, guilds, and fraternities were comparatively rare in Wales. They were nearly all slenderly endowed, usually with tenements and small acreages of land in and around the towns, and with stocks of sheep and cattle or small sums of cash in the rural parishes.[1]

There were in all some forty-seven religious houses in Wales before the dissolution, i.e. about one to every twenty parishes, as compared with one to every ten parishes in England. Not one was rated at more than £200 a year, and the clear annual value of their total endowments, as listed in the *Valor Ecclesiasticus* at £3,178, was worth less than that of the single great house of Westminster (£3,470). They varied considerably in the sources of their income, though all of them, except the seven houses of canons, depended chiefly on their landed estates, and the thirteen Cistercian houses, especially, were by Welsh standards landowners on a big scale. Monastic lands were in the hands of tenants except for a small fraction kept in hand to meet the needs of the now very small numbers of monks—there were probably no more than 250 men and women in religious orders in the whole of Wales—and their household servants. There is no conclusive evidence that Welsh monastic landlords were trying to draw back land into their own hands for direct exploitation early in the sixteenth century as some English houses are known to have been doing.[2] Among their tenants conditions of tenure varied widely, but, broadly speaking, the usual four classes of tenants were recognized: freeholders, copyholders, tenants-at-will, and leaseholders. There had been a growing tendency for leaseholds to

[1] *Ibid.*, pp. 284–6 and Appendix A (for beneficed clergy); pp. 287–8 (unbeneficed clergy); and pp. 288–95 (chantries etc.).
[2] See *supra*, p. 77.

displace other tenancies in the fifteenth and sixteenth centuries. But the custom was far from prevalent even on the eve of the dissolution, and most surviving Welsh leases show that there had been a rush to secure them in 1535 and 1536. Unlike many of the earlier sixteenth-century leases, which were usually entered into for a term of lives, many of these late leases were for long terms, ranging from forty to one hundred years, and may have represented an attempt by landlords and tenants to reap the maximum benefit in the form of high entry fines and security respectively in the brief space at their disposal. Late as many of these leases were, they were almost without exception confirmed when the Crown took over, and evidence from the early seventeenth century shows that some of the pre-dissolution leases were still valid.[1]

## 2. *The dissolution of the monasteries*

Welsh houses, like those of England, were surveyed by commissioners appointed by the Crown in 1535 and their possessions recorded in the *Valor Ecclesiasticus*. None was valued at more than £200 and all should have been dissolved under the terms of the first act for the dissolution of the religious houses. In fact, three—Whitland, Strata Florida, and Neath—were reprieved for a short time on payment of fines to the Crown; and others, like Ewenni or Malpas, which were daughter priories of the large English monasteries of Gloucester and Montacute, survived until the dissolution of the mother house. The Welsh friaries, all of which were meagrely furnished and held only the scantiest possessions in land, much of it leased to local laymen, disappeared in 1538. The commandery of the Knights of St John at Slebech, Pembrokeshire, and the possessions of the order in north Wales survived until 1540. Finally, the chantries and similar endowments were appropriated in 1549, after an abortive proposal of 1545. The chantry certificates place the total value of the assets of Welsh chantries at just over £950. Even allowing for the very considerable degree of concealment and embezzlement which took place at the time of the dissolution, it is clear that chantry property was not very extensive in Wales and much of it was already being diverted for secular purposes even before 1549.[2]

The broad pattern of the subsequent disposal of these confiscated properties was, as might be expected, much the same for Wales as for England. In the years immediately after the dissolution the intention of the government seems patently to have been to retain most of its

---

[1] *Exchequer Proceedings concerning Wales in Tempore James I*, ed. T. I. Jeffreys Jones, Cardiff, 1955, pp. 29, 35, 92, 109, 119, 226, 292, 309.
[2] Details in Williams, *Conquest to Reformation*, pp. 288–95.

newly won assets in its own hands. The process of leasing began in 1537 and rapidly gained momentum in 1538-9 when the bulk of the leases were concluded, though others continued to be made in smaller numbers during the remaining years of Henry VIII's reign. The possessions thus leased consisted for the most part of vacant sites, demesne lands, and rectories not already farmed out by the monks. Rents were based on the assessments made in 1535 and the term of years was always twenty-one. The majority of these early leases were entered into by members of the royal household or men in close touch with it. Some had no connection with Wales at all, but many of them were drawn from local Welsh families, like Morgan Wolfe, the king's goldsmith but a Monmouthshire man by origin, who took out leases of properties formerly belonging to Chepstow and Abergavenny priories. Three of those concerned with monastic visitations would appear to have taken advantage of inside information and contacts to acquire leases—John Price (Brecon Priory), Edward Carne (Ewenni Priory), and John Vaughan (Grace Dieu, Pembroke, and Whitland).

Whatever its original intentions may have been, the Crown found itself obliged, from about 1539 onwards, to begin selling its interests in the former monastic lands. The first official statement of the terms, i.e. twenty years' purchase, comes in December 1539, and the first sales in Wales are recorded in 1540, the earliest being the sale of the priory of Cardigan together with three of its rectories to William Cavendish, auditor of the court of Augmentations, on 26 February.[1] This was followed by a number of other sales in the same year; then followed a relatively quiet period until the crisis of the years 1544-6, when heavy war expenditure forced Henry to make many more sales. At first the Crown was anxious to dispose only of small, isolated tenements and sought to attach the lucrative but burdensome military tenure to them. Under the pressure of necessity, however, smaller properties were offered in free socage or burgage, and large blocks of the more valuable granges were disposed of. Similar financial embarrassments forced Edward VI and Mary to sell further parcels of monastic land, and it is clear that by Elizabeth's reign a large part of it had been alienated. Close examination of the disposal of former monastic lands in the diocese of Llandaff, which broadly speaking covered the two counties of Glamorgan and Monmouth, and contained within its borders much the heaviest concentration of monastic possessions in Wales, shows that by the end of Henry VIII's reign about 50-60 per cent had been disposed of. A further 20-30 per cent followed during the next two reigns, so that by Elizabeth's accession less than a quarter remained in the queen's

[1] LP xv, 282 (108).

hands. This compares broadly with similar estimates made for some English counties, and the picture for the rest of Wales seems not to differ significantly.

Only a very small amount of this property found its way back to the Church or to educational foundations. The new dioceses of Gloucester and Bristol founded by Henry VIII benefited to some slight extent by being allowed to take over some of the former interests in south Wales of the abbeys of Tewkesbury, Gloucester, and St Augustine's, Bristol; and grammar schools were founded at Brecon, Carmarthen, and Abergavenny with buildings and/or endowments partly from the former priory of Abergavenny, friaries at Brecon and Carmarthen, and the collegiate church of Abergwili.[1] Nor was a very large amount of monastic land given away or disposed of on highly favourable terms. The only really significant gift of it in Wales was that made to the earl of Worcester as early as March 1537 when the site and the possessions of Tintern Abbey in south Wales were bestowed upon him.[2] The rest was bought for hard cash, for rarely less than the market rate of twenty years' purchase, and in some instances for considerably more, as for example when Sir Edward Carne, a trusted royal servant, none the less in 1543 paid twenty-three years' purchase for lands in Colwinston and twenty-seven years' purchase for the site of the Austin Friars' house in Newport.[3]

At first sight it might seem that many Welsh properties were bought by large-scale speculators. But closer inspection usually reveals that even men like Henry Audley or Sir Thomas Heneage were for the most part agents who were subsequently given licences to alienate land to local buyers. In fact, the biggest buyers of Welsh monastic land were local gentry who made application direct to the court of Augmentations on their own account. In some instances, they were men already leasing the site and some of the demesne of former monasteries, some of whose larger estates they now wished to purchase—Sir John Williams at Cwm-hir, John Scudamore at Dore, John Price at Brecon, Rice Mansel at Margam, John Bradshaw at St Dogmael's, Edward Carne at Ewenni, and Nicholas Arnold at Llanthony, are the most notable examples. The only individuals who could thus benefit were those who had ready cash or who could raise it quickly. Quite often they were men who had done well out of service to the Crown, or in trade, or at the law, or by all or a number of these means. To acquire their new estates they were often able to raise impressive sums; Rice Mansel, for instance, put up no less than £2,600 in all for the estates

---

[1] LP xvi, 503 (30), 1226 (5); xvii, 1154 (60), 556 (25); xviii, i, 226.
[2] LP xii, i, 795 (16).
[3] E 318, 243.

of Margam Abbey between 1540 and 1556.[1] In general it is probable that many of these purchasers, though not without an eye to business, were more concerned with prestige than profits. There is very little evidence that they were unduly oppressive or inequitable in their treatment of under-tenants; at all events there are very few of the protracted lawsuits that might have been expected to ensue in so litigious an age if they had been. Often, indeed, the boot was on the other foot, with new monastic proprietors or lessees complaining of being unable to get former monastic tenants to fulfil obligations.[2] Nor can they be said to have constituted a 'new' gentry. Certainly the purchase of extensive monastic holdings might help to establish a new family in a county, as it did the Barlows of Slebech, the Bradshaws of St Dogmael's, or the Steadmans of Strata Florida. But in general, the families that benefited most, the Herberts, the Somersets, the Devereux, the Carnes, the Gunters, or the Morgans of Monmouthshire, were already well established and rising clans. Their stake in monastic property did not create, but helped to emphasize, the differences between them and less successful families. It has often been suggested that their acquisitions from this source, especially when paid for at the market price, helped to ensure the permanence of the English Reformation, yet it is noteworthy that in Wales, at least, some of the families who did best out of the dissolution were also among the most tenacious upholders of the Roman religion, the Somerset earls of Worcester being among the foremost recusants in the whole realm.

By Elizabeth's reign almost all the surviving Crown leases of former monastic possessions relate to rectories and tithe.[3] Examined decade by decade over the whole reign they reveal some interesting trends. During the years 1558–70 profits anticipated from such leases seem to have been sufficient for the Crown to try to offset the effects of inflation by exacting high entry fines, averaging about four years' rent and rising to as high as six years'. Between 1570 and 1580 entry fines were still fairly high, averaging about three years' rent. During the whole period down to 1580 the term of a lease was invariably twenty-one years. In the decade between 1580 and 1590 the market hardened against the Crown; entry fines were down to an average of about two years, and leases for three lives began to appear, though those for twenty-one years were still more common. By the time of the agri-

---

[1] *Penrice and Margam Manuscripts*, ed. W. de G. Birch, 1893–1904; cf. G. Williams, 'Sir Rhys Mansel of Penrice and Margam', *Morgannwg*, VI, 1962.
[2] *Records of the Court of Augmentations relating to Wales and Monmouthshire*, Cardiff, ed. E. A. Lewis and J. C. Davies, 1954, *passim*; *Exchequer Proceedings (Equity) concerning Wales*, ed. E. G. Jones, Cardiff, 1939, *passim*.
[3] *Records...Augmentations*, part II.

cultural crises of the 1590's leases for three lives began to predominate and entry fines were down to an average of about one year. The lessees continued to be local gentry in the main, though it was comparatively rare for a family to maintain an unbroken lien on the lease of any rectory. Where urban tenements, notably parcels of the former chantries, were still being leased, complaints of their decayed and ruinous state were not infrequent.

### 3. *Lay pressure on the secular clergy, 1536–58*

The transfer of such enormous assets from monastic to lay owners threatened to put the possessions of the secular clergy in almost equal danger. It had been proved that the patrimony of the Church could be despoiled with impunity and advantage; a large part of the property of the secular clergy was already farmed out to a laity which regarded them as being hardly less grossly over-endowed than the monks had been; and the nature of Protestant doctrine, particularly Puritan versions of it, rendered it sharply critical of the worldly wealth of the clergy.[1] As the pace of economic and doctrinal change began simultaneously to quicken the secular clergy came under increasingly heavy pressure. They were perhaps at their most defenceless during the reign of Edward VI, when they could hope for no protection by the government. In three of the Welsh dioceses we have clear evidence of attempts by the laity to extend their control over the possessions of the bishops and chapters. At Llandaff, Bishop Kitchen (1545-66) had a bad reputation for having granted away to the Mathew family of Radyr his marcher rights over the lordship of Llandaff and for selling and leasing land to the prejudice of his successors. While we can only guess what pressures on the part of the local gentry Kitchen had to contend with, we are left in no doubt of the part of the dominant Salusbury family in the diocese of St Asaph. Here the efforts of the vigorous Marian bishop, Thomas Goldwell (1555-9), make it plain that this family, which for a generation or two had been the outstanding family in the diocese, had exercised its influence to such an extent as almost to turn the endowments of the deanery and archdeaconry of St Asaph, not to mention the chapter seal, into its own private property. At St David's during the same period no small part of the violent contentions between Bishop Ferrar (1548-55) and clergy and laymen of his diocese, which ended in his being imprisoned at the order of the Privy Council, arose out of Ferrar's attempts to undo some of the unduly favourable leases and concessions made by his predecessor, William Barlow (1536-48). They brought him into conflict with some of the most powerful

[1] Christopher Hill, *The Economic Problems of the Church*, 1956.

families in the south-west, above all the Devereux. In all these episodes the possessions of the cathedrals and the higher clergy were as much the subject of the laity's attention as those of the bishops. In many instances the laity's task was made easier by weakness or even collusion on the part of friends, relatives, or dependants among the cathedral clergy. At Llandaff, where leading canons had in 1538–9 been implicated in the spoliation of the treasures of their own cathedral, the chapter was found by a commission of enquiry to have made favourable leases to friends, and the archdeacon confessed to having removed the chapter seal contrary to the bishop's will. Similar accusations were brought against some of the canons at St David's, and there, too, there were unedifying squabbles over custody of the chapter seal, while at St Asaph Bishop Goldwell later accused Sir John Salusbury of having entered into "very corrupt and simoniacal pacts and agreements" with the former dean and of appending the chapter seal to forged leases.[1]

Mary's reign brought some relief to the bishops. There were even attempts at St Asaph and Llandaff to make good some of the earlier spoliation. But Mary's appeal for the restitution of monastic land brought no better response in Wales than it did elsewhere. Her policy of depriving many of the parish clergy for heresy and removing them for marriage gave rise to a series of disputes over the validity of leases of tithe and glebe agreed upon by the deprived clergy. About seventy to eighty Chancery suits of this period for England and Wales give some indication of the ways in which a clergyman about to be deprived had leased his benefice in such a way that a "great part of the profits of the same might come to the relief of himself, his wife, and children."[2] Such juggling with leases was not to be wondered at. Chancery suits for the period before the Reformation record many disputes concerning the leasing of tithe and glebe and embody numerous allegations of forgery, tampering with seals, ante-dating, and the like. The rapid changes of religious policy, repeated attacks on ecclesiastical property, and the inflationary spiral, all taught men to anticipate disaster and to think only of their own interest in their freehold. Many of the economic problems of the clergy of Elizabethan and Stuart times and the solutions they were obliged to find to them are in embryo much older than is often supposed.

[1] Lawrence Thomas, *The Reformation in the Old Diocese of Llandaff*, 1930, pp. 75–82; *An Inventory of the Early Chancery Proceedings concerning Wales*, ed. E. A. Lewis, 1937, pp. 130–2, 274;. Glanmor Williams, 'The Protestant Experiment in the Diocese of St David's', *Bull. BCS*, xv, 1953, pp. 212–24; XVI, 1954, pp. 38–48; Glanmor Williams (ed.), *Glamorgan County History*, IV, 1974, pp. 212–18.

[2] Lewis, *Early Chancery Procs.*, *passim*; cf. *Early Chancery Proceedings, List of*, x, 1936.

## 4. *Economic tensions, 1558–1640*

The reigns of Elizabeth and the first two Stuarts were a period of sustained tension between the economic interests of the clergy and laity, in which religious conviction reinforced the latter's ambitions to curtail the privileges and property rights of the former. The events of the century had immeasurably weakened the clergy's position and given the laity reason to anticipate that continued pressure would bring them further gains. Elizabeth's own attitude towards the clergy was ambivalent: while she was determined for political reasons to preserve the authority of the hierarchy, she missed no opportunity to milch the bishoprics of many possible sources of revenue.[1] Her lay subjects were not loth to follow her example, and from all four Welsh dioceses there are protests by the bishops against the rapacious pressures of greedy laymen, typified by Sir John Wynn of Gwydir, whom the best of the Welsh bishops, William Morgan, described as "a sacrilegious robber of my church, a perfidious spoiler of my diocese." One of the favourite devices of such laymen was the commission of concealment, i.e. a royal commission to enquire into ecclesiastical possessions such as those of former monasteries or collegiate churches which allegedly ought to have passed into the hands of the Crown but which were said to be illicitly detained. The instigators of such a commission generally hoped to derive some reward for their efforts in the form of a lease of the concealed lands brought to light by them. The bishops of St David's suffered particularly badly from such commissions when they were deprived of their interests in the former collegiate church of Llanddewibrefi and came near to losing their rights in the other college of Abergwili. The fortunate Queen's farmer who was allowed to rent these possessions for £40 a year was reputed by 1600 to be making a profit of close on £400 on his bargain. It is true that the Stuart kings were more disposed to defend the interests of their bishops than Elizabeth had been, but even so the bishops of early Stuart Wales were as doleful in their complaints of the impoverishment of their sees by lay rapacity as their Elizabethan predecessors had been—and with reason.[2]

The surviving chapter records for the dioceses of Llandaff and St

[1] Gordon Donaldson, *The Scottish Reformation*, 1960, p. 172, n. 2, for refs.

[2] D. R. Thomas, *The History of the Diocese of St Asaph*, 1908, I, p. 101; A. G. Edwards, *Landmarks in the History of the Welsh Church*, 1913, pp. 104 *sqq*; E. J. Newell, *Llandaff*, 1902, pp. 145–51; Glanmor Williams, 'Richard Davies, Bishop of St David's, 1561–81', *Hon. Soc. Cymmrodorion*, 1948, pp. 147–69; CPSD, *passim*; Thos. Richards, *A History of the Puritan Movement in Wales, 1639–53*, 1920, ch. 1; Glanmor Williams, 'The Collegiate Church of Llanddewibrefi', *Ceredigion*, IV, 1963; idem, 'Bishop William Morgan ...', *J. Merioneth Hist. and Rec. Soc.*, VII, 1976, pp. 347–72.

David's[1] show the eagerness of laymen to enter into leases of episcopal and capitular property, in both glebe and tithe. Most of the lessees were local gentry, though there was also a sprinkling of lawyers and merchants, particularly among those who appear to be related to the lessors. Leases of Llandaff capitular possessions were dominated to a large extent by the families of Herbert and Morgan, but those of St David's, with its much wider geographical spread, show a greater variation. The records themselves, of course, reveal little of the pressures exerted or the inducements offered to obtain such leases, though it may be significant that the registrar of St David's recorded in 1563 that he had no record of any lease before 1559, "such hath been the alteration and misorder in these later days of our predecessors," and it is certainly noticeable that before the act of 1571 preventing leases for longer than three lives or twenty-one years, a number of St David's leases had been entered into for terms ranging from thirty to seventy years. But we know from other sources what kind of pressures bishops and chapters were in general subjected to and there are indications from Welsh bishops' comments that things were not different in Wales. Bishop Richard Davies of St David's (1561-81) attacked the "insatiable cormorants" in his own diocese, "greedy for Church spoils and contemptuously intolerant of the Church's rulers." His successor, Marmaduke Middleton (1581-93), complained how all the best prebends in his diocese were leased out for long terms, and there were comparable complaints from the dioceses of Llandaff, Bangor, and St Asaph.[2] Middleton also bemoaned that the endowments of a large number of the rectories and vicarages within his diocese were leased out, and averred that the incumbents of livings worth £10 and even £30 were glad to take £6 13s. 4d., or even less, "and yet bound in bonds that they cannot avoid it without their undoing." Parsonages impropriate to the bishop and chapter, "the chiefest part of the revenues of the see," were all leased out so that "almost none" would return for fifty years to come. Middleton is not the best of witnesses and his sweeping statements cannot safely be taken at their face value. Yet there is corroborative evidence from his own chapter's records and those of Llandaff and other sources that such endowments were regularly leased.

On the subject of lay impropriations Welsh bishops were outspokenly critical. Many of these livings were "the very best things in all the whole diocese," but were regarded by the impropriators solely as a source of profit to themselves. Where there was an endowed vicarage

[1] National Library of Wales, LlCh 4; SDCh, B, 1-4.
[2] SP 12, 65, i; BM Lansdowne MS 120; Thomas, *St Asaph*, I, pp. 98-100; Glanmor Williams, 'Bishop William Morgan', *op. cit.*, pp. 347-42; cf. *infra*, p. 159, n. 1.

they squeezed the incumbents hard trying to cut down on their income and making no allowance in lieu of former oblations and other "superstitious offerings" which had formerly accrued to them. The parish of Llanbadarn Fawr in Jacobean times affords an outstanding example of their methods. In this enormous parish of 180 square miles, with its 2,400 communicants, the farmer's issues were alleged to be worth over £1,000 a year while his rent was £120. He paid £20 to the vicar and had also allowed £40 or £50 in tithes to make up for the loss of former oblations, but had withdrawn this concession, with the result that the vicar took him to the Exchequer Court.[1] Where there was no vicarage endowed and no vicarial tithes, but only a stipendiary curate, the farmer could do even better. Here it was usual for his rent to remain at its customary level when a lease was renewed, and in so far as the Crown reaped a profit at all it did so by means of entry fines. Meantime the customary stipend, often small in pre-Reformation times, was grossly inadequate for a married clergy in an inflationary age, and was maintained unchanged from decade to decade, while the impropriator stood to gain handsomely from rising prices. Richard Davies's report on his diocese in 1570 speaks of many churches of this kind. In a return for St David's diocese in 1583, out of seventy-nine curates' stipends listed, eleven only were worth £10 or more and thirty-three were worth £5 or less—it was hardly a matter of surprise that seven of the curates should be fugitives from their cures. A similar report on Llandaff in 1603 listed seven curacies out of thirty-one as worth more than £5 a year, and four were without anyone to serve them at all. The parishioners of Churchstoke, situated in one of the most fertile spots in north Wales, yielding a yearly revenue of £160 for a rent of £6 or £7, so it was claimed, in a bill of complaint alleged that the farmers had for years paid their stipendiary curates less than twenty nobles a year. The result was that the ministers were "unlearned, poor, bare and needy fellows," forced to leave their wives and children to the mercy of the parish, "such a mischief and inconvenience... happening in the parts of Wales so often," that their lordships of the Exchequer should attend thereto. The chancel of the church there, like that of many others in the possession of impropriators, was in a ruinous condition on account of their unwillingness to spend money in fulfilling their obligations as rectors to maintain the chancel in good repair.[2]

[1] SP 12, 66, 26, i; D. R. Thomas, *The Life and Work of Bishop Davies and William Salesbury, etc.*, 1902, pp. 37–44; Jeffreys Jones, *Exchequer Procs. James I*, pp. 103, 119, 224.

[2] SP 12, 65, i; BM Harleian MS 595; J. Jones, *op. cit.*, pp. 123, 293, 333; W. H. House, 'Contest for a Radnorshire Rectory in the Seventeenth Century', *Hist. Soc. Church Wales*, VII, 1957; G. Gruffydd, 'Bishop Godwin's Injunctions for...Llandaff, 1603', *ibid.*, IV, 1954.

Nor was the process of impropriation and annexation everywhere at an end even as late as the first decade of the seventeenth century, judging by the comment of Bishop Parry of St Asaph, who in 1611 wrote to Salisbury that the miserable state of his diocese, lacking a learned resident ministry, might be made all the worse by the many efforts being made and bribes being offered to procure annexations.

Along with the leasing of the endowments of benefices went the eager acquisition of rights of advowson. A record from the diocese of St Asaph for the years 1536-8 shows that the practice of granting away rights of next presentation to livings within the bishop's gift was prevalent at least as early as Henry VIII's reign, and later records from Llandaff and St David's showed that it remained usual throughout our period.[1] Bishops rarely parted with these rights except for a consideration, and laymen's motives for acquiring them were usually self-interested: either they wished to place relatives or clients in employment, or they intended to extract a favourable lease or some other simoniacal agreement from the incumbent they presented. The more creditable motives of raising the standards of the ministry associated with the acquisition of advowsons by Feoffees for Impropriations, though they made some impact upon Wales and the border English counties, were not given much encouragement in a country so little touched by Puritan influences as Wales was.[2]

## 5. *The reaction of the clergy*

In face of all this pressure from laymen, clerics were not, of course, entirely defenceless or invariably the losers. If only they could maintain their sources of income intact they stood to benefit as much as anyone else from the rise in prices. It was thought reasonable in 1583 to estimate the benefices of St David's diocese as being then worth three times what they had been valued at in 1535 for the *Valor Ecclesiasticus*, though the incumbents not surprisingly maintained that they were hardly worth double the earlier estimate, especially since so many of them were leased out anyway. At St Asaph four years later, livings were reckoned to be worth five or six times what the *Valor* rated them, but this estimate comes in too partisan an account to be wholly reliable. Scattered fragments of information from the early seventeenth century certainly point to a striking increase in the value of the tithe-yield from Welsh parishes, and this may be reflected in the much larger number of graduates and preachers who were being ordained in

[1] NLW, SA, M, 21; Cf. p. 000, n. 1 *supra*.
[2] Howse, *loc. cit.*; C. Hill, 'Puritans and "the Dark Corners of the Land",' *Trans. RHS*, 5th Ser., XIII, 1963, pp. 91-3.

Welsh dioceses by Stuart times as compared with the pre-Reformation era or even the early Elizabethan period, when Welsh livings were said to be too poor for the most part to attract men with such training.[1] Nevertheless, it is doubtful whether the resident clergy in Wales gained more than a small fraction of this increased prosperity. Most of the cathedral dignitaries and the best rectories were held by non-resident absentees and their endowments were normally leased out, or were impropriate, to laymen. Even where this was not so, the lesser tithes of natural increase, where the largest increments were likely to accrue, were notoriously the most difficult to collect.

Almost inevitably, therefore, the consequence of frequent and bitter exchanges between the clergy and laity was that the former tended to become as shameless in their methods as their adversaries. The example was set at the top and spread down from the head to members. Even the best of the bishops did not entirely escape the taint, while the administration of some rapidly degenerated into avarice and corruption. Most of them were men of middle-class origin and hardly any, apart from Rudd of St David's (1594–1615), had private income of any consequence. Obliged to maintain state and hospitality appropriate to their station on their miserably inadequate incomes, they were querulous and persistent in their expostulations, though only Carleton of Llandaff (1618–19) had the unabashed frankness to admit that he accepted his unwelcome "promotion" there because "the favours of princes are not to be rejected."[2] *Commendams* and pluralism, common in Wales since the fifteenth century, were normal among all the higher clergy, and even Laud as bishop of St David's proved no exception. Some took to systematically acquiring some of the better rectories in their gift, the most notorious offender being Hughes of St Asaph (1573–1600). Allegations of simony and greed were made, probably with justice, against a number of them. It comes as no surprise that Marmaduke Middleton, deprived of his see in 1593, should be accused of simony and many other extortions and corrupt practices, but some of the best bishops have their reputations hardly less tarnished in this respect, among them Lewis Bayly, author of *The Practice of Piety* and bishop of Bangor (1616–31), and Richard Davies of St David's (1561–81). The unusually well documented activities of Davies and his precentor, Thomas Huet, show that even men who had a conscientious regard for their office were obliged to provide for themselves and their families by unashamed nepotism in granting rights of next presentation

---

[1] Williams, *Conquest to Reformation*, pp. 327–31; *Idem*, 'The Episcopal Registers of St David's, 1554–65', *Bull. BCS*, XIV, pp. 45–54, 125–38; NLW, SD, BR, 3; Richards, *Puritan Movement*.

[2] CPSD 1611–18, p. 500.

to livings, leasing of prebends, and conferring livings.¹ The temptation of *sauve qui peut* was made the stronger by short episcopates and frequent changes. Pressed by poverty, high taxation, and rising living-costs, they took what they could in the way of high entry fines and other short-term gains. They cut down on overheads like residence, repairs, and hospitality; palaces, parsonages, chancels, the cathedrals themselves, were allowed to fall into disrepair and even ruin.²

So that when in Charles I's reign, under Laud's direction, a determined drive was made to safeguard what remained of the Church's property and to recover from profane hands as much as possible, it was directed nearly as much against some of the practices of the clergy as against those of the laity. Bishops were required not to be absentee landlords nor to prejudice their successors' rights or possessions before being translated. These were eminently salutary regulations as far as Welsh dioceses were concerned, where short-term bishops were all too usual, though neither of Laud's appointments to his old diocese of St David's, Field (1627-35) and Manwaring (1636-53), did much to comply with his wishes. On the other hand there are a few small signs of the changing times to be discerned in the contemporary ecclesiastical records. The chapter of Llandaff in 1626, considering the "great decay" of the church, piously resolved not to renew the lease of the rectory of Eglwysilan but to "convert the entire profits and annual rent (being not minished by taking any fine) to the best use and most valuable advantage" of the church of Llandaff. Encouraged perhaps by a concession in its favour from Charles I over a lease, in 1629 it refused rent from so great a figure as the earl of Worcester on the grounds that it was not certain just how much of its possessions the sum was being tendered for; and in 1634 it carefully entered into its records royal letters forbidding the negotiation of leases for a term of lives by the whole chapter or individual members of it. The bishop of St David's had already laid down as early as 1629 that the chapter was not to lease for a term of lives or to agree upon any leases in his absence.³ Laud in 1637 settled on the bishop the perpetual annexation of two rectories *in commendam*. In the still poorer dioceses of north Wales he was also active, settling commendams on the bishop of St Asaph and providing him with a new palace. In Bangor, where

[1] St Ch. 5, G15, 23, 580, 25; H. R. Trevor-Roper, *Archbishop Laud, 1573-1645*, 1962 ed., p. 188; Williams, *Hon. Soc. Cymmrodorion*, 1948, pp. 163-4.

[2] Gruffydd, *Hist. Soc. Ch. Wales*, IV, pp. 18-19; W. T. Morgan 'Two Cases concerning Dilapidations to Episcopal Property etc.', *National Library Wales J.*, VII, 1951, pp. 149-54.

[3] NLW, LlCh, 4, pp. 106, 111, 126-8; SDCh, B, 4, p. 30; Williams, *Glam. County History*, IV, pp. 239-45.

"everything was let for lives, down to the very mill that grinds his corn," by his predecessors, the bishop was required to make a survey of all the lands of his see; and, moreover, in 1637 the archdeacon of Anglesey was promoted to be bishop of the diocese as a reward for having recovered for the see concealed lands to the value of £1,000.[1] But this was a quite exceptional piece of good fortune for the Church. Much of its property was gone beyond recall and more still was to be lost in the vast upheaval that was soon to shake it and the whole realm to their foundations.

[1] Trevor-Roper, *Laud*, p. 189; Hill, *Economic Problems*, pp. 312, 315.

# 3

# FARM LABOURERS

## A. THE LABOURING POPULATION

"...I think it fit to begin with the poorer sort, from whom all other sorts of estates do take their beginning. And therefore of our poor thus much:...as well the poor as the rich proceed from the Lord...the rich cannot stand without the poor...and the humble thoughts which smoke from a poor man's cottage are as sweet a sacrifice unto the Lord as the costly perfumes of the prince's palace."[1]

In these words Robert Reyce opened his description of the social order in Suffolk, in the early years of the seventeenth century; and his homily may serve to remind us of a field of study still largely unexplored by English historians.

The reason for the comparative neglect of the Tudor and Stuart farmworker is not far to seek. No one has written his signature more plainly across the countryside; but no one has left more scanty records of his achievements. No diaries, no letters, no account books; few lawsuits, a handful of wills and inventories, an inchoate mass of manorial surveys, subsidy assessments, royal commissions, and parish registers: these, with the observations of a few contemporaries, are almost all we have to go on.

Yet the history of the Tudor farmworker is surprisingly full of interest and variety. The work of labourers in the cornlands of Hertfordshire was quite unlike that of shepherds on the Yorkshire Wolds, hopmen in the Weald of Kent, neatherds on the Cumberland mountains, or warreners in the cony country of Wiltshire. The lives of farmhands who lived with their master in the farmhouse bore little resemblance to those of labourers who lived with their wives and children in cottages in the village street. The economic standing of a skilled farmworker with a holding of his own and unstinted pasture rights on the common waste was altogether different from that of a disinherited day-labourer with no property but his wages, and a mere hovel of sticks and dirt to live in. If all the relevant material could be studied, the Tudor farmworker's story would, indeed, furnish sufficient information for a book. In the space of a single chapter only the bare outlines of the subject can be traced.

[1] Robert Reyce, *Suffolk in the XVIIth Century: the Breviary of Suffolk by Robert Reyce, 1618...*, ed. Lord Francis Hervey, 1902, pp. 56, 57.

The first problem confronting the student of Tudor farmworkers is that of definition. For the bulk of the labouring population the question does not arise; but in the topmost rank of the working community there was sometimes no sharp distinction between the better-off labourer working his own holding and supplementing his income with seasonal wage-work, and the poor husbandman whose holding was insufficient to support his family and who turned to occasional wage-work to augment his resources. All that can be said is that the employment of the former tended to be regular, and of the latter spasmodic. This distinction is sometimes difficult to observe in practice; but the difficulty affects only a marginal section of the working community, though it should be borne in mind in interpreting the figures given below.

For an estimate of the size of the labouring population, in proportion to that of the country as a whole, we must turn to the subsidy assessments of 1524, the Hearth Tax Returns of the 1660's, two occupational censuses of the early seventeenth century, and a sample of manorial surveys.[1] In the subsidy of 1524 people were assessed on lands, goods, or wages, and in rural parishes most of those in the latter category can probably be regarded as farm servants. In forty-four parishes scattered throughout Devonshire the average proportion so assessed was 36 per cent, though in some places it rose as high as two thirds. In Lincolnshire it was about one third, ranging from 28 per cent on the sparsely populated wolds to 35 per cent in the marshland, and 41 per cent in the middle marsh. In Leicestershire, by contrast, only about 20–22 per cent of the rural population were assessed on wages, though here there was even wider diversity between different parishes, and in some places the proportion was as high as 90 per cent.

In the Hearth Tax Returns poor people were usually returned as "not chargeable," and most people so described were probably labourers. In Kent, the proportion so accounted was one third: ranging from 16 per cent on the thinly settled sheep pastures of Aloesbridge hundred in Romney Marsh, to 44 per cent in the populous countryside

[1] W. G. Hoskins and H. P. R. Finberg, *Devonshire Studies*, 1952, pp. 419–20; W. G. Hoskins, *Essays in Leicestershire History*, 1950, pp. 129–30; Joan Thirsk, *English Peasant Farming*, 1957, pp. 41, 74, 83, 98, 149; A. J. and R. H. Tawney, 'An Occupational Census of the Seventeenth Century', EcHR, v, 1934–5, pp. 39 and n., 46 *sqq.*; information on Kentish Surveys (1562–1639) and Hearth Tax Returns kindly given by Dr Felix Hull; PRO LR, 2, 230, ff. 42–3, 223–34; SP 14, 44, 28; SP 14, 47, 75; Bradford Corporation, Cunliffe-Lister MSS (2), Bdle 29; Lancs. RO, DDM. 14.7, DD Pt. 39, DD F. 112, DD He. 61.5; Carlisle, Dean and Chapter Records, Hugh Todd's Account of Rentals (1490); Cumb. RO, Surveys of Dacre Lands (1589); Yorks. Arch. Soc., MS Collns., DD.121.31; *Yorks. Arch. Jnl*, XXXI, 1934, pp. 245, 246; Yorks. Arch. Soc., Rec. Ser., CIV, p. xxiii. Most of the surveys relate to 1570–1640; three to 1651 (Yorkshire); one to 1490 (Cumberland); cf. also VCH *Wilts.*, IV, 1959, p. 57.

round Maidstone, Ashford, and the Wealden cloth villages, and 51 per cent in the rich cornlands of Downhamford hundred, between Sandwich and Canterbury.

Between the 1524 subsidy and the Hearth Tax Returns, two county 'censuses' were compiled, one for Gloucestershire in 1608, and another for part of Northamptonshire in 1638. In the latter, the proportion of agricultural labourers in the ten hundreds of the eastern division of the county was probably about 31 per cent.[1] In Gloucestershire, where an exceptionally large number of people were employed in the cloth industry, farmworkers formed only one fifth of the population, although labouring people as a whole comprised nearly 30 per cent of the total. From this latter census it is also clear that the actual number of farmworkers in Gloucestershire, between the ages of 20 and 60, was about 3,500, out of a total male agricultural population of about 8,000.[2]

The evidence of manorial surveys is more difficult to interpret. It is probably safe to assume, however, that most rural tenants with holdings of less than five acres occasionally, at least, augmented their income by working as wage-labourers. (The Act of 1589, it will be recalled, stipulated that no cottage should be erected with less than four acres of land attached.) On the fifty-one manors in the sample here analysed, nearly thirty-seven per cent of tenants occupied smallholdings of this kind. As between different farming regions, the proportions varied from only 19 per cent on the fell-side manors of the north to 34 per cent in mainly arable clayland areas, 35 per cent in marshland manors, and almost 70 per cent in the fens. (In this last area, however, commons were unusually extensive and the arable exceptionally fertile, and smallholdings do not necessarily represent labourers' tenements.)

Taken together, these various sources suggest that in the Tudor and early Stuart period the labouring population probably formed about one quarter or one third of the entire population of the countryside. The figure was lowest in moorland areas, a little higher on wolds and downs, and a good deal higher in fertile corn-growing districts. In unenclosed heath- and forest-lands, it was probably higher still, especially at the end of the period. The foregoing evidence does not

[1] Tawney, *op. cit.*, p. 39 and n. I have reckoned half the "servants" of unspecified occupation together with all the "labourers" as agricultural employees; but the interpretation of these categories is doubtful.

[2] Tawney, *op. cit.*, pp. 46 *sqq.* I have reckoned two thirds of the 430 knights, esquires, and gentry in the census as engaged in agricultural pursuits. I have also counted half the 750 servants and half the 283 servants of unspecified employment as probably engaged in farm-work. These proportions may be either too high or too low; but on any estimate they can hardly affect the relevant percentages by more than two or three either way.

cover such areas; but contemporaries like Hartlib and Norden expressed this opinion, and their statements are supported, as we shall see, by other evidence from manorial surveys and Exchequer Commissions.[1]

The size of the labouring population did not remain constant, however. Between the opening and closing decades of the period, it almost certainly expanded, both absolutely and relatively, till by the end of the seventeenth century labourers, cottagers, and paupers were said to comprise as much as 47 per cent of the entire population.[2] The consequences of this expansion of the working population were far-reaching. As the number of labourers increased, the pressure on land also increased, and smallholdings were either divided up amongst children, and subdivided again till they shrank to mere curtilages, or else bequeathed to the elder son alone, so that the younger children were left propertyless. As the period proceeded, therefore, a growing army of landless, or almost landless, labourers appeared, dependent on wages alone for their livelihood, often forced to wander from place to place till they found employment, or else to hire themselves out at the autumnal labour fairs held in many market towns. At the same time, largely because the development of commercial farming and the progress of regional specialization in agriculture greatly intensified the *demand* for seasonal or occasional labour, a new population of migrant labourers gradually came into being, principally recruited from among the ranks of these disinherited peasants. In all probability the labouring population had always been more mobile than we realize: droving and transhumance were, after all, long-standing practices in pastoral areas, from Wales and Northumberland to Romney Marsh and the Weald; the enclosure movement and the dissolution of the monasteries, moreover, had set many labourers adrift from their moorings; and the expansion of urban areas, especially London, attracted an increasing influx of labourers from rural parishes all over the kingdom.[3] But the appearance of an army of migrant wage-

---

[1] Cf. *Samuel Hartlib, his Legacie*, 1652, p. 42. Hartlib's remarks, however, on the fewness of commons in Kent need qualification in view of the extensive woodlands in the county, where, according to Cobbett in the nineteenth century, a similar economy prevailed. For Norden's opinion, see *Harrison's Description of England in Shakspere's Youth*, ed. F. J. Furnivall, Part IV, New Shakspere Soc., 6th Ser., VIII, 1881, p. 180. [Quoted hereafter as Harrison, *op. cit.*].

[2] D. C. Coleman, 'Labour in the English Economy of the Seventeenth Century', EcHR, 2nd Ser., VIII, 1955–6, p. 283; cf. C. W. Chalklin, *Seventeenth-Century Kent*, 1965, p. 247.

[3] Cf. E 134, 7 Car. I, M 15; E 134, 3 Car. I, M 35; Gloucester City Lib., MS 16064, f. 14; R. U. Sayce, 'The Old Summer Pastures', Pt. II, *Mont. Coll.*, LV, i, 1958, p. 71; SP 14, 138, 11. For the mobility of the rural population in Leicestershire, see W. G. Hoskins, *Essays in Leicestershire History*, 1950, pp. 131–2.

earners in the Tudor countryside was essentially a different phenomenon, and it was directly attributable to the demands of commercial farming and the growth of the labouring population.

We must not exaggerate either the novelty or the extent of these new developments, however. Judged by modern standards, the working population of Tudor and early Stuart England was still relatively small. England still remained an overwhelmingly peasant community: a land of small family farms where outside labour was only occasionally employed at peak periods. On the holdings of yeomen and husbandmen in Gloucestershire, for instance, masters outnumbered men by at least two to one: only one husbandman in ten employed any servants at all, and scarcely one in 350 more than two. In Kent and other counties, even substantial landed families, like the Tokes of Godinton Place, sometimes employed nephews and cousins of neighbouring branches of the family, when in need of farm servants or stewards.[1] Despite the development of capitalist farming and the virtual extinction of serfdom,[2] the structure of farming society yet remained intensely patriarchal, even on sizeable estates. In many counties, from Cumberland to Cornwall and Kent, it continued to be so till long after the Civil War and the Revolution of 1688.

## B. HOLDINGS AND COMMON-RIGHTS

In most parts of England the labourer's landed property, like that of other country people, was of two kinds: his individual holding, and his common rights in the village fields, meadows, and wastes. Individual cottage-holdings, according to the Act of 1589, were supposed to consist of not less than four acres of land, and many examples of tenements of this size and larger existed. William Hobson, for example, a labourer of Wheldrake in the vale of York in James I's reign, inherited a farm of six acres from his father, consisting of a house, barn, homestead, and garth of one acre, together with arable strips amounting to

---

[1] Tawney, *op. cit.*, pp. 52, 53; E. C. Lodge, ed., *The Account Book of a Kentish Estate, 1616–1704*, British Academy, Records of Social and Economic History, VI, 1927, *passim*. Professor and Mrs Tawney's figures relate only to *known* employers; on any showing, however, it is not likely that more than one husbandman in six employed a servant.

[2] For bondmen and manumission under the Tudors see A. Savine, 'Bondmen under the Tudors', RHS, NS, XVII, 1903, pp. 235–89. Savine's opinion is that even in the early sixteenth century bondmen formed little more than 1 per cent of the population, although he shows that Tudor villeinage was "not in all cases a harmless fiction ..." (pp. 248, 263). His evidence relates almost entirely to the first half of our period. Exchequer Special Commissions and Depositions show that bondmen not infrequently bequeathed property worth £30 or £40.

four acres in the east and north fields of the village, and a further acre of arable land in the Flatt. His neighbour Richard Penrose rented a similar tenement, with five and a half acres of arable in the four common fields of the village, a quarter of an acre of meadowland, and a house, a barn, a homestead, and a small garth. Two generations earlier, Robert Plommer of Nassington, in Northamptonshire, was renting a cottage with a garden and an acre of land belonging to it, together with twenty selions of arable and an acre of meadowland in the village fields. Robert Sharpe, his neighbour, lived in a cottage with a garden and a close of one acre, "lying between the king's lands" there, with nearly four acres of meadowland belonging to it.[1]

In general, however, labourers with as much as four or five acres of land were exceptionally fortunate. A study of holdings of five acres and less listed in manorial surveys of the period suggests that the lot of most village labourers was very different. Out of about 650 small-holdings on forty-three manors scattered over thirteen counties, only 7 per cent covered four or more acres; a further 26 per cent, each consisting of a cottage and garden with toft, croft, close, or orchard attached, comprised under one acre; and 41 per cent consisted of little more than a cottage and garden.[2] Even assuming that all the four-acre holdings belonged to labourers (some may have been worked by husbandmen), and taking account of holdings of over five acres, it seems probable that the tenements of at least two labourers out of three consisted of little more than a garden, with possibly a small close or two attached. As the period advanced, moreover, the proportion of labourers with very small tenements almost certainly increased. There can be little doubt that, between 1500 and 1640, the labourer's share of the cultivable area of the country as a whole was declining.

As between different counties, the size of labourers' holdings varied widely. In the marcher counties cottagers often seem to have been relatively fortunate, barely half of them renting less than one acre of land, and one in five more than two acres. In east Northamptonshire the relevant proportions were 56 and 17 per cent, and in Yorkshire and Lancashire 61 and 24 per cent. In the southern parts of Sussex, however, three labourers in four cultivated holdings of less than one acre; and in some of the densely populated manors of East Anglia nearly four out of five. Only a tiny minority of labourers on these eastern manors—some 3 per cent—farmed the statutory holding of four acres or more.

---

[1] PRO LR, 2, 230, ff. 279, 281; Northants. RO, Westmorland Apethorpe Colln., 4, XVI, 5 (1551).

[2] See Table 1 and note thereto for names of manors. In interpreting the evidence of surveys, however, it must be remembered that they tell us nothing about the sub-letting of holdings.

On the manor of Hartest, near the Suffolk wool town of Lavenham, there were, in 1608, no fewer than "40 small and poor copyholders, the best of them not having above two acres, the most of them being cottingers, and 35 other poor households that have no habitation of their own, nor cow nor calf..." It was in such areas, as Dr Thirsk has pointed out elsewhere, that labourers were forced to turn to by-employments like spinning and weaving to eke out a living.[1]

Table 1. *The size of labourers' holdings (percentages)*[a]

|  | Cottage with garden or croft, etc., only | Under 1 acre | 1–1¾ acres | 2–2¾ acres | 3–3¾ acres | 4 and 5 acres |
|---|---|---|---|---|---|---|
| Cumberland | 60 | 12 | 10 | 5 | 8 | 6 |
| Yorks. and Lancs. | 31 | 30 | 14 | 7 | 8 | 9 |
| West Midlands | 16 | 33 | 28 | 8 | 6 | 8 |
| Sussex and Hants. | 20 | 57 | 8 | 6 | 5 | 5 |
| Eastern Counties | 73 | 5 | 10 | 7 | 2 | 3 |
| Northants. | 4 | 52 | 26 | 0 | 4 | 13 |
| All areas | 41 | 26 | 13 | 6 | 7 | 7 |
| Fell parishes | 47 | 18 | 13 | 3 | 7 | 11 |
| Forest parishes | 10 | 34 | 30 | 2 | 10 | 15 |
| Plain parishes (Sussex) | 22 | 50 | 8 | 8 | 8 | 5 |
| Plain parishes (Cumb.) | 60 | 12 | 10 | 5 | 8 | 6 |
| Before 1560 | 11 | 31 | 28 | 7 | 11 | 11 |
| 1600–10 | 35 | 36 | 13 | 6 | 5 | 5 |
| After 1620 | 40 | 23 | 14 | 8 | 7 | 8 |

[a] The first section of the table covers 651 labourers' holdings in forty-three manors; the second 356 holdings in twenty-four manors; the third 447 holdings in twenty-eight manors. For the surveys used, see pp. 397, n. 1, 401, n. 1, 402, n. 1, 404, n. 1. The manors covered are: North Bersted, Falmer, Preston, Stanmer, St Leonards, and Tarring (Sussex); West Linton, Bowness, Drumburgh, Cardurnock, Glasson, Easton, Rockcliffe, Aikton, Orton, and Wetheral (Cumb.); Hoff and Drybeck (Westm.); Castleton and Butterworth (Lancs.); Elloughton, Wheldrake, Sheriff Hutton, Temple Newsam, Wensleydale, Pickering, Grassington, Ellingtons, Healey, Howsham, and Swine (Yorks.); Church Aston and Longford (Salop); Hallow (Worcs.); Hartest (Suffolk); Great Wigborough and Salcott Wigborough (Essex); Prior's Barton (Hants.); The Lea in Mitcheldean and Gotherington (Glos.); Nassington and Apethorpe (Northants.); Great Abington (Cambs.).

[1] SP 14, 40, 21; Joan Thirsk, 'Industries in the Countryside', in *Essays in the Economic and Social History of Tudor and Stuart England*, ed. F. J. Fisher, 1961, pp. 75–7.

Quite as diverse was the average size of holdings in different agricultural regions.¹ In both the coastal plain of Cumberland and the coastal plain of Sussex nearly three quarters of the labouring population rented less than one acre of land apiece, and only one fifth more than two acres; scarcely one labourer in twenty worked the statutory acreage. In such districts, especially in the north and Midlands, it was not uncommon for two or more labouring families to share a single cottage, dividing the croft or garden between them.² In some of the fell-side villages of Yorkshire and Lancashire, labourers were a little more fortunate, though there too nearly two thirds held under one acre; while in valleys like Garsdale a rising population, coupled with gavelkind tenure, compelled peasants to turn to by-employments, such as stocking-knitting, to supplement the resources of their dwindling holdings. In woodland areas, by contrast, or on manors where wasteland was still abundant, many labourers were relatively well off. In the vale of York with its extensive royal forests, and in the vale of Pickering with its neighbouring marshes and moorlands, about half the working population rented at least one acre of land. On a group of woodland manors in Sussex, Northamptonshire, Staffordshire, and the marcher counties, the proportion was well over half, and one labourer in four worked at least three acres. In Kinver Forest one cottage holding amounted to no less than eleven acres and another to thirty; whilst at the enclosure of Deerfold Forest in Herefordshire all cottagers were allotted at least four acres of land, "that so they may be able to maintain their families and not continue a great charge and burden to the several townships."³

Important though the labourer's individual smallholding was, the vital factor in his fortunes was his rights of common.⁴ Pre-eminent among these privileges were his grazing rights on common pastures, which in moorland and woodland districts were often extensive. On the forest manor of Feckenham in Worcestershire all the inhabitants, including labourers, enjoyed common at all times of the year, for all kinds of beasts without number, whether sheep, swine, geese, or cattle. At Alberbury in Shropshire, in Elizabeth's reign, the tenants had common pasture in the village woodlands for all cattle without stint, and for 100 hogs without rate of pannage. In Northamptonshire the

---

¹ For a map of agricultural regions, see *AHEW*, IV, p. 4.

² Cumb. RO, Surveys of Dacre lands, 1589. For examples of shared holdings in a Midland county, cf. Northants. RO, Westmorland Apethorpe Colln., 4, XVI, 5.

³ E 134, 10–11 Car. I, H 22 (for Garsdale); E 178, 4959 (for Kinver Forest); Hereford City Library, L.C. Deeds, Bdle 5571 (1611).

⁴ Cf. Chalklin, *op. cit.*, p. 22.

fifty-two cottagers of Nassington were allowed to pasture three cattle and ten sheep each on the common lands of the village, and were able "to live in such idleness upon their stock of cattle [that] they will bend themselves to no kind of labour; for there is few of the 52 cottagers but has as much cattle in the Forest [of Rockingham] over and above the rate aforsesaid as any husband [man] in the town..." In thickly populated vales and plains, however, the labourer's pasture rights were often being restricted, challenged, or extinguished in this period. At Broughton near Stokesley, in the vale of Cleveland, where at one time each of the poorer inhabitants had been suffered to pasture ten or twenty cattle, sheep, or horses on the common, their privileges were threatened by enclosure in Charles I's reign. At Sutton on Derwent, near York, the "gressmen" or cottagers, who comprised nearly two thirds of the village farmers, were in the mid-sixteenth century allowed to put only one beast each on the common between Lammas and Martinmas; while at Kirkby Moorside, where in 1560 every inhabitant had kept at least one or two kine, the poor cottagers seem to have lost their common rights altogether by 1570.[1]

Rights of pasture were not the only communal benefits enjoyed by labourers. They also claimed privileges in the shrubs, woods, undergrowth, stone-quarries, and gravel-pits of the common: for building and repairing their houses, for making gates, fences, and hurdles, and for fuel for cooking and heating. In some parishes, like Kennington in east Kent, commoners were allowed to take loam and sand for making bricks for their cottages, and turves "for amending their highways..." In some, like Cartmel in Furness, they were permitted to lop and crop underwood for the browse of their cattle in wintertime. At Burnley and Ightenhill in Lancashire they might dig what coal they pleased from the pits on the common, for use in their cottages. In parts of Holmesdale and the Weald of Kent labourers possessed an almost unlimited supply of top and lop in the woods and copses, and of fallen wood after winter storms. On the peat-moors of the Pennines, the Cheviots, and Devonshire, on the mosslands of the Lancashire plain, on the sandy heaths of Surrey and Hampshire, cottagers often took what turf, bracken, and furze they pleased. On Cattell Moor, near Wetherby in Yorkshire, the "poorest sort" of inhabitants, "through the whole year, as they had occasion to use them, have usually gotten all such elding or fuel (*viz.*, whins and brake)...as they did usually burn... within their houses," carrying them home "on their back..." Wherever woodland or commonland was short, however, as in much of

[1] Worcs. RO, 705, 78 (1590 or 1591); C 2, Eliz., A 8, 58; Northants. RO, Westmorland Apethorpe Colln., 4, XVI, 5 (1551); E 134, 9 and 10 Car. I, H 37; Yorks. Arch. Soc., Rec. Ser., CXIV, 1947, p. 64; E 164, 37, f. 386.

Leicestershire and the East Riding, common rights of this kind were closely restricted and the labourer's lot in winter weather was hard.[1]

Labourers also shared in the wild bird- and animal-life of the common. In the parishes of the Isle of Axholme poor people possessed rights of fishing and fowling. In Hatfield Chase they were said to have almost lived off the abundance of rabbits breeding on the commons. Until the enclosure of the royal forests, they frequently poached the king's deer, sometimes maiming a young kid so that its dam was forced to feed it where it lay, till it became "as fat as brawn," and then returning "in a dark night" to cut its throat and carry it home.[2] In many parishes poor people also appropriated hares, fish, wood-pigeons, and birds' eggs; together with beech-mast from the copses, for their pigs; crab-apples and cobnuts from the hedgerows; brambles, whortles, and juniper berries from the heaths; and mint, thyme, balm, tansy, and other wild herbs from any little patch of waste. Almost every living thing in the parish, however insignificant, could be turned to some good use by the frugal peasant-labourer or his wife.

All these customary rights of rural labourers were more or less carefully regulated by village by-laws and manorial customs. At Cartmel, for example, villagers were not permitted to cut rushes on Windermoor before 26 September; those with meadow on the common were ordered to mow the same on 1 or 2 July; and no one was allowed to gather nuts before Nutday, 1 September, or shear his bracken for thatching, bedding, or burning before Brackenday, 2 October.[3] Judged by modern standards of individual freedom, restrictions of this kind may seem petty and repressive; but in a society where resources were strictly limited and the sense of community intense, they were both natural and necessary. The labourer's rights of common formed part of a carefully integrated economy, whose balance could rarely be altered without serious consequences for the commoners themselves. When we read of old William Hall, of Amble in Northumberland, solemnly striking the village boundary stone with his staff in the presence of his two sons, or of Mistress Clarke compelling her grandson to sit on it with "his bare buttock" that he might "remember the same so long as he should live," we sense something of the importance of communal privileges in the

---

[1] E 178, 3960 (1615); A. P. Brydson, *Some Records of two Lakeland Townships*, 1908, p. 162; PRO DL, 43, 4, 12; E 134, 20–21 Eliz., M 10; *Lancs. and Ches. Rec. Soc.*, XXXII, p. 139; SP 14, 58, 7; E 134, 41 and 42 Eliz., M 22; William Burton, *The Description of Leicestershire*, [1622], p. 2.

[2] *Yorks. Arch. Jnl*, XXXVII, 1951, p. 386; BM Lansdowne MS 897, ff. 50–1; cf. SP 14, 31, 74.

[3] Lancs. RO, DDCa.7.3 (mainly late seventeenth- and early eighteenth-century customs).

aspirations of the village.[1] Poor though they seem, those rights alone added a few simple graces to an otherwise bare existence, and bred in the labourer a sense of hope and independence. For the cottager with ample common rights, there was profound truth in Sir Henry Wotton's dictum:

> How happy is he born and taught
> That serveth not another's will.

## C. ENCLOSURE AND ENCROACHMENT

Such an economy was peculiarly vulnerable, however, to the new economic forces of the period, and it is no accident that the fiercest opposition to the Tudor enclosure movement stemmed from poor commoners. In using the word 'enclosure' it is important to differentiate between two distinct phenomena: first, large-scale enclosure of common fields and commons, usually undertaken by wealthy tenants or proprietors without the poor commoners' consent, and often involving depopulation; secondly, small-scale enclosures of common-land, consisting of a few roods of land only, usually undertaken by poor commoners themselves, and involving no depopulation. In contemporary usage 'enclosure' often covered both kinds of activity. Here it is confined, in the interests of clarity, to the former, while the latter is designated 'encroachment'. For the labouring community, enclosure and encroachment had diametrically opposite, though often complementary, consequences.

The effect of enclosure upon the lives of poor commoners was notorious. At its worst, where arable land was forcibly converted to pasture, enclosure led to the eviction of whole villages, and compelled their inhabitants either to seek employment elsewhere or to join the swelling army of perhaps 20,000 vagrants already roaming the Tudor countryside.[2] Where depopulation did not occur, the effects of enclosure might still be revolutionary. As the complaints of labourers themselves in countless lawsuits indicate, it could hardly fail to undermine the way of life to which they and their forebears had, for generations, been accustomed. When two hundred poor inhabitants of Oakley, Brill, and Boarstall in Buckinghamshire were threatened in 1611 with the enclosure of their common, they complained that they would "be utterly undone and have small or no means to relieve

---

[1] E 134, 13 Jas. I, M 4.
[2] This is probably a conservative figure. Gregory King estimated the number of vagrants at 30,000 in the late seventeenth century.—Andrew Browning, ed., *English Historical Documents, 1660–1714*, 1953, p. 517.

themselves." At Preston in Holderness the parishioners asserted in 1601 that, if their pasture was turned over to new usages, it would lead "to the utter undoing of the poorer sort, for that they shall thereby be enforced to leave off their tillage for want of pasture for their draught oxen." As a result of the enclosure of commonland at Easingwold in James I's reign, "the poor sort" of villagers were "utterly overthrown in the best means of their livelihood," for they "had no other means or relief at all whereupon to live..." When the Lord President of the Council of the North visited the area, "a great multitude...of people assembled...to make complaint," and an inhabitant of the neighbouring village of Crayke "cried to the said Lord President and commissioners to take pity of the poor inhabitants thereabouts..." Wherever enclosure took place, similar stories abounded: in Warwickshire, in Monmouthshire, on Sedgemoor, in the Isle of Axholme, in the Lincolnshire fenland, in the West Riding of Yorkshire, in County Durham.[1]

The realization that their whole way of life was at stake was a prominent factor in the peasant risings of the period. It is important not to overestimate the labourer's part in these rebellions. Magnates like the Northumbrian Percys and knightly families like the Yorkshire Constables were also behind them. Quarrelsome local gentry, like the Nortons of County Durham, were only too eager to array themselves "in warlike manner, with weapons as well invasive as defensive," and "in most riotous and disordered manner" break into their neighbours' cony-warrens. Rebel leaders were sometimes drawn, not from the ranks of countrymen at all, but from those of tanners "of good estate," carpenters "placed in very good service," or artisans and tradesmen of towns like Louth. Both the Gillingham Forest riots and those of the forest of Dean, in Charles I's reign, seem to have been led by a certain Henry Hoskins, a substantial yeoman whose Dorset followers included nearly fifty urban tradesmen and weavers, but only twenty-five countrymen, of whom no more than two were labourers.[2]

Nevertheless, much of the initiative behind these risings indubitably

---

[1] SP 14, 54, 15; C 2, Eliz., C 16, 55; SP 14, 116, 133; E 178, 4852; CSPD 1640–1, p. 371; CSPD 1625–49, p. 617; CSPD 1636–7, p. 257; *Yorks. Arch. Jnl*, XXXVII, 1951, p. 386; Joan Thirsk, *English Peasant Farming*, 1957, p. 111; PRO DL, 44, 440; E 134, 16 Jas. I, E 25.

[2] LP XII, i, pp. 166–7, 82; Req. 2, 106, 55; D. G. C. Allan, 'The Rising in the West, 1628–1631', EcHR, 2nd Ser., v, 1952, pp. 78, 80; SP 14, 28, 64; LP XII, i, pp. 173–5; E 159, 472. Trin. 8 Car., rot. 38. Hoskins received the maximum fine of £200, and was evidently a substantial farmer. I am indebted to Dr T. G. Barnes for references to the Gillingham Forest riots. For further information on labourers' risings, see D. G. C. Allan, *Agrarian Discontent under the early Stuarts and during the last Decade of Elizabeth*, London M.Sc. (Econ.) thesis, 1950.

came from labouring peasants. In the Northern Rebellion of 1536 poor commoners gathered in hundreds to throw down enclosures and defend their tenurial privileges in Cumberland and Westmorland. In the Midland risings of James I's reign, multitudes of "the meaner sort of our people" assembled and armed themselves in Northamptonshire, "sometimes in the night and sometimes in the day," alleging sundry villages had been depopulated and "divers families undone." Nor were these riotous activities confined to the menfolk: women, and even children, joined in them with equal vigour, arming themselves with stones and bedposts, and breaking down newly erected enclosures.[1]

Although rarely successful, such risings at least drew the attention of the government and the church to the labourers' problems. The policy of the Crown was necessarily ambivalent; but both Tudors and Stuarts were firmly set against depopulation, and often tempered their natural severity against rebels with compassion "towards the simplicity of such offenders." The attitude of ecclesiastics, though in the fifteenth century they had themselves often enclosed, was also animated by a tradition of opposition to depopulation, stretching from Latimer and Grindal to Abbott and Laud. The outlook of the gentry was more divided. Many were themselves responsible for enclosure, and, as the poor of Cockfield in Durham complained, did not "spare to enclose us up even to our own doors..." Others, however, like the Scotts of Scots' Hall in Kent, endeavoured to protect their poorer tenants, and when "certain rich men who had great stock of cattle" transgressed their common rights, commanded "the said greedy-minded tenants" to "desist from their said oppression..." In many cases, there is reason to think, it was primarily new or minor gentry and self-assertive tenants who were the real culprits, while the indigenous or greater gentry endeavoured to restrain them in the interests of the poor.[2]

Nevertheless, from almost every point of view, enclosure increased the dependence of labourers on their landlords. Where they were compensated with land in severalty, their allotment was usually too small to support their livestock. Where they were compensated in kind, like the poor of Conisborough who received an allowance of milk in lieu of their cattle-rake on Firsby Moor, they had to walk to the farmhouse each Sunday, vessel in hand, to collect it.[3] Where they lost

---

[1] Cf. LP XII, i, pp. 182, 234, 304 *et passim*; SP 14, 73, pp. 139, 140, 147; SP 14, 35, 52; LP VIII, p. 393; SP 16, 116, 37. See also E 134, 13 Jas. I, E 18 and M 17, though it is not clear whether these cases refer to labourers or other peasants.

[2] Cf. R. H. Tawney, *The Agrarian Problem in the Sixteenth Century*, 1912, pp. 371 sqq., 420–1; SP 14, 73, pp. 139–47; SP 14, 142, 23; *Cumb. and Westm. Antiq. and Archaeolog. Soc.*, NS, XLIII, 1943, p. 178; E 134, 26 Eliz., E 11; C 2, Jas. I, G 5, 70; E 134, 10 Car. I, E 47.

[3] E 134, 21 Jas. I, M 14.

their rights altogether, they became mere wage-earners, tied to the wayward favour of a possibly temperamental employer. Wherever the labourer of the enclosed village turned, he was forcibly reminded of his loss of independence. The sole purpose of his existence was to serve "another's will."

Meanwhile *encroachment* was producing a very different effect on the labouring community. Largely under the impulse of peasant-workers themselves, and as a consequence of their steady nibbling at the remaining areas of uncultivated commonland, a new wave of settlement was taking place in this period. Driven partly by the depopulation of old-established villages, partly by the rapid rise of population and morcellation of their ancestral tenements, and in part by the attraction of new industries like mining and smelting, many labourers were drifting away from the old centres of rural population in this period, and resettling themselves, wherever land remained unappropriated, in royal forests, on sandy heaths, and beside wooded spaces.[1] While some villages were enclosed and depopulated in the fertile arable plains, new settlements began to appear round small commons, greens, and forstals; old hamlets received an influx of fresh blood, and extended their boundaries further into the waste. Not all the new encroachments were originated by new settlers; many consisted of small parcels of land added to already ancient holdings. But although contemporaries may have exaggerated the phenomenon, the existence of a new wave of settlement by squatters in search of living-space is undeniable.

In Kingswood Forest in Gloucestershire, for instance, John Norden found in 1615 "very many cottages raised upon the forests, maintained under the toleration of the statute for erecting houses near mineral places: but in this forest are far more erected than the necessity of the coalmines requireth..." In the moorland forest of Wensleydale, about 1610, one contemporary averred that, within his own memory, the number of forest inhabitants had increased, while another stated that

---

[1] The increasing population of these areas was also connected with the prevalence of gavelkind inheritance (e.g., in Kent and in the Pennine dales) and possibly borough-English customs, leading to excessive subdivision of tenements (cf. SP 14, 45, 94; E 134, 10–11 Car. I, H 22; Thomas Robinson, *The Common Law of Kent, with an Appendix concerning Borough English*, 1822, pp. 9, 17, 42 *sqq.*, 391 *sqq.*; Joan Thirsk, 'Industries in the Countryside', p. 77). For the influence of industries like mining and smelting on the populations of forest areas and wastes, cf. E 134, 22 & 23 Eliz., M 17 (Benwell, Northumberland); SP 14, 84, 46 (Kingswood Forest, Glos.); E 134, 16 Car. I, M 36 (Forest of Dean); E 178, 4533 (Cannock Chase). Quite apart from private forests and unappropriated wastes, there were probably at least one hundred royal forests and chases at this time: SP 14, 32, 26, lists over eighty in thirty-two English and five Welsh counties.

many of the new settlers were poor people and lived "very hardly." In Galtres Forest, a few years later, the "poorest sort" of people were said to be especially numerous, and in Easingwold manor alone there were 150 poor commoners. In Feckenham Forest in Worcestershire, in 1573, five hundred inhabitants brought a suit before the court of Requests and asserted that the population of the Forest was then "above five thousand people." In the Forest of Dean "many townships, parishes, and hamlets adjoining unto and depending on the forest"

Table 2. *Distribution of population in rural Kent: analysis of the Compton census, 1676*[a]

(Acres per head of population)

|  | East Kent | Mid Kent | West Kent | All Kent |
| --- | --- | --- | --- | --- |
| Weald | 14·5 | 6·2 | 9·6 | 7·7 |
| Chartland | 7·4 | 6·9 | 7·2 | 7·2 |
| Upper downland | 10·8 | 9·4 | 12·1 | 10·7 |
| Lower downland | 7·1 | 5·7 | 8·1 | 6·1 |
| Northern marshlands | 15·7 | 25·1 | 16·2 | 18·3 |
| Romney Marsh | 44·2 | — | — | 44·2 |
| All agrarian regions | 9·8[b] | 7·3 | 9·9 | 9·1[c] |

[a] The census is edited by C. W. Chalklin in *A Seventeenth Century Miscellany*, Kent Arch. Soc., Records Publication Committee, XVII, 1960, pp. 153–74. Urban parishes and parishes covering more than one agrarian region have been omitted from the calculations. The census appears to list inhabitants over sixteen only, and in estimating the total population I have followed Mr Chalklin's suggestion of an average of forty children to sixty adults (pp. 155, 157). The table covers nearly two thirds of the area of the county and about half the total population. It is not possible to calculate any valid figures for the Isle of Thanet and the Forest of Blean, owing to *lacunae* in the material and to subsequent boundary changes.

[b] Excluding Romney Marsh.

[c] Including Romney Marsh (excluding Romney Marsh, the figure is 8·8).

were said, about 1640, to be "full of poor people, and that such poor people have much increased and multiplied..." In Nottinghamshire many new cottages were erected on wasteland and some settlements were so "pestered" with squatters that "they are hardly able to live one by another..." In Rossendale Forest, in Lancashire, the same process seems to have been at work, and "the whole system of landholding was in a state of continuous dissolution" as a consequence. In Kent, the forest parishes of the Chartlands and the Weald were among the most thickly settled in the county, and the parishioners were often forced to take to by-employments, such as clothing and iron-working, to make a living. According to James I's surveyors, the inhabitants of forests were everywhere "increasing in such abundance" that they would soon thrust one another out of their possessions by violence, from mere "want of habitations." Wherever a Jacobean traveller like Norden crossed "great and spacious wastes, mountains, and heaths" he observed "many such cottages [of poor people] set up..."[1]

The character of these new and expanding forest communities is plain enough. They usually consisted, on one hand, of a small core of substantial peasant labourers, with sizeable holdings of their own, decidedly better off than common-field labourers, and probably identifiable with the indigenous settlers of the original community. On the other hand, they often included a much larger body of new squatters and "beggarly people," who had little legal right to the land they appropriated, but "adventured upon" the erection of their cottages —like two Kentish squatters at Longbridge Leaze, Willesborough— "for that they were destitute of houses, and had seen other cottages upon the same waste, built by other poor men."[2] Not infrequently these hovels existed for two or three generations before they were tracked down by manorial surveyors, and their owners forced to pay rent.

By and large, the new forest communities were squatters' settlements, and were formed of scattered hamlets rather than nucleated villages. They often consisted solely of husbandmen and labourers, without either squire or parson to diversify their social structure, or to keep them in order. According to the Londoner John Norden, their inhabitants were "given to little or no kind of labour, living very hardly with oaten bread, sour whey, and goats' milk, dwelling far from any church or chapel, and are as ignorant of God or of any civil course of life as the very savages amongst the infidels..."[3] For "the people bred amongst woods," he remarked, "are naturally more stubborn and uncivil than in the champion countries." As each generation came and went, they became more and more inbred, more and

---

[1] SP 14, 84, 46; E 134, 7 Jas. I, E 34; SP 14, 116, 133; Req. 2, 66, 84; E 134, 16 Car. I, M 36; SP 16, 185, 86; G. H. Tupling, *The Economic History of Rossendale*, Chetham. Soc., LXXXVI, 1927, pp. 95, 97; Joan Thirsk, 'Industries in the Countryside', p. 79; PRO LR, 2, 194, f. 35; Harrison, *op. cit.*, p. 180; cf. SP 16, 44, 45; SP 14, 144, 24; G. E. Fussell, *The English Rural Labourer*, 1949, pp. 3-4; Hoskins and Finberg, *op. cit.*, p. 327. So late as 1656 Cromwell sent to suppress "near 400 cabins of beggarly people" in the Forest of Dean.—Allen, *loc. cit.*, p. 84. For the distribution of the population in Kent, see Table 2.

[2] E 178, 3960; Allan, *op. cit.*, p. 84. They may have trusted to the widespread belief that a cottage erected on the waste overnight constituted a lawful piece of property: cf. Hoskins and Finberg, *op. cit.*, p. 327; Fussell, *op. cit.*, p. 10.

[3] Quoted in Harrison, *loc. cit.*

more tenacious of their real or supposed customs and common-rights, and gradually more alienated from the common-field villages whence their inhabitants originally migrated.[1] Their greens and inns became the resorts of cattle-drovers and wayfaring badgers; their woods and dingles the haunts of vagabonds, gipsies, and bandits; their cottages the meeting places of millenarian sects. For the government and for local justices, their expanding population raised many a problem in preserving peace and providing work.[2] By the inhabitants of established villages their disorderly habits were regarded with fear and aversion, and their encroachment on the waste with jealousy. In the Forest of Dean they were described as people of very lewd lives and conversations, leaving their own "countries" and "taking this place for a shelter as a cloak to their villainies."[3] But for many a poor labourer forest hamlets afforded not only a footing, but a certain freedom denied to the farmworker of the village, whose life was lived under the shadow of the manor-house. For these workers the sixteenth century was an age not only of depopulation, but of settlement on heaths and wastes: and on these wastes, as we shall see, there was still opportunity for many an enterprising labourer to make a comfortable living.

### D. COTTAGE HUSBANDRY AND PEASANT WEALTH

For a picture of the husbandry of rural workers, it is necessary to turn to the inventories of goods drawn up for probate purposes after their death. Only the uppermost layers of the labouring population possessed sufficient property to leave inventories; but those who were too poor to do so probably possessed little farm property worth valuing, so that the pattern of cottage husbandry presented in the inventories is in fact substantially complete.[4] In the following account, the terms 'cottager' and 'cottage farmer', which in contemporary usage were applied to labourers and husbandmen indiscriminately, are used of labourers only. Like the term 'peasant labourers', they refer to those workers whose livelihood was based partly on their holdings and who were wealthy

[1] John Norden, *Surveyor's Dialogue*, p. 215. Of the Knaresborough Forest commoners, it was said in James I's reign: "they observe their customs curiously" and "are the most headstrong people in that country..."—SP 14, 37, 107.
[2] The policy of disafforestation and attempts to 'suppress' new cottages and forbid the entertainment of "inmates and undersetters" helped to foment the labourers' revolts of the early seventeenth century.—SP 14, 120, 35; cf. SP 14, 37, 102; SP 14, 124, 137; Helmingham Hall MSS, D.L's' and J.P's' Committee Book, *passim;* and see Allan, *op. cit.*, pp. 77 sqq.
[3] SP 16, 44, 45 (?1626), and cf. E 178, 3960; E 134, 18 Jas. I, H 15; SP 16, 143, 41.
[4] A small but increasing proportion of labourers who left inventories possessed no farmstock.

enough to leave inventories. For this study, the inventories have been grouped in six broad regions: northern lowlands, northern highlands, eastern England, the west country, the woodland areas of the Midlands, and the fielden areas of the Midlands. For all except the last area and the west country, the inventories have been subdivided into two periods, those between 1560 and 1600, and those between 1610 and 1640.[1]

In all regions, the basis of the labourer's farming was livestock.[2] Only a small proportion of cottage farmers possessed no stock what-

Table 3. *Peasant labourers' cattle*[a]

| Region | Period | Percentage of peasant labourers possessing | | Number of cattle per 100 labourers |
| | | Cows, calves and heifers | Other cattle | |
| --- | --- | --- | --- | --- |
| Northern lowlands | 1560–1600 | 74 | 26 | 227 |
| | 1610–1640 | 88 | 12 | 161 |
| Northern highlands | 1560–1600 | 84 | 16 | 197 |
| | 1610–1640 | 87 | 13 | 163 |
| Eastern England | 1560–1600 | 82 | 18 | 122 |
| | 1610–1640 | 79 | 11 | 153 |
| Midland forest areas | 1560–1600 | 92 | 8 | 142 |
| | 1610–1640[b] | 93 | 7 | 237 |
| Midland fielden areas | 1590–1640[b] | 91 | 9 | 153 |
| West of England | 1590–1640 | 90 | 10 | 82 |

[a] Based on probate inventories. For the term 'peasant labourers' see p. 177.
[b] Including a few inventories of the 1660's for Northants.

[1] For the west country and Midland fielden areas there are insufficient labourers' inventories before 1600 for separate analysis. In selecting the inventories I have in general included: (*a*) all those described as belonging to labourers, (*b*) all those which belonged to country people whose social status is not described and were valued at under £5 before 1570, under £10 during the 1590's, and under £15 during 1610–40. I have not always followed this rule blindly in the north-west, where money-values were lower and labourers fewer, and where farmers with inventories of these values were sometimes obviously not labourers. Some inventories of small value evidently belonged to retired yeomen or others living with their family, and these also have been excluded. Most of the Northants. inventories unavoidably relate to the 1660's, since few before 1640 have survived. Any rules of selection are bound to contain an arbitrary element; but the fact that in Hertfordshire (where social status is usually described) Stuart labourers not infrequently left property worth more than £15 suggests that these limits are, if anything, set rather too low than too high. But I do not think they are likely to be very wide of the mark either way.

[2] See Table 4.

ever: about one in twenty before 1600 and one in seven or eight thereafter. In all parts of the country the staple item in the worker's stock-farming was cattle.[1] In the north of England about 75 per cent of cottage farmers possessed cattle, in eastern England about 70 per cent, in the Midlands 60 per cent, and in the west of England 55 per cent. The great majority owned no more than one or two beasts each, and the number of labourers with more than five never exceeded 6 per cent except in the woodland areas of the Midlands, where in the seventeenth century it rose to 16 per cent. For every hundred peasant labourers, there were something like 80 cattle in the west country, 140 in the eastern counties, 150 in Midland fielden areas, 180 in the northern highlands, and 190 or more in the lowland areas of the northern counties and the woodland areas of central England.

The great bulk of this livestock consisted of milch kine, heifers, and calves: nowhere less than two thirds, and generally more than four fifths. Only a few labourers, chiefly in the north, interested themselves in breeding or fattening livestock for the expanding Tudor meat-market; still fewer either possessed or needed draught beasts. The primary agricultural concern of the labourer was to provide milk, cheese, and butter for his own family, while he or his wife disposed of surplus produce at the butter-cross in the neighbouring market town. Sometimes an exceptionally pushing or resourceful labourer, with a well fitted-out dairy, manufactured cheese or butter specifically for the local market. Richard Gurleye of Knebworth in Hertfordshire, for instance, died possessed of as many as twenty cheeses in his store-rooms, and Robert Wood of Nuneaton left more than seventy. But people like Wood and Gurleye comprised only a fraction of the working population: except in a few favoured districts, the husbandry of Tudor cottagers reflected only to a limited degree the agricultural specialities or the commercial opportunities of their region.

Next in importance to the labourer's cattle were his sheep. In eastern England the proportion of peasant labourers who possessed sheep was only 19 per cent; in the west the figure rose to 45 per cent, in the Pennines to 48 per cent, and in the Midlands to 55 per cent. Most labourers' flocks, if such they can be called, were exceedingly small, often of less than three sheep, and rarely of more than nine. Everywhere, however, there were a few labourers, generally shepherds with little or no other stock of their own, who possessed twenty or more sheep. It was a well-recognized custom for shepherds to be allowed a few lambs from their master's flock each year, to be run on their employer's sheep-pastures.[2] In this way many a poor shepherd in

[1] See Table 3.
[2] See, for example, BM Harleian MS 98, f. 31v.

Table 4. *Peasant labourers' livestock*[a]

| Region | Period | No stock | Cattle | | | | Sheep | | | Horses | | | | Pigs | | | | Poultry |
|---|---|---|---|---|---|---|---|---|---|---|---|---|---|---|---|---|---|---|
| | | | 0 | ½-2 | 3-5 | 6+ | 0 | 1-8 | 9+ | 0 | ½-1½ | 2-3 | 3+ | 0 | 1 | 2-3 | 4+ | |
| Northern lowlands | 1560-1600 | 7 | 13 | 53 | 27 | 6 | 77 | 16 | 6 | 57 | 27 | 10 | 6 | 67 | 23 | 0 | 10 | 30 |
| | 1610-40 | 6 | 32 | 37 | 27 | 4 | 72 | 10 | 18 | 61 | 29 | 0 | 0 | 80 | 14 | 6 | 0 | 39 |
| Northern highlands | 1560-1600 | 3 | 13 | 53 | 33 | 0 | 47 | 27 | 13 | 63 | 33 | 3 | 0 | 93 | 0 | 3 | 0 | 47 |
| | 1610-40 | 13 | 29 | 39 | 23 | 3 | 56 | 13 | 8 | 59 | 39 | 3 | 0 | 85 | 15 | 0 | 0 | 30 |
| Eastern England | 1560-1600 | 0 | 22 | 67 | 11 | 0 | 78 | 11 | 11 | 100 | 0 | 0 | 0 | 45 | 22 | 22 | 11 | 56 |
| | 1610-40 | 21 | 39 | 45 | 10 | 6 | 84 | 11 | 5 | 76 | 21 | 0 | 3 | 58 | 21 | 17 | 4 | 29 |
| Midland forest areas | 1560-1600 | 9 | 38 | 33 | 29 | 0 | 54 | 24 | 21 | 63 | 17 | 12 | 8 | 54 | 17 | 25 | 4 | 42 |
| | 1610-40[c] | 16 | 47 | 11 | 26 | 16 | 37 | 31 | 32 | 79 | 11 | 0 | 10 | 63 | 16 | 11 | 10 | 16 |
| Midland fielden areas | 1590-1640[c] | 13 | 32 | 44 | 18 | 0 | 44 | 25 | 25 | 88 | 6 | 6 | 0 | 50 | 32 | 12 | 0 | 12 |
| West of England | 1590-1640 | 15 | 45 | 40 | 15 | 0 | 55 | 30 | 10 | 70 | 25 | 5 | 0 | 70 | 20 | 10 | 0 | 35 |

[a] Based on probate inventories; for the basis of selection of inventories, see p. 178, n. 1. For the term 'peasant labourers' see p. 177.
[b] Small discrepancies in percentage totals are due to the fact that some inventories do not specify the *number* of livestock owned by the labourer. The references to 'half-beasts' and 'half-horses' arise from the custom, in some areas, of sharing stock. There are too few inventories for Midland fielden areas and the west of England for separate analysis of the period before 1600.
[c] Including a few inventories of the 1660's for Northants.

the Midlands, and a few in the north and south, built up a stock of twenty or thirty sheep; while, very occasionally, a labourer like Henry Joyce of Winwick in Northamptonshire possessed nearly one hundred, or, like John Power of Longstock in Hampshire, as many as eight score. By such means a few Tudor and Stuart labourers were still able to work their way up in the social scale, step by step, till they reached the ranks of the yeomanry.

Pigs were not so ubiquitous an adjunct of the labourer's cottage in the sixteenth century as they became in the nineteenth; in the west of England and the Pennines they were still a rarity. Until labourers began to grow potatoes, they were rarely in a position to rear and fatten swine. In Midland and eastern England, however, about 40 or 50 per cent of peasant-workers kept swine, and bacon flitches hung from many a cottage chimney and roof-tree. In the forest areas of the Midlands a few labourers had as many as six pigs, no doubt fattened on mast in nearby woodlands, or on the waste products of dairies.

Horses were kept by only a minority of the peasant-labouring population, in most areas by less than one third. They were relatively numerous in the north of England where 40 per cent of cottage farmers kept horses, and least common in the eastern counties (12 per cent). Most labourers had little need for plough-animals of their own, or else, when they required them, either borrowed those of a neighbouring farmer for a day or two, or employed the common draught-team bequeathed to the parish by a former vicar or landowner. (Charitable bequests of this kind were not uncommon, and suggest that more labourers might have grown crops if they had possessed draught animals.)[1] In the woodland areas of the Midlands, it is true, near horse-markets like Stratford on Avon and manufacturing districts like Birmingham, a few well-off labourers seem to have been breeding horses: there was a growing demand for packhorses in these areas, and labourers' inventories often mention mares-with-colts or -with-fillies. The typical labourer's horse, however, served much the same purpose as the peasant's donkey in modern Ireland: it was employed, as inventories and lawsuits suggest, in carrying turf and bracken in packs, panniers, and 'nets', slung across its back; in carting hay, corn, and wood; and in conveying the labourer's wife and neighbours to the nearest market town.[2]

Hens or geese were kept by about one third of the labouring population. The proportion was rather higher in East Anglia, Cornwall, the

---

[1] See R. H. Tawney, *The Agrarian Problem in the Sixteenth Century*, 1912, p. 109; E 134, 8 Eliz., E 2; and cf. Req. 2, 29, 62 (26 Elizabeth) for a bequest of heifers and calves.
[2] Cf. C 3, 185, 47 (n.d., c. 1560–70).

East Riding, and Furness; rather lower in the lowland areas of Cumberland and Lancashire, in Hertfordshire and Somerset, and in the fielden areas of the Midlands. Only a few cottagers kept ducks or turkeys, and scarcely any owned bees; most labourers must have eaten all their food unsweetened, for few can have afforded the luxury of sugar.

Between the earlier and later parts of the period, so far as the evidence of probate inventories reveals, a number of significant changes seem to have occurred in the pattern of labouring stock-farming as a whole. On one hand, the number of *really poor* labourers—i.e. without *any* livestock of their own—rose from 5 per cent (of those who left inventories) to 13 per cent; the proportion with no cattle increased from 13 to over 30 per cent in the north, from 22 to 39 per cent in the east, and from 38 to 47 per cent in the Midlands; the numbers of small stockmen, with only one or two beasts, dropped from 53 to 38 per cent in the north, from 67 to 45 per cent in the east, and from 33 to 11 per cent in the Midlands; the percentage of labourers without any pigs or poultry increased, and in most areas the numbers with only one or two pigs, or three or four sheep, or a single horse, declined.[1] Over against this picture of declining fortunes, it seems that in most districts the *better-off* labourers, with herds of four or more cattle, were able to maintain their position: while in the Midland forest areas their numbers actually increased from 4 per cent to nearly 40 per cent. In the northern lowland areas, moreover, an increasing number of labourers began to keep poultry, and the number with sizeable sheep flocks rose threefold. In the dales and fells of the north a clear increase occurred in the proportion of labourers who kept horses and pigs; in the eastern counties a number of labourers began to keep horses and a few seem to have begun breeding them; in Midland forest parishes, the proportion of better-off pig farmers rose from 4 per cent to 10 per cent, and the average sheep flock rose from eight to twelve.

What do these facts and figures suggest? They seem to show that, as the period advanced, two distinct developments were taking place in the pattern of labourers' stock-farming. In the first place, as the population rose and land-hunger increased, most peasant labourers were keeping fewer cattle, and turning their attention instead to other kinds of livestock requiring less extensive grazings. Secondly, while the *better-off* labourers were able to increase their stock, the agrarian fortunes of the *poorer* peasant workers were declining, and the number of

[1] It may be thought that these changes were due to a growing habit among poorer labourers of leaving inventories; but I see no evidence for such a habit. In fact, the lower ranks in the sample were not usually poorer in *total* wealth than before but in *agricultural* wealth; instead of investing in stock, they were turning to by-employments to augment their income, and were also investing more in domestic goods.

labourers with *no* stock increased. In other words, the smaller labouring stockman was gradually being squeezed out in favour of the larger: the larger man was working his way up into the ranks of the husbandmen, and the small peasant was becoming a mere wage-worker.[1] In both these developments we can trace the influence of deep-seated economic forces: in each case the determining factor was the diminishing supply of land.

Arable husbandry played a far smaller part in cottage farming than stock-husbandry. Few workers possessed either sufficient land or sufficient capital to grow corn or other crops on even the smallest scale. The great majority of labourers purchased their grain requirements in the local market town week by week, or from the travelling badgers and mealmen who frequented the country districts of Tudor England. Of those labourers whose inventories were drawn up in the corn-growing season, less than one third left any sown land, and in the Midlands only one seventh. Very occasionally, a labourer in the vale of York kept as much as seven acres of land under the plough; but elsewhere the figure did not rise above three acres. In the country as a whole, the sown area (excluding inventories listing no crops) averaged little more than one acre, declining from seven roods before 1600 to four thereafter; the average was slightly higher in the north of England, where the pressure on land was less acute, rather lower in the Midlands and the east, and very low in the west country. Barley, the poor man's usual breadcorn, seems to have been the most frequent crop, followed by peas, wheat, and oats. The labourer was usually accustomed to vary his sowing, however, and he often planted a little of each kind of grain, with perhaps a small quantity of rye and beans as well, and in some districts, such as Hertfordshire, the Pennines, and the East Riding, a small garth or croft of hemp, or occasionally flax. Quite probably, if later custom is any guide, the worker's corn was sometimes literally planted, grain by grain with a dibber, with a correspondingly good yield, no doubt, at harvest-time.[2]

In marketing their produce, labourers rarely went beyond their local town. Corn was usually sold soon after harvest in order to pay

[1] It may be argued that these conclusions are influenced by the basis of selection of inventories (see p. 178, n. 1), and that the apparent decline of poor stockmen's fortunes is because the £15 datum for the 1630's is set too low. But this would not explain the rising fortunes of the better-off. I believe the interpretation in the text is correct, more particularly since it tallies with other lines of argument, such as the shrinkage in size of most labourers' holdings, the restriction of common-rights, and the fact that stockless labourers were usually most numerous in 'advanced' agricultural areas like the eastern counties.

[2] This was a nineteenth-century custom in Surrey.—George Bourne, *Memoirs of a Surrey Labourer*, 1911, p. 150.

rent, and butter and eggs were disposed of weekly at the nearest market-cross. A few labourers, it is true, especially in forest districts, seem to have definitely oriented their production towards the private market, and to have ventured on individual contracts with butchers, drovers, and cheese-factors. In Hertfordshire, an important barley county, a number of labourers engaged in malt dealings. In Kent, Thomas Strowde and Joseph Mayowe of Marden "dealt together in the working and sale of... wood:" purchasing timber from local gentry, hiring other workmen to help them hew and cleave it, and reselling it in the form of boards, laths, pales, faggots, roundwood, and "checker-timber" to the wheelwrights, carpenters, and spoon-makers of the area. But in fact such men were exceptional. As a rule, labourers lacked either the education to keep accounts, or the experience and 'credit' necessary to deal as private traders; they were frequently defrauded by more knowledgeable people as a consequence. The partnership of Mayowe and Strowde came to an untimely end because Mayowe kept no note of his dealings, "being a mere layman and illiterate." A note on the inventory of a Hertfordshire labourer records that £20 was owing to him "upon bonds and bills, which is all lost by ill debtors." A "man of power and credit" in Dorsetshire was able to extort a composition far short of his just debt from a local labourer who had sold him forty-one sheep, and eventually, "by taking advantage of his poverty and want, and... unableness to follow suits," compelled the labourer "to leave his own country of Dorsetshire, and live in service in Devonshire..." In fact, as William Harrison indicated, marketing was one of the labourer's most serious problems, for the worker was either forced to dispose of his produce in an unfavourable market in order to raise ready money for his rent, or else to risk his whole farmstock in a single private contract, with the possibility of ruining his family in the upshot.[1] The changing market conditions of the period were undoubtedly responsible, in part, for the gradual decline in the fortunes of the smaller labourer peasant.

We must now re-examine the probate inventories with a view to reconstructing the pattern of wealth as a whole among peasant labourers. The subject is most easily approached by posing four separate questions. First, what was the proportion of cottage farmers to the farming community at large? Analysis of about 3,600 inventories, between 1540 and 1640, scattered over seventeen counties, suggests that labourers' inventories comprised about 8 per cent of the total. The number of

[1] Req. 2, 28, 5; Req. 2, 30, 30; Herts. RO, inventory of Robert Pearman of Ardeley, Herts., 1619; C 2, Jas. I, H 18, 64; Harrison, *op. cit.*, Part I, New Shakspere Soc., 6th Ser., 1, 1877, pp. 296–7.

cottage farmers naturally varied widely between different regions. It was more than twice as high in the lowland zone (9 per cent) as it was in the highland zone (4 per cent). As between different agricultural regions, it was exceptionally high in the woodland parishes of the lowland zone, where it varied from 7 per cent in the 1560's to 18 per cent in the 1590's, falling away again to 12 per cent in the 1630's. It was lowest in the fielden parishes of both zones, where it rarely exceeded 6 per cent and sometimes dropped to *nil:* not so much because labourers were few in such areas as because most of them were too poor to leave inventories.

Secondly, what was the proportion of cottage farmers to the *labouring* population as a whole? If, as has been said, labourers' inventories comprised about 8 per cent of the total number, and if, as we saw earlier, labourers comprised about one third of the whole population, it seems that perhaps one labourer in four was sufficiently well-off to leave an inventory. Allowing for the fact that about one tenth of those workers who left an inventory possessed no farm stock, and assuming that those who left no inventories were too poor to bequeath any stock worth speaking of, we shall not be far wrong in thinking that cottage farmers, as distinct from rural craft-workers and labourers dependent solely on wages, comprised something like one quarter of the farmworking population as a whole: a figure which roughly tallies with the number of labourers who possessed holdings of two or more acres.[1] There can be little doubt that the proportion of cottage farmers varied widely in different parts of the country; but no valid figures can be arrived at until we know more accurately the proportion of labourers in each county. It is safe to say, however, that they formed a higher percentage of the farmworking population in the woodland areas of Hertfordshire, Somerset, and the Midlands than in East Anglia, the north, and, in all probability, other parts of the west country.

Thirdly, what was the pattern of personal wealth, amongst labourers, in each region and period? It is not possible to calculate any very reliable averages, owing to the basis of selection necessarily adopted for this study;[2] but the overall pattern is clear enough nevertheless.[3] In the Pennine fells and the lowland areas of the far north, cottage farmers were relatively few and never well-off, but not often totally indigent, and the labouring community was relatively equalitarian in its social structure. In the fielden parishes of the Midlands, the vale of York, and East Anglia, labourers were usually poor (most of them far too poor to leave inventories), though a very small sprinkling left property worth £30, £40, and even £50. In the forest parishes of the Midlands, few peasant labourers in the earlier part of the period were

[1] Cf. Table 1.     [2] See p. 178, n. 1.     [3] See Table 5.

either very poor or very rich, and most left property worth £5–£10; after 1610, however, a substantial proportion of the working population left goods valued at more than £30, and the general level of labouring wealth was higher than in any other region. In the woodland parishes of Hertfordshire wealthy peasant labourers were also numerous, and few cottagers were very poor, though none left as much as £40. In Somerset, where the inventories also relate mainly to woodland parishes, there were no very wealthy labourers, although in the early seventeenth century many left a comfortable cottage estate of £7–£12. Thus in the north of England cottage farmers were relatively few and, though never well-off, rarely destitute; in the Midland fielden areas they were more numerous, but mostly very poor; in the forest areas they were very numerous, but not infrequently quite well-to-do.

Table 5. *The pattern of peasant labourers' wealth*[a]

|  | Percentage of wealth invested in domestic goods | | Average value of domestic goods | |
|---|---|---|---|---|
|  | 1560–1600 | 1610–40 | 1560–1600 | 1610–40 |
|  |  |  | £ s. d. | £ s. d. |
| Northern lowlands | 18 | 29 | 10 0 | 1 9 4 |
| Northern fells | 34 | — | 1 6 8 | — |
| Midland fielden areas[b] | 35 | 46 | 2 16 6 | 3 12 8 |
| Midland forest areas[b] | 44 | 39 | 2 9 6 | 4 10 0 |
| Hertfordshire | 59 | 69 | 4 3 9 | 7 9 10 |
| Eastern counties | — | 48 | — | 3 18 4 |
| Somerset | — | 65 | — | 5 17 0 |
| All England | 40 | 50 | 2 5 3 | 4 9 6 |

[a] Based on probate inventories; for the basis of selection of inventories (in some degree affecting the reliability of the 'Average Value of Domestic Goods'), see p. 178, n. 1.

[b] Including a few inventories of the 1660's for Northants.

Lastly, what was the proportion of personal wealth invested by labourers in farm goods and household goods respectively, in each region and period? In the country as a whole, the domestic proportion rose from 40 per cent to 50 per cent as between the Tudor and Stuart periods, and the agricultural percentage dropped in the same ratio. (The tendency to invest a higher proportion of wealth in domestic goods seems to have characterized all levels of society in this period.) In the north-country lowlands, household property comprised only 18 per cent of total wealth before 1600, and 29 per cent thereafter;

while in the dales and fells it was approximately 34 per cent before 1600. In the fielden areas of the Midlands the proportions were 35 per cent and 46 per cent for the two periods; in the woodland areas of central England, 44 and 39 per cent; and in Hertfordshire 59 and 69 per cent. For the eastern counties and Somerset no reliable figures can be computed for the period before 1600, but for the Stuart period the East Anglian proportion closely approached the Midland fielden figure, and the Somerset percentage that of Hertfordshire. The average value of household goods during the latter part of the period thus ranged from under 30s. in the northern lowlands to £3 13s. in the fielden areas of central England, £3 18s. in East Anglia, £4 10s. in Midland forest parishes, £5 17s. in Somerset, and £7 10s. in Hertfordshire.[1] In other words, it was relatively low in the fielden areas of England and comparatively high in the woodland districts.

In explanation of this varying pattern of wealth in different regions of England, no single factor of universal application can be adduced. Each part of the country was affected by influences largely peculiar to itself, and before stating any general conclusions, it is necessary to depict the broad economic characteristics of each region.

In the north, in both field and fell parishes, cottage inventories were relatively few because of the general poverty of the region, and because there was comparatively little demand for agricultural labour. The typical agrarian unit in the north, especially on the fells, was the small family farm, on which outside help was rarely required. Among farm-workers themselves, the sharing of holdings, livestock, crops, and implements—as is shown by references in inventories to 'half-tenements,' 'half-beasts,' and 'half plough teams'—suggests that labourers also cultivated their holdings on a family basis. The comparatively equalitarian structure of the labouring community in the north was largely due, no doubt, to the relative poverty of the small farmer in the area and his general lack of interest in the market.

The poverty of the labouring population in the fielden areas of East Anglia, the Midlands, and the southern parts of the vale of York arose from different causes. In all three areas, though in varying degrees, the *demand* for labour was relatively intense (especially in the arable areas of Norfolk), but cottage-holdings were often small, and common-land, except near wolds, fens, or forests, was scarce. The working population was therefore numerous, but labourers' inventories were relatively few and their value small. Many workers had evidently won what little wealth they possessed only by taking up by-employments, such as thatching, spinning, and hemp-weaving. Their domestic

---

[1] The scale of valuation evidently tended to be higher in the south, but not to this degree.

goods, though two or three times as valuable as in the far north, were generally modest. Only where a man of exceptional energy or good fortune built up a healthy herd of cattle and took advantage of the unrivalled commercial facilities of a county like Norfolk, or, like Henry Joyce of Winwick, bred a large sheep flock on the pastures of Northamptonshire, was the labourer likely to prosper. In such cases a man might justly style himself 'husbandman' in his will, although his neighbours still remembered his lowly origins and described him as 'labourer' in his inventory.

In the woodland areas of the Midland and Hertfordshire the picture was quite different. Here peasant labourers formed an exceptionally large section of the population; and although the local demand for labour was mainly seasonal and many of the workers were intensely poor squatters, many others possessed valuable holdings and common rights and were remarkably well-to-do. Some, like Robert Pearman of Ardeley, farmed as much as nine acres of arable land. Others, like Robert Wood of Nuneaton, rented stretches of pastureland and made a living by cheese-making. Others again, like Thomas Hall of Fillongley, built up sizeable sheep flocks. Many also engaged in by-employments, such as wood-turning, carpentry, forestry, and charcoal-burning; a few became carriers for Black Country manufacturers; a few were gardeners, gamekeepers, and petty maltsters in Hertfordshire. Nearby, there were many busy market towns in Hertfordshire, many sheep- and cattle-fairs in the Midlands, a rising industrial region round Birmingham, and the largest commercial city of the kingdom in London. There can be little doubt that a significant minority of labourers, especially in Hertfordshire and Warwickshire, exploited these commercial opportunities, for their inventories mention debts owing to them, in all probability for goods sold by private contract. The two regions differed significantly in only one respect. In the Midlands, well over half the typical labourer's wealth was sunk in his farming stock, whereas in Hertfordshire almost two thirds consisted of household property. It is tempting to attribute the difference to the influence of metropolitan wealth and the higher standard of living generally credited to south-eastern counties; but the explanation would be misleading, since purely domestic wealth was insignificant in value in other eastern counties, such as Suffolk, and relatively high in some counties remote from London, such as Somerset. More probably, with more ample commons at their disposal, Midland forest labourers were able to add to their stock more readily than their cousins in Hertfordshire, who depended increasingly on by-employments and work in neighbouring arable areas for their livelihood.

Until many more local studies of the economic structure of rural communities have been undertaken, the conclusions suggested by this study can only be tentative. Nevertheless, the broad economic pattern seems clear. Over the country as a whole, the wealth of peasant labourers appears in general to have reached a peak in the latter part of Elizabeth's reign, and to have tended to decline during the first half of the seventeenth century. Although well-off peasant labourers became more numerous, the proportion of labourers' inventories declined, the middle ranks of the labouring community became poorer, while the lower ranks ceased to possess any stock of their own, and sank to the level of a landless proletariat. In other words, the labouring class was becoming increasingly differentiated within itself.

Perhaps the most striking conclusion emerging from the inventories is the difference in the condition of labourers between forest and fielden areas. In the latter the decline in the wealth of peasant labourers was much more striking than in the former. By Charles I's reign a very few fielden cottagers of exceptional force of character were still able to make fortunes of £50 or even £150, and so work their way up into the ranks of the husbandmen; but the vast majority were slowly sinking in the social scale, and in many villages the poor stockman virtually ceased to exist. In the woodland parishes of Hertfordshire and Somerset, by contrast, the decline in labouring wealth was slight, and in the forest areas of Warwickshire and Northamptonshire the worker's fortunes actually seem to have improved; the number of labourers dependent solely on wages probably increased, but well-off labourers certainly became wealthier and more numerous. Beneath these distinctions it is not difficult to trace that gradual disinheritance and increasing dependence of the fielden labourer, due to a rising population and enclosure, which has already been remarked, and the consequent resettlement of poor peasants in unappropriated wastes and forests. As Cobbett found in the early nineteenth century, a rich land was apt to breed poor labourers, whilst a poor or wooded countryside often promised them prosperity.[1]

Both probate inventories and other sources suggest that labouring society was less rigid in its structure than might have been supposed. It is abundantly evident that the fortunes of peasant workers and their families fluctuated from one generation to the next almost as much as those of other people. A labourer like Henry Feltnes of Mereworth in Kent was descended from a yeoman grandfather farming sixty acres of his own land at Speldhurst; whilst a labourer like Christopher Tomlinson of Wilton near Pickering in the North Riding was able to amass a fortune of £40, purchase a second farmhold at Great Driffield, and bequeath it as a jointure to his widow. Indeed, it was not unknown for

[1] Cf. William Cobbett, *Rural Rides*, Everyman edn., 1957, I, pp. 247-8, 256.

labourers who were still technically 'bondmen in blood' to bequeath property worth £30 or £40.¹ Where labourers still owned smallholdings, prudent marriage alliances often helped to make their fortunes; where they held extensive common rights, they sometimes built up substantial flocks or herds from quite modest beginnings; where neither condition obtained, they might still augment their resources by turning to spinning, weaving, wood-turning, charcoal-burning, or some other by-employment. It was the conjunction of all three circumstances in woodland areas—large holdings, generous commons, numerous by-employments—that enabled enterprising labourers to better their lot at a time when the labouring community, as a whole, was being gradually disinherited and impoverished.

## E. BY-EMPLOYMENTS

Of the labourer's other sources of income, by-employments were therefore of considerable importance. Of those labourers wealthy enough to leave an inventory, nearly two thirds took up some kind of by-industry: the figure varying from under one half in the northern lowlands to nearly four fifths in the woodland parishes of Somerset, Hertfordshire, and the Midlands.² Most of these industries were connected either with forest and woodland crafts, or with the spinning and weaving of flax, hemp, or wool. There were, of course, countless other local industries, such as glove-making in Dorset, lace-making in Buckinghamshire, and rush-mat-making in Cornwall; but only the principal employments can be mentioned in this brief survey.³

Woollen industries probably occupied the spare hours of at least one quarter of the cottage-farming population in England as a whole, and nearly half of that in the Midlands: generally in spinning and carding wool or in knitting stockings, only occasionally in weaving cloth. In parts of Suffolk, where poor people were exceptionally numerous, labourers' wives often used to "go spinning up and down the way"

---

¹ Req. 2, 206, 12; York Probate Registry, will and inventory of Christopher Tomlinson, 1610; cf. Req. 2, 226, 30 for an account of an Elizabethan yeoman of Huntingdon sinking to the level of wage-labourer; E 178, 7064; cf. Savine, *op. cit.*, pp. 277–9.        ² See Table 6.

³ The following paragraphs are based largely on probate inventories, in addition to the sources cited below. For Cornish mat-making, see Richard Carew, *The Survey of Cornwall*, 1602, p. 18. I have omitted extractive industries, because in some counties inventories and Exchequer special commissions and depositions suggest that some mining and quarrying was undertaken by labourers not engaged in agriculture. In Devon, Hooker seems to suggest such a division between farm-labourers and tin-miners (*Devonshire Association*, XLVII, 1915, p. 342). In south Wales, however, probate inventories show that mining and farming were closely connected. Cf. also Joan Thirsk, 'Industries in the Countryside', p. 73.

with a distaff in their hands. In populous Pennine valleys like Garsdale and Dentdale, and in parts of Wales, both men and women knitted stockings as they walked from house to house and village to village. In the two townships of Sowerby and Warley, near Halifax, a great part of the 400 copyholders were said, about the year 1600, to live by "spinning, weaving, dighting cloth, or work pertaining to clothing..." In the poor heathy areas of west Surrey at least 1,100 "poor workfolk" depended for their livelihood, in Charles I's reign, on the clothiers of Wonersh and Godalming, "besides a great number in the county [of Hampshire] adjoining." In Hertfordshire, too, despite the assertion of certain inhabitants that tillage offered a "better means to set the poor children on work," many of the better-off labourers spun and carded wool, no doubt for the clothiers of Hatfield and the neighbouring parts of Essex and Suffolk.[1] Wherever travellers went, in scores of parishes in Tudor England—in Dorset, Somerset, Gloucestershire, Warwickshire, Northamptonshire, East Anglia, the Pennines, or the Weald of Kent— they would have heard spinning-wheels turning, or seen the distaff twirling, in countless farm labourers' cottages.

Spinning and weaving of hemp and flax were not so widely undertaken, although together (so far as inventories indicate) they occupied the spare hours of nearly one third of the labouring population. Hemp-spinning was particularly widespread in the far north and in east Yorkshire: generally, no doubt, for the coarse sheets and pillow-cases used by the poorer classes, sometimes for sacks, ropes, and fishing nets. Elsewhere, except in the Northamptonshire forests, Lincolnshire, East Anglia, and Somerset, comparatively little hemp seems to have been grown or woven by Tudor farm labourers, although in the eighteenth century it was widely cultivated by labourers in the Welsh Marches and elsewhere.[2] Flax-spinning was undertaken by labourers in most parts of the country, except the eastern counties; it was especially common in the lowland parishes of the north and in the woodland areas of Hertfordshire and the Midlands.

[1] Cf. HMC, *Reports*, XIII, ii, p. 266 (*temp*. Restoration); Reyce, *op. cit.*, p. 57; E 134, 10–11 Car. I, H 22; Leeds, TN, Hx, E, f. 6; SP 16, 177, 56 and 56. i; SP 14, 96, 39; C 2, Jas. I, M 12, 41 (which relates how a Hatfield, Herts., clothier in 1616 employed fifty poor children and many other poor townsfolk). Until Gilbert White's time the women of Selborne "availed themselves greatly by spinning wool for making of *barragons*...chiefly manufactured at Alton..."—*The Natural History of Selborne*, Everyman edn., 1945, p. 17.

[2] Cf. Henry Best, *Rural Economy in Yorkshire in 1641, being the Farming and Account Books of Henry Best of Elmeswell in the East Riding*, Surtees Soc., XXXIII, 1857, p. 106; *Yorks. Arch. Jnl*, XXXVII, 1951, p. 386, referring to a stock of £400 worth of hemp to be set aside to employ the poor of Axholme in making sackcloth, in compensation for loss of fishing and fowling rights due to enclosure in Charles I's reign; Joseph Plymley, *General View of the Agriculture of Shropshire*, 1803, pp. 177–8.

Forest industries were more localized. In the wooded districts of central England one peasant labourer in three, and in Hertfordshire two in three engaged in some kind of woodcraft. Many labourers in woodland parishes possessed tools for felling, hewing, cleaving, sawing, adzing, and carting timber. They must often have spent their spare days, and probably much of the wintertime, in making spiles, pales, poles, gates, posts, rails, and laths for fencing and walling. In Gillingham Forest in Dorset some labourers made parts for weavers' looms; on the borders of Hampshire and Surrey they carved wooden bottles; around Wymondham in Norfolk wooden taps and handles; near the South Downs in Sussex shepherds' crooks; in the Weald of Kent 'checkerwork' objects and wooden spoons; in Staffordshire wooden trenchers and 'treenware'; and in the Forest of Arden they made brooms and besoms.[1] Sometimes farm labourers were also small village carpenters; sometimes coopers or turners; sometimes wheelwrights, cartwrights, or ploughwrights. Some of these crafts, it is true, such as the wheelwright's, called for lengthy training, and were more generally undertaken by townsmen; others, however, like those of the wooden spoon- and bottle-makers, seem to have been the traditional arts of a small dynasty of local labouring families. All over the country, woodland wares must have been exported in considerable quantities in this period to the neighbouring fielden districts, and in both Hertfordshire and the Midlands labourers acted as packmen or carriers of their neighbours' products. Forest areas were the natural workshops of an agrarian civilization largely dependent on wooden tools and implements for its work: the number and variety of local crafts, often highly specialized and recondite, was legion.

Other by-employments, such as potting, tiling, nailing, coaling, and iron-smelting, which required plentiful supplies of fuel, were also centred in woodland districts. In Cannock Chase and the Weald of Sussex and Surrey some labourers burnt charcoal for the forges and furnaces of local ironmasters. In Gloucestershire many hamlets "adjoining unto and depending on" the Forest of Dean were "full of poor people" employed in the ironworks. On Dartmoor the 'venville men' cut and burned turf-coal, and were said in 1610 to have carried not less than a hundred thousand horse-loads "out of the forest every year to the parishes about the said forest," both for domestic use and for "the blacksmiths thereabout, [who] use no other coal to work withal." On the borders of Staffordshire and Warwick-

[1] Req. 2, 30, 30; E 159, 472, Trin. 8 Car., rot. 38 (for a Gillingham Forest slay-maker). Wymondham was a noted market for small woodware objects. Was 'checkerwork' possibly an early form of the well-known 'Tunbridge-ware'? 'Treenware' was wooden or 'tree' ware—usually domestic utensils.

Table 6. *Labourers' by-employments: percentage of labourers engaged in different rural industries*[a]

| | Spinning or weaving | | | Woodland crafts | Other by-employments | All by-employments |
|---|---|---|---|---|---|---|
| | Wool | Hemp | Flax | | | |
| Northern lowlands | 17 | 20 | 20 | 0 | 10 | 46 |
| Northern fells | 25 | 19 | 9 | 0 | 22 | 59 |
| East Riding | 8 | 35 | 14 | 8 | 22 | 68 |
| Midland fielden areas | 38 | 0 | 13 | 13 | 13 | 56 |
| Midland forest areas | 41 | 9 | 18 | 36 | 27 | 77 |
| Hertfordshire | 41 | 4 | 26 | 59 | 22 | 78 |
| Eastern counties | 11 | 11 | 0 | 32 | 26 | 58 |
| Somerset | 33 | 0 | 11 | 22 | 22 | 78 |
| All areas | 23 | 15 | 14 | 17 | 19 | 60 |

[a] Based on labourers' probate inventories. Many labourers, especially in Hertfordshire and Midland forest areas, engaged in more than one by-employment, so that the percentages in the final column do not equal the sum of those in the previous columns. The low percentages for the eastern counties are probably due to the fact that a larger proportion of labourers who engaged in spinning and weaving were too poor to leave inventories.

shire, and occasionally in Yorkshire and Lancashire, labourers took up nail-making and other smiths' work; around Newcastle-under-Lyme they engaged in both nailing and potting. In the neighbourhood of Bernwood Forest, in Buckinghamshire, villagers apparently dug tile-earth and potters' earth, and in James I's reign scores of "poor women and little children" were employed "for the greater part of the whole year" in making woad, without which employment they would have been forced to "starve or wander begging..." "Amongst those who inhabit[ed] in the cottages on the outwood" of Wakefield in Yorkshire, there was, in 1709, "a manufactory of earthenware pots of all sorts;" the inhabitants paid the lord of the manor 4d. per 1000 for their right to make bricks.[1] All over England there were hundreds of local 'manufactories', of which little or no trace remains today, save perhaps in an occasional place-name like Kilnwood or Collier Street in the woodland parishes of counties like Kent.

The factors underlying the location of these rural by-employments

[1] E 178, 2098; C 2, Jas. I, N 1, 5; SP 14, 58, 7; SP 14, 54, 15; Yorks. Arch. Soc., Rec. Ser., CI, 1939, p. 184.

have been discussed elsewhere by Dr Thirsk; the foregoing evidence fully bears out her thesis. For the most part, country industries were established in areas at one time well-wooded, now largely given over to dairying or pasture farming. As a result of the custom of partible inheritance and possibly also of Borough English, both characteristic of these areas, and the migration of labourers from common-field villages, the population of woodland districts rose rapidly during the sixteenth century, and by the mid-seventeenth century regions like the Weald of Kent were among the most thickly settled in the country.[1] Yet it was precisely in these districts, with their pastoral economy, that the local demand for agricultural labour was relatively slight, or at best spasmodic.[2] During the slack months, therefore, labourers naturally took up those employments for which woods and forests furnished at once the fuel supplies and the raw materials.

The importance of by-employments in raising the labourer's standard of living has already been emphasized. Wherever peasant industries were combined with agriculture, farmworkers tended to be relatively wealthy. In Hertfordshire, where labourers often engaged in two or three employments at once, they were better-off than in almost any other county. In Gloucestershire, too, where "many families… were almost equally interested in farming and manufacturing," labourers were sometimes comfortably off.[3] It was in regions where rural industries were divorced from agriculture, as apparently in some of the mining villages of Derbyshire and wool villages of Suffolk, or where they were absent altogether, as in Herefordshire, that labourers were very poor.[4] The income which a working family derived from any particular by-employment may have been small; but it was often sufficient to pay the rent of their cottage-holding, and it enabled them to lay aside a small surplus against times of dearth or unemployment. It was an evil day for farmworkers when rural industries left the countryside and returned to the towns.

[1] Joan Thirsk, 'Industries in the Countryside', pp. 70 *sqq*.; cf. E 134, 10–11 Car. I, H 22 (for the connection between gavelkind, a rising population, and by-employments in Garsdale). See also Table 2.

[2] For the "persistent chronic unemployment" of agricultural workers in Stuart England, cf. D. C. Coleman, 'Labour in the English Economy of the Seventeenth Century', EcHR, 2nd Ser., VIII, 1955–6, pp. 283–8.

[3] A. J. and R. H. Tawney, 'An Occupational Census of the Seventeenth Century', EcHR, V, 1934–5, p. 42; Gloucestershire probate inventories.

[4] In a sample of over sixty Herefordshire inventories, none related to labourers. It was the absence of local industry that led Rowland Vaughan to found a "commonwealth" of tradesmen living on the products of his estate, which by 1604 had been joined by 2000 "mechanicals."—N. Jackson, 'Some Observations on the Herefordshire Environment in the 17th and 18th Centuries', *Woolhope Naturalists' Field Club*, XXXVI, i, 1958, pp. 32, 36. See also p. 190, n. 3.

## F. WORK, WAGES, AND EMPLOYERS

By-employments, nevertheless, benefited only a section, possibly only a minority, of the labouring population as a whole. The mainstay of all but a few labourers, apart from the income from their holdings, was their work as wage-labourers on a farm. Contemporaries and historians have sometimes seemed to describe farmwork in terms implying unrelieved hardship and monotony. Sir Thomas More, for instance, remarked in *Utopia* that "almost everywhere the life of workmen and artificers" involved "continual work, like labouring and toiling beasts," from "early morning to late in the evening..."[1] There is a good deal of truth in such statements; but a glance at a few estate account books and diaries may serve to modify More's somewhat over-pessimistic picture, and illustrate the great variety of farming tasks undertaken by Tudor and Stuart farmworkers.

Amongst the labourers employed by Nicholas Toke of Godinton, a landowner of East Kent in Charles I's reign, were gardeners, bailiffs, lookers, haywards, thatchers, carpenters, masons, shepherds, ploughmen, ploughboys, and mole-catchers. The squire's cherry orchards at Great Chart were tended by "Old James," his hop-gardens by one of his head-labourers, Tom Finn, and his sheep in Romney Marsh by Barnaby Punyer. His wage-accounts include payments for washing and shearing sheep in marsh and upland; for ploughing, harrowing, and sowing the arable lands at Great Chart; for mowing, reaping, binding, and carrying hay and corn; for felling timber, digging stone and gravel, setting quicks, mending hedges, scouring drills and ditches, and for work "about the ponds." In Berkshire, at a slightly earlier period, the account book of Robert Loder of Harwell, yeoman, records the wages paid to William Weston, his carter, John Austen his harrower, Dick [?Cottes] his shepherd, John Andrews his ploughboy, and Joan Colle and Alice Keates his two maids. Many sums were paid out each year for thatching, hedging, reaping, mowing, cocking, threshing, winnowing, and 'ruddering'; for pilling hemp, gathering walnuts, picking cherries, pulling hops, carrying fruit and pigeons to market, and managing the watermeadows. In the north of England, on the estates of the Shuttleworths near Burnley and Bolton, the steward or bailiff records payments to Roger Harper for mowing rushes, to Nicholas Pendleburie for clipping sheep, to "wife Turner and her folks" for clipping and washing, to Robert Houlden for scouring watercourses, to "divers women of Bolton" for turf-gathering, to fourteen persons at Hoole for dressing hemp, to John Hackings for

---

[1] *The Utopia of Sir Thomas More*, ed. J. H. Lupton, 1895, p. 141; cf. pp. 301 *sq.*

walling on Broadheale Moor, to a man for watching and warding cattle at Burnley Fair, to three women for weeding in the garden, and to "Mr James Andertone's man"—for bringing a porpoise.[1]

This variety in the labourer's work was neither eclectic nor haphazard, however: it was closely related to the rhythmic pattern of the seasons. On John Clopton's farm at Great Wratting in Suffolk the month of March was largely spent in ploughing; April was taken up with "fallowing" and grafting crab-stocks; August with reaping and "pitching cart;" September and October with picking apples, making cider, and sowing wheat and rye; and the winter months with pruning apple trees, cleaving logs, ploughing and sowing the arable lands, and threshing and dressing 'bullimong'. On Nicholas Toke's estates, the winter months were spent in ploughing and sowing the fields, dunging the meadows, felling timber and bushes, topping and clearing oats, scouring the river, and "drilling in the new hop-garden;" the months of March and April in lambing, hedging, "diking," "sharping and carrying" hop-poles, and setting and poling hops. May and June were spent in mole-catching, mowing hay, washing and shearing sheep, and carrying and spreading marl; July and August in burning lime, weeding barley, dressing and hoeing the hop-gardens, mowing bracken, making hay, and thatching the barn at Yardhurst; September in reaping tares and wheat, cutting and binding 'podware', stacking and stripping hop-poles, and "driving and spreading marl;" and October and November in ploughing, felling, diking, 'clodding,' clearing the ponds, dressing the hop-grounds, and cutting timber.[2]

Some further insight into the variety of the labourer's work may be gained from a study of his work-tools. For men who were boarded in the house, the farmer himself usually seems to have supplied the necessary implements; but outworkers and day-labourers were often expected to bring their own gear with them—sometimes their own horse and cart too—when they came to work on the farm each morning. In a sample of some 300 labourers' probate inventories, more than sixty different kinds of work-tools and farm-gear are mentioned: ploughs, harrows, spades, rakes, shovels, skoppets, and dung-forks for preparing and manuring the ground; scythes, sickles, pitch-forks, pease-hooks, flails, sieves, and riddles for harvesting, threshing, and sifting grain; carts, 'courts', cars, barrows, wains, and drays for carrying

---

[1] Lodge, op. cit., pp. xxxii–ix et passim; G. E. Fussell, ed., *Robert Loder's Farm Accounts, 1610–1620*, Camden Soc., 3rd Ser., LIII, 1936, passim; John Harland, ed., *The House and Farm Accounts of the Shuttleworths of Gawthorpe Hall...*, Parts I and II, Chetham Soc., XXXV, 1856, and XLI, 1856, passim.

[2] Essex RO, B 7, B.38.1502, John Clopton's Diary, entries relating to 1649–50; Lodge, op. cit., passim.

corn, hay, dung, furze, and turf; mattocks, bills, axes, hatchets, saws, augers, adzes, drags, chains, wedges, and a dozen other implements for grubbing, hedging, felling, cutting, carting, and preparing wood. Not to mention the ladders and apple baskets for use in the orchard; the crooks and shears and bells for the sheep; the "doggchyne" for the labourer's sheep dog; the small metal or wooden bottles for his own drink; and the bridles, saddles, nets, packs, and panniers for his horse or mare. A well-furnished labourer, like Richard Perkins of Acton Beauchamp in Herefordshire, might possess a rake, a shovel, two trowels, a bill-hook, three sheaf-picks, a hair sieve, a wire sieve, four ladders, a hand-barrow, two hurdles, a manger, and various coils of rope; together with an axe, a hatchet, two augers, a handsaw, a hammer, a pair of puncheons, a crowbar, and a "little pewter bottle." Altogether, Perkin's gear was worth nearly £1, although the whole of his worldly wealth did not amount to £5. All his tools were carefully listed by the neighbours who drew up his inventory; for they had doubtless been purchased at some expense from the wheelwright or blacksmith of the next market town, or perhaps from some travelling iron-merchant from the Black Country.[1] They were the symbols of his calling, as well as the tools of his trade.

The work of labourers on the farm was not only characterized by variety, however, but by an increasing tendency for certain men to specialize in particular crafts. Many of the tasks so far mentioned, and much of the work allotted in particular to women and children, such as stone-gathering, weeding, rush-cutting, treading hay, and picking apples, required little skill.[2] On small yeoman-farms, moreover, only one or two labourers were employed, and there was little scope or necessity for division of labour. But there were numerous farm-tasks, such as ploughing, shepherding, and dairywork, that were highly technical arts requiring careful training, and were undertaken by certain expert men and women only. Skills of this kind did not, of course, originate in this period; but with the progress of commercial farming and regional specialization in husbandry, agricultural tasks themselves became more highly specialized, and on large farms the number of specialist labourers was sometimes remarkable. On the sheep-farms of the earl of Winchilsea at Watton in Holderness, for example, the number of shearers alone ran to forty or fifty. On monastic demesnes, quite minor houses like Cockersand or Conishead employed forty or

---

[1] Judging from inventories, however, only one labourer in three possessed any farm—or work—gear; but it should be remembered that inventories do not always list gear in detail, and many workers needed only the tools of their particular craft.

[2] Harland, *op. cit., passim.*

fifty hinds and labourers, and a small nunnery like St Sexburga's in Sheppey maintained a carter, a carpenter, a thatcher, a horsekeeper, a maltster, two cowherds, and three shepherds; the average number of agricultural labourers or 'hinds' on the estates of seventy small houses dissolved in 1536 was nineteen. On the home-farms of Nicholas Toke in Kent there were carters, shepherds, haywards, ploughmen, gardeners, thatchers, carpenters, hopmen, and overseers of the orchards. And on the co-operative peasant farms of common-field villages it was not unusual for the community to employ its own shepherd, cowherd, swineherd, moorman, hayward, and "fen-clerk."[1]

The development of these specialist labouring skills exerted a profound influence on the structure of the labouring community as a whole. Without doubt it helped to accentuate that distinction between forest and fielden settlements which has already been remarked. In many fielden parishes, with their emphasis on arable husbandry, the supply of work was relatively abundant and farms were large enough to employ a sizeable labour force; the structure of society was intensely patriarchal, manorial organization was rigid, and the working population was relatively static. On the farms of Nicholas Toke, for instance, a number of ancient village families, like the Gillams and Punyers, were employed from one generation to the next almost *en masse:* sons, sisters, daughters, and brothers evidently worked side by side; as their children grew up, they were taken to work each morning by their fathers, and gradually trained up, over the years, to follow in their footsteps as ploughmen or shepherds.[2] In parishes like these, labourers could afford to stick to the particular farm-crafts in which they had been trained; certain arts became traditional in certain families, and a kind of rigid pattern or hierarchy of skills came into being. Many tasks on the farm acquired their own peculiar customs and *mystique;* the farmer was careful to enquire into a new employee's "true knowledge in his art;"[3] and few labourers, for their part, would have consented to divagate

---

[1] Best, *op. cit.*, pp. 96–7 (Best confuses the earl with his cousin, Lord Finch; Finch was the family name); LP XII, i, p. 1; R. H. Tawney, *The Agrarian Problem in the Sixteenth Century*, 1912, p. 21n.; David Knowles, *The Religious Orders in England*, III, 1959, p. 262; Lodge, *op. cit., passim;* Lancs. RO, DDCa 7.3. (relates to Cartmel in 1703); E 134, 5 Jas. I, E 12; *Yorks Arch. Jnl*, xxxv, 1943, pp. 298, 300; E 134, 9 Jas. I, E 4; E 134, 17–18 Eliz., M 6.

[2] Lodge, *op. cit.*, pp. xxxiii, xxxvii, xxxix, *et passim;* cf. Lancs. RO, DDM 1.1 (Heskin rental, 1572), ff. 12, 15, 19. Richard Jefferies described these same patriarchal influences in agricultural society, in the nineteenth century, in *The Toilers of the Field*, 1892, pp. 49–54.

[3] Cf. BM Harleian MS 98, f. 25, in which Paul D'Ewes of Stowlangtoft, Suffolk, engages Ambrose Clarke of Bury, gardener. For a modern account of the customs and *mystique* of the horseman's art, see G. Ewart Evans, *The Horse in the Furrow*, 1960, especially chapters I–VI.

from their particular calling and take up that of another man. In these areas, as Richard Jefferies remarked of labourers in the nineteenth century, "work for the cottager must be work to please him; and to please him it must be the regular sort to which he is accustomed, which he did beside his father as a boy, which *his* father did, and *his* father before him; the same old plough or grub-axe, the same milking, the same identical mowing, if possible in the same field. He does not care for any new-fangled jobs. He does not recognize them, they have no *locus standi*—they are not established."[1]

In forest areas, by contrast, labourers were compelled to be more versatile and more adventurous. The influence of kinship and the tendency for certain crafts to become traditional in certain families may have been little less apparent; but the supply of work was less plentiful, and the labourer was often forced to look for employment elsewhere. In this way a sizeable population of migrant workers came into being, occupying the winter months at home, in woodland crafts or other by-employments, and, as seed-time or harvest came round, seeking work on the arable farms of fielden villages. In Kent the high wages paid by corn-farmers "invite[d] many stout workmen hither from the neighbouring country to get in their harvest: so that you shall find, especially on Sundays, the roads full of troops of workmen with their scythes and sickles, going to the adjacent town to refresh themselves with good liquor and victuals." In Yorkshire, when reaping began, Henry Best of Elmswell used to send to Malton to hire "moor-folks" from the Cleveland Hills, and set up boards and bedsteads in his folks' chamber, his kiln, and any other "convenient house," for their accommodation. In Pembrokeshire George Owen gathered a labour force of as many as 240 people to get in his corn harvest.[2] If we may judge from contemporary account books and from later evidence, the same practice obtained in the arable districts of Norfolk, Suffolk, and Sussex, and in other areas where a seasonal demand for additional labour existed, whether for haymaking, harvesting, hop-picking, or any other kind of farmwork.[3]

---

[1] Richard Jefferies, *Field and Hedgerow*, 1904, p. 198.
[2] HMC, *Reports*, XIII, ii, p. 280 ('An account of some remarkable things in a journey between London and Dover', n.d., but from internal evidence c. 1664); Best, *op. cit.*, p. 48, and cf. pp. 110, 115; G. Owen, *The Taylors Cussion*, ed. E. M. Pritchard, 1906, I, ff. 31–34.
[3] Cf. Harland, *op. cit., passim;* Bradford Corporation, Cunliffe Lister MSS (2), Bdle 1 (2); William Marshall, *The Rural Economy of Norfolk*, 1787, I, pp. 184 *sqq*. Since the population increased perhaps 50–75 per cent in this period, and at the same time corn exports rose rapidly, areas like Cambridgeshire, Hertfordshire, Thanet, Holderness, Norfolk, and the Thames basin became major granaries for England and parts of Europe, and required a large population of seasonal labourers.

It is of course important not to exaggerate the differences between the two kinds of community. Many labourers neither remained rooted in one village for life nor became truly migratory, but hired themselves out from year to year at the autumnal hiring-fairs, where they stood in rows in the market-place, with ribbons in their caps to indicate their craft, waiting for some farmer to engage them.[1] Neither is it possible to mention here the special characteristics of the working population in fen and fell areas, where wage-labour, however, was generally less in evidence.[2] The foregoing account stresses only the distinctive tendencies in the two principal types of labouring community, and indicates the dominant trends of the future. Quite certainly those trends helped to foster a relatively free and mobile society in heath and wood parishes, and a relatively static and subservient one in the parishes of the fielden plains.

Labourers' wages are discussed elsewhere in this volume by Dr Bowden, and only a brief commentary is called for here. The figures Dr Bowden has worked out show that, on a group of college estates in the south and east Midlands, farm wages increased in money terms three-fold between 1500 and 1640, rising on the average from 4d. *per diem* to 1s. *per diem*, without allowance for meat and drink. The cost of living, however, rose sixfold in this period, and the labourer's real wages therefore dropped by 50 per cent. In the north of England wage-rates were rather lower than on these estates, and in the west and south somewhat higher; but in all areas the general trend was similar.[3]

[1] Cf. Richard Blome, *Britannia*, 1673, p. 70. For examples of hiring agreements between masters and men, see BM Harleian MS 98, ff. 25, 30, 31v., 32; Hereford City Library, LC Deeds 3731.

[2] Some marshland areas (as in Kent) were very thinly populated in any case (see Table 2); moorland areas were sometimes characterized by the same features as forest regions, however. See also p. 203, n. 4.

[3] I am indebted to the Price History Committee of the Economic History Society for permission to utilize the material on which these statements are based. Cf. also J. E. Thorold Rogers, *A History of Agriculture and Prices in England*, IV, 1882, chapters XVII and XXVII; V, 1887, chapters XXIII and XXVIII. The above rates for agricultural labourers resembled those paid to building labourers: cf. E. H. Phelps Brown and Sheila V. Hopkins, 'Seven Centuries of Building Wages', *Economica*, NS, XXII, 1955, pp. 195–205. For other information on wages, see J. E. Thorold Rogers, *Six Centuries of Work and Wages*, 1903, pp. 388 *sqq.*; N. C. P. Tyack, *Migration from East Anglia to New England before 1660*, London Ph.D. thesis, 1951, Part II, pp. 153–68; E. M. Leonard, 'The Relief of the Poor by the State Regulation of Wages', EHR, XIII, 1898, pp. 91–93; Sir William Beveridge, 'Wages in the Winchester Manors', EcHR, VII, 1936–7, pp. 22–43 (between 1208 and 1453). For information on wage-assessment, the reader is referred, *inter alia*, to articles in EHR, IX, XII, XIII, XV, XLI, LVII; in EcHR, I; and to HMC, *Reports*, XII, iv, pp. 460–62, and *Report on the Records of The City of Exeter*, 1916, pp. 50–1.

The consequences of this decline in the wage-labourer's economic position are obvious; they became ever more serious, moreover, as the working population multiplied, and the number of labourers dependent solely on wages for their livelihood increased.

Nevertheless, these figures do not tell the whole truth about rural wages. They refer only to basic rates for regular tasks like hedging and ditching. Specialized tasks and seasonal work were more highly paid, and most labourers received a number of perquisites, gifts, and allowances in addition. On large farms, like those of Nicholas Toke, there was in fact a great deal of variation in the actual economic fortunes of farm employees. Most of Toke's permanent labourers seem to have lived in the manor-house or one of the farmsteads, and their annual wages ranged from 20s. to 30s. for a newly engaged lad, to £2 10s.-£3 for women workers, £3-£7 10s. for most of the men, £8 for Pack the bailiff, £10 for Masters the gardener, and £15 (probably including meat) for one of the lookers in Romney Marsh.[1] For day labourers, with no allowance for meat and drink, the usual rate was 1s. a day; but in the mid-seventeenth century 1s. 1d. was paid for haymaking, 1s. 2d. for ploughing, 1s. 3d. for work about the ponds, 1s. 4d. for lading water, 1s. 2d.-1s. 6d. for felling timber, 1s. 6d. for reaping, 1s. 9d. for hedge-mending, and 2s.-2s. 6d. for thatching.[2] For men employed upon piecework it is difficult to arrive at reliable comparisons; but occasionally they earned higher wages than workers engaged by the year. For ploughing, piece-rates varied from under 1s. an acre for a boy to 1s. 4d. for working fallow and barley land, and as much as 5s. 6d. an acre, presumably for work on specially intractable soils. For harrowing, pieceworkers received 1s. 4d. an acre; for hay-making 1s. 8d.; for reaping fodder 4s.-5s.; and for reaping wheat 3s. 4d.-5s. 6d. Hedging and ditching were paid at 2d.-9d. a rod; "making quickset" at 1s. the rod; shearing sheep at 1s.-1s. 4d. the score, and washing sheep at 2d. or 3d. the score.[3] Such rates may seem to suggest that Nicholas Toke's estates were run on unusually generous lines, and they lend colour to Thomas Baskerville's remark that Kentish labourers received "the best wages...of any in England." But in fact, though well above the levels fixed by the local justices and the wage-rates actually paid in the Midlands and Lancashire, Toke's payments were not unique. In Baskerville's own county of Berkshire one of Robert Loder's men

[1] These figures relate to the mid-seventeenth century; Master's wages may also cover purchases for the garden, and the looker's an allowance for food.
[2] Some of these rates were probably paid to men working specially long hours, or using their own carts or horses. In Yorkshire Henry Best's field-workers started work by 7 o'clock, or 6 o'clock when carrying corn from the wolds, and worked till half an hour after sunset.—Best, *op. cit.*, p. 52.
[3] Lodge, *op. cit.*, pp. xxxii–vii

received in 1617 the "exceeding great wages" of £13 9s. 4d.: a sum which Nicholas Toke certainly never paid to any of his resident labourers in Kent.[1]

On most farms, labourers' wages were also supplemented by various allowances and perquisites. At Holme on Spalding Moor, in the vale of York, Marmaduke Dolman allowed his herdsman the milk of three kine, in addition to his annual stipend. In Suffolk, Paul Dewes agreed to give one of his workers five combs of rye and five of barley annually, together with a house and farmhold. In Berkshire, Robert Loder allowed his shepherd several bushels of malt or "four sheep's wintering," and his carter a load of bushes or "a hog's keeping all the year." In Kent, during the Civil War, Nicholas Toke paid his labourers' monthly tax-assessments for them. In Norfolk, the Southwells and Townshends sometimes allowed their shepherds and sheep-reeves a number of lambs and fleeces, a provision of corn, and a rent-free cottage and land. In most districts there were also customary allowances of clothing: harvest gloves for the men, boys, and girls on the estates of Nicholas Toke; a new shirt for the men and a new smock for the maids, each year with their wages, on Robert Caton's farm at Cark in Cartmel; a pair of shoes for his boy, and shoes and knitting wool for his maid, on Robert Loder's near Abingdon.[2]

Where labourers lived in the farmhouse or were boarded out in other workers' cottages, the value of their food and drink also has to be taken into account. Robert Loder estimated the annual cost of meat and drink for each of his three men and two maids at £9 16s. 6d. in 1614, and £11 18s. 6d. in 1616. Nicholas Toke allowed one of his sheep-lookers in Romney Marsh £10 a year for his board and £36 a year for the diet of two men and two boys.[3] Such men were clearly well-fed, often, it appears, at their master's own table, and probably a good deal more generously than in their own cottages. At haysel and

---

[1] *Ibid.*, pp. xxxiii–iv, xxxvi; HMC, *Reports*, XIII, ii, p. 280 (relating to *c.* 1664); Harland, *op. cit., passim;* Price History Committee's wage-material, transcripts of Stowe estate records; Fussell, *Loder's Farm Accounts*, p. 137. According to Baskerville, writing about 1664, Kentish labourers received 4s.–5s. an acre for reaping wheat *plus* 2s. a day for meat and drink; but he probably exaggerated.

[2] E 134, 6 Car. I, M 29; BM Harleian MS 98, f. 30, and cf. ff. 31v, 32 (1628, 1629); Fussell, *Loder's Farm Accounts*, pp. 23, 49, 107, 123, 137; Lodge, *op. cit.*, pp. xxxiii, xxxvi, 137; K. J. Allison, 'Flock Management in the Sixteenth and Seventeenth Centuries', EcHR, 2nd Ser., XI, 1958, p. 110; cf. also Best, *op. cit.*, pp. 96–7; *Yorks. Arch. Jnl*, XXXVI, 1944, p. 446; Lancs. RO, inventory of Robert Caton and his wife, of Cark in Cartmel, Lancs. (1590); cf. Essex RO, D.Dk.M.135, Foulness bailiff's account (1424).

[3] Fussell, *Loder's Farm Accounts*, pp. 108, 122; Lodge, *op. cit.*, p. xxxvii. There was no farmhouse on Toke's marsh estate, and his men probably lodged in one of the 'removable houses' of the kind mentioned in Kentish inventories at this time.

harvest time they and the outworkers were granted an additional allowance for beer, which on Toke's farms sometimes amounted to as much as 1s. a day. And when all the harvest had been gathered in, they were invited by the farmer to a great feast of boiled beef and bacon, puddings and apple-pies, and hot cakes and ale.[1]

Nevertheless, we must not make the fortunes of the wage-worker appear too rosy. The labourer with a good master, or with adequate seasonal work and suitable by-employments for the winter months, was relatively well-off. But the chronic problem of the labouring community as a whole was an inadequate supply of work.[2] For many thousands of rural workers every slack period or harvest failure brought unemployment and hunger. Neither the Privy Council nor the local justices were unsympathetic to their necessities; and somehow or other, by charity, or poor relief, or poaching, they and their children managed to procure the means of subsistence. But behind the laconic sentences of conciliar enquiries and justices' reports there must have been countless unrecorded tales of human suffering and tragedy.

Relationships between masters and men are largely a matter of personality. In all ages there are good and bad employers, in the sixteenth century no less than our own day. When a Stuart farmer complained that his "men can work if they list, and so they can loiter," or a Tudor labourer left behind him a list of unpaid wages due from a succession of employers, it may prove little about working conditions in general or the characteristic attitudes of masters and men.[3] Our present concern is not with these personal considerations, but with the economic and social conditions underlying them.

On most farms the social conditions in which Tudor farm-labourers worked were still intensely 'feudal' or patriarchal. In the north of England the abiding strength of feudalism is well known. Although the characteristic Pennine farm was a small family holding worked with little outside assistance, the territorial dominion of the monastic houses and of magnates like the Percys and the bishops of Durham was a social force of immense power in the lives of the poor.[4] In the south

[1] Lodge, op. cit., p. xxxv; Best, op. cit., p. 93; cf. Carew, op. cit., p. 68. Even a close-fisted yeoman like Robert Loder spent £2 16s. "extraordinary" on "our feast" in 1614.—Fussell, Loder's Farm Accounts, pp. 68, 107. According to Baskerville, Kentish labourers were sometimes allowed 2s. per diem for meat and drink at harvest time, though probably he exaggerated.—HMC, XIII, ii, p. 280.
[2] Cf. p. 194, n. 2.
[3] Fussell, op. cit., p. 59; Worcester Diocesan Registry, inventories of William Nurthall of Halesowen (1544-5), John Hyende of Blockley (1560).
[4] According to a Jacobean puritan, Northumbrian people were "merely led by the example of their masters, which is for the most part papistry or atheism..."—SP 14,

of England, feudalism, though different in quality, was in many ways little less firmly entrenched. It is only necessary to glance at the probate inventory of a Kentish squire or a Hertfordshire corn-farmer, with its detailed description of the manor- or farm-house, to sense the autocratic influence of south-country landowners in the lives of their rural labourers. William Smyth's Caroline farmhouse at Three Houses in Hertfordshire, for instance, comprised a hall, kitchen, chambers, garrets, buttery, and men's chambers within doors; and a mealhouse, henhouse, hayhouse, brewhouse, beer-cellar, stables, and barns round the yard: it was a microcosm, in fact, of each aspect of rural and labouring life. The Rudstones' Elizabethan manor-house at Boughton Monchelsea in Kent consisted of a great hall, dining-room, parlour, court-room, gallery, nursery, buttery, kitchens, chambers, and garrets looking southwards over the Weald; and adjoining them, grouped round the courtyards, a milkhouse, stilling-house, wheat-loft, brewhouse, fish-house, boulting-house, bakehouse, workhouse-chamber, barns, and stables.[1] Quite clearly, farms of this kind resembled, in Norden's phrase, virtually independent "commonwealths"; their rulers wielded very considerable power in the local community, and the life of the labourer was entirely bound up in their agricultural and social routine.[2] It is no accident that the political theory of patriarchalism received its most extreme enunciation, not in the north of England, but in Kent, in the writings of Sir Robert Filmer of East Sutton—the next village to Boughton Monchelsea.

Of the labourer's working conditions on these farms something has already been said. It was from these conditions that a distinctive ideal of conduct, governing the relationships between masters and men, took its rise. From Henry VIII's reign to that of Charles I it is possible to trace the development of a definite social code by which high-minded employers believed they should regulate their conduct towards employees: a code that governed not only the social and spiritual welfare of their own labourers, but that of all the poor in their neighbourhood generally. When their labourers were ill, farming squires like Nicholas Toke and John Clopton assisted them in their expenses

92, 17; cf. LP XII, i, pp. 82, 166, 167, 234. For evidence of the fewness of wage-labourers in Georgian Westmorland see A. Pringle, *General View of the Agriculture of the County of Westmorland*, [1813], p. 333, and cf. p. 301; according to J. Bailey and G. Culley, *General View of the Agriculture of the county of Northumberland*, 1813, p. 164, there were few servants kept in Northumbrian farmhouses.

[1] MSS of Michael Winch, Esq., at Boughton Monchelsea Place: inventory of Belknap Rudstone. I am indebted to Mr Winch for a transcript of this document.

[2] "And is not every manor a little commonwealth, whereof the tenants are the members, the land the body, and the Lord the Head?"—Quoted in R. H. Tawney, *The Agrarian Problem in the Sixteenth Century*, 1912, p. 350 n.

and paid other workers or women to nurse them; when their wives were in childbed, they sent their own wives to attend their labour; when disputes with other villagers arose, they endeavoured to mediate between them; when their rights in the local commonland were challenged, they took up their cause in the court of the manor, or filed a bill in their behalf in Chancery or Requests.[1] In 1529, when Sir Thomas More heard of the "loss of our barns and our neighbours' also," he instructed his wife to "take all the household to church and thank God, both for what He has given and for what He has taken from us," and "to make some good ensearch what my poor neighbours have lost and bid them take no thought therefor; for if I should not leave myself a spoon," he added, "there shall no poor neighbour of mine bear no loss by any chance happened in my house." At the end of the period Sir George Sondes of Lees Court in Kent considered that it was "the master's part" not only to find work for the labourers of his own parish and to relieve and feed the poor at his table, but also to see them "perform the outward duties of God's service, as prayer and going to church, and to show them the way by his own godly example:" calling upon his servants to do the same, and attending family prayers in his own house "once, if not twice every day." For a period of some thirty years Sondes spent "at least a thousand pounds a year" on his labourers and workmen, and relieved upwards of twenty poor people weekly: providing each week a bullock of about fifty stone, a quarter of wheat, and a quarter of malt for his household.[2] There is no reason to suppose that these philanthropic customs were universally adopted; but even where they did not obtain, they were sometimes held up as an ideal.

On many farms, however, the semi-feudal conditions underlying ideals of this kind were beginning to give way to a specifically commercial nexus between masters and men. On large arable farms especially, where many labourers were employed in production for the market, and where it was imperative for farmers to keep an eye fixed firmly on prices and profits, the frictions between masters and men were often acute. In the vale of York, the earl of Strafford's steward remarked to his patron in the 1620's that "nothing is more unprofitable than a farm in tillage in the hands of servants, where the master's eye is not daily upon them." (It would be interesting to know the opinion of his labourers.) In the corn-growing area of Berkshire Robert Loder was continually complaining of his "unruly servants,"

[1] Cf. Lodge, *op. cit., passim;* Essex RO, B, 7 B.38.1502, John Clopton's Diary, *passim;* Req. 2, 223, 40; C 2 Jas. I, G 5, 70.
[2] LP IV, p. 2651, and cf. II, p. cclxxvi, citing More's *Utopia;* Harleian Miscellany, X, pp. 49, 51.

and nicely calculating the less and more of their wages and expenses: for "all workmen almost (it is to be doubted) will play legerdemain with their masters and favour themselves..." In the arable plain of Lancashire, James Bankes, a London goldsmith-turned-corn-farmer, at the age of seventy counselled his son to "make no more tillage to get corn than to serve your house, for I have been hindered by keeping servants in getting of corn that I have rather desired to die than to live, for they care not whether end goeth forward so that they have meat, drink, and wages; small fear of God is in servants, and thou shalt find my counsel just and most true." As Richard Jefferies pointed out in the nineteenth century, short terms of service and frequent changes of employment (which were little less characteristic of many arable districts of Stuart England) necessarily deepened the social gulf between masters and men.[1]

Partly as a result of this manifest animosity between labourers and employers, a new attitude to the working community as a whole was emerging in this period. As labourers increased in numbers and came more and more to depend on wages alone for their livelihood, some farmers came to think of them as mere employees, to be taken on or dismissed at pleasure, as commercial prudence alone dictated. They ceased to think of their labourers as their own "folk" and neighbours, and began to regard their responsibility towards them as something of a problem, and even a nuisance. In Suffolk, Robert Reyce remarked severely on "the corrupt and froward judgement of many in these days, who esteem the multitude of our poor here to be a matter of heavy burden, and a sore discommodity;" he felt himself bound to remind his countrymen that "as well the poor as the rich proceed from the Lord, and that the rich cannot stand without the poor..."[2] In Norfolk, poor people seem to have felt very bitterly "how little favour" the local gentry "bear to us poor men," and threatened to "go to their [sc. the gentry's] houses and get harness and victuals and kill those who will not join us, even their children in the cradles; for it were a good turn if there were as many gentlemen in Norfolk as there be white bulls."[3]

Once again, it is important not to exaggerate either the novelty or the extent of these changing attitudes. In point of fact, people like Loder were often more generous than their critical or plaintive comments suggest. But the change itself can hardly be gainsaid. And it is

---

[1] Fussell, *Loder's Farm Accounts*, p. 25, and cf. pp. 36, 59, 68, 71, 90, 108, 118; Sheffield Central Library, Strafford Letters, no. 17; J. H. M. Bankes, 'James Bankes and the Manor of Winstanley, 1596–1617', *Hist. Soc. of Lancs. and Ches.*, XCIV, 1943, p. 75; Richard Jefferies, *The Gamekeeper at Home*, 1948 edn., p. 32.

[2] Reyce, *op. cit.*, p. 56.

[3] LP XV, p. 354, quoting depositions of four local men against John Walter of Griston. The phrases occur in a projected speech to rioters in 1540.

not without significance that it was most marked in the economically advanced eastern counties, and in those arable and fielden districts where cottage holdings were smallest and labourers were perforce most dependent on their masters' favour. By many of their contemporaries in the seventeenth century farmworkers were ceasing to be thought of as respected members of a distinct social order, with peculiar rights and privileges of their own; they were coming to be regarded, instead, as a class of pariahs, and spoken of collectively, and a little condescendingly, as "the poor." It would not be many years before they were described as the "rude forefathers of the hamlet."

## G. DOMESTIC LIFE

The farmworker's cottage has often been described as a one-room hovel of sticks and dirt, and for the majority of landless labourers the description is probably not far off the mark. A glance at a few probate inventories, however, will show that not all farmworkers were so ill-housed as we might expect. Out of about three hundred inventories, approximately one quarter afford some description of the layout of labourers' cottages. It would not be safe to assume that the rest were too poor to be worth describing, since rooms were mentioned only to facilitate the description of goods; but the number of cottages whose rooms *were* described probably provides a rough, if exaggerated, indication of the proportion of relatively well-housed labourers in each region. In the Welsh Marches and the north-west the proportion of cottages with more than one room was almost *nil;* in the East Riding it was nearly one third, in the east Midlands nearly two thirds, and in Hertfordshire more than nine tenths. In forest parishes the proportion was nearly twice as high as in fielden parishes, although the number of small, two-roomed cottages was greater, and three- and four-roomed houses were rather less numerous. Houses with five or more rooms were naturally rare in any region, although a few, probably former yeomen's houses, had six, seven, and even eight rooms. As the period progressed, the standard of housing definitely improved, and by 1640 four labourers in five (of those who left inventories) lived in cottages with at least three rooms.[1]

Of the cottages described in the inventories, nearly all contained a hall or 'house' as their principal living-room, with at least one chamber, either at the end of, or more usually above, the hall, though the exact position is not always specified. Many also had a parlour, generally indistinguishable in function from the chamber. In Hertfordshire the space above the hall was often boarded off into lofts for sleeping

[1] See Table.

quarters and storage; the term 'loft' was rarely used in labourers' inventories in other areas, but some of the 'chambers' in the Midlands would probably have been called mere lofts in Hertfordshire. Cooking was generally done in the labourer's hall or 'house', for even in 1640 few cottages had separate kitchens. Opening off one end of the hall, there was usually a buttery, and a number of the larger cottages also boasted a milkhouse, dairy, or cheese-chamber. In the yard often stood some kind of outhouse, usually a barn, occasionally a stable, woodhouse, or some other kind of 'hovel', although in more than half the inventories describing the cottage building no kind of outhouse is mentioned.[1]

Table 7. *Labourers' houses—1*

| | Percentage[a] of labourers' houses with | | | | |
|---|---|---|---|---|---|
| | 2 rooms | 3 rooms | 4 rooms | 5 rooms | 6 or more rooms |
| 1560–1600 | 44 | 28 | 11 | 17 | 0 |
| 1610–20 | 22 | 22 | 34 | 11 | 11 |
| 1630–40 | 21 | 41 | 23 | 9 | 6 |
| Fielden parishes | 17 | 43 | 25 | 8 | 8 |
| Forest parishes: | | | | | |
|   Midlands | 33 | 39 | 17 | 0 | 11 |
|   Herts. | 36 | 16 | 28 | 20 | 0 |
| All regions | 27 | 32 | 24 | 10 | 7 |

[a] Based on all labourers' inventories in which rooms are specified (about eighty in a sample of 300). These probably cover only one sixteenth of the labouring population as a whole; most of the remainder probably inhabited one-room houses, but it is not always safe to assume so, since rooms were listed only to facilitate the description of goods. A few inventories relating to the 1660's for Northants. are included.

Quite clearly not every Tudor and Stuart labourer was condemned to live in a miserable one-roomed cabin. But probate inventories, it must be remembered, represent only the upper levels of the labouring population. How did farmworkers fare who were too poor to leave an inventory? For a description of their houses we are indebted to a few scrappy remarks by contemporary travellers and topographers. In Cornwall, according to Richard Carew, the older cottages were built with "walls of earth, low thatched roofs, few partitions, no planchings [*sc.* floor-boards] or glass windows, and scarcely any chimneys other

[1] See Table 8.

Table 8. *Labourers' houses—2*

| | Hall or house | Chambers | | | Parlours | | | Kitchen | Buttery | Lofts | | Milkhouse, dairy, or cheese-room | Other rooms[b] | Out-houses[c] | |
|---|---|---|---|---|---|---|---|---|---|---|---|---|---|---|---|
| | | 1 | 2 | 3 | 1 | 2 | | | | 1 | 2 | | | 1 | 2 |
| Fielden parishes | 92 | 67 | 13 | 9 | 38 | 9 | 25 | 33 | 0 | 0 | 17 | 17 | 25 | 4 |
| Forest parishes: | | | | | | | | | | | | | | |
| Midlands | 94 | 56 | 22 | 0 | 61 | 0 | 22 | 28 | 0 | 0 | 11 | 17 | 33 | 6 |
| Herts. | 100 | 64 | 24 | 0 | 4 | 0 | 12 | 32 | 20 | 16 | 16 | 12 | 40 | 0 |
| All regions | 96 | 63 | 20 | 3 | 32 | 3 | 20 | 32 | 8 | 6 | 15 | 15 | 33 | 3 |

Percentage[a] of labourers' houses with

[a] See note to Table 7.
[b] Entry, backhouse, firehouse, little house, 'other room', or shop.
[c] Barn (fourteen instances), stable, woodhouse, hovel (five instances), outhouse, kiln.

than a hole in the wall to let out the smoke..."¹ In Suffolk, according to Robert Reyce, the mean person or cottager "thinks he doth very well if he can compass in his manner of building to raise his frame low, cover it with thatch, and to fill his wide panels (after they are well splinted and bound) with clay or culm enough well tempered, over which it may be some of more ability, both for warmth, continuance, and comeliness, do bestow a cast of hair, lime, and sand made into mortar and laid thereon, rough or smooth as the owner pleaseth." Elsewhere the poorer worker's cottage was probably little better. Sometimes, as in Cumberland and Northumberland, it was built of stone and clay; sometimes, as in Devon and Leicestershire, of cob or earth; occasionally, as on the North Downs, of flints and clunch; most often, however, of wattle and daub over a wooden frame, thatched with straw, reeds, or bracken. The common belief that a cottage erected on the waste overnight entitled its builder to undisputed possession, and the fact that few, if any, labourers' cottages of the period are known to survive, provides the most eloquent evidence of their flimsy construction.²

In heath and forest areas, poor cottages like these were being erected in great numbers in this period.³ For labourers turned adrift from other districts, woodlands afforded both living-room and building materials. And not infrequently, statutes notwithstanding, the judges at assizes ordered local landlords to allow such poor men to retain "quiet possession" of their hovels merely "in regard of [their] misery."⁴ In all probability, however, the story of two Kentish labourers who built themselves cottages on Longbridge Leaze, in the valley of the Stour, in James I's reign, was typical of many others. Because "they had erected

[1] Richard Carew, *Survey of Cornwall*, 1602, p. 66. Carew is actually referring to husbandmen's cottages in "times not past the remembrance of some living;" but by his own day those of husbandmen had generally improved, and probably the above description is more applicable to those of labourers of his time. He does not mention labourers' houses as such. See also G. E. Fussell, *The English Rural Labourer*, 1949, pp. 6–12 for further information regarding cottages; much of Mr Fussell's evidence, however, relates to husbandmen's or yeomen's, not labourers', houses.

[2] Reyce, *op. cit.*, p. 51; Bailey and Culley, *op. cit.*, p. 27 (published 1813, but referring to the older Northumbrian cottages); CSPD 1629–31, p. 562; *Cumb. & Westmorland Antiq. & Arch. Soc.*, NS, LIII, 1953, pp. 150, 151. In Cumberland, labourers' clay houses were said to take three or four hours to build; they were "rude earth and timber shanties that would not readily burn." For further information on labourers' houses see M. W. Barley, *The English Farmhouse and Cottage*, 1961, *passim*.

[3] Cf. PRO LR, 2, 194, f. 35. Many cases regarding "spoils of woods" in the Exchequer Special Commissions and Depositions also bear witness to cottage encroachment in woodland areas at this time; cf. also SP 14, 124, 137.

[4] Cf. T. G. Barnes, *Somerset Assize Orders, 1629–1640*, Som. Rec. Soc., LXV, 1959, p. 25.

the said cottages without any authority or lawful licence given them," and only "for that they were destitute of houses and had seen other cottages upon the same waste built by other poor men," the two men were fined by the parishioners of Willesborough in the court leet, forced to pay "recompense" for repair of the parish church, and ordered by three justices of the peace, themselves goaded into activity by the Exchequer, to pull down their hovels "according to his Majesty's commission." The two outcasts then wandered abroad, no doubt, till they found some other corner of land where they might squat down unmolested and unobserved.[1]

The furniture in labourers' cottages was often listed in great detail in probate inventories. It varied much in kind and value in different parts of the country. James Caddie of Cleator, in Cumberland, who died in the winter of 1597, left furniture valued at no more than 4s., although his cattle and sheep were worth nearly £4. John Cuthbertson of Wormington, who died in 1635, was rather better off, and left three chests, two chairs, two stands and coolers, three pots, three pans, an iron pot, a grate, a pair of tongs, and the "old bedclothes which the children lie on, at small value." In general, however, there were very few labourers in Cumberland, Westmorland, or north Lancashire whose domestic goods were worth more than £2. There was evidently very little money to spare in the north for anything but farmstock and the barest domestic necessities.

In the East Riding of Yorkshire a number of labourers lived in almost equally poverty-stricken circumstances. A labourer of Reedness, William Waterhouse, whose property was worth £6 5s. when he died in 1632, possessed only a cupboard, a little table, a chair, a single pot, one pan, and one "reckon." But a number of labourers' houses in this region were surprisingly well-furnished. William Heptinstall of Carleton, dying in 1611 worth £18, left in his dining parlour a livery table, a cupboard, two chairs, a little stool, two forms, two glass windows, various painted cloths, nineteen pewter dishes, two salts, four saucers, five porringers, two candlesticks, six cushions, and a carpet. His three lodging chambers were well supplied with beds, linen, and chests (together with crooks, pitchforks, and swine-grease); and in his kitchen, buttery, and 'firehouse' stood an impressive array

---

[1] E 178, 3960. The record of the case is very stained and partly illegible, but I believe the above account represents the gist of it, though possibly these two men were not actually fined. The Leaze was crown property. Village by-laws (cf., e.g., E 134, 18, James I, H 15, regarding Holme on Spalding Moor, Yorks.) often specified that only cottages of "ancient toft and croft" should have common rights, and new houses should have "no common at all." This jealousy over common rights naturally tended to divide local communities between the old and new settlers.

of pots, pans, bowls, chafing-dishes, skimmers, grid-irons, barrels, stands, liquor-tubs, flasks, flaskets, copper ladles, brewing vessels, and an iron range.

In Suffolk and Norfolk few labourers were so well off as William Heptinstall. On the whole, their domestic goods were rather meagre. A number of agricultural craftsmen, however, such as thatchers and daubers, lived in comparative comfort, and few labourers who were rich enough to leave inventories lived so hardly as in Cumberland.

In the Midlands, the counties to the north and west were markedly poorer than those to the south-east. In Derbyshire, Staffordshire, Shropshire, and Worcestershire, only one labourer in twelve left domestic goods worth more than £4; in Warwickshire and Northamptonshire, by contrast, one labourer in two. In forest parishes cottages were sometimes well-furnished, and the household property of a relatively wealthy peasant labourer, Robert Wood of Nuneaton, was valued in 1617 at nearly £11. Robert Wood lived in a seven-roomed farmhouse with kitchen, milkhouse, two chambers, two parlours, and a wainscoted hall. He had evidently made his money by weaving and cheese-making. When he died in the summer of 1617 he possessed nearly eighty cheeses stored in two chambers over 'the entry', and his milkhouse contained cheese-vats, milk-benches, butterpots, barrels, puncheons (or casks), and various brazen vessels. In his kitchen stood a cheese-press, a churn, a wash-tub, three pails, two looms, two spinning-wheels, and a number of meal-sieves, boulting-tubs, and brass and iron pots. In the chamber and parlours were beds and bedding, napkins, sheets, and a hand-towel; in his own bedroom a valuable joined bedstead and feather bed; and in the hall a set of pewter dishes, salts, cups, and candlesticks. Clearly Robert Wood was tiptoeing his way up into the ranks of the husbandmen; but he was still regarded by his neighbours as a farm-labourer when they came to compile his inventory.

In the west of England, as in the Midlands, the remoter counties were much the poorest. In Cornwall the labouring population was relatively small, and the household goods of farmworkers were generally meagre. John Tregellest of Cubert, for instance, who died in 1637, left only a table-board, a form, a coffer, three dishes, and an old coverlet and bedstead worth in all only 14s. 9d., or less than one third the value of his solitary cow, four sheep, one lamb, and labouring tools. In the wooded parishes of Somerset and Gloucester, on the other hand, though labourers were rarely as well off as in the east Midlands, two out of three left domestic goods worth over £4. The household gear of Philip Wilkins of Chillington was valued at nearly £5 when he died in the autumn of 1634. Like Robert Wood of Nuneaton, though in a smaller way, he had made his money by making cheese and butter, no doubt for sale in the neighbouring dairy markets of Yeovil and Ilminster. His goods included a cheese-rack, a cheese-stean (a stone weight or vessel), a cheese-stock, a butter-barrel, a skimmer, and various buckets, pails, and barrels; his furnishings comprised a press, two forms, two coffers, two dustbeds, a little bedstead with coverlet, blankets, feather-bolsters, and pillow; together with the usual array of pothooks, platters, porringers, brazen crocks, kettles, a cup, a salt, and a candlestick.

In Hertfordshire, peasant-labourers' cottages were particularly comfortable. Their furnishings were usually worth at least £7 in the early seventeenth century, and occasionally more than £25. Even a labourer with no farm stock, and only his wages and work as a woodman to support him, like Thomas Carter of Pirton, sometimes left household property valued at nearly £10. One of the wealthiest Hertfordshire labourers was William Layfield of Shenley, who died in the spring of 1612 leaving property worth no less than £38 11s. 2d. Layfield's income, apart from his wages, came partly from dairying and bee-keeping, partly from a small piece of arable land recently sown with wheat, and partly from work in the neighbouring woods and from spinning flax and wool. In his hall stood a cupboard, table, form, bench, joined stool, wicker-chair, two little chairs, three cushions, and a collection of pewter spoons, brass pots and kettles, tin dripping pans, and posnets. In the chimney-space hung his wife's cob-iron, frying-pan, bellows, tongs, spit, grid-iron, and trivet. In the milkhouse and buttery were bowls, tubs, firkins, cheese-moots, powdering-troughs, boulting-hutches, and a butter-churn; in his own chamber there were beds, chests, boxes, a clothes-press, and a bedstead worth no less than £5; together with eight pairs of sheets, four table-cloths, a dozen table-napkins, two cupboard-cloths, and four towels. The comfort of William Layfield's home evidently owed much to the diligence of his wife: for not only would she have been responsible for the butter- and cheese-making, but for spinning flax and hemp for her prized store of sheets, towels, cloths, and napkins. There can have been few idle moments for the busy fingers of Mistress Layfield.

For the domestic goods of labourers too poor to leave inventories, we are dependent on a few comments of topographers. According to Carew, the bedding of poor people in Cornwall consisted of nothing but straw and a blanket, and the rest of their substance "a mazer and a pan or two." The Elizabethan Harrison, referring to earlier generations, remarks that if servants "had any sheet above them, it was well, for seldom had they any under their bodies to keep them from the pricking straws that ran oft through the canvas [of the pallet] and rased their hardened hides." John Taylor, the water-poet, describes a poor weaver's cottage at Hastings as offering

> ...no lodging but the floor,
> No stool to sit, no lock upon the door,
> No straw to make us litter in the night,
> Nor any candlesticks to hold the light.

According to Bishop Hall, the "thatched spars" of a poor man's cote were

> ...furred with sluttish soot
> A whole inch thick, shining like blackmoor's brows
> Through smoke that through the headless barrel blows.
> At his bed's feet feeden his stalled team,
> His swine beneath, his pullen o'er the beam.

None of these descriptions, however, comes from the pen of labourers themselves; *they*, no doubt, would have distinguished many varying degrees of poverty and cleanliness in the cottages of their fellow workers, such as the casual glances of poets and gentlemen failed to observe.[1]

Labourers living in the farmhouse were often relatively well-off. Until Charles I's reign, they usually fed at their master's table, and were lodged in simply furnished folks' or servants' chambers, or else on boarded bedsteads put up in barns and outhouses at harvest time.[2] Their life was often hard, but not necessarily any more so than that of a hop-picker in a modern Kentish hutment. John Doggett's folks' chamber at Albury in Hertfordshire, for instance, contained two bedsteads, with flock beds, bolsters, and blankets; Thomas Granwine's at Sandridge four beds, together with bedding, valued at £6; John Gybbe's at Rickmansworth two beds and a coffer. On some farms seasonal workers, instead of being boarded in the house, were lodged in the cottages of local widows and labourers, their diet being paid for by the farmer who employed them.[3]

Probate inventories also sometimes afford us a brief description of the labourer's clothing. Generally speaking, it was worth about 7 per cent of his total wealth: rather more in poor districts like the north-west (12 per cent), rather less in prosperous areas like the south Midlands (5 per cent). In Cumberland, in the early seventeenth century, the labourer's apparel was worth on the average about 10s.; in the north

---

[1] Carew, *loc. cit.*; Fussell, *op. cit.*, pp. 9, 11, 8; Harrison, *op. cit.*, Part I, p. 240. Carew actually refers to husbandmen of previous generations; but by his own day husbandmen were better housed and his remarks would probably be more applicable to labourers.

[2] Best, *op. cit.*, p. 48.    [3] Harland, *op. cit.*, *passim*

and west Midlands about 8s.; in East Anglia 13s. 4d.; and in Warwickshire, Hertfordshire, and Somerset, usually about £1, sometimes as much as £2.¹ Only very occasionally do inventories describe the labourer's clothing in any detail. The apparel of George Sprott of Abbey Holme in Cumberland is said to have included a leather doublet and a pair of blue breeches; that of John Hyende of Blockley in Gloucestershire a new coat, a new shirt, a shift, a jerkin, and an old ragged coat; that of John Fessher of Portbury in Somerset, two coats, two jackets, a doublet, three pairs of hose, and a cap, in all worth £1. On working days labourers often wore cloths made of sack-cloth, canvas, or skins; their holiday wear might consist of a suit of woollen cloth, containing six yards of material and lasting them perhaps two years. At the end of each year of service, their master might provide them with a new smock or shirt, and a pair of shoes and stockings, and at harvest time with a pair of gloves.²

The labourer's food, like his furniture and clothing, varied much from region to region. The staple articles of his diet were bread, pies, and puddings. Judging by probate inventories and the reports of local justices, the poor man's breadflour was usually made from barley, occasionally, however, from oats, wheat, and rye.³ During times of dearth, and at all times amongst the very poor, mixed grain was often used: either oats, peas, beans, and acorns, or else beans, peas, oats, tares, and lentils, and no doubt other mixtures. In the East Riding, according to Henry Best, "poor folks put usually a peck of peas to a bushel of rye, and some again two pecks of peas to a frundell [*sc.* two pecks] of massledine [*sc.* wheat and rye], and say that these make hearty bread." In Norfolk, during the dearth of 1623, "the poorer sort" were forced to mix buckwheat with their barley-flour, although, according to the justices, they had not formerly been "acquainted with [it], and therefore shew much loathness to use [it]."⁴

During the greater part of the period, as already remarked, very few cottagers grew their own breadcorn. The great majority depended for their supplies on small weekly amounts bought in local market towns,

¹ To some extent, however, these figures are affected by local differences in the value of money.
² SP 16, 537, 17; Fussell, *Loder's Farm Accounts*, pp. 70, 107, 123; Lancs. RO, inventory of Robert Caton and his wife, of Cark in Cartmel, Lancs. (1590).
³ Sir William Ashley, in *The Bread of our Forefathers*, 1928, seems to me greatly to over-emphasize the importance of rye as the standard breadcorn at this time: justices' reports, *inter alia*, frequently indicate that barley was the staple grain among the poorer classes. See also vol. 3 of this paperback series, p. 24.
⁴ Harrison, *op. cit.*, Part I, p. 153; Fussell, *English Rural Labourer*, p. 30; Best, *op. cit.*, p. 104; SP 14, 138, 35.

or on occasional purchases from some itinerant "badger of the Forest."¹ In Somerset, for instance, nearly seven thousand labourers and artisans obtained their weekly corn and meal from the two small markets of Bruton and Wincanton. In Derbyshire many poor workmen and miners attended the great corn mart in the county-town, to which barley was brought by way of the Trent from as far afield as East Anglia and even Danzig. At Bury St Edmunds, in James I's reign, "four millers at the least weekly... brought every day in the week three or four horseloads of meal of rye and barley, to the great relief and comfort of the poorest sort of people, who being very many in number, can buy meal of them by the penny and twopence, and such small sums... and employ part to bread, part to make a pudding for the relief of them and their children."² In consequence of this increasing dependence on local markets, periods of dearth struck the labouring population with growing severity. When prices rose, they were not able to compete with brewers and maltsters for the available supplies of barley, and, as the reports of justices to the Privy Council indicate, they were often reduced to extreme misery.³

Next to bread, the principal items in the labourer's diet were cheese, lard, milk, and occasionally butter. Judging from probate inventories, cheese was frequently to be found in labourers' store-rooms, and it was certainly more widely eaten than inventories themselves suggest. Even the tin-miners of Devon, the poorest of the poor, reckoned some kind of hard cheese in their diet. Together with butter and lard, "skimmed cheese" (as Baxter called it) probably formed the only fat and protein elements in the poorer farmworkers' meals.⁴

Of the various kinds of butchers' meat eaten by farmworkers, the most usual was swine-flesh. Though few labourers kept pigs of their own, many had flitches of bacon hanging in their roof or chimney, presumably cured by their wives and purchased from neighbouring smallholders when they slaughtered their own animals. Beef was eaten by labourers who fed at their master's table, but in the inventories of out-labourers it is rarely mentioned.⁵ The cottager's own cattle were primarily milch-beasts, or if, on occasion, fatting animals, they were usually destined for the market. A whole beef would have lasted a labourer's household several months, and would probably have required an expenditure on salting and storing beyond his means.

¹ Worcester Diocesan Registry, inventory of Chrystyan Darby, 1545 (of Old Swinford, Worcs.).
² SP 16, 187, 51; SP 14, 137, 33.i, and cf. 33 and SP 14, 138, 18.
³ Cf. Harrison, *op. cit.*, Part I, pp. 297–300; and see 'The Marketing of Agricultural Produce', pp. 576–7, 582–6, *infra*.
⁴ Fussell, *English Rural Labourer*, p. 28; *Devonshire Association*, XLVII, 1915, p. 342.
⁵ Harland, *op. cit.*, II, p. 244 *et passim*.

Mutton is not referred to in any of the three-hundred labourers' inventories analysed for this study: judging by references to wool in store, the farmworker's sheep were valued rather for their wool-clip than for their capabilities as mutton-producers, though their carcases may have been sold to local butchers.

Except in areas where wildfowl or deer were plentiful, other kinds of meat were rarely eaten by labourers. Occasionally, a cottager may have slaughtered one of his hens or ducks, and possibly, at feast times, a goose. But the labourer's own fowls were invariably too few to have formed a regular part in his diet, and it is improbable that he purchased much in the open market. He or his wife were more likely to be found among the sellers than the buyers at the poultry-cross of the neighbouring town. In the vicinity of parks and deer-forests, however, labourers not infrequently varied their fare with a haunch of venison. There was certainly a good deal of illicit deer-hunting in forests like Galtres in Yorkshire and in royal parks like Knole, Postern, Leigh, and South Frith in Kent. In Hatfield Chase, on the borders of Yorkshire and Lincolnshire, the poor were said at one time to have "almost lived" off the abundance of deer and rabbits, before the Chase was enclosed in Charles I's reign.[1]

The rest of the labourer's food came mostly from his own garden or from the wild places of the parish. Roots like radishes, carrots, and parsnips, green vegetables such as cabbage and lettuce, and probably herbs like mint, sage, balm, and parsley were commonly grown in cottage gardens; their value was too slight to be worth mentioning in inventories, but occasionally a labourer kept a load of roots in his loft, worth 3s. or 4s. In some cottage gardens there were also a few apple trees (the crop is occasionally mentioned in inventories); and by the end of the seventeenth century turnips and potatoes were being grown by the poor. For the rest, the labourer gathered brambles and herbs in the hedgerows; juniper berries on Lakeland fells and Surrey downs; sloes and bilberries on southern heaths and chartlands; chestnuts and cobs in Kentish woods and hazel copses; and wild nuts of various kinds, when the annual Nutday came round, on north-country manors like Cartmel.[2] In a land with a population of only four or five millions, and at a time when many heaths and moors were still partially uninhabited, wild life of all kinds was more abundant than it is today, and rural labourers profited accordingly.

The labourer's drink, like his food, differed much according to his neighbourhood and his own resources. Some labourers had plentiful

[1] BM, Lansdowne MS 897, f. 51; LP XIII, ii, pp. 542-3, and cf. XIII, i, p. 106.
[2] Harrison, op. cit., Part I, p. 259; Lancs. RO, DDCa.7.3; cf. Fussell, English Rural Labourer, p. 33.

supplies of milk from their kine, a few from sheep. Some evidently brewed their own ale and beer. In East Anglia and the south and west of England they drank cider; in the Welsh Marches mead and metheglin. According to Norden, poor heath-dwellers drank "sour whey and goats' milk;" according to Richard Baxter "skimmed milk and whey-curds." Few farm-workers were so poor as the Devon tin-miner, whose drink was "commonly the dew of heaven, which he taketh either from his shovel or spade, or in the hollow of his hand." In the hayfields and at harvest time, at any rate, there was no lack of beer and ale for even the poorest day-labourers.[1]

Fuel supplies varied greatly from county to county and according to the extent of the village waste. In mining areas like Kingswood Forest and the Forest of Dean, or in parts of Derbyshire, Lancashire, and Northumberland, labourers not infrequently burnt coal. In woodland parishes and in royal forests and chases rights of fuelboot and top and lop were sometimes valuable; in parts of Kent labourers took fallen branches and brushwood whenever they pleased. In northern fell parishes, on the barren heathlands of Surrey and Hampshire, and on west country moorlands, they dug turf or peat. Elsewhere, if wood and coal were lacking, furze, bracken, thorn-bushes, and elder-scrub were widely utilized. Over much of England, however, particularly in the Midland champion areas and on chalk downlands, the labourer's fuel problem was often acute. The long winter months can have brought little joy to labourers on the Yorkshire Wolds or in the woodless parishes of Leicestershire, where people burned straw and cow-dung, or in those Wiltshire villages where groups of cottagers were forced to cook their daily meals by the meagre heat of a single common fire.[2]

Taken as a whole, the proportion of wealth invested in domestic property by the wealthier labourers markedly increased as the Tudor and Stuart period proceeded. As already remarked in England as a whole this proportion expanded from 40 per cent before 1600 to 50 per cent thereafter: rising in the northern lowlands from 18 to 29 per cent, in the common-field villages of the Midlands from 35 to 46 per cent, and in the woodland parishes of Hertfordshire from 59 to 69 per cent. The average value of the labourer's domestic property, in the

[1] *Ibid.*, pp. 28, 31–35 (but much of Mr Fussell's evidence relates to yeomen or husbandmen, not labourers); Thomas Westcote, *A View of Devonshire in MDCXXX*, 1845, p. 53; Harrison, *op. cit.*, Part III, p. 180; HMC, *Reports*, XIII, ii, p. 280; Lodge, *op. cit.*, p. xxxv.

[2] This account is based on village by-laws and disputes in Exchequer Special Commissions and Depositions in PRO; cf. also SP 14, 58, 7; Burton, *loc. cit.* In Cambridgeshire sedge was used, locally called 'stuff-reek'.—*A sad Relation of a dreadful Fire at Cottenham,* 1676, p. 3.

reigns of James I and Charles I, ranged from about £1 10s. in the northern lowlands to £3 10s. in Midland field parishes, £4 in East Anglia, £4 10s. in Midland forest parishes, £6 in Somerset, and £7 10s. in Hertfordshire.[1] To some extent, these varying levels reflect local differences in the value of money; but they also indicate real differences in home comfort. One telling indication of the rising standard of living amongst the better-off labourers may be mentioned. The furniture of early Tudor cottages was evidently rough carpentry work, of small value, quite possibly constructed by the labourer himself: whereas by Charles I's reign many a cottager possessed at least one article of *joined* furniture, properly constructed by a trained craftsman, carefully described by the neighbours who drew up his inventory, and lending a new touch of modest luxury to his home.

Amongst the poorer labourers, however—that anonymous majority who were too indigent to leave any wills or inventories—there can have been few luxuries. We know little enough about them, and the comments of contemporaries were often vague and undiscriminating. But all the evidence suggests that their economic fortunes were declining; that their cottages were cramped and poverty-stricken; and that their lives were rich in nothing but hungry children.

## H. THE CHANGING PATTERN OF LABOURING LIFE

Until the end of the sixteenth century the labouring community was still an essentially peasant society. With infinite local variation in detail, and in spite of the growing number of very small holdings, it was still characterized by a certain unity of outlook, and that unity was based, in the main, on distinctively peasant preconceptions. Hitherto, it has been primarily the economic aspects of that community that have engaged us; it now remains to penetrate, if possible, into the mind of the peasant-labourer himself, and to envisage, as far as may be, his aspirations and ideals. The evidence is necessarily slight, since cottagers rarely recorded their own thoughts and can only be observed through the eyes of outsiders; but, such as it is, it may enable us to visualize the labourer as a human being, instead of an economic abstraction, and to sense the difference in his outlook from that of the rural wage-worker of today. We may do so most simply by posing a series of questions: what was the characteristic attitude of peasant-labourers to their land, their stock, their families, their work, their pastimes, and their religion?

Land is the basis of all peasant societies, and the traditional attachment of the labouring peasant to his own farmhold and common-

[1] See Table 5.

rights can be sensed in many Tudor and Stuart lawsuits. At Pontefract in 1611, for instance, the poorer tenants kept certain proposed land-dealings in which they were involved "very secret" from the other party concerned, lest "their offers should be refused, and so in the end be turned to their prejudice."[1] At Leeds in Kent, when it was rumoured in 1608 that the tenants' leases would not be renewed, it "went so near...the heart" of one "poor and simple man, as he lived but few days after, leaving behind him a poor wife lying bedrid, and 3 small children, having no other dwelling, nor means but the alms of the parish to live on." Of the lengths to which poor commoners were prepared to go in defence of their common-rights, mention has already been made; so late as the nineteenth century, the tenants of Southowram, near Halifax, refused to give their landlord permission to enclose a few yards of waste land near his lodge at Stonyroyd.[2]

The attachment of labourers to their farm property is equally evident. It comes to light in many probate inventories of the period, with their carefully listed details of each cottager's stock and crops. It also appears in a number of Chancery disputes relating to the property of Tudor and Stuart farm labourers, of which one concerning Richard Veredy, a labourer of Sedgeley in Staffordshire, in Elizabeth's reign, may be taken as typical. Veredy, "a very poor man and having a wife and seven children, all at his own only cost and charges," possessed one single "horse of his own, being worth to be sold fifty shillings, and did use to let out the said horse to hire by the day to divers persons...as well for his own relief as for the necessity of his neighbours, which was a good stay of his living and the greatest part of his substance." One day, a certain Mistress Annes Gestone, "naming herself to be a surgeon and coming and going divers times to the said town of Sedgeley," requested to hire the horse for a period of four days. Riding it away into Worcestershire, with its saddle, bridle, and pillow, she there sold it to John and Joan Moole, and pocketed the proceeds. Thereupon, Richard Veredy "made great move and labour to seek out the said Annes," and followed her as far as Droitwich, where he found John and Joan Moole and offered them the full price they had paid Annes Gestone for the horse, in order to regain his one animal.[3]

The regard of peasant labourers for their families, and the strength of family ties in labouring households, comes to light in the scrupulous

---

[1] SP 14, 65, 75 (relating to 1611). The other parties were Sir Henry Savile, jr., Sir Henry Slingsby, and Thomas Blande, on behalf of the king.

[2] SP 14, 37, 35; J. Lister, 'Some Local Star Chamber Cases', *Halifax Antiq. Soc.*, 1927, pp. 199–200.

[3] C 3, 185, 47; for other cases relating to poor people and their animals, cf. C 3, 20, 83 and Req. 2, 242, 30.

care with which they endeavoured to provide for them in their wills. Of many examples which might be adduced, four must suffice. John Perry of Brinklow, in Warwickshire, who died in 1634, left his property to his son, with the request that he should provide his widow with "all needful, sufficient, and convenient meat and drinks, apparel and lodging, landresses and all other necessaries decent and meet for a woman of her age, state, and condition." John Goosy of Old, in Northamptonshire, dying in 1613, left "the cottage-house where I now dwell in, with...the timber and hovels in the yard," and "all the outhouses and floors to that cottage belonging" to his second son Thomas; half his cattle and goods to his daughter Avice, together with "a little house called the stable, to be in, if she need, so long as she lives unmarried;" £10 in money to his third son Edward, to be paid within six months by his brother Thomas; but nothing to his eldest son Robert, because he had already received the lease of "a quartern land in Naseby, and a great brass pot." Robert Pearman of Ardeley in Hertfordshire, dying in 1619, left all his property to his wife, so long as she remained a widow, but if she remarried, it was to be equally divided between his two sons: Robert was to have the east end of the house, the north half of the barn, the "little garden-place fenced in with faggots behind it," and two acres of the family holding in the common fields: Edward was to have the west end of the house, the little garden attached, the south half of the barn, and the other half of the family holding; while the orchard and well were to be held in common between them. Finally, Thomas Smith, a poor widower of Great Amwell, who died in 1567, left "one cow and one bullock, and my daughter Joan" to his brother-in-law in Cheshunt; "one cow and one bullock, and my son John" to his cousin in Hertford; and "the residue of my goods and movables, and the residue of my children," to his neighbour John Rolfe, whom he entreated to look after all his children, and receive all his property, if his kinsmen refused the care of them.[1] Quite clearly labourers like these regulated their conduct towards dependants by the recognized social customs of their order, and went to considerable lengths to keep their children out of the workhouse, even to the extent of 'bequeathing' them along with their goods and cattle. Neither is it without significance that they were careful to provide, more or less equally, for *all* their dependants: for the tyranny of primogeniture did not usually hold sway in the cottages of the labouring peasantry.

[1] Smith's will is quoted in C. M. Matthews, 'Annals of the Poor: taken from the Records of a Hertfordshire Village', *History Today*, v, 1955, p. 701; the rest are in the relevant county record offices. Smith is not stated to be a labourer, but the conditions of his will suggest he was either a labourer or possibly a husbandman.

The attitude of labourers to their work has already been referred to. In the sixteenth century, quite as much as in the twentieth, farmworkers were "masters of many complicated and exquisite crafts—land-drainage, shepherding, forestry, hedge-laying, thatching, plowing—and the repository of much knowledge, part-traditional and part acquired by experience and acute observation, of the vagaries of nature."[1] They did not think of themselves as *labourers* merely, but rather as ploughmen, horsemen, hopmen, shepherds, hedgers, cowmen, reapers, shearers, thatchers, foresters, threshers, or experts in any of the other score or more of skilled crafts on the farm. The detailed lists of their work-tools in probate inventories—the bills, scythes, shovels, skoppets, dung-picks, spittles, and trowels; the axes, hatchets, handsaws, augers, mattocks, chisels, and other implements—suggest something of that "unsuspected fame amongst their own people" which many a skilled labourer of the period enjoyed in his own community.[2]

The pleasures and pastimes of farm-labourers were closely interwoven with their work. Many of the old country songs seem to have been connected with agricultural tasks, such as ploughing, milking, and churning. Labourers, no doubt, played a major part in the Plough Monday plays of the period. Wandering pipers were sometimes paid a few pence by Yorkshire farmers to play through the long spring days to the sheep-clippers on the Wolds.[3] Cornish labourers, according to a Georgian topographer, used to sing to their plough-oxen "in a sort of chaunt, of very agreeable modulation, which, floating through the air from different distances, produces a striking effect both on the ear and imagination..."[4] The great feast of the year, the harvest-home, celebrated the successful completion of the year's work, when the farmer invited "all the work folks and their wives that helped them that harvest" to a supper of boiled beef, apple pies and cream, and hot cakes and ale.[5] Although not directly connected with farm-work, sports such as wrestling, hurling, and vaulting, at which "the meaner sort who labour hard all the week" were encouraged by the Stuarts "to refresh their spirits," also served to "inseme their bodies with hardenes and strength," and to fit them for the heavy labour of the fields.[6] Even a purely political occasion, like the restoration of Charles

[1] Quoted from F. Brett Young, *Portrait of a Village*, 1937, by F. A. Walbank in *The English Scene*, 1947 edn., p. 67, and referring to a modern Midland village.

[2] The words quoted in the text are from George Bourne, *The Bettesworth Book*, 1920, p. 7. 'Spittles' are small spades or spuds.

[3] Best, *op. cit.*, p. 97; cf. *Montgomeryshire Collections*, LV, Part I, 1958, p. 80.

[4] Quoted in W. H. Hudson, *A Shepherd's Life*, Everyman edn., 1949, p. 100.

[5] Best, *op. cit.*, p. 108.

[6] *Devonshire Association*, XLVII, 1915, p. 342; S. R. Gardiner, *The Constitutional Documents of the Puritan Revolution, 1625–1660*, 1906 edn., pp. 99, 101.

II, coinciding as it did with traditional Maytime games, was welcomed in Kent with "a kind of rural triumph, expressed by the country swains in a morris dance, with the old music of tabor and pipe,... with all agility and cheerfulness imaginable..."[1] Unlike the leisure pastimes of today, the recreations of Tudor and Stuart labourers were not merely a means of escape: they formed a kind of inherited art or ritual, centring round their daily occupations, and based upon the ordinary sights and sounds of the village.

No less closely bound up with the work of Tudor and Stuart labourers was their religion. In the frequent recitation of the Psalms in church, for instance, the sights and sounds of the village fields where they worked were continually re-echoed. "I will take no bullock out of thine house," they would have heard, "nor he-goat out of thy folds. For all the beasts of the forest are mine, and so are the cattle upon a thousand hills." Or, again: "Thou crownest the year with thy goodness, and thy clouds drop fatness...The folds shall be full of sheep; the valleys also shall stand so thick with corn, that they shall laugh and sing." Or, yet again: "So we, that are thy people, the sheep of thy pasture, shall give thee thanks for ever, and will alway be shewing forth thy praise from generation to generation." For the peasant-labourers of Stuart England, the vivid imagery of the Bible must have come with an immediacy it has largely lost for the urban worker of today. Was not King David himself once a shepherd boy, and Ruth a poor gleaner in the fields of Boaz? It may be that farmworkers did not regularly attend their parish church, but, when they did, the pastoral poetry of the Bible came native with all the warmth of familiarity.[2]

The survival of many distinctly peasant attitudes and aspirations amongst the labourers of Tudor England was of course not fortuitous. The aspirations remained, because the social institutions and traditions essential to their existence also remained, largely intact. The abiding force of local loyalty, of manorial custom, and of feudal authority, was still sufficient, in a changing world, to maintain the vitality of many peasant preconceptions.

The force of local loyalty, if gradually (and perhaps temporarily) being undermined by the increasing mobility of the labouring population, was still immensely powerful. For the great majority of labourers the local community was still the natural sphere of life and thought, and a place, despite its jealousies, "where much affection and pity of neighbours doth reign." The past events of their lives they still reckoned, not by the regnal or dominical year, but by some local "commotion

---

[1] Alan Everitt, *The Community of Kent and the Great Rebellion, 1640-60*, 1966, p. 318.
[2] Cf. Peter Laslett, *The World we have lost*, 1965, pp. 71-3.

in the time of the reign of the late King Edward VI."[1] The narrowness of their environment was often such that, when a handful of Suffolk labourers were sent across the county border into Essex, during the Civil War, to a military rendezvous at Saffron Walden, they soon found themselves in a "strange country" and "benighted." Even the administration of the new Elizabethan poor law, which might have been expected to create a sense of class solidarity, only served to root the typical labourer more deeply in his own community. When local jealousy between towns and villages could force the justices of two counties to spend weary hours in determining whether a single "poor impotent person" should be cared for by Dunster or Tiverton, it was not surprising if the sense of class loyalty among farmworkers remained rudimentary. The inhabitants of the two places were quite as likely to fight with one another as with their employers and landlords.[2]

Closely bound up with the strength of local loyalty was the continuing force of manorial custom. The custom of the Tudor village was no vague body of tradition, but a rigorous, detailed, and precise *corpus* of local law. It regulated the lives of all the people on the manor; it sometimes governed the usage of the remotest corner of the parish, even to the empty mountain tops of Lakeland fells. Customs of inheritance, rules of cultivation, stints for sheep and cattle, maintenance of paths and hedges, rights of fuelboot, houseboot, and hayboot, precautions against fire: these and countless other matters affecting the welfare of labourers came within the purview of the manorial court. According to the Court Book of Billington in Lancashire, for instance, no one was to dig turves on the Moor before 12 May; no one was to "play at the ball" or any other unlawful game, such as quoiting and pitching, in Chapel Garth; the nests of crows or magpies on local farmhouses were to be pulled down, and their young destroyed; and every tenant paying a rent of 10d. annually was to plant, near his house, at least one apple- or crab-tree, one birch, six alders, and four quick-staves yearly. At Burton Agnes in the East Riding, a Book of Pains and Orders for 1632 laid down that no man should allow his servant to keep above four shorn sheep and lambs; that no one should keep any geese from 3 May till average-time (viz. till after harvest); that no kine, oxen, or other horned beasts should be tethered in west field or middle field; and no one should cut or cart away more whins (viz. furze) than he could carry upon his back. At King's Langley in

[1] LP XII, i, p. 234; Cecil Torr, *Small Talk at Wreyland*, 1926, pp. 43-4 (quoting document of 1602 referring to the Cornish Rising of 1549; the words cited are from the deposition of a yeoman, but would have been no less typical of a labourer).
[2] Alan Everitt, *Suffolk and the Great Rebellion, 1640-1660*, Suffolk Records Society, III, 1961, p. 94; Barnes, *op. cit.*, pp. 6, 11, 50, and cf. p. 24.

Hertfordshire no inhabitant was allowed to leave any timber, dung, or wood on the king's highway; no one was to receive any "foreigner" into his house without first giving security; no one was to put any cattle in the lanes or highways, except in charge of a keeper; no one was to pick any cherries or other fruit growing on the lord's waste in Chipperfield; and every villager with lands adjoining the river was to cut down the water-weeds adjoining his property, once a year.[1]

That such orders were duly enforced, with more or less strictness, is clear from any number of court-rolls of the period. At Whitmore in Staffordshire Thomas Stevenson was fined in the manor-court for putting horses and mares into his neighbour's field in the night-time, and Richard Blackeshawe for chasing the sheep of other tenants "with his doggys." At Wentworth Woodhouse in Yorkshire Robert Lowden was presented for not sending his servants to the common work, Francis Burton for tethering his horses in the sown fields, Gilbert Crowden for driving six oxen through the hardcorn field, Thomas Swift for plowing a common balk in the Barron Field going towards Lanehead, and seventeen persons for not having their swine duly ringed. At Little Crosby, in Lancashire, Ellen Davie was fined 3d. for tethering horses in the Town Field, Elizabeth Rice 4d. for "carting down a butt of meadow and treading corn," Margaret Brough 6d. for putting more cattle than her stint into the Town Field, and Margaret Rice, worst offender of all, 3s. 4d. for reviling the jury in open court.[2]

Judged by modern notions of individual freedom, such repressive customs may appear pettifogging; but for the peasant labourer they were rather a protection against overmighty neighbours than a restriction. Their readiness to defend them is shown by the records of many a Tudor lawsuit; and even today the empty court-room of an Elizabethan manorhouse like Boughton Monchelsea Place, with its bare wooden benches ranged round the whitewashed walls, still conveys some impression of the stark, yet not entirely unwelcome, authority of manorial custom in the peasant labourer's life.

The protection of the manor-court would have been of little avail, however, without the feudal authority of the gentry to uphold it. So much has been written, not without reason, about rack-renting and enclosing landlords, that it is easy to forget that, unless vital economic

[1] Lancs. RO, DD Pt, Box 22, Billington (1559–66); C. V. Collier, 'Burton Agnes Courts, Miscellanea II', Yorks. Arch. Soc., Rec.Ser., LXXIV, 1929, pp. 87, 93, 94, 95; Herts. RO, 20737, m. 1 and dorse.
[2] William Salt Library, Stafford, D 1743, M 130 and M 123 (1569 and 1597); Sheffield Central Library, Wentworth Woodhouse Muniments, C 7, 80, 99, 122, 85 (1626, 1629, 1653, 1666, 1641); Lancs. RO, DD BL.48.35 (1667).

interests were at stake, rural squires were as anxious to preserve the customary order as their tenants and labourers. Only a fraction of the 800 or so gentry of counties like Suffolk, Kent, and Somerset, and probably only a small proportion of the 300 or so of counties like Leicestershire and Wiltshire, were in any way concerned with enclosure. As the Civil War was to show, the great majority of the gentry and peasantry, in their almost morbid anxiety to preserve the traditional fabric of local society, generally stood side by side.

The kind of feudal protection, in the widest sense, afforded by a well-disposed squire to the labourers of his neighbourhood might be illustrated from many examples. Three instances, all drawn from the county of Kent, must suffice. At Sellindge, in the east of the county, when the local parishioners' title to certain lands was disputed by one Alexander Lewknor about 1586, Squire Ralph Heyman undertook, and paid half the charges of, a lawsuit to re-establish their rights, and the whole charge of a second suit two years later, when two labourers' leases of these lands were challenged by a wealthy local yeoman. In the next parish of Brabourne, about 1574, when "certain rich men who had great stock of cattle did go about to break the...custom [of the common]," Sir Thomas Scott, "being then lord of the said manor of Brabourne...caused the court-rolls of the said manor to be produced and read unto divers...of the said tenants," and, in the interests of the poorer inhabitants, commanded "the said greedy-minded tenants" to "desist from their said oppression and surcharge of the said common..." At Barham, in Charles I's reign, when Goodwife Gilnot was "accused to be a witch," and was likely to lose her good name and her livelihood, Squire Henry Oxinden wrote to his brother-in-law, a justice of the peace, requesting "that you will not lightly believe such false and malicious reports as you hear, or may hear, alleged against this woman, whom I believe to be religiously disposed. Certain I am," he added, "she hath undergone a great deal of labour to bring up her charge of children, and hath taken no small care to have them instructed up in the fear of God, and therefore it is the more pity to have her labour under so great a scandal. And for so much as the neighbours healp [sic] themselves together, and the poor woman's cry, though it reach to heaven, is scarce heard here upon earth, I thought I was bound in conscience to speak in her behalf..." Quite clearly, men like Heyman, Oxinden, and Scott, all of them representatives of ancient Kentish families, took their responsibilities to their local community seriously.[1] The economic gulf between them and their farmworkers was already wide; but they were still as interested in farming as their

---

[1] Req. 2, 223, 40; C 2, Jas. I, G 5, 70; Dorothy Gardiner, ed., *The Oxinden Letters, 1607–1642*, 1933, p. 222.

own labourers; they still spoke or understood the local Kentish dialect; and they still believed in old notions of social duty and 'hospitality'.

During the seventeenth century, however, the unity of peasant labouring society, and the protection afforded to the labourer by the customary order of society, were beginning to break down. That unity had no doubt never been complete, and its basis was not finally destroyed till the eighteenth or nineteenth century. But it was probably in the latter half of our own period, with the growth of population, the decline in real wages, and the progress of commercial farming, that some of the most distinctive changes in labouring society took their rise. By the time the Civil War broke out, the labouring community was manifestly split by a twofold cleavage within its own ranks.

In part this cleavage was an economic one. As the labouring population increased, the pressure on land became continually more acute, an ever-growing army of landless labourers came into being, and the distinction between rich and poor labourers became more pronounced. A minority of farmworkers, still possessed of sizeable holdings or valuable common rights, were enabled to profit by the new commercial openings of the age and work their way up into the ranks of the husbandmen; while the middle and lower ranks of cottagers were slowly losing their landed rights and sinking to the level of mere wage-workers. The former were able to add new rooms to their cottages, invest an increasing proportion of their income in domestic comforts, purchase a few pieces of good joined furniture, and leave a modest competence to their sons and widows. The latter inhabited flimsy cots and hovels, fed "very hardly with oaten bread, sour whey, and goats' milk," lived very close to the poverty line, and in time of dearth sank far beneath it.[1]

The cleavage in labouring society was not only economic, however. It also consisted in a growing distinction between working communities in forest and in fielden areas. In the nucleated villages characteristic of the latter, forms of society were often deeply rooted, social classes were relatively stable and distinct, manorial customs fairly rigid, political habits comparatively orderly, and the labourer's outlook deeply imbued with the prevalent preconceptions of church and manor-house. In these fielden areas labourers often tended to remain rooted in the same district from one generation to the next: working on the same farm, specializing in the same crafts, passing on the same customary skills to their children, and more or less freely accepting their dependence on squire and parson. Few of them were really well-off,

[1] Harrison, *op. cit.*, Part III, p. 180; and see 'The Marketing of Agricultural Produce', in vol. 4 of this paperback series, pp. 125–6, 131–5.

their holdings were usually small, and their common rights often negligible; but the very poor were less numerous than in remote woodland settlements, and manorial charity was probably more abundant.

In the isolated hamlets characteristic of forest settlements, by contrast, the roots of society were often relatively shallow, the population was largely composed of a single social class, the customs of the manor were sometimes vague or difficult to enforce, the instincts of the poor were anything but law-abiding, and the authority of church and manor-house seemed remote. In these areas, labouring society frequently consisted, on one hand, of a core of indigenous peasants with sizeable holdings and a relatively high standard of living; and, on the other, of an ever-growing number of very poor squatters and wanderers, often evicted from lately enclosed fielden villages, "given to little or no kind of labour...dwelling far from any church or chapel, and...as ignorant of God or of any civil course of life as the very savages amongst the infidels..."[1] In consequence of their semi-vagrant origins, many forest labourers were less rooted in their own community than their fielden cousins; more willing to migrate at certain seasons in search of employment elsewhere; more independent and eager to take up the cudgels in their own defence; and more prone to pick up new ways and new ideas. It was primarily in heath and forest areas, visited as they were by travelling badgers and tinkers, that the vagrant religion of the Independents found a footing in rural communities;[2] it was principally thence, there is reason to think, that the godly (or not so godly) troops of the Parliamentarian armies were recruited during the Civil War. It was also in heaths and forests that the millenarian leaders of the Interregnum, the Methodist preachers of the eighteenth century, and later messianic sects like that of John Nichols Tom in East Kent, found many of their most devoted adherents.[3]

Essentially the difference between fielden and forest societies was that of a relatively static and a relatively mobile way of life. Of the

[1] Harrison, *op. cit.*, Part III, p. 180; cf. SP 16, 176, 55 for an account of Irish vagrants in Somerset in 1630, and Carew, *op. cit.*, p. 67, for poor Irish people flocking into Cornwall.

[2] During the sixteenth century the Familists spread their doctrines in Cambridgeshire by going round as travelling basket makers, musicians, etc. (Ronald Knox, *Enthusiasm*, 1950, p. 171). During the Interregnum, Gerrard Winstanley, the well-known Independent and Digger, wished to take in "all the commons and waste ground in England" for the poor (W. Schenk, *The Concern for Social Justice in the Puritan Revolution*, 1948, p. 102).

[3] P. G. Rogers, *Battle in Bossenden Wood*, 1961, pp. 201 *sqq*. Tom's supporters came from the Forest of Blean; after the collapse of his movement (in a battle in 1838 in which twelve lives were lost), a church was built at Dunkirk specifically to 'civilize' the area.

latent jealousy between them, the last embers continued to smoulder on until the closing years of the nineteenth century. In Oxfordshire, at the end of Queen Victoria's reign, the hamlet people of 'Lark Rise', though then bereft of all their common rights, still maintained an attitude of independence and mild animosity towards the parent village of 'Fordlow', with its parish church, its Tory parson, and its decrepit little manor-house; while the labourers of the village itself, still sunning themselves in the fading rays of parish gentility, retorted by calling the hamlet children, "That gypsy lot from Lark Rise."[1]

Hand in hand with the break-up in the unity of labouring society itself went a decline in the protection afforded to the labourer by the customary social order. There was of course no sudden or universal change in that order; traditional ideas of social duty still lingered on for generations after the end of the period. But in some districts, at least, a definite decline in the sense of responsibility to dependants and a widening psychological gulf between gentry and peasantry was coming into evidence. In newly enclosed parishes, and in the eastern counties with their relatively advanced economy and acute land-hunger, these developments seem to have been particularly pronounced. In Norfolk some poor people apparently felt "that the gentlemen had all the farms and cattle in the country in their hands, and poor men could have no living..." In Suffolk a sharp linguistic division between gentry and peasantry was already emerging, and the "honest country toiling villager" would "many times let slip some strange different-sounding terms, no ways intelligible to any of civil education..." In Essex the abominable Lord Rich actually wished "none else to be put to school, but only gentlemen's children," since the poor were fitted for nothing but to be unlettered ploughmen and artificers: a sentiment which Archbishop Cranmer, to his credit, indignantly repudiated.[2]

With the Civil War these social cleavages were suddenly deepened. The reins of traditional authority were inevitably relaxed, the bonds of society weakened, and the gentry driven into harsh repressive measures to restore order. The strict enforcement of military discipline, moreover, and the herding together of social classes in cramped quarters with the king or with Fairfax, unavoidably accentuated those status symbols by which rich and poor were distinguished. With rival

[1] Flora Thompson, *Lark Rise to Candleford*, 1957 edn., pp. 188 *et passim*. 'Lark Rise' was Juniper Hill in north Oxfordshire, and 'Fordlow' the village of Cottisford.
[2] SP 14, 28, 64; LP XII, i, p. 482; Reyce, *op. cit.*, p. 55; R. H. Tawney, *The Agrarian Problem in the Sixteenth Century*, 1912, p. 135. Cranmer retorted that "the poor man's son by painstaking will be learned, when the gentleman's son will not take the pains to get it..." Rich was an Essex landowner; the "other gentlemen" with him are not named by Professor Tawney.

armies plundering the countryside, and with thousands of estates under sequestration, many labourers could not tell to whom their rents, and their loyalty, were due.[1] With many squires taking up arms for Charles I or Parliament, and leaving their home locality for years on end, the direct interest of many landlords in farming ceased, and absenteeism became, first a military necessity, then a social habit. As a consequence, an attitude of supercilious contempt for social inferiors developed, amongst both cavaliers and puritans, which must have filled old-fashioned squires like Sir George Sondes with shame and dismay. In a word, the Civil War and the Interregnum dealt a death-blow to the age-old conception of society as a hierarchy of interdependent orders, and went far to replace it by the notion of society as a series of independent and necessarily antagonistic classes.

From the Civil War onwards, the preconceptions of labouring society thus became increasingly alienated from those of the country at large. In all the cant of contemporary demagogues about "the people," Hodge was the one individual whose aspirations were never considered: it was scarcely proper that he should have any. Even the well-meant lucubrations of his few champions, like William Walwyn, displayed no real understanding of his problems: the wish of that London silk-merchant "that there was neither pale, hedge, nor ditch in the whole nation" must have struck village labourers, of all people, as strangely absurd.[2] But for another two centuries Hodge's feelings necessarily remained unspoken and unknown; for his was a way of life whose secret springs became more and more unintelligible to polite society. Yet nowadays, in the mid-twentieth century, as we watch the autumnal sunshine cast lengthening shadows across the meadows of a Pennine valley, or the deserted cattle-pastures of a Wealden farm, it is but just to remember how much we still owe to the labours of the Tudor and Stuart farmworker. For the fact that "things are not so ill with you and me as they might have been, is half owing to the number who lived faithfully a hidden life, and rest in unvisited tombs."[3]

---

[1] Cf. Alan Everitt, *The County Committee of Kent in the Civil War*, University of Leicester, Dept. of English Local History, Occasional Papers, no. 9, 1957, pp. 41–2; HMC, *Reports*, VII, p. 553.

[2] Schenk, *op. cit.*, p. 50. Winstanley's well-known Digger experiment at St George's Hill in Surrey, where he attempted to found an ideal labouring community, was bitterly opposed by local people, who smashed his followers' tools, tore down their houses, and pulled up their corn and vegetables.—*Ibid.*, p. 102.

[3] The quotation is from the concluding sentence of George Eliot's *Middlemarch*.

# 4

# SELECT BIBLIOGRAPHY, 1500–1640

Alcock, L., and Foster, I. Ll. (eds.). *Culture and Environment*. London, 1963.
Allan, D. G. C. *Agrarian Discontent under the early Stuarts and during the last Decade of Elizabeth*. University of London M.Sc. (Econ.) thesis, 1950.
—— 'The Rising in the West, 1628–31', EcHR, 2nd Ser., V, 1952.
Allen, J. Romilly. 'Old Farmhouses with Round Chimneys near St David's', *Arch. Camb.*, II, 1902.
Allison, K. J. 'Flock Management in the Sixteenth and Seventeenth Centuries', EcHR, 2nd Ser., XI, 1958.
—— 'The Sheep-Corn Husbandry of Norfolk in the Sixteenth and Seventeenth Centuries', AHR, V, 1957.
—— *The Wool Supply and the Worsted Cloth Industry in Norfolk in the Sixteenth and Seventeenth Centuries*, University of Leeds Ph.D. thesis, 1955.
Ambler, L. *Old Halls and Manor Houses of Yorkshire*. London, 1913.
Ascoli, Georges. *La Grande-Bretagne devant L'Opinion Française au XVIIe Siècle*. Travaux et Mémoires de l'Université de Lille, NS, Fascicule 13, 1, Paris, 1930.
Ashley, Sir William J. *The Bread of our Forefathers*. Oxford, 1928.
Ashton, T. S. *An Economic History of England: the Eighteenth Century*. London, 1955.
—— *Economic Fluctuations in England, 1700–1800*. Oxford, 1959.
Aylmer, G. E. *The King's Servants*. London, 1961.
—— 'The Last Years of Purveyance, 1610–1660', EcHR, 2nd Ser., X, i, 1957.
Bacon, Nathaniel. *Annalls of Ipswiche*. Ipswich, 1884.
Bailey, J., and Culley, G. *General View of the Agriculture of the County of Northumberland*. London, 1813.
Bankes, Joyce (ed.). *The Memoranda Book of James Bankes, 1586–1617*. Inverness, 1935.
Barley, M. W. *The English Farmhouse and Cottage*. London, 1961.
Barnes, D. G. *A History of the English Corn Laws from 1660 to 1846*. London, 1930.
Barnes, T. G. *Somerset Assize Orders, 1629–1640*. Som. Rec. Soc., LXV, 1959.
Bates, E. H. *The Particular Description of the County of Somerset, 1633*. Somerset Rec. Soc., XV, 1900.
Batho, G. R. 'The Finances of an Elizabethan Nobleman: Henry Percy, Ninth Earl of Northumberland', EcHR, 2nd Ser., IX, 1957.
—— *The Household Papers of Henry Percy, ninth Earl of Northumberland*. Camden Soc., XCIII, 1962.
Beale, John. *Herefordshire Orchards, a Pattern for all England*. London, 1657.
Bean, J. M. W. *The Estates of the Percy Family, 1416–1537*. London, 1958.
Bell, H. E. *An Introduction to the History and Records of the Court of Wards and Liveries*. Cambridge, 1953.
Bennett, M. K. 'British Wheat Yield Per Acre for Seven Centuries', *Economic History*, III, 1935.
Beresford, M. W. 'Glebe Terriers and Open-Field Buckinghamshire', *Records of Bucks.*, XVI, 1953–4.
—— 'Habitation versus Improvement. The Debate on Enclosure by Agreement', *Essays in the Economic and Social History of Tudor and Stuart England*, ed. F. J. Fisher. Cambridge, 1961.
—— 'A Journey to Elizabethan Market Places', chapter VI in *History on the Ground*. London, 1957.

Beresford, M. W. *The Lost Villages of England*. London, 1954.
—— 'The Lost Villages of Medieval England', *Geog. J.*, CXVII, 1951.
—— 'The Lost Villages of Yorkshire', *Yorks. Arch. J.*, XXXVIII, 1952.
Best, Henry. *Rural Economy in Yorkshire in 1641, being the Farming and Account Books of Henry Best of Elmeswell in the East Riding*, ed. C. B. Robinson. Surtees Soc., XXXIII, 1857.
Beveridge, Lord. 'British Exports and the Barometer', *Economic J.*, XXX, 1920.
—— 'The Yield and Price of Corn in the Middle Ages', *Economic History*, II, 1927.
—— 'Wages in the Winchester Manors', *EcHR*, VII, 1936–7.
—— 'Weather and Harvest Cycles', *Economic J.*, XXXI, 1921.
Beveridge, Lord, and others. *Prices and Wages in England from the Twelfth to the Nineteenth Century*. London, 1939.
Bickley, W. B. *Abstract of the Bailiffs' Accounts of Monastic and other Estates in the County of Warwick*. Dugdale Soc., II, 1923.
Bindoff, S. T. *Ket's Rebellion, 1549*. Hist. Assoc. Pamphlet, General Series 12, 1949.
—— *Tudor England*. London, 1950.
Birch, Walter de Gray. *A Descriptive Catalogue of Penrice and Margam Manuscripts*, Series I–IV. London, 1893–5.
Blagrave, J. *The Epitomie of the Art of Husbandry*. London, 1669.
Blake, W. T. 'Hooker's Synopsis Chorographical of Devonshire', *Devon Assoc.*, XLVII, 1915.
Bland, A. E., Brown, P. A., and Tawney, R. H. *English Economic History. Select Documents*. London, 1914.
Blith, Walter. *The English Improver Improved*. London, 1652.
Blome, Richard. *Britannia*. London, 1673.
Bouch, C. M. L., and Jones, G. P. *The Lake Counties, 1500–1830*. Manchester, 1961.
Bourne, George. *The Bettesworth Book. Talks with a Surrey Peasant*. London, 1920.
—— *Memoirs of a Surrey Labourer: a record of the last years of Frederick Bettesworth*. London, 1911.
Bowden, P. J. 'The Home Market in Wool, 1500–1700', *Yorks. Bull. of Econ. and Soc. Research*, VIII, ii, 1956.
—— *The internal Wool Trade in England during the Sixteenth and Seventeenth Centuries*. University of Leeds Ph.D. thesis, 1952.
—— 'Movements in Wool Prices, 1490–1610', *Yorks. Bull. of Econ. and Soc. Research*, IV, 1952.
—— *The Wool Trade in Tudor and Stuart England*. London, 1962.
Brace, H. W. *History of Seed Crushing in Great Britain*. London, 1960.
Bradley, Harriet. *The Enclosures in England—an Economic Reconstruction*. New York, 1918.
Brenner, Y. S. 'The Inflation of Prices in Early Sixteenth Century England', *EcHR*, 2nd Ser., XIV, 1961.
—— 'The Inflation of Prices in England, 1551–1650', *EcHR*, 2nd Ser., XV, 1962.
Brett-James, N. G. *The Growth of Stuart London*. London, 1935.
Brown, E. H. Phelps, and Hopkins, Sheila V. 'Seven Centuries of Building Wages', *Economica*, NS, XXII, 1955.
—— 'Wage-rates and Prices: Evidence for Population Pressure in the Sixteenth Century', *Economica*, NS, XXIV, 1957.
—— 'Builders' Wage-rates, Prices and Population: Some Further Evidence', *Economica*, NS, XXVI, 1959.
Browning, Andrew (ed.). *English Historical Documents, 1660–1714*. London, 1953.
Brunskill, R. W. 'An Appreciation of Monmouthshire Houses', *Mont. Coll.*, LIII, ii, 1954.

Brydson, A. P. *Some Records of two Lakeland Townships—Blawith and Nibthwaite—chiefly from original documents.* Ulverston, 1908.
Burton, William. *The Description of Leicestershire.* London, 1622.
Caley, J., and Hunter, J. (eds.). *Valor Ecclesiasticus temp. Hen. VIII....* (6 vols.). London, 1810–34.
Camden, W. *Britannia,* trans. R. Gough. 3 vols., London, 1789.
Campbell, Mildred. *The English Yeoman Under Elizabeth and the Early Stuarts.* New Haven, 1942.
Carew, Richard. *The Survey of Cornwall.* London, 1602.
Carpenter, H. J. 'Furse of Morhead', *Devon Assoc.,* XXVI, 1894.
Cave, T., and Wilson, R. A. (eds.). *The Parliamentary Survey of the Lands and Possessions of the Dean and Chapter of Worcester.* Worcs. Hist. Soc., 1924.
Chalklin, C. W. 'The Compton Census of 1676: the dioceses of Canterbury and Rochester', *A Seventeenth Century Miscellany.* Kent Arch. Soc., Records Publication Committee, XVII, 1960.
—— 'The Rural Economy of a Kentish Wealden Parish, 1650–1750', AHR, X, 1962.
—— *Seventeenth Century Kent.* London, 1965.
Charles, B. G. 'The Second Book of George Owen's Description of Pembrokeshire', *Nat. Lib. Wales J.,* V, 1947–8.
Charman, D. 'Wealth and Trade in Leicester in the early Sixteenth Century', *Leics. Arch. Soc.,* XXV, 1949.
Cheke, Val. *The Story of Cheese-making in Britain.* London, 1959.
Chippindall, C. L. W. H. (ed.). *A Sixteenth-century Survey and Year's Account of the Estates of Hornby Castle, Lancashire.* Chetham Soc., NS, CII, 1939.
Cipolla, C. M. 'La prétendue "révolution des prix." Réflexions sur l'expérience italienne', *Annales E.S.C.,* 10e année, 4, 1955.
Clapham, Sir J. *A Concise Economic History of Britain from the Earliest Times to 1750.* Cambridge, 1949.
Clark, G. N. *The Wealth of England from 1496 to 1760.* Oxford, 1947.
Clarkson, L. A. 'The Organization of the English Leather Industry in the Late Sixteenth and Seventeenth Centuries', EcHR, 2nd Ser., XIII, 1960.
Clay, J. M. *Yorkshire Monasteries: Suppression Papers.* Yorks. Arch. Soc. Rec. Ser., XLVIII, 1912.
Clay, T. *Briefe, Easie and Necessary Tables of Interest and Rents Forborne.* London, 1624.
Cliffe, J. T. *The Yorkshire Gentry on the Eve of the Civil War.* University of London Ph.D. thesis, 1960.
Coleman, D. C. 'Industrial Growth and Industrial Revolutions', *Economica,* NS, XXIII, 1956.
—— 'Labour in the English Economy of the Seventeenth Century', EcHR, 2nd Ser., VIII, 1955–6.
Collier, C. V. 'Burton Agnes Courts, Miscellanea II', Yorks. Arch. Soc., Rec. Ser., LXXIV, 1929.
Collis, I. P. 'Leases for Term of Years, determinable with Lives', *J. Soc. Archivists,* I, 1957.
*Considerations Touching Trade, with the Advance of the King's Revenue...,* 1641.
Cooper, J. P. 'The Counting of Manors', EcHR, 2nd Ser., VIII, 1956.
—— 'The fortune of Thomas Wentworth, Earl of Strafford', EcHR, 2nd Ser., XI, 1958.
Cordingley, R. A. 'British Historical Roof Types and their Members', *Ancient Monuments Soc.,* NS, IX, 1961.
—— 'Stokesay Castle, Shropshire: The Chronology of its Buildings', *The Art Bulletin* (U.S.), XLV (2), 1963.
Cornwall, J. C. K. *The Agrarian History of Sussex, 1560–1640.* University of London M.A. thesis, 1953.

Cornwall, J. C. K. 'English Country Towns in the Fifteen Twenties', EcHR, 2nd Ser., XV, i, 1962.
—— 'Farming in Sussex, 1560–1640', *Sussex Arch. Coll.*, XCII, 1954.
Cox, J. C. (ed.). *The Records of the Borough of Northampton*, II. Northampton, 1898.
Craig, Sir J. *The Mint. A History of the London Mint from A.D. 287 to 1948.* Cambridge, 1953.
Cramer, J. A. (ed.). *The Second Book of the Travels of Nicander Nucius of Corcyra.* Camden Soc., XVII, 1841.
Creighton, C. *A History of Epidemics in Britain from A.D. 664 to the Extinction of Plague.* Cambridge, 1891.
Crook, Barbara. 'Newnham Priory: Rental of Manor at Biddenham, 1505–6', *Beds. Hist. Rec. Soc.*, XXV, 1947.
Cross, M. Claire, 'An Exchange of Lands with the Crown, 1587–8', *Bull.* IHR, XXXIV, 1961.
Cunningham, W. *The Growth of English Industry and Commerce in Modern Times*, II. Cambridge, 1919.
Daniel-Tyssen, J. R. 'The Parliamentary Surveys of the County of Sussex', *Sussex Arch. Coll.*, XXIII, 1871.
Darby, H. C. *The Draining of the Fens.* Cambridge, 1940.
—— (ed.). *Historical Geography of England before A.D. 1800.* Cambridge, 1936.
Darby, H. C., and Saltmarsh, J. 'The Infield-Outfield System on a Norfolk Manor', *Economic History*, III, 1935.
Davies, D. J. *The Economic History of South Wales prior to 1800.* Cardiff, 1933.
Davies, Elwyn. (ed.). *Celtic Studies in Wales.* Cardiff, 1963.
Deane, Phyllis, and Cole, W. A. *British Economic Growth. 1688–1959.* Cambridge, 1962.
Defoe, Daniel. *A Tour through England and Wales.* Everyman edn., London, 1959.
Dendy, F. W. 'The Ancient Farms of Northumberland', *Archaeologia Aeliana*, 2nd Ser., XVI, 1894.
Denney, A. H. *The Sibton Abbey Estates: Select Documents, 1325–1509.* Suffolk Rec. Soc., II, 1960.
Dexter, R., and Barber, D. *Farming for Profits.* London, 1961.
Dickens, A. G. 'Estate and Household Management in Bedfordshire, c. 1540', *Beds. Hist. Rec. Soc.*, XXXVI, 1956.
—— *The Register or Chronicle of Butley Priory, Suffolk, 1510–35.* Winchester, 1951.
Dietz, F. C. *English Government Finance, 1485–1558.* University of Illinois, Studies in the Social Sciences, IX, 3. Urbana, 1920.
—— *English Public Finance, 1558–1641.* New York, 1932.
Dodd, A. H. *Studies in Stuart Wales.* Cardiff, 1952.
Edwards, Ifan Ab Owen (ed.). *A Catalogue of Star Chamber Proceedings relating to Wales.* Cardiff, 1929.
Eland, G. (ed.). *Thomas Wotton's Letter-Book, 1574–1586.* London, 1960.
Ellis, Sir Henry (ed.). *Speculi Britanniae Pars: an Historical and Chorographical Description of the County of Essex by John Norden, 1594.* Camden Soc., IX, 1840.
Elsas, M. J. 'Price Data from München, 1500–1700', *Economic History*, III, 1935.
—— *Umriss einer Geschichte der Preise und Löhne in Deutschland vom ausgehenden Mittelalter bis zum Beginn des Neunzehnten Jahrhunderts*, I, II. Leiden, 1936–49.
Elton, G. R. *The Tudor Constitution.* Cambridge, 1960.
—— *The Tudor Revolution in Government.* Cambridge, 1953.
Emerson, W. R. *The Economic Development of the Estates of the Petre Family in Essex in the Sixteenth and Seventeenth Centuries.* University of Oxford D.Phil. thesis, 1951.
Emery, F. V. 'West Glamorgan farming circa 1580–1620', *Nat. Lib. Wales J.*, IX, X, 1955–6, 1957–8.

Emmison, F. G. *Tudor Secretary: Sir William Petre at Court and Home*. London, 1961.
Ernle, Lord. *English Farming Past and Present*. New (sixth) edn., London, 1961.
Evans, A. 'Battle Abbey at the Dissolution', *Huntington Lib. Qtrly.*, IV, 1941-2.
Evans, Elwyn. 'Two Machynlleth Toll-Books', *Nat. Lib. Wales J.*, VI, 1949-50.
Evans, G. Ewart. *The Horse in the Furrow*. London, 1960.
Everitt, Alan. *The Community of Kent and the Great Rebellion, 1640-60*, Leicester, 1966.
—— *The County Committee of Kent in the Civil War*. Leicester, Dept. of English Local History, Occasional Papers, 9, 1957.
—— *Kent and its Gentry, 1640-1660: a political Study*. University of London Ph.D. thesis, 1957.
—— *Suffolk and the Great Rebellion*. Suffolk Rec. Soc., III, 1961.
Farrer, W. *Chartulary of Cockersand Abbey*, III, iii. Chetham Soc., NS, LXIV, 1909.
Feaveryear, A. E. *The Pound Sterling. A History of English Money*. Oxford, 1933.
Felix, D. 'Profit Inflation and Industrial Growth', *Qtrly. J. of Economics*, LXX, 1956.
Fiennes, Celia. *The Journeys of Celia Fiennes*. ed. C. Morris. London, 1947.
Finberg, H. P. R. 'An Early Reference to the Welsh Cattle Trade', AHR, II, 1954.
—— *Gloucestershire Studies*. Leicester, 1957.
—— 'The Gostwicks of Willington', *Beds. Hist. Rec. Soc.*, XXXVI, 1956.
—— *Tavistock Abbey*. Cambridge, 1951.
Finch, Mary. *The Wealth of Five Northamptonshire Families, 1540-1640*. Northants. Rec. Soc., XIX, 1956.
Fisher, F. J. 'Commercial Trends and Policy in Sixteenth Century England', EcHR, X, 1939-40.
—— 'The Development of the London Food Market, 1540-1640', EcHR, V, 1935.
—— 'London's Export Trade in the Early Seventeenth Century', EcHR, 2nd Ser., III, 1950.
Fisher, H. A. L. *The History of England, 1485-1547*. London, 1906.
Fishwick, H. (ed.). *The Survey of the Manor of Rochdale*. Chetham Soc., NS, LXXI, 1913.
Folkingham, W. *Feudigraphia*. London, 1610.
Fowler, J. T. *The Coucher Book of Selby Abbey, II*. Yorks. Arch. Soc., Rec. Ser., XIII, 1893.
Fowler, R. C. 'Inventories of Essex Monasteries in 1536', *Essex Arch. Soc.*, NS, X, 1909.
Fox, Sir Cyril. *A Country House of the Elizabethan Period in Wales: Six Wells, Llantwit Major, Glamorganshire*. Cardiff, 1941.
—— 'The Round-chimneyed Farm-houses of Northern Pembrokeshire', *Aspects of Archaeology in Britain and Beyond, Essays presented to O. G. S. Crawford*, ed. W. F. Grimes. London, 1951.
—— 'Three Rounded Gable Houses in Carmarthenshire', *Arch. Camb.*, 1951.
Fox, Sir C., and Raglan, Lord. *Monmouthshire Houses: A Study of Building Techniques and Smaller House-Plans in the Fifteenth to Seventeenth Centuries*. 3 vols. Cardiff, 1951-4.
Fussell, G. E. 'Adventures with Clover', *Agriculture*, LXII, 7, 1955.
—— 'Cornish Farming, A.D. 1500-1910', *Amateur Historian*, IV, 8. 1960.
—— *The English Rural Labourer*. London, 1949.
—— 'Four Centuries of Cheshire Farming Systems, 1500-1900', *Hist. Soc. Lancs. & Cheshire*, CVI, 1954.
—— 'Four Centuries of Farming Systems in Derbyshire, 1500-1900', *Derbyshire Arch. & Nat. Hist. Soc.*, LXXI, 1951.
—— 'Four Centuries of Farming Systems in Dorset, 1500-1900', *Dorset Nat. Hist. & Arch. Soc.*, LXXIII, 1952.
—— 'Four Centuries of Farming Systems in Hampshire, 1500-1900', *Hants. Field Club & Arch. Soc.*, XVII, iii, 1949.

Fussell, G. E. 'Four Centuries of Farming Systems in Shropshire, 1500–1900', *Salop Arch. Soc.*, LIV, i, 1951–2.
—— 'Four Centuries of Nottinghamshire Farming', *Notts. Countryside*, XVII, 2, 1956.
—— 'History of Cole (*Brassica* Sp.)', *Nature*, 4471 (9 July), CLXXVI, 1955.
—— *Robert Loder's Farm Accounts, 1610–1620*. Camden Soc., 3rd Ser., LIII, 1936.
Fussell, G. E., and Goodman, Constance. 'The Eighteenth-century Traffic in Milk Products', *Economic History*, III, 1937.
Gardiner, Dorothy (ed.). *The Oxinden Letters, 1607–1642*. London, 1933.
Gardiner, S. R. (ed.). *The Constitutional Documents of the Puritan Revolution, 1625–1660*. 1906 edn., Oxford.
Gay, E. F. 'Inclosures in England in the Sixteenth Century', *Qtrly. J. of Economics*, XVII, 1903.
—— 'Inquisitions of Depopulation in 1517 and the Domesday of Inclosures', RHS, NS, XIV, 1900.
—— 'The Midland Revolt and the Inquisitions of Depopulation of 1607', RHS, XVIII, 1904.
—— 'The Rise of an English Country Family: Peter and John Temple, to 1603', *Huntington Lib. Qtrly.*, I, 1938.
—— 'The Temples of Stowe and Their Debts: Sir Thomas Temple and Sir Peter Temple, 1603–1653', *Huntington Lib. Qtrly.*, II, 1938–9.
Gerard, J. *The Herball or Generall Historie of Plantes*. London, 1597.
Glass, D. V. 'Gregory King's Estimates of the Population of England and Wales, 1695', *Population Studies*, III, 1950.
Gough, R. (ed.). *Description des Royaulmes d'Angleterre et d'Escosse composé par Etienne Perlin, Paris 1558*. London, 1775.
Gould, J. D. 'Mr Beresford and the Lost Villages: a Comment', AHR, III, 1955.
—— 'The Inquisition of Depopulation of 1607 in Lincolnshire', EHR, LXVII, 1952.
Grafton, Richard. *A little Treatise conteyning many proper Tables and Rules, very necessary for the use of all men*. 1602 edn., London.
Gras, N. S. B. *The Evolution of the English Corn Market...*, Cambridge, Mass., 1926.
Gray, H. L. *English Field Systems*. Harvard Historical Studies, XXII, 1915.
Green, Mrs J. R. *Town Life in the Fifteenth Century*. London, 1894.
Habakkuk, H. J. 'The Long-term Rate of Interest and the Price of Land in the Seventeenth Century', EcHR, 2nd Ser., V, 1952.
—— 'The Market for Monastic Property, 1539–1603', EcHR, 2nd Ser., X, 3, 1958.
Haldane, A. R. B. *The Drove Roads of Scotland*. London, 1952.
Hallam, H. E. 'Some Thirteenth-century Censuses', EcHR, 2nd Ser., X, 3, 1958.
Hallett, G. *The Economics of Agricultural Land Tenure*. London, 1960.
Hamilton, E. J. 'American Treasure and Andalusian Prices, 1503–1660', *J. Econ. & Bus. Hist.*, I, 1928–9.
—— *American Treasure and the Price Revolution in Spain, 1501–1650*. Harvard, 1934.
—— *Money, Prices, and Wages in Valencia, Aragon, and Navarre, 1351–1500*. Harvard, 1936.
—— 'The Decline of Spain', EcHR, VIII, 1938.
Hammarström, D. I. 'The Price Revolution of the Sixteenth Century: Some Swedish Evidence', *Scand. Econ. Hist. Rev.*, V, 1957.
Hammersley, G. 'The Crown Woods and their Exploitation in the Sixteenth and Seventeenth Centuries', *Bull. IHR*, XXX, 1957.
Harland, John (ed.). *The House and Farm Accounts of the Shuttleworths of Gawthorpe Hall...*, Parts I and II. Chetham Soc., XXXV, XLI, 1856.
Harris, A. 'The Agriculture of the East Riding of Yorkshire before the Parliamentary Enclosures', *Yorks. Arch. J.*, CLVII, 1959.

Harrison, William. *Harrison's Description of England in Shakspere's Youth*, ed. F. J. Furnivall, New Shakspere Soc., 6th Ser. I and VIII. London 1877 and 1881.
Hartlib, Samuel. *Samuel Hartlib his Legacie*. London, 1652.
Harvey, N. 'Farm and Estate under Elizabeth the First', *Agriculture*, LX, 1953.
Hasbach, W. *A History of the English Agricultural Labourer*. London, 1908.
Hasted, Edward. *History of Kent*. Canterbury, 1797–1801.
Havinden, M. 'Agricultural Progress in Open-field Oxfordshire', AHR, IX, 1961.
Hembry, P. M. *The Bishops of Bath and Wells, 1535–1647: a social and economic study*. London University Ph.D. thesis, 1956.
Hemp, W. J., and Gresham, Colin. 'Park, Llanfrothen and the Unit System', *Arch. Camb.*, XCVII, 1942.
Henman, W. N. 'Newnham Priory: a Bedford Rental, 1506-7', *Beds. Hist. Rec. Soc.*, XXV, 1947.
Hervey, Lord Francis (ed.). *Suffolk in the Seventeenth Century. The Breviary of Suffolk by Robert Reyce, 1618*. London, 1902.
Hexter, J. H. *Reappraisals in History*. London, 1961.
Heylyn, Peter. *A Help to English History*. 1709 edn., London.
Hill, C. *Economic Problems of the Church, from Archbishop Whitgift to the Long Parliament*. Oxford, 1956.
Hill, J. W. F. *Tudor and Stuart Lincoln*. Cambridge, 1956.
Hilton, R. H. *The Social Structure of Rural Warwickshire*. Dugdale Soc. Occasional Paper, 9, 1950.
—— 'Winchcombe Abbey and the Manor of Sherborne', *Gloucestershire Studies*, ed. H. P. R. Finberg. Leicester, 1957.
Hirst, L. F. *The Conquest of Plague*. Oxford, 1953.
Hobsbawm, E. 'The General Crisis of the European Economy in the Seventeenth Century', *Past and Present*, V, VI, 1954.
Holdsworth, W. S. *An Historical Introduction to the Land Law*. Oxford, 1927.
Hopkins, E. *The Bridgewater Estates in North Shropshire in the First Half of the Seventeenth Century*. University of London M.A. thesis, 1956.
Hoskins, W. G. *Devon*. London, 1954.
—— 'English Provincial Towns in the early Sixteenth Century', RHS, 5th Ser., VI, 1956.
—— *Essays in Leicestershire History*. Liverpool, 1950.
—— 'Harvest Fluctuations and English Economic History, 1480–1619', AHR, XII, 1964.
—— *Industry, Trade, and People in Exeter, 1688–1800*. Manchester, 1935.
—— *The Midland Peasant*. London, 1957.
—— 'The Reclamation of the Waste in Devon', EcHR, XIII, 1943.
—— *Two Thousand Years in Exeter*. Exeter, 1960.
Hoskins, W. G., and Finberg, H. P. R. *Devonshire Studies*. London, 1952.
Howells, B. E. 'Pembrokeshire Farming circa 1580–1620', *Nat. Lib. Wales J.*, IX, 1955-6.
Hudson, W. H. *A Shepherd's Life*. Everyman edn., London, 1949.
Hughes, H. 'Notes on the Architecture of some old houses in the neighbourhood of Llansilin, Denbighshire', *Arch. Camb.*, XV (5th Ser.), 1898.
Hughes, H., and North, H. L. *The Old Cottages of Snowdonia*. Bangor, 1908.
Hulbert, N. F. 'A Survey of the Somerset Fairs', *Som. Arch. and Nat. Hist. Soc.*, LXXXII, 1937.
Hull, F. *Agriculture and Rural Society in Essex, 1560–1640*. University of London Ph.D. thesis, 1950.

Hurstfield, J. 'Corruption and Reform under Edward VI and Mary: the Example of Wardship', EHR, LXVIII, 1953.
—— 'The Greenwich Tenures of the Reign of Edward VI', *Law Qtrly. Rev.* LXV, 1949.
—— 'Lord Burghley as Master of the Court of Wards', RHS, 4th Ser., XXXI, 1949.
—— 'The Profits of Fiscal Feudalism', EcHR, 2nd Ser., VIII, 1955.
—— *The Queen's Wards: Wardship and marriage under Elizabeth I.* London, 1958.
Jackson, J. N. 'Some Observations upon the Herefordshire Environment of the Seventeenth and Eighteenth Centuries', *Woolhope Nat. Field Club*, XXXVI, i, 1958.
James, M. E. *Estate Accounts of the Earls of Northumberland, 1562–1637.* Surtees Soc., CLXIII, 1955.
Jefferies, Richard. *Field and Hedgerow. Being the Last Essays of Richard Jefferies.* London, 1904.
—— *The Toilers of the Field.* London and New York, 1892.
Jevons, W. S. *Investigations in Currency and Finance.* 2nd edn., London, 1909.
Jevons, H. S. *The Causes of Unemployment, the Sun's Heat, and Trade Activity.* London, 1910.
—— 'Trade Fluctuations and Solar Activity', *Contemporary Rev.*, August, 1909.
Johnson, A. H. *The Disappearance of the Small Landowner.* New edn., London, 1963.
Jones, Emyr G. (ed.). *Exchequer Proceedings (Equity) concerning Wales, Henry VIII–Elizabeth.* Cardiff, 1939.
Jones, E. L. 'Eighteenth-century Changes in Hampshire Chalkland Farming', AHR, VIII, 1960.
Jones, Francis. 'An Approach to Welsh Genealogy', *Trans. Cymmrodorion Soc.*, 1948.
Jones, S. R., and Smith, J. T. 'The Houses of Breconshire, Part I', *Brycheiniog*, 1963.
Jones, T. I. Jeffreys (ed.). *Exchequer Proceedings concerning Wales in Tempore James I.* Cardiff, 1955.
Kennedy, J. *The Dissolution of the Monasteries in Hampshire and the Isle of Wight.* London University M.A. thesis, 1953.
Kenyon, G. H. 'Petworth Town and Trades, 1610–1760: Part I', *Sussex Arch. Coll.*, XCVI, 1958.
Kerridge, E. 'Agriculture, c. 1500–c. 1793', VCH *Wilts.*, IV, 1959.
—— *The Agrarian Development of Wiltshire, 1540–1640.* University of London Ph.D. thesis, 1951.
—— 'The Floating of the Wiltshire Watermeadows', *Wilts. Arch. & Nat. Hist. Mag.*, LV, 1953.
—— 'The Movement of Rent 1540–1640', EcHR, 2nd Ser., VI, 1953.
—— 'The Notebook of a Wiltshire Farmer in the early seventeenth century', *Wilts. Arch. & Nat. Hist. Mag.*, LIV, 1952.
—— 'A Reconsideration of some Former Husbandry Practices', AHR, III, 1955.
—— 'The Returns of the Inquisitions of Depopulation', EHR, LXX, 1955.
—— 'The Revolts in Wiltshire against Charles I', *Wilts. Arch. & Nat. Hist. Mag.*, LVII, 1958–9.
—— 'Ridge and Furrow and Agrarian History', EcHR, 2nd Ser., IV, 1951.
—— 'The Sheepfold in Wiltshire and the Floating of the Watermeadows', EcHR, 2nd Ser., VI, 1954.
—— 'Social and Economic History of Leicester', VCH *Leics.*, IV, 1958.
—— *Surveys of the Manors of Philip, First Earl of Pembroke, 1631–2.* Wilts. Arch. and Nat. Hist. Soc., Records Branch, IX, 1953.
King, G. *Natural and Political Observations and Conclusions upon the State and Condition of England.* 1696.
Klotz, E. L., and Davies, G. 'The Wealth of Royalist Peers and Baronets during the Puritan Revolution', EHR, LVIII, 1943.

Knocker, H. W. 'Sevenoaks: the Manor, Church and Market', *Arch. Cant.*, XXXVII, 1926.
Knowles, D. *The Religious Orders in England*, III. Cambridge, 1959.
Knox, Ronald. *Enthusiasm: a Chapter in the History of Religion*. Oxford, 1950.
Koenigsberger, H. G. 'Property and the Price Revolution (Hainault, 1474-1573)', EcHR, 2nd Ser., IX, 1956.
Lambarde, William. *A Perambulation of Kent*. 1826 edn., Chatham.
Lamond, E. (ed.). *A Discourse of the Common Weal of this Realm of England*. Cambridge, 1954.
Laslett, T. P. R. 'The Gentry of Kent in 1640', *Camb. Hist. J.*, IX, 1948.
Leadam, I. S. *The Domesday of Inclosures, 1517-18*. 2 vols. RHS, 1897.
Le Hardy, W. *County of Buckingham: Calendar to the Sessions Records, I, 1678-1694*. Aylesbury, 1933.
Leland, J. *Itinerary in England*, ed. L. Toulmin Smith. 5 vols. London, 1906-8.
Lennard, R. 'The Alleged Exhaustion of the Soil in Medieval England', *Econ. J.*, CXXXV, 1922.
—— 'English Agriculture under Charles II: The Evidence of the Royal Society's "Enquiries"', EcHR, IV, 1932.
—— *Rural Northamptonshire under the Commonwealth*. Oxford Studies in Social and Legal History, V, 1916.
Leonard, E. M. 'The Inclosure of Common Fields in the Seventeenth Century', RHS, NS, XIX, 1905.
—— 'The Relief of the Poor by the State Regulation of Wages', EHR, XIII, 1898.
Lewis, E. A. (ed.). *An Inventory of the Early Chancery Proceedings concerning Wales*. Cardiff, 1937.
—— 'The Toll-Books of some North Pembrokeshire Fairs (1599-1603)', *Bull. BCS*, VII, 1934.
Lewis, E. A., and Davies, J. Conway (eds.). *Records of the Court of Augmentations relating to Wales and Monmouthshire*. Cardiff, 1954.
Lipson, E. *The Economic History of England*, III. London, 1947.
Lisle, E. *Observations in Husbandry*, II. London, 1757.
Lister, J. 'Some Local Star Chamber Cases', *Halifax Antiq. Soc.*, 1927.
—— *Yorkshire Star Chamber Proceedings*, IV. Yorks. Arch. Soc., Rec. Ser., LXX, 1927.
Lloyd, Nathaniel. *A History of the English House from primitive times to the Victorian Period*. London, 1931.
Lodge, E. C. *The Account Book of a Kentish Estate, 1616-1704*. Records of the Social and Economic History of England and Wales, VI. London, 1927.
Low, David. *On the Domesticated Animals of the British Islands*. London, 1845.
Lyte, Henry. *A Niewe Herbal or Historie of Plantes...translated out of French by H.L.* London, 1578.
McGrath, P. V. *The Marketing of Food, Fodder, and Livestock in the London Area in the Seventeenth Century*. University of London M.A. thesis, 1948.
Malfatti, C. V. *Two Italian Accounts of Tudor England*. Barcelona, 1953.
Markham, Gervase. *Cheape and Good Husbandry*. 1623.
—— *Markham's Farewell to Husbandry*. London, 1625.
Marshall, William. *The Rural Economy of Norfolk*. London, 1787.
—— *The Rural Economy of the Southern Counties*. 2 vols., London, 1798.
Mascall, L. *The Government of Cattell....* London, 1620.
Matthews, C. M. 'Annals of the Poor: taken from the Records of a Hertfordshire Village', *History Today*, V, 1955.
Maxey, E. *A New Instruction of Plowing and Setting of Corne, Handled in Manner of a Dialogue betweene a Ploughman and a Scholler*. London, 1601.

Meekings, C. A. F. *Dorset Hearth Tax Assessments, 1662-1664*. Dorset Nat. Hist. and Arch. Soc., Occasional Publications, Dorchester, 1951.
Mercer, E. 'The Houses of the Gentry', *Past and Present*, v, 1954.
Miller, H. 'The Early Tudor Peerage' (thesis summary), *Bull*. IHR, XXIV, 1951.
―― 'Subsidy Assessments of the Peerage in the Sixteenth Century', *Bull*. IHR, XXVIII, 1955.
Minchinton, W. 'Bristol—Metropolis of the West in the Eighteenth Century', RHS, 5th Ser., IV, 1954.
Moore, H. L. *Economic Cycles: their Law and Cause*. New York, 1914.
―― *Generating Economic Cycles*. New York, 1923.
More, Sir Thomas. *The Utopia of Sir Thomas More*, ed. J. H. Lupton. Oxford, 1895.
Mortimer, J. *The Whole Art of Husbandry*. London, 1707.
Morton, J. *The Natural History of Northamptonshire*. London, 1712.
Mousley, J. E. 'The Fortunes of Some Gentry Families of Elizabethan Sussex', EcHR, 2nd Ser., XI, 1959.
Munby, L. *Hertfordshire Population Statistics, 1563-1801*. Hitchin, 1964.
Nalson, John. *An impartial Collection of the great Affairs of State*. I. London, 1682.
Nef, J. U. 'A Comparison of Industrial Growth in France and England, 1540-1640', EcHR, VII, 1937.
―― 'Mining and Metallurgy in Medieval Civilisation', *The Cambridge Economic History of Europe*, ed. M. Postan and E. E. Rich, II. Cambridge, 1952.
―― 'Silver Production in Central Europe', *J. Polit. Econ.*, XLIX, 1941.
―― *The Rise of the British Coal Industry*. London, 1932.
―― 'The Progress of Technology and the Growth of Large-scale Industry in Great Britain, 1540-1640', EcHR, V, 1934.
Norden, John. *Speculum Britanniae. An Historical and Chorographical Description of Middlesex and Hartfordshire*. London, 1723.
―― *The Surveyors Dialogue*. London, 1607.
Notestein, W., Relf, F. H., and Simpson, H. (eds.). *Commons Debates, 1621*. 8 vols. New Haven, 1935.
Oschinsky, D. 'Medieval Treatises on Estate Accounting', EcHR, XVII, 1947.
Owen, George. *Description of Pembrokeshire*, 2 vols. ed. H. Owen. London, 1892.
―― *The Taylors Cussion*, ed. E. M. Pritchard. London, 1906.
Owen, G. Dyfnallt. *Elizabethan Wales. The Social Scene*. Cardiff, 1962.
Owen, L. 'The Population of Wales in the Sixteenth and Seventeenth Centuries', Hon. Soc. Cymmrodorion, 1959.
Page, F. M. *Wellingborough Manorial Accounts, A.D. 1258-1323*. Northants. Rec. Soc., VIII, 1936.
Palmer, A. N. *History of Ancient Tenures of Land in the Marches of North Wales*. Wrexham, 1883. Second edition in collaboration with Edward Owen, 1910.
Parenti, G. *Prime ricerche sulla rivoluzione dei prezzi in Firenze*. Florence, 1939.
Parker, L. A. 'The Agrarian Revolution at Cotesbach, 1501-1612', *Studies in Leicestershire Agrarian History*, Leics. Arch. Soc., XXIV, 1948.
―― 'The Depopulation Returns for Leicestershire in 1607', *Leics. Arch. Soc.*, XXIII, 1947.
―― *Enclosure in Leicestershire, 1485-1607*. University of London Ph.D. thesis, 1948.
Parliament. House of Commons. *Journals*, I, II, 1547-1642.
Pearce, Brian. 'The Elizabethan Food Policy and the Armed Forces', EcHR, XII, 1942.
Peate, I. C. *The Welsh House, A Study in Folk Culture*. Liverpool, 1944.
Pelc, J. *Ceny w Krakowie w latach 1369-1600, Badania z dziejow spolecznych i gospodarczych*. Lwow, 1935.
Pierce, T. Jones (ed.). 'An Anglesey Crown Rental of the Sixteenth Century', *Bull*. BCS, X, 1940.

Pierce, T. Jones (ed.). *A Calendar of Clenennau Letters and Papers*. Aberystwyth, 1947.
—— 'The Law of Wales—the last Phase', *Trans. Cymmrodorion Soc.*, 1963.
—— 'Notes on the History of Rural Caernarvonshire in the Reign of Elizabeth', *Trans. Caernarvons. Hist. Soc.*, 1940.
—— 'Pastoral and Agricultural Settlements in Early Wales', *Geografiska Annaler*, XLIII, 1961.
Platt, Sir Hugh. *The Jewell House of Art and Nature*.... London, 1594.
Plattes, G. *A Discovery of Infinite Treasure Hidden Since the World's Beginning*. London, 1639.
Plot, R. *The Natural History of Oxfordshire*.... Oxford, 1677.
Plymley, Joseph. *General View of the Agriculture of Shropshire*. London, 1803.
Pollard, A. F., and Blatcher, M. 'Hayward Townshend's Journals', *Bull*. IHR, XII, 1934–5.
Postan, M. M. 'Some Economic Evidence of Declining Population in the later Middle Ages', EcHR, 2nd Ser., II, 1950.
—— 'The Chronology of Labour Services', RHS, 4th Ser., XX, 1937.
—— 'The Fifteenth Century', EcHR, IX, 1939.
Pribram, A. F. *Materialien zur Geschichte der Preise und Löhne in Österreich*. Vienna, 1938.
Pringle, A. *General View of the Agriculture of the County of Westmorland*. London, 1813.
Public Record Office, London. *Acts of the Privy Council, New Series, 1542–1630*.
Pugh, R. B. *Antrobus Deeds before 1625*. Wilts. Arch. & Nat. Hist. Soc., Records Branch, III, 1947.
—— *The Crown Estate, An Historical Essay*. London, 1960.
Pugh, T. B. (ed.). *The Marcher Lordships of South Wales, 1415–1536*. Cardiff, 1963.
Purvis, J. S. 'A Note on Sixteenth-century Farming in Yorkshire', *Yorks. Arch. J.*, XXXVI, 1944.
—— *A Selection of Monastic Records and Dissolution Papers*. Yorks. Arch. Soc. Rec. Ser., LXXX, 1931.
Ramsay, G. D. (ed.). *John Isham, Mercer and Merchant Adventurer: Two Account Books of a London Merchant in the Reign of Elizabeth I*. Northants. Rec. Soc., XXI, 1962.
Rathbone, A. *The Surveyor in Foure Bookes*. London, 1616.
Rea, W. F. 'The Rental and Accounts of Sir Richard Shireburn, 1571–77', *Hist. Soc., Lancs. & Cheshire*, CX, 1959.
Rees, W. *A Survey of the Duchy of Lancaster Lordships in Wales, 1609–13*. Cardiff, 1953.
Reid, Rachel R. *The King's Council in the North*. London, 1921.
Rew, R. H. *An Agricultural Faggot. A Collection of Papers on Agricultural Subjects*. Westminster, 1913.
Richards, Thomas. *A History of the Puritan Movement in Wales, 1639–53*. London, 1920.
Richardson, H. *Medieval Fairs and Markets of York*. St Anthony's Hall Publications, 20. York, 1961.
Richardson, W. C. *History of the Court of Augmentations, 1536–1554*. Baton Rouge, 1961.
—— *Tudor Chamber Administration, 1485–1547*. Baton Rouge, 1952.
Robinson, Thomas. *The Common Law of Kent; or, the Customs of Gavelkind. With an Appendix concerning Borough English*. London, 1822.
Rodgers, H. B. 'Land Use in Tudor Lancashire: the Evidence of the Final Concords, 1450–1558', *Trans. Inst. British Geographers*, XXI, 1955.
—— 'The Market Area of Preston in the Sixteenth and Seventeenth Centuries', *Geographical Studies*, III, i, 1956.
Rogers, J. E. T. *A History of Agriculture and Prices in England*. Oxford, 1866–1900.
—— *Six Centuries of Work and Wages*. London, 1894.

Rogers, P. G. *Battle in Bossenden Wood*. London, 1961.
Rowse, A. L. *The England of Elizabeth*. London, 1950.
—— *Tudor Cornwall, Portrait of a Society*. London, 1941.
Royal Commission on Ancient Monuments in Wales and Monmouthshire. *Anglesey Inventory*. London, 1937.
—— *Caernarvonshire Inventory*, 3 vols. London, 1956–64.
Royal Commission on Historical Monuments. *Monuments threatened or destroyed: a Select List*. London, 1963.
Royal Commission on Land in Wales and Monmouthshire. *Report*. London, 1896.
Royce, D. (ed.). *Landboc sive Registrum Monasterii...de Winchelcumba...*, II. Exoniae, 1903.
Russell, J. C. *British Medieval Population*. Albuquerque, 1948.
Rye, W. B. *England as seen by Foreigners*. London, 1865.
Sabin, A. *Some Manorial Accounts of Saint Augustine's Abbey, Bristol*. Bristol Rec. Soc., XXII, 1960.
Salter, E. Gurney. *Tudor England through Venetian Eyes*. London, 1930.
Salter, H. E. *Cartulary of Oseney Abbey*, VI. Oxford Hist. Soc., CI, 1936.
Saltmarsh, J. 'A College Home-farm in the Fifteenth Century', *Economic History*, III, 1936.
—— 'Plague and Economic Decline in England', *Camb. Hist. J.*, VII, 1941.
Savine, A. 'Bondmen under the Tudors', RHS, NS, XVII, 1903.
—— *English Monasteries on the eve of the Dissolution*. Oxford Studies in Social and Legal History, ed. P. Vinogradoff, I, 1909.
Sayce, R. U. 'The Old Summer Pastures, Pt II', *Mont. Coll.*, LV, i, 1958.
Schenk, W. *The Concern for Social Justice in the Puritan Revolution*. London, 1948.
Scott, W. D. Robson. *German Travellers in England, 1400–1800*. Oxford, 1953.
Simiand, F. *Recherches anciennes et nouvelles sur le mouvement général des prix du XVIᵉ au XIXᵉ siècle*. Paris, 1932.
Simpson, A. *The Wealth of the Gentry, 1540–1660: East Anglian Studies*. Cambridge, 1961.
Skeat, Rev. W. W. (ed.). *The Book of Husbandry by Master Fitzherbert*. English Dialect Soc., 1882.
Skeel, Caroline. 'The Cattle Trade between Wales and England...', RHS, 4th Ser., IX, 1926.
Slack, W. J. *The Lordship of Oswestry, 1393–1607*. Shrewsbury, 1951.
Smith, J. T. 'The Long-house in Monmouthshire: a Reappraisal', *Culture and Environment*, ed. Alcock & Foster, 1963.
—— 'Medieval Roofs: A Classification', *Arch. J.*, CXV, 1958.
Smith, P. 'The Long-house and the Laithe-house', *Culture and Environment*, ed. Alcock & Foster, 1963.
—— 'Plas Teg', *J. Flints. Hist. Soc.*, XVIII, 1960.
Smith, P., and Gardner, E. M. 'Two Farmhouses in Llanbedr', *J. Merioneth Hist. and Rec. Soc.*, III, iii, 1959.
Smith, P., and Owen, C. E. V. 'Traditional and Renaissance Elements in some late Stuart and early Georgian Half-timbered Houses in Arwystli', *Mont. Coll.*, LV, 1958.
Smith, R. A. L. *Canterbury Cathedral Priory, A Study in Monastic Administration*. Cambridge, 1943.
Smith, W. J. (ed.). *Calendar of Salusbury Correspondence, 1553–1700*. Cardiff, 1954.
Somerville, R. *History of the Duchy of Lancaster*, I, 1265–1603. London, 1953.
Speed, Adolphus. *Adam out of Eden...*, London, 1659.

Speed, Adolphus. *The Husbandman, Farmer, and Grazier's...Instructor...or Countryman's Guide*. London, [1705 or later].
Spratt, J. *Agrarian Conditions in Norfolk and Suffolk, 1600–1650*. Univ. of London M.A. thesis, 1935.
Steer, F. W. (ed.). *Farm and Cottage Inventories of Mid-Essex, 1635–1749*. Chelmsford, 1950.
Stone, L. 'The Anatomy of the Elizabethan Aristocracy', EcHR, XVIII, 1948.
—— 'The Elizabethan Aristocracy—a Restatement', EcHR, 2nd Ser., IV, 1952.
—— 'Elizabethan Overseas Trade', EcHR, 2nd Ser., II, 1949.
—— 'The Fruits of Office: The Case of Robert Cecil, first Earl of Salisbury, 1596–1612', *Essays in the Economic and Social History of Tudor and Stuart England*, ed. F. J. Fisher, Cambridge, 1961.
—— 'The Nobility in Business, 1540–1640', *The Entrepreneur*, Harvard University, 1957.
—— 'State Control in Sixteenth-century England', EcHR, XVII, 1947.
Straker, E. 'Ashdown Forest and its Inclosures', *Sussex Arch. Coll.*, LXXXI, 1940.
Straton, C. R. *Survey of the lands of William, first earl of Pembroke*. Roxburghe Club, 2 vols., 1909.
Summerson, Sir J. N. *Architecture in Britain 1530 to 1830*. London, 1953.
Supple, B. E. *Commercial Crisis and Change in England, 1600–1642*. Cambridge, 1959.
Sylvester, D. 'The Open Fields of Cheshire', *Hist. Soc. Lancs. & Cheshire*, CVIII, 1956.
Sylvester, D., and Nulty, G. *The Historical Atlas of Cheshire*. Chester, 1958.
T., R. Gent. *The Tenants' Law, or the Laws Concerning Landlords, Tenants and Farmers*. London, 1666.
*Tables of Leases and Interest...*, London, 1628.
Tawney, R. H. *The Agrarian Problem in the Sixteenth Century*. London, 1912.
—— *Business and Politics under James I: Lionel Cranfield as Merchant and Minister*. Cambridge, 1958.
—— 'The Rise of the Gentry, 1558–1640', EcHR, XI, 1941.
—— 'The Rise of the Gentry: A Postscript', EcHR, 2nd Ser., VII, 1954.
Tawney, A. J. and R. H. 'An Occupational Census of the Seventeenth Century', EcHR, V, 1934–5.
Tawney, R. H., and Power, Eileen (eds.). *Tudor Economic Documents*, 3 vols. London, 1924.
Taylor, H. *Old Halls of Lancashire and Cheshire*. Manchester, 1884.
Thirsk, Joan. *English Peasant Farming*. London, 1957.
—— 'Industries in the Countryside', *Essays in the Economic and Social History of Tudor and Stuart England*, ed. F. J. Fisher. Cambridge, 1961.
—— 'The Isle of Axholme before Vermuyden', AHR, I, 1953.
—— *Tudor Enclosures*. Hist. Assoc. Pamphlet, General Ser., 41, 1959.
Thomas, D. R. *The History of the Diocese of Saint Asaph*. 3 vols. Oswestry, 1908.
Thomas, Lawrence. *The Reformation in the Old Diocese of Llandaff*. Cardiff, 1930.
Thompson, Flora. *Lark Rise to Candleford*. 1957 edn., London.
Thorpe, S. M. *The Monastic Lands in Leicestershire on and after the Dissolution*. University of Oxford B.Litt. thesis, 1961.
*Topographer and Genealogist*, I. London, 1846.
Torr, Cecil. *Small Talk at Wreyland*. 1926 edn., Cambridge.
Trevor-Roper, H. R. 'The Elizabethan Aristocracy: an anatomy anatomized', EcHR, 2nd Ser., III, 1951.
—— *The Gentry, 1540–1640*. EcHR Supplement, 1, 1953.
Trow-Smith, R. *A History of British Livestock Husbandry to 1700*. London, 1957.

Tupling, G. H. 'An Alphabetical List of the Markets and Fairs of Lancashire recorded before the Year 1701', *Lancs. and Ches. Antiq. Soc.*, LI, 1936.
—— *The Economic History of Rossendale.* Chetham Soc., NS, LXXXVI, 1927.
—— 'Lancashire Markets in the Sixteenth and Seventeenth Centuries', *Lancs. and Ches. Antiq. Soc.*, LVIII, 1947.
—— 'The Origin of Markets and Fairs in Medieval Lancashire', *Lancs. and Ches. Antiq. Soc.*, XLIX, 1933.
Tyack, N. C. P. *Migration from East Anglia to New England before 1660.* University of London Ph.D. thesis, 1951.
Upton, A. F. *Sir Arthur Ingram, c. 1565–1642.* London, 1961.
Utterström, G. 'Climatic Fluctuations and Population Problems in Early Modern History', *Scand. Econ. Hist. Rev.*, III, 1955.
Verlinden, C. and Others. 'Mouvements des prix et des salaires en Belgique au XVIe siècle', *Annales E.S.C.*, 1955.
Wales. A Bibliography of the History of Wales. Cardiff, 1962. See also Supplement I, *Bull.* BCS, 1963.
Walford, Cornelius. *Fairs, Past and Present: a chapter in the History of Commerce.* London, 1883.
Walker, F. *Historical Geography of South-West Lancashire before the Industrial Revolution.* Chetham Soc., NS, CIII, 1939.
Wallen, W. C. 'Tilty Abbey', *Essex Arch. Soc.*, NS, IX, 1904–5.
Watkin, Dom Aelred. 'Glastonbury 1538–9 as shown by its account rolls', *Downside Review*, LXVII, 1949.
Wedgwood, C. V. *The Great Rebellion: II, The King's War, 1641–1647.* London, 1958.
West, T. *The Antiquities of Furness.* Ulverston, 1805.
Westcote, Thomas. *A View of Devonshire in MDCXXX.* Exeter, 1845.
Westerfield, R. B. *Middlemen in English Business, particularly between 1660 and 1760.* Transactions Connecticut Academy of Arts and Sciences, XIX, Connecticut, 1915.
White, Gilbert. *The Natural History of Selborne.* Everyman edn., London, 1945.
Wiebe, G. *Zur Geschichte der Preisrevolution des XVI und XVII Jahrhunderts.* Leipzig, 1895.
Willan, T. S. *The English Coasting Trade, 1600–1750.* Manchester Economic History Series, XII. Manchester, 1938.
—— *River Navigation in England, 1600–1750.* London, 1936.
Willan, T. S., and Crossley, E. W. (eds.). *Three Seventeenth-Century Yorkshire Surveys.* Yorks. Arch. Soc. Rec. Ser., CIV, 1941.
Williams, Clare. *Thomas Platter's Travels in England, 1599.* London, 1937.
Williams, Glanmor. *The Welsh Church from Conquest to Reformation.* Cardiff, 1962.
Williams, N. J. *The Maritime Trade of East Anglian Ports, 1550–1590.* University of Oxford D.Phil. thesis, 1952.
—— 'Sessions of the Clerk of the Market of the Household in Middlesex', *London and Middlesex Arch. Soc.*, XIX, ii, 1957.
—— *Tradesmen in Early-Stuart Wiltshire.* Wilts. Arch. and Nat. Hist. Soc., Records Branch, XV, 1960.
Williams, W. Ogwen. *Calendar of the Caernarvonshire Quarter Sessions Records.* Cardiff, 1956.
Wilson, Rev. J. M. (ed.). *Accounts of the Priory of Worcester for the year 13–14 Hen. VIII, A.D. 1521–2.* Worcs. Hist. Soc., 1907.
Winchester, Barbara. *Tudor Family Portrait.* London, 1955.
Wolffe, B. P. 'The Management of English Royal Estates under the Yorkist Kings', EHR, LXXI, 1956.

Wood, E. B. (ed.). *Rowland Vaughan, His Booke*. London, 1897.
Wood-Jones, R. B. *Traditional Domestic Architecture in the Banbury Region*. Manchester, 1963.
Woodward, G. W. O. *The Benedictines and Cistercians in Yorkshire in the sixteenth century*. Trin. Coll., Dublin, Ph.D. thesis, 1955.
Woodworth, Allegra. 'Purveyance for the Royal Household in the Reign of Queen Elizabeth', *American Philosophical Soc.*, NS, xxxv, 1946.
Worlidge, John. *Systema Agriculturae; the Mystery of Husbandry discovered: . . . 2nd edn. with additions by the author*. London, 1675.
Wright, T. *Three Chapters of Letters relating to the Suppression of the Monasteries*. Camden Soc., 1843.
Wynn, Sir John. *History of the Gwydir Family*. Cardiff, 1927.
Wynn of Gwydir. *Calendar of Wynn of Gwydir Papers, 1515–1690*. Aberystwyth, 1926.
Youings, J. A. *Devon Monastic Lands: Calendar of Particulars for Grants, 1536–58*. Devon and Cornwall Rec. Soc., NS, I, 1955.
—— 'The Terms of the Disposal of the Devon Monastic Lands, 1536–58', EHR, LXIX, 1954.
Young, F. Brett. *Portrait of a Village*. London, 1937.

# 5

# LANDLORDS AND ESTATE MANAGEMENT IN ENGLAND, 1640–1750

### A. THE CIVIL WAR AND INTERREGNUM

#### 1. *Private landowners*

*(a) War and sequestration*

The economic impact of the Civil Wars on English landed society is usually discussed almost exclusively in terms of the composition fines that many royalists had to pay to recover their estates from sequestration, and of the confiscation and sale of the estates of an unfortunate minority of them. However, even for those royalists who experienced them, composition and confiscation were not necessarily the most serious consequences of the war. Both they and many landowners who had supported parliament as well as others who had tried to avoid taking any active part in the hostilities were also affected in numerous other ways. They suffered from unprecedentedly heavy taxation, from falling rents, from damage to their property, from interruption of their income as a result of sequestration and other causes. Nevertheless, up to the time of writing, there has been no full and systematic investigation of any of these effects of the war, so that some of the generalizations which follow are necessarily based on rather fragmentary sources and may possibly need to be modified in the light of future research.

To start with, it is probable that only a minority of the landowning class participated actively in the war at all, although in some counties it was a bare majority, and undoubtedly the more important county magnates found it harder to maintain their neutrality than did the mass of the county gentry.[1] Most of those who did take part limited their voluntary contributions to such proportions of the family plate as they felt could conveniently be spared, and to the cost of equipping themselves and a few servants to join one of the armies. To this the wealthier ones added the gift, or more often the loan, of one or two hundred pounds. For those few, and they seem mostly to have been on the royalist side, who spent really large sums in raising and maintaining regiments, or in supporting the garrisons they commanded, such expenditure must have contributed significantly to their post-war financial

---

[1] In Yorkshire, a county deeply involved in the war, Cliffe found that out of the 679 families he identified as gentry, 370 took sides; but amongst the families with incomes of over £1,000 p.a. the proportion was 50 out of 73 – J. T. Cliffe, *The Yorkshire Gentry from the Reformation to the Civil War*, London, 1969, pp. 5, 28, 352.

embarrassment. Sir Henry Carey of Cockington, Devon, for instance, who eventually had to sell a great deal of land, calculated his military expenditure on behalf of the king in both the first and the second Civil Wars at £15,000, whilst his loans added a further £1,600 to this total.[2] But only in very few cases can military spending have been the principal cause of a family's difficulties, because those who spent largely in this fashion usually suffered even heavier losses in other ways.

Indeed it was just because both sides found that the flow of voluntary contributions was inadequate to support the war that they were forced to resort to regular taxation. Although it was by no means the only tax, the main prop of parliament's financial system after 1643, as of the republican governments of the 1650s, were the 'assessments', which were at first levied on a weekly basis, later on a monthly one. These were a new type of levy, different in kind from the old subsidies, but above all their novelty lay in the enormous amount of money which was demanded. The county of Suffolk, for instance, had been asked to pay £8,000 by way of Ship Money in the year 1639, but by the latter part of 1643 £5,000 was expected per *month*, and a year later £7,500, again per month. At the level of the village, in 1643 the inhabitants of Sherington (Bucks.) were faced with the prospect of raising £4 2s. 6d. per month, five times what they had paid to the two subsidies granted to the king in 1641, whilst by 1645 they were expected to pay £6 15s., or more than half as much again, as their share of the £120,000 per month required from the kingdom as a whole. At the end of the 1640s and in the early 1650s the assessments were again back at the high levels of £120,000 or £90,000 per month, and only in 1655 were they again reduced to £60,000.[3] The assessments, moreover, were explicitly a tax imposed on the landowners rather than the occupiers, and if a tenant paid what was due on account of his farm he was entitled to deduct it from his rent. A few owners, for instance Lord Dacre at Herstmonceaux, succeeded in shifting part of the burden onto tenants from the beginning (in his case one-third), but not until the later 1640s did many of them begin to insert covenants into their leases or letting agreements binding the tenants to pay a proportion of the tax: one-fifth or one-sixth on Lord Petre's Essex estate, about one-fifth on Sir Roger Twysden's Kentish properties, between a quarter and two-thirds on various holdings of the earl of Southampton's Hampshire estate.[4] Nor

[2] PRO, SP 29/78, item 98. For other examples of the expenditure incurred by royalist commanders, see M. Coate, *Cornwall in the Great Civil War and Interregnum*, 2nd edn, Truro, 1963, pp. 120–1, 123–4 and app. 6 and 7.

[3] C. Holmes, *The Eastern Association in the Civil War*, Cambridge, 1974, p. 137; A. C. Chibnall, *Sherington: The Fiefs and Fields of a Buckinghamshire Village*, Cambridge, 1965, pp. 217, 219. The ordinances imposing the assessments are printed in C. H. Firth and R. S. Rait, eds., *The Acts and Ordinances of the Interregnum*, 3 vols., London, 1911 (hereafter Firth and Rait), *I* and *II, passim*.

[4] T. Barrett Lennard, 'Extracts from the Household Account Book of Herstmonceaux Castle', *Sussex Arch. Coll.*, XLVIII, 1905, p. 131; Essex RO, D/DP E.26; BL, Add. MS 34,167, f. 32 *et seq.*; L. Stone, *Family and Fortune: Studies in Aristocratic Finance in the Sixteenth and Seventeenth Centuries*, Oxford, 1973, pp. 235–6.

in truth was this a great deal of help, since it could only be done at the cost of allowing a reduction in rent or of forgoing an increase which might otherwise have been obtained. During the first Civil War parliament's taxes could, of course, only be levied in areas controlled by its armies, but the king imposed assessments of a similar type in the areas he controlled and nominally these seem to have been heavier still. The royalist assessment on Cornwall in 1643, for instance, was £750 per week compared to the £625 per week that the parliamentary ordinance envisaged for the county, although in practice the king seems to have been much less successful in securing payment in full from the areas he controlled than was parliament.[5]

But how great a proportion of their income landowners actually paid in taxes in these years is a more difficult question. The rate at which those in Buckinghamshire were asked to pay amounted to 2s. in the pound of pre-war rent incomes, in Kent it was the equivalent of 2s. 6d., and in Cornwall the 1643 royalist assessment seems to have implied a land tax of nearly 4s. in the pound,[6] but such figures do not tell us much about the real weight of taxation, which depended on the extent to which wartime conditions had depressed estate incomes. Even in counties as remote from the fighting as Kent land values were adversely affected, and in some parts of the country were affected very seriously indeed, whilst landlords whose tenants abandoned their farms were put in the position of having to pay tax on land which was yielding them no income at all.[7] With rent receipts drastically reduced, real poundage rates were in fact a great deal higher than the nominal ones. Furthermore, many areas were for several years not firmly under the control of either side, but changed hands two or more times during the struggle, or were subject to the incursions of raiding parties from the garrisons of both king and parliament. Landowners in such areas were quite likely to find themselves called on to pay taxes to both sides. The earl of Salisbury's estate at Marston and Petworth in Gloucestershire, for instance, was in a particularly exposed situation in this respect, and the bailiff's account for the years 1643-6 is full of payments made to satisfy the demands first of one party, then of the other. Thus in 1645 we find the entry: "To the Parliament for 2 monthes contribution 26$^L$ being imposed – 20 0s. 0d", and a little further on, "To Capt. Jones for Prince Maurice his use 3 months contribution – 20 0s. 0d". Some at least of what was described as plundering by its victims was, in the view of those who authorized it, simply the forcible collection of taxes from areas where they did not normally or continuously exercise control. Certainly in disputed areas a considerable proportion of the taxes owed were paid in

---

[5] Coate, *op. cit.*, p. 58; J. Engeberg, 'Royalist Finances during the English Civil War, 1642–1646', *Scand. Ec. Hist. Rev.*, XIV, 1966, pp. 89–92; J. S. Morrill, *Cheshire 1630–1660: County Government and Society during the English Revolution*, Oxford, 1974, pp. 104, 135.

[6] A. M. Johnson, 'Buckinghamshire 1640 to 1660', unpub. Univ. of Wales, Swansea, Ph.D. thesis, 1963, pp. 127–8; A. M. Everitt, *The Community of Kent and the Great Rebellion*, Leicester, 1966, pp. 159–60; Coate, *op. cit.*, p. 104.

[7] D. Gardiner, ed., *The Oxinden and Peyton Letters 1642–1670*, London, 1937, pp. 67–8.

kind by the delivery of farm produce to armies or garrisons, as the accounts of the parliamentary garrison of Chalfield House in Wiltshire illustrate very clearly.[8] Whether contributions levied in kind, under a threat that force would be used if they were not forthcoming, should be regarded as taxation or plunder is perhaps only an academic point.

A further difficulty in the way of generalization about the weight of taxation is that, even within a given county, estates of equal value did not necessarily pay equal tax. Complaints from royalists that they were unfairly assessed so that their parliamentarian neighbours might escape more lightly are heard from widely separated parts of the country, but lands might be inequitably assessed for other reasons. For instance, the assessors found that they could collect the money more easily if they parcelled the tax out among the more substantial farmers, and did not bother at all with the poorer ones from whom it was difficult to get money.[9] Finally, much depended on the sources of a landowner's income, since the assessments were essentially a tax on rents, and other forms of estate revenue usually escaped. So for all these reasons it is not surprising to find that the available case studies show wide variations in the proportion of estate income absorbed by taxes. In relatively peaceful Kent the farming squire Nicholas Toke of Godinton paid no more than 5 per cent of his income in taxes over the period 1645–60 as a whole, but he was a tenant for some of his land and so would not have been liable for the tax on the rented portion of it. In Sussex Sir Thomas Pelham of Laughton paid out just over 7 per cent of his income from rents during the years 1643–9, but he also enjoyed a large income from iron works which he operated himself, and which in some years equalled or even exceeded his rents, and on that he appears to have paid no tax at all. Other landowners, however, even in the protected south-east, paid considerably higher proportions. On the Essex estate of Lord Petre allowances to the tenants for taxes paid by them came to £603 on a rent roll of some £3,800 in 1648–9, nearly 16 per cent; by 1651–2 some of the tenants were paying their rents clear of taxes, but the allowances to the remainder amounted to nearly 21 per cent of their rents. The Hare family apparently paid just over a quarter (26.3 per cent) of the rental of their Norfolk estate in the years 1643–5, and in the six counties of the Eastern Association as a whole Holmes found proportions ranging from 15.6 per cent to 35.3 per cent. From Bedfordshire and Northamptonshire, which were more seriously affected by the war than any of the foregoing counties, Habakkuk cites the case of the Gery family, who were paying a quarter of their modest income in taxes during the first years of the first Civil War, and still as much as one-eighth during the 1650s. Where

---

[8] HMC, *Salisbury*, XXII, pp. 475–9; J. H. P. Pafford, 'Accounts of the Parliamentary Garrisons of Great Chalfield and Malmesbury', *Wilts. Arch. & Nat. Hist. Soc., Records Branch*, II, 1940, esp. pp. 9, 45, 69.

[9] Coate, *op. cit.*, app. 3, p. 359; Gardiner, *op. cit.*, pp. 22–3; CCC, I, p. 252.

conditions were particularly unfavourable to landlords, owing to both an unusually heavy fall in land values and the levying of taxes by both parties, the proportion of estate income absorbed in taxation could be higher still. On the Studley estate in Oxfordshire it was no less than 71 per cent of the rental over the years 1642–6, as stated in a paper which, according to the owner, "my bailife doth affirme upon his oath to be a true accounte and if this may not sattisfie he will be ready upon reasonable warninge to make oath of it before any judge in England".[10]

On some estates rents were reduced to enable the tenants to pay the assessments themselves, but this was only one of several factors that were reducing estate incomes in the 1640s. Rents in some districts were affected by dislocation of the normal channels of trade and marketing for farm produce. Early in 1643, for instance, the inhabitants of Melbourne told those of Derby that the forces of Sir John Gell had been seizing the horses of country people taking their produce to town, which had "caused divers of them to throw their sacks of corn upon the way and return home so that we cannot come into your market to sell our corn".[11] Almost everywhere the repair and maintenance of farm buildings and other forms of fixed capital was neglected, and the prolonged absence of tenants and their labourers whilst they served with the armies was also serious. Women could, and frequently did, run farms at this period, but nevertheless many rents must have fallen into arrears in circumstances similar to those of a farm on the earl of Bridgewater's Shropshire estate, whose tenant in 1650 was, according to the surveyor, "a poor widow, her husband killed at Montgomery fight". The departure of the landowners themselves must have meant a sharp decline in the level of managerial effectiveness, especially on the smaller estates where no professional steward was employed, at the very moment when wartime conditions greatly magnified difficulties of managing an estate. As the correspondence between Sir Thomas and Lady Knyvett shows, the wife of an absentee owner was likely to find tenants throwing up their farms, pressing for reductions in rent, ignoring husbandry covenants, and encroaching on their landlord's rights in other ways, and she would have to deal with them as best she could without the experience of a lifetime spent in handling estate matters. Some managed very well, but there is no doubt that many tenants successfully took advantage of the situation.[12]

[10] Everitt, *op. cit.*, p. 160; E. C. Lodge, ed., *The Account Book of a Kentish Estate, 1616–1704*, Oxford, 1927, p. xxvi; BL, Add. MSS 33,144–5; Essex RO, D/DP Z.30/29, A.62/1; Holmes, *op. cit.*, p. 271 n. 46; H. J. Habakkuk, 'English Landownership, 1680–1740', EcHR, x, 1940, pp. 8–9; BL, Egerton MS 2,978, ff. 62–3.

[11] Derbs. RO, D 803M/29, f. 49.

[12] M. James, *Social Problems and Policy during the Puritan Revolution*, London, 1930, pp. 61–6; E. Hopkins, 'The Bridgewater Estates in North Shropshire during the Civil War', *Shrops. Arch. Soc.*, LVI, 2, 1960, p. 310; B. Schofield, *The Knyvett Letters*, London, 1949, esp. pp. 134, 137, 151, 156.

Another factor which received a great deal of publicity at the time was plundering. There is no doubt that practically everywhere individuals suffered very severely at the hands of marauding soldiers, and an immense volume of minutely detailed evidence on the nature and extent of the losses incurred is preserved in the Commonwealth Exchequer papers in the form of accounts submitted by villages across the length and breadth of England.[13] Taking the country as a whole it is hard to be sure how much it all amounted to, and the evidence suggests that in areas where fighting was neither intense nor continuous, and in areas where the generally better paid and disciplined parliamentary army usually had the upper hand, it was not very widespread. But in areas which were disputed between the two sides for a considerable part of the war, where garrisons living off the country were numerous, or through which armies on the march frequently passed, plundering did affect more than isolated individuals. Worst affected seem to have been the area around Oxford, a swathe of country stretching from Hampshire and Wiltshire in the south up through Gloucestershire and the Welsh border counties to Cheshire, and parts of the north, in some districts of which the evils associated with the presence of armies had lasted ever since the invasion of the Scots in 1639. As far as the working farmer was concerned, the most serious aspect of plundering was that he was liable to lose his livestock. This was obviously serious in pastoral districts, and in some of them, relatively sheltered Norfolk as well as exposed Northamptonshire and Buckinghamshire, the prevailing insecurity seems to have caused farmers temporarily to switch from animal husbandry to growing grain.[14] But the loss of animals was hardly less of a disaster to the arable farmer who was heavily dependent on his horses; if deprived of them he would be unable to do his ploughing, get his crops in from the fields, or take them to market. As early in the war as February 1643 an intelligence report reached Sir Samuel Luke that Rupert's seizure of horses in Oxfordshire was having the consequence that in some places "the inhabitants are constrayned to ioyne 3 or 4 of them [together] to make upp a teame".[15] Besides seizure of farm stock the theft of stored foodstuffs was the most common crime committed by the soldiers, but they might take anything they could carry away and cause a great deal of damage to what they could not. The hamlets of Lea and Marston in Warwickshire, in no way untypical of thousands of other small places, recorded the loss at

---

[13] PRO, SP 28. However, it should be noted that the village accounts only record losses experienced at the hands of parliamentary troops and the Scottish army: royalist plundering, which was more important to the inhabitants of the south-west and parts of the Midlands, is not included. The accounts also cover expenditure on free quarter, deliveries in kind to the armies, and tax payments.

[14] P. A. J. Pettit, *The Royal Forests of Northamptonshire: A Study in their Economy, 1558–1714*, Northants. Rec. Soc., XXIII, 1968, pp. 176–7; Schofield, *op. cit.*, p. 151; F. P. Verney, *Memoirs of the Verney Family during the Civil War*, 2 vols., London, 1892, II, pp. 156–7.

[15] *The Journal of Sir Samuel Luke, vol. I*, Oxon. Rec. Soc., XXIX, 1950, p. xiii.

the hands of the Scots of a wide variety of household goods, including numerous articles of clothing, hats, gloves, shoes, bedding, cushions, books, a brass candlestick, and a looking glass. A possible index of the extent of the material impoverishment which this type of plundering caused to many rural communities is provided by Bettey's finding that the proportion of the total wealth of deceased Dorset farmers held in the form of household goods fell from 41 per cent in the 1630s to 34 per cent in the 1640s.[16]

Nevertheless, in most places the taking of free quarter by troops was probably a more serious matter than either plundering or regular taxation, although of course quartered troops were often themselves plunderers. In the districts where it occurred its incidence was wider, for soldiers might be quartered on virtually everyone in a neighbourhood, rich or poor, either repeatedly for short periods, or sometimes for weeks or months at a time, until they were literally eaten out of house and home. The inhabitants of Chesham Magna (Bucks.), for instance, had a troop of 120 horse billeted on them continuously from 12 December 1644 until April 1645, and at 1s. 8d. per man per day this involved them in providing £1,493 worth of goods and services. Chesham Magna was a largish place, but what could be involved for a small one is illustrated by the experience of Lea and Marston (War.) when the Scots arrived some time in 1645. Four hundred and thirty-three soldiers with about the same number of horses were distributed among thirty-five households, and although the largest landholders accommodated most of them, not only those described as labourers, but even Elizabeth Gisbourne, "a poore widow", had to take their share. Fortunately, this particular horde of locusts passed on after only three days. In most parts of the country the receipts which the unwilling hosts received for what they had provided were never honoured.[17] The role of free quarter in depressing the ability of tenants to pay their rents was the more important, since it afflicted the rural population over a much wider geographical area and lasted over a longer period than did plundering, and it was still giving rise to complaints at the beginning of the next decade. Thus in his account for Michaelmas 1650 the steward of the earl of Bridgewater's Shropshire estate reported of one holding that "nothing was made of this farm these two years, it being eaten up and destroyed by Colls Willis, Vaughan, Hosiers and other troops".[18]

The combined impact of all these side effects of seventeenth-century warfare on rent receipts was clearly considerable. The tenantry of course bore the brunt of them in the first instance, but inevitably the landlords had to

[16] PRO, SP 28/182; J. H. Bettey, 'Agriculture and Rural Society in Dorset 1570–1670', unpub. Bristol Univ. Ph.D. thesis, 1977, p. 339.
[17] PRO, SP 28/182; Holmes, *op. cit.*, pp. 152–6; Johnson, thesis, pp. 142–4; Morrill, *op. cit.*, p. 107.
[18] Hopkins, *op. cit.*, p. 310. See also CCC, *I*, pp. 363–4.

accept that part of the burden would be shifted onto them. As one tenant, who was three years in arrears with his rent, reminded the dean and chapter of Westminster, after presenting them with an account of his losses from plundering and free quarter and of his expenditure on emergency repairs, "most landlords as your Honours well know have used and do use to bear out their tenants in most of those extraordinary payments and pressures, otherwise tenants and families must be undone". The extent to which sufferers were in fact borne out by their landlords differed from estate to estate, but an unusually explicit statement of policy in this respect is that made in October 1646 by the earl of Salisbury's steward with reference to the manor of Tarrant Rushton in Dorset: "I allow the same to all tenants uppon rack rents...beinge a 3rd part of quarteringe and contribution if it exceed not the rent, but noe plunder." And apart from making such allowances owners could not normally recover more than a small fraction of the unpaid arrears of rent – on the largest estates amounting to thousands of pounds – which their tenants owed them. The Verneys could obtain none at all from those of their outlying estates in Oxfordshire and Berkshire, whilst the earl of Salisbury, whose arrears totalled £12,187, or more than a year's pre-war income, by 1644–5, and still exceeded £7,000 in 1650–1, was obliged to write off some £8,500 worth over the years 1643–56 and had great difficulty in securing payment of what he was not prepared to forgive.[19]

In fact, for obvious reasons, complete series of estate rentals for the 1640s are less common than for any other seventeenth-century decade, and most of those that do survive relate to areas where disruption from the war was minimal. On the Essex estate of Lord Petre, and on that of Sir Thomas Pelham of Laughton in East Sussex, rents had to be reduced on only a few farms and there is no evidence of an unusually high level of arrears,[20] but this was not the universal experience even within the south-east. In less protected areas few estates can have escaped entirely unscathed. There is a good deal of evidence that reductions in rent of one-third were nothing out of the ordinary – by 1645 the Verneys' steward in Buckinghamshire was very happy if he could let for as much as two-thirds of the pre-war rent – and it was not until 1647, 1648, or even later that rent levels returned to normal. Where damage and dislocation were most acute tenants were able to pay their landlords little or nothing for years on end, and sometimes threw up their farms altogether, so that holdings were left unoccupied or at best were used only for occasional grazing. Abandoned farm land was reported from places as far apart as the neighbourhood of Carlisle, Skawton, and Walton in the

[19] Westminster Abbey, Muniments no. 8,221; HMC, *Salisbury*, XXII, pp. 387–8; J. P. F. Broad, 'Sir Ralph Verney and his Estates, 1630–1696', unpub. Oxford Univ. D.Phil. thesis, 1973, pp. 15–17; Stone, *op. cit.*, pp. 151, 161.
[20] For the Petre rentals, BL, Add. MS 5,505, ff. 63–6; Essex RO, D/DP E.9, E.22/2, A.62/1. For those of Sir Thomas Pelham, BL, Add. MS 33,144.

North Riding, Brigstock Park in Northamptonshire, Middle Claydon in Buckinghamshire, Blagdon in Somerset, and Hardwick in Gloucestershire. The lessor of a church estate at the last of these places reported that events had "caused the tennts to throw up their leases it lying between Gloycester & Worcester and they forced to pay contribuc̄on to both garrisons besides ffree quartering continually to the one partie or the other whereby the said tennts were disabled to pay their rents". He had, he said, received nothing from them for three and a half years.[21] In some places a hardly less disastrous situation, from the landlords' point of view, prevailed even after the end of the fighting. Thus in 1645 John Ponsonby, Esq., promised his tenants at Kirk Leavington, Yorkshire, to make them allowance not only for the tax payments they made but also for the expenses they incurred in quartering troops, and in the event these proved to be so great in the two years or so following that Ponsonby's rental for 1648 recorded that "their charges did far surmount the full value of the said lands" so that no rent at all had been received from them. The Yorkshire estate of Lord Fairfax of Emley was another which suffered very severely during the war years. By 1645 some of the tenants had to be forgiven a whole year's rent and their future rent reduced by half, the rest had their rent reduced by a third, and all assessments still had to be paid by the landlord. "My lord", wrote the distraught steward, "this cuts off a great part of your revenue, and yet I fear your tenants are so impoverished, that they will scarce be able to pay what is now set down." Things were hardly less bad on dozens of other Yorkshire estates, and on the properties of the earl of Northumberland, which lay mostly in Northumberland itself, it was reported to their owner in 1646 that the tenants had suffered so severely that a 50 per cent reduction in rent would hardly be enough to enable them to pay the other half for several years ahead.[22] Conditions on estates in the north-east may well have been worse than almost anywhere else, but impressive evidence of reduced rents comes from sequestered estates in several other parts of the country. In March 1647 the local authorities in the Wirral reported to the Committee for Compounding that the annual value of thirty-one properties in their care had fallen from £4,144 before the war to only £2,247, that is, by 45.7 per cent, whilst a year later on twenty-seven estates in Gloucestershire the reported fall was from £6,542 per annum to only £3,142 (52 per cent). Almost certainly the

[21] Broad, thesis, pp. 17–18; CCC, *I*, p. 232; R. Bell, *Memorials of the Civil War Comprising the Correspondence of the Fairfax Family...* 2 vols., London, 1849, *I*, p. 212; Pettit, *op. cit.*, pp. 176–7; HMC, *Salisbury*, *XXII*, p. 381; Westminster Abbey, Muniments no. 32,967; James, *loc. cit.*; H. B. Newman, 'The Sequestration of the Royalists' Estates during the Civil War', unpub. Harvard Univ. Ph.D. thesis, 1949, pp. 77, 85, 183–93. See also the comments, relating mainly to 1647–8, from the county committees of Glos., Rutland, Lincs., Durham, and Northumb. in CCC, *I*, pp. 76, 81, 82, 99, 238.

[22] Clwyd RO, Glynde MSS D/G 650; Bell, *op. cit.*, *I*, pp. 211–12; J. W. Clay, *Yorkshire Royalist Composition Papers*, Yorks. Arch. Soc. Rec. Ser., xv, 1893, *passim*.

rents on sequestered lands were further depressed than were rents in general, but nevertheless the comments of the local committees on the rentals from which these figures are derived make it clear that the fact of sequestration was of less importance in pulling them down than were the factors outlined above which affected all estates alike, whether or not they were sequestered. It is true that rents recovered fairly quickly in most places, and indeed were not uncommonly higher by the 1660s than they had been in 1640, but this should not blind us to the realities of the rent falls of the war period.[23]

However, for many landowners the fall in rents was overshadowed by the fact that they were not in possession of their estates anyway, since they had been sequestered either by the king or by parliament. Naturally, the adherents of the losing side were the main sufferers in this respect: delinquents (as active royalists were called) were subject to complete sequestration, and Catholics, whether or not they had actively supported the king, were subject to sequestration of two-thirds of their estates.[24] In some cases they were thus dispossessed for as long as ten years. But whilst the war still continued, royalists and Catholics were not the only ones to suffer in this way, for the king also seized the properties of his opponents in the areas he controlled. Royal sequestration was, moreover, harsher than that of parliament, since there never seems to have been any provision for the support of dependants, although, like that of parliament, it does seem to have respected trust terms.[25] Royalist control in the north was ended by the summer of 1644, but in much of Wales, the Welsh border counties, the south-west, and around Oxford it survived late into 1645 or even 1646, so that supporters of parliament with estates in those districts were sometimes deprived of incomes for as long as three years and more. Even before the end of 1642 the Cornish royalists, on their own initiative and without any orders from the king, were sequestering the estates of opponents in the county, and the accounts of the royalist sheriff of Cornwall include the names of forty-five sequestered persons from Lord Robartes downwards. By May 1643, if not before, the marquess of Newcastle was ordering the sequestration of prominent parliamentarians in the north.[26] It should be remembered that a royalist whose property did not fall under

[23] CCC, I, pp. 60–1, 85–8. See also some similar figures for sequestered estates in Wiltshire – ibid., pp. 76–8.

[24] The basic sequestration ordinance was not passed until 22 Mar. 1643, but parliament had enunciated the general principle that the delinquents should pay the cost of the war as early as Sept. 1642 and the estates of some prominent royalists (including Lord Capel) had been seized during the autumn – Firth and Rait, I, pp. 106–17; S. R. Gardiner, History of the Great Civil War, 4 vols., London, 1897–1905, II, pp. 17–18; A. Kingston, Hertfordshire during the Great Civil War, London and Hertford, 1894, p. 22.

[25] For an example of royalist sequestration being lifted on the owner's proving that the estate had been vested in trustees, see Verney, op. cit., II, pp. 212–13. See also Engeberg, 'Royalist Finances', pp. 92–4.

[26] Coate, Cornwall, pp. 103–4; C. B. Phillips, 'County Committees and Local Government in Cumberland and Westmorland, 1642–1660', Northern Hist., v, 1970, p. 38 n. 35.

parliamentary control until towards the end of the war and who was able to compound promptly would have been deprived of his rents for a much shorter period than a parliamentarian with estates in the west.

However, neither side ever succeeded in sequestering the estates of anything approaching the total number of those who had actively opposed them. Parliament probably caught up with most delinquents and Catholics in areas like East Anglia where its control was very strong, but even there the small Cambridgeshire estate of the Catholic Lord Petre escaped notice until as late as July 1650.[27] In counties like Lancashire, Yorkshire, and Cornwall, where the mass of the gentry were royalist and would not inform the authorities about each other's delinquency, numbers of them avoided the attention of the county committees for years after the end of the war, or even until the act of indemnity in February 1651/2 finally removed the danger of sequestration altogether.[28] The total number of landowners whose estates were sequestered by parliament cannot be known accurately, but since considerably more were sequestered than were eventually obliged to compound, probably at least a quarter and possibly an even higher proportion of the entire class was affected.[29] The proportion varied locally, of course, according to the political complexion of the area. In Suffolk, with very few royalists, fewer than 10 per cent of the gentry suffered, in Cumberland and Westmorland the proportion was well over half, whilst in Kent it was over 60 per cent, and it must have been higher still in an overwhelmingly royalist county like Cornwall.[30] Nor was sequestration the only reason why landowners might be deprived of their incomes in the Civil War period. There were those 'neuters' who happened to live under the power of one side whilst their estates lay under the power of the other, and, whilst avoiding sequestration, yet found that it was impossible to carry on the administration of their estates in such conditions or to transmit rents even if they could be collected. Thus on the Shropshire properties of the earl of Bridgewater, who lived at Ashridge in Hertfordshire, collection of rents seems to have come to a complete halt during the war and not to have been fully resumed until 1647. Thus for several years the earl received no income from this very important part of his estate and in consequence was forced into serious debt: by the time he died in 1649 his own debts amounted to £26,950 and in addition he had burdened his successor with annuities payable out of the estate

[27] CCC, I, p. 277.
[28] Coate, *op. cit.*, pp. 265–6; Newman, thesis, pp. 151–3. As late as 1648 Hesilrige reported from Newcastle that few of the local gentry who had fought against parliament had yet been sequestered.
[29] H. J. Habakkuk, 'Landowners and the Civil War', EcHR, 2nd ser., XVIII, 1965, pp. 147–8. This author demonstrates that the proportion of the gentry and aristocracy who eventually compounded, together with those whose estates were confiscated, was roughly one-quarter.
[30] A. M. Everitt, *Suffolk and the Great Rebellion, 1640–60*, Suffolk Rec. Soc., 1960, p. 11; C. B. Phillips, 'The Gentry in Cumberland and Westmorland, 1600–1665', unpub. Lancaster Univ. Ph.D. thesis, 1973, pp. 46, 315–22, 327, 337–8.

to various individuals who had advanced him money. Another landowner who lived in the south (at Petworth), far removed from the bulk of his estates, was the earl of Northumberland. His northern properties were sequestered for a time by the royalists in 1643–4, but it was mainly a result of the acutely disturbed conditions which prevailed in the far north from well before the outbreak of the Civil War in England until long after the royalist defeat at Marston Moor that he received no rents from his estates for the five years up to Michaelmas 1646. By that time his loss of income totalled £37,984 11s.[31]

There were, however, a number of factors which blunted the effects of sequestration on the victims. First, the parliamentary sequestration ordinance of August 1643 provided that up to one-fifth of the income from sequestered estates might be paid to the wife and children of a delinquent by way of maintenance. Complaints by individual royalists or their families that county committees were not making these payments promptly, in full, or even at all, are quite frequently found. But in general it seems that the payments were made as the ordinance laid down, and they must have saved many royalists from complete destitution.[32] Secondly, the difficulties of administering the sequestered properties meant that the county committees were often ready to lease the estates back to the owner, or to his wife, or to someone acting as his agent, usually at a rent well below its full value. Thus the two-thirds part of Lord Petre's Essex estate which had been sequestered was let to his nominee at a rent of £1,500 per annum, even though it was worth something over £2,500 per annum.[33] By no means all sequestered persons were so fortunate as to secure such leases, but the practice seems to have been sufficiently widespread to arouse concern in London that sequestration revenues were being seriously reduced and delinquents deprived of the most obvious incentive to compound.[34]

It was also very important for many families that in all its dealings with delinquents and their estates parliament was prepared to honour the terms of family settlements, provided that these had been made before the war. Consequently sequestration was imposed only on property legally in the possession of the delinquent himself, and any part of the estate that was vested in trustees for the payment of debts or the raising of portions for younger children could normally escape it. Probably quite a significant minority of delinquent families succeeded in limiting the extent of sequestration in this way. The trusts they brought forward were doubtless normally genuine enough, though some may have been forged and others were probably obsolete and in reality had already been fully performed, even though the

---

[31] Hopkins, *op. cit., passim*; HMC, *Third Report*, app. p. 86; Phillips, 'County Committees', p. 38 n. 35.
[32] Firth and Rait, *I*, p. 258; Newman, thesis, pp. 210–13.
[33] Essex RO, D/DP Z.30/29, 31.
[34] Newman, thesis, pp. 118–19, 243–4; CCC, *I*, pp. 63, 74, 84.

term of years was still outstanding in law and so available for use as a deception. But having used genuine trusts to recover part of their estates most landowners are likely to have used all or part of the income accruing to them to maintain themselves and their families, rather than to perform the trusts themselves.[35]

So for an unknown proportion of royalists the practical effects of sequestration were somewhat reduced by one or another of these means. Yet landowners whose incomes were even partly interrupted for a considerable period were likely to find themselves in financially deep water because it was difficult or impossible for them to reduce their outgoings to the extent that their incomes had been reduced. Even if they did cut down their living expenses to the bare minimum, economize drastically on the education of the younger children, and postpone the marriage of the older ones, there were often other items over which they had no control. If debts or annuities were charged on their estates, the creditors or annuitants would not in the long run willingly abate their claims just because of the misfortunes of the debtor, although many do seem to have shown some temporary forbearance, and they would keep careful account of unpaid arrears, which after a few years would begin to mount up to a frightening sum. With interest on mortgages normally at 8 per cent in the 1630s and 1640s, the principal of a debt on which no interest had been paid for six years would have increased by roughly half. Such accumulations of unpaid interest and annuities were often the most serious result of sequestration, and might be enough to turn what had been a manageable level of debt in 1642 into a crushing one that could be discharged only by a substantial sale of land. It was largely for this reason that the fourth Lord Petre, who eventually recovered his estate without having to pay a composition fine, was nevertheless forced to sell £21,500 worth of property, about one-seventh of his entire estate, between 1652 and 1663.[36] But it was not the owners of large estates like Lord Petre who suffered worst from sequestration. A royalist with several geographically dispersed properties would almost certainly escape the 1640s less seriously scathed than one with land in one single locality: if he had estates in the west these would escape sequestration for several years longer than those in the east, and small outlying properties might be missed by the sequestrators altogether. The small landowner who was totally deprived of his whole estate at a single blow might indeed be in a parlous state. One can sense the desperation which inspired Richard Conquest, who returned from the king's quarters to his estate at Houghton Conquest in Bedfordshire to try to collect some rent and "swore he would destroy man, woman, and child if he had it not".[37]

---

[35] For examples of the use of a trust, respectively to recover lands from sequestration and to keep sequestration at bay, see C. Clay, 'The Misfortunes of William, Fourth Lord Petre', *Recusant Hist.*, XI, 2, 1971, pp. 96–7; and Broad, *op. cit.*, pp. 43–7.

[36] C. Clay, *op. cit., passim*.

[37] J. Godber, *History of Bedfordshire, 1066–1888*, Bedford, 1969, p. 248.

But both large and small landowners were likely to find that sequestration had had adverse consequences for their estates which could not be righted quickly and easily even when they had regained possession. Their woodlands and timber trees had often been felled. Repairs and maintenance had probably been neglected so that farm buildings were becoming ruinous, fences and gates dilapidated and falling down, ditches and water courses choked up and liable to flood. The state as landlord of sequestered properties did not always neglect its duty in respect of repairs, but the instances where it fulfilled them adequately, as in Cheshire, seem to have been the exception rather than the rule. And as for the tenants, in wartime conditions they would often be in no position to fulfil their responsibilities, and, even if they were, the situation made it possible for them to break their covenants with impunity, whilst the inability of the county committees (down to 1650) to grant them more than annual tenancies gave them no incentive to do otherwise. If sequestration lasted a long time the extent of deterioration might be serious and make it essential for the restored landlord to invest considerable sums at the very time he could least afford to do so. Damage done to the land itself by ploughing up pasture, improper cropping, or neglect of the normal manuring procedure might reduce the value of a farm just as much as neglect of repairs but would be even less easy to put right, since it would take time as well as the expenditure of capital. Consequently it might be several or even many years before an estate which had been maltreated whilst under sequestration yielded its owner the same rent as before the war.[38]

Landowners in the 1640s also experienced heavy capital losses from damage done to their houses, parks, home farms, and woods. Attacks on the houses of gentry believed to be hostile were a marked feature of the behaviour of partisans on both sides from the very beginning of the war, and in fact began even before Charles had raised his standard at Nottingham. In the early months the occasion for these attacks was often a search for arms in the house of a 'suspected person' which then got out of hand and turned into a general despoiling of the owner's possessions, as at the house of the Countess Rivers at St Osyth's, of the earl of Bridgewater at Ashridge, and at Knowle and Barham Court in Kent. However, once the fighting had begun, opportunities for plundering country houses became much more numerous, and as one district after another became the seat of serious hostilities so the houses of the local gentry of either or both sides suffered. Thus when the earl of Essex invaded Cornwall in the late summer of 1644 Jonathan Rashleigh's Menabilly and the residences of other royalists were sacked by his troops.[39] How many

---

[38] Everitt, *Community of Kent*, pp. 169–70; D. Gardiner, *Oxinden and Peyton Letters*, pp. 70–1, 90; Newman, thesis, pp. 262–3; Morrill, *Cheshire*, pp. 112–17; CCC, *I*, pp. 170–1, 230, 235, 252, 321, 382; *II*, p. 1,053.

[39] *Old Parliamentary History*, 24 vols., London 1751–61, *XI*, pp. 336, 383; Earl of Clarendon, *History of the Great Rebellion*, 7 vols., Oxford, 1849, *II*, p. 346; S. R. Gardiner, *op. cit.*, *II*, pp. 12–13; Kingston, *op. cit.*, pp. 35–6; Everitt, *Community of Kent*, pp. 111–15; Coate, *op. cit.*, pp. 153–4.

gentry and aristocratic families had their houses pillaged, and all – or at least the most valuable part – of their possessions stolen or destroyed, cannot be estimated with any accuracy, but it was clearly a very large number, probably running into thousands rather than hundreds. The only section of the landed class to escape this form of loss would have been those parliamentarians whose residences were safely in the parts of East Anglia and the south-east never invaded by the king's forces. The landed magnates whose country palaces were looted of their contents sometimes experienced losses running into thousands of pounds, those of Lord Arundell at Wardour Castle and the earl of Northampton at Castle Ashby being especially notorious, but they could usually sustain them better than lesser owners. Those who suffered the worst damage from these attacks were probably those country gentlemen who derived a substantial proportion of their income from farming their own demesne land, for they not infrequently involved the virtual wiping out of the home farm as a productive unit. Sir Robert Harley, for instance, lost a flock of 800 sheep, besides cattle and a stud of 30 brood mares, when the royalists attacked Brampton Bryan in 1643. At Menabilly in 1644 Jonathan Rashleigh lost 500 sheep, 100 lambs, 18 draught oxen, 20 milch kine, and a bull, 90 bullocks, 40 horses, and 80 hogs, which he valued at a total of £1,310; his stock of wool worth £300; stored and standing grain and hay worth £750; and husbandry implements, wains, and other equipment worth a further £100. Losses on a similar scale were suffered by a Mrs Jane Crosland of Helmsley (Yorks.) at the hands of the parliamentary forces besieging the castle there. She drew up a list to send to the Committee for Compounding which included considerable stores of grain, hay, peas, and malt; no fewer than 930 stooks of hardcorn, 940 stooks of barley, and 500 of oats; 500 sheep, 20 oxen, 54 cattle of other types, 15 horses, 12 swine, and much else besides. Lest the committee refuse to believe this huge loss, she had her list signed as a true account by her family, servants, and thirty-six local inhabitants including the two constables.[40] Quite apart from the capital cost of restocking, a home farm denuded of animals and equipment would cease to yield its owner any income.

Another way in which a house might suffer harm was as a result of its use as a garrisoned strong-point. Occupation of a house by soldiers for a period of months or even years was bound to result in a good deal of damage, even when the troops were friendly and were there with the owner's consent, let alone in the opposite case. However, the consequences were likely to be a good deal more serious if the garrison were attacked by the enemy, and worse yet if it was subjected to prolonged bombardment or determined storm. Damage would not then be limited to furnishings and such relatively minor matters as wainscoting or windows: it might undermine the basic

[40] J. Webb, *Memorials of the Civil War...as it Affected Herefordshire and the Adjacent Counties*, 2 vols., London, 1879, *I*, p. 319; Coate, *op. cit.*, app. 3, pp. 359–60; J. W. Clay, 'Yorkshire Royalist Composition Papers', pp. 92–6.

structure, and at worst leave the place an uninhabitable heap of ruins. In fact the number of country houses that were partially or wholly destroyed during and after the war seems to have been considerably larger than is usually appreciated. Some suffered this fate during the concluding stages of a siege, as did the marquess of Winchester's great Basing House (Hants.), Sir John Strangeways's Abbotsbury (Dorset), and Shelford House (Notts.). Some were demolished or burnt to prevent the enemy using them as strong-points, as in the case of Viscount Campden's splendid house in Gloucestershire, and Hawkesley and Frankley houses (Worcs.), all three destroyed by the royalists in the few weeks before Naseby. Some, like Sir John Bankes's Corfe Castle, were 'slighted' by the parliamentarians after the war was over; more suffered the fate of Sir Walter Earle's Charborough (Dorset), which was burned as an act of terror and revenge; others caught fire accidentally whilst being looted; a few, on lands confiscated and sold in the 1650s, were knocked down by their new owners, as happened to Sir John Stawell's Somerset seat of Cothelstone.[41] No one has yet attempted to compile a complete list, but the evidence available in the local histories of the Civil War suggests that at least 150 to 200 houses of major local importance were more or less reduced to ruins, and the true total may well have been very much higher. These were not, of course, equally distributed over the whole country and the casualties were concentrated in the areas where there was much fighting, such as Shropshire, where a survey of readily available literature reveals at least twelve, Nottinghamshire and Dorset, where there were at least nine each, and Worcestershire, where there were at least eight.[42] That members of parliament realized that all too many houses were being destroyed, and that this was likely to have adverse effects for the economies of the localities in question, is suggested by the terms of their refusal to sanction local proposals to demolish High Ercall in Shropshire and several houses in Sussex, all of which had been used as strongholds by the royalists.[43] But besides those totally ruined, many hundreds more manor houses, possibly even a matter of thousands, required more or less extensive repairs after what they had been through. During the decade or so after the cessation of hostilities in England in 1646, making good the damage their houses had suffered must have been a major financial preoccupation of the gentry. The cost of necessary repairs

[41] A. R. Bayley, *The Great Civil War in Dorset*, Taunton, 1910, pp. 129, 227–8, 305; G. N. Godwin, *The Civil War in Hampshire*, London, 1904, pp. 359–61, 366; J. W. Willis Bund, *The Civil War in Worcestershire*, Birmingham and London, 1905, pp. 152, 158–9; A. C. Wood, *Nottinghamshire and the Civil War*, Oxford, 1937, pp. 102–3; G. D. Stawell, *A Quantock Family*, Taunton, 1910, p. 404.

[42] A. Stackhouse, *The Garrisons of Shropshire*, Shrewsbury, 1867; W. J. Farrow, *The Great Civil War in Shropshire*, Shrewsbury, 1926; Wood, *op. cit.*; Bayley, *op. cit.*; Willis Bund, *op. cit.*

[43] W. Phillips, 'Sequestration Papers of Sir Richard, First Baron Newport', *Shrop. Arch. & Nat. Hist. Soc.*, 2nd ser., XII, 1900, p. 20 n. 1; C. Thomas-Stanford, *Sussex in the Great Civil War and Interregnum*, London, 1910, p. 161.

to Cranbourn House in Dorset, for instance, which had received a moderately severe ransacking by the royalists and then played host to a succession of parliamentary detachments, was estimated to be £666 15s.[44]

*(b) Composition fines and confiscations*
Parliament began allowing royalists to recover their sequestered estates on payment of a fine in the early part of 1644. However, in the first half of that year the king's party still had prospects of ultimate victory, and right down to the time of Naseby, or even the fall of Bristol, a recovery might have seemed possible, so that the number of applications to compound was not very large until 1646 and 1647. Yet even then not all were ready to yield. In April 1647 the Committee for Compounding told the county committees that because, contrary to instructions, they were allowing the owners of sequestered properties to lease them at undervaluations, the owners were not coming forward to compound, or if they did tender a petition, they did not prosecute it, "hoping for a turn of things whereby they may preserve their estates to do more mischief". The year of the second Civil War, 1648, naturally saw a sharp decline in the number of compositions, but in the following year, after the failure of the risings had provided a convincing demonstration of the strength of the new regime, and had also produced a fresh crop of sequestrations, the tide of applications was renewed. After the execution of the king even the landowners of the most strongly royalist areas like Cornwall were ready to compound, and by the summer of 1652 the whole business was almost completed.[45]

The earliest applicants applied direct to parliament for permission to compound and were then referred to the Goldsmith's Hall committee for their fine to be set. However, as the numbers involved grew and the composition procedure became firmly established, compounders approached the committee direct in the first instance, and matters were handled by it without the intervention of parliament.[46] The amount of the fine was calculated as a proportion of the capital value of the delinquent's estate, ranging from a nominal tenth to a nominal two-thirds for the various categories of offender. Now the latter of these rates would at first sight appear to have been ruinously high. The actual weight of the fines was, however, substantially reduced by the rule whereby the estate of the delinquent compounding at one-tenth should be valued at twenty years' purchase, the estates of those fined one-sixth should be reckoned at eighteen years'

---

[44] HMC, *Salisbury, XXII*, p. 396.

[45] CCC, I, p. 63; V, pp. v–ix; P. Hardacre, *The Royalists during the Puritan Revolution*, The Hague, 1956, pp. 20–3, 64–7; Coate, *op. cit.*, p. 237.

[46] By an act of parliament of March 1649, however, the committee of the Northern Association at Newcastle was directed to compound directly with royalists from the northern counties – CCC, I, pp. vii–viii, 201–4; CJ, VI, p. 153.

purchase, of those fined one-third and a half at fifteen, and of those fined two-thirds at only twelve. As a result the compounder at one-third, for instance, had to pay five, and the compounder at one-sixth only three, years' value of their property. A further point of importance is that in practice most delinquents compounded at the lower rates of one-tenth and one-sixth, and relatively few at the higher ones. The parliamentary regulations about fines varied from time to time, but fines of a quarter were mostly imposed on the rebels of 1648 in the south-east; fines of one-third were imposed on members of parliament and on members of the clerical and legal professions; fines of a half on the even more limited group of prominent royalist leaders who had been specifically named by parliament; and the fines of two-thirds were reserved only for a handful of the most incorrigible delinquents.[47] Besides, many royalists who would otherwise have had to compound at higher rates were permitted to pay fines at the lower because they were covered by the 'articles' agreed upon as the surrender terms of various royalist garrisons, such as Exeter, Truro, Oxford, and Ashby de la Zouch, in late 1645 and early 1646. These 'articles' invariably provided that the defenders might compound at the minimum rate of one-tenth. The Committee for Compounding not infrequently showed itself inclined to ignore the undertaking contained in surrender articles, but luckily for the compounders the army felt that its honour was involved, and the Committee for Relief on Articles of War was prepared to uphold them. Fairfax himself intervened on behalf of those who had surrendered to him on a number of occasions. One of those who benefited from his intervention was Lord Poulett, together with his son Sir John Poulett. The fines originally fixed on them had been at the rate of one-half, and amounted to £10,432 and £9,400 respectively, but, after their right to the benefit of the Exeter articles had been established, Lord Poulett's fine was reduced to £2,743 and his son's to £3,760 12s.[48]

Numerous royalists who were not covered by articles of war nevertheless appealed to the Committee for Compounding for a reduction in their fines. All sorts of grounds might be adduced for such a reduction, for instance that no allowance had been made for debts charged on the estate, or for damage or depreciation resulting from the war, or that they had overvalued the property through mistaking the nature of the tenancies on it. The committee does seem to have treated appeals very fairly, and although some grounds for appeal such as war damage and depreciation were never accepted as valid,

---

[47] CCC, *I*, pp. vi–viii, x–xii, 35, 58, 139–40; *V*, pp. ix–x; P. G. Holiday, 'Royalist Composition Fines and Land Sales in Yorkshire 1645–1665', unpub. Leeds Univ. Ph.D. thesis, 1966, pp. 121–2; Habakkuk, 'Landowners and the Civil War', p. 132. According to Holiday, of 216 fines imposed on Yorkshire landowners, 200 were at either one-tenth or one-sixth, 2 were discharged, 2 were at unknown rates, and only 12 were at higher rates.

[48] CCC, *V*, pp. xvi–xvii; Coate, *op. cit.*, pp. 226–33; Hardacre, *op. cit.*, pp. 71–3.

where the grounds were acceptable and the facts established, then reductions do normally seem to have been granted. As an example one may cite the cases of several landowners from the Welsh border counties who protested that their estates had been overvalued because the committee had reckoned their rents to be of the same nature as the 'old rents' of the west country, whereas in fact they represented a considerably higher proportion of the full rack value than did the latter. The fines of these owners were accordingly lowered: in the case of Sir Richard Lee from £4,913 17s. to £2,813.[49]

A number of other factors served to mitigate the impact of the composition fines. The landowner was fined only on his actual interest in his estate, and where this interest amounted to less than a fee simple the fine was reduced accordingly. Life tenants were fined only half the full rate that would otherwise have been imposed on them; and where property was held in jointure or by trustees for the payment of debts or portions to other members of the family, the owner would be liable to be fined only on the value of the reversion. These concessions, based on parliament's respect for the terms of family settlements, extended, however, only to property which had been settled before 20 May 1642. As the political situation deteriorated in early 1642, and acute political crisis and uncertainty gradually turned into the real likelihood of war, many landowners of both parties (and of neither) had made settlements of their property, often limiting their own interest in it to a life tenancy and making provision for their younger children, possibly to guard against the very eventuality that now arose for many of them. When they came to compound, the date borne by their settlement was to make a great difference to their fine.[50]

Another factor was the opportunity royalists had to undervalue or conceal their assets. The composition fines were calculated on particulars of their estates submitted by themselves, and it was quite impracticable for the Committee for Compounding to check their accuracy and completeness. All that could be done to try to limit the extent of undervaluation and concealment was to threaten that if they came to light they would have to be compounded for at a higher rate, and to offer informers a share of the proceeds from their discoveries in such matters. How much undervaluation and concealment actually went on is not easy to judge, since only unsuccessful attempts ever came to light in the official records, but judging by the concern of the authorities they clearly believed that the amount was considerable. Thus from Cornwall alone the local committee returned a list of twenty-seven important delinquents who they alleged had undervalued their estates by a

---

[49] CCC, V, pp. xxii–xxiii; W. Phillips, op. cit., pp. 25–34; E. R. O. Bridgeman and C. G. O. Bridgeman, 'The Sequestration Papers of Sir Orlando Bridgeman', Shrops. Arch. & Nat. Hist. Soc., 3rd ser., II, 1902, pp. 31–6, 38–9.

[50] Habakkuk, 'Landowners and the Civil War', p. 133; CCC, I, p. 140; The Memoirs of Sir Hugh Cholmley, privately printed, 1778, p. 73.

third, a half, or even two-thirds. Certainly in the early days at least it seems to have been believed by the royalists that their valuations would not be scrutinized too closely. In September 1646, for instance, Sir Ralph Verney was advised that "the particular should be drawn according to the rents before these troubles. Most do otherwise and hitherto without prejudice...the general opinion is that if anything near the yearly value be given, it will not be excepted against." In October 1650 new regulations offered to all who 'discovered' their own undervaluations within a strictly limited time the opportunity of compounding for them at the same rate as their original composition; otherwise they would have to pay at a higher one after all. This led numerous delinquents to 'rectify' their former statements. But many undervaluations were never discovered: in Yorkshire, where about 20 per cent of all compounders have been shown by Holiday to have undervalued their estates, less than half of them were discovered at the time. Probably it was easier to conceal or undervalue property in an overwhelmingly royalist area, where a man's neighbours, who knew the extent and value of his property, were in the same boat as himself, than in areas where royalists were in a minority and where neighbours could be less trusted not to inform against him. Even in royalist districts it would be easier to conceal personal estate, commercial assets, and even timber (particularly if it was in the form of small copses and in the hedgerows rather than large woods) than it would be to conceal land. The easiest way to undervalue property was to declare farms to be let at rack rents when in fact they were let on beneficial leases for which fines had been taken: this deception had a good chance of passing undetected in districts where the two forms of tenure were found side by side, or where beneficial leases were not usually met with. So, whilst the extent of undervaluation and concealment is likely to have varied from one part of the country to another, it was probably sufficiently widely practised, and frequently enough attended with success, to reduce significantly the amount of the fines paid by a substantial number of royalist families.[51]

Two further factors somewhat lessened the impact of composition fines, although unlike the foregoing they did not actually reduce them. First, many royalists succeeded in delaying the payment of the full amount of their fines for a considerable time. The rule was that half the fine had to be paid over before the sequestration was lifted and the owner put back into possession, so the delinquent had every incentive to pay it promptly, and apparently only those in severe financial difficulties allowed more than a few months to elapse between the time the fine was fixed and payment of the first instalment. The second half of the fine was then supposed to be paid within six weeks of the first, but here it seems that a large minority did not pay on time. Though some delayed because of their financial problems, others

[51] CCC, *I*, pp. viii–ix, xvi; *V*, pp. x, xxvii–xxviii; Broad, thesis, p. 55; Holiday, thesis, pp. 92–7; Habakkuk, 'Landowners and the Civil War', pp. 134–6.

were clearly deliberately trying to postpone payment as long as they could. Theoretically resequestration ought to have followed any failure to pay the second instalment of the fine when it was due, but in practice, because of the other preoccupations of the central and local committees, it did not do so, at least until an interval of many months or years had elapsed. Dilatory compounders postponed payment by making petitions for a reduction in the amount of the fine, or by spinning out negotiations about how it should be paid, but when in early 1652 the Committee for Compounding demanded immediate payment of outstanding arrears, and recalcitrants faced the possibility of outright confiscation if they did not comply, most of them did so fairly promptly.[52] Delay in payment of the fine in respect of property of which the delinquent did not actually have possession but to which he was reversioner, and in respect of property the title to which he was contesting at law, was, however, permitted by the Committee for Compounding. The fine only had to be paid when possession of the property had finally been obtained. The procedure here was to enter on the petition a 'saving to compound' for the future, which then safeguarded the delinquent against a later accusation that he had concealed his expectant interests. In many such cases, of course, possession was not obtained before 1660, and no fine was ever paid.[53]

Secondly, it was possible to avoid having to find the whole amount of the fine in cash by conveying rectories or annuities (which were used by the government to augment clerical salaries) in satisfaction of part. This was not in fact at all a good bargain for the royalist, since they were only accepted at the rate of ten years' purchase, even though, for the purposes of fixing the fine in the first place, all property was valued at a much higher rate, and it amounted to a sale on very poor terms. Altogether under 10 per cent of the total of composition fines were discharged in this way, but some individuals used it to pay off very considerable sums. Thus Sir Henry Thynne of Cause Castle, Shropshire, discharged about half his fine of £7,160 by settling some £360 per annum. Such men probably found their short-term financial problems significantly eased by this means, and since the rectories they conveyed away were restored to them in 1660, they recovered part of their fine, whereas those who paid the whole in cash got nothing back.[54]

So, all in all, it does seem that composition fines were a less serious imposition on royalists than at one time was supposed, and if Habakkuk's findings for Bedfordshire and Northamptonshire royalists are typical, then the weight of the fines was really very light indeed. Most of the thirty-two families that he studied paid less than two years' purchase of the true value of their estates, and many of them not more than one. Even the earl of

---

[52] CCC, I, pp. x, 84, 128; Holiday, thesis, pp. 109–21.  [53] CCC, V, p. xxviii.
[54] CCC, II, pp. 910–12, 990; V, pp. xxiv–xxv; Bridgeman and Bridgeman, op. cit., pp. 15, 19.

Northampton, who was fined at the rate of one-third, paid less than two years' value.[55] Certainly to any landowner whose estates had experienced serious war damage, or who had been deprived of his income over a long period of years by sequestration, a composition fine tended to be quite overshadowed by other losses. A good illustration of this is provided by the earl of Thanet, who was an early compounder and so not out of possession of his estate for very long, but whose composition fine was the very large one of £9,000. By comparison he reckoned his losses at just over £6,000 in horses, farm stock, stored crops, faggots and other types of wood, and other such things seized by the sequestrators or soldiers. In addition, he lost an enormous quantity of plate and all the furnishings and other contents of his London house and of his two large and splendid country mansions at Hothfield in Kent and Wiston in Sussex. The latter of these seems to have suffered especially severely, for the earl singled it out as having been "totally defaced". These losses he estimated at no less than £32,000. Finally, large amounts of timber, valued by the earl at £20,000, had been felled by the parliamentarians. Even if we accept the virtual certainty that Thanet exaggerated the extent of the damage he had suffered, it is apparent that it was much more serious than his fine.[56] Another county magnate who paid a very heavy fine (£9,846) was Sir Richard Leveson, and in his case too this was dwarfed in significance by the scale of his other losses, even if allowance is made for exaggeration. He had been sequestered for three years, and had lost his entire personal estate of all types, which he reckoned at £24,000, whilst the "demolistion" of Lilleshall, his principal seat in Shropshire, the burning of the stables at another house, the defacing of his mills, and the destruction of his pales and park represented a further £6,000 worth of damage. In the case of the Kentish landowner Sir George Sondes, his fine was only £3,450, whilst he reckoned his loss of goods and stock at £20,000, besides being kept out of his estate for seven years by sequestration. Similarly, the Cornish royalist Sir Richard Vyvyan of Trelowarren recorded that his composition cost him only £1,850 out of a total of £9,982, of which the major part was unrecovered military expenditure. To that other Cornishman, Jonathan Rashleigh, his fine was even less important. His property had suffered very severely indeed during the earl of Essex's invasion of his county, his two houses had been thoroughly ransacked, and his home farm completely stripped. He estimated all his losses during the 1640s and 1650s at over £17,700, of which £9,940 was accounted for by the despoiling of his houses and his farm, and only £1,100 by his composition fine.[57]

---

[55] Habakkuk, 'Landowners and the Civil War', p. 136.
[56] CCC, II, pp. 839–40; V, p. xi; F. Hull, 'The Tufton Sequestration Papers', *Kent Records*, XVII, 1960, pp. 43, 57–62.
[57] CCC, II, pp. 867–8, 990; 'Sir George Sondes his Plain Narrative', *Harleian Misc.*, X, 1808, pp. 42–3; Coate, *op. cit.*, app. 3, pp. 357–60; app. 7, p. 368.

Proposals to confiscate and sell the estates of the leading royalists had been discussed in parliament on several occasions in the 1640s, but it was not until 1651 that the policy was actually implemented. By then most of the property of the church and the crown had been sold and still the government had not solved its financial difficulties. So to raise the sorely needed money it turned to the lands of those royalists who could not compound because they were exempted from pardon and in exile, or were Catholics, or were unable to raise the money, or would not do so out of loyalty to the monarchy. It was important for the royalists involved that the government's primary motive was to raise money rather than to deprive them of their estates, since it meant that few obstacles were placed in the way of those who tried to recover their confiscated property. As long as someone paid the price demanded for the land, the government was not, in most cases, concerned with the identity of the purchaser. This was made explicit by a provision in the third act of sale that, notwithstanding the confiscation, the owner could recover his estate by compounding for it for one-third of its value. A resolution of the Commons apparently extended this to those included in the second act as well.[58]

Altogether three acts of sale were passed: the first in July 1651 contained 71 names, including those of the most prominent royalist leaders; the second in August 1652, which was an interim measure containing 29 names; and a third in November 1652 containing 680 names, many of whom were quite minor figures included because of their Catholicism.[59] A substantial minority of these men were able to raise money quickly enough to compound for their lands within the thirty-day period which the third act allowed to them. Of the 61 Yorkshire gentry included in the acts of sale, 13 were able to compound for their whole estates, and five more compounded for part, so that altogether 29 out of 211 confiscated properties were recovered in that way. Compounding under the third act of sale was very much more expensive than compounding in the normal way. It meant paying a full six years' purchase, which was a much higher rate than was paid by the ordinary delinquent, and paying it on a valuation drawn up by the government's own surveyors, not on one produced by the owner himself, so that there was no opportunity for undervaluation or concealment. Nevertheless, there was no difference in principle between compounding under the act and on any other basis. Indeed, recent investigations have made it clear that the fate of many, even most, of the royalist landowners whose estates were put up for sale differed from that of the mass of sequestered royalists in degree rather than in kind. They too recovered their estates for a price, only the price was higher

---

[58] Hardacre, *op. cit.*, pp. 94–7; P. G. Holiday, 'Land Sales and Repurchases in Yorkshire after the Civil Wars, 1650–1670', *Northern Hist.*, v, 1970, pp. 70–3, 78.

[59] Firth and Rait, *II*, pp. 520–45, 591–8, 623–52.

and for those who were not able to compound the course they had to follow was rather different.[60]

The procedure laid down for the sale of the delinquents' lands was very much the same as for other brands of confiscated property. For a start, tithes and impropriated rectories were altogether excluded from the sales, since they were to be reserved for the support of the clergy. Also excluded were a few estates which had been granted to deserving parliamentarians and army officers, either as rewards or as compensation for their losses in the war. Everything else was vested in a body of trustees: it was to be surveyed and valued; and then, after a thirty-day pre-emption period for immediate tenants, it was to be sold to the highest bidder, but not for less than ten years' purchase for lands in possession. In fact, however, the lands confiscated from the delinquents offered even less attractive investment opportunities to would-be purchasers than did those of the crown and church, since many of them were entailed on the issue of the owner or otherwise settled so that they could not be sold outright.[61] Holiday found that over 40 per cent of the confiscated estates of the Yorkshire gentry which were still offered for sale after the pre-emption period could be sold only for the lifetime of the owner.[62] Besides, because of the geographical distribution of the king's supporters and of Catholicism, a large number of the confiscated lands were in counties remote from London. A large number of them, too, were small and widely separated from each other, both of which characteristics made them unattractive to the moneyed men of London, who were perhaps the most obvious group of potential buyers. In the event, the City men could do considerably better, and run less risk, by lending money to royalists to enable them to recover their own properties. Of the other groups of possible purchasers the army officers had already been largely satisfied out of the crown lands, whilst the rest of the gentry in the localities where the confiscated estates lay seem to have been reluctant to buy the holdings of distressed neighbours in such circumstances, even if they could afford to do so. Some local gentry clearly overcame their scruples in this matter, but many more probably held back. Then there were the sitting tenants on the estates for whom the thirty-day pre-emption period was provided, but, as on crown and church lands, and presumably for the same reasons, few of them actually bought their tenancies, except apparently occupiers of urban and suburban property in London and Middlesex.[63] There remain, however, two groups

---

[60] Holiday, 'Land Sales and Repurchases', pp. 74–6; J. Thirsk, 'The Sale of Delinquents' Estates during the Interregnum and the Land Settlement at the Restoration', unpub. London Univ. Ph.D. thesis, 1950, ch. 3, *passim*; *id.*, 'The Sales of Royalist Lands during the Interregnum', EcHR, 2nd ser., v, 1952–3, pp. 192–5.

[61] All three acts specifically excepted from their terms any interests in the estates enjoyed by persons other than those named, provided they had been created by settlements made before 20 May 1642, and except for the right of jointure of the owner's wife. See Firth and Rait, *II*, pp. 523, 593, 643.      [62] Holiday, 'Land Sales and Repurchases', p. 76.

[63] *Ibid.*, pp. 76, 79, 81; Thirsk, 'Sales of Royalist Lands', pp. 199–200, 203.

who, having a strong vested interest in the confiscated lands, could be expected to bid for them, and in the event did secure most of them: the ex-owners themselves, or occasionally their heirs or other close relatives, and, in the case of heavily indebted owners, their creditors.

In an early study of the sales of confiscated royalist property Chesney concluded that the main beneficiaries were London business men and speculators, but more recent studies by Thirsk and Holiday have clearly demonstrated that those whom Chesney identified in this way were in fact acting as agents for the dispossessed owners. Agents were not used for the sake of secrecy, for there was no need of this, but for convenience. The whole business had to be transacted in London, and it required a familiarity with the workings of the Commonwealth bureaucracy. Besides, the royalist attempting to buy back his own estate needed to raise money by borrowing, and because of the advantage of paying the purchase price in 'doubled' bills, he needed the loan partly in the form of government paper.[64] Such a loan would be much more easily negotiated by an agent who knew the City financiers and was known by them than by the royalist himself. Most of these agents were Londoners, and some of them were acting on a very large scale: the best-known of them, John Wildman, contracted for the purchase of forty separate confiscated properties in twenty-four counties. At any rate it was largely through them that the royalists succeeded in recovering their lands, and though the extent of their success was not the same in all areas, taking the country as a whole it was considerable. In general, unless they were already heavily indebted or in enforced exile abroad, large owners were more successful than small, partly because their credit was better, and partly because entails were more general among them, so that they frequently had only to buy their own life interest in their estates rather than the fee simple. Thirsk found that only 25 per cent of confiscated estates sold in Essex, Hertfordshire, Kent, and Surrey were recovered by their owners at this stage, but that the proportion rose to 39 per cent in Berkshire, Hampshire, Oxfordshire, and Sussex. It may also be added that both these figures would be higher if they included properties recovered by composition under the third act of sale. However, it was only a minority of those named in the three acts whose estates lay in the south-east, even if some of the wealthiest were among them. Far more lived distant from London, especially in the north and to a lesser extent the south-west, and there, if Holiday's investigations for Yorkshire are typical, the extent of recovery was much greater: 67 per cent of the Yorkshire properties were regained by their owners by composition or purchase. The lower proportions recovered in the south-east seem to reflect the fact that more of the prominent royalist leaders who were in exile had their estates there, and it may also have been because proximity to London did make them more attractive as investments to moneyed purchasers. In the south-east buyers who were neither owners nor creditors acquired just

[64] For 'doubled bills', see below, pp. 284-5.

over half (53 per cent) of the confiscated properties, whereas in Yorkshire they obtained fewer than one-fifth (18 per cent), but in neither area were speculators, buying in order to resell quickly at a profit, at all prominent. In both the south-east and Yorkshire the proportion of confiscated land which went to satisfy the creditors of the former owners was much the same, 11 and 12 per cent respectively.[65]

Almost all the royalists who recovered any land before the Restoration did so by composition or purchase from the trustees, and very few by subsequently buying it at second hand, since if they could not raise the money when the opportunity first arose they could rarely find it later. Consequently, in 1660 a considerable proportion of the estates confiscated in the three acts of 1651-2 were still in the hands of purchasers or their successors: in the south-east as many as three-quarters; in Yorkshire about one-third. As is well known, parliament, to whom Charles had referred the lands question in the Declaration of Breda, did not enact any general measure to dispossess the purchasers in favour of the former owners. Confiscated rectories and tithes which had not been sold, and estates which had been granted as rewards to leading parliamentarians, were returned to them; a handful of peers, headed by the duke of Newcastle, secured private acts in their own favour, and in a few more cases the House of Lords ordered that the delinquent should be reinstated, which seems to have been equally effective. But the great majority of those involved were left to take legal proceedings to recover their lands. Lawsuits involved the delinquents in expense, which they could ill afford after being kept out of their lands so long, as well as uncertainty and delay. Nevertheless, in the end they were almost universally successful unless their properties had gone to satisfy their creditors, as in the case of the notoriously indebted earl of Cleveland; or they had themselves confirmed the sale, which some had done for a consideration in order to salvage something from the wreck of their fortunes, in which case the transaction was regarded as 'voluntary' and the delinquent had no remedy at all. Thirsk found that in the south-east, out of 130 properties which had been confiscated and sold, and whose subsequent history could be traced, no fewer than 126 were eventually recovered by their owners. Holiday found the proportion for Yorkshire nearly as high, whilst in Cumberland and Westmorland, according to Phillips, out of fourteen families named in the three acts of sale only one was permanently parted from its estates. On the other hand, not all the families who recovered their lands were able to retain them. Some of those who had repurchased them from the trustees in the early 1650s had already been forced to sell part again before 1660, and in later years there were yet further sales by them and by those who recovered after the Restoration.[66]

[65] H. E. Chesney, 'The Transference of Lands in England, 1640-60', RHS, 4th ser., xv, 1932; Holiday, 'Land Sales and Repurchases', pp. 76-8, 80-2; Thirsk, 'Sales of Royalist Lands', pp. 192-5, 204-5; id., thesis, pp. 123-33.

[66] Holiday, 'Land Sales and Repurchases', pp. 82-92; J. Thirsk, 'The Restoration Land Settlement', JMH, xxvi, 1954, passim; id., thesis, p. 270; C. B. Phillips, thesis, ch. 11.

How extensive these resales of recovered property eventually were is extremely difficult to know because of the problems of tracing the history of so many families, often of quite modest wealth and of only local importance, over a period of several decades. However, the question is only part of the wider one of the long-term social and economic consequences of the Civil Wars for the landowners, for we have seen that it was not only those whose estates were confiscated, or even only those who had to compound, who were likely to have fallen into financial difficulties from which they might find it very difficult to extricate themselves.

### (c) The long-term consequences

The financial obligations which the misfortunes of the 1640s and 50s imposed on landed families were usually met in the first instance by borrowing. Those who had to repurchase an estate did not have much choice, since until they had recovered possession after payment of the full price they could not raise money out of it in any other way. Nor did most of those who had to compound, for although they gained possession after paying only half their fine, the other half was due to be paid within a further six weeks, which was not long enough to permit any alternative. However, we have seen that many compounders did not comply with this requirement and succeeded in putting off payment of the balance of the fine for a considerable time, and this certainly gave them a greater choice of how to raise the money. Sales of property were impossible as long as an estate was under sequestration, but even when the owner was in a position to sell, he was likely to go to great lengths to avoid doing so because of the very low level of land prices which prevailed during the disorder and uncertainty of the years of war and revolution, and which continued into the early 1650s, when the market was flooded with confiscated estates. Even creditors were unlikely to press for lands to be sold when values had fallen so far that their security might no longer cover the principal of their debt.[67]

But borrowed money would probably have to be paid back sooner or later. One way of doing this would be to realize capital by selling timber, but only a small minority of owners had large woods, and many of those that did found that much of their timber had been felled during the war or whilst their estates were under sequestration. Another way was to raise fines from the tenants in return for the grant of leases for ninety-nine years determinable on lives, or other long terms. This was indeed the most obvious course for those whose estates lay in the western and Welsh border counties where these leases were usual, since the collapse of estate administration during the war and the legal inability of sequestrators to grant long leases meant that there was often a large backlog of 'dropped' lives, with some holdings out of lease altogether, so that a large crop of fines could be harvested. Some landowners in areas where farms were usually let at rack

[67] Habakkuk, 'Landowners and the Civil War', pp. 137–9.

rents may also have resorted to the sale of long leases, although doing so would, of course, reduce the income available to them and their successors for a long way into the future. Other expedients could only make a significant contribution to a landowner's financial difficulties in the medium or long term. Rents could be raised again as economic conditions returned to normal, but unless an estate had been seriously underrented in 1640 it would not normally be possible to raise them much above the pre-war level, for the secular trend of rents was no longer so favourable to the landlord as it had been earlier in the century. Investment in improvements might, however, increase productivity sufficiently for further rent increases. Great landowners like the Hattons, Comptons, and Griffins in the Midlands invested in enclosure in the 1650s, and on a smaller scale the Lancashire recusant squire William Blundell spent some of his scanty resources on marling and liming his lands. In Buckinghamshire Sir Ralph Verney, whose annual income was then about £2,000, invested £1,000 or more in enclosing some 500 acres at Middle Claydon (1654–6), which permitted an immediate increase in rent from 5s. to 15s. an acre, and in rebuilding many of his tenants' houses. He also increased the area available for letting at the expense of the home farm, and racked his tenants to the utmost.[68] Finally, in addition to any such measures a family might take, there would have to be rigid economies at home to cut expenditure to the minimum. In most cases frugal living was 'voluntary', even if in practice unavoidable, but sometimes, in order to ensure that an owner kept within a sufficiently tight budget, his creditors (usually as a condition of extending or continuing their loans) obliged him to make over a proportion of his income to a trust out of which his debts would be discharged. The fourth Lord Petre was twice obliged to accept such a trust before he got clear of his Civil War debts, in 1652 and again in 1674, and on both occasions he had to make over to the trustees over three-quarters of his income.[69]

Yet it seems that sooner or later a high proportion of landed families who had been actively royalist, or were Catholics, together with others who were neither, were obliged to sell at least some land. The four most recent and most detailed case studies of landowners who had been treated by parliament as hostile, the Eyres of Hassop, the Constables of Everingham, the fourth Lord Petre, and the Verneys of Claydon, all reveal sales, although not on a scale sufficient to undermine their social position.[70] And although it may

[68] *Ibid.*, p. 138; M. Blundell, ed., *Cavalier: Letters of William Blundell to his Friends*, London, 1933, pp. 31–2, 41, 99–100; Broad, thesis, ch. 7.
[69] C. Clay, 'The Misfortunes of William, Fourth Lord Petre', pp. 107–9; Essex RO, D/DP F.50, 65.
[70] R. Meredith, 'A Derbyshire Family in the Seventeenth Century: The Eyres of Hassop and their Forfeited Estates', *Recusant Hist.*, VIII, 1965; P. Roebuck, 'The Constables of Everingham: The Fortunes of a Catholic Royalist Family during the Civil War and Interregnum', *ibid.*, IX, 1967; C. Clay, *op. cit.*; Broad, thesis, chs. 2–4.

be objected that these and other families whose histories are known and include the sale of property are not a representative selection, it should be remembered that all were relatively wealthy, with incomes large enough to give them some room for manoeuvre, with estates at least partly protected by family settlements, and with relatives or friends able to help financially or by exerting influence in appropriate quarters. Thus they represented that section of the royalist party which was best able to withstand the financial shocks of the period.

The petty squires, whose resources were much smaller, almost certainly suffered more severely than the greater gentry and the peerage, and consequently the extent of land sales among them was probably proportionately greater. As one contemporary remarked specifically of the less well-to-do recusant gentry, there was little hope "for the poor people who want both money and friends".[71] But although there is every reason to suppose that the extent of sales was greater amongst these families than amongst the more important and richer ones, bias in the survival of records has ensured that very much less is known about them and their experiences. On the other hand, the evidence clearly shows that few landowners had to sell a significant amount of land unless they had already been in some financial difficulty before the wars began. It may, therefore, seem appropriate to argue that in reality their sales were made to discharge those debts and were not really caused by the events of the 1640s at all, even though these may have been the last straw. Certainly this was true enough in some cases, but in others where it seems at first sight to be appropriate, closer examination shows that it would be a serious misinterpretation. The origin of the debts of the fourth Lord Petre lay before the outbreak of war, it is true, in the lavish provision made for the large families of the second and third lords, who had died in quick succession, and in the misfortune of a crown wardship from 1638 onwards. Yet what made these debts a really serious burden and forced the sale of land between 1652 and 1665 was the interruption of income for a considerable number of years so that unpaid arrears of annuities and interest built up and greatly increased the size of the debt to be paid off. In this case the Civil War was not the last straw, but a goodly proportion of the whole load, and without that addition it is unlikely that sales would have been necessary at all.[72] Much the same was probably true for many other families who were forced to sell in order to discharge pre-war debts: without the war they could have supported the burden without sales or at least without such large sales. This is not to argue that the Civil War rather than the pre-war debts should be seen as the main cause of the sales, but that the two causes cannot really be separated.

A reasonable guess at the extent of the sales brought about more or less

---

[71] Quoted by Roebuck, *op. cit.*, p. 85.
[72] Habakkuk, 'Landowners and the Civil War', pp. 139–42; C. Clay, *op. cit.*, *passim*.

directly by the Civil War would be that down to, say, 1680 they amounted to 15 per cent of the possessions of that section of the gentry and aristocracy who were either actively royalist or Catholic, which in turn composed less than a quarter of the whole class in number but possibly accounted for as much as a quarter of its wealth.[73] Not all compounders had to sell any land at all, but on the other hand families, such as the Petres and Verneys, who never compounded did have to. There may also have been regional differences, sales being more prevalent in some districts than others: in the far north-west, for instance, the landowners seem to have got away from the upheavals of the time relatively lightly, sales of land were not extensive, and there is very little evidence of delayed sales in the post-Restoration period.[74] Nevertheless, if anything the guess is unduly conservative. But no figure that can reasonably be suggested is high enough to warrant writing of a social revolution, especially when it is considered that these sales were spread over a period of several decades. What occurred was the disappearance from landed society of a few families, usually ones whose fortunes in 1640 were already so far undermined that they would eventually have collapsed anyway and for whom wartime losses, composition fines, or the costs of repurchase were the final straw rather than the main cause of their difficulties. Beyond this there were some shifts in the relative wealth and power of certain individual families within counties, whilst in the second half of the seventeenth century the volume of land coming up for sale was rather higher than it would otherwise have been, which must have facilitated the acquisition of property by new families. The fact that there was not an unusual degree of change in the composition of landed society as a result of the war is demonstrated for one county by Everitt's findings that in Kent the rate at which new landed families replaced old between 1640 and 1688 was no higher than it had been between 1590 and 1640.[75]

Why was it that in terms of social change the events of the 1640s and 50s had such limited consequences? A major factor was clearly that the victorious party deliberately did not try to destroy the royalists' position as landowners. The statement of policy which laid down the principle that the king's supporters might recover their estates from sequestration on payment of a fine promised that parliament would be "as carefull to prevent their ruin, as to punish their delinquencies", and, as we have seen, this promise was fulfilled in the respect shown to the terms of settlements and the moderate

[73] According to Habakkuk, about 3,225 persons compounded for their delinquency, and some 780 more were included in the acts of sale, though not all were landowners, whilst Gregory King reckoned that there were (in 1688) 15,560 families of the rank of gentry and above – Habakkuk, 'Landowners and the Civil War', p. 147. But those who did compound or were subject to confiscation undoubtedly included a high proportion of major owners richer than the average squire.

[74] C. B. Phillips, thesis, ch. 11.     [75] Everitt, *Community of Kent*, p. 323.

rates at which the fines were levied.[76] Even in the case of those whose estates were actually confiscated the government made little or no effort to prevent the owners from recovering them. A second factor was the existence of numerous ties of family and friendship which linked together those who had fought for the king and those who had fought against him or had remained neutral, ties which existed because the war was not a struggle of one region against another, still less of one class against another. Once the fighting was over, hard-pressed royalists often derived useful support from their parliamentarian or neutral connections. Sometimes this might be in the form of influence and protection: the Verneys, for instance, made the most of their connection with the earl of Warwick in their efforts to secure the release of their estate from sequestration in 1646–7. But frequently it took the form of financial support in the shape of loans. A good example is provided by Rowland Eyre, a Derbyshire Catholic, whose estates were included in the third act of sale and who was obliged to repurchase his life interest for £14,932. The actual purchases were mostly made in the name of a parliamentarian neighbour and old friend, the earl of Rutland, who continued to act as one of Eyre's trustees until the Restoration. And most of the money required to complete them came from three creditors, all active parliamentarians, who were respectively a relative, a neighbour to one of Eyre's outlying estates in Leicestershire, and a Derbyshire neighbour who may also have been a business associate.[77]

In most cases relatives and friends were probably able to lend to a royalist only to help him over the immediate crisis of composition or repurchase, and were not in a position to leave the debt outstanding indefinitely, which would explain the apparent shift of royalist borrowing onto the London money market in the 1650s. Rowland Eyre never seems to have needed to borrow in London at all, but others who began in the same way as he did subsequently paid off family and local creditors by doing so. Sir Philip Constable of Everingham was another Catholic royalist who had to rescue his estates from the third act of sale, at a cost of over £8,000. He began by borrowing locally in York and from his son-in-law Richard Shireburne of Stonyhurst, Lancashire, but by the early 1650s London had become his main source of capital. The same pattern is shown by the borrowings of the fourth Lord Petre, who avoided having to compound but nevertheless accumulated large debts as a result of many years of sequestration. In October 1652 Petre owed a total of £17,200 on bond and mortgage, of which £11,800 had been borrowed from friends, neighbours, or relations, whilst only £3,000 definitely (and a further £1,000 possibly) was owed to a City man. During

[76] CCC, V, p. vii. And see above, pp. 257–8, 262–3, 266–7.
[77] Broad, thesis, pp. 56–67; Meredith, *op. cit.*, pp. 32–46. For other examples, see Everitt, *Community of Kent*, pp. 227–8, and G. Ridsall Smith, *Without Touch of Dishonour: The Life and Death of Sir Henry Slingsby*, Kineton, 1968, pp. 107–8.

the following years, however, the relative importance of these two main sources of credit altered as Petre paid off most of these old loans and raised a series of new ones in London from a group of lenders which included Gilbert Crouch, a prominent agent for the repurchase of confiscated estates. And so we should add, as a further factor limiting the changes in landed society brought about by the Civil War, that the existence of a money market sufficiently well developed to satisfy the huge demand for loans from embarrassed royalists and others in the aftermath of war was of the greatest importance in reducing the amount of land that had eventually to be sold. Not only was a sufficient volume of funds forthcoming to meet the demand for loans, but the development of the principle of the equity of redemption meant that mortgage borrowers did not have to fear that their creditors would foreclose to recover the principal of their debt provided that they were able to maintain interest payments. Landowners could thus support a much higher level of debt without having to sell property than they could have done somewhat earlier. The fall in interest rates over the period was also important in this respect: before 1651 most, if not all, private borrowers had to pay 8 per cent on loans, but thereafter only 6 per cent.[78]

Long-term mortgages, together with the rigid economies necessary if interest payments were to be met, enabled many families to carry their Civil War debts for decades. The Constables of Everingham were still struggling with their debts in the 1670s, with Sir Marmaduke confined to £150 a year for his personal expenditure out of a total estate income of some £2,150 a year. Similarly, the Petres were not clear of serious debt until the 1680s.[79] Some families, we are told, were still in difficulties in the early eighteenth century as a result of debts originating in the Civil War period, and were finally obliged to sell up fifty or even seventy years after the debts had been incurred.[80] But in such cases one is bound to question how far it is meaningful to ascribe the final crash to the factors which originally gave rise to the debt rather than to those which subsequently prevented its discharge. After all, other families were likewise in serious trouble in the 1650s and 60s, and yet were richer and more powerful than ever by the beginning of the eighteenth century. How do we explain the widely varying experiences of families which emerged from the trials of the 1640s in an apparently similar situation? In some cases it may have been due to differences in the care with which they managed and improved their estates. In Kent, where there were little fighting, few active royalists, and few heavy composition fines, Everitt notes that families which were prepared to economize and concentrate on the care of

[78] Habakkuk, 'Landowners and the Civil War', pp. 149–50; Roebuck, *op. cit.*, pp. 75–81; C. Clay, *op. cit.*, pp. 108–10.

[79] Roebuck, *op. cit.*, pp. 82–3; C. Clay, *op. cit.*, p. 111.

[80] H. J. Habakkuk, 'The English Land Market in the Eighteenth Century', in J. S. Bromley and E. H. Kossmann, eds., *Britain and the Netherlands*, London, 1960, pp. 158–9; E. Hughes, *North Country Life in the Eighteenth Century: The North-East, 1700–1750*, London, 1952, p. 1.

their estates invariably survived the Civil War period, but neither in Kent nor elsewhere were all families prepared to do this.[81] Probably more important was the way in which the family history worked out in the half-century that followed. Was the family fortunate in such matters as marriages to heiresses, inheritances from relatives, and the number of younger children to be provided for? If it was, then it seems that within a generation or so debts resulting from the Civil Wars were usually paid off, and damage of other sorts made good. But if it was not, and the financial consequences of family history tended to reinforce the effects of the Civil War rather than to cancel them out (as in cases where families had to support long-lasting jointures and had numerous children to provide for), then the fortunes of the family do seem to have been permanently impaired and sometimes to have collapsed altogether.

The Staffordshire magnate Sir Richard Leveson had been an ardent royalist who had not only had to pay the very large fine of £9,864 but also suffered substantial loss in other ways, all of which on top of considerable pre-war debts forced him to sell the whole of his large Kentish estate (1646–8). However, he had been able to preserve his main properties in Staffordshire and Shropshire, and despite this set-back to the family's prosperity its recovery was rapid. Sir Richard died childless in 1661, and his next two successors also died prematurely, without leaving families of younger children or widows to burden the estate, which thus passed unencumbered to old Sir Richard's great-nephew William Gower. The latter took the name Leveson-Gower and proceeded first to marry a daughter of the earl of Bath, who brought him a good portion, and then, owing to the unexpected death of his nephew Sir Thomas Gower, in 1689 to inherit the Yorkshire estate of the Gowers. When Sir William Leveson-Gower died in 1691 he left his heir an estate enlarged by purchase as well as by inheritance, a newly rebuilt mansion at Trentham, and savings of £50,000.[82]

A similar story of successful recovery is provided by the Radcliffes, created earls of Derwentwater in 1688. Sir Edward Radcliffe's estates were included in the second act of sale; however, because they were entailed, and because his wife had lands of her own which were not confiscated and on which money could be raised, buying them back did not pose great problems. But the cost was considerable, and the property had suffered damage during the war which included the destruction of the family residence on Lord's Island. Nevertheless, the later seventeenth century was a period of increasing prosperity for the family. This was partly due to the rising profits of their lead mines on Alston Moor, but also to the marriage of Sir Francis Radcliffe to the heiress of Sir William Fenwick of Meldon, who brought him large

---

[81] Everitt, *Community of Kent*, pp. 277–8.
[82] J. R. Wordie, 'A Great Landed Estate in the Eighteenth Century', unpub. Reading Univ. Ph.D. thesis, 1967, pp. 32, 36–7, 130–2, 136.

properties in Northumberland. Moreover, in successive generations potentially burdensome families of younger brothers and sisters followed what seems to have been a common path in Catholic landed families, that of celibacy. When the second earl inherited his estate in 1696 he was one of the wealthiest men in the northern counties, with an estate of more than £6,000 a year encumbered with nothing worse than a few family annuities.[83]

Sir Ralph Verney of Middle Claydon (Bucks.) did not lose a great deal of income from sequestration, nor did he have to pay a composition fine, but his estates lay in an area disputed between the two sides throughout the war, and they suffered very severely in consequence. As a result he was unable to maintain interest payments on the large debt, over £10,000, which he had inherited, and the accumulation of unpaid arrears, on top of the original principal, created a critical financial situation in the later 1640s. Between 1648 and 1664 Sir Ralph had to sell virtually all his outlying properties, amounting to roughly a third of his pre-war estate. However, he was greatly helped in his efforts to stabilize his financial position by having an eldest son of marriageable age, for whom he secured as a wife the heiress of a City merchant in 1662, and by a succession of premature deaths within the family which eliminated the need to make any jointure payments to widows and greatly reduced the financial burden of providing for younger children. Indeed, both Sir Ralph's eldest son and his grandson predeceased him, so that after his death in 1696 the estate passed to his younger son John, who had had a long and successful career as a Levant merchant, had married three wealthy wives, acquired some lands of his own, and still retained sufficient liquid resources to clear the inherited lands of the last traces of debt. This unexpected injection of mercantile wealth greatly revived the fortunes of the Verneys, and in the eighteenth century they acquired an Irish peerage, and were able to make large additions to their estates and later to spend lavishly on politics and buildings. Their subsequent ruin, as a result of the extravagance of the second Earl Verney, was in no way connected with their mid-seventeenth-century difficulties.[84]

Rather less fortunate were the Eyres of Hassop (Derbs.). Their estate had also been confiscated, and, although it had been successfully recovered, this had only been achieved at the cost of a very large debt (well over £15,000 in 1653). This in turn had forced them to sell several thousand pounds' worth of property, and to grant beneficial leases to tenants on lands which were retained. At the end of the century, however, the family was still in financial difficulties. A combination of over-generous marriage portions to daughters, a long-lasting jointure, and an expensive lawsuit not only prevented recovery but eventually obliged Rowland Eyre to sell yet more property in the 1690s.[85]

[83] R. Arnold, *Northern Lights*, London, 1959, pt 1.     [84] Broad, thesis, chs. 1–5.
[85] R. Meredith, *op. cit.*; *id.*, 'The Eyres of Hassop, and Some of their Connections from the Test Act to Emancipation', *Recusant Hist.*, IX, 1967, pp. 17–18.

Even so, the Eyres retained the bulk of their estates, whereas the Lords Stourton were eventually forced to sell virtually everything.

Like Sir Richard Leveson, the eleventh Lord Stourton was in debt before the war began, suffered sequestration, was obliged to compound, and experienced the destruction of his seat during the fighting. However, unlike Leveson, his estate was heavily encumbered by family financial commitments which made recovery impossible. His father had made over nearly half the estates to his two brothers for their lifetimes, leaving him less than £1,500 a year, out of which he was expecting difficulty in providing for his four younger children even before the disasters of the 1640s came upon him. Stourton married his eldest son to a sister of the fourth Lord Petre in 1641, and intended to use her £6,000 portion to settle his debts and to provide for the other children. However, only half of it had been paid before the outbreak of war, and Lord Petre first delayed payment of the other half, and then produced grounds for denying his legal liability to pay it at all. Stourton sued for it, and though he eventually won his case it dragged on until 1665, and meanwhile the loss of the expected money on top of all his other difficulties reduced him to dire straits. Instead of being able to pay off his debts he had to sell land at a poor rate during the war, and to borrow still more. Despite eventual victory in the suit against Petre the debts of the family gradually accumulated until the estate was mortgaged for almost its entire value, and shortly after the thirteenth lord succeeded to it in 1685 the selling began. Between 1688 and 1714 almost everything the family owned, in Wiltshire, Somerset, and Dorset, was sold off piecemeal, leaving the thirteenth lord and his successors only the small manor of Bonham.[86]

The almost total ruin of the Stourtons may have had relatively few parallels amongst the great landed magnates who had been involved in the troubles of the mid seventeenth century, although it certainly had many more amongst the lesser gentry. Yet even if we accept that few landed families were utterly ruined by the Civil Wars, it remains indisputable that many were hit very hard. If the historian considers it his task to portray as nearly as possible the realities of the past, and not merely, as has sometimes been the tendency in the last generation or so, to concentrate on highly generalized problems of economic and social change to the virtual exclusion of everything else, then he cannot ignore misfortunes that befell thousands of families and must have dominated their lives and thoughts for many years, even if in the end those misfortunes were not so severe as to cause their ruin and their disappearance from the ranks of their class. The Civil Wars plunged numerous families into acute financial crisis, and they emerged from the two middle decades of the century stripped of their reserves of readily realizable assets, burdened with debts, with the value of their estates impaired, and not

[86] Lord Mowbray, *History of the Noble House of Stourton*, 2 vols., London, 1889, *I*, pp. 492–5; C. Clay, *op. cit.*, pp. 92–3, 101–3; Wilts. RO, 383/761, 763.

infrequently having suffered other losses which might range from the destruction of their houses to lost educational or marriage opportunities for their children. Few landed families involved to any extent in the events of 1640 to 1660 can have avoided some period when unaccustomed economies were necessary. For a fair proportion it meant a period of real hardship, even as much as one or two generations of financial stringency as debts were gradually discharged and the yield of their estates gradually increased by careful management. We have seen that serious financial difficulties for some families persisted into the 1670s and beyond. If these are not accounted long-term effects, a reincarnated royalist might well be entitled to ask how long is the long term?

## 2. Institutional landowners

### (a) The crown

Despite the sales which had taken place in the earlier part of the seventeenth century, in 1640 the crown remained a landowner on a very large scale. It still held at least some land in almost every county in England, and although the yearly value of properties let out to tenants was no more than £50,000–£55,000,[87] since most of them were leased out on terms very favourable to the latter, their extent was much greater than this figure might suggest. Besides, the crown also held the royal forests, which together made up an enormous acreage despite the pitifully small income they yielded.

Most of these lands, except the forests, were sold by parliament under an act of 1649, in order to discharge arrears of pay owed to the army.[88] This act laid down that the minimum rate at which they were to be sold was thirteen years' purchase of their full improved value if they were in possession, six and a half years' purchase for those on lease for one life or seven years, and correspondingly lower rates for those leased out for longer terms. In practice almost all crown lands were leased, often for very long terms, so that only a very small proportion of them commanded the full thirteen years' purchase. Nevertheless, crown property was put on the market at a rather higher rate than were other confiscated estates, almost certainly because the act had made its purchase the only way in which the army could recover its arrears, so that purchasers were unlikely to jib at the price demanded.[89] On the other hand, even thirteen years' purchase was well

---

[87] PRO, E 407/78/5 gives the total of the crown's landed income as £116,461 p.a. However, fee farm rents accounted for something more than £60,000 p.a. of this, for rents to about this value, which represented the bulk, but not quite the whole, of those belonging to the crown, were sold in the 1670s.

[88] A series of separate acts followed in the early 1650s authorizing the sale of the forests and other properties excluded from that of 1649 – Firth and Rait, *II*: the relevant acts will be found commencing on pp. 168, 358, 412, 583, 614, 691, 720, 783, 993.

[89] The act for the sale of episcopal lands had laid down a minimum of 10 years' purchase (1646); that for capitular lands, 12 years' purchase (1649); those for the royal fee farm rents, 8 and 10 years' purchase (1650); and those for delinquents' lands, 10 years' purchase (1651, 1652) – Firth and Rait, *I*, p. 902; *II*, pp. 87, 360, 499, 528, 594, 644.

below the value of freehold land in normal circumstances, and the real price paid by many purchasers was considerably less even than that. Army debentures were transferable, and many of the rank and file were unable to wait any longer before they received their money. They were thus forced to sell them for what they would fetch, which was inevitably substantially less than their face value.[90] So officers and well-to-do civilians were able to obtain enough debentures to make a desired purchase at a considerable discount, and only a very small proportion of the total price of crown lands was actually paid in cash. In fact, of all the confiscated properties sold off by the Long Parliament, only in the case of the royal fee farm rents, which were put on the market under a separate act passed in 1650, was a substantial part paid for in ready money as opposed to the various forms of paper held by government creditors.[91]

The act of 1649 provided that immediate crown tenants, except those of parks and chases, should have the right of pre-emption over their tenancies, but few of them took advantage of this. In all probability they lacked the necessary capital, and those that possessed it considered that the purchase of a parliamentary title to the freehold was an excessively risky speculation, and preferred to remain as tenants to the new owners.[92] Pre-emption rights were also granted to the original holders of debentures, and only thereafter was the field open to those who had acquired debentures at second hand. This was a provision secured by the army officers in order to restrict competition from civilian purchasers, who could only have acquired debentures from others, so as to ensure that they would be able to snap up the best properties as they came up for sale. The officers themselves found a way round this restriction, which would otherwise have hampered their own freedom to make purchases with debentures acquired from their men. Instead of having the debentures assigned to them, they got the men to sign letters of attorney making their officers trustees to make purchases on their behalf, with separate agreements that the officers should buy out their interests in the properties acquired at a later date. Largely for these reasons there was not a great deal of competition between buyers of crown land. Certainly the great bulk of the property went to military purchasers, and even after resales such people retained three-quarters of it. Altogether there were about 450 military buyers, almost all of them officers, of whom most got properties of no more than modest size. Only a handful of grandees obtained really large estates, among whom Lambert with Nonsuch Palace and the great manor of Wimbledon was the most prominent. It is significant that many of the most important men in the army avoided buying crown land altogether, even though it meant

[90] C. H. Firth, *Cromwell's Army*, London, 1902, pp. 204–7.
[91] H. J. Habakkuk, 'Public Finance and the Sale of Confiscated Property during the Interregnum', EcHR, 2nd ser., xv, 1962–3, pp. 71–5.
[92] Coate, *Cornwall*, p. 271; S. J. Madge, *The Domesday of Crown Lands*, London, 1938, p. 251; I. Gentles, 'The Debentures Market and Military Purchases of Crown Land, 1649–60', unpub. London Univ. Ph.D. thesis, 1969, pp. 113–21.

selling debentures worth hundreds of pounds at a heavy discount, and this confirms other evidence that crown property was regarded as an even worse risk than other forms of confiscated land.[93]

Few of the purchasers of crown land came into an estate which they could actually occupy themselves and set about improving, because almost all of them were encumbered with long leases yielding very low rents. However, once these leases had expired, they or their heirs could look forward to very greatly increasing the yield of their properties, and a substantial number of them would eventually have found themselves (had there been no Restoration) in possession of estates as valuable as those possessed by many of the local gentry. And into the ranks of the gentry those who were not of gentry origin anyway would doubtless have been quickly assimilated. It should be remembered that a century earlier many of the purchasers of monastic lands had had to wait many years, generations even, before the outstanding leases expired, and only then had their descendants reaped the full benefits of their acquisitions. In the event, however, few purchasers of crown land had more than a bare ten years in possession. At the Restoration some of them, notably officers who had actually marched with General Monck or who had corresponded with him or Sir George Booth, and immediate crown tenants who had bought their own holdings, received leases on moderate terms by way of compensation for their loss of ownership. The majority, however, were dispossessed within a few months.[94]

(b) *The church*

On the eve of the Civil War the landed estates of the church were also still very extensive, despite the depredations of the Tudor monarchs, and although at present no figures are available it is probable that they amounted to almost, if perhaps not quite, 5 per cent of the cultivated area of the country. Certainly they were much larger than those of the crown, if the royal forests be excluded from the count. However, like the crown lands, most of them were leased out to laymen at very low rents, generally in large blocks to gentlemen and substantial freeholders, who in turn let to cultivating sub-tenants. It is true that church landlords secured fines for the grant of these leases, but they were almost invariably lower than those lay owners would have insisted upon in similar circumstances. This was mainly because of the weak bargaining position of individual bishops, deans, prebendaries, and the like, who enjoyed

---

[93] I. Gentles, 'The Sales of Crown Lands during the English Revolution', EcHR, 2nd ser., XXVI, 1973, *passim*; Madge, *op. cit.*, pp. 213–19.

[94] *Cal. Treasury Books, I*, pp. 65, 70; Madge, *op. cit.*, p. 270. Purchasers who could claim that they would suffer hardship if dispossessed could appeal to a commission established in Oct. 1660 to deal with such matters. The reasons why parliament did not pass the legislation on behalf of the purchasers, which so many of them had confidently expected, are discussed by H. J. Habakkuk, 'The Land Settlement and the Restoration of Charles II', RHS, 5th ser., XXVIII, 1978.

possession of their estates for life only,[95] and partly because of their anxiety to avoid arousing the perennial anti-clericalism of their gentry lessees. As a result, a substantial part of the profits deriving from the ecclesiastical estates was diverted into the pockets of the latter.

Despite the hostility of the parliamentarians to the established church in general and to episcopacy in particular, it was not until after the Civil War was over that the Long Parliament passed ordinances for the confiscation of the estates of the bishops and the deans and chapters. During the war years the property of individual churchmen who had aided the royal cause had been sequestered, in the same way as that of lay delinquents, but as late as September 1645 it was specifically stated in the Commons that where personal delinquency could not be alleged against its holders church property was still unsequestered.[96] Confiscation and sale were mooted in September 1645, and again about a year later. On this second occasion the proposal was actually implemented as far as the episcopal estates were concerned, but it was not until early 1649 that parliament's financial difficulties made it necessary to sell the capitular lands as well. In neither case, however, did the properties sold amount to the whole wealth of the previous owners, since tithes, which made up a substantial part of some ecclesiastical endowments, and advowsons were excepted from the sales so that they might be used to support the preaching ministry so much desired by the Puritans.[97] The nominal price obtained for what was disposed of amounted to something over £675,000 for the bishops' lands and about £1,170,000 for those of deans and chapters, but unfortunately these figures tell us very little about the extent of the properties in question.[98] Partly because so much church land was burdened with leases, and partly because of changing political conditions, the purchase rates at which it was sold varied widely from one type of estate to another, and for the same type of estate from one time to another, so that one is unable to establish what the average may have been, and it is therefore impossible to convert the capital figure into one for annual value.

The episcopal lands were in fact the first of all the various forms of confiscated property which parliament put on the market, and it was for their sale that the method of 'doubling' was invented, which was subsequently applied in the case of all the other confiscated lands other than the main estates of the crown. The state of parliamentary finances by the latter part of 1646 faced those responsible for handling them with severe problems. Parliament owed very large debts incurred during the war, which would have to be honoured if it was to retain any sort of credit at all, and the sale of confiscated

[95] For the implications of this, see C. Clay, '"The Greed of Whig Bishops"? Church Landlords and their Lessees, 1660–1760', *PP*, no. 87, 1980.
[96] CJ, IV, p. 275.
[97] W. A. Shaw, *A History of the English Church during the Civil Wars and under the Commonwealth*, 2 vols., London, 1900, *II*, pp. 205–15.   [98] Habakkuk, 'Public Finance', p. 87, Table 1.

lands was the only possible way in which this could be done. However, the title to confiscated property would obviously depend on the political survival of the regime, and since this was rather uncertain the property could not be regarded as a very secure investment, which in turn could make it difficult to sell at a respectable price. But beyond this parliament was desperate to raise fresh supplies of money to meet present and future needs, and so was unwilling to apply the proceeds of the sales wholly to the redemption of past debts. 'Doubling' offered a solution to all three difficulties. It offered government creditors a way of recovering what they had lent, for the value of their public faith bills had greatly depreciated in view of the improbability that they would be redeemed in the foreseeable future, or at all. It offered the government itself a way of inducing people to buy the risky confiscated lands, and of raising additional funds at the same time as old debts were discharged. The creditors were informed that, if they would advance as much more again as the government already owed them (i.e. the nominal value of their public faith bills together with the accumulated interest), then their 'doubled' bills would be secured on the lands about to be sold, and when the sales actually took place, then they would be accepted at face value towards their purchase.[99] Of course, many of the original creditors, in so far as they still retained their bills (and many certainly did not), were not interested in buying land. Nevertheless, these provisions made it possible for them to dispose of the bills at a rather better price than they had previously fetched, and, if they could afford to double them, at a considerably better price. Those who were interested in land, together with a crowd of financial speculators and agents, moved in to buy up bills and a vigorous market in them developed. However, they did not, save for one or two brief periods, change hands at anywhere near par, which presumably reflects the fact that the rates at which confiscated lands were being sold were not felt to give the purchasers sufficient allowance for risk. Certainly few buyers were prepared to pay the whole of the purchase price of what they acquired in cash. Of the £627,425 realized by the sale of bishops' lands down to November 1652, only £17,501 represented cash sales; and in the case of the capitular lands the proportion was even smaller.[100]

In November 1646 it had been laid down for bishops' lands that the minimum price for those in possession was to be ten years' purchase of the 1641 value.[101] As there had been a general fall in land values since then, this meant that in reality parliament was asking for more than ten years' purchase of current values. On the other hand, since doubled bills could be obtained at a substantial discount, the real cost to the purchaser was less than the nominal rate in proportion to the extent of the discount, which was usually at least a quarter. But even if the minimum price at which bishops'

[99] Firth and Rait, I, p. 884.  [100] Habakkuk, 'Public Finance', pp. 74–5, 81–2, 87.
[101] Firth and Rait, I, p. 902.

lands could be bought amounted to a real rate of ten years' purchase of current values, this was far lower than was normal for property in the mid seventeenth century.[102] And certainly, once sales got under way they proceeded briskly enough, despite the facts that most of the properties were encumbered with long lease terms and the confiscation ordinance had specifically confirmed the validity of church leases granted before 1 December 1641.[103]

Such properties offered the purchaser only a fixed annual rent, usually very low in relation to their value, with a more or less remote prospect of being able to charge a fine for renewing the lease, or of being able to occupy the premises himself when it finally expired. However, the hurriedly undertaken 'surveys' upon which the sale valuations were based must almost invariably have understated the true value of the properties, thus offering purchasers the prospect of a good bargain despite the existence of the leases. At any rate, by April 1648 two-thirds of the episcopal estates had already been sold or contracted for, and most of them went for significantly more than the minimum price. Eleven or twelve years' purchase was apparently the most usual rate, and there was eager competition for the more desirable properties. Thus Henry Oxinden had two rivals for the archiepiscopal woodlands in Kent which he had hoped to buy at the end of 1646, whilst when Sir Edward Harley was contracting to buy the bishop of Hereford's palace and five of his Herefordshire manors in 1649, three others were interested.[104] As for the capitular lands, the ordinance of April 1649 which authorized their sale fixed a minimum price of twelve years' purchase of their current value for lands in possession, or fifteen years' purchase for those who bought without doubling. However, these rates were certainly too optimistic, for less than two months later parliament, "taking into consideration how expedient it is for this Commonwealth, that speedy sale be made of the premises, for the present raising of moneys", reduced them to ten and thirteen years' purchase respectively.[105] According to Edmund Ludlow, "most" of the capitular lands were in the event sold at rates well above the statutory minimum, at fifteen, sixteen, or even seventeen years' purchase.[106] But clearly he can have been referring only to lands in present possession, since rates such as he mentions would have been much too high for land encumbered with leases even in normal circumstances in the seventeenth century. We may therefore safely assume that he meant "most" of only that relatively small proportion of the estates which were clear of leases, and

---

[102] See below, p. 300.   [103] Firth and Rait, *I*, p. 882.

[104] D. Gardiner, *Oxinden and Peyton Letters*, pp. 94–104; T. W. Webb, *Military Memoir of Colonel John Birch*, Camden Soc., 1873, pp. 154–5.

[105] The act of 25 June 1649 also reduced the minimum rates for reversions after the expiry of leases to the same as those for bishops' lands – Firth and Rait, *II*, pp. 87–8, 103, 155–6.

[106] C. H. Firth, *The Memoirs of Edmund Ludlow*, 2 vols., London, 1894, *I*, p. 231.

which, like the corresponding part of the episcopal estates, sold particularly well.

Little is yet known about the purchasers of the capitular lands, but Gentles, to whom we owe much of what is known about the fate of the crown lands in the Interregnum, has recently completed a study of the sale of the episcopal properties also.[107] Among the 807 persons who came into possession of the bishops' lands at first hand or by subsequent resale, provincials (most of them gentry, very few occupying tenants) outnumbered Londoners in a ratio of roughly 4:3, but the average size of the latter's purchase was larger and they acquired very nearly half (48 per cent) of the property by value. City merchants, who had lent heavily to the parliament from 1642 onwards, and were taking advantage of the opportunity to recover their debts, were one very prominent group of purchasers, and another was those actually in the service of the state, whether as MPs, civil servants, or army officers, for they too were often owed money for arrears of pay or expenses incurred on behalf of parliament during the war. A few speculators purchased in order to resell at a profit, but, as with other categories of confiscated land, most of those whose activities at first sight suggest speculation were in fact acting as agents for those who found it difficult to come to London in person. Some, however, combined the two functions: John Blackwell, captain in one of Cromwell's regiments and son of one of the officials responsible for the sales, for instance, and John Casbeard. The latter was a Bristol attorney who had at one time been employed as a surveyor of episcopal lands. He bought considerable quantities of church property in Somerset and elsewhere in the west, some of which he kept for himself. In other transactions, however, he was acting as a speculator, buying only to sell again, whilst in yet others he was acting as an agent for the tenants, or for other people less knowledgeable or less well placed than himself.[108] Professional dealers in confiscated land were, however, only just beginning to appear at this stage, and these were operating on a small scale compared to those who emerged in the early 1650s when the crown and royalist lands came on the market. As amongst the purchasers of crown land, most buyers did not obtain very extensive properties, though Lambert's acquisitions in Surrey were paralleled by the large northern estate built up by Sir Arthur Hesilrige out of lands formerly belonging to the bishop of Durham, and for which he paid a nominal price of nearly £20,000.

Gentles also found that among the civilian purchasers of crown land Londoners were predominant, again obtaining 48 per cent of the civilians' total where the origin of the purchaser could be established, and that among provincials those below the level of gentry acquired relatively little.[109] It does, therefore, seem that a very real contrast can be made between the

---

[107] I. Gentles, 'The Sales of Bishops' Lands in the English Revolution, 1646–1660', EHR, xcv, 1980, upon which most of the following paragraph is based.

[108] D. Underdown, 'A Case concerning Bishops' Lands', EHR, LXXVIII, 1963, pp. 24–7.

[109] Gentles, thesis, p. 115.

purchasers of church lands and the civilian purchasers of crown lands on the one hand, and those of delinquents' lands on the other, since among the latter Londoners were not very numerous and it was principally the provincial gentry who were the beneficiaries. This seems to have been mainly because the delinquents were actively trying to recover their property, and, for the Londoners advancing them loans, to enable them to do so was obviously a safer investment than outbidding them for their own estates. There is, however, also a clear contrast to be made between the fate of the church lands and the crown lands as a whole. Some army officers obtained large amounts of the former: Colonel Birch, the parliamentary governor of Hereford, for instance, who obtained the lordship of six episcopal manors in that shire.[110] But the arrangements which were made to secure army arrears ensured that the bulk of soldiers' purchases of confiscated property were made out of crown lands, whereas the civilians amongst the new ruling élite dominated the purchase of church lands.

In 1660 the church was restored its lands, but the government was well aware that much hardship, and consequently much dangerous resentment, would be caused if the churchmen insisted on enforcing their rights to the letter. A royal injunction was therefore issued to all bishops, and to deans and chapters, ordering them to deal generously with former tenants of their lands, "giveing them not only the priviledge of preemption [for leases] before any others, but useing them with all favour and kindness", and on no account to evict them. And the injunction continued that for the present no other leases should be granted except to those who had been purchasers, or with the purchasers' consent.[111] Further, a royal commission was established to treat with the purchasers of both church and crown lands. The commissioners were to ascertain the terms on which purchases had been made, what profits the purchasers had derived from the lands, and what they had laid out on improving them. They would then be able to assess which of them would suffer hardship and loss if they were to be dispossessed outright, and consequently deserved sympathetic treatment, and which of them had recouped all that they had laid out. It is generally assumed, although there has been no detailed investigation of the problem, that most of the latter category of purchasers lost their lands without any compensation at all. So also did those who had acquired the actual residences of church dignitaries, the episcopal palaces and castles with their parks and home farms, the deaneries, and so on.[112] But those who could claim to have suffered serious hardship seem to have been fairly treated, and in many cases to have received at least partial compensation in the form of a lease on easier terms than were

[110] Webb, *op. cit.*, pp. 154–5.
[111] *CSPD 1660–1*, p. 310; W. R. Stephens and F. T. Madge, *Documents relating to the History of the Cathedral Church of Winchester in the Seventeenth Century*, Hants. Rec. Soc., 1897, pp. 115–16.
[112] Thirsk, 'The Restoration Land Settlement', pp. 319–20, 326–7. See also Habakkuk, 'The Land Settlement', pp. 216, 219–20.

usually available. The commissioners investigated the purchasers' complaints and, where enquiries suggested that they were justified, brought pressure to bear on the restored owner to take a more lenient course. They were clearly concerned to encourage the churchmen to have second thoughts about hard decisions, and if possible to reach agreement with purchasers on their own, and they only intervened directly where this proved impossible. Thus they wrote to the new bishop of Durham about one purchaser, "recommending him to your lordship, presumeing that you will treat him in such a mannor as may best comply with his majesties condiscension; if the peticioner desires noething from you but what is in your power lawfully to doe though you bee yourselfe a looser of some perticuler benefitt and advantage which in rigour might be insisted upon".[113] As a result of mediation, backed by power to impose a solution in the last resort, the commission was able to resolve disputes between owner and purchaser so successfully that within a year of the king's return the land settlement had ceased to be a political issue. What proportion of purchasers did in the end remain on their lands as lessees is unknown, but it was probably a substantial minority.[114]

B. THE EVOLUTION OF LANDED SOCIETY AFTER THE RESTORATION

1. *Introduction*

Considerable difficulties confront the historian attempting to establish what changes occurred in the structure of landowning society between the mid seventeenth and the mid eighteenth century. There are no comprehensive surveys of landownership such as the 'New Domesday' of 1873, and the records of taxes levied upon land are not of much use for this purpose in the period with which we are concerned. As for the estimates made by contemporaries concerning the numbers and wealth of the various sections of the landed community, they are of uncertain reliability and difficult to interpret even when they are not mutually contradictory.

These estimates have, nevertheless, been pressed into service, by F. M. L. Thompson and J. P. Cooper, in two brave attempts to measure changes in the social distribution of property over the post-medieval centuries as a whole. A principal purpose of their efforts was to discover whether or not they could confirm the long-established historical generalization that from the later seventeenth century onwards there was a steady concentration of property ownership into fewer and fewer hands, and this they succeeded in doing, albeit somewhat insecurely. Their writings suggest that the share of the great proprietors owning more than 10,000 acres remained roughly stable

[113] G. Ornsby, *The Correspondence of John Cosin, Part II*, Surtees Soc., LV, 1870, pp. 18–20. For other examples of cases dealt with by the commissioners, see PRO, SP 26/36, ff. 103–4, and *CSPD 1660–1*, pp. 502–3, 544, 596–7.   [114] Thirsk, 'The Restoration Land Settlement', p. 320.

at between 15 and 20 per cent from the mid fifteenth to the end of the seventeenth century, but by 1750 had begun to edge up towards the 24 per cent (of a significantly larger cultivated acreage) at which it stood in 1873.[115] The estates of small owners with under 300 acres had, it would seem, declined somewhat from the peak of one-third which they had attained around the middle of the seventeenth century, possibly by as much as between 2.5 and 3.5 million acres out of the 11 to 13 million they had held at that time. Between these two extremes the mass of middling landowners, holding between 300 and 10,000 acres, must have held, if some allowance is made for the institutional estates,[116] significantly less than half the cultivated acreage in the mid seventeenth century but possibly somewhat nearer half by the mid eighteenth. These calculations probably err on the side of caution in assessing the drift of property towards the larger owners. Furthermore, they almost certainly conceal a considerable shift of property within the very broad category of middling landowners, which as defined above extends from those living the lives of leisured county magnates down to men whose resources for supporting their gentility were hardly greater than those of a well-to-do farmer. Indeed, if the proportion of the cultivated area held by the owners of over 10,000 acres increased after the later seventeenth century, then since the latter were so very few in number – not more than a few hundred at most – it is almost impossible to believe that this was not merely the tip of an iceberg. Concealed from view must surely have been an increase in the proportion held by those towards the top of the 300–10,000-acre band at the expense of those in its lower parts. But even so the Thompson–Cooper estimates make it clear that there was no mass takeover of the property of any one section of society by another. As Cooper has observed, "some more complex process of change within and between groups must be envisaged".[117]

For a start, it is clear that, whatever the process may have been, it did not operate in an identical fashion in all parts of the kingdom. Relatively few regional studies of landownership have yet been attempted for this period, and those that are available vary much in the depth and thoroughness with which they were undertaken, and the precise time span to which they refer. Nevertheless, they leave no doubt that, within a national trend towards the concentration of property into fewer hands, in some areas the tide was running more powerfully than the global estimates would suggest, whilst in others it was relatively weak. This, of course, is hardly surprising in view of the wide differences in the social structure of landowning society between

---

[115] F. M. L. Thompson, 'The Social Distribution of Landed Property in England since the Sixteenth Century', EcHR, 2nd ser., XIX, 1966; J. P. Cooper, 'The Social Distribution of Land and Men in England, 1436–1700', EcHR, 2nd ser., XX, 1967.

[116] The institutional owners probably held about 6 to 7 per cent of the cultivated acreage.

[117] Cooper, op. cit., p. 435.

one area and another at the beginning of the period, and differences in the extent to which they were exposed to the principal economic forces at work in the century after the Civil War. So far, however, no sizeable areas have yet come to light where a contrary trend was at work, although there were undoubtedly limited districts, such as the immediate vicinity of London and some of the major manufacturing towns, where this did occur; and in the very different economic conditions which prevailed in the generation after 1790 it may well have been, temporarily, another story. In Bedfordshire and Northamptonshire Habakkuk found that after 1680 the drift of property was very strongly in favour of the great estate and the large landowner; that the lesser gentry and owner-occupiers were in serious economic difficulties; and that as they sold out they were not being replaced by other owners of a comparable socio-economic standing, but that their properties were mostly falling to established magnates or incomers of great wealth building up large new estates. An increase also occurred in the holdings of the larger owners in Warwickshire between 1660 and 1730, mainly, it would seem, by those already established in the county before the former date. Something similar seems to have been happening in the north-east by the eighteenth century, although it was new landowners rather than old who replaced the indigenous gentry and peasantry. In the north-west again a similar but apparently less pronounced drift of property into the hands of the large owners took place, but new recruits to the middling and lesser gentry were more prominent and the peasantry maintained their position almost completely. In Devon, on the other hand, no very marked aggrandizement of the larger estates occurred, the middling and lesser gentry and the freeholders remained numerous, and relatively few incomers appeared at any level of landed society. In Lincolnshire, too, the established great estates experienced relatively little growth, but many outsiders were buying their way into the county and building up new properties large and small, and a great many local men deriving their wealth from professional occupations, commerce, or farming were purchasing on a small scale. The net effect was thus to leave the structure, as opposed to the personnel, of landed society more or less unaltered. Finally, in Wiltshire and parts of the adjacent counties there seems likewise to have been a very active land market, but with many wealthy outsiders accumulating big agglomerations of property, so that the balance of ownership was tipped firmly in favour of the great proprietors.[118]

---

[118] Habakkuk, 'English Landownership'; A. M. Mimardière, 'The Warwickshire gentry, 1660–1730', unpub. Birmingham Univ. M.A. thesis, 1963, ch. 1; Hughes, *North Country Life... The North-East*, pp. xviii–xix, 1–13, 79; J. V. Beckett, 'Landownership in Cumbria, c. 1680–c. 1750', unpub. Lancaster Univ. Ph.D. thesis, 1975; W. G. Hoskins, 'The Occupation and Ownership of the Land in Devonshire, 1650–1800', unpub. London Univ. Ph.D. thesis, 1938, ch. IV; B. A. Holderness, 'The English Land Market in the Eighteenth Century: The Case of Lincolnshire', EcHR, 2nd ser., XXVII, 1974. The observations on Wiltshire are based upon my own unpublished research.

## 2. Demographic factors

The process of change may have brought about somewhat different results in almost every region, but everywhere its ingredients were very much the same. Two principal sets of factors, indeed, were at work: demographic ones operating through the system of intergenerational inheritance, and the socio-economic ones which determined who was selling and who was buying land. These cannot be entirely separated, for at many points they will be found to overlap and either to reinforce or to offset each other. Nevertheless, for the sake of clarity the remainder of this section will be mainly concerned with the demographic influences, whilst the following one is devoted principally to the socio-economic.

The demographic climate of the period we are concerned with was very different from that which had prevailed down to the early part of the seventeenth century and was to prevail again later, and though the detailed evidence at present available relates only to the peerage, there is every reason to suppose that their experience was shared by the whole landowning community. As a result of a slight increase in mortality (especially child mortality), a slow rise in the age of marriage, and a significant fall in fertility, the class was gradually tending towards biological extinction in the second half of the seventeenth century, and the generation born in the first quarter of the eighteenth century failed to reproduce itself by a considerable margin. The average size of family amongst the peerage fell from 5.04 for those born between 1600 and 1624 and so producing their children between about 1625 and 1665, to only 3.83 for those born a century later and giving birth between the mid 1720s and the mid 1760s. When these figures are combined with appropriate assumptions about the likelihood of children surviving their fathers, it emerges that throughout the period about a quarter of all marriages would produce female heirs only, the proportion increasing slightly with the passage of time. During the later seventeenth and early eighteenth centuries a further fifth of the peerage marriages would have left no surviving children at all, and this fraction would have risen to nearly a quarter by the end of our period.[119] The proportion of landowners who left only daughters or no children would not have been so high as the 45 per cent implied by these two fractions combined, because of the frequency with which widowers remarried, although this was becoming less universal as time passed. But even so it was, according to Bonfield, about a third (34.2 per cent) for those dying in the later seventeenth century and at the beginning of the eighteenth, and as high as 40.6 per cent for those dying towards the middle of the eighteenth.[120] The proportion of those whose estates passed to their

[119] T. H. Hollingsworth, 'The Demography of the British Peerage', suppl. to *Pop. Stud.*, XVIII, 1964, esp. Table 19; J. Goody, 'Strategies of Heirship', *Comp. Stud. in Soc. & Hist.*, XV, 1973, pp. 16–18.

[120] Hollingsworth, *op. cit.*, Table 14; L. Bonfield, 'Marriage Settlements and the "Rise of Great Estates": The Demographic Aspect', EcHR, 2nd ser., XXXII, 1979, p. 491.

daughters, or to relatives beyond their own immediate family, was, however, lower still, for many of those who died without sons to succeed them did have younger brothers, to whom a sense of family tradition might incline them to leave their possessions in preference to their own daughters,[121] even if a family settlement did not oblige them to do so.

Nevertheless, inheritance of property by means of heiresses and from collateral relatives must have been extremely common (more common, it would seem, than at any other period since the end of the Middle Ages),[122] and certainly all those who have studied the economic and social history of the aristocracy and gentry in the seventeenth and eighteenth centuries appear to agree that marriage and inheritance were the most important determinants of the fortunes of individual families. At all levels of landed society owners enlarged their estates by this means, often in a spectacular fashion. Thus the Claverings of Chopwell, county Durham, substantial gentry but hardly county magnates, with an estate of perhaps £600–£700 a year at the beginning of the eighteenth century, received an addition of 50 per cent or more to their rent roll when they inherited the compact 500-acre Potter Newton estate near Leeds from the Hardwick family as a result of John Clavering's marriage to the Hardwick heiress at some date in the 1680s. Even more striking was the case of the Berkshire gentry family of Pleydell, whose relatively modest estate at Shrivenham yielded only £300–£400 a year, but who rose into the top rank of county families as a result of the marriage of Thomas Pleydell (d. 1670) to Mary, daughter of Sir George Pratt, a landowner on a considerably larger scale. Mary was not the Pratt heiress at the time of her marriage, but both Pratt himself and his only son died within a year or so of each other in the early 1670s, and under the terms of the former's will the whole of his estate, worth well over £2,000 a year in Berkshire, Gloucestershire, and Wiltshire, passed to his wife for her to dispose of as she thought fit. She settled the major part of it, including the Pratt mansion house at Coleshill, on Mary's issue by Thomas Pleydell, another Thomas, and divided the rest between him and Mary's children by a second

[121] It did not do so in all cases: Sir John Arundell of Lanthorne, writing in 1697, considered it "a barbarity not to prefer my own child before any [other] relation" – G. Oliver, *Collections Illustrating the History of the Catholic Religion*...London, 1857, pp. 206–7.

[122] According to D. Thomas, 'The Social Origins of the Marriage Partners of the British Peerage', *Pop. Stud.*, XXVI, 1972, Table 7, p. 105, the proportion of peers marrying within the peerage who married heiresses was 32.8 per cent for those born in 1700–19 and 25.4 per cent for those born in 1720–39; of those marrying outside the peerage, 46 per cent and 31.9 per cent respectively. For later cohorts, whose marriages fell well outside our period, the proportions fell continuously into the nineteenth century. However, for reasons explained above, these figures do not provide a guide to the proportion of families inheriting property via marriage to an heiress. In the case of the landowners of Glamorgan studied by Martin no fewer than 45 out of the 83 families she was able to trace failed in the male line between 1660 and 1760, and in 26 out of the 45 the property passed through a daughter or daughters to other families – J. O. Martin, 'The Landed Estate in Glamorgan, c.1660–1760', unpub. Cambridge Univ. Ph.D. thesis, 1978, p. 219.

husband. Thus when Lady Pratt died in 1697 the Pleydells found themselves enjoying a landed income in excess of £2,000 a year, and Mary's grandson Sir Mark Stuart Pleydell was in due course (1738) able to buy out his cousin's share in the remaining Pratt lands for £6,000.[123] In the same way, at the very top of the social pyramid, it is beyond question that the very largest agglomerations of property, and the most impressive improvements in the wealth and standing of established landowners, were the result of one already affluent family absorbing the possessions of one, two, three, or more others by inheritance. Thus the great west-country estates of the earls of Ilchester represented a union of those of the Fox and Strangways families, brought together by the marriage of the first Lord Ilchester to the Strangways heiress in 1744. The first of these, built up by the financier Sir Stephen Fox in the late seventeenth century and situated mainly in Wiltshire and Somerset, had been worth about £6,500 a year at Sir Stephen's death in 1716. The second belonged to a long-established line of major Dorset gentry. They were centred on their great mansion at Melbury, but extended into both Somerset and Devonshire as well, and were worth considerably more (because of the income from fines charged upon the renewal of leases) than the annual rental of £6,681 at which they were valued in 1729.[124]

Examples such as these can be replicated almost indefinitely, and yet because they illustrate only one of the ways in which the inheritance system operated there is no doubt that they give a greatly exaggerated impression of the extent to which the ownership of land was coming to be concentrated into fewer hands. For if it was common for one family inheriting the estates of another to retain the inheritance intact, and to hand it down from eldest son to eldest son in the same way as paternal property, this was definitely not the general practice, and the alternatives seem to have been no less common. The former pattern was perhaps most often found where an inheritance was the result of a marriage alliance with a woman who was already known to be an heiress, deliberately entered into by the bridegroom's family in order to secure material advantage, and by the bride's in order that their estate passed into approved hands and would eventually descend to a representative of their own blood. Another type of 'planned' inheritance which usually resulted in a permanent addition to the estates of the heir and his descendants was where the cadet line of a landed family with several or many branches died out and its property passed back to the main branch. This might happen under the terms of an entail created when the cadet had

[123] Herts. RO, Panshanger Collection, T. 4,933; R. Thoreby, *Ducatus Leodiensis*, Leeds, 1816 edn, pp. 120–1; Berks. RO, D/EPb E.5: ledger A, f. 1 *et seq*., and T. I, bdle D, purchase deed of 7 June 1738; Wilts. RO, 490/75: abstract of title of the estates of Sir Mark Stuart Pleydell.

[124] C. Clay, *Public Finance and Private Wealth*, Oxford, 1978, pp. 328–9; Dorset RO, D.124. Family (box 226, bdle 2): marriage settlement dated 9 Sept. 1744, and booklet headed "1749 [sic] Strangways Family Estates..."

originally been endowed, or, even though the last survivor of the cadet line had freedom of action in respect of his property, because of the persistence of clan loyalty over the generations.

However, by no means all inheritances were in any sense 'planned' or arranged between branches of a single clan, and indeed unplanned and unexpected ones must have been equally or even more common. Many women who in the end turned out to be heiresses to landed property or great moneyed fortunes had not been such at the time of their marriage, a point which should be borne in mind when it is asserted that marriage to heiresses in successive generations is an indication that a family had a 'policy' of allying itself with women who were due to come into property. Thus the ultimate result of the decision of Lord Chancellor Cowper, later first Earl Cowper, to marry Mary Clavering as his second wife in 1706 was the inheritance by his descendants in 1762 of an estate in lands and money worth over £3,000 a year. Yet at the time of the marriage Mary was poorly endowed for the wife of such a great man and had no expectations for the future, and Cowper specifically stated that he had married her because he thought she would make him a good housekeeper as he grew older. Similarly, the marriage of Cowper's son, the second earl, to Henrietta, daughter of the earl of Grantham in 1732, was the means whereby over £4,000 a year in crown annuities and over £100,000 in paper securities came into his family. Yet in 1732 Henrietta had not been an heiress, and Cowper's motives for the match had been so far from mercenary that when he tried to persuade his brother to marry for money, the latter had retorted: "It was so small a motive with you in your choice that you can recommend it to no one, your choice was directed by affection."[125] A few deaths in quick succession from infectious disease could, and quite often did, bring to an unexpected end a line whose future had only months before seemed perfectly assured. Thus the Gloucestershire baronet Sir Robert Cocks of Dumbleton had seven children, including three sons, of whom five survived the perilous months of infancy. However, he lost three of these, and his wife, "by the same fatal sickness, a fever and sore throat" within little more than a fortnight in 1749, and in the end, when he himself died in 1765, shortly followed by his only surviving daughter, unmarried at the age of eighteen, his estate passed to a cousin, Charles Cocks of Castleditch, Herefordshire.[126] In other cases families became extinct even though several sons survived well into adult life, because as a result of relative poverty, indolence, disinclination, or congenital mental or physical defects none of them ever got around to marrying. There were thus innumerable instances in which one family inherited the property of another as a more or less unexpected windfall, often from quite close relatives, but sometimes

[125] C. G. A. Clay, 'Two Families and their Estates: The Grimstons and the Cowpers from c. 1650 to c. 1815', unpub. Cambridge Univ. Ph.D. thesis, 1966, pp. 260–4, 417–18 and n. 17, 18.
[126] S. Rudder, *A New History of Gloucestershire*, 2 vols., Cirencester, 1779, I, pp. 420–2.

from very distant connections indeed – as heirs general on the basis of a marriage contracted generations before, or as ultimate beneficiaries under some settlement of whose existence they were hardly aware. Thus in 1720 the estates and the title of seventh Viscount Fairfax of Gilling passed to a remote cousin, descended from a younger son of the first viscount who had died eighty-four years earlier, and who had been the twentieth remainderman in a settlement drawn up in 1699.[127]

Now when such windfall inheritances came to those who already had substantial estates of their own they were unquestionably regarded by their recipients as being in a different category from paternal property, or lands acquired from another family by a mutually agreed marriage strategy. If they came free of serious financial encumbrances, and the finances of the recipient family were in a sound condition, they might be treated as permanent additions to the main estate, but even in such circumstances this was not invariably so. It was, for instance, not uncommon (if and when it became legally possible) for them to be used to provide for younger children, or as a capital fund upon which the new owner could call at will for his own purposes, whether by sale or mortgage. When Lord Lexington wished to raise an unusually large marriage portion for his daughter Bridget upon her marriage to the heir of the duke of Rutland in 1717, for instance, he financed it by conveying to Rutland (with a prior agreement that they be sold, as they duly were the following year for £33,585) all the lands which had come to him through his wife, the heiress of Sir Giles Hungerford, in 1693.[128] However, land descending in one of the ways now under discussion was in practice often heavily encumbered, as indeed was land passing from one family to another in accordance with a prior agreement. Nor, of course, were all recipients financially sound. Lands acquired in this way were therefore commonly sold, sooner or later, thus in the long term adding nothing to the territorial possessions of the family which had inherited them, although they might well provide a financial buffer which made it possible for the latter to avoid sales of their paternal property. In the long run, therefore, the result of the large number of cases in which established landowners inherited additional estates through heiresses and from collaterals seems to have been as much the fuelling of the land market, whilst preserving intact the hereditary property of many owners who otherwise would have been forced to sell, as it was the concentration of property into the hands of a diminishing circle of great proprietors.[129]

A second reason why the latter effect was so relatively muted was that where owners without direct heirs had legal power to dispose of their property as they chose, they often wished to ensure that it retained a separate

---

[127] H. Aveling, 'The Catholic Recusancy of the Yorkshire Fairfaxes', pt II, *Recusant Hist.*, IV, 2, 1957, p. 92; pt III, *ibid.*, VI, 1, 1961, p. 14.

[128] Wilts. RO, 490/73.

[129] See also below, pp. 323–5.

existence and that their mansion houses continued to serve as family seats. Thus if they had a choice of relatives on whom they could settle property, they tended to avoid any who were already major proprietors, since, if it passed to such a person, it would be liable to lose its identity and become merely a subordinate part of a larger whole, attracting no particular attention from its owner. Thus Sir Harbottle Luckyn of Messing Hall (Essex), who died unmarried in 1737, deliberately avoided bequeathing his estate to his closest kinsman, Viscount Grimston, on the grounds that the latter "hath [already] a very plentiful estate", and provided that if the Luckyn line failed altogether, so that the Grimstons were the only possible heirs, then the property was not to be settled on the viscount or his eldest son, but on his younger son.[130] A preference for younger sons on the part of owners who were free to direct the descent of their estate because of the failure of their blood seems, indeed, to have been very common, and numerous examples could easily be cited. To provide but one, when the last of the Petres of Stanford Rivers (Essex) died in 1762, he left his estate of about £1,000 per annum, not to his closest surviving kinsman, the ninth Lord Petre, who already owned an estate of £6,000 a year in Essex and at least £4,500 more in Devon, Somerset, and Gloucestershire, but to his second son, with a proviso that if the latter were to inherit the main Petre estate, then Stanford Rivers should go to the third son.[131] It may indeed be the case, as Martin has suggested, that this desire to preserve the separate identity of their estates was more common amongst large landowners than amongst the lesser gentry, in which case the accumulation of estates through heiresses was probably (and in contradistinction to the impression given by some well-known examples) of more importance towards the base of the pyramid of landowning society than in its upper reaches.[132]

### 3. The land market

#### (a) Yeoman farmers and petty gentry

We may now come to consider how the structure and personnel of landed society changed as a result of the sale and purchase of land. To start with, it is clear that landed families with incomes of many hundreds of pounds a year or more were sufficiently well off to weather the effects of adverse economic conditions, provided of course that other things were equal and they were not already up to their ears in debt. They generally drew most of their income from rent-paying tenants who provided them with a buffer against a fall in income proportionate to the fall in agricultural profits in times of depression, for the tenants had to maintain rent payments as far as they could, even at the expense of their own savings, consumption, and

[130] Herts. RO, Gorhambury Collection, IX.B.37; *VCH Herts.*, Genealogical Volume, p. 182.
[131] Essex RO, D/DP F.256/12.    [132] Martin, thesis, pp. 224–8.

reinvestment in their farms. Besides, such landowners normally had a large enough margin between incomings and unavoidable outgoings to ride out fluctuations between them. It was only the smallest gentry and owner-occupiers who were likely to be caused serious difficulties by a series of bad farming years or a spell of heavy taxes on their own, and even amongst them it is difficult to establish how frequently such things really were fatal, for detailed accounts kept by such families rarely survive. In all likelihood it was not often. Undoubtedly, large numbers of yeoman farmers and petty gentry did sell out within the period with which we are concerned, especially during the most acute episodes of agricultural depression, but it was probably almost always those who were already in financial difficulties who succumbed most easily to outside economic pressures. It is impossible to establish it definitively, but it seems likely that an equally important effect of difficult economic conditions upon this section of landed society was that it made it less easy or even impossible for them to save, thereby depriving them of funds for expansion. Amongst them strict primogeniture was far from universal, especially in the seventeenth century, and the tendency of fathers to provide younger sons with land meant that some measure of continuous expansion was necessary for the holdings of the group even to remain stable. If fathers were unable to endow younger sons with property specially purchased for that purpose, as many could and did in prosperous times, then they were likely to provide for them by breaking pieces off their inherited possessions. Thus, if the land purchases of the group faltered, then its holdings would inevitably start to suffer from attrition.

Difficulties in accumulating savings at relatively low levels of income, however, also inevitably made it more common for small landowning families to incur debt in order to provide for those sons who were not set up on a piece of land, and for daughters. This in turn meant a steady increase in the number of those who were encumbered with interest payments to creditors. They would thus become more vulnerable to the next bout of agricultural depression, and liable to share the fate of Richard Willoughby of West Knoyle, Wiltshire. Willoughby was a small squire who sold out in 1732, during the depths of a notorious period of agricultural difficulty, and it is clear that at the root of his problems lay the fact that he was committed to paying out more than two-thirds of the £470 per annum his estate could be expected to produce even when all his rents were being paid in full. Part of this was going to his mother for her jointure, the rest in interest on a mortgage incurred to discharge the portions of his five sisters.[133]

Small owners also lacked a source of economic strength enjoyed by the larger ones in that in general they found it less easy to borrow if they began to get into difficulties. For lesser proprietors in the more remote parts of the

[133] Wilts. RO, 383/359, 716, 862. Willoughby also had some income from the renewal of copyhold fines, but on an average it cannot have exceeded £40 a year.

country, Cumbria for instance, it does not seem to have been at all easy to raise loans, even in the first half of the eighteenth century, simply because local lenders were few and the London money market was far beyond their geographical horizons. Things were certainly easier in the more advanced agricultural regions, and altogether different in rapidly advancing areas of rural industry such as south Staffordshire and north Worcestershire, and in the vicinity of prosperous port towns like Liverpool or Bristol.[134] However, everywhere raising small sums, say £100 or less, on the mortgage of freehold property was likely to prove difficult because the legal costs and the trouble the lender might experience in ensuring that the borrower's title to the security was sound made it hardly worth while to those with money to lay out. Ironically, it was easier for copyholders because their title was so much easier to prove. This frequently obliged small owners to borrow on bond, which in turn was difficult for people in their position because it involved reliance upon a man's personal credit as opposed to the credit of his estate. By contrast, the wider horizons of the major gentry and aristocracy gave them the necessary contacts to find whatever credit they needed. Moreover, mortgages for substantial sums on large estates were much sought after as investments, and were never difficult to obtain even at times when heavy government borrowing forced up interest rates generally, however large the principal sum required. The rise in the selling prices of landed estates from the 1710s onwards increased the value of the security that landowners had to offer and so enabled them to borrow larger sums than before, whilst the continuous if slow and irregular fall in the rate of interest between the mid seventeenth and the mid eighteenth century enabled them to service their borrowings more easily. Substantial owners thus acquired a wider margin of safety which further increased their resilience in the face of financial difficulties. In the second quarter of the eighteenth century they could normally raise money at 4 per cent, sometimes even at $3\frac{1}{2}$ per cent. They were thus able, for the same cost in interest charges, to support a debt half as large again as had been possible for their ancestors in the third quarter of the seventeenth century, when 6 per cent had generally been the going rate on mortgages, and twice as large as had been possible in the 1630s and 40s.

For the smaller owners, including the petty gentry, the eighteenth-century rise in land values may, on the contrary, have increased their propensity to sell because it provided even those whose finances were perfectly sound with a powerful inducement to do so. Men whose primary interest was in

[134] J. V. Beckett, 'English Landownership in the Later Seventeenth and Eighteenth Centuries: The Debate and the Problems', EcHR, 2nd ser., xxx, 1977, pp. 572–3; M. B. Rowlands, *Masters and Men in the West Midland Metalware Trades before the Industrial Revolution*, Manchester, 1975, pp. 43–4, 46–7; B. L. Anderson, 'Provincial Aspects of the Financial Revolution of the Eighteenth Century', Bus. Hist., xi, 1969.

Table 9. *Movement of land prices*

| Period | Normal spread of prices | Remarks |
| --- | --- | --- |
| 1646–50 | 14–16 years' purchase | Abnormally low |
| 1650–64 | 18–20 years' purchase | Recovering |
| 1665–89 | 16–18 years' purchase | Falling |
| 1690–1703 | 20–2 years' purchase | Rising |
| 1704–13 | 17–19 years' purchase | Falling |
| 1714–20 | 21–5 years' purchase | Rising steeply |
| 1721–30 | 25–8 years' purchase | Rising steeply |
| 1731–43 | 26–30 years' purchase | Rising more slowly |
| 1744–62 | 24–30 years' purchase | Fluctuating sharply with war and peace |
| 1763–72 | 30–5 years' purchase | Rising steeply |
| 1773–83 | 22–8 years' purchase | Falling heavily |

*Note*: This table gives an approximate indication of the rates at which land changed hands in areas where prices were neither exceptionally high nor exceptionally low.
*Source*: C. Clay, 'The Price of Freehold Land in the Later Seventeenth and Eighteenth Centuries', EcHR, 2nd ser, XXVII, 1974.

commercial farming and in maximizing their money income from agriculture will have understood perfectly well that, with purchase rates at between twenty-five and thirty years' purchase (as they were by the 1730s), it could be exceedingly advantageous to sell, especially where the purchaser was content to let the seller remain as a rent-paying tenant with a long lease. This was because a sale would provide them with the capital to increase the scale of their operations, either by a higher level of stocking on an existing acreage or by taking over a larger one. Similarly, for those who needed resources to develop some other economic activity which they had hitherto pursued in conjunction with small-scale landowning, such prices provided a fine opportunity. The famous Samuel Whitbread, for instance, raised part of the capital for the brewery he established in 1742 by the sale of a small estate in Gloucestershire which had come to him through his mother, and which fetched £600. And on a larger scale Mathew Boulton raised capital for his industrial enterprises, including the hardware partnership with Fothergill and the development of Watt's steam engine, by the sale of his Packington estate for £15,000 in 1772.[135] Indeed, sales for such reasons must have become increasingly common as the eighteenth century wore on. This was partly because of the increasing diversification of economic activity, the rise of new

[135] P. Mathias, *The Brewing Industry in England, 1700–1830*, Cambridge, 1959, p. 261; J. E. Cule, 'Finance and Industry in the Eighteenth Century: The Firm of Boulton and Watt', *Ec. Hist.* (Suppl. to *Ec. J.*), IV, 1940, p. 320.

forms of manufacture and new branches of commerce, and the continued expansion of old, in most of which the entrepreneurs were usually men who also owned at least some land, either inherited or purchased out of the fruits of their enterprise.[136] It was also partly due to the demographic conditions which appear to have prevailed amongst the mass of the population, as well as amongst the well-to-do, which ensured that land passed from family to family, via inheritance by heiresses and through collaterals, with unusual frequency.[137] As a result, particularly in the economically more advanced parts of the country, it often came into the hands of those who were not farmers or gentry with deep roots in the countryside, but were employed in trade, industry, or the professions; or who lived, in an urban setting, the lives of leisured gentlemen on incomes derived from the funds.[138]

Such people might remain as small absentee landlords for long periods, even for generations, but for them landholding was not a way of life as it had been for their predecessors. They did not make the mansions on their estates into family homes, but allowed them to deteriorate into mere farmhouses or become altogether ruinous, a symptom of social change which contemporary observers did not fail to notice.[139] And still more important, they did not see their property as a treasured inheritance but as a useful capital asset. This was a crucial distinction, for it meant that they were always liable to sell in order to mobilize funds for other purposes. Some of them, having no emotional attachment to their property, nor even any particular liking for country life, might do so simply in order to increase their net income by exchanging land for a higher-yielding asset, or even because they did not wish to be troubled with the problems of managing a landed estate. Thus William Abel, who in late middle age in 1715 had inherited East Claydon (Bucks.) from a cousin, three years later offered the property to Lord Fermanagh, owner of a much larger estate in the immediate vicinity, with the comment that his state of health was such "that for the future...I must (as my phisicians tell me) give over all business which requires action, or causes the least uneasiness imaginable. I am sure a country life with a country estate requires the one, and can't be without the other." He further announced his intention to retire to London and, with the help of a congenial coffee house, there seek "inaction and quietness...the injoyments of old age".[140]

[136] For instance, see the extent of landholding amongst the ironmasters of the west Midlands and the potters of north Staffordshire at this time – Rowlands, *op. cit.*, pp. 112–13; and L. Weatherill, *The Pottery Trade and North Staffordshire, 1660–1760*, Manchester, 1971, pp. 54–5 and ch. 9.

[137] See above, sect. B.2.

[138] For the increasing number of moderately well-to-do professional, commercial, and leisured 'pseudo gentry' inhabiting the towns by the later seventeenth century, see A. M. Everitt, 'Social Mobility in Early Modern England', *PP*, no. 33, 1966, pp. 70–2.

[139] See, for instance, Rudder, *Gloucestershire*, I, p. 440; A. Young, *General View of the Agriculture of the County of Essex*, 2 vols., London, 1807, I, p. 45.

[140] F. P. Verney and M. M. Verney, *Memoirs of the Verney Family during the Seventeenth Century*, 2nd edn, 2 vols., London, 1907, II, p. 488; M. M. Verney, *Verney Letters of the Eighteenth Century*, 2 vols., London, 1930, II, pp. 55–6.

An increase in the amount of land in the hands of small absentee owners did not occur everywhere to the same degree, and in some areas, such as the district where Wiltshire, Dorset, and Somerset meet, it can be detected only to a very limited extent,[141] whilst in the remote and backward north-west it apparently did not happen at all.[142] Elsewhere, however, especially in much of the Midlands and Home Counties, the increase was striking. At Wigston Magna, near the busy town of Leicester, a village where in many respects peasant proprietorship was still vigorous, one-third of the land belonged to non-resident owners by the mid eighteenth century. At Sherington (Bucks.) the proportion had risen from 12 per cent in 1650 to over two-thirds by 1760.[143] Such developments were not necessarily accompanied by great increases in the size of the units of landowning, though they usually involved some degree of concentration, but they clearly represented an important change in the structure of society. Moreover, if a large owner in the district was interested in adding to his estate, or if a moneyed man intent on creating a new one appeared there, then the way forward was made considerably easier. Thus the evidence relating to the estate in Hertfordshire built up by the successful lawyer Sir Harbottle Grimston illustrates how often land sold to a wealthy buyer had first passed, usually by marriage or inheritance, from the families of yeoman farmers or indigenous gentry to non-resident landholders. Grimston purchased some 2,893 acres for a total of £54,183 in over seventy separate transactions (1651–83), and almost exactly two-thirds by area was acquired from this type of seller.[144]

To conclude, the swelling tide of sales by smaller owners to men of great resources which characterized this period in some, though not in all, districts was due in part to the difficulty experienced by peasant farmers in managing on small resources in changing technical and marketing conditions. But it occurred also, especially in the eighteenth century, because both peasants and small owners who were anything but peasants did not resist the temptation to sell out at good prices.

When we turn to consider the land purchases of the yeomen and the farming gentry we must remind ourselves that, although this period is clearly characterized by recurrent bouts of agricultural depression, conditions were worse in some areas than in others. Not all types of farming were afflicted to the same degree by the scourge of overproduction and underconsumption which lay at the root of the problems of the agricultural sector in this period, whilst those farmers who succeeded in raising their productivity by adopting one or other of the innovations described in the regional chapters doubtless

---

[141] This observation is based on a study of the title deeds of the numerous small and middling-sized parcels of land purchased by the Hoares of Stourhead from 1718 onwards – Wilts. RO, 383/*passim*.     [142] Beckett, thesis, chs. 4, 5.
[143] W. G. Hoskins, *The Midland Peasant*, London, 1957, pp. 219–20; Chibnall, *Sherington*, pp. 237–8.     [144] C. G. A. Clay, thesis, pp. 15, 20–8, and app. II.

protected their incomes better than those who did not. However, in the 1670s, 1680s, and mid 1700s, districts of mixed farming and pastoral husbandry alike seem to have suffered from prices which, for many farmers, covered costs of production barely or not at all. Thus although land was to be had at bargain rates (sometimes for as little as fourteen years' purchase) by those farmers and farming gentry who did contrive to make money, that is, the largest producers, well placed for markets, on easily worked soils upon which advanced methods had already been introduced, these were probably the times when demand from the farming sector was at its weakest – and sales by its members most extensive.[145] Quite apart from the current difficulties of so many, the uncertain future prospect for farming profits and the demand for credit from financially embarrassed neighbours seem to have encouraged those who had savings to lend money rather than buy land. Studies of places as far apart as Sussex, the east Midlands, and Cumbria show that the most successful families of this time had considerable sums so laid out. These sometimes ran into hundreds of pounds; Robert Walthew of Pemberton in Lancashire, a yeoman on the threshold of gentry status, had as much as £2,750 out at interest when he died in 1676.[146] In the chronic depression of the second quarter of the eighteenth century it was the areas in which profits were mainly dependent upon the sale of grains that were most seriously affected by price movements, though the devastation caused by the cattle plague at that time ensured that the pastoral districts were not entirely unscathed. But in the intervening periods some groups of farmers undoubtedly enjoyed great prosperity: grain producers, if they had a surplus, during the years of poor harvests and high prices in the 1690s; graziers during much of the first quarter of the eighteenth century. And many of them invested in land purchase, especially the graziers, whose scale of operations and profits (in good times) tended to be larger than that of other farmers.

The steady increase in the price of land between the 1710s and about 1740[147] should, theoretically, have encouraged small owners to use accumulated capital in one (or both) of two alternatives to buying land, either of which would certainly have paid higher dividends in a strictly financial sense. One was to use available funds to stock a larger area by taking more land on lease. The other was to plough back farming profits into the existing acreage by investing in new farm buildings, drainage, digging and spreading

[145] For land changing hands at a mere fourteen years' purchase, see Broad, thesis, pp. 83–5 (1646); Hughes, *North Country Life... The North-East*, p. xvi (1665); C. G. A. Clay, thesis, app. 1 (1675).

[146] G. E. Mingay, *English Landed Society in the Eighteenth Century*, London, 1963, p. 87; G. H. Kenyon, 'Kirdford Inventories, 1611 to 1776', *Sussex Arch. Coll.*, XCIII, 1955, p. 82; B. A. Holderness, 'Credit in English Rural Society before the Nineteenth Century', AHR, XXIV, 1976, pp. 101–4; Beckett, thesis, pp. 156–7; J. J. Bagley, 'The Will, Inventory and Accounts of Robert Walthew of Pemberton', *Lancs. & Cheshire Rec. Soc.*, CIX, 1965.

[147] See Table 9. p. 300.

marl or chalk, buying in fertilizer, buying better seed or improved livestock, and the like. The extent to which they actually did so is uncertain, but the gradual increase in the size of farms, and the fact that it now seems well established that the farming gentlemen and larger yeoman farmers were the leaders in the spread of more advanced agricultural methods, indicate that it may have been considerable. On the other hand the financial advantages of both tenancy and investment in improvements, given the high purchase rates that had to be paid for land from the 1710s onwards, did not deter small buyers from enthusiastically entering the land market when, after the end of the period, farming profits boomed once again.

However, demand for land from the farming sector never depended wholly upon the profitability of farming. Farmers and petty gentry derived income from non-agricultural sources, from the provision of services to the communities in which they lived, and from commercial and industrial undertakings, and these might flourish at times when their farming operations did not. Even more important, they received portions in money with their wives, married heiresses, and received legacies from relatives, so that some of them would always have money available for the purchase of land, even when all around their brethren were financially at their last gasp. Thus at no time did the demand for land from the farming community die away altogether, and at some times in some places it was as insistent as ever it had been, with single closes, groups of open-field strips, and small holdings changing hands at a rapid rate. As we shall see, however, over considerable expanses of countryside the remorseless growth of established large estates and the creation of new ones out of numerous small units had virtually extinguished this type of land market by the middle of the eighteenth century. Taking the kingdom as a whole, the yeoman family rising steadily into the gentry by buying land was a much less characteristic figure in rural society between 1640 and 1750 than it had been in the preceding period. Plenty of individual examples of this phenomenon may be found in our period, but, save in the far north-west, the far south-west, parts of the Welsh border counties, and perhaps in a few limited districts elsewhere, it was not a significant factor in the evolution of landed society during this time.

*(b) Piecemeal purchases by substantial owners and moneyed newcomers*
The difficulties which so many landowners periodically experienced, especially between the later 1660s and about 1710, and again in the 1720s and 30s, in collecting their rents in full and even in maintaining the nominal value of their rent rolls necessarily served to depress the demand for land from substantial owners too. So did the heavy land taxes imposed in the aftermath of the Civil Wars, intermittently in the 1660s and 70s, and continuously from 1692 to 1713. Particularly in the grain-growing parts of the lowland zone, where the agricultural depressions tended to be most severe, and in the south,

east, and Midlands, where the land tax was levied at full rate, not only were the resources available to landowners reduced, but, no less important, a serious question mark arose over the future value of land. As long as the rise in agricultural prices had been more or less continuous, and taxes on land had been so light as to be of little consequence, land had been a truly gilt-edged investment, and, indeed, one whose value could be counted on to appreciate, not necessarily from year to year, but certainly from decade to decade. But at least from the time of the Civil War, and probably from somewhat earlier, its value was only too likely to drop, and could drop quite heavily and suddenly. This made it very much less suitable as a temporary haven for savings for which a future use was clearly foreseen, and the buying of land, whether in small parcels or large, for this purpose was very much less characteristic of the period after 1660 than it had been before 1640, and especially before 1620. From about or soon after the middle of the seventeenth century onwards, if established landowners bought land at all, they generally bought in order to hold indefinitely.

However, it must be stressed that, contrary to what is sometimes believed, established gentry or aristocratic landowners were not concerned to expand their acreage indefinitely. Such an attitude was confined to those who were self-consciously creating a new estate out of the profits of some non-agrarian activity, and, indeed, only to the minority who had overweening social pretensions or political ambitions. It is true that a strong ideology prevailed amongst the landed classes that property inherited from a father and grandfather ought not to be sold as long as there was a direct male heir to inherit (an important proviso), but few owners were prepared to sink all their spare cash in the purchase of additional land. There were so many other uses for any surplus of income over ordinary expenditure that the majority of country gentry, with no outside resources available to them, were not often able to buy land in any quantity, and if they could afford to they were usually unwilling to forgo the satisfactions to be had from the expenditure of money in other ways. Moreover, the rather small minority of landowners who were able to save significant sums were increasingly inclined to lay out their surplus in other ways. Lending money at interest on bond, or for larger sums on mortgage, to other proprietors within the county or to local merchants, was the normal investment outlet for all but the wealthiest families, at least in the first half of the period. For those whose contacts and way of life enabled them to look beyond their own locality to the London money market the range of alternative securities was widening steadily, especially between about 1690 and 1720, but in practice few landowners were involved in this as investors until well into the eighteenth century. Thus, according to Mimardière, amongst the gentry of Warwickshire, who numbered several hundreds, only twenty-four persons, representing nineteen different families (all well-to-do), held Bank of England stock at any time between 1694 and 1730, and half of them acquired it only after 1720, whilst only ten individuals representing eight families held East India stock. Ownership of short-term government securities was a little more widely diffused, but even so only one member of the lesser gentry could be shown to have invested outside his home county.[148]

Of course, if the opportunity arose for a landowner to acquire a piece of land which abutted directly on the main part of his estate, or would serve to consolidate his property, rendering his ownership of a particular manor or parish more 'entire', then if he could afford the price he would generally be inclined to buy it. If the acquisition was sufficiently important, an owner might even be prepared to borrow for the purpose. As we shall see, it did not make financial sense for an owner to mortgage simply in order to expand the acreage of an estate.[149] However, to do so in order to acquire land which lay within a few hundred yards of his house or which his family had long coveted because it represented a last outpost of alien ownership within his little kingdom was another matter, for the motive was not a financial one but connected with the maintenance or improvement of a social or political position, or simply with psychological satisfaction and a desire for neatness and order. As Lord Ilchester's chief agent commented to his master in such an instance in 1767, "if we can't purchase on terms we would, we must purchase on the best we can, as from its contiguity [the farm in question] is extremely desirable, and to have a disagreeable neighbour, so near, would be superlatively vexatious".[150] Yet land which lay even just out of sight of his house and grounds might not seem a worthwhile acquisition to the landowner conscious of the poor financial return it would yield. Thus in April 1748, after he had just bought thirty-four acres of a stretch of woodland then on the market, Lord Bristol told his son: "as to buying any of the other woods of the said estate, as they all lye behind and are covered by the said West-wood from being visible to any eye standing in the park, they are wholly unnecessary to answer any further purpose of ours, at least of mine". What he had acquired would, he had calculated, pay only 2 per cent on its purchase price, and he had bought it only because its possession by the family would serve "to encrease the beauty of our prospect from this park".[151]

Bristol was certainly not unique in setting his face against virtually any extension of his estate. He, and others, like the third Viscount Lonsdale, who came to share his jaundiced view of landed investment, were, after all, only following the dictates of the commonsense aphorism, coined in a later period by the earl of Derby, but almost equally valid for the eighteenth century and even for the later seventeenth: "there is a limit beyond which most men do not desire to extend their holdings of what is essentially an unremunerative

[148] Mimardière, thesis, ch. 6, sect. iii.   [149] See below, pp. 314–15.
[150] BL, Add. MS 51,346, f. 176: G. Donisthorpe to Lord Ilchester, 9 May 1767.
[151] *Letter Books of John Hervey, First Earl of Bristol*, 3 vols., Wells, 1894, III, p. 356.

investment".¹⁵² The apparent increase in absenteeism in this period may, moreover, have increased the number of owners who ceased to bother about the enlargement of their properties. So too, in all probability, did the growing number of those whom the peculiar demographic tendencies of the period left without male heirs, and whose estates were destined to pass to distant cousins, and whose inclination to sacrifice their own purchasing power (by exchanging liquid cash or some relatively high-yielding security for relatively low-yielding land) for the sake of posterity was thereby much diminished.

On the other hand, amongst those landowners who were both resident upon their estates and had an heir in whom they had a real interest – and at any one time they were certainly the majority at all levels of society – the fashion grew for 'ring fence' estates. This undoubtedly owed a good deal to the increasing professionalization of estate administration as the period wore on, which in turn was partly the result of the transfer of land into the hands of new owners who often (though not always) had a more businesslike approach to the management of their land than those they replaced. However, it probably owed more to the increasing tendency to employ the modern type of land steward, who saw his task not just as that of a mere rent collector but as an active manager whose business it was to improve his employer's property to the utmost. Particularly important was the development of accurate mapping and of estate surveys which were concerned with expounding the agricultural conditions prevailing upon each farm, potentialities for future improvement, and general economic prospects, rather than with just recording tenancies and their financial obligations. Such surveys seem to have been relatively unusual before the early eighteenth century, and they are not found in large numbers before the second half of it. Doubtless their appearance was as much or more a symptom of interest in improvement than a cause of it, but nevertheless, by pointing out to an owner the extent of the advantages to be gained by acquiring particular pieces of land in order to improve his existing farms, they must often have provided an impetus to expansion. More influential still in this context were professionally drawn estate maps, of which the first examples date from the end of the sixteenth century,¹⁵³ and which by the eighteenth century had come to be regarded by the owners of larger properties as an essential aid to competent management. They provided the proprietor with a bird's-eye view of the layout of his farms, which made clear, with an immediacy that

---

¹⁵² D. Spring, 'Introduction', in J. Bateman, *The Great Landowners of Great Britain and Ireland*, Leicester, 1970, p. 9. Investment in land was "unremunerative" because it yielded so much lower a rate of return than the alternatives, and though the gap had widened by the mid nineteenth century, it was already a large one in the later seventeenth, as contemporaries were well aware: see the comments of Sir Stephen Fox in 1667, Dr Prideaux in 1674, and Nathaniel Pinney in 1691 – C. Clay, *Public Finance and Private Wealth*, p. 161; HMC, *Fifth Report*, app., p. 375; R. Grassby, 'The Rate of Profit in the Seventeenth Century', EHR, LXXXIV, 1969, p. 748.

¹⁵³ F. G. Emmison, *Catalogue of Maps in the Essex Record Office*, Chelmsford, 1947.

no written survey could attain, where islands and promontories of land in alien ownership lay intermixed with his own, where indentations in his frontier demanded to be filled in, and where salients running out into the estates of others provided a basis for expansion.

Personal satisfaction to the owners in the creation of fully consolidated estates was often as important as any rational calculation of the financial advantage that might ultimately derive from them. This is illustrated by the fact that consolidation was consistently pursued by proprietors who showed no interest at all in undertaking the reorganization of tenancies which their purchases had made possible. The Earls Cowper in Hertfordshire provide an example of this[154]; and doubtless there were other landowners besides Sir John Griffin Griffin of Audley End (1719-97), who not only had his estate mapped especially to show the prospects and possibilities for rounding out his property, but kept the map itself not in his estate office but in his own dressing room.[155] Nevertheless, if an acquisition would contribute towards making possible an enclosure or some other major rationalization of farm layout, then it would be worth while as an investment, even if it had to be bought at an exorbitant price. This was because the high rate of return obtainable from capital used to improve land would more than offset the fact that the rate of return on the land purchased was very low. Improvements paid so well in part because the estate did not become liable to reassessment for land tax as a result of them. More important, however, was the relatively low cost of most types of improvements to land, and the very large increases in productivity they made possible. In 1775 the agricultural writer Nathaniel Kent reckoned that improvements generally paid four times the 3 per cent which was the most that could be expected from a land purchase as such, and that they might well pay much more. Indeed, Chambers and Mingay have estimated that the gross return to the landowner on investment in enclosure was, on average, as high as 15-20 per cent for the period 1760 to 1813, although this figure may be inflated by the inclusion of the wartime period of soaring agricultural profits and continuously rising rents after 1793, and thus is not a safe guide to the return on mid-eighteenth-century schemes.[156] Especially in parts of the country where unenclosed land remained, therefore, the more substantial landowners did have a sound economic motive for expanding their estates at the expense of their smaller neighbours. Thus one landowner was told, à propos of a holding at Wilton (Yorks.), whose possession would complete a long process of consolidation: "By purchasing this farm you may have it in your power to inclose and

[154] C. G. A. Clay, thesis, pt II, passim.
[155] J. D. Williams, 'A Study of an Eighteenth-Century Nobleman... Sir John Griffin Griffin...', unpub. London Univ. Ph.D. thesis, 1974, pp. 306-7, 384.
[156] N. Kent, Hints to Gentlemen of Landed Property, London, 1775, pp. 9-10; J. D. Chambers and G. E. Mingay, The Agricultural Revolution, London, 1966, p. 84.

make land worth 15 shillings an acre that is now in tillage and only lett att 5."[157] Whether or not enclosure by act of parliament reduced the amount of land in the hands of small owners after 1760, there can be no doubt that the prospects of achieving enclosure by unity of possession, or by agreement once the number of proprietors had been reduced to the point where achieving this posed few problems, was a major cause of its diminution in many parts of the country in the preceding century. To give a concrete example, in 1732 Henry Hoare paid £12,700 for the purchase of the lordship of West Knoyle (Wilts.) and the principal farm there. West Knoyle's arable land was unenclosed open field and the manor had several hundred acres of common on the slopes of the nearby downland, making it a perfect target for the improving landlord if only he could gain control of a large enough proportion of its total acreage. Thus in the next few years Hoare bought up eleven separate small- and medium-sized holdings in the parish, at a total cost of over £2,900, and in 1742 succeeded in negotiating an enclosure agreement with the remaining life-leaseholders.[158]

Piecemeal purchases in order to consolidate established estates, whether for social or economic reasons, thus remained a significant factor in the land market, although more so in some areas than in others. But inevitably the lesser gentry with money incomes of only a very few hundred pounds a year could rarely afford to make any important additions to their estates at all, since even in the improbable event of their being able to save a considerable fraction of their incomes, the sums they would be able to accumulate in this way would not be large enough, especially when purchase rates rose (but landed incomes did not) from the 1710s onwards.[159] On the other hand, the owners of large estates, with a much greater absolute margin between income and unavoidable expenditure, could usually find the price of a single farm or a few fields without much difficulty. Many, perhaps most, major county families made at least a small handful of consolidating purchases in each generation, and some were continually buying on a small scale. Thus between 1693 and 1744 two generations of the Colchester family of Westbury (Glos.) spent some £10,530 on thirty-one separate purchases from twenty-eight different sellers, half of which were for £100 or less. Similarly, two successive owners of the Mildenhall estate in Suffolk, Sir Thomas Hanmer and his nephew Sir William Bunbury, made no fewer than sixty distinct additions to their property there at a total cost of over £18,700 over the forty years after 1724: five of these involved sums over £1,000, but again many were under £100.[160] What is more, large landowning families seem to have been able to extend their estates in this way even when their overall

[157] E. Riding RO, DDHO/59/15: William Wright to the Hon. Beaumont Hotham, 13 Feb. 1742/3.
[158] Wilts. RO, 383/297–9, 590–4, 862, 864, 873, 874; 598/1.
[159] See Table 9 above, p. 300.
[160] Glos. RO, D.36/E5; W. Suffolk RO, Bunbury Collection, E.18/454/13.

financial position was not very strong. Even the often desperately straitened Viscount Grimston was able to make at least ten purchases, adding some 262 acres at a cost of £3,619 16s. to his Gorhambury estate during his long tenure of it (1700–56).[161]

Men who had made money in business, government service, or one of the professions, and were intent upon establishing themselves in landed society, also tended to build up estates by means of piecemeal purchases. Such newcomers may have been less numerous than they had been in the century before the Civil War, but they still continued to invade county society at all levels throughout the period, and at any rate amongst those who made large fortunes the propensity to buy land seems to have been as great as ever. Amongst the only modestly successful the unpromising prospects in the agricultural sector of the economy in the later seventeenth century, and the sharp fall in the rate of return to be expected from land as prices surged upwards after 1713 to reach twenty-five years' purchase or more by the later 1720s,[162] undoubtedly caused some diversion of funds into alternative and higher-yielding investments. Money deposited with goldsmith bankers, mortgage lending, the securities of the major joint stock companies, and government stock all came to look more attractive than landed property to many such people. At twenty-five years' purchase, land yielded no more than 4 per cent gross or little more than 3 per cent net of outgoings; at thirty years' purchase, only $3\frac{1}{3}$ per cent gross or perhaps $2\frac{3}{4}$ per cent net. By comparison, even in peacetime in the eighteenth century 4 per cent was usually to be obtained from a mortgage, and the income was subject to no deductions. The very rich, however, tended to use such outlets as a medium-term haven for their savings, until the time came when they were ready to move into land. The availability of such outlets made it unnecessary for them to invest their money in property as they accumulated it, rendering it possible to postpone the all-important step until their own affairs made the moment propitious, and in the meantime to keep their investment income at the highest possible level. Men who had pursued active careers as merchants, financiers, lawyers, or as military or naval commanders did not usually relish the prospect of burying themselves deep in the countryside, and as often as not seem to have bought land rather for the sake of their posterity than for themselves. At any rate, especially by the eighteenth century, it became increasingly common for them to postpone making any major purchases of land until late in their careers. As a result it was not infrequent for them to be still engaged in converting their fortunes from paper securities into landed property when they died, leaving their heirs or executors to complete the process. To take a particularly dramatic case, the first duke of Marlborough died leaving an estate worth only £2,344 per annum around his seat of Blenheim Palace in Oxfordshire, but he bequeathed

[161] C. G. A Clay, thesis, app. III.   [162] See Table 9 above, p. 300.

£400,000 in trust for the purchase of lands to be settled on his right heirs.[163] Sooner or later, however, even if it was in the second or even the third generation rather than the first, almost all the major fortunes built up within this period were invested in land.

A few wealthy individuals are still to be found buying a series of quite distinct estates, widely separated from each other, usually because political considerations were uppermost in their minds. During the 1690s, for instance, the banker Charles Duncombe bought lands in Huntingdonshire, Bedfordshire, Buckinghamshire, and Wiltshire, as well as making his famous purchase of the Helmsley estate in the North Riding of Yorkshire for £92,000.[164] However, this pattern, whether on a large or a small scale, does not seem to have been common even in the later seventeenth century and was certainly very unusual by the middle of the eighteenth. A much more common approach was to concentrate on the acquisition of farms and manors within one, or at most two, limited districts, and gradually to build up a consolidated estate around a country residence. Men often commenced with one substantial purchase, and then devoted the rest of their effort to ensuring that nothing else that came up for sale in their chosen locality escaped them. A large number of small acquisitions might thus go to create even a middling-sized estate. The Puritan lawyer Sir Harbottle Grimston, for instance, acquired the nucleus of his Gorhambury estate in 1652 with the purchase of the house and some 1,582 acres of land for £12,760. Then during the next thirty years or so he spent another £39,000 on the purchase of a further 2,768 acres, involving seventy transactions, in only nine of which did the purchase price reach into four figures. Another example of the same type of estate building is represented by the Hoares of Stourhead. In 1718 Henry Hoare the elder bought the manor of Stourton in Wiltshire and that of Stourton Caundle in Dorset for £14,000 and £9,000 respectively. He and his son Henry 'the magnificent' then added to these twin nuclei whenever opportunity offered, and by the death of the latter (in 1785) had between them spent in excess of £146,000 on making fifty-six separate additions to the former and fifteen to the latter. Neither Grimston nor the Hoares bought anything that lay more than six miles from the house at the centre of their original purchase, and the vast majority of their acquisitions lay within a radius of three or four miles.[165]

This very gradual but continuous process of expansion and consolidation by the larger estates, both old-established and new, had a cumulative impact upon the structure of landed society, for it steadily reduced the pool of farms and small holdings within the means of those groups in rural society beneath the gentry. In some areas, indeed, a shortage of properties suitable for small

[163] BL, Blenheim Papers, F.1.64a.
[164] Wilts. RO, 490/249: abstract of title to lands in Downton.
[165] C. G. A. Clay, thesis, pp. 10–11 and app. II; Wilts. RO, 383/*passim*.

purchasers had undoubtedly developed by the last third of the eighteenth century. At least this is suggested by the 'Terramania' which developed in parts of the Midlands, Yorkshire, and elsewhere, in the years on either side of 1770, and again in the late 1780s and 90s, when, under the influence of high farming profits, those buying in order themselves to occupy the land were prepared to pay up to forty or even fifty years' purchase for it.[166]

It is true that large estates were quite commonly reduced in size by the sale of substantial blocks of land in order to discharge financial encumbrances which had accompanied property inherited from another family, or to pay off marriage portions with which a previous generation had charged the paternal estate. However, such sales did not serve to counteract the development under discussion, for in this period large owners needing to sell did not normally break up the estates they had decided to dispose of into their constituent farms. Least of all did they break them up into the various components from which they had been constructed, for these had almost inevitably lost their separate identity. When large owners did sell, in other words, they tended to sell in larger units than they bought, and the properties they disposed of tended to go to men who were themselves of considerable substance. Thus, when in 1730 Henry Hoare of Stourhead sold the Kentish estate worth some £362 per annum which he had inherited through Susannah Colt, he sold in only two lots property which Susannah's father, grandfather, and great-uncles had acquired bit by bit from sixteen separate sets of sellers over a period of roughly thirty years. Similarly, when Admiral Sir Edward Hughes sold the 325-acre Epcombes estate near Hertford to the fourth Earl Cowper late in the eighteenth century for £9,633, he was selling as a single unit a property which had been put together as a result of thirteen separate transactions with twelve different sellers, most of them the work of Hughes's father in the years 1713–34.[167] It is true that manors were sometimes dismembered altogether, but except in cases where the manorial rights were worth relatively little anyway, this was not very often done save by urban-based speculators or the utterly bankrupt.

Generally landowners preferred to sell in large units, not because these fetched higher rates than did small (the contrary was in fact normally the case), but because the larger sum that might be fetched by piecemeal sales was not larger by a sufficient margin to compensate for the greater trouble and delay involved, and the discredit reflected upon the seller in the eyes of his fellow landowners. The absence of a powerful financial incentive for division almost throughout the period with which we are concerned undoubtedly reflected the rather feeble demand for land from the farming sector. When the greatly improved prosperity of commercial farming

[166] W. Marshall, *The Rural Economy of the Midland Counties*, 2 vols., London, 1790, I, pp. 14–15; id., *The Rural Economy of Yorkshire*, 2 vols., London, 1788, I, pp. 30–2.
[167] Kent AO, U.499 T.8–17, 40; Wilts. RO, 383/708, 978.

eventually produced a much stronger demand for land in small parcels from working farmers, and correspondingly enhanced purchase rates, the advantages of selling piecemeal came to outweigh the disadvantages for an increasing number of sellers. Thus in the last third of the century, but especially towards the very end of it, it becomes increasingly common to find large estates being sold off in lots, sometimes in dozens or even scores of lots. In 1777, for instance, the earl of Abingdon attempted to sell his Wiltshire estate, consisting of over 3,000 acres, in a single lot, but without success, for in 1788 he was offering a somewhat larger property in 60 lots, and what remained unsold of that was offered again in 1790 divided up into no fewer than 146 lots.[168]

Down to 1750 there is no doubt that the trend was towards rounding out and consolidating the larger estates, but equally there can be little question that there were regional inequalities in the extent to which this occurred. It was most marked in those parts of the Midlands, the central south, and the south-east which were most attractive to newcomers and where the seats of the established aristocracy and gentry were most thickly clustered, since, for reasons that have already been considered, piecemeal additions were more often made to the home estates of wealthy families than to either their distant appanages or to the estates of lesser owners. It was much less marked in districts within those regions, such as south-eastern Essex and between the Charnwood Hills and the rivers Trent, Tame, and Anker (i.e. around the meeting point of Leicestershire, Warwickshire, Staffordshire, and Derbyshire), where for geographical or historical reasons there were few major gentry families, resident or otherwise.[169] It was also less pronounced in the north and the south-western peninsula where many of the largest estates were held by absentees who rarely visited them, who gave them relatively little attention compared to that they bestowed upon the smaller but often more valuable properties upon which they resided, and who were not much concerned with their enlargement. As for the mass of the gentry in those areas, most of them were petty squires whose slender resources normally precluded land purchase altogether.

(c) *Major purchases by substantial owners*
Most substantial landowners were able to make occasional small additions to their inherited properties, but major purchases were hardly ever made out of the surplus income of an agricultural estate alone, unless there were unusual circumstances, such as the availability of savings accumulated during a long minority when expenditure would have been reduced to a fraction of its normal level. It was, for instance, the fund built up by his trustees during his twenty-year-long minority which enabled the ninth Lord Petre to

---

[168] Wilts. RO, 490/1,152; 845/uncatalogued sale particulars of the Abingdon estate.
[169] Young, *Agriculture of Essex*, I, p. 44; Marshall, *Midland Counties*, I, pp. 4–5, 13–14.

purchase the manor of Fithlers and the Childerditch and Tillingham estate (both in Essex) for £2,900 and £29,207 respectively in 1759 and 1766, thereby making the first important additions to the family property since before the Civil War.[170] Even landowners with truly enormous rent rolls of £5,000 or £10,000 a year, or even more, were not necessarily able to afford to buy on a large scale out of income even if they wished to. Many of them were heavily encumbered with jointure payments (sometimes more than one) to their mothers or to the widows of previous holders of the estates, annuities to other relatives and old servants, and debt charges, some of which might have been incurred as a result of their own or their predecessor's extravagant spending but which no less characteristically represented undischarged portions. On top of all this some might also have made over part of their estates to eldest sons when they got married. A landed magnate's net income was thus often a great deal less than his gross income, and in extreme circumstances might amount to only a small fraction of it.

In order to be able to finance really substantial estate expansion out of the savings accumulated from rent income, a man needed not only to have a very large rent roll, but also one which was not heavily encumbered with family charges. He also needed to have the self-discipline, which the gentlemanly upbringing of the period was unlikely to inculcate, to keep his current expenditure well below what his net income would bear. Such landowners were definitely the exception, and there do not seem to have been many of them at any one time. However, an example is provided by John Holles, duke of Newcastle, in the early years of the eighteenth century. His inherited rent income, after sales of land to discharge debts which had come to him along with the estates, was about £25,000 a year, to which the profits of his post of Lord Privy Seal added a couple of thousand more. Between 1701 and 1711 he made a series of major purchases in Lincolnshire, Cambridgeshire, Bedfordshire, Middlesex, and elsewhere, altogether adding about £13,000 per annum to his rental at a cost of some £250,000. Clearly, it is impossible that all of this huge sum could have been derived from surplus estate income — and, indeed, part of the price of some properties was left outstanding as a mortgage charge upon them — but most of the rest apparently was.[171] In theory, landowners who had not accumulated savings in the past, but anticipated being able to make them in the future, could by borrowing raise the funds necessary to finance a purchase. However, since throughout the period the interest payable on mortgages exceeded the return obtainable from land, to buy on a large scale by this means would involve a heavy drop in income and still leave a capital sum to be discharged at some

---

[170] Essex RO, D/DP T.33 and 150.
[171] O. R. F. Davis, 'The Wealth and Influence of John Holles, Duke of Newcastle, 1694–1711', *Renaissance and Modern Stud.*, IX, 1965; *id.*, 'The Dukes of Devonshire, Newcastle, and Rutland', unpub. Oxford Univ. D.Phil. thesis, 1971, pp. 173–6.

future date, unless a property was capable of considerable improvement within a short period. It was therefore rarely done, save as a short-term expedient until other funds could be mobilized, except by the improvident, or by those nursing political ambitions who wished to strengthen their electoral influence in a particular district and were prepared to pay over the odds to do so. Established landowners who made land purchases that were large in relation to their existing estates almost always turn out either to have had access to income derived from sources other than agricultural rents; or to have received an injection of capital from another family via marriage or inheritance; or, often as a result of the latter, to have possessed land away from their main estates which they decided to sell in order to buy nearer at hand.

Those landowners with a sufficiently substantial non-agricultural income to finance major land purchases were undoubtedly very few in this period. It is often said that office at court, as a government minister, or in the bureaucracy was an important element in the finances of a substantial number of the aristocracy and gentry. But in fact not many posts offered remuneration sufficiently generous to enable a man to make large additions to his estate. In the time of George I, for instance, there were only about thirty posts in the royal household whose total emoluments exceeded £1,000 a year, and after the deduction of taxes and customary fees the profit of many of these will have been reduced to three figures. The number of posts anywhere worth £2,000 a year or more was very few indeed: no more than a handful in the household, another in the Treasury, the Exchequer and the revenue, and at the summit of the judiciary, together with the principal commanders of the armed forces and the army paymasters.[172] Moreover, most if not all of these were obtainable only if a man was prepared to make office-seeking his career, whilst, once obtained, they required more attention to business than most great landowners were prepared to give. They tended, therefore, to be the preserve either of cadet members of important families, who, though highly born, had nevertheless to make their own way in the world, or of the heirs to relatively modest estates who so totally transformed their economic and social position that they are scarcely less to be regarded as 'new men'. They were rarely themselves the heads of major families. The most spectacularly successful of those who built up great estates out of the profits of the army paymastership in this period, James Brydges (the fourth son of a Herefordshire baronet) and Henry Fox (the younger brother of Lord Ilchester), provide examples of the first. The second are represented by such prominent political figures as Sir Thomas Osborne, earl of Danby and eventually duke of Leeds, Lord Chancellor Cowper, and Sir Robert Walpole,

---

[172] J. M. Beattie, *The English Court in the Reign of George I*, Cambridge, 1967, pp. 5, 209–14; S. B. Baxter, *The Development of the Treasury*, London, 1957, *passim*. I am grateful to Professor G. S. Holmes for information about bureaucratic salaries in the early eighteenth century.

each of whom enlarged beyond all recognition inherited paternal estates in Yorkshire, in Hertfordshire and Kent, and in Norfolk respectively.

That handful of already really large landowners who used their wealth as a road to office and power, such as the earl of Sunderland from the 1670s onwards, or the Pelham duke of Newcastle from the 1710s onwards, almost always found that the income they derived from the offices they held was quite inadequate to offset the direct and indirect costs incurred in attaining and holding onto them. Anyway, most of the offices which fell to the lot of established landowners were not sufficiently lucrative to support a policy of territorial aggrandizement, and the income from them was likely to be in large part absorbed by the higher living expenses which periodic attendance at Court rendered unavoidable. They bestowed honour and prestige, but in financial terms they were unlikely to do more than provide a useful supplement to estate income, albeit one which served to provide partial insulation against the consequences of a depressed agriculture and falling rent receipts. The best that even peers could realistically hope for was something such as a lordship of the king's bedchamber, worth £1,000 a year; a commissionership of the Admiralty or Treasury, worth not very much more than the official salary of £1,000 a year and £1,600 a year respectively; a colonial governorship; or a pension of comparable value.[173] More was only to be had by the occasional individual whose personal standing with the sovereign was sufficiently good, or whose political importance was sufficiently great, for him to obtain a plurality of lucrative posts or an unusually large supplementary pension. As for a landowner of lower social standing, if he obtained a place at all he was more likely to get one worth only a few hundreds. An unusually fortunate gentleman in this respect was Sir Charles Hotham, a Yorkshire baronet, who as a young man on the Grand Tour had become friendly with the future George II, then prince of Wales. He was a groom of the bedchamber (at £400 per annum) from 1727 to 1738, special ambassador to Berlin in 1730, and held several army colonelcies which raised his income from office to £2,247 per annum in 1736, somewhat more than he received from the family estate when he inherited it. Altogether Sir Charles, and after his death his trustees, spent some £6,925 on the purchase of land, but even so this yielded only some £300 a year, which was little more than one-tenth of what the paternal property then produced.[174]

The total income accruing to landowners from industrial and urban sources undoubtedly increased considerably in this period, and for the first time colonial property began to pass into the hands of families domiciled in England. Nevertheless, although they were enjoyed by considerable

[173] For the official remuneration of these posts, see *Cal. Treasury Books, passim.*

[174] P. Roebuck, 'Four Yorkshire Landowning Families', unpub. Hull Univ. Ph.D. thesis, 1969, pp. 53, 74–5, and Tables 11 and 14 in vol. II; *id., Yorkshire Baronets, 1640–1760*, Hull, 1980, pp. 74–93.

numbers of landowners in certain areas, receipts from mining and quarrying were generally too unreliable and intermittent, and gains from West Indian sugar estates and from urban development were enjoyed by too few, to make a major contribution to the expansion of the possessions of the established landowning class.

The number of substantial planters in the British West Indies was already quite large by 1713, but at least down to the middle of the eighteenth century their profits did more to finance the acquisition of estates by those who had hitherto held little or no land in England. It was only gradually that marriage, inheritance, and the movement of the most successful creole families back to the motherland gave the aristocracy and gentry a quantitatively significant financial stake in the empire, although individuals such as the Helyars of East Coker (Somerset), the Coddringtons of Doddington (Glos.), and the Lowthers of Moulds Meaburn (Westmor.) had come into possession of valuable plantations from or even before the early years of the century. Robert Lowther, for instance, had been a relatively minor squire with an income of only a few hundreds of pounds a year until his wife brought him the inheritance of a plantation in Barbados. Sales of sugar shipped home to England realized an average of £1,300 a year over the period 1705–45, and it was on the strength of his possessions on the island that he secured its governorship worth at least another £2,000 a year (1711–20). He was thus able to buy a large estate adjoining his own for £30,400 in 1727, adding some £1,200 a year to his rent roll, and after his death in 1745 his trustees made other major purchases, including a property in Cleveland (Yorks.) for over £28,000. When the whole of his accumulated fortune had been invested in this way the family estate was worth £4,420 a year.[175]

As for urban property, a fair number of gentry families, especially amongst those seated in the Home Counties whose forebears had been London business men, owned small but valuable properties in the City which had been acquired before the family had begun to buy land in the country. However, many of these were destroyed in the fire of 1666 and were rebuilt on terms which precluded any increase in rent until well into the following century. And this, together with the sluggish movement of rents in the inner City in the middle decades of the eighteenth century, the accuracy of land tax assessments in London, and the high rate of depreciation on urban property, combined to make such estates no more of an adequate basis for expansion than was purely agricultural property.[176] Possession of substantial areas of suburban land which could be developed for housing for the first time was,

---

[175] J. H. Bennett, 'William Whaley, Planter of Seventeenth-Century Jamaica', *Agric. Hist.*, XL, 1966, pp. 113–23; V. Harlow, *Christopher Coddrington, 1668–1710*, Oxford, 1928, pp. 217–20; Beckett, thesis, ch. 8.

[176] C. G. A. Clay, thesis, pp. 176, 360–4; B. A. S. Swann, 'A Study of Some London Estates in the Eighteenth Century', unpub. London Univ. Ph.D. thesis, 1964, ch. IV.

on the other hand, another matter. Among the earliest of the great landowners to benefit on a large scale were the earls of Salisbury, who had a number of separate sites along the Strand and St Martin's Lane, which they had been developing from well before the Civil War, and which by 1720 yielded £3,263 per annum out of a total estate income of £8,715 per annum. Another was the earl of Southampton, whose housing developments in Bloomsbury to the north of Holborn were yielding only about £970 per annum in the 1640s, but over £3,000 per annum by 1669. A third was the earl of Bedford, who was developing the Covent Garden area from the 1630s onwards. In the case of the Salisburys this urban income helped the family to avoid total catastrophe during a period of prolonged financial crisis in the late seventeenth and early eighteenth centuries, but possession of Covent Garden and the former Southampton estate in Bloomsbury was probably what enabled the fourth duke of Bedford to finance an enormous enlargement of his estate in Bedfordshire after 1732. At the latter date Bedford's total rental was £32,545, of which roughly a third came from his metropolitan properties, and the amount was growing steadily as development was pushed ahead. Thirty years later the rental of Covent Garden and Bloomsbury was approaching £19,000 a year, exclusive of fines: this alone was a larger income than was enjoyed by all but a handful of the greatest aristocrats in the land.[177] By the middle decades of the eighteenth century the growth of the London 'West End' in the area north of St James's Park had added considerably to the list of landowners with substantial urban interests, but even so only a diminutive fraction of the class was involved.[178]

Coal mining was by far the most important source of industrial income to landowners between 1640 and 1750, and in parts of the north-east, the north-west, south Lancashire, south Yorkshire, and the north and west Midlands a significant minority of them were involved, either as lessors of the mining rights on their estates or as active operators of mines on their own or on leased property. Even before the Civil War some 8 per cent of the gentry of Yorkshire and 5 per cent of those of Lancashire had coal-mining interests, and the proportion was undoubtedly higher a hundred years later.[179] However, the number of families to whom coal mining was really important was very much smaller than such figures might seem to suggest. Many of the shallow seams exploited at this period were fairly quickly worked out, whilst deeper workings involved considerable capital outlay and

[177] Stone, *Family and Fortune*, pp. 92–113, 234–40; Godber, *Bedfordshire*, pp. 300–1; D. J. Olsen, *Town Planning in London*, New Haven and London, 1964, pp. 39, 220–1.

[178] The dukes of Portland, the Grosvenors, and the Berkeleys of Stratton were three great magnates who came to draw large incomes from their West End estates by the end of our period. By 1768 the Grosvenor income from the Mayfair estate was some £3,450 a year – *Survey of London*, XXXIX, London, 1977, p. 33.

[179] Cliffe, *Yorkshire Gentry*, p. 57; B. G. Blackwood, 'The Economic State of the Lancashire Gentry on the Eve of the Civil War', *Northern Hist.*, XII, 1976, p. 64.

not infrequently gave rise to drainage problems which might be technically difficult and exceedingly costly to solve. Mining profits were thus liable to fluctuate wildly over quite short periods, to dry up altogether, or quite suddenly to turn into losses. Especially for those landowners who preferred to work their own pits, rather than lease them out for a rent and a royalty, it was all very much of a gamble, and one in which a man of limited resources could easily lose more than he could afford. For most of them, therefore, mineral income was something of a windfall which continued only for a limited number of years at a time. Reasonably steady and substantial receipts over long periods were only to be had by those such as the first and second Lords Gower in Shropshire and Staffordshire, whose estates were large enough to include a wide range of coal-bearing sites, and who could afford the capital required to open a succession of large-scale workings which could then be leased out as going concerns on favourable terms.[180] Really big profits accrued only to that tiny minority of coal-owning landlords who invested large sums not only in the mines themselves but also in ancillary facilities; who operated them directly through their own employees; and who reinvested the profits in the same field over a period of generations.[181] Such were the Willoughbys in Nottinghamshire in the seventeenth century; the Lowthers of Whitehaven (Cumb.) in the later seventeenth and eighteenth centuries; and the earls of Scarborough and the Tempests on the Wear, and the Curwens of Workington (Cumb.), in the first half of the eighteenth.

Windfall profits accruing to 'occasional' coal-mining families may sometimes have been invested in land purchase, though it seems they more often went on a more lavish style of living, but before 1750 there were not many save those in the last category discussed above who were enabled to make major additions to their estates. A striking example of the use of mineral income to buy land is provided by the Lowthers of Whitehaven, whose coal receipts rose from under £1,000 a year in the 1690s to about £9,000 a year by 1750. Between 1675 and 1705 Sir John Lowther spent some £12,000 on land or mining rights in Cumberland and Westmorland. Then in the next generation (1705–55) his son Sir James laid out over £80,000 more, mostly in Cumberland, but including the manor of Laleham in Middlesex. Likewise, on the north-eastern coalfield the Tempest family, from their seat at Old Durham, purchased lands worth over £36,500 between 1734 and 1767, and even larger properties later in the century.[182] As for industrial activities other

---

[180] Wordie, thesis, pp. 161 et seq.

[181] The suggestion made by Mingay in *English Landed Society*, p. 192, that, as the eighteenth century went on, it became more common for landowners to lease out their mines and industrial premises has not been fully supported by more recent work in the field.

[182] J. V. Beckett, *Coal and Tobacco: The Lowthers and the Economic Development of West Cumberland, 1660–1760*, Cambridge, 1981, pp. 19–20, 45, 79–81, 220–6; Durham RO, Catalogue of Londonderry MSS.

than coal mining, such as iron working, glass making, lead and copper production, and stone and slate quarrying, they undoubtedly yielded a useful supplement to the income of a handful of landowners in various districts, but even less commonly than coal mining were they large or reliable enough to provide the financial basis for major territorial acquisitions. A relatively rare exception to this generalization is provided by the experience of the earls of Rutland, whose profits from their Derbyshire lead mines soared upwards in the 1670s to reach £8,296 in 1675. This boom proved to be temporary, for by 1688 the figure had fallen back to £2,731 and after 1696 was generally below £1,000 a year, but by then some part of the gains had been safely turned into permanent additions to the estate in Leicestershire and in Derbyshire itself.[183] More typical of the scale of profits generated by landowners' investment in industry at this time was the average of about £320 per annum over the years 1675–84, and already fallen to £200 per annum by 1693, which the Archers of Umberslade (War.) received from the iron mill they worked at Ruin Clifford.[184] Most industrial premises out on lease would, moreover, have brought in less than even the lower of these two figures, and a high proportion of those country gentlemen upon whose estates such activities were carried on probably benefited to the extent of only a few score pounds a year.

It was argued many years ago by Sir John Habakkuk that the capital sums which landowners, or their eldest sons, received upon the occasion of their marriages from their brides' families were generally invested in the purchase of additional property, and that this was an important factor in the expansion of many estates.[185] Unquestionably, very large sums passed from one family to another in this way. By the first half of the eighteenth century it was not unusual for £10,000 to £15,000 to be offered with the hand of the daughter of a prominent peer, or that of a wealthy business man seeking an alliance with a distinguished landed family. Five thousand pounds became no unusual portion for the daughter of an untitled county magnate, and less than £800 to £1,200 would hardly do if the daughter of a respectable gentleman of local importance was to secure an appropriate match.

Now if marriage portions had been generally invested by the recipients in the purchase of permanent additions to their estates, this would certainly have been a major factor in the evolution of landed society. However, all the detailed studies which have been made since Habakkuk wrote confirm that, at least amongst established landowners, it was the exception rather than the rule for them to be spent on land. The most common use to which portions were put in these circles was undoubtedly to discharge encumbrances

---

[183] Davis, thesis, pp. 140, 188–90.
[184] Mimardière, thesis, pp. 183–6.
[185] H. J. Habakkuk, 'Marriage Settlements in the Eighteenth Century', *Trans. RHS*, 4th ser., XXXII, pp. 22, 28.

on the estates of the recipients' families. Examples of this are legion, and the fact that a landowner in difficulties could rid himself of debt in this way made an heir of marriageable age (or the landowner's own freedom to marry) the most valuable financial asset he possessed.[186] Not uncommonly it was actually laid down in the marriage settlement, or in an associated agreement, that all or part of the portion must be used to pay off debts. This was the case, for instance, when the heavily indebted William Grimston of Gorhambury (Herts.) married Jane Cook, the daughter of a wealthy London waxchandler, with a portion of £10,000 in 1706; or again when the equally ensnared fourth Lord Cornwallis married Lady Charlotte Butler, daughter of the earl of Aran, in 1700.[187] If there were no encumbrances on the estate, then the money was often kept to provide a fund out of which provision could in due course be made for the heir's younger brother and sisters, or even for the younger children of the marriage which had just been celebrated. In the period before the one with which we are concerned such a reserve fund probably was often invested in land which could subsequently be resold when the capital was required. As we have already noted, the uncertain course of land prices, and the more ready availability of alternative securities, meant that this was rarely done by the second half of the seventeenth century. Instead, if no immediate use for the portion money could be found, it was usually left as an outstanding mortgage upon the estate of the girl's family, yielding an income to her husband in the form of interest at the going rate. When the capital was eventually required, the security could simply be assigned to another lender through the services of a broker.

It was these mortgages, which by then had often passed through several hands, which so often formed the core of the debt that the bride's family would seek to pay off when their eldest son came to get married. Even if the girl's father was able to pay the portion in cash it became increasingly common for it to be invested in paper securities. As early as 1664 the first draft of the marriage articles of the eldest son of the earl of Thanet and Elizabeth Boyle, daughter of the earl of Cork, provided for the £10,000 portion to be secured initially by a recognizance in Chancery and then to be laid out on mortgages as it was paid over.[188] In the eighteenth century provisions that the money should be used for the purchase of Bank stock or other government securities also begin to make their appearance, though few if any of these seem to antedate the 1720s. But whether the portion was left outstanding on the estates of the new relatives, or invested in paper

[186] For two illustrative examples, see the negotiations for the marriage of the earl of Sunderland's heir in 1681 and 1694, and for that of the duke of Newcastle in 1716–17 – J. P. Kenyon, *Robert Spencer Earl of Sunderland*, London, 1958, pp. 77, 267–8; R. A. Kelch, *Newcastle: A Duke without Money: Thomas Pelham-Holles 1693–1768*, London, 1974, pp. 44–7.

[187] Herts. RO, Gorhambury Collection, IX. A. 96; Dorset RO, D.124.Deeds. Yorks. (box 134): deed dated 12 Apr. 1700.

[188] Kent AO, U.455 T 282. These articles were, in the event, cancelled and replaced by others.

securities, it would yield a higher net income than if it had been laid out on land. Scarcely less important, it would also be very much more liquid, thereby providing a useful degree of financial flexibility which the landowner who had no capital assets other than his land necessarily lacked.

Doubtless the fathers of brides-to-be always hoped that the portion money they provided would be turned into permanent additions to their sons-in-law's estates, which would thus eventually pass to their own grandchildren. However, it was rarely possible for them to insist on it, and a clause specifying that it should be so used is not often found in the marriage articles and post-nuptial settlements of the established landed class. There was, after all, no purpose in demanding that a portion be used to buy land if an estate was subject to encumbrances: since the rate of return on land was below the rate of interest on borrowed money, it would add more to a family's income from land to use the money to pay off the latter. In the period between the Civil War and the mid eighteenth century the increase in land values was not sufficiently great or sufficiently sustained for owners to count on rising rents to pay off major capital charges out of income, as had perhaps been the case before about 1620 and was to be the case again after 1760. Sums large in relation to annual income could thus normally be discharged (other than by realizing part of the capital invested in the estate itself) only by determined economies or by an injection of funds from some outside source, and in the case of most families the heir's marriage portion was the only one ever likely to be at their disposal. There was thus every reason to suppose that the use of portions to discharge encumbrances, rather than to buy land, would add more to the net income of future generations as well as to that of the present generation. How uncommon it was for portions to be spent on land by established landowners, at least by the later part of the period, is suggested by an assertion of the countess of Cork and Orrery to Henry Hoare, whose daughter Sukie had married her eldest son in 1752 with a portion of £25,000. The fact that they had sunk £19,000 of this in land, she wrote, "gave her daughter in law an advantage very few have received...that of having the greatest part of her portion laid out to increase the inheritance which is to descend to her husband, to herself, and her children". This she contrasted with "the general custom of [fathers] taking the whole portion of the woman who comes into the family for [their] own use".[189]

It is likely, however, that the practice of investing a marriage portion in land was more common in the case of younger sons who were not due to inherit any paternal estate, encumbered or otherwise, but who were fortunate or socially elevated enough to secure well-portioned brides. It was probably very much more common where the recipient family was 'moneyed' rather than landed, for in such cases the purchase was part of the process whereby

[189] Wilts. RO, 383/909.

a fortune made in business or otherwise was converted into an estate. Thus when, in 1702, Henry, son of Richard Hoare, the founder of the banking firm, married Jane Benson, the daughter of a London merchant, with £10,000 portion, it was stipulated that £8,000 of this be laid out on freehold land. Then a generation later, after the Hoares had acquired the nucleus of the Stourhead estate but were still in the very early stages of building it up, the agreements made prior to the marriages of Henry Hoare II to Ann, daughter of Lord Masham (1726), and after her death to Susannah Colt, the daughter of an East India merchant (1728), both contain similar clauses: in the first case for the whole of the £10,000 portion, in the second for £4,000 out of £11,000.[190]

A more common background to the land purchases of the established owners was a substantial accession of wealth by inheritance through an heiress or from collateral relatives. Inheritances of this sort were often heavily encumbered with financial obligations, but they were not necessarily so, and a sudden increase in income without a corresponding increase in commitments might provide a sufficient flow of funds to pay for some additions to the estate. Especially if a substantial sum in paper investments was acquired by inheritance it was likely that major land purchases would follow, and it was indeed very probable that it would be a condition of inheritance that all the capital should be reinvested in this way. Thus when the earl of Grantham died without a male heir in 1754, dividing his residual personal estate worth £108,791 between his two daughters, his will required that it should in due course be laid out on land. Eventually, owing to the premature death of one of them, the whole passed to the survivor and her husband, the third Earl Cowper, and financed a massive programme of land purchases in Hertfordshire later in the century.[191] But even if only lands had been inherited, unless the new acquisitions comprised a large and well-consolidated estate which could be satisfactorily managed from a distance, or lay close enough to the family's own seat to be administered as part of the paternal estate, then their sale and the reinvestment of the proceeds in more conveniently placed properties was (as we have seen) a likely consequence, even though this might not happen until a generation or more had elapsed.[192]

The sale of property held at a distance, whether in the possession of the family for centuries or inherited only a year or two before, was indeed probably the commonest set of circumstances in which established landowners were able to make substantial purchases. Indeed, for most such families it provided the only means whereby they could ever afford to enter the land market on a large scale. The frequency of purchases financed in this way almost certainly increased during the period with which we are concerned, especially in the latter half of it. This was partly because of the demographic

[190] Wilts. RO, 383/527, 708, 764.
[191] C. G. A. Clay, thesis, pp. 260–3, 284–7. [192] See above, p. 296.

factors already discussed which meant that inheritances through heiresses and from collaterals were more common than either earlier or later, and partly because of the growing fashion for consolidated 'ring fence' estates.[193] Much of the apparent aggrandizement of large estates in the period after about 1680 to which Habakkuk, Mingay, and others have drawn attention was in reality consolidation and expansion in one area at the expense of holdings in another. This is a fact which partially explains why so many examples can be found of great landowners selling at a time when many of the factors which had tended to precipitate sales earlier on – rapid inflation down to 1640, the gross conspicuous consumption of the Jacobean age, the difficulty of borrowing long term and the high cost of borrowing on any terms, and the after-effects of the Civil War – were losing force. In other words, a great deal of what was in effect exchange was going on between the larger landowners. Sometimes, indeed, it actually took the form of exchanges as such, not just of small parcels of land to facilitate farm reorganization, but of complete estates. At some date in the later seventeenth century, for instance, Samuel Baker of Fairford (Glos.) exchanged Alderton for Meisey Hampton with the judge Sir Mathew Hale, who was building up a substantial estate to the north-east of Bristol.[194] Direct exchanges, however, were rarely practicable, so that sales and repurchases were more normal. Thus when Robert Middleton of Chirk Castle, Denbighshire, inherited property in and around Hatfield and Welwyn in Hertfordshire, through his marriage to one of the daughters and co-heiresses of Sir John Reade of Brockett Hall (Herts.), he promptly sold it to Lord Chancellor Cowper, who was building up a large estate in the district, and put the £10,545 it fetched towards the price of a property immediately adjacent to his Welsh seat (1721). Another example is provided by the considerable additions, worth £1,070 per annum, made to the Holkham (Norfolk) estate by Thomas Coke, earl of Leicester, between 1718 and 1746, many of which, in view of Coke's financial difficulties, had to be financed by sales of out-county properties. The result was that the Coke family estates, which had been spread out over five counties when he inherited them, became increasingly concentrated in Norfolk.[195]

This type of selling and buying created a considerable amount of activity on the land market but did not substantially increase the area held in large units of ownership. Indeed, the reorganization movement did not necessarily imply any growth at all in the size of the individual estates involved, and since a family not infrequently seized the opportunity presented by a decision to sell (which might require a private act of parliament) to use part of the money to discharge outstanding encumbrances, it could conceivably have concealed a tendency for large estates to shrink. Whether or not this was

---

[193] See above, pp. 307–10. [194] Rudder, *Gloucestershire*, I, p. 219.
[195] Herts. RO, Panshanger Collection, T.1,810; R. A. C. Parker, *Coke of Norfolk: A Financial and Agricultural Study 1707–1842*, Oxford, 1975, pp. 1, 27, 37–9.

so, it should be borne in mind that a higher degree of estate consolidation, providing opportunities for more effective supervision of the tenantry, and for enclosure or other forms of improvement such as bigger or better-laid-out farms, might (if the opportunities were taken) go a long way to offset the effects upon gross income of any reduction in size. Likewise, lower management expenses could make a noticeable impact upon net receipts. Nevertheless, it is probable that a single-minded concentration by historians of landed society upon the additions which established landlords made to their main estates, without due consideration for sales elsewhere, has given an exaggerated impression of their landed gains. Because so many of their major purchases were counterbalanced by sales, it was probably not these which were most important in concentrating property into fewer hands, despite the superficially impressive evidence they appear to provide of the 'rise' of successful families. Rather it was their slow, piecemeal expansion, as they absorbed single fields and single farms on the perimeters of their estates as time and chance brought them on the market, which was the major factor in the gradual transformation of English landownership.

## C. THE MANAGEMENT OF ESTATES

### 1. *Types of tenancy*

(a) *Customary tenure and life leasehold*

In the England of the mid seventeenth century customary tenures were still widespread and important, although the proportion of the rural population holding their land in this way was very much smaller than it had been a hundred years earlier.[196] In the sixteenth and early seventeenth centuries, on manors all over the country, tenants who had thought that they enjoyed the protection of custom had discovered that in law they were mere tenants-at-will. In some places, where the land was especially valuable, they had been evicted and their holdings enclosed and then relet as large farms at much higher rents. Perhaps more commonly, after futile legal wrangling, they had been obliged to accept the new situation. They continued to occupy their lands, but as non-customary leaseholders they invariably had to pay more for them. Even where tenures had been undeniably customary there had been innumerable disputes between manorial lords and their tenants about what exactly local custom prescribed, and in particular how much the tenants could be made to pay for their tenancies. By the middle of the seventeenth century, however, these controversies were dying down, in part because few tenants remained whose customary status could be challenged,

---

[196] The classic discussion of customary tenures in the period before 1640 is R. H. Tawney, *The Agrarian Problem in the Sixteenth Century*, London, 1912. His views have been criticized by E. Kerridge, *Agrarian Problems in the Sixteenth Century and After*, London, 1969.

and few manors where ambiguous customs had not been spelt out one way or another. It was also in part because the common law had clarified many formerly contentious issues. Disputes over fines still occurred in some districts, especially the north, in the 1650s and 60s,[197] but little is heard of them thereafter, for both in terms of the common law and the custom of particular manors, the position of those who still held by customary tenure was clearly understood and accepted by all parties by the later seventeenth century. It may therefore be said of the period 1640–1750 that, except at the very beginning of it, neither the security of customary tenants nor the extent of their financial obligations was a live social issue.

What proportion of landholders did still hold by customary tenures in the later seventeenth century is, however, almost entirely obscure. It might have been as many as one-third, but because small farms and cottage holdings were more often let in this way than were the more substantial ones, the proportion of the cultivated area subject to this form of tenure was certainly smaller. In any event, there were marked regional variations in its relative importance. In Kent, for instance, customary tenants were comparatively few, and most country people either occupied their own freeholds or held on non-customary terms, on a yearly basis or by a lease for a term of years. In neighbouring Surrey and Sussex, by contrast, they were still numerous. Likewise in the east Midlands customary tenure was relatively unusual, though it became more common as one moved westwards towards the Welsh border. In the south-west it was common, although, as we shall see, declining markedly as the period wore on, whilst in the north there were some districts, such as the Lancashire plain, where it had virtually disappeared, at least by the early eighteenth century, although in many others it predominated almost to the exclusion of other forms of tenancy.

As is well known, by far the most common form of customary tenure was copyhold. Copyholders paid low annual rents, known as rents of assize, quit rents, reserved rents, or by some other local name, rents which may have represented the full value of the land in the remote past, but which in this period amounted to only a very small fraction of it. The relationship they might bear to rack rents may be illustrated by the situation prevailing on Lord Waldegrave's manor of Radstock (Somerset) in the late seventeenth century. The 'improved' values of the various holdings ranged from £3 a year up to £40, but the reserved rents from a mere 6d. to £2 3s.[198] These rents were, however, everywhere fixed by custom and the manorial lord could not increase them. However, on every change of tenancy, whether by descent or by alienation, the copyhold tenant also paid a lump sum known as a fine, which might either be 'certain', that is, also fixed by custom, or alternatively 'arbitrary', which meant that it was subject to negotiation. Generally, too, the death of the tenant necessitated the rendering of a heriot,

[197] C. B. Phillips, thesis, ch. 5.   [198] Somerset RO, DD/Wg/box 8/3.

that is, the most valuable piece of movable property on the holding – in practice usually one of the farm animals – or a sum of money in lieu. Everywhere attendance at the manor court was obligatory. Changes in tenancy had to be registered there, and it was the 'copies' of the records of the proceedings in those courts which provided copyholders with their title deeds. Especially in the western part of the country many copyholders were also subject to a variety of minor financial obligations of an archaic nature, such as farlieus, reliefs, kind rents in the form (for instance) of a capon or two at Christmas, and even vestigial labour services. These did not, however, very often add much to the value of a copyhold estate to its lord. The customs which governed the terms upon which copyholders actually enjoyed their estates differed in detail, and sometimes in substance, from one manor to the next, but there were only two important variants of copyhold which need to be distinguished in the present context. In the eastern part of the country, and in most of the Midlands, copyhold was normally hereditary, as were the various forms of customary tenure found in the north.[199] The fines payable were sometimes fixed, sometimes arbitrary, but even in the latter case a long series of legal decisions in the Court of Chancery and elsewhere had firmly established that they must be 'reasonable' and that the lords could not pitch them so high as to defeat the custom of inheritance. In practice, therefore, even arbitrary fines seem rarely to have been more than one year's, or at most two years', improved value of a holding, and those which had become fixed in the fifteenth century or earlier were usually very much less, perhaps no more than one or two years' reserved rent. In the western part of the country, west, that is, of a frontier zone running from Cheshire and Derbyshire, through Warwickshire, Oxfordshire, and Hampshire, the normal form of customary tenure was copyhold for lives, subject to fines which, because the tenant had no right of inheritance after his grant had expired, were not subject to any provisos about being reasonable. The lord, in other words, was perfectly entitled to demand whatever he liked, and, as the saying went, to 'sell' his copyholds to the highest bidder.[200]

In practice, however, at least in this period, there was less difference between the two types of copyhold than this account might suggest, and contemporary authorities on the subject did not lay as much emphasis on the distinction as some historians have done.[201] On manors where copyhold

---

[199] In parts of the north customary tenure was still sometimes called 'tenant right', although legally this tenure, which had formerly involved the obligation to perform military service on the Scottish border, had become extinct before 1640. In this period the most important difference between so-called tenantright and other northern customary tenures, and those found elsewhere, was the fact that those who held by the former were liable to fines on a change of lord as well as on a change of tenant – S. J. Watts, 'Tenant-Right in Early Seventeenth-Century Northumberland', *Northern Hist.*, VI, 1971. [200] Kerridge, *op. cit.*, pp. 35–44.
[201] See, for instance, the article on copyhold in Giles Jacob, *A New Law Dictionary*, London, 1729 edn.

for lives prevailed, grants were generally for the lives of three named persons, for instance, the tenant himself and two of his children, although in some places such as Culmstock in Devon the custom was for only two lives, and in others, as on many of the manors belonging to the bishops of Worcester, for four lives.[202] In reality, however, these copyholds were effectively for one more life than the number formally granted, since it was very general for the widow of each male tenant dying in possession to enjoy 'free bench' as long as she remained unmarried and, by the customs of some manors, chaste as well. This meant that a grant for three lives would probably last for four before it ran its full course. As we have seen, there was no legal compulsion upon the lord to make a new grant to the heir after the last life or widowhood had expired, or indeed to make a new grant on customary terms to anyone, but in practice neither lord nor tenant normally allowed copyhold grants to expire. As soon as one or two of the lives had 'dropped' the tenant would apply for a renewal. In other words, he offered to surrender the outstanding portion of his grant in return for another one incorporating a replacement life or lives, for which the fine would be appropriately less than for a full three-life grant. Copyhold tenancies were thus generally kept 'filled up', and fresh three-life grants 'out of hand' to entirely new tenants were relatively unusual. This system ensured that the tenants enjoyed what was in effect hereditary tenure, provided only that they were able to pay their fines, and it furnished the lords with a more regular income from the latter than if they had received them only upon the final extinction of all outstanding lives.

Moreover, when it came to negotiations over the amount that was to be paid by way of a renewal fine the tenant for lives was in a very strong position. The first problem which faced the lord was to ascertain how much the holding was truly worth. To the small squire with only a single manor upon which he himself lived, and whose farms and fields he had known from boyhood, this might not present very great difficulties, but for the owners of large estates, especially if they were absentees, it was not so easy. Most copyholds had been out on lives for generations; and with numerous renewals involved, often of very small farms, anything more than a cursory inspection of each might be impracticable. They had, therefore, to rely mainly upon the values recorded in their survey books, which, because undertaking any form of survey was a complicated and expensive task, were invariably out of date, in extreme cases such as the Devonshire estate of Lord Petre in the early eighteenth century, by as much as a hundred years.[203] Nor, in any event, were surveys of customary estates surveys at all in the modern sense; rather they were compilations derived from written evidences, and whilst they provided the owner with a clear guide to what tenancies were outstanding, even the acreages, let alone the annual values, ascribed to each

---

[202] Exeter Cathedral Library, 4,030; Worcs. RO, 009: BA 2,636/9, ff. 81-2.
[203] BL, Add. MS 28,251, f. 372.

bore a very uncertain relationship to reality. In a period when it could no longer be taken almost as axiomatic that rental values had risen substantially since the last time a fine had been assessed, tenants would usually be able to conceal the fact of any increase which had taken place, whilst they would always make the most of any grounds upon which they could claim a reduction. Besides, if the lord and the tenant could not agree upon a fine, then, apart from simply waiting for the tenancy to fall into hand as the remaining lives (and the widowhood) dropped one by one – which might be many years, decades even, during which no fine would be forthcoming – the lord's only recourse was to make a reversionary grant to someone else. This could be very difficult to do to advantage, for it would be a highly speculative bargain for the purchaser, who could not know when he would gain possession or what condition the holding would be in when he eventually obtained it. He would not, therefore, be likely to offer more than a tenant in possession. Copyhold renewals inevitably involved much hard bargaining over the amount of the fine, but in this period when rental values were stable or falling rather than rising, there was no doubt where the balance of advantage generally lay, particularly on the estates of absentees. In practice, therefore, the fine for renewing a single life was rarely more than two years' value, at least until the 1720s, after which an increasing number of landlords were successful in pushing up the rate around which negotiations were conducted to two and a half years' value.[204] Until well into the eighteenth century, therefore, copyholders for lives paid no higher fines than did many copyholders of inheritance.

In theory it was, as we have seen, open to a manorial lord to refuse to renew his copyholds at all, to allow all outstanding grants to expire so that the land reverted to the status of demesne, and then to let it out on non-customary and financially more advantageous terms. Of course, some life copyholds were continually falling into their lords' hands, because lives dropped unexpectedly, and because some tenants could not afford to renew or, having no direct heirs, did not bother to do so. But for an estate owner to make a policy of not permitting renewals meant sacrificing income from fines in the short and medium term, and this was something which in practice few, save moneyed newcomers to landed society, could afford to do. However, the financial return from land which had been 'sold' for fines, was considerably lower than that from land let at rack rents, that is, rents representing the full economic value of the land.[205] The advantages of

[204] C. Clay, 'Lifeleasehold in the Western Counties of England 1650–1750', AHR, XXIX, 2, 1981, where these points are discussed in the context of leases for ninety-nine years determinable on lives (see below). Fining rates for renewing one life in copyhold and leasehold estates seem usually to have been identical.

[205] This did not, however, mean that the purchaser of land for which fines were taken was securing a lower return on the capital he had invested, because the purchase rates for land let in this way were lower than for land let at rack rent.

changing from one system to the other were very much less clear-cut in a period when rents were often falling than they had been before 1640 or were to be after 1760 when rents were almost continuously rising. In difficult times those who received their incomes mainly from fines were less immediately vulnerable to downward pressure on the farming profits of their tenants. A large part of the total income to be received from a letting had been paid over as a capital sum at the very beginning, and the rent thereafter payable was so low in relation to the earning capacity of the farm that the tenant was not likely to fall into arrears, especially as, by so doing, he would be liable to eviction from the tenancy he had purchased. Moreover, unlike the proprietors of estates let at rack rents, those who received their incomes mainly from fines did not have cause for constant concern about whether their tenants were maintaining their farms in good order, since, unless the latter had any reason to believe that they would be refused a renewal, or were on the point of bankruptcy, they had as much interest as the landlords in maintaining soil fertility, undertaking repairs, etc. And as for tenants in difficulties, there was not the same need to come to their rescue in order to avoid the loss of income that would arise if a rack-rented farm fell vacant. If a life holder was unable to carry on he would sell the outstanding part of his grant for what it would fetch, and the purchaser would assume responsibility for paying the rent.[206] Agricultural depression would eventually affect the owner of an estate let for fines and lives, because the sums he was able to obtain for renewals would fall as land values declined. However, in the short and even the medium term he was less vulnerable than if he depended on rack rents, since on average each holding would not come up for renewal more than once in every nine or ten years.[207] These are probably the reasons why relatively few owners made any systematic move away from the system of fines in the later seventeenth and early eighteenth centuries, whereas in the later eighteenth century, when land values were rising strongly, many made the change.

What many owners of manors on which copyhold for lives prevailed did do in the period 1640–1750 was to make a change from customary to non-customary lettings, whilst leaving the old fining system, and indeed most of the other conditions of tenancy, unaltered. This was easily achieved, and could be carried through almost without financial penalty. The normal form of lease on non-customary land in the western and south-western parts of the country where copyhold was usually for lives was a demise for ninety-nine years determinable upon three lives, that is, for ninety-nine years or the lives of three named persons, whichever was the shorter. Copyholders in these

[206] C. Clay, 'Lifeleasehold', pp. 86–7.
[207] In practice the intervals between renewals could well have been even longer. H. Phillipes, *The Purchaser's Pattern*, London, 1663, pp. 21–3, considered that leases for three lives were equivalent to grants for twenty-seven years at the very lowest reckoning.

areas who applied for renewals, to which it must be remembered they had no *right*, could therefore simply be offered a lease instead of a fresh customary grant. The change in form made little immediate difference to them, for the fine was either the same or lower,[208] and in practice they must often have received some additional consideration for agreeing to it. As for the other conditions upon which the leases were granted, they seem normally to have been very close, if not identical, to the terms upon which customary land was let in the manor in question. On many manors in the south-west the leaseholders continued to be liable to heriots, and on some to perform suit of court as well.[209] The only significant loss to the tenant was the widowhood, which lay in the future, and this would be a serious matter only to those who were unable to renew. For everyone else the insertion of his wife's name as one of the lives ensured that she would not be left unprovided for. The lord, however, gained two advantages. He got rid of the custom of widowhood, which was sometimes abused by tenants who had failed to renew making death-bed marriages as a means of providing for children. He also gained a more effectual means of enforcing the conditions of tenure. Copyholders who did not fulfil their obligations in respect of repairs, or who exceeded their customary rights in such matters as subletting or ploughing up meadow and pasture, had either to be dealt with through the unreliable mechanism of the manor court, or by means of a full-dress legal action to terminate the tenancy altogether. In the case of leaseholders, however, the conditions could be spelt out more explicitly in a series of covenants, breach of which could bear a monetary penalty to which a tenant would automatically become liable if he overstepped the mark.[210] Besides, if in the future the owner should wish to change the conditions of tenancy he would be able to do so, whereas under copyhold he was obliged to accept whatever was customary. Particularly in the south-west, therefore, from the mid or later seventeenth century onwards, a continuous process of changeover was under way from copyhold for lives to leases for ninety-nine years determinable upon lives, occurring first, it would seem, on the smaller estates belonging to resident gentry, and only later on the larger estates of the absentees. It apparently began first and proceeded most rapidly in Devon, perhaps because of the preponderance of small estates there, so much so, indeed, that by 1750 there was little copyhold left in the county. This could not be said of other parts of the region at that date, but throughout it customary tenure was certainly in rapid retreat well before the end of the period.[211]

[208] It was sometimes lower because of the loss of the widowhood.
[209] C. Clay, 'Lifeleasehold', pp. 90–3.
[210] J. H. Bettey, 'Marriages of Convenience by Copyholders in Dorset during the Seventeenth Century', *Dorset Arch. Soc.*, XCVIII, 1976; E. Laurence, *A Dissertation on Estates upon Lives and Years*, London, 1730.
[211] W. G. Hoskins, 'The Occupation of Land in Devonshire, 1650–1800', *Devon & Cornwall N. & Q.*, XXI, 1941; J. H. Bettey, 'Agriculture and Rural Society in Dorset', unpub. Bristol Univ. Ph.D. thesis, 1977, pp. 183, 212.

In a few districts, notably south Lancashire and Cheshire, leases were generally granted for three lives 'absolute' rather than for ninety-nine years determinable upon lives,²¹² but in most practical respects these two forms of leasehold were the same, and the conditions of tenure seem likewise to have been very close to those prevailing on customary land in the area. The most characteristic feature of Lancashire leasehold, indeed, was the great frequency with which labour services were required. Sometimes these were astonishingly varied: thus in 1717 Hillary Ashton of Outrawcliffe, yeoman, owed an annual rent of 21s. and 2 days' ploughing, 2 days' harrowing, 2 days' carrying of dung and one of stone, 1 day "weeding in the garden", "getting four wiskets-ful of bent", 2 days' shearing, "clipping and washing of sheep as needful", delving and dressing 40 loads of turves, and keeping a dog!²¹³ Such lease terms clearly derived from a time when the leasehold had indeed been held on customary terms, although in other instances the services may rather have been imposed in imitation of customary tenure where leases were granted of land being taken into cultivation for the first time in the sixteenth and seventeenth centuries.

Nowhere could it said that the terms upon which copyholders and life leaseholders occupied their farms were in any way onerous, and few restrictions were laid upon their freedom of action. The former, in particular, had almost unfettered freedom to manage their land as they liked, subject to particular local customs and the general proviso, well established in the common law, that they must not commit 'waste', that is, do anything, whether by deliberate action or negligence, which would reduce the lord's reversionary interest in the freehold of their property.²¹⁴ When spelled out in the form of lease covenants these conditions amounted, first and foremost, to a requirement that the premises be kept in good repair; secondly, that although they might take from the trees growing on their land whatever timber or wood they needed for the maintenance of their buildings, fences, gates, and equipment, and for domestic fuel, they might not cut either for sale. This was, of course, a constant temptation to the tenants, and an owner or his steward had to have a sharp eye to prevent them doing so: covenants apart, the law was quite clear that the timber of both copyhold and leasehold belonged to the landlord, but the facts of a particular case might be difficult to establish, and disputes over real or alleged cutting of timber for sale were common on any estate with many lifeholders. Thirdly, and again a frequent bone of contention, tenants were not to plough up old pasture without permission. It was also common for tenants to be required to plant a certain number of timber trees, usually oak, ash, or elm, in their hedgerows every

---

²¹² Another form of lease for which fines rather than rack rents were taken were leases for twenty-one years, renewable every seven years. These were common on the estates of the church, but were relatively unusual on lay properties.

²¹³ R. Sharpe France, 'The Registers of Estates of Lancashire Papists 1717–1788', *Lancs. & Cheshire Rec. Soc.*, XCVIII, 1943, pp. 22–3.

²¹⁴ Jacob, *New Law Dictionary*, loc. cit.

year, a provision which was essential if there was to be a constant succession of timber available for repairs in the future. Some landlords also demanded that their lessees use on the premises all the farm manure produced there, but this requirement was by no means universal.[215] It seems to have been less common in the south-west than elsewhere, and it may have been impossible to insist on it where units of cultivation did not coincide with units of tenure and farms often consisted of land held from more than one lessor or were part leasehold and part the lessees' own freehold. Neither manorial custom, nor the covenants inserted into leases for ninety-nine years determinable upon lives, ever seem to have entitled landlords to regulate their tenants' husbandry practices in detail in the way that many owners of non-customary land in the eastern part of the country were, at least in theory, able to do. Of course, in open-field districts a degree of communal agricultural discipline was generally exercised by the manor court. The terms, at any rate of leasehold tenure, were slightly more limiting in the Welsh border counties than they were in the south-west, but in neither area did they amount to much more than the minimum which the common law took for granted.[216]

Inevitably customary estates and those let for lives and ninety-nine years determinable upon lives received less day-to-day attention from landlords or their stewards than did those let for rack rents. Indeed, on large properties owned by absentees, such as that belonging to Lord Petre in south Devon, the tenants seem to have been left almost entirely to their own devices.[217] Resident owners usually, if not always, kept a closer eye on them, but it was not unusual for copyholders and life leaseholders to have almost no contact with their landlord save on rent days, and also when the dropping of a life entitled the latter to a heriot and made negotiations for a renewal necessary. Indeed, although there was no question that in law they were tenants, yet in reality many of them were themselves a species of landed proprietor. The small customary and life-leasehold properties may usually have been occupied by the tenants themselves, but the larger ones were perhaps as often as not sublet,[218] sometimes in smaller parcels, to working farmers. These regarded the tenant as in every way their landlord, paid him their rent, and had no financial obligations to the ultimate owner of the land and sometimes no direct contact with him at all. Nor did the owner have much control over this subletting, for, provided that the tenant did not sublet for more than a year at a time, he was not normally obliged to obtain the former's consent.

[215] Devon RO, 123M/L, *passim*; Wilts. RO, 383/*passim*; Bristol City RO, AC/WO/12 (31, 32); AS/22/2, 28/2, 32/2, 39/1, 49/1; Somerset RO, DD/PT box 20; Wordie, thesis, pp. 361–2; D. Hey, *An English Rural Community: Myddle under the Tudors and Stuarts*, Leicester, 1974, pp. 80–1.

[216] Jacob, *New Law Dictionary*, sub "lease". [217] BL, Add. MS 28,251, f. 372.

[218] On the Northcote estate in Devon, for instance, subletting was 'virtually the rule' on life leaseholds in the mid eighteenth century. I am indebted to Patrick Keeley of Jesus Coll., Oxford, for this information.

On many manors, indeed, especially where hereditary tenures prevailed, custom permitted lettings of up to three years without the need to secure a licence, and some were even more favourable. At Edgmond (Salop.), for instance, the copyholder could sublet for three successive terms of three years each, and if he was prepared to go through the formality of a surrender in the manor court and pay a fine of half a year's value, he could lease for up to twenty-one years. Small wonder, therefore, that from the landlord's point of view such properties were, as Sir John Lowther (d. 1675) put it, with reference to customary holdings in Cumberland, estates "more in show than in substance".[219] For all that radical agitators of the 1640s and 50s, who wanted to see copyholds transformed into their tenants' freeholds, claimed it to be a servile and degrading tenure, few if any were unwilling to acquire customary land on that account. The financier Richard Hill, for instance, was not deterred from buying copyhold as he built up his Shropshire estate in the early eighteenth century. It is true that the death of one of the lives by which he held provoked his steward to write that it was "a tenure which I never affected", but this was not on account of any servility attached to it but merely because renewal fines and heriots made it "an estate yt is never payd for".[220] In fact, the readiness with which the title to copyhold land could be proved, and the simplicity and cheapness with which it could be conveyed by means of surrender and admission in the manor court, meant that it was a particularly suitable form of property for the man of modest means to buy as an investment. Numerous urban business men, professional men, and their widows thus acquired copyhold or, in the west, life leasehold. Nor did country gentlemen, or even titled aristocrats, hesitate to buy either in the process of expanding their estates, even though they thereby became tenants, customary or otherwise, to manorial lords whose social standing was sometimes far inferior to their own. By the middle of the eighteenth century, for instance, Earl Cowper had come into possession of copyhold in about half a dozen Hertfordshire manors, and was therefore tenant not only to his fellow peer the earl of Salisbury at Hatfield but to one undistinguished country squire at Hertingfordbury and, after 1767, to another at Stondon.[221] Thus by no means were all copyholders in any sense peasants, and indeed with the passage of time an increasing proportion of customary land passed into the hands of estate owners who let it out along with their own freeholds, their farms not infrequently consisting in part of the one and in part of the other. Particularly in the western counties of the kingdom many of the lesser gentry depended very heavily upon income from land held by copy or ninety-nine-year leases determinable upon lives, and some owned little freehold, or even none at all.

By the middle of the eighteenth century the amount of land held under

[219] Salop. RO, 81/599, ff. 12–13. Lowther is quoted by C. B. Phillips, thesis, ch. 5.
[220] Salop. RO, 112/2,686–7.   [221] Herts. RO, Panshanger Collection C.1,810–11, 3,387.

customary tenure was certainly much smaller than it had been in 1640. One factor in this decline was the conversion in the west of copyhold for lives to leasehold for ninety-nine years determinable upon lives, but there were others. Because the financial return to landlords from the possession of customary land was so poor on manors where the custom was for hereditary tenure, they were much more ready to sell it than they were to part with freehold, and families who wished to raise capital often found this the least painful way of doing so. The reversion of a customary holding was always worth more to the tenant in possession than to anyone else, and so the best bet was not to sell a manor encumbered with many copyholders as a single unit but to offer the latter individually the chance of enfranchising their holdings, thereby extinguishing the copyhold altogether. Some landowners enfranchised in order to discharge debts, as did Ralph Sadleir and his nephew Lord Aston in south Gloucestershire from 1652 onwards, and William Vernon at Hertingfordbury in the 1670s and 1680s. Others did so in order to mobilize funds for purchases elsewhere, as did the first Viscount Lonsdale in the far north-west in the later seventeenth century, and others again in order to maximize a capital gain (or, like the financier Sir Stephen Fox in Wiltshire in the 1680s, to minimize a loss) after having bought land as a speculation.[222] It is difficult, however, to assess on how large a scale copyhold was being converted into freehold in this way, but it was probably considerable. In addition, purchases by lords of manors of their tenants' copyhold interests, and the consequent conversion of customary land into demesne, also contributed to a reduction in the amount of the latter. We have noted earlier in this chapter the growing fashion for ring-fence estates, the tendency of major county families to buy small parcels of land on the fringes of their estate whenever they came up for sale, and the creation of large estates out of numerous small purchases by men of great resources. And inevitably it was not only freehold but also customary land which was thereby swallowed up, for having once acquired the lordship of a manor it was natural for an owner to regard the extension of its demesne as a desirable objective. Thus whilst building up his estate in Hertfordshire between 1652 and 1683 Sir Harbottle Grimston made at least seventeen separate purchases of copyhold on his own manors, adding nearly 290 acres to his demesnes, a process which his eighteenth-century successors continued until by the end of it little copyhold remained in either the manor of Gorhambury or that of Redbourn.[223]

(b) *Tenancies-at-will*
In the western parts of the country estate owners did not often let their non-customary land for rack rents, although large demesne farms were

[222] Sadleir/Aston purchases ex inf. J. S. Moore; Herts. RO, Panshanger Collection, C.835–49; Beckett, thesis, ch. 6; C. Clay, *Public Finance and Private Wealth*, pp. 206–8.
[223] C. G. A. Clay, thesis, app. II–IV.

sometimes tenanted on that basis even when all the other holdings on the estate were out on lives. East of the Pennines, and east of a line running roughly from the Peak District to the Solent, however, at least by the later seventeenth century, landlords almost always took rack rents. Within this zone leases for terms of years were the characteristic form of tenure in East Anglia and the south-east, although yearly tenancies were also common, especially for the smaller farms. Such leases might be for any number of years up to twenty-one, with terms of seven, nine, twelve, and twenty-one being perhaps most frequently found. Longer terms were unusual and found only in exceptional circumstances,[224] for instance, where a tenant had at his own expense brought land into cultivation for the first time, or where an owner wished to provide for an old servant. In the Midlands and the north-east yearly tenancies were more usual, and in some parts of the former were all but universal even for the largest farms. Nevertheless, in many respects the contrast between the tenancies prevailing in the two parts of the country was more apparent than real, for, as we have seen, life leaseholders in the western half of the country frequently sublet their holdings, and the sub-tenants almost invariably enjoyed yearly tenancies and paid rack rents. Many of those who actually cultivated the land in the western areas thus occupied on terms indistinguishable from those applying to yearly tenants in other parts of the country.

Tenants who occupied their farms on a yearly basis might either hold 'at will' or 'from year to year', and we shall see that there were important differences between these two tenancies. Tenants-at-will had no written agreement with their landlords, but that did not mean that the latter could turn them out whenever they liked. Only a tenant 'at suffrance', for instance, one who had received legally valid notice to quit, whose notice had expired, but who had nevertheless been permitted to remain on a temporary basis, was liable to instant ejection. There might be one or two such tenants on a large estate at any one time, but substantial areas of land would never be held in that way save for very short periods in highly peculiar circumstances.[225] Tenancies-at-will could only be determined by the landlord at the end of the harvest year so that the tenant was enabled to gather in the grain crops he had planted, and, in the event of an eviction, the law required that he receive a full quarter's notice so as to give him time to find another farm. If he was obliged to quit with an unharvested crop still in the ground,

[224] Save that on crown lands it was common for leases to be granted for thirty-one years.

[225] For instance, on the Petre estate in Essex in 1728 2 tenancies were at suffrance out of 98. Perhaps the most common circumstance in which large numbers of tenants might be found holding at suffrance was immediately after the death of a landlord who had granted them leases for the duration of his own life only. Such leases were rarely granted after the middle of the seventeenth century, for settlements of property almost invariably gave life tenants the power to lease for terms up to 21 years or 99 years determinable upon three lives. However, for an example of the mass termination of leases as a result of the death of the stepmother of the then owner (1636), see E. Hopkins, 'The Re-Leasing of the Ellesmere Estates, 1637–42', AHR, x, 1962.

spring-sown turnips, for instance, the landlord would have to compensate him. Moreover, even though in law the tenant-at-will's security did not extend beyond the next Michaelmas rent day, in practice it was usually as good as that of a tenant by lease. Landlords who let most of their estates at will often prided themselves that no tenant who paid his rent and otherwise behaved himself need ever fear for his farm. Indeed, on the Leveson-Gower estate in Staffordshire and elsewhere many tenancies-at-will were in practice hereditary in the same family of tenants.[226] If such owners wished to reorganize their holdings, they generally waited until farms fell vacant by natural means. Nor, indeed, was this anything more than elementary self-interest, for any owner who gained a reputation for arbitrary evictions would find it impossible to get good tenants and would soon discover that his farms were being exploited by their occupants for the maximum short-term advantage. The mass termination of tenancies-at-will was certainly very rare and probably only happened when a large-scale enclosure scheme was about to be implemented, but in such circumstances leaseholders were no better off, at least once enclosures came to be carried out under the authority of an act of parliament, for the acts invariably voided outstanding lease terms.

Nor did tenants-at-will in practice have to fear constant increases in their rent, even in those times and places when economic conditions made it feasible for landlords to demand more from those holding land from them. Indeed, the fact that he could in theory raise the rents of tenants without leases suddenly and without warning whenever conditions seemed to warrant it was a trap for the greedy or short-sighted landlord which most of them were sensible enough to avoid. The nature of the trap is made very clear by what occurred on one estate in the Lincolnshire fenland in the early 1720s. Some years before, the holdings had been occupied by substantial tenants who had property of their own in the nearby Wold country, and who rented parcels of land in the Marsh in order to fatten their sheep for the market. When the rents were raised they threw up the farms rather than pay the increases, and their places were taken by a "meaner set of people" who were unable to use them in the same way, kept them overstocked, failed to manure them, and neglected the dykes and drains. They had few or no reserves of capital to fall back on (unlike their predecessors, who had been perfectly capable of surviving losses for several years), so that when difficult times returned several of them soon failed, leaving their holdings badly run down, difficult to relet, and anyway worth less than they had been in the beginning.[227] However, in a century characterized by long periods of low prices and low farming profits the boot was more often on the other foot, and the fact that the tenant without a lease was not bound to continue paying

---

[226] Jacob, *New Law Dictionary*, sub "lease"; Wordie, thesis, p. 363; G. E. Mingay, 'The Size of Farms in the Eighteenth Century', EcHR, 2nd ser., XIV, 3, 1962, pp. 476–7.
[227] LAO, Tyrwhitt Collection 2/2/21.

an agreed rent for a specified number of years meant that he could at any time request an abatement or a permanent reduction in his rent with the threat, open or implied, that he would leave if it was not forthcoming. "For my parte", wrote Lord Irwin's chief tenant and bailiff at Birdsall (Yorks.) to his master's head agent in March 1690, demanding in effect that he be allowed to remain in arrears with his rent, "if my lord be soe very haisty to call of me for moneys faster than I can possably gett it, I must be forced to give his Lordshipp his land into his own hand. For if times continue as they are att this time the very best of us all must leave farming whilst wee have something to live of."[228] Such a threat from a small farmer might not cut much ice, but the tenant of a large acreage was in a very strong position, because it might be very difficult to replace him during the depths of an agricultural depression, especially if the circumstances of his departure had gained his landlord a reputation in the local alehouses of insisting on very hard bargains. Thus when Lord Fitzwilliam's steward at Milton (Northants.) reported that a tenant who considered his rent too high had given notice to leave at Lady Day 1689, he added: "but where to gitt a tent yt will give ye rent I knowe not".[229] If it did prove impossible to relet a farm immediately, an owner could rarely make much profit from it himself. Indeed, to make anything at all he would have to lay out large sums on the purchase of livestock and equipment, which might be inconvenient or worse. "I have a gret deale of money owing mee for rent", lamented one owner in 1688, "[but] my tenants tell mee corne is so low yt they cannot raise it and to put them out and tack it in hande wolde ruin mee." At about the same time Sir Stephen Fox's Somerset bailiff reckoned that farms in hand would at best yield a bare half of the rent, and when one of the principal tenants seemed to be on the point of giving in his notice he wrote urgently to his employer. "It will be a great loss to yor Honor to lose such a tenant as Penny is", he told him, and in due course Penny received the concessions necessary to induce him to stay. In 1712, a bad year for farmers sandwiched between several much better ones, a tenant agreed to take the largest farm (278 acres) on the Peper Harrow estate in Surrey at £120 a year only on condition that the rent would be automatically reduced by £10 a year when the price of grain was below 5s. a bushel at Guildford market. And in a later period of agricultural depression, in 1733, the earl of Uxbridge's agent in Nottinghamshire could persuade tenants to continue to hold their farms only by guaranteeing that if times did not improve they would have as much rent allowed to them "as their necessities required".[230]

There were other reasons, moreover, why the lot of the tenant-at-will was

[228] Leeds Archives Dept, TN/BL/C.6.   [229] Northants. RO, F (M) C.685.
[230] Northants. RO, F (M) C.674; Dorset RO, D.124.Estate. Somerset (box 173, bdle 1): T. Allen to Sir S. Fox, 8 Mar. 1681, 24 Oct. 1687, 31 Jan. 1687; GMR, Middleton MS 145, box 1: survey of Peper Harrow, etc., 1715; Staffs. RO, D.603 C.50 XVII.

in some respects preferable to that of the tenant by lease. He was not required to meet the cost of repairs, and although in practice when these were necessary he (or on a large farm his employees) would normally provide the labour, using materials supplied by his landlord, he did not have to make everything good before he left, as did the lessee. In law, indeed, he was not even liable to repair damage arising from his own negligence, although if he declined to bear a share of the cost he could presumably expect his tenancy to be terminated. Repairs were a relatively heavier burden on small farms than on large, and the tenant-at-will's freedom from liability for them was certainly an important reason why small holders generally preferred to avoid leases for terms of years. In April 1716 Richard Hill's bailiff told his employer (from Whitchurch, Salop.) that "tenants at rack in this country will not be tied to any repairs", and he continued significantly that "as for takeing leases, they do not at present seem forward thereto". The landlord's position vis-à-vis tenants-at-will was, indeed, much weaker than might be supposed, and an estate occupied in this way required very careful supervision. The tenants were subject to no covenants, and though they could be directed in detail in matters of husbandry in a way which (in the last resort) the holder of leases could not, if they did misbehave the landlord could not exact monetary penalties or proceed against them for damages. He could only, unless they agreed to make some kind of restitution in order to retain his favour, evict them. Thus in 1728 when Lady Hungate's steward failed to find any lease or tenancy agreement for a tenant who had been discovered to have indulged in a variety of agricultural misdemeanours, he was forced to tell his employer that he must be regarded as a tenant-at-will and "consequently not liable to be called to account for running the farm so prodigously out of order". Similarly, when a tenant of Lord Cardigan's quitted his farm, leaving it in a state of disrepair, the steward wrote to say that he was perfectly within his rights, although "if he had been a tenant for a term of years, the case would then have been altered".[231]

(c) *Tenancies from year to year and by lease for years*
Unlike the tenancy-at-will, the letting from year to year was regulated by a formal agreement between landlord and tenant, either verbal or written. Written agreements might be individually drawn up for each tenant like full leases, or (as on Lord Scarborough's Lincolnshire estate) the occupiers might merely sign a declaration in a 'contract book' to abide by a set of rules which applied to all farms in a particular village.[232] These agreements enabled owners to bind their tenants to covenants which either prescribed or forbad certain forms of action, breach of which might incur a monetary penalty

---

[231] Jacob, *New Law Dictionary*, loc. cit.; Salop. RO, 112/2,698; N. Riding RO, ZDV (F) VI/11; J. Wake and D. W. Webster, eds., *The Letters of Daniel Eaton*, Northants. Rec. Soc., 1971, p. 67.
[232] T. W. Beastall, *A North Country Estate*, London and Chichester, 1975, p. 94.

in the form of an increase in rent, or liability to forfeit a bond entered into by the latter to observe the terms they had accepted. The major burden of repairs, at any rate to the buildings, although not necessarily the maintenance of gates, fences, and ditches, etc., remained the landlord's. Technically, annual lettings could be terminated by either party at the end of any agricultural year, but in practice tenants from year to year, like tenants-at-will, often remained in possession for very long periods. One farm at Eastington (Glos.) belonging to the Woolnough family of Bristol was occupied on a year-to-year basis by father and son for half a century down to 1748, and in 1723 Mrs Thirlwall of Warwick Hall described her principal tenants in Hexham (Northumb.) as holding "on lease parole, from year to year, as long as they are pleased".[233]

Leases for terms of years might likewise be either verbal or written, although the latter were very much more common. Nominally the law did not countenance a 'lease parole' of more than three years' duration, but longer ones were certainly to be met with. A survey of the estates of Thomas Talbot of Longford (Salop.), for instance, refers to the letting of two farms, each of over a hundred acres, by leases parole for twenty-one years from 1685.[234] The expedient of a verbal lease for large holdings was probably adopted when avoidance of the clerical and legal expenses involved in engrossing a proper parchment lease was an important consideration, although in some districts it was undoubtedly the custom to use them for small parcels of land. However, whether written or not, the lease transferred to the tenant a right to the use of the premises (on the conditions and subject to the restrictions laid down) for the term agreed upon, which the landlord could not revoke, although if he wished to regain possession he could always offer to buy back an outstanding lease term for a valuable consideration. Indeed, even if the lessee was in breach of one of the covenants which entitled the landlord to a monetary penalty or to re-enter the holding, he could only enforce his right by taking or at least threatening legal action. On the other hand, the tenant was in law obliged to continue to hold the land and to pay the rent for the whole term, even if it no longer suited his purposes or had ceased to afford him as good a profit as he had expected. For this reason, when the outlook for farming profits was uncertain, tenants became reluctant to tie themselves to long leases unless they were offered highly favourable bargains. Thus in August 1690, during a period of very low prices for virtually all agricultural products, Sir Thomas Hales was informed that his principal tenant at Brymore near Bridgwater (Somerset) would not take a further lease for more than a single year unless his rent was reduced.[235] Certainly during the

---

[233] Bristol City RO, AC/WO 14(17)b; 'Register of the Estates of Roman Catholics in Northumberland', *Surtees Soc.*, CXXI, 1918, p. 80.
[234] Jacob, *New Law Dictionary, loc. cit.*; Salop. RO, 81/599.
[235] Somerset RO, DD/BR/e.l.y. 5/6.

chronically difficult times of the second half of the seventeenth century there was a pronounced tendency towards shorter lease terms and for leases to be replaced by annual tenancies. Thus on the Verney estate in Buckinghamshire leases had commonly been for twenty-one years in the 1620s, but by the 1660s Sir Ralph found it difficult to persuade tenants to accept a given level of rent for more than a year at a time. Only the return of better times in the 1690s made three-year agreements possible once again. Similarly, on the Grimston estate in north-eastern Essex and at Rishangles in Suffolk, the eleven-year leases which its owner favoured in the 1650s and 1660s gave way to shorter terms of nine, seven, five, or even three years from about 1670 onwards as agricultural depression steadily increased its grip on the area. After the early 1690s, however, the Grimstons rarely executed leases for under nine years and most of their grants were for longer terms.[236] The period of low grain prices in the 1730s and 1740s apparently saw a similar move towards shorter lettings in grain-growing areas, although it must have been less pronounced, for less evidence of it has come to light. However, it is clearly detectable on the Kingston estates in Nottinghamshire, and in Essex the Lords Petre, who normally let their principal farms on leases for twenty-one years, made almost no fresh grants for terms of years between the late 1720s and the mid 1740s.[237] However, after 1750 any such development must have been reversed, for tenants no longer had anything to fear from the movement of prices, although before the end of the century the accelerating rate of their increase had created a situation in which a growing number of landlords came to perceive it to be in *their* interests to keep lettings short so as not to deny themselves the opportunity for regularly reviewing the levels of rent upon their estates.

(d) *The conditions of rack-rent leases*

As for the covenants in rack-rent leases and letting agreements, generalization from the enormous numbers surviving in every Record Office in the country is inevitably difficult. However, it is safe enough to say that the general tenor of them remained the same throughout the period, although with the passage of time they tended to become more prolix, as both restrictions and injunctions were spelt out in greater detail. There was also a tendency for the number of both to increase, and the very short, simple leases containing only two or three clauses sometimes found (usually on smaller estates) in the earlier part of the period appear to have become markedly less common by the end of it. To some extent this increasing elaboration reflects changes in methods of husbandry and the advent of new crops and cropping systems, but quite as much it reflects the growing influence of attorneys upon estate

[236] Broad, thesis, pp. 250–2; C. G. A. Clay, thesis, pp. 58–9, 60–4.
[237] See *AHEW*, vol. V, pt 1, p. 115; Essex RO, D/DP E.26, 27; T.182.

management, for the same increases in length and complexity are to be found in other types of legal documents, for instance conveyances and settlements.

Throughout the country, wherever leases at rack rent were granted, the overwhelming majority of them included the same core of covenants (albeit with very different wording in different districts), whose purpose was to ensure that the premises were no less valuable at the end of the term than they had been at the beginning. In other words, tenants were bound to treat the land and buildings in the same way that common prudence would lead them to treat their own freeholds. Their leases very rarely required them to do more than this, and before 1750 landlords scarcely ever seem to have attempted to use lease covenants as means of making their tenantry change their ways in a progressive direction. Leases were almost invariably conservative rather than radical in their purport, and, indeed, to a large extent the conditions upon which landlords let their farms were a mere reflection of local convention in agricultural and tenancy matters. The 'custom of the country' imposed a powerful restraining hand upon the landlords' freedom of action in these respects because it dictated what occupiers and potential occupiers were prepared to accept. Tenants for vacant farms, except perhaps for the very largest, did not normally come from very far afield. Owners and their stewards would be unlikely to seek beyond the neighbouring market towns for them, and strangers from an altogether different neighbourhood would tend to be unacceptable, even if they presented themselves, because of the difficulty they would have in providing satisfactory references.

Landlords invariably tried to ensure that those to whom they let their land had a reputation for industry and honesty, and the capital to stock it properly, but it was difficult for them to make the necessary enquiries in far-off districts outside their counties where they had no personal contacts. Occupiers were thus almost always local men, used to local farming ways and local conditions of tenure, and any attempt to introduce radical changes to either would undoubtedly have made farms more difficult to let. Moreover, the average country gentleman was still almost as likely to take the custom of the country for granted as were his tenants, and therefore tended to use it as the basis for his estate policy. This was obviously less true of the owners of great estates spreading across several counties, but such men rarely paid much attention to the details of their management, whilst the age of the 'improving' type of steward, bent on rationalizing estate administration and imposing greater uniformity in the interests of efficiency, was barely under way by the middle of the eighteenth century.[238]

Signs of a modern approach to management, such as surveys which consisted of a full report on the economic potentialities of each holding, rather

---

[238] Edward Laurence's book *The Duty of a Steward to his Lord*, perhaps the most influential of the early treatises on estate management, and in some ways a harbinger of the new approach to the subject, was not published until 1727.

## THE MANAGEMENT OF ESTATES

than just a list of tenants' names, acreages, and rents, and a standard form for all tenancy agreements and leases, are not often found before the end of the period covered by this volume. Sir Mark Pleydell, a Berkshire proprietor, was using a printed form of lease as early as the 1740s, but he was unusual.[239] Even the moneyed man building up a new estate by purchase and, in the process, getting rid of tenants in order to make himself a park, consolidating small holdings into large farms, enclosing open field and common pasture, and the like, did not necessarily change the terms upon which the surviving tenants held their land. In the area around St Albans (Herts.) Sir Harbottle Grimston brought about very considerable changes in the structure of occupancy as he simultaneously enlarged and reorganized the original nucleus of his Gorhambury estate between the 1650s and the 1680s, but his leases closely resembled those of the owners from whom he had purchased. He invariably repeated his predecessors' covenants in effect, even when he did not use their exact wording, which he sometimes did; and his successors did the same well into the eighteenth century.[240]

It would not be unjustified, therefore, to see the main purpose of lease covenants in this period as being to ensure that the tenant adhered to normally accepted local usage in matters of husbandry, and to provide the landlord with a basis for claiming financial compensation or the right to terminate the tenancy if he did not do so. Adherence to local usage is implicit in the requirement found in so many leases that certain tasks be performed in a "proper" or "husbandlike" but otherwise undefined manner, or be carried out in "the usual course of husbandry". It is also implicit in the use of dialect phrases to describe what was expected of the tenants. In many leases granted in east Kent, for instance, they were required to leave, at the end of their terms, so many acres of land "podware grotten" fit for sowing with wheat the following year: that is, so many acres of beans, peas, or vetches ploughed under.[241] However, often the fact that the lease covenant was simply demanding what would have been considered normal even if there had been no lease is quite explicit. Thus Dame Jane Bacon's twenty-one-year lease of Pray farm (near St Albans, Herts.) granted in 1647 laid down that during the last year of the term the landlord might enter into and commence cultivation of the part of the arable left fallow for the next year's sowing "according to the custom of the country". Similarly, in 1725 a London upholsterer leased a small property not far away in Redbourn (Herts.), obliging the tenant "to keep the ordinary seasons for tilling and sowing

[239] G. E. Mingay, 'The Eighteenth Century Land Steward', in E. L. Jones and G. E. Mingay, eds., *Land, Labour and Population in the Industrial Revolution*, London, 1967, p. 5.

[240] C. G. A. Clay, thesis, pp. 47–56.

[241] See, for instance, Kent AO, U.449, T. 17, 19, 21, 38, 48: leases of properties in various parishes east and south-east of Canterbury by William, Lord Cowper; Thomas Mays; George Ward; Edward Harvey; Epiphanius Holland; William Brodnax; Margaret Ley; and other landlords.

according to the course of good husbandry and the custom of the country". In Wiltshire, in a lease of 1703, Lord Stourton covenanted one of his tenants not to plough any arable land "but in husbandly manner and according to the custome and usage of the place". And in Yorkshire in 1729 Sir John Ingilby's tenant of Haveray Park was bound to fallow his ploughland with lime after he had used it for growing corn "according to the custom of the country thereabouts".[242]

It was very general for rack-rent leases and tenancy agreements to set a limit to the number of grain crops that might be taken consecutively from land being used as arable. This was usually no more than two, sometimes only one, as on some (but not all) of the farms on the Essex estate of the Lords Petre in the second quarter of the eighteenth century. The lease of Little Boynton Hall granted in 1729, for instance, laid down that only two crops might be taken successively, and that the second was to be either peas or tares and "no other grain whatsoever". However, on some soils, landlords such as the duke of Grafton on his Northamptonshire estate in leases granted in 1725, and the duke of Bedford on his estate at Thorney (Cambs.) in the 1740s, permitted three.[243] Thereafter it was very common, even in leases granted in the middle decades of the eighteenth century, for the tenant to be obliged, by an uncompromisingly worded covenant, to give the land a summer fallow.

Mention of the new fodder crops which were coming into use during the seventeenth century is very rare before the end of that century, and they are specifically referred to in only a small minority of leases even in the late eighteenth. Clover, sainfoin, trefoil, ryegrass, etc. are most often mentioned in passing as one of a range of permissible alternatives to 'natural' grass when land was to be laid down to temporary or permanent pasture, and turnips likewise appear in a context which suggests that their use was already well established in the locality. The lease of Breakspear's farm in Sopwell (Herts.) granted by Sir Samuel Grimston in 1699, for instance, prohibited the tenant from growing barley save on a tilth or next after a crop of turnips.[244] Very rarely indeed do any of these crops appear in a context which gives any reason to suppose that a landlord is binding his tenantry to methods which were new to them.

By the eighteenth century the occasional landlord may be found insisting on specific rates of seeding for fodder crops, and this may very well represent an attempt to raise standards within an established system of husbandry. In an agreement of March 1742, for instance, the duke of Bedford required

[242] Herts. RO, Gorhambury Collection I.H.5 and II.D.38; Wilts. RO, 383/721; Leeds Archives Dept, Ingilby MS 2,168.
[243] Essex RO, D/DP E.26, f. 219v; Northants. RO, Grafton Collection G.3,884 ML 1,291/2; Bedford RO, Russell Collection R4/4,016.
[244] Herts. RO, Gorhambury Collection IV.D.10.

David Vesey, one of his tenants at Thorney (Cambs.), to lay down land with "good highland hay seed" at the rate of at least four pounds per acre.[245] On the other hand, such a covenant could equally well be inserted in times of difficulty when profit margins were narrowing, in order to ensure that a tenant did not skimp sowings of which the benefit might in large part accrue to a successor. Indeed, unless the history of an estate can be studied in considerable detail it is rarely possible to be certain what significance should be attached to the wording of leases, and although the necessary evidence seems to survive for a fairly large number of estates, only a handful have yet been the subject of scholarly investigation.[246]

The explicit prescription of any of the more advanced husbandry courses is exceedingly rare in leases granted before the last quarter of the eighteenth century, although as early as 1751 one of the tenants on the Coke estate at Holkham (Norfolk) was covenanted to a six-course rotation of corn, corn, turnips, corn, grass, grass; and from 1754 tenants on the Massingberd estate at S. Ormsby (Lincs.) were bound to a four-course alternate system.[247] However, even in such cases it cannot be taken for granted that the landlord was doing more than writing into his leases what had become the common standard of good husbandry in the locality.[248] Nor did the initiative for specific reference to a new crop or a new course of husbandry necessarily come from the owner or his steward. Thus the lease of Panshanger farm (near Hertford), granted in 1711 by guardians on behalf of the young son of a London merchant named Elwes, forbad the tenant to take more than two crops of grain consecutively, but noted, in terms strongly suggesting that the proviso had been inserted at the behest of the tenant, that turnips were not to be accounted as one of the crops. Likewise, the first time a clause referring to a progressive husbandry course appeared in any of the leases granted by the Lords Grimston to their Hertfordshire tenants it was permissive and not mandatory, and there can be little doubt that it was inserted at the insistence of the three gentleman-farmer brothers who were taking the farm (1779). Rather than requiring them to use any particular form of husbandry, it

[245] Bedford RO, Russell Collection R.4/4,016.

[246] The estates which have received more or less adequate investigation for the late seventeenth and early eighteenth centuries are, at the time of writing (1979), those of the Cokes, earls of Leicester in Norfolk; the Earls Cowper in Herts. and Kent; the Grimstons in Herts. and Essex; the Leveson-Gowers in Staffs. and Salop.; and the Verneys in Bucks. See Parker, *Coke of Norfolk*, Oxford, 1975; C. G. A. Clay, thesis; Wordie, thesis; Broad, thesis. See also B. A. Holderness, 'The Agricultural Activities of the Massingberds of South Ormsby, Lincolnshire, 1638–c. 1750', *Midland Hist.*, I, 3, 1972.

[247] Parker, *op. cit.*, p. 55; Holderness, 'Agricultural Activities', pp. 23–4. It should be noted, however, that it is much less rare for leases to *imply* that tenants are *already* following systems other than the traditional rotation of crop, crop, fallow.

[248] In the case of the Massingberds, however, it seems that they themselves had introduced the new crops to the neighbourhood where their estates lay – Holderness, 'Agricultural Activities', pp. 22–3. See below, sect. C.2(*b*).

modified the strict insistence, found in the majority of leases throughout both the seventeenth and eighteenth centuries, that no more than two crops of corn might be taken without the land being given a summer fallow, by declaring "clover or barley after turnips and a shed of pease or beans sown in drills and twice horse-hoed to be deemed fallow".[249] However, it is perfectly clear that on the Grimston estate at least (and no doubt on many others) tenants did not in practice adhere to an old-fashioned course of crop, crop, fallow, even when in theory that is what their leases bound them to. It seems that how they actually farmed must have been thrashed out between the agent and each individual tenant, with a highly restrictive wording retained in the lease in order to provide the owner with protection against an unscrupulous or financially desperate lessee out to exploit his farm for a quick return. Presumably a special 'permitting' clause was inserted only when a tenant wished to be quite certain of his legal position, or intended to adopt practices not generally known in the district.

Less universal than clauses placing restrictions upon the cropping of the arable, but nonetheless common, were covenants requiring tenants to lay dung or some other fertilizer upon their land at a specified rate per acre. Thus the lessee of Hole's tenement in Thorverton (Devon) in 1666 was required to lay upon every acre he ploughed 9 hogsheads of "good stone lyme", or 200 seams of black dung, or 50 seams of soap dung. Similarly, once he had taken two crops from it, the tenant of a farm at Mayfield in Sussex was to amend his land with "four cart loads of well burnt chalk lime or two hundred loads of marl" per acre (1745).[250] Such covenants may have been more common in some districts than in others, for they are especially often found in contexts which indicate that convertible husbandry was being practised, and, as we shall see, there were undoubtedly variations over time in the frequency of their appearance. However, landlords invariably placed restrictions on the amount of land which might be used as arable at any one time, either by inserting a maximum acreage or by prohibiting the ploughing up of pasture unless an equivalent area was laid down to grass. Alternatively, the ploughing of particular fields might be forbidden, or there might even be a complete ban on the ploughing up of any land which was not arable at the time the lease was granted, backed by a crushing financial penalty. But it is unlikely that such a seemingly draconian clause as the last was intended to be taken at face value by most landlords even in the mid seventeenth century, let alone in the mid eighteenth, and, like covenants appearing to bind tenants to a three-course system of crop, crop, fallow, it was essentially a safety device to protect a farm against an unscrupulous lessee. Indeed, it was often tempered by the insertion of a let-out phrase: no land might be ploughed unless a licence to do so was obtained from the owner

---

[249] Herts. RO, Panshanger Collection C.3,298; C. G. A. Clay, thesis, p. 147.
[250] Exeter City RO, 71/13/1/27; E. Sussex RO, Glynde MS 3,039.

or his steward. But even in the absence of this, what was actually permitted was undoubtedly a matter for negotiation and, as we shall see, owners might find it necessary to be less strict about this matter at some times than at others. A ban on the ploughing up of meadow, which might be worth anything up to four times as much as arable, would unquestionably be intended literally, but otherwise it was generally accepted that even land that was normally kept under grass would benefit from the occasional ploughing. However, if an owner was prepared to permit a tenant to break up grassland contrary to the wording of his lease, he was normally careful to insist that it was done in a manner of which he approved. The granting of permission thus often stipulated the course of husbandry the farmer was to pursue on the land in question in much more detail than is normally found in leases themselves. The intention behind all clauses restricting the amount of land a tenant could use as arable was to ensure that, whether the holding was being managed under convertible husbandry or not, he did not unilaterally alter the balance of his system further towards grain crops and away from livestock than had been accepted as appropriate by both parties at the beginning of the term. For if, in the last few years of his lease, or in order to take advantage of a period of high grain prices, a tenant cropped a greater acreage than he could provide with manure, he would be able to make money for himself whilst simultaneously running down the capacity of his farm to pay its rent in the future.

Clearly, tenants were more likely to mine the soil in this way in periods of agricultural depression, and in such times more explicit restrictions on their cropping practices might seem to have been called for. However, if landlords were then more anxious to insert additional restrictions into their leases, tenants were the less willing to agree to the changes and, because of their scarcity value, better able to resist them. In order to ensure that lessees did not try to alleviate their own financial difficulties at their expense, landlords had therefore in general to rely upon existing covenants and their own and their stewards' vigilance in enforcing them. At any rate, there is no clear sign that the number of restrictive covenants increased in times of unusually low farming profits, although a tendency for the monetary penalties attached to breach of covenants to be increased is detectable. At the beginning of the period the penalty for the unauthorized ploughing up of pasture was commonly an increase in rent of £1 or £2 per acre for the remainder of the term, but by the second quarter of the eighteenth century £3 or even £5 per acre was not unusual. Since there had, if anything, been a fall in the price of grain in the interim, these higher figures represented a substantially greater deterrent, even if allowance is made for increases in productivity. Breaking up pasture without permission was indeed the cardinal sin of the tenant farmer in this period, more serious by far than the neglect of buildings, since the damage caused would take not only money but also time to put right. On poorly supervised estates tenants may sometimes have been able to get away with it, but on properly managed ones they emphatically could not. Even amidst the harassments and distractions to which he was subject as a result of the Civil War, Thomas Knyvett was able to find time to write to his wife about the composition that was to be extracted from an outgoing tenant "for his missowing the park, contrary to covenants" (1643). Three-quarters of a century later (1725) two of the duke of Newcastle's lessees at Hepple (Northumb.) who had ploughed up pasture after their request to do so had been rejected similarly found themselves in trouble. And in 1732 we find Sir John Ingilby taking legal action against one Yorkshire tenant who, contrary to a clause in his lease, had broken up four closes of pasture and planted them with rape. A final example, which illustrates how sharp-eyed the owner of a great estate could be about his property, is provided by the second Viscount Grimston. He was out riding one day in 1762 when he noticed that a recently deceased tenant had ploughed up a field which he felt sure should have remained under grass. Upon returning home he had immediate recourse to his copy of the man's lease, and, finding that the ploughing was indeed unauthorized, wrote promptly to his executor to demand redress.[251]

It was also general for tenants to be required, at the end of their terms, to leave an appropriate portion of their land ready for an incoming successor to commence arable operations. What this involved obviously depended on the nature of local husbandry practice, but either they would have to rest it with a summer fallow, and then give it one or more ploughings so that it was ready for sowing immediately after Michaelmas, or (where convertible farming prevailed) they would be obliged to lay it down to grass several years before the end of the term so that it would be ready for breaking up again early in the new tenancy. Thus a twenty-year lease of Horsefrith Park (Writtle, Essex) granted by Lord Petre in 1656 required the tenant to lay down 115 acres, roughly a third of the total acreage, not less than four years before the grant expired.[252] The alternative, in some districts, to requiring an outgoing tenant to make preparations for his successor was to provide for the latter to enter onto part of the property before the old lease had finally expired, thus allowing him to do what was needed himself. Such a dovetailing of tenancies seems to have become increasingly common as the eighteenth century wore on, and the clauses regulating it increasingly lengthy and complicated. This probably reflects the spread of more elaborate field courses which occurred during the period, for as the range of crops in common use widened there was less and less of a clear break in the agricultural calendar between one year and the next. For unless a proper procedure had been spelt

[251] Schofield, *Knyvett Letters*, pp. 117–18; Nottm Univ. Library, Ne E.60; Leeds Archives Dept, Ingilby MS 1,660: memo. dated 17 Dec. 1733, and MS 2,078; Herts. RO, Gorhambury MSS I.F.26: Lord Grimston to C. de Laet, Apr. 1762.   [252] Essex RO, D/DP E.26, f. 67v.

out, when a farm changed hands upon the expiry of a lease a landlord might find it very difficult to get rid of an old tenant without substantial loss. This the steward of the Hales estate in Somerset discovered in the autumn of 1690 when faced by the unwillingness of one occupier to continue paying the old rent. He found a replacement who agreed to take the farm from the following Michaelmas, provided that part of it was sown with clover in the spring of 1691, but the sitting tenant (as he was legally entitled to do) refused to permit this unless he received "a valuable consideration", and thereby succeeded in frustrating the attempt to replace him.[253]

When a new lessee took over a farm the landlord invariably ensured that it was put into good repair, or alternatively allowed the tenant a sum of money to cover the cost of doing what had been agreed to be necessary. Thereafter the latter was normally expected to maintain the holding himself, and in due course hand it back to the owner in as good condition as he had received it. A minority of leases excepted damage by fire and tempest from the tenants' obligation, but even where this was not specifically stated it is unlikely that in practice lessees would be expected to rebuild if they suffered really serious loss in this way: indeed, they would probably not be able to afford to do so. It was an almost universal practice for the landlord to allow the tenant rough timber for repairs if it was to be had from trees growing on the farm, but usually tenants were strictly prohibited against helping themselves to it. It was common, but not universal, for them to be allowed timber even if it was not to be had on the holding. Beyond this, practice differed from district to district, but other material generally had to be supplied at the tenants' expense, and they almost always had to provide the necessary labour. However, even the latter was not an invariable requirement, and the precise division of financial responsibilities in respect of repairs could vary from farm to farm even on the same estate. In such cases it must have been settled by negotiation between landlord and tenant, in the same way as the rent was, prior to the grant of each lease. Thus on the estate of the Earls Cowper in Kent in the first half of the eighteenth century some tenants had to meet all costs of repairs save that of providing timber, whilst others were totally discharged of all such costs unless the damage resulted from their own negligence. Others still fell into an intermediate group. Under leases of 1705 and 1711, for instance, the tenant of Wingham Court farm was freed from any liability for repairs to the buildings save for bearing the cost of the carriage of timber for not more than three miles, but was left to see to the hedges, fences, gates, and bridges, for which the landlord was to provide posts, pales, rough timber, and 10s. a year towards the costs of workmanship. On another farm, Overland in the parish of Ash, under leases of 1720 and 1731, the tenant was responsible for the maintenance of hedges and ditches,

---

[253] Somerset RO, DD/BR e.l.y. 5/6: J. Jeanes to Sir Thomas Hales, 26 Oct., 29 Oct., and 28 Nov. 1690; and 5/9: J. Morgan to Hales, 2 Apr. 1698.

and some (but not all) gates and fences. However, towards the repair of the buildings he had only to replace glass windows, provide straw for rethatching, and meet the costs of carriage of other materials from not more than eight miles.[254]

Tenants were invariably forbidden to fell trees except when specifically authorized to do so, and although they were normally allowed to take domestic fuel and wood for repairing their equipment, the cutting of 'lops and tops' for sale was strictly prohibited. They were also frequently bound to plant a stated number of saplings each year to secure a succession of timber in the future. They were not to remove hay, straw, or dung off the premises, or, where the removal of the two former was permitted, it was conditional upon laying on the land an equivalent amount of manure brought in from outside. In the draft lease of one large farm in Bedfordshire drawn up in 1739 the dowager Baroness Gowran specified that for every ton of hay sold, four loads of manure were to be spread.[255]

Finally, it should be noted that tenants at rack rent were normally forbidden to sublet without their landlord's permission, and a minority of owners inserted a covenant obliging the lessee actually to live on the premises, although this may have been done only in areas where it was fairly common for occupiers to rent more than one holding. The subletting of rack-rented farms, or part of them, was not in fact unusual, and was an obvious course of action for a widow left to manage on her own, or for executors looking after the affairs of orphaned infants. In general, however, it was less common than in districts where most landlords let for ninety-nine years determinable upon lives, and the owners usually took good care to ensure that the sub-tenant was obliged to observe the covenants imposed upon the lessee, and that he was not paying so much rent that he would be obliged to abuse the farm to make a living.

The number and range of formal conditions which landlords imposed on their tenants depended in part upon the size of the holding, and on the nature of farming in the locality. Leases of small parcels of land, especially those on which there were no buildings, could be much shorter than those of full-sized farms. Likewise, leases in districts which were entirely pastoral did not require covenants intended to prevent the overcropping of arable for short-term gains. Particular local conditions or practices naturally demanded the insertion of appropriate clauses not found in the leases granted in areas into which those practices did not extend. For instance, where the night-time folding of sheep which grazed by day on rough downland pasture was essential for maintaining the fertility of the arable, it was necessary for owners to ensure that the flocks which fed on their pastures deposited the dung on their ploughland and not on that of some other owner. Thus in the leases

---

[254] The leases of the Cowper farms in Kent are to be found in Kent AO, U.449 T. 1, 17, 19, 21, 28, 32, 33, 38, 39, 41, 48, 49, 50. Those cited in the text are in T. 41 and 48 and T. 21 respectively.
[255] Bedford RO, Ashburnham MSS, R.O. 1/127.

of his farms in the environs of Folkestone (Kent), granted in the years after 1716, the London merchant Sir Jacob Des Bouverie regularly specified the number of sheep to be folded on his land: 80, 100, 300, and so on, according to the size of the holding.[256] To take another example, where hedges were numerous and provided an important source both of firewood and timber, as in much of Hertfordshire, covenants concerning their upkeep were exceedingly detailed.[257]

No less important in determining the contents of the lease was the type of owner to whom the estate belonged. On small estates where the owner was resident and kept a close watch on matters, covenants were often relatively few, their multiplication rendered unnecessary in the landlord's eyes by the degree of personal supervision he exercised. On the other hand, absentee owners of small, detached holdings who were unable to exercise any personal supervision at all, and at best depended upon the occasional services of an attorney in a nearby town, often issued very detailed leases. So did many moneyed men, conscious of the rate of return they were obtaining on the capital they had invested in land purchase: in 1722 Sir Jacob Des Bouverie drew up a list of no fewer than seventeen clauses to be inserted in all the leases to be granted on his new Kentish estate.[258] As for the established great landowners, managing their estates through the services of a full-time professional steward, if they granted leases at all they too tended to have a full range of covenants.

(e) *Rents and the terms of tenancy*

A discussion of rent trends is beyond the scope of this chapter, but there were a variety of ways in which change in the terms upon which farms were let could alter the 'real' rent paid for a holding over and above any change in the money rent, or, indeed, alter it even though the money rent remained unchanged.[259] One of these was an alteration of the distribution of the tax burden between landlord and tenant. The normal arrangement was for poor rates and other parochial and county dues to be met by the tenant, whilst 'great taxes' imposed by parliament or 'extraordinary taxes' (as they were still regarded in the early part of the period) were the responsibility of the owner. The various forms of land tax levied from the 1640s onwards were specifically designed by the legislature to fall upon owners, rather than upon tenants, and although they were usually paid by the latter in the first instance, if there was nothing in their leases to the

---

[256] Kent AO, U.270 E. 10.
[257] Herts. RO, Gorhambury MSS, *passim*.   [258] Kent AO, U.270 E. 10.
[259] In the early seventeenth century it was still not uncommon for a substantial proportion of the rent of a farm let out at rack to be paid in kind, but this practice did not survive the falling product prices of the decades after 1660. By 1700 only trivial payments in kind are found, save on college estates. The colleges normally sold their leases for fines, but they were bound by parliamentary statute to require one-third of their reserved rent to be paid in grain.

contrary they were entitled to claim them back by withholding an appropriate sum out of their rent. During the two decades or so after the Civil War, when land values were still rising in many areas, a minority of owners succeeded in getting their tenants to pay the whole, or at least a proportion, of the parliamentary taxes due on account of their farms instead of having their money rents increased. On Lord Petre's estate in Essex, for instance, the tenants were generally paying one-fifth of their taxes in the later seventeenth century.[260] Some of those who succeeded in increasing their tenants' financial obligations in this way worded the relevant covenants very carefully so that, come revolution, counter-revolution, or restoration, no dispute about the legality of the impositions should throw into question the division of liability laid down in the lease. Thus one of Lord Petre's leases executed in 1647 bound a tenant to pay the whole of all tenths, fifteenths, etc., "ordinary and extraordinary...as well to our sovreign lord the King his heirs and successors as to any other person", whilst another of 1650 committed the tenant to pay a proportion of all extraordinary taxes levied "by the supreme government of England for the time being".[261] By the 1670s and later, however, worsening agricultural conditions in many areas made it very difficult for owners to continue to insist upon tenants' carrying the full burden of great taxes, and sometimes, in order to avoid the need to reduce the nominal rent, they even agreed to relieve their lessees of liability to pay parochial due. Thus in one Wiltshire lease of 1703 Lord Stourton undertook to pay all taxes and (perhaps with an eye to a possible French invasion) all costs and damages caused by legal or illegal quartering of soldiers, whilst in another he freed the tenant from "all taxes, burthens and payments whatsoever" except for tithes and the performance of personal offices such as overseer of the poor or surveyor of the highways.[262]

It may have been rather unusual for owners to relieve their lessees of local taxes, and leases containing such clauses seem mostly to date from the worst periods of depression, but it was not until after the middle of the eighteenth century that most of them could even contemplate making it a standard condition of letting that the occupiers pay a full 4s. land tax themselves. Before this, individual tenants might be induced to take on the liability, or, as in the case of one of Lord Bruce's Bedfordshire tenants in 1728, two-thirds (or some other fraction) of it. Alternatively they might agree to pay the tax, provided that it did not rise above a certain rate. By the 1730s, for instance, some of the tenants on the Goodricke estate at Great Ribstone (Yorks.) were covenanted to pay so long as the rate did not rise above 2s. in the pound: above that level, in other words in wartime, the landlord was to meet the cost.[263] A general shift of the burden of the land tax onto the shoulders of the tenants did not, however, get under way until the 1760s or later.

[260] See also above, p. 247.  [261] Essex RO, D/DP E.26, ff. 70v, 74v.
[262] Wilts, RO, 383/737 and 721: leases of Stourton and Colcott farms.
[263] Quoted by Parker, *Coke of Norfolk*, p. 3 n. 12.

Another way in which a change in the conditions of a tenancy could alter the real rent was by concessions, or the withdrawal of concessions, about the breaking up of pasture or cropping practices generally. These would have an important bearing on the level of a tenant's profits in the short run, and if one was having difficulty in paying his rent, permission to sow an increased acreage with grain might make all the difference. Thus in July 1689 one of Lord Fitzwilliam's Northamptonshire tenants asked leave to plough three more fields, telling the steward that he had made a loss for the previous two or three years and that unless he was permitted to do this he would not renew his tenancy. The steward passed the request on to his master with the comment that "Times are bad for ye tents, I believe never worse. He is a good husband and a good tent. therefore I would not have yr Honr pt with him for a little."[264] Contrariwise, when economic conditions were more favourable owners could not merely afford to be less accommodating about requests of this kind, since it would be much easier to get a replacement tenant, but could tighten up on matters of cropping and ploughing. They could thereby oblige tenants involuntarily to sacrifice their own short-term profits to increase the long-term value of the land.

Also important in affecting the real burden of rent upon the tenant were reductions or increases in the extent of his financial responsibility for the repair and maintenance of the fixed capital. Under the most usual arrangements in leases for terms of years, repairs were a substantial part of any tenant's outgoings, and in periods when farming profits were under pressure, some landlords tended to agree to shoulder a larger proportion of these costs so as to render a reduction in money rent unnecessary. However, it remains obscure on how large a scale this actually occurred in any of the episodes of agricultural depression within this period. There seems little doubt that throughout it the majority of lessees for years formally remained responsible for the bulk of repair costs, but on the other hand in an indeterminate number of cases landlords relieved them in whole or in part even though they were in no way obliged to do so under the terms of their agreement. Thus on the Grimston estate in Essex, the 1698 lease of Weeks' Lodge does not specifically exempt the tenant from doing repairs, yet when a new one was granted in 1710 it is noted in the rental that although the rent was to remain the same, the tenant was now "to be at ye full charge of repairs during his lease". Clearly this owner had assumed the responsibility for repairs during the difficult years of the first decade of the eighteenth century, and was handing them back now that times had improved. To take another example (also from Essex), in 1724 one of Lord Petre's leases mentioned that the stable, hayhouse, and little cowhouse "being all in one building" were utterly rotten,

---

[264] Northants. RO, F (M) 1. 703. For another example, Wake and Webster, *Letters of Daniel Eaton*, p. 96.

and that although the tenant was obliged by his previous lease to keep them in good order, nevertheless his lordship would pull them down and rebuild them.[265] In matters of repairs, as in many other matters, the legal position and the realities of estate management did not necessarily coincide. When the profitability of farming improved markedly in the second half of the eighteenth century, however, there is no doubt at all that landlords who had at some stage accepted a legal liability to bear all or part of the cost of repairs on their leased properties divested themselves of it as rapidly as they could. As the old leases fell in and new ones were granted, tenants had to take it on, instead of, or in addition to, an increase in money rent. On the Kent estate of the Earls Cowper, for instance, the varied arrangements referred to above had been abandoned by the 1770s, and almost every new lease by then imposed the full cost (except for rough timber) upon the lessees.[266]

Responsibility for the maintenance and improvement of soil fertility was also something which was, up to a point, shifted backwards and forwards between landlord and tenant to bring about alterations in the real rent of the holdings on an estate. Primary responsibility for this was invariably the tenant's, for he was always expected to put back into the land the equivalent in manure of what he had extracted from it. However, by requiring their tenants to go beyond this and to spend money on dunging, marling, liming, or sanding at a specified rate per acre in order to bring about a long-term increase in the value of the farm, landlords could obtain what was in effect a concealed increase in rent. But such requirements would probably have to be withdrawn when the tenants' profit margins were shrinking, and for much of this period it was a more characteristic state of affairs for owners to be supporting rents by providing their tenants with extra fertilizer at their own expense. Sir Ralph Verney sometimes did this on his Buckinghamshire estate in the later seventeenth century; in the later 1690s Sir Samuel Grimston was meeting the cost of laying chalk on a number of his farms in north-east Essex; and in 1741 Lady Abergavenny agreed to do the same in respect of liming to be undertaken by one of her Sussex tenants. The costs involved could, moreover, amount to a significant fraction of a year's rent: in 1736, for instance, Lord Bruce allowed £36 to the tenant of a Bedfordshire farm renting at £100 *per annum* towards the provision of manure at the start of a new twenty-one-year lease.[267] For all these reasons, therefore, fluctuations in 'real' or total rents were considerably greater than the rather slight movements, whether upwards or downwards, which are revealed by a study of money rents alone.

---

[265] C. G. A. Clay, thesis, p. 64; Essex RO, D/DP E.26, f. 198v.
[266] See above, pp. 349–50, and refs. cited in n. 254.
[267] Broad, thesis, pp. 242–5; Essex RO, D/DH vi.A.41, 51, 72, 96, 115; Kent AO, U.269 E. 326/1: agreement for lease, dated 8 Oct. 1741; Bedford RO, Russell MSS box 251: lease dated 8 Mar. 1736.

## (f) The importance of leases

As much of what has already been written will have made clear, the formal terms of a tenancy were not necessarily the most important factor in determining the nature of the relationship between landlord and tenant. Over a wide range of issues leases and tenancy agreements provided owners with a legally enforceable weapon of last resort against an unscrupulous or recalcitrant occupier, but in normal circumstances they provided no more than a loose framework within which dealings between landlord and tenant could be conducted. This, and the fact that their terms tended to mirror locally accepted agricultural usages, meant that in practice it probably did not make a great deal of difference to either party whether or not leases existed, unless or until a serious dispute between them arose. In fact, it must be very doubtful whether in any given district tenants-at-will, yearly tenants, and tenants with leases for years held their land on significantly different terms. Certainly the set of instructions to the steward of a Sussex estate (c. 1730) telling him what to require of tenants-at-will differs very little in content from the conditions imposed in the typical lease.[268] The degree of tenant responsibility for repairs was perhaps the most important respect in which there generally was a difference, but, as we have seen, even this did not exist everywhere.

By the last third of the eighteenth century the existence of leases was regarded as of the highest importance by agricultural writers and by some landlords, because it encouraged tenants to invest their own capital in improving their farms by giving them a guarantee that they would not be deprived of the fruits of their investment by eviction or a prompt increase in rent. Thus in a letter of October 1772 Edward Gibbon defended to a friend his grant of an unusually long lease of thirty years to a farmer on his Hampshire estate "on the following grounds 1. The giving the tenant a durable interest to use my land like his own..."[269] Undoubtedly leases for years were regarded in a similar light at an earlier period, although the sources do not often carry the suggestion that they were primarily granted for that reason, and we may note that Edward Laurence in his widely read *The Duty of a Steward to his Lord* (1727) does not recommend them in such a context. Some evidence from the eighteenth century suggests that rents may have been adversely affected in the long run by the absence of leases, but although tenants' unwillingness to invest their own money in farms held at will might account for this, it is not the only possible explanation.[270] Anyway, tenants-at-will often were prepared to improve at their own expense and to trust their landlords not to take advantage of it to their detriment: they did

---

[268] Sussex Arch. Soc., RF 15/25: memos. c. 1730.
[269] J. E. Norton, ed., *The Letters of Edward Gibbon*, 3 vols., London, 1956, I, p. 341.
[270] C. G. A. Clay, thesis, ch. XIII.

so on the Leveson-Gower estate in Staffordshire in the eighteenth century, for instance. And such trust rarely seems to have been misplaced. When Richard Hill contemplated raising the rent on one newly acquired farm in Shropshire in 1716, his steward told him categorically that it would be unjustified, since any increase in the value of the holding was entirely due to marling undertaken by the tenant at his own expense. When the same steward terminated some tenancies in pursuit of his employer's strategy of consolidating small holdings to create larger farms, he softened the blow to the farmers involved by promising them compensation for the improvements they had made.[271]

It is therefore by no means clear whether leases were regarded as so important in this period, either by owners or by tenants, as the emphasis placed on them by somewhat later writers would lead one to believe. Whether or not they existed on a particular estate depended in part upon its whereabouts in the country, and in part upon the preferences of individual landowners and the traditions of individual estates. Thus on the Grimston estate near St Albans (Herts.) leases were normally granted to all the principal tenants throughout this period, whilst on the estate built up by Lord Chancellor Cowper to the west of Hertford in the early part of the eighteenth century leases were seldom or never issued. This was despite the facts that the two estates lay only about ten miles apart and were of comparable size, and that lands which went to make up the Cowper property had often been under lease at the time of their purchase.[272] A far more important factor in estate management than the existence or otherwise of leases was the degree of supervision over his property exercised by the owner or his steward, and the attitude of the former towards those dependent upon him for a livelihood. Certainly on well-run estates a continuing personal dialogue between landlord and tenant, not of course always an amicable one, but a dialogue nonetheless, had more influence upon how the latter farmed his land, and even upon the extent of his financial obligations, than did the wording of any written documents.

This has no doubt been true at all periods in English history, but it was particularly so in one as marked by frequent and prolonged periods of agricultural depression as was the century after the Civil War. In these periods owners who insisted on their legal rights to the last iota would in many areas be rewarded, sooner rather than later, by untenanted farms and a disastrously depleted rent roll. It was simply no use, in the economic conditions which prevailed for so much of the century, for them to insist that a lessee should continue to pay in full what had become an unrealistically high rent for the whole of his lease term, if to do so would force him to run down the farm or to go bankrupt or (the most likely result) to do first one and then the

[271] Wordie, thesis, pp. 88–90; Salop. RO, 112/2,698 and 2,389.
[272] C. G. A. Clay, thesis, pp. 146–9, 340–2.

other. It was no use insisting that he do all the repairs that his lease required of him if he could only afford to do so by parting with livestock essential to the proper running of the farm. Nor was it sensible to seize a known and trusted tenant's stock and evict him as soon as he began to accumulate arrears if a replacement was unlikely to be any more successful in making the farm pay.

## 2. Beyond the formal agreement

### (a) Financial forbearance in time of trouble

Landowners who lived on their estates could see the nature and the intractability of the economic problems faced by their tenants clearly enough, even if their own financial difficulties sometimes led them to adopt desperate measures in order to try to survive an immediate crisis. Indeed, those whose home farms provided them with an important fraction of their income would be experiencing directly and at first hand the pressures which were afflicting their tenants. Thus in November 1655 Sir Ralph Verney told one of his creditors: "You shall have your interest to a farthing, but when I call for rent, my tenants protest they can make nothing either of their cheeze or cattle, & I know 'tis too true, & corne is also att so low a rate, that I know not what wee shall doe."[273] Urban-dwelling absentees, however, might need reminding of the realities of life in the countryside, and in every era of agricultural depression letters from distraught stewards flooded down to London, endlessly repeating the same chorus. In June 1683 Lord Fitzwilliam heard from Northamptonshire that "I feare wee shall have a great deale of land come into our hands next Lady Day: for Mr Blythe has given his warning... & Mr Norton his; & I feare many more will do ye like: I feare yor Honr must abate a great deale of rent." In November 1696, at the time of the recoinage crisis, Edward Mellish, a Yorkshire landowner living in the capital, was warned that things were so bad that a similar situation could easily develop on his property: if severity was used towards his tenants over the payment of their rents, wrote his steward, the estate would be left unoccupied. In October 1703 another Yorkshire steward told Sir John Ingilby that he had forced several tenants to take sheep and cattle to market to sell in order to discharge their arrears, but that they had not had a penny bid for them and that no one had even asked the price. He added for good measure that they could hardly be expected to give them away. Nearly forty years later (1741) a letter in almost identical terms reached the owner of an estate on the Welsh border. His steward informed him that "Severall of your tenants took cattle to the fair last Monday but sold not one so that I could not get one farthing [from them]." In 1750, when the cattle plague was sweeping through Lancashire, the local agent of the Molyneux family told

[273] M. M. Verney, *Memoirs of the Verney Family during the Commonwealth*, London, 1894, p. 120.

their chief steward that two more tenants who had lost all their livestock had been to see him to give in their notice, notwithstanding the fact that their leases had several years to run. He had dissuaded them and promised to intercede on their behalf, insisting that unless some consideration was given to them to get them back on their feet they could not carry on. If nothing was done, and they left, he made it clear that no other takers could be expected, in which case "their farms must lie to the crows".[274]

In this period landlords could not for long lose sight of the fact that both in the short term and the long their own interests and those of their tenants at rack rent coincided extremely closely. They could not prosper unless their tenants prospered, and if their tenants were in difficulties they could not expect to escape unscathed. The best way to deal with the situation was to help their tenants weather the storm, and if they refused to do so they would almost certainly pay a heavier price in the end. Most owners who paid any attention at all to their estates understood perfectly well that competent farmers, possessed of adequate capital to stock their land, were the most valuable assets their estates possessed. "I have nothing I desire so much as to have good tenants", declared the Lincolnshire landowner Burrell Massingberd in 1722,[275] and it was worth extending much forbearance to enable those who had proved themselves to be such to survive periods of crisis. Tenants who fell behind with their rent owing to their own incompetence or folly would invariably receive short shrift. On the other hand, those who had shown themselves to be good husbandmen and had hitherto been prompt in paying their rents would receive much consideration from most landowners. If their difficulties were the result of some particular misfortune they might expect to be allowed a substantial rebate out of their year's rent, or to receive a loan to get them back on their feet. When serious flooding ruined the crops of scores of his tenants at Thorney (Cambs.) in 1708–9, the duke of Bedford allowed rebates of up to half a year's rent to 137 of them. And Bedford, like innumerable other owners up and down the country, had perforce to help those of his tenants whose livestock were wiped out by the cattle plague in the 1740s. In February 1748 it was reported to him that total losses on the Thorney estate amounted to 890 beasts with a sale value of £2,898. The government's compensation for compulsorily slaughtered stock came to only £1,091 12s. 6d., and the duke agreed to allow them half as much again out of his own funds. However, his agent informed him that this would not be enough to avoid "fatal consequences to the estate", and pressed him to increase the sum, although whether he did so or not is uncertain. Among

[274] Northants. RO, F (M) 1. 496; Nottm Univ. Library, ME 74/13: R. Nicholson to E. Mellish, 11 Nov. 1696; Leeds Archives Dept, Ingilby MS 1,707: E. Ridsdale to Sir J. Ingilby, 1 Oct. 1703; UCNWL, Nannau 3,582: J. Williams to the Hon. R. Williams, 9 July 1741; GMR, LM 778/35/20.

[275] LAO, MM VII/2/32: B. Massingberd to Mr Loft, 1 Feb. 1722.

the landowners who preferred to make loans in such circumstances were Sir Stephen Fox, who advanced hundreds of pounds to his Somerset tenants in the early stages of the vicious depression of the 1680s, and the earl of Nottingham when his estates at Foulness (Essex) suffered damage from flooding in 1724.[276] When one bad year succeeded another, and the problem of the tenantry was a chronic inability to make a profit on their husbandry, landlords generally allowed their tenants, at least their larger tenants, to accumulate arrears as long as there was any hope that they would one day succeed in paying them off. In the 1680s some Throckmorton tenants in Warwickshire came to owe their landlord four and a half, or even five and a half years' rent before they were finally evicted at the beginning of the next decade. In certain circumstances owners might even be prepared to write off all or part of such accumulated debts in order to allow valued tenants to start afresh. Sir Stephen Fox was content for several of his larger tenants whose security was good to remain several years behindhand with their rent in the later 1680s and early 1690s, and in about 1691 he agreed to write down the amounts owing by proportions ranging from £33 5s. 6d. out of £56 12s. 9d. in one case to £64 0s. 8d. out of £464 0s. 8d. in another.[277]

*(b) Positive action to support the rental*
Besides being willing to help, or at least to bear with, tenants who were temporarily failing to make ends meet, some owners also adopted positive measures to try to ensure that their rents would be better paid in the future. Various possible courses of action were open to them, although not all of them would necessarily be appropriate on any given estate.

If the land was in the hands of numerous small tenants, a policy of combining them so as to create large holdings was almost certain to yield dividends in the long run. Small farms almost always let for more shillings per acre than large, reflecting the greater competition for them amongst potential tenants and the proportionately heavier investment in buildings and the like. But this was offset by the fact that repair costs were heavier and small holders at rack rent could hardly ever be expected to assume full responsibility for them. "By pcells it amounts to more", wrote the agent of the Mansell family in 1697 of an estate he had just succeeded in leasing *en bloc*, "but it will be much more advantageous for ye landlord to have one able tenant yt will keep house, hedges, & ditches in repair & rent well pd, than to let it out in pcells from yeare to yeare to poore tenants sometimes never paying but [i.e. and] certainly never repairing hedge nor ditch."[278]

---

[276] Bedford RO, Russell MSS R.5/4,337/1 and R.4/4,032; C. Clay, *Public Finance and Private Wealth*, pp. 200–1; Leics. RO, Finch MSS DG.7/2/43.
[277] Mimardière, thesis, pp. 139–40; Dorset RO, D.124.Estate. Somerset (box 173, bdle 3): documents relating to arrears 1690, 1691, 1693.
[278] NLW, Penrice and Margam MSS L.333.

Indeed, even more important than the matter of repairs was the fact that large holdings could be let to a quite different type of tenant, able to bring more capital to his undertaking, likely to farm in a superior fashion and to be able to market what he produced to greater advantage, more capable of withstanding hard times, and for all these reasons much less likely to fall into arrears. Richard Hill's Shropshire bailiff voiced a commonly held and, from the landlord's point of view, a perfectly justified impatience with small family farmers when he apologized for the arrears owing from the estate at Weston-under-Redcastle by saying: "I doubt it will be noe other way while that estate is let into soe many hands" (June 1722).[279]

Serious obstacles, however, lay in the way of any owner who was minded to try to bring about a radical restructuring of the occupancies on his estate in a short time. Evictions in order to attain this end caused intense ill feeling, and this in itself was a considerable deterrent even to landlords who lacked an active social conscience. The impact upon the local poor rates also had to be considered. Evicted families could not in this period simply be forced out of the parish, and if insufficient work was available for them to earn a living as wage labourers, they would have to be supported at the ratepayers' expense. Even by the third quarter of the eighteenth century the poor rates had become a sufficiently serious financial burden in many places for some of the most widely read authorities on estate management to be hostile to the creation of very large farms at the expense of small, and even to recommend that in certain circumstances they be broken up to create more family-sized holdings.[280] Anyway, the number of potential takers for farms of 200 or 300 acres or more, which would require a capital of several hundred pounds to stock, was relatively small. By proceeding too quickly a landlord therefore courted the risk of being unable to let his newly created 'capital farms', or at least of being unable to let them for as much rent as he had counted on. Generally owners had of necessity to proceed cautiously, making changes only when small farms fell vacant by natural means, and the occupiers of the larger ones felt ready to manage an additional acreage. Deliberate creation of large farms all at one go was probably unusual save where substantial areas of waste were being enclosed for the first time.[281]

A second way in which landowners could try to deal with the problem of tenants unable to make adequate profits from their farming was by laying out money on improvements, receiving interest on their capital in the form of a narrower gap between gross rental and actual receipts, or by avoiding a reduction in rents that would otherwise have been necessary. Consolidation of farms, indeed, normally involved some investment by the landlord, even

---

[279] Salop. RO, 112/2,408.
[280] Laurence, *Duty of a Steward to his Lord*, p. 3; J. Mordant, *The Complete Steward*, 2 vols., London, 1761, I, pp. 359–61; Kent, *Hints to Gentlemen of Landed Property*, pp. 204 et seq.
[281] For the subject of this paragraph, see also Mingay, 'The Size of Farms', *passim*.

if no enclosure was involved, for one large holding required different buildings, domestic and agricultural, than were to be found on its constituent components. The types of improvement most commonly undertaken in this period inevitably varied from district to district, and have already been referred to in the regional chapters. A further discussion of this form of investment from the landlords' point of view will be found in the final section of this chapter.

A third way open to landlords who wished to tackle the difficulties of their tenants at the roots was to induce them to make changes in the way they carried on their farming. Normally this consisted of introducing them to new crops, field courses, or manures which would increase the productivity of their land without a fundamental alteration in the nature of their husbandry. However, in certain circumstances some of them did go further, and tried to persuade them to make a more or less complete change in land use. A change from corn growing to animal husbandry was not normally possible for poor men, because they could never raise the capital to buy enough livestock to commence operations. However, in many areas it was the practice for the landlords to let out milch kine, whether in large herds or small numbers, on the same basis as they let land, and dairying was therefore a feasible proposition for smallholders. Indeed, it was a particularly suitable form of economic activity for them, since the processing of butter and cheese occupied the labour of female members of their families in a way that most other branches of husbandry could not. Thus in the 1650s Sir Ralph Verney tried to introduce the small tenants on his Buckinghamshire estate to dairy farming, albeit unsuccessfully. Another example, again from a time when violently fluctuating grain prices were making it difficult for those growing grain on a small scale not only to pay their rents but even to feed their families, is provided by the Yorkshire estate of the absentee owner Stamp Brooksbank. In March 1729 his agent told him that he had suggested to the villagers at Healaugh and Catterton that they should turn to dairying. Unperturbed by their reaction – "like old cart horses, one can't thrust 'em out of their old beaten tracks; they'l not be persuaded to try experiments" – he advocated rewording their leases when they came up for renewal, although clearly envisaging that this be done in such a way as to encourage rather than compel them to adopt his advice.[282]

Certainly those who sought to raise the standard of their tenants' farming usually proceeded by proffering informal advice and by example, rather than by manipulating the terms of leases or tenancy agreements. That there was a flow of ideas from gentleman landowners, who read modern farming books and corresponded about farming methods with their friends, and from estate stewards to ordinary working farmers in this way, even in the seventeenth

[282] M. M. Verney, *Verney Family during the Commonwealth*, pp. 120–2; Leeds Archives Dept, HE 37(a): T. March to S. Brooksbank, 14 Aug. 1728, 17 Nov. 1728, 16 Mar. 1729.

century, is unquestionable.[283] The nature of the exchanges means that the historian is only occasionally able to eavesdrop upon them, but an example is provided by what befell when the duke of Bedford's agent in the west visited his employer's estate at Bridport (Dorset) in 1745. He found much of the land badly out of heart, and discovered that although their soil was a stiffish clay, the tenants never made any use of the sea sand freely available on a nearby beach. He therefore recommended it to them as a fertilizer, and though their response was guarded, he was able to report that one of the principal occupiers had agreed to try it on an acre or two.[284]

Farmers, especially small farmers, tended to be suspicious of unfamiliar methods unless their own eyes convinced them that they were worth while, and innovations undoubtedly spread more rapidly where they had an example to copy. Frequently this was provided by the home farm of a gentleman, whether or not he was their landlord, who kept a substantial part of his acreage in hand and derived an important fraction of his income from the sale of produce. Model farms whose primary purpose was to promote better methods among the tenantry are rarely if ever found within the period with which we are concerned. A good example of a home farm having a long-term influence upon the estate tenants is provided by that of the Massingberds of South Ormsby in the Lincolnshire Wolds. Drayner Massingberd introduced sainfoin to his own fields in 1672, and by the 1680s was moving towards a fully fledged convertible husbandry in which it was a key element. By the 1690s his son and successor, Burrell Massingberd, was letting sainfoin land to some tenants and selling seed to others, and by the 1720s the crop was clearly well established on the estate. In the early eighteenth century Burrell likewise introduced clover, coleseed, and turnips, and the use of the first and the last was likewise in due course taken up by his tenants.[285] On very large estates only a small fraction of the tenantry could be influenced by what the owner did on the land he farmed himself, but tenant farms temporarily in hand because of difficulty in finding suitable occupiers and thus under the direct supervision of the steward for several years on end sometimes fulfilled a similar function. There were one or two such on most estates of any size at almost any time in the 1730s and 1740s: on the duke of Bedford's property at Thorney in Cambridgeshire in 1745 there were no fewer than six, together some 640 acres.[286] Methods at Thorney were relatively advanced, but a year or two earlier the duke's steward in Devon had written to the head agent à propos a holding he was managing there: "I should be glad if you'd please to send down the coleseed to sow on Cassell Parks, and don't doubt but it will be the means of introducing it into this

[283] See vol. 3, of this paperback series, pp. 264ff.
[284] Devon RO, Bedford MSS W.1,258M/LP2/4.
[285] Holderness, 'Agricultural Activities of the Massingberds', pp. 19–23.
[286] Bedford RO, Russell MSS R.5/4,311–14.

country, which will in time turn out to his Grace's interest, by the improvement it will make in the estates."[287]

It has been stressed elsewhere in this volume that high-yielding industrial crops such as flax, hemp, woad, madder, saffron, liquorice, and tobacco provided a vital supplement to the incomes of many farmers, especially those on relatively small acreages, who found that the prices of their traditional staples were too low for them to yield a decent living. However, all of them took a great deal out of the soil, and from the landlords' point of view they were at best controversial innovations. Certainly some authorities, such as Edward Laurence (1727), took the view that their cultivation was altogether inappropriate on ordinary farms.[288] Thus if some owners encouraged their tenants to grow them, others did the opposite to the extent of inserting covenants in their leases severely restricting their cultivation, or even forbidding it altogether. Even towards the end of the seventeenth century some major proprietors were still exceedingly severe about the range of crops they were prepared to permit their tenants to grow. Daniel Finch, the future second earl of Nottingham, for instance, wrote to his Essex steward in 1680 in uncompromising terms: "You must take particular care that they covenant not to sow coleseed or oade etc., nor indeed any thing save only wheat, barley, rye, oates and pease etc. and lett this be a standing rule in all agreemts that you shall at any time hereafter make for us."

More typical of the eighteenth century was the clause in a draft lease of 1721 whereby the dowager countess of Winchelsea forbad one of her Kentish tenants to sow either woad or flax in the last three years of a seven-year term; or that in the twenty-one-year lease of 1720 in which Mary Lady Forrester permitted a Shropshire occupier to sow only a single acre of flax. The cultivation of such crops on small parcels of land specifically let out for that purpose, and consequently commanding a very high rent, was, of course, quite another matter. In 1722, for instance, when one Gloucestershire owner leased a plot for flax growing, the rent she was able to obtain was no less than £4 per acre, about eight times as much as even enclosed arable was likely to command.[289]

(c) *Landlords, cottagers, and the provision of employment*

The growing of industrial crops might also be another matter if a landowner held property in a township where cottagers were numerous and industrial occupations to employ them were lacking. In such places the cost of poor relief might rise high enough to threaten rent levels, especially in years when

---

[287] Devon RO, Bedford MSS W.1,258M/LP5/2.
[288] Laurence, *Duty of a Steward to his Lord*, pp. 30–1.
[289] Leics. RO, Finch MSS DG.7/2/32; Kent AO, U.449 T. 21: unexecuted lease of Hoath farm, 1721; Salop. RO, 1,224/LW.18: lease of Jervis's tenement, dated 24 Aug. 1720; Clwyd RO, Rhual MSS D/HE 134: memo. of lease, dated 1 Jan. 1721/2.

food was dear, for the poor rates were in effect a tax on rents. It is true that most leases and letting agreements bound the tenants to pay them, but any substantial increase in the latter's outgoings would inevitably have an adverse effect upon the amount they were able, or at any rate willing, to pay for their land. It was therefore very much in the landlords' interest to keep the rates as low as possible. There were two quite distinct ways they could go about this. One of these was to try to ensure that the number of families living in the village was no larger than was necessary to meet the labour requirements of the larger farmers holding land there. To this end cottages would often be pulled down as they became vacant rather than relet, and any land or common rights attached to them added to one of the bigger tenancies. Indeed, some landowners were even prepared to evict the occupants of cottages in order to speed up the process, although many, probably most, had a strong enough sense of responsibility for the welfare of the poor (at least on their home estates) for this not to be particularly common. Even if they were numerous, cottages were rarely worth much to a landowner as a source of rent, and the cost of keeping them in repair was such that land was often worth more without them. It was a common opinion, according to Nathaniel Kent (1775), to regard them as "incumbrances and clogs to...property".[290] Thus the mid-eighteenth-century surveyor of the Wiltshire manor of Pewsey, upon which there were many cottages, remarked that, "were it not for the consideration that poor people must have habitation somewhere", the owner would do best to get rid of them instead of wasting his timber on repairs.[291] The fact that cottagers also tended to cause damage when they illicitly helped themselves to fuel from the hedgerows and when they cut down branches of timber trees was another reason why their presence in any number often reduced rather than enhanced the value of an estate. Owners determined to keep poor rates down by limiting the number of potential claimants for relief would also take care to ensure that no outsiders secured a valid settlement in the parish, for once this was obtained the ratepayers would be obliged to support them and their families if they became destitute. If seasonal or casual labour over and above normal needs was required it could be imported from outside the parish, and unauthorized settlement by squatters on common land would be strictly prohibited. Prevention of permanent immigration from elsewhere was the purpose of a clause in the lease of a farm in West Knoyle (Wilts.), granted by the banker-landowner Henry Hoare in 1758, by which the tenant covenanted not to hire any servant for more than eleven months at a time without special licence from his landlord. West Knoyle belonged almost entirely to Hoare, who had enclosed most of it and radically reorganized the

[290] Kent, *Hints to Gentlemen*, p. 230. This was a view with which Kent vehemently disagreed.
[291] Wilts. RO, Savernake MSS: Correspondence: "Observations on the particulars of... Pewsey", c. 1765.

farms in the 1740s, and from thenceforth it became more and more of a 'closed' village.[292]

However, if the number of cottagers was clearly larger than the landlord and his principal tenants could provide with work in the ordinary course of events, and if it was impracticable to reduce their numbers, the alternative was to try to create additional employment so that as few as possible of them would be in need of relief. And quite apart from the matter of the rates, this was a policy dictated by common humanity, an emotion to which the great majority both of owners and of stewards were at least periodically subject. "I beg your Lordship would let old Guelder keep his cow", wrote the earl of Cardigan's steward at Deene (Northants.) in 1725 when a reallocation of pasturage amongst the cottagers was under discussion, "for he is very old and infirm and past his work, & I think cannot live a great while." And in a similar vein Richard Hill's agent told his master that although one Shropshire smallholding was worth more rent than its tenant was paying, yet the latter was "an old lame man and his wife old soe not capable of managing as others might do", and accordingly no increase was insisted upon during their lifetimes.[293] All the industrial crops were more labour-intensive than conventional forms of husbandry: some of the gentlemen who introduced woad onto their land in the early part of the seventeenth century avowedly did so in order to employ the poor,[294] and their successors continued with it at least in part for the same reason. Some of the crops had the additional advantage that they provided labour at times of the year when other forms of agricultural work were scarce. Coleseed did this; so did potatoes. The latter were also controversial amongst landowners, and in the north, where they were most widely met with before 1750, a prohibition upon their cultivation for sale was frequently enforced. Thus in 1729 a Cheshire tenant, Humphrey Mainwaring, was limited to growing only as many "as shall be absolutely necessary for the relief and support of his own family" in his seven-year lease of that date. However, their value to the poor, both as a source of employment and of cheap food, began to persuade an increasing number of owners to take a more lenient approach even by the middle of the eighteenth century. In 1758, for instance, it was reported to Sir John Heathcote that on an estate near his own in Lincolnshire the steward who had formerly restricted their planting was now permitting them to be cultivated without restraint.[295]

In some pastoral areas, where the labour requirements of a stock-raising or stock-fattening husbandry were particularly low, the growing of cereal

[292] Wilts. RO, 383/864: lease of farm at W. Knoyle, dated 23 Oct. 1758; and 297–9, 359.
[293] Wake and Webster, *Letters of Daniel Eaton*, pp. 12, 15; Salop. RO, 112/2,388–9.
[294] Joan Thirsk, *Economic Policy and Projects*, Oxford, 1978, p. 22.
[295] Salop. RO, 484/294: lease of lands in Dunham Massey, dated 1 Dec. 1729; LAO, 3 Anc. 7/3/12. See also C. S. Davies, *The Agricultural History of Cheshire*, Manchester, 1960, p. 131.

crops could fulfil the same purpose. In about 1673 Sir John Lowther declared that he grew grain on the lands he kept in hand in Cumberland not because he made any profit from it but because the ploughing, harrowing, carting, and threshing involved created much needed employment for the local poor.[296] And everywhere it was of course true that the more of his household supplies he produced on his own home farm or purchased in local rather than faraway markets, and the more of his servants he recruited locally, the fewer of the landowner's poorer neighbours and dependants would want employment. Even minor squires had half a dozen servants, excluding farm labourers. A major country family with an income of about £2,000 a year would certainly employ at least twenty full-timers, indoors and outdoors, from a housekeeper to kitchen maids, gardeners, stablehands, and the farm bailiff, although the number would be more or less according to the number of children to be looked after, the size of the gardens, whether or not the owner kept a pack of hounds, and so on. On the eve of the Civil War Sir Henry Slingsby kept 24 (16 men and 8 women) at his house in Yorkshire; the second Earl Cowper about 22 at Cole Green (Herts.) in 1742; and John Mytton about 26 at Halston Hall (Salop.) in 1756. The owner of a really large estate yielding an income of many thousands a year, and living in one of the great private palaces of the realm, gave work to many more. Thus in 1682 the earl of Devonshire had about 70 on his payroll at Chatsworth, and the earl of Rutland no fewer than 81 at Belvoir at about the same time, whilst in the mid eighteenth century the duke of Dorset had well over 50 at Knowle. Exceptionally great magnates of this period are sometimes found with 100 or more.[297] In addition, all landowners employed the services of a wide variety of skilled craftsmen and unskilled labourers as their occasions demanded, both in general husbandry work and in building, as well as in the provision of transport services.

The consumption of victuals by the family itself and all its employees was enormous. A handbook for the aspiring country gentleman published in 1717 suggested that a household of 25 to 30 would each week get through

> one small bullock, or part of a large one, containing about 350 or 400 pound weight; three sheep of about 150 pound each, or two larger; besides...fish, lamb, veal, bacon, etc. and fowls; about four bushels of wheat for bread and flour: about half a hogshead of stale-beer; near a hogshead of ale, and about two hogsheads of small-beer. The stale-beer brew'd after the rate of 10 or 12 bushels of malt to the hogshead...ale and small-beer brew'd together at 9 bushels the hogshead.[298]

[296] A. B. Appleby, *Famine in Tudor and Stuart England*, Liverpool, 1978, p. 160.
[297] G. Jacob, *The Country Gentleman's Vade Mecum*, London, 1717, pp. 46–7; D. Parsons, ed., *The Diary of Sir Henry Slingsby, Bart*, London, 1836, pp. 24–5; Herts. RO, Panshanger MSS A.2; Shrewsbury Public Library, Deed 13,667: list of servants at Halston, 1756; G. Scott Thomson, *Life in a Noble Household, 1641–1700*, London, 1937, p. 130; Davis, thesis, pp. 157 *et seq.*; V. Sackville-West, *Knole and the Sackvilles*, London, 1958 edn, p. 166.
[298] Jacob, *Country Gentleman's Vade Mecum*, p. 46.

All told, an important landowner resident upon his estates would, according to the scale of his domestic establishment, generate from several hundreds to as much as several thousands of pounds of purchasing power in the community of which he was inevitably the centre. To put it another way, much, though of course by no means all, of the rent income collected from the countryside surrounding the owner's mansion passed directly back into the hands of the tradesmen, farmers, labourers, etc. who provided a high proportion of the good and services which the owner and his family consumed. The increasing number of landowning families who lived away from their estates in London, York, Bath, or elsewhere, for part or even all of the year, and the growing number of manor houses downgraded to the status of mere farmsteads as a result of the consolidation of estate ownership, thus inevitably had an adverse effect upon employment in many localities. Rents were remitted away from the district in which they were collected, and to a considerable degree the demand for labour was transferred from the countryside to London, and to those particular districts which provided the capital with the bulk of its foodstuffs.

Whether or not landlords ever promoted mining or other forms of industrial activity on their estates primarily in order to provide opportunities for wage labour, there is no doubt that they welcomed its existence in part on this account. Thus in 1729 Lord Widdrington wrote with satisfaction about the opening of a new mine on one of his northern properties: "it is very plain that £100 a year more rent is added to the estate, besides what advantage may be made by the tenants being employed in leading great quantities of coal, which ever since I knew the estate has been the only means of enabling those who had small and dear takes to pay their rents". They were also generally ready to encourage their smallholders and cottagers to take advantage of any other by-employment which the locality offered. When Richard Hill found that many of the small tenants on his Shropshire estates were having trouble in paying their rent in 1721 he enquired of his steward whether they "did not have industry enough" to supplement their farming incomes by providing carting services.[299] But diversification into other forms of economic activity by major tenants whose farms provided them with more than enough to do was frowned on. For instance, in April 1703 Lord Fitzwilliam wrote with reference to one Northamptonshire tenant who had recently been up to London with his waggon, "I am sorry he neglects his farme so as to undertake such journeys. This time of the year is usually a busie time with the farmers... Wricraft will do as John Webster and Woollaston did, to gett ready money, carted away their time & neglected their farmes, which made them have bad cropps, & so were undone, & beggered my farmes besides."[300]

[299] J. W. F. Hill, ed., *The Letters and Papers of the Banks Family of Revesby Abbey*, Lincoln Rec. Soc., 1952, p. 103; Salop. RO, 112/2,387.
[300] Northants. RO, F (M) C. 1,262. See also Mordant, *Complete Steward*, I, pp. 414–16.

Where landlords were not prepared to go out of their way to provide work for their villages, they might be prepared to offer smallholders and cottagers in arrears with their rent, or in difficulties in any other way, the opportunity to work off their debts by undertaking paid work on their home farms or about their estates. Thus in 1736 it was agreed that Thomas Jacques, a Yorkshire tenant of Sir Tancred Robinson, who was a year behindhand with his rent, was to saw wood at 1d. per yard and help with repair jobs in other ways, in order to clear his account with his landlord.[301] And by an extension of the same principle landlords would sometimes try to ensure that if and when any extra labour was required over and above that provided by their permanent employees, whether in their own concerns or those of their tenants, it was shared out among as many of those in need as possible. Thus in 1652 Sir Ralph Verney requested his steward to confer with other major employers in the vicinity of Claydon "so that all men that can work, want work, and are without work, shall be given work according to theire abilities".[302] And more than a century later Mordant enjoined estate stewards as a general principle:

Whether it be cutting wood, hedging, ditching, trenching, draining, or any other labour, where there is more money to be earned than by other common labour... he should partly dispose of it according to the labourers necessity; not letting one do all that work which brings in the most money, and another... whose exigencies require the same or more be no partaker... when he or they are as capable of doing the work as the other.[303]

Finally, the landowner's own charitable giving could be used as an arm of estate policy, for not only could he satisfy his conscience and an inherited tradition of generosity by making small doles to the poorest villagers at Christmas time, but he could also secure a settlement for the children of cottagers in some other parish by paying an apprenticeship premium on their behalf. By this means he could relieve his ratepayer tenants of liability for their support, and that of their offspring, in the future.

### (d) Different landlords, different approaches

For much of this period economic conditions were such that for landowners able to see beyond the next rent day, financial self-interest reinforced ancient traditions of paternalism towards those who occupied their land, whereas in the century of booming rents and intense tenant competition for farms before 1640 it had more often run directly counter to them. Not that these traditions had become by any means moribund in the mid seventeenth century: indeed, they still had much life in them in the later nineteenth. Nevertheless the extent to which owners showed sympathy for tenants under pressure, their willingness to evict, and the degree of help they were prepared (or indeed

---

[301] Leeds Archives Dept, NH2,249B: Journal of Husbandry, under June 1736.
[302] M. M. Verney, *Verney Family during the Commonwealth*, p. 121.
[303] Mordant, *Complete Steward*, I, p. 342.

able) to provide naturally varied from estate to estate. So too did their attitude towards the raising of rents, at times and in places where economic circumstances made this a feasible proposition, and the extent of their willingness to push through schemes of enclosure or farm reorganization whose implementation adversely affected the well-being of some of their tenants. To a degree the varying attitudes of landlords reflected differences in their socio-economic status and the nature of their estates. Minor gentry, resident on their property, personally well acquainted with those to whom they let their land, and not so grand as to be immune from the influence of public opinion, had obvious reasons for behaving with restraint in dealings with their tenants. At the other end of the scale, great territorial magnates enjoyed so powerful an economic position that they were inviolable to attempts at blackmail by their tenants, and could often afford (financially) to contemplate with relative equanimity the prospect of empty farms which the pursuit of harsh and unbending policies towards their tenants might threaten. However, throughout the seventeenth and eighteenth centuries such people tended to be extremely sensitive to the reputation in which they were held in the localities where their estates lay. This might derive from a sense of personal or family pride, concern to secure political loyalty, or (especially by the eighteenth century) desire to be certain of votes at election time. Undoubtedly great landlords were sometimes ruthless with their tenantry, but when they were it was almost certainly the exception, not the rule. In 1624 the earl of Salisbury actually dismissed one of his agents in Dorset for being so assiduous in promoting his employer's immediate financial interests that he had provoked ill feeling on a scale which had begun to prejudice his wider concerns there. Towards the end of the seventeenth century the third earl of Clare (d. 1689) laid it down in his will that arrears of rent due to him should be collected only as far as his executor "shall judge of my tenants' abilities, not [being] willing they should be harassed for what they are unable to pay". Nor was his successor, the duke of Newcastle, an unduly oppressive or exacting landlord: at any rate on one occasion he admitted rather shamefacedly to his wife, "You think I am always too favourable to the tenants and maybe I am so." As a final example we may take the vastly wealthy Henry Fox, Lord Holland, who in 1761 asserted flatly that in no circumstances would he raise the rents on an estate whose purchase he was contemplating. And later still in the eighteenth century Arthur Young considered it to be common for the estates of great families to be under-rented for various reasons, of which one was their sense of "magnificence".[304]

In truth, however, the easy-going approach to their estates shown by so many (though not all) great landlords was as often a symptom of neglect

---

[304] Bettey, thesis, pp. 245–8; Davis, thesis, p. 181; BL, Add. MS 51,409: Lord Bolingbroke to H. Fox, 25 June 1761; A. Young, *A Six Months Tour through the North of England*, 4 vols., London, 1770, *IV*, p. 344.

as it was of conscious paternalism or political calculation. Most great men were not particularly interested in the details of their own business and financial affairs, and they did not necessarily employ agents who were either competent or honest. The second Earl Cowper's Hertfordshire steward in the 1740s had been promoted from footman, just the sort of appointment satirized so effectively by Mordant in his treatise on estate management published in 1761.[305] During the course of the eighteenth century the rise of the professional steward, well educated, with a considerable knowledge not only of agricultural techniques, but also of surveying, land law, and accounting, undoubtedly improved the quality of management on estates large enough to justify his employment. Nevertheless, as we have already observed,[306] professional stewards made their main impact after 1750, and down to the middle of the century such men were still not very numerous and only a minority of great estates had yet fallen under their care. The fact that middling gentry owners seem on the whole to have been more severe in their dealings with their tenants than the great magnates may be partly because they were less able to afford to be indulgent, but it was also partly because they generally managed their estates themselves and indeed often made it their principal concern.

On small estates owned by absentees, who often regarded them purely as a source of income and took no interest in their management, tenants were likely to be left very much to themselves: to sink or swim as best they could in hard times, and to get away with very favourable bargains in good ones. Thus Edward Gibbon senior so neglected his small property at Lenborough (Bucks.) over a period of several decades that when his son inherited it in 1771 he discovered that his lands rented at 23s. an acre whilst those of Lord Verney, with which they lay intermixed, were let for 29s.[307] As for the *nouveaux riches*, the moneyed men building up new estates out of the profits of careers in trade, law, or government service, they were often none too sensitive to the local animosity aroused when they applied their business acumen to estate management. Such people could be expected to take the opportunity provided by the financial difficulties of their tenants in times of depression to oust those whose holdings might be profitably combined together to make larger farms, as Sir Harbottle Grimston seems to have done on his Gorhambury (Herts.) estate in the later seventeenth century. They were more likely to push ahead with enclosure schemes, even if it meant displacing some of their tenants, as did Henry Hoare on the manor of West Knoyle (Wilts.) in the years after he purchased it in 1732.[308] They were also more likely to raise rents if there was the slightest possibility of getting away with it.

[305] C. G. A. Clay, thesis, p. 337; Mordant, *Complete Steward*, I, pp. 208–10.
[306] See above, pp. 307, 342–3.
[307] Norton, *Letters of Edward Gibbon*, I, pp. 277–8.
[308] C. G. A. Clay, thesis, pp. 49–51; Wilts. RO, 383/297–9, 359.

## THE MANAGEMENT OF ESTATES 371

Yet exceptions to all the generalizations made in the preceding paragraphs are easily found. Not all great landowners shared the attitudes of considered leniency or benign neglect assumed by most of their fellows. In the 1680s, according to the steward of a neighbouring estate, Lord Fitzharding promptly evicted those of his Somerset tenants who got into difficulties. Likewise, in March 1703 Lord Fitzwilliam issued curt instructions to his Northamptonshire steward: "Pray take away fro<sup>m</sup> such tenants as run in arreare their grounds...& dispose of those grounds to other tenants."[309] Nor were all new owners vigorous improvers. Some, like Lord Chancellor Cowper in Hertfordshire in the early eighteenth century, did virtually nothing to disturb the *status quo* on the estates they were building up. Others, like the financier Richard Hill, were interested in the rationalization of farm layout and other forms of improvement, but were prepared to proceed slowly and with consideration for those who lived on their land. Even the demanding and abrasive Sir Jacob Des Bouverie was capable of occasional acts of kindness towards tenants on the Kentish estate which otherwise he managed with single-minded attention to its profitability as an investment.[310]

Landowners with a very similar position in society are, in other words, to be found acting in very different ways, and even the same individual was not necessarily consistent in his approach to estate management. In 1655 the Kentish gentleman Sir George Sondes recorded, in what was undoubtedly intended to be a frank disclosure of his estate policy, that

I do not know that I let a farm to any tenant for more than I thought...it was really and honestly worth, nor for more than (had I been to have taken a farm) I would have given for it myself...Notwithstanding corn is so cheap, I give any tenant I have liberty to leave his farm...I never did, or ever will, force any tenant to keep his farm...I have never arrested or imprisoned any tenant for his rent, nor willingly used any severe course, if I could indifferently be satisfied any other way. I have scarce demanded my rents of late because of the cheapness of corn, but have made all the shifts I could to get money for my occasions, and spared my tenants, that they might not be forced to put off their corn at too mean rates.[311]

In contrast, his contemporary Sir Ralph Verney of Claydon (Bucks.), like Sondes head of a leading county family resident on his estates, was a harsh landlord, not lenient to those in arrears, unprepared to make any concessions to his tenants unless forced to do so, and determined to secure the highest rents he possibly could. By his own confession he was accustomed to demand a higher figure when letting a farm than the one he was prepared to accept.[312]

---

[309] Dorset RO, D.124.Estate. Somerset (box 173, bdle 1): Thomas Allen to Sir S. Fox, 1 Dec. 1690; Northants. RO, F (M) C. 1,258A.

[310] C. G. A. Clay, thesis, pp. 212–20; E. M. Jancey, 'An Eighteenth-Century Steward and his Work', *Shrops. Arch. Soc.*, LVI, 1, 1957–8, p. 39; Salop. RO, 112/2,388–90; G. E. Mingay, 'Estate Management in Eighteenth-Century Kent', *AHR*, IV, 1, 1956, pp. 108–9.

[311] Quoted in T & C, p. 143.

[312] Broad, thesis, pp. 247–9, 252.

The financial circumstances and personality traits of individual owners, or in the case of estates whose management was left largely to the discretion of an agent, the personality and degree of professional competence of the steward, were probably the most important factors determining the nature of management upon an estate. In 1654 William Blundell of Little Crosby told a correspondent that the custom of the country required his fellow landowners of south Lancashire to treat sitting tenants kindly in respect of the grant of new leases, but he noted that in practice the interpretation of this precept was "variable according to the landlord's humour, affection, etc."[313] The build-up of debt, as often the result of providing marriage portions for daughters and younger sons as of extravagance, was probably the most common cause of a change from inefficient estate management or indulgence towards the tenantry to the opposite. We have seen in an earlier section[314] that Verney had become heavily enmeshed in debt as a result of the Civil War, and another example from the following century is provided by Sir Leeke Okeover. The latter's attitude towards his Norfolk tenants at a time (1748) when they had suffered heavy losses from the cattle plague was so unbending that it provoked even his own steward to remonstrate: "I think you are very sevear for your rent & consider the misfortune of the countrey but very littell." Okeover's finances, however, gave him no leeway for generosity, and a few years later he was obliged to flee to France to escape his creditors.[315]

### 3. Landlords' investment in their estates

No landlord could treat his estate merely as a source of income to be exploited, at least for any length of time. Something had to be ploughed back into it if it was not to become completely run down, but it is very difficult to discover what proportion of estate income was characteristically reinvested in this period. Indeed, it is difficult enough to discover how much individual owners reinvested. Estate accounts covering a run of years survive in considerable numbers, especially from the eighteenth century, but even though the old 'charge–discharge' method of accounting had almost disappeared by 1700, they are rarely cast in a form from which expenditure upon repairs and improvements can reliably be deduced. Even when the accounts contain a separate heading under which such expenses are ostensibly gathered together, contemporary book-keeping practice was not sufficiently rigorous to ensure that all the relevant items were in fact placed there. Some are almost invariably to be found scattered haphazardly under other heads, whilst others may be omitted altogether.

---

[313] T. E. Gibson, ed., *Crosby Records: A Cavalier's Note Book*, London, 1880, pp. 254–5.
[314] See above, sect. A.1(c).
[315] Derbs. RO, D.231 M/E.4,587, 4,589, 4,592; also Calendar of Collection D.231 M, introduction, p. ii.

The value of timber provided off the estate (which might otherwise have been sold) would not normally be accounted for at its full cost, and often not at all: a serious omission, since where buildings were concerned this was likely to represent the largest single item of expenditure upon materials. Moreover, other materials forthcoming from the estate itself might well be treated in the same way, and these might include not only thatching, but the locally available brick substitutes, and even bricks and tiles themselves if they were made in the landlord's own kiln. Nor is it likely that all the labour costs incurred would be appropriately attributed. Permanent estate employees would be put to a wide variety of tasks during the course of the year, ranging from the normal routines of husbandry on the home farm through work in the kitchen garden to the discharge of essentially domestic errands. For instance, on one Shropshire estate in the mid eighteenth century the owner's standing orders for the employment of his servants directed that when the waggoners were not engaged in discharging their primary duty they were to do ordinary farm work, including the maintenance of the hedges and digging potatoes.[316] The contribution of many such workers to the maintenance or improvement of their employer's fixed capital might be small or it might be considerable, but it is normally impossible to ascertain, and it is likely to be only additional labour, specially hired for a particular purpose, which appears in the accounts under 'repairs and improvements'. And an understatement of labour costs, too, is a serious matter, for in most forms of improvement other than building they were overwhelmingly the most important element. Thus Thomas Manley remarked in 1669, "What wayes soever we take to pursue improvements, labour is almost the whole charge: pasture is to be mended by dung, sea-sand, clover, cinque-foyle, or the like; tillage by dung, sand, lime, chalk, marl, burning the turf or stubble, etc. in most of which labour is the principall charge."[317] Finally, there is a third category of cost which early modern accountants would be most unlikely to notice, and whose omission might be the most serious of all: that is the amount of fine or annual rent which the owner of the land sacrificed in order to compensate tenants who undertook repair or improvement work at their own expense.

Thus unless the very greatest care is exercised there is likely to be a degree, sometimes a very considerable degree, of underestimation in any conclusions drawn from contemporary records about the rate of landlord reinvestment. And even if all the considerations mentioned are borne in mind, it may not be possible to make appropriate allowance for them. In general landlords probably ploughed back more into their estates than they have commonly been given credit for. Certainly statements that individual owners reinvested such diminutive proportions of their income as a mere 1 or 2 per cent or

[316] Shrewsbury Public Library, Deed 13,667 (Halston, 1756).
[317] T. Manley, *Usury at Six Per Cent Examined*, London, 1669, p. 10.

less are almost certainly misleading. That may have been all they laid out in cash, but it is inconceivable that it was the sum total of their real expenditure. If it had been, then their property would have been deteriorating rapidly. Hedges, fences, and gates inevitably required periodic repairs, and the relatively flimsy wooden construction of so many farm buildings must have ensured a much more rapid rate of decay than in more recent times. In 1775 Nathaniel Kent reckoned that, having once been put into good repair, large farms might be kept so at an average cost of 7 per cent of their rent, small farms (upon which the buildings made up a higher proportion of the value) at 10 or 11 per cent.[318] These he claimed were figures based upon practical observation, but whilst they may have been correct for some parts of the country, they are likely to have been too high for others. Different types of farming each demanded a different range of buildings, and consequently there were considerable regional variations in the size of repair bills. Nor were standards of domestic housing uniform. Thus in the pastoral vale country of north Wiltshire Lord Bolingbroke could plausibly claim that repair costs were relatively low "because the tenants ask but for few out houses, and are contented with bad ones for themselves to live in". He was doubtless exaggerating when he said that "a farm of £50 a year in Kent has more building & requires more repairs consequently than any farm I have...[in Wiltshire]...of £200 pr annum", but the difference was large enough for his claim to go uncontradicted by his correspondent.[319] Besides, fifty or a hundred years before, farms had fewer buildings and lower standards of maintenance may have prevailed: certainly the agricultural buildings portrayed in seventeenth-century landscapes are rarely either substantial or in good order, and although this may partly reflect artistic preference for the picturesque, the limited amount of scholarly investigation which has been undertaken seems to confirm the general accuracy of the impression thus created. Nevertheless, taking the country as a whole, the cost of keeping farms in good enough repair to hold their rent can scarcely have fallen below 4–5 per cent of the gross income they were capable of yielding, and was probably rather higher. And in the last resort this cost was inescapably the landlord's. As we have seen, he did not necessarily have to meet it directly, but paying it indirectly via an allowance in the rent cost him almost as much, though it certainly saved him trouble. If an owner did skimp his expenditure on repairs for any significant period, either through negligence or financial stringency, then sooner or later he would be obliged to make up for it with an expensive campaign of estate expenditure to put to rights everything that had gone wrong in the meanwhile.

It is probable, indeed, that on all save the very best-administered estates, the proportion of the landlord's income laid out on repairs fluctuated sharply

[318] Kent, *Hints to Gentlemen of Landed Property*, pp. 207–8.
[319] BL, Add. MS 51,409: Lord Bolingbroke to H. Fox, 20 and 29 June 1761.

from generation to generation, and over even shorter periods, according to the interests and circumstances of each successive owner. Thus, according to Mingay, on the Nottinghamshire estates of the duke of Kingston cash expenditure on repairs was roughly 4 per cent of rent income in the 1740s, but no more than 1.4 per cent in the 1750s.[320] And undoubtedly this pattern generally prevailed in respect of expenditure on improvements in the sense of additions to fixed capital, although it must be said that, if it is difficult to ascertain total expenditure on repairs and improvements in this period, in most cases it is virtually impossible to separate the two with any confidence.[321] On most estates the deployment of substantial sums on improvements seems to have occurred only occasionally, and long periods might elapse during which such expenditure dwindled to the barest trickle. Difficulty in reletting a farm during a period of agricultural depression might oblige an owner to provide it with a new set of buildings, or a new dwelling house. As one estate agent commented (c. 1723), à propos the need to make some badly run-down holdings more attractive, "beggarly houses will bring none but beggarly tenants".[322] Indeed, when they felt that they were in a strong bargaining position potential tenants would often insist upon some new building as a condition of accepting the rent the owner demanded.[323]

However, whether the total volume of landlord investment actually rose in difficult times is much less certain. The prospect of poor prices for the foreseeable future may well have deterred them from undertaking any improvements other than those whose benefits would accrue immediately, with the result that there was rather a change in the form of investment, which may indeed have masked a drop in total outlays. Certainly some late-seventeenth-century writers, Manley for instance, thought that poor market prospects were inhibiting landlords from investing more.[324] Alternatively, an owner faced with serious financial difficulties might deliberately pursue a policy of heavy investment for a few years in order to increase his estate income. Many of them, we have already noticed in another context, certainly did this in the aftermath of the Civil War.[325] Another example is provided by the first Viscount Grimston. When he first inherited the Gorhambury estate in 1700 he was so heavily in debt, because of encumbrances laid upon it by his predecessor, that he could barely afford to undertake even the most necessary repairs. However, once the immediate crisis was over he began to plough back considerable sums, and although no total figures are available, the scale of his improvements is indicated by the fact that in 1723 he laid out over £500 on just one single farm at a time when the total income

[320] G. E. Mingay, 'The Agricultural Depression, 1730–1750', EcHR, 2nd ser., VIII, 1956, p. 330.
[321] This remains true of estate accounts from a much later period; see B. A. Holderness, 'Landlord's Capital Formation in East Anglia, 1750–1850', EcHR, 2nd ser., XXV, 1972, p. 435.
[322] LAO, Tyrwhitt Collection 2/2/21: notes on the Lincs. estate by Thomas Lowe, c. 1723.
[323] For instance, LAO, Monson Collection 7/13/60; E. Riding RO, DDWA/12/1(e).
[324] Manley, loc. cit.          [325] See above, sect. A.1(c).

from his estates was less than £4,000 a year gross.³²⁶ Sometimes the opposite set of circumstances, that is, a temporary surplus of income over outgoings, might also lead to an unusually high level of expenditure on the estate. Thus when the estates of the Hotham family in the East Riding were inherited by a small child in 1738, the trustees who managed it on his behalf invested much larger sums on both repairs and new building on tenant farms than previous owners had felt able to afford.³²⁷ Quite apart from the inherent shortcomings of the figures themselves, the sums invested by individual landowners over relatively short periods do not, therefore, tell us very much about the average rate attained by the class as a whole. What this may have been remains almost completely obscure. Holderness has suggested that "it will be very surprising if the generality of *rentier* estates is found to have laid out more than five per cent of gross rents at most" in the creation of fresh capital assets (as opposed to repairs and maintenance), and no better estimate is yet available.³²⁸

It seems probable that estates upon which a high level of expenditure upon improvements was maintained over a long period were relatively few. Indeed, the only properly documented example of this which has yet come to light is provided by the Holkham estate of the Coke family in Norfolk, where roughly £24,000, or about 8 per cent of the gross rent received, was laid out in this way over the years 1722 to 1759. This was over and above what was spent on running repairs, which accounted for rather more than as much again, and financed the enclosure of open-field strips; the ploughing up, fencing, hedging, and marling of rough grazing land; and the construction of new farm buildings as existing holdings were reorganized and new ones created from scratch.³²⁹ The Coke property lay on poor, sandy heathland, and these, along with other thin, quick-draining soils, for instance on the chalk and limestone uplands, were those which benefited most directly from the new crops and husbandry courses being introduced in this period. Formerly incapable of producing grain on anything but an occasional basis, and thus used mainly as sheepwalk, they could now be made to support a highly productive mixed husbandry, provided that the necessary capital to develop them was forthcoming. There may, therefore, have been other great landowners with estates in areas like Salisbury Plain, the Sussex Downs, or the Yorkshire Wolds, who pursued a similar policy of almost continuous improvement, at least by the later decades of the period. Where the new forms of husbandry could be introduced without all the preliminary investment required in the districts just mentioned, however, or where they could not be introduced at all, investment in improvements was almost

---

³²⁶ C. G. A. Clay, thesis, pp. 143–4.    ³²⁷ Roebuck, thesis, pp. 99–102.
³²⁸ B. A. Holderness, 'Capital Formation in Agriculture', in J. P. P. Higgins and S. Pollard, eds., *Aspects of Capital Investment in Great Britain, 1750–1850*, London, 1971, p. 178.
³²⁹ Parker, *Coke of Norfolk*, pp. 40–57.

inevitably more spasmodic. Thus on the Leveson-Gower property in Staffordshire, the second Earl Gower laid out perhaps £2,000 on the enclosure of Lightwood Forest between 1733 and 1736, but, this apart, over the whole of the 1730s and 1740s his cash outlays on the estate fluctuated between £247 in 1734 and £47 in 1742. They averaged only £112 a year on a rental which rose from £1,500 to £1,800 a year during the two decades in question.[330]

When landowners laid out money on improvements they did so either to forestall a decrease in rent or to secure an increase. The rate of return they secured from their investment naturally varied greatly, according to the nature of the scheme, the competence and economy with which it was carried out, the course of prices, and so on, but in the first half of the eighteenth century it seems usually to have been between 6 and 12 per cent a year. Major undertakings, such as the enclosure of large areas of waste or open-field arable, or the floating of a large water meadow, might yield more, but higher rates were probably the exception rather than the rule. When Sir Stephen Fox laid out £425 on new farm buildings on his estate at Chiswick (Middx) in the first decade of the century, he reckoned on a 6 per cent return. In 1726 Sir More Molyneux was advised that the enclosure of thirteen acres of common land on his Lancashire estate would, after the expense of ditching and marling it had been met, "make near double interest", meaning nearly 10 per cent.[331] Similarly, in 1749 one of the duke of Bedford's agents recommended expenditure of £200–250 upon Fitzford Barton, a farm in Devon then rented at £70 a year, which would, he thought, enable the rent to be raised to £100 after five or six years. This again implies expectation of a return of the order of 10 per cent.[332]

The long-term fall in the rate of interest on borrowed funds was probably not directly relevant to the progress of agricultural improvement, for few owners borrowed for this purpose in the period with which we are concerned. On the other hand, the upward movement in the price of land may very well have been. In the later seventeenth century, and even during the War of the Spanish Succession, land in most areas could be bought at well below twenty years' purchase. Often, indeed, it could be had for eighteen or even sixteen times its value, so that a purchaser could secure a financial return of 5 or 6 per cent gross (perhaps 4 or 5 per cent net of all outgoings), besides the social return which ownership of an enlarged estate inevitably conveyed. By the 1730s, however, twenty-eight to thirty years' purchase was no uncommon price, so that the yield to the buyer had dropped

---

[330] Wordie, thesis, pp. 74, 312.

[331] "Double interest" means, in this context, double the legal maximum rate of interest, which after 1714 was 5 per cent.

[332] BL, Add. MS 51,324, ff. 124, 147; GMR, LM 778/28/29; Devon RO, Bedford MSS W1,258/L2/12.

to only $3\frac{1}{2}$–$3\frac{1}{3}$ per cent gross (3 per cent or less net). The disparity between the rate of return to be obtained from buying more land and investing capital in the improvement of land already held had therefore widened very greatly, and widened yet further in the third quarter of the century. Land prices seem to have fallen back somewhat in the 1740s, but they rose higher than ever in the 1760s and early 1770s, in many areas to well over thirty years' purchase, thrusting the rate of return on purchases even lower, whilst more buoyant rents tended to push up the return on improvements. In the book he published in 1775 Nathaniel Kent considered that improvements could be expected to yield three or four times the return to be obtained from buying land.[333] These developments ought to have increased the propensity of owners to plough surplus funds back into their estates. On the other hand, neither the timing nor the extent of any increase in the rate of landlord investment can be properly established, so that it is impossible to know how important these developments may have been. Indeed, since even the unsatisfactory evidence from which generalizations about such investment in the eighteenth century have been attempted is not available for the later seventeenth, the assumption that there was an increase before 1750 is insecurely based.

[333] C. Clay, 'The Price of Freehold Land in the Later Seventeenth and Eighteenth Centuries', EcHR, 2nd ser., XXVII, 1974; Kent, *Hints to Gentlemen*, pp. 9–10.

# 6
# LANDLORDS AND ESTATE MANAGEMENT IN WALES, 1640–1750

Welsh landowners in these years were generally poor by English standards. The different income groups adopted by Habakkuk to distinguish the categories of great landowners (over £3,000 a year), substantial squires (£800 to £2,000), and landed gentry (£800 and under) within mid-seventeenth-century English landed society have to be adjusted downwards when considering such propertied ranks in a Welsh context: the great landowners were those of £2,000 and over, and the substantial squires those with rentals between £500 and £2,000, while the gentry stretched further down the social pyramid than did their English counterparts.[1] Indeed, it has been rightly stressed that in economic terms many Welsh gentry belonged properly to the ranks of the yeoman-freeholders. What sustained and legitimized their anxious, proud claims to gentility were their ancient pedigrees rather than their insufficient fortunes.[2] For, if wealth in land as well as noble descent was important for a nobleman in seventeenth-century Wales, a small freeholder, for his part, could claim gentry status solely on the strength of his pedigree. So low down the economic scale did Welsh gentry reach that certain of their members, like those of Pembrokeshire in the 1730s, acted as chief or high constables in their respective hundreds.[3]

The poverty of Welsh landowners was attested by certain contemporaries aware of the lack of suitable men for local office. The celebrated observation of Major General Berry to Secretary Thurloe that in Wales "You will sooner find 50 men of £50 per ann. than five of an hundred", if impressionistic,

---

I would like to express my thanks to Professor Glanmor Williams, Professor G. E. Mingay, Dr Prys Morgan, Dr Hugh Dunthorne, and Dr Joanna Martin for their reading of the manuscript and their helpful comments. Mr G. B. Lewis of the Geography Department, Swansea, constructed the map and Mrs Rhiannon Brown identified the location of certain mansions. The staffs of a number of record offices and libraries rendered ready assistance, but in particular I am indebted to those of the Manuscripts Department at the National Library of Wales and at Carmarthen Record Office for their invaluable help and guidance.

[1] H. J. Habakkuk, 'English Landownership, 1680–1740', EcHR, x, 1940, p. 3; Keith Williams-Jones, *A Calendar of the Merioneth Quarter Sessions Rolls, I, 1733–65*, Aberystwyth, 1965, p. lxi n. 2.

[2] F. Jones, 'An Approach to Welsh Genealogy', *Hon. Soc. Cymmrodorion*, 1948, p. 432; Gwyn Thomas, 'A Study of the Changes in the Tradition of Welsh Poetry in North Wales in the Seventeenth Century', unpub. Oxford Univ. D.Phil. thesis, 1966, p. 4; D. Defoe, *A Tour of the Whole Island of Great Britain*, 4th edn, 4 vols., 1748, II, p. 379; W. R., *Wallography: or the Britton Describ'd*, London, 1682, published in a later edition in 1738 under the title *Welch Travels*.

[3] Pembs. RO, Quarter Sessions Order Book, 1738–48: entry for 15 Apr. 1735; Thomas, *op. cit.*, p. 150.

Fig. 1. Wales: Distribution of various gentry seats.

nevertheless revealed a sound grasp of realities.⁴ Again, it was remarked by certain prominent Anglesey landowners in 1676 that the burdensome office of sheriff might well prove ruinous to the many men of small estates of that county, "the choice of men of better estates in this county for that office being not many as we all well know". Fertile and accessible areas, of course, boasted richer gentry than did less favoured ones. It was thus observed in the 1650s how Merioneth was "far inferior to Denbighshire for greatness and number of gentry".⁵

The mid- and late-seventeenth-century rentals assembled in the appendix to this chapter show that there were few large owners in Glamorgan and Anglesey, and this was doubtless true of other Welsh counties. The substantial squires were more numerous but still relatively sparse. In remote Anglesey during the personal government of Charles I they were confined to the houses of Prysaeddfed, Rhosmor, and Bodeon, with annual incomes of £700–£800, and to the lesser ones of Monachdy and Llugwy, of £500.⁶ The Glamorgan substantial squires were predictably richer: eleven houses in 1645 had yearly incomes of between £1,000 and £2,000 while a further eleven were between £500 and £1,000.⁷ By far the most numerous category were the gentry proper. Thus below the five substantial squires listed for Anglesey came twenty families of £100 to £500. Again, the twenty-two substantial Glamorgan 'county' squires were surrounded by many more 'parish' gentry: some eight were recorded as between £300 and £500, and "men from £10 to £200 – more than 100 men in the county". At about £60 to £100 a year the gentry and yeoman freeholders in all areas of Wales shaded imperceptibly into one another. The clear economic distinction obtaining in England between gentry as rentiers and yeomen as owner-occupiers was blurred by the tendency, already noted, for small freeholders to style themselves "gent." on the basis either of claims to ancestry or that they simply considered themselves such and desired the recognition of others.⁸

What impact did the Civil War have upon the predominantly royalist Welsh landowners? There was no cataclysmic disintegration of Welsh estates and redistribution of land nor a general extinction of the old county families. In Glamorgan, for example, there was very little change in the composition of landownership in 1677 from what had obtained in 1645.⁹ The number

⁴ *Thurloe State Papers*, London, 1742, *IV*, p. 316, cited by A. H. Dodd, *Studies in Stuart Wales*, 2nd edn, Cardiff, 1971, p. 2. See pp. 14–15 for the level of income of Welsh landowners.

⁵ NLW, Carreglwyd MSS, ser. ii, MS 58, undated but of the seventeenth century; Dodd, *op. cit.*, p. 14; W. J. Smith, ed., *Calendar of Salusbury Correspondence*, Cardiff, 1954: Salusbury MS 395.

⁶ Huntington Library, San Marino, Calif., EL 7,155.

⁷ R. Symonds, *Diary of the Marches of the Royal Army during the Great Civil War*, Camden Soc., OS LXXIV, 1859, pp. 216–17.

⁸ For the situation in Glamorgan, see M. I. Williams, 'Agriculture and Society in Glamorgan 1660–1760', unpub. Leicester Univ. Ph.D. thesis, 1967, p. 45.

⁹ A. H. Dodd, *Life in Wales*, London, 1972, p. 92. For 'List of Glamorganshire Gentry" drawn up in 1677, see PRO, SP 29/398, ff. 283–4, quoted in I. G. Jones, 'Glamorgan Politics from 1660 to 1790', in *The Glamorgan County History*, *IV*, ed. Glanmor Williams, Cardiff, 1976, p. 380.

of confiscated estates in Wales of private royalists who were unable or ineligible to compound for their delinquency totalled a mere thirty-three or so; the majority lay in the border counties, especially Monmouthshire, and fell within the third Act for Sale (4 August 1652) which confiscated the lands of minor royalists and largely comprised recusants who, but for their religion, would have been allowed to compound.[10] Not all thirty-three estates were actually sold, and it is likely from what happened elsewhere in Britain that of those which were alienated most were regained later.[11] The limited research so far undertaken into the Welsh situation reveals that the lands of John Robinson of Gwersyllt in Denbighshire and Monachdy in Anglesey were repurchased, though at a ruinously high cost, and that the estate of John Morgan of Trawsfynydd, Merioneth, was purchased in 1654 from the Commonwealth by Sir Richard Lloyd of Esclus (near Wrexham), a Welsh lawyer who (in the light of the address of Morgan to him – "your assured loving kinsman") may well have been instrumental in assisting Morgan in the recovery of his property.[12] The lands in south Wales of the earl of Worcester and of John Barlow of Slebech were restored after 1660. Although this happened infrequently, confiscated property, like, for example, the extensive Hawarden estate, could be permanently alienated.[13]

Most Welsh landowners paid a fine to compound for their delinquency, thereby releasing their estates from sequestration. As Habakkuk has argued, it is the possible repercussions that these fines had on the 'voluntary' sale of lands in order to raise money to pay them that is vital in determining the amount of property that permanently changed hands in these years. Fines were commonly levied on Welsh estates at a tenth or a sixth of capital values and a few at a third. Thus most paid a fine amounting to two or three years' annual value of their properties. Some of the more influential royalists like the earl of Carbery in south Wales and Sir John Owen of Clenennau in the north escaped lightly, thanks to the intervention on their behalf of powerful kinsmen and friends from the opposite camp.[14]

Many less favoured families were embarrassed by the weight of these fines, although precisely how many sold parts of their estates to raise money to

[10] C. H. Firth and R. S. Rait, eds., *Acts and Ordinances of the Interregnum, 1642–60*, 3 vols., London, 1911, II.

[11] J. Thirsk, 'The Restoration Land Settlement', *JMH*, XXVI, 4, 1954, p. 323; P. G. Holiday, 'Land Sales and Repurchases in Yorkshire after the Civil Wars, 1650–1670', *Northern Hist.*, V, 1970, p. 89; A. H. Dodd, 'The Pattern of Politics in Stuart Wales', *Hon. Soc. Cymmrodorion*, 1948, p. 71.

[12] Dodd, *Studies in Stuart Wales*, p. 199; NLW, Peniarth MSS 1,481, 1,461, 1,460, 1,435–51, 1,464, 1,413, 1,502, 1,480, 1,538; NLW, Puleston MSS 1,483–99.

[13] A. G. Veysey, 'Col. Philip Jones, 1618–74', *Hon. Soc. Cymmrodorion*, 1966, pt 2, p. 337; NLW, Badminton, ii, MS 11,749; F. Green, 'The Barlows of Slebech', *W. Wales Hist. Rec.*, III, p. 43; NLW, Hawarden MSS 331, 335, 337, 341, 342, 346, 348; A. H. Dodd, 'Flintshire Politics in the Seventeenth Century', *Flints. Hist. Soc.*, 1953–4, pp. 38–9.

[14] H. J. Habakkuk, 'Landowners and the Civil War', *EcHR*, 2nd ser., XVIII, 1965, pp. 130–2; F. Jones, 'The Vaughans of Golden Grove, I: The Earls of Carbery', *Hon. Soc. Cymmrodorion*, 1963, pt 1, p. 118; A. H. Dodd, 'Caernarvonshire in the Civil War', *Caerns. Hist. Soc.*, XIV, 1953, pp. 28–9.

meet them is problematic. Small owners' estate records simply do not survive, and the crucial possibility is that these were the most likely to have to sell despite the likely disincentive of a glutted land market. Again, sales made in these years may well have been a consequence (as in the case of those of Sir William Thomas, MP, of Carnarvon) of essentially pre-Civil War difficulties.[15] A few fragmentary pieces of evidence do point, however, to the sale of lands stemming directly from the burden of fines. A mid-eighteenth-century pedigree book stated that "William Thomas Esq. [of Danygraig, Swansea] father of the late William Thomas suffered much for his loyalty to King Charles I in the Civil Wars and was obliged to sell part of his estate at Llandilotalybont [Glam.] in order to prevent it being sequestered." (He was fined £786 in 1646.)[16] Again, the imprisonment in 1646 of Sir Nicholas Kemeys of Cefn Mably, Glamorgan, meant that he could not prosecute his composition "for want of liberty to raise money by sale of lands".[17] Although some at least, and perhaps a sizeable number, were forced to sell, others who were financially strained, like, for example, Sir Philip Jones of the Llanarth and Treowen estates, Monmouthshire, resorted instead to borrowing by mortgaging their lands or entering into bonds. Still others relied for financial help on family or friends or, like Sir John Stepney of Prendergast, Pembrokeshire, on the local corporation.[18]

Some land came on the market from the sale of church and crown property. Much church property was to be irretrievably lost during the upheaval of these years.[19] The alienation of crown lands in Wales was the continuation of a practice that had been going on since Elizabeth I's reign and was a response to financial exigencies. Particularly heavy alienations occurred in the reign of Charles I and under the Commonwealth when manors and other land revenues of the crown were sold for ever, for two or three lives, or for terms of years. Thus in the Commonwealth period land revenues from properties in all Welsh counties, amounting to about £4,500 a year, were granted to various purchasers.[20]

[15] Habakkuk, 'Landowners and the Civil War', p. 139; CCC, IV, p. 2,740; Dodd, 'Flintshire Politics', p. 33.

[16] NLW, Castell Gorfod MS 8: pedigree book of Gabriel Powell of Swansea. This reference was kindly given me by Dr Prys Morgan of Swansea. CCC, II, pp. 1,175–6.

[17] CCC, II, p. 1,276.

[18] NLW, Kyrle Fletcher MSS, pcl A, no. 19: letter of 10 Dec. 1648; NLW, *Calendar of the Wynn (of Gwydir) Papers, 1515–1690*, Aberystwyth, 1926, MSS 2,104, 2,105; Carmarthen RO, Derwydd H.44; F. Green, 'The Stepneys of Prendergast', *W. Wales Hist. Rec.*, VII, 1917–18, p. 132.

[19] A. H. Dodd, 'The Church in Wales during the Reformation Period', *Welsh Church Congress Handbook*, 1953, pp. 38–9.

[20] NLW, MS 9,475E: "Twelfth Report of the Commissioners appointed to inquire into the state of...Land Revenues of the Crown, 25 May 1792"; Llanfair Brynodol MS 68: "An Account of the Land Revenue belonging to the Crown in Wales when sold by Oliver Cromwell as part of the estate of Charles Stuart".

The limited amount of land entering the market led to the founding of a number of new landed families as well as adding to the patrimonies of existing ones. Thus leading parliamentarians like Colonel Philip Jones and his 'creatures' built up estates in south Wales while in the north parliamentary men like George Twistleton, Colonel John Carter, John Glynne, Colonel John Jones, and John Peck bought royalist lands.[21] As stressed, however, there was no real upset in the balance of landed property. Nevertheless, many landowners suffered temporary financial difficulties. A few never recovered and were forced to sell out after 1660. What were the reasons for such indebtedness? Besides having to borrow money on interest to pay their fines, many were further impoverished by the assessments levied on them first by the king and later by parliament, assessments which far exceeded the usual level of taxation. Many petitions were presented from north and south Wales complaining of the burden of taxation and, allowing for the exaggerated nature of such appeals, it is clear that the gentry were feeling the pinch.[22] Landowners sometimes lightened their burdens by passing on demands to their poorer landless neighbours, including their tenantry. Thus Thomas Salusbury informed Thomas Bulkeley of Baron Hill in August 1642 that the gentry of Denbighshire and Flintshire in raising £1,500 for the royal cause were to "make themselves savers as much as they could" by persuading the common people to contribute.[23]

Such additional taxation bore extra heavily upon Welsh landowners because of the economic dislocation of this exporting region resulting from the royal embargo on the all-important droving trade with London and the interference with the sale of Welsh cottons at Shrewsbury. Landowners suffered from the disruption in trade and the general commotion accompanying hostilities both directly through their own farming activities and (more important) indirectly through the failure of tenants to meet their rents, as, for example, on the Trevalun estate, Denbighshire, in 1642, and in Merioneth in 1643.[24] Tenants' ability to pay their rents was particularly hampered in those areas where forays for cattle, horses, sheep, and other provisions were made by the armies of both sides. Although the limited campaigning area meant that the problem was not widespread, where it did occur the effects

[21] Veysey, *op. cit.*, pp. 316–39; H. Thomas, *A History of Wales 1485–1660*, Cardiff, 1972, pp. 234–6; *CJ*, VII, pp. 656, 663, 684, 691, 697; Dodd, *Studies in Stuart Wales*, pp. 125–6; A. H. Dodd, 'The Civil War in East Denbighshire', *Denbs. Hist. Soc.*, III, 1954, p. 79; Dodd, 'Flintshire Politics', pp. 38–9.

[22] NLW, Crosse of Shaw Hill MS 1,123; B. E. Howells, ed., *A Calendar of Letters relating to North Wales*, Cardiff, 1967, pp. 61–2: Llanfair Brynodol letters, no. 62; NLW, Plymouth MS 1,368.

[23] Smith, *op. cit.*: Llewenny MS 265; see also Dodd, 'Caernarvonshire in the Civil War', p. 17.

[24] NLW, *Calendar of the Wynn Papers*, MS 1,724: copy of a petition (1643) by the inhabitants of north Wales to Charles I for safe conduct of the clothiers and drovers through the royalist forces; Clwyd RO, DG. 3,275: letter of 23 July 1642 from the Trevalun estate agent; NLW, Dolfriog MS 64: letter of 3 Feb. 1643 from Kathrin Wynne.

could be devastating. The siege of Montgomery Castle in 1644, for instance, resulted in heavy losses of rent from Lord Herbert's tenants.[25] Of course, plundering not only reduced landowners' incomes by interrupting the payment of rents. It could have a more injurious effect in damage done to the fabric of houses, loss of personalty (especially jewels and plate), and confiscation of livestock on home farms. A few royalist owners like those of Mathafarn (Mont.), Ynysmaengwyn and Caergai (Mer.), Picton Castle (Pembs.), Crosswood (Cards.), Gwydir (Caerns.), and Montgomery Castle suffered heavy losses of this nature.[26]

Although many Welsh landowners were financially embarrassed, for most of them these difficulties were only temporary and did not lead to ultimate alienation of their estates. But properties were often mortgaged in the sixties and seventies as a direct consequence of such debts, and it was particularly fortunate that owners at this time could avail themselves of the long-term mortgage. Such temporary discomforts were experienced, for example, by the earl of Carbery, by Robert Anwyl of Park, Merioneth, and by Major General Rowland Laugharne of St Bride's, Pembrokeshire, all staunch royalists.[27] A handful of families, however, failed to recover. Such casualties included the royalists Richard Dutton of Cefn y Wern, Denbighshire (he sold out to Thomas Myddelton of Chirk Castle in 1653), Colonel Edward Lloyd of Llanvorda, Denbighshire (the estate was sold by his son in 1675 to Sir William Williams), Captain Ellis Sutton of Gwersyllt Issa, Flintshire (he sold out in or before 1684 to Sir Jeffrey Shakerley, a former royalist officer), Bevis Lloyd of Carreg y Pennil, Denbighshire (he sold the estate to Chirk Castle in 1672), and the Roundhead Simon Thelwall of Plas y Ward, Denbighshire (part of the estate was sold by his grandson in 1679).[28]

According to Habakkuk and Mingay, there was a marked tendency within

[25] W. J. Smith, ed., *Herbert Correspondence*, Cardiff, 1963, pt 2, pp. 118–19, no. 179: certificates of losses of Lord Herbert.
[26] Dodd, *Life in Wales*, p. 92; significantly, the Philippses of Picton Castle were to complain in a later Chancery suit of the temporary financial embarrassment arising from Gerard's plundering the castle in 1643 – see F. Jones, 'The Pageantry of Picton', in B. Morris, ed., *The Slebech Story*, Haverfordwest, 1948, p. 62.
[27] F. Jones, 'The Vaughans of Golden Grove, I: The Earls of Carbery', pp. 120–1; H. F. J. Vaughan, 'Private Papers of Richard Vaughan, Earl of Carbery', *Arch. Camb.*, 1881, p. 220; 'Wales at the Restoration', *Old Wales*, III, 1907, p. 22; NLW, Wigfair MS 3, letter no. 10: of 1 Mar. 1671 of Sarah Gwynne of Park; A. L. Leach, *The History of the Civil War (1642–49) in Pembrokeshire*, London, 1937, pp. 215–16; NLW, MS 4,989D.
[28] G. R. Thomas, 'Sir Thomas Myddelton ii: 1586–1666', unpub. Univ. of Wales M.A. thesis, 1968, p. 296; NLW, Brogyntyn MS 2,566: letter book of Edward Lloyd of Llanvorda, letter of 28 Oct. 1680 to R. Evans; W. M. Myddelton, ed., *Chirk Castle Accounts, 1666–1753*, Manchester, 1931, pp. 127 n. 696, 133 n. 748, 56–7 n. 276; T. Pennant, *Tours in Wales*, ed. J. Rhys, 3 vols., Caernarvon, 1883, I, pp. 391–2; NLW, Wynnstay Old Misc. Rental, vol. IV: purchases of part of Plas y Ward from Edward Thelwall. Since this chapter was prepared, the Wynnstay rentals have been scheduled and numbers assigned to them. Details concerning these may be found in the "Schedule of Wynnstay Archives", vol. I, at NLW.

English landownership from the Restoration to the mid eighteenth century for land to gravitate towards the large estates while at the same time there was an appreciable decrease in the area owned by the lesser gentry and freeholders.[29] As we shall see, this model has recently been questioned by a number of historians. As far as Wales was concerned, these years certainly witnessed the growth of large estates of £2,000 and over. But the development was a much slower one and the decline of the smaller gentry and freeholders was very limited. The large owners benefited as they had always done from their relatively greater success in the marriage market. But now, Habakkuk has argued, they could hold on to such advantages by the new device of the strict settlement, which made estates far more secure than they had been previously.[30] Despite Clay's qualifications as to the reality of this advantage in being able to carry off the richest heiresses, my impression is that they did not operate significantly enough within Welsh landed society to prevent the greatest owners from benefiting in many instances over their lesser landed neighbours in the 'success' of their marriages. Welsh owners of substantial estates often extended them in these years by arranging suitable matches, and one aspect of this policy was the increasing extent to which marriages were made with English families.[31] The claim made by Habakkuk that the more numerous marriages to brides who were not heiresses but who had large dowries once again worked in favour of the large owners has also been questioned by Clay.[32] He contends that too much has been made of the importance of marriage portions in extending the estates of the large owners through purchase. Martin has shown that as far as Glamorgan estates were concerned, the bride's dowry was often put to uses other than the purchase of land, and this may well have been so for other Welsh areas.[33] On the other hand, the fact that large portions were sometimes laid out in paying off debts meant that certain estates were rescued from being broken up.[34]

While marriage and inheritance, therefore, worked in favour of the large properties, it is likely, as Clay argues, that the vital importance of the marriage and inheritance factor in these years sprang not so much from the

[29] Habakkuk, 'English Landownership', pp. 2–5; G. E. Mingay, *English Landed Society in the Eighteenth Century*, London, 1963, p. 50.

[30] H. J. Habakkuk, 'Marriage Settlements in the Eighteenth Century', RHS, 4th ser., XXXII, 1950, pp. 27–8.

[31] C. Clay, 'Marriage, Inheritance, and the Rise of Large Estates in England, 1660–1815', EcHR, 2nd ser., XXI, 3, 1968, pp. 503–7. For heiresses of great estates in Glamorgan, see J. O. Martin, 'The Landed Estate in Glamorgan, circa 1660–1760', unpub. Cambridge Univ. Ph.D. thesis, 1978, pp. 226–8.

[32] Habakkuk, 'Marriage Settlements', p. 28; Clay, *op. cit.*, pp. 507–9.

[33] Martin, thesis, pp. 234–7.

[34] *Ibid.*, p. 236; F. Jones, 'The Old Families of Wales', in *Wales in the Eighteenth Century*, ed. D. Moore, Swansea, 1976, pp. 38–9; see, e.g., NLW, Slebech MSS 7,465–6: marriage settlement of 13 Apr. 1708 between John Barlow and Ann Harcourt.

legal innovations of the late seventeenth century as from the remarkable failure of male heirs, which meant that estates were being concentrated within fewer families through marriage and inheritance.[35] The important point to stress here is that such a failure of male heirs occurred in all ranks of landed society, and so marriage and inheritance led to the rise of small as well as large landowning families. There was an unusually high failure rate of male heirs in the Welsh counties of Merioneth, Anglesey, Brecknock, and Glamorgan in these years.[36] However we may account for such a failure, marriage with heiresses was the cause of many of the small Welsh mansions lying empty in these years. Such seats had not been swallowed up through purchase by the 'Leviathans' – rather there was a tendency for all landed categories to benefit from failure of male heirs within certain families.

If marriage and inheritance largely accounted for the pattern of landownership in these years, nevertheless some land came on the market. Clay has argued that much of the land for sale was the consequence of female or indirect inheritance, but it is not yet possible to comment whether this was true for Wales or not.[37] What we do know is that most of the land entered the market because of the indebtedness, for one reason or another, of various owners. Habakkuk and Mingay point to the difficulties of the lesser gentry in the face of the adverse economic conditions of these years. They draw attention to the burden of the land tax, the limited sources of their income together with the fact that a rising proportion of this went on ostentation, and the absence of elaborate settlements on their estates as particular reasons for failure. On the other hand, they argue, the greater owners possessed positive advantages assisting them to ride out short-term difficulties, in particular their more diversified sources of income, such as money from government offices and pensions and revenue from industrial resources.[38] Two recent studies by Holderness and Beckett on Lincolnshire and Cumbria respectively have questioned whether there was a general trend causing the

[35] Clay, *op. cit.*, p. 517.
[36] Williams-Jones, *op. cit.*, I, p. lxiv; J. E. Griffith, *Pedigrees of Anglesey and Caernarvonshire Families*, Horncastle, 1914: e.g. the houses of Castellior (p. 96), Penhesgin Issa (p. 53), Penmynydd (pp. 106–7), Ty Marian Heilin (p. 63), Plas Gwyn (p. 104), Pencraig (p. 51), Rhosmor (p. 132), Llangadwaladr (p. 116), Presaddfed (pp. 29, 95–6), Tre'rgof (p. 40), Tre'r Ddol (pp. 132, 137, 126), Bodychen (pp. 98–9), Caerau (p. 74), Plas Ucha (p. 38); see also NLW, Ty Coch MS 11, quoted in W. Ogwen Williams, 'The Social Order in Tudor Wales', *Hon. Soc. Cymmrodorion*, 1967, pt 2, pp. 168–9; Theophilus Jones, *History of the County of Brecknock*, 2 vols., Brecknock, 1805–9, II, p. 349n. Martin, thesis, pp. 218–19, discusses this in its Glamorgan context. For such a failure of male heirs in south-west Wales, see my forthcoming book *Patriarchs and Parasites: The Gentry of South-West Wales in the Eighteenth Century*, Univ. of Wales Press.
[37] Clay, *op. cit.*, pp. 510–15. It is claimed that female or indirect inheritance had only a small impact on the Glamorgan land market – Martin, thesis, pp. 275–6. The same holds good for south-west Wales – see my forthcoming *Patriarchs and Parasites*.
[38] Habakkuk, 'English Landownership', pp. 8–11; Mingay, *op. cit.*, pp. 78–85.

lesser owners to be more seriously affected than the greater and, as a result, having to sell their estates.[39]

There was certainly no substantial decline in the numbers of the lesser gentry and small freeholders within Welsh areas. It is likely that in Wales as in Cornwall and Cumberland the land tax was relatively light.[40] Moreover, in the event of certain owners finding the tax too heavy, it is possible – from what happened on the Abermarlais estate (Carms.) at the turn of the eighteenth century – that they shifted it onto their tenants, though, in turn, abatements were made in the rents.[41] The less drastic falls in dairy and livestock than in arable prices once again meant that small owners were less critically placed in Wales as, indeed, Mingay indicates, was the case with their counterparts in other pastoral regions of western Britain.[42] A further element here was the fact that the small peasant owners in this 'highland zone' were physically and psychologically adjusted to privation and thus it would have taken disastrous seasons indeed to have pushed them into giving up their cherished way of life.[43] Finally, many of the smaller Welsh owners, like those of Pembrokeshire and Glamorgan, were engaged in mining activities.[44]

From this last observation, it is clear that it was not just the greater landowners who were assisted in riding out hard times with the profits from their industrial undertakings. The other advantage supposedly enjoyed by the greater owners in the buildup of their estates was access to funds from government offices. Although men like John Campbell of Stackpole Court in Pembrokeshire (who held a couple of prestigious offices between 1736 and 1754) and Thomas Mansel of Margam (who likewise held important offices between 1704 and 1714) reaped substantial rewards, most of the larger Welsh owners were not considerable office holders.[45] It is unlikely that profits from government office gave them any significant advantage over their lesser

[39] B. A. Holderness, 'The English Land Market in the Eighteenth Century: The Case of Lincolnshire', EcHR, 2nd ser., XXVII, 4, 1974, pp. 557–76; J. V. Beckett, 'English Landownership in the Later Seventeenth and Eighteenth Centuries: The Debate and the Problems', EcHR, 2nd ser., XXX, 4, 1977, pp. 567–81.

[40] *The Case of the Salt Duty and Land-Tax Offered to the Consideration of Every Freeholder*, 1732, pp. 16–17, quoted in Mingay, *op. cit.*, pp. 81–2.

[41] Carmarthen RO, Glasbrook coll., Foley of Abermarlais and Ridgeway: abstract of the estate of Francis Cornwallis, Esq., 1703.

[42] Mingay, *op. cit.*, p. 100. Martin, thesis, pp. 39–42, 298, stresses this factor in explaining the survival of small owners in Glamorgan, and my comments rely heavily on her work.

[43] For the view that the staying power of the English peasantry as a whole rendered it unlikely that many of them would have been voluntary sellers in these years, see F. M. L. Thompson, 'Landownership and Economic Growth in England in the Eighteenth Century', in E. L. Jones and S. J. Woolf, eds., *Agrarian Change and Economic Development*, London, 1969, pp. 47–8.

[44] F. S. A., *Family Records of the Allens of Cresselly*, 1905: letter of John Allen to Margaret Allen, 23 Nov. 1752; for an examination of this aspect in relation to Glamorgan, see Martin, thesis, pp. 165–7, 175, 297–8. Once again, Dr Martin's comments influenced my thinking on this subject.

[45] I am indebted to Dr Martin for information on Thomas Mansel. For John Campbell, see PRO, T 38/161: Civil List Expenses 1746–50, bks 1, 2.

neighbours. Indeed, as was the case with John Campbell, the necessary expense involved in costly electioneering and the 'social' demands of such high positions must have considerably offset the financial gains of office.[46]

We are left asking, Did the larger owners enjoy *any* advantages? There is some truth in the contention that they possessed the advantage of making the best marriages. Furthermore, their estates were not so easily broken up as those of the small gentry. Richard Vaughan of Gray's Inn – with reference to an estate probably in Carmarthenshire – reminded his brother in 1712 that "it is not usual to limit small estates upon marriage so strictly that the husband and wife joining cannot destroy it".[47] This lack of elaborate settlements on English and Welsh estates may have mattered a great deal in the failure of certain of the smaller Welsh gentry at a time when contemporaries were criticizing them for attempting to keep up with the growing ostentation of the age. Thus Ellis Wynne of Lasynys wrote in 1703: "And the small freeholders around them [the knights] must either vainly follow or give bail for them, resulting in their own ruin, the loss of their possessions, and the sale of their patrimony, or expect to be hated and despised, and forced to every idle pursuit."[48] Finally, as Martin argues for Glamorgan, the greater gentry, by virtue of their social and political prominence, had the indulgence of their creditors.[49]

If the lesser gentry certainly did not collapse as a class there were nevertheless a sizeable number of small properties of the minor 'parish' gentry and yeoman freeholders coming on the market because of financial difficulties. David Williams, "who sold away the estate of Betws" (near Ammanford, Carms.), was in 1698 in "a beggar's state", while Leyson Thomas, yeoman of the small freehold of Llanfyrnach, outside Brecon, who sold the estate to a mortgagee in 1676, was afterwards "forced to live by fishing and fowling".[50] Francis Jones has indicated how "the Golden Grove MS. and other genealogical compilations of the period 1680–1700 reveal the words 'he sold all' with a tragic frequency".[51] If the land market was more active earlier in the eighteenth century, there was certainly no lack of land sales in the later decades. Demand had not dried up by the 1750s; indeed, there is some indication that demand from outside was increasing from the 1770s. Nor was there any shortage of supply. In 1779 Richard Morris was lamenting how the newspapers were "shamefully stuff'd with continual advertisements for sale of Welsh estates; several of which I remember to have seen in a

[46] NLW, MS 1,352B, f. 296: letter of 14 Jan. 1744.
[47] Carmarthen RO, Cawdor/Vaughan MS 102/8,029: letter of 2 Dec. 1712.
[48] Ellis Wynne, *Gweledigaetheu y Bardd Cwsc*, London, 1703, tr. R. C. Davies, *The Visions of the Sleeping Bard*, London and Caernarvon, 1897, p. 78.
[49] For creditors' indulgence to John Myddelton of Chirk after 1733, see Mingay, *op. cit.*, p. 126; Martin, thesis, p. 279.
[50] NLW, Castell Gorfod MS 8, f. 48; BL, Harleian MS 4,181. Both references were kindly provided by Dr Prys Morgan.
[51] F. Jones, 'Approach to Welsh Genealogy', p. 397.

flourishing condition...said [sic] effect of dissipation!"[52] All this meant that by the end of the century William Williams, a land agent, was bewailing the fact that in Caernarvonshire, because of marriage and purchase, "we but seldom meet with affluent freeholders who heretofore were as parents to the indigent", and others made similar observations for Pembrokeshire and Glamorgan.[53]

Contemporaries certainly pointed to encumbered properties falling to 'Leviathans' in the early eighteenth century. Thus a survey of the lordship of Ruthin in Denbighshire observed: "At the time of Richard Myddelton [he died in 1716] most of the freeholds of this lordship have gone into the hands of great men."[54] Thomas Pennant listed thirty-five deserted seats in Merioneth in the early 1770s, and added ruefully: "most of them now swallowed up by our Welsh Leviathans".[55] Examples of greater owners who purchased lesser estates in their respective areas include Sir Edward Mansel of Margam (between the 1660s and the 1690s), the Morgans of Tredegar Park (Mon.), the Wynns of Wynnstay (Denbs.), the Myddeltons of Chirk (Denbs.), and the Bulkeleys of Baron Hill (Anglesey).[56]

Yet the greater landowners did not monopolize the market. There were a number of local gentry, country attorneys, and land agents buying estates. Given the distance from the loan markets of London, many small men still looked upon land as a pure investment quite apart from its prestige value. The fact that the great estates in Wales were few meant that in areas removed from the dominance of a great family the smaller gentry and freeholders were in a good position to make purchases. The activity of small men is seen, for example, in Pembrokeshire, where a number of gentry laid out money on mortgages and no doubt foreclosed in a number of instances.[57] Demand down to the mid century was chiefly from within the region. The isolation of the principality and the fact that the limited area of fertile soils and the

---

[52] Quoted in P. R. Roberts, 'The Decline of the Welsh Squires in the Eighteenth Century', *Nat. Lib. Wales J.*, XIII, 1963–4, p. 164.

[53] NLW, MS 821C: Survey of Caernarvonshire in 1806 by William Williams, with reference to the district of Dolbenmaen; R. Fenton, *A Historical Tour through Pembrokeshire*, London, 1811, p. 558; G. J. Williams, *Iolo Morganwg*, Caerdydd, 1956, I, pp. 20–1. This last reference was kindly provided by Dr Prys Morgan.   [54] NLW, Ruthin MS 2,084.

[55] NLW, MS 2,532B, f. 28, quoted in F. Jones, 'Approach to Welsh Genealogy', p. 430.

[56] NLW, Margam and Penrice MSS 1,350–1, 1,353–4, 1,356–60, 1,369–70, 1,373–5, 1,377, 1,382–4, 1,388, 1,390, 1,393, 1,395, 1,427, and many others; Tredegar Park MSS 374, 376, 382; Roberts, *op. cit.*, pp. 157–8; NLW, Chirk Castle papers, F. 10, 166(i), E. 3,236; Myddelton, *op. cit.*, p. 98 n. 525; NLW, Ty Coch MS 11; UCNWL, Baron Hill MSS 1,926–8: sale of real estate of Francis Bulkeley of Porthamel (who shot himself in 1714 because of debt) to the third Lord Bulkeley for £21,600.

[57] H. J. Habakkuk, 'The English Land Market in the Eighteenth Century', in *Britain and The Netherlands*, ed. J. S. Bromley and E. H. Kossmann, London, 1960, p. 170; Beckett, *op. cit.*, p. 570; Martin, thesis, pp. 260–1, where the point about smaller owners purchasing in areas removed from the dominance of great families was first made for Wales; D. W. Howell, 'The Landed Gentry of Pembrokeshire in the Eighteenth Century', unpub. Univ. of Wales M.A. thesis, 1965, I, pp. 25–6.

climate together restricted the uses to which the land could be put meant that hardly any London merchants and other moneyed outsiders were looking for land in Wales. And with the level of demand probably constituting the crucial determinant of the secular trend of freehold land prices, rates were consequently lower in Welsh areas than those which prevailed in the southern and Midland counties of England.[58]

It is clear that there was a certain amount of consolidation of the large estates in these years even if the smaller ones survived in large numbers. The Wynnstay estates brought in £19,623 in 1736, Chirk Castle £5,876 in 1742, Stackpole Court £3,132 in the early 1760s, Picton Castle £3,897 in 1736, Margam and Penrice £4,715 in 1729, and Golden Grove just over £3,000 in 1751.[59] The owners of these and other large properties were clearly in a position to live grandly, but many (like their English counterparts) spent beyond their incomes. A certain quantity of 'natural' indebtedness resulted from family settlements, as on the Stackpole Court estate consequent upon the marriage settlement of John Campbell in 1725, and, again, on the Penrhos estate, Anglesey, whose family was "ruinat'd" when the jointure rent charge which William Owen settled on his wife in their marriage settlement came into operation upon his death in 1733.[60] But extra debts were incurred through wanton extravagance in the vulgar pursuit of social prominence. The serious financial problems of both the Myddeltons of Chirk Castle and their arch-opponents, the Wynns of Wynnstay, in the early eighteenth century arose from costly electioneering.[61] A spendthrift life tenant or heir could similarly play havoc with estate finances. For example, the disastrous marriage of Anne, heiress of Golden Grove, Carmarthenshire, in 1713 led to heavy mortgaging of lands to meet the importunate demands of her prodigal husband. In addition, lawsuits were vexatious, troublesome, and expensive, as Sir Erasmus Philipps of Picton Castle was to be painfully aware round 1690.[62]

[58] Freehold land prices for Welsh areas have been assembled from a wide range of estate records. The following represents no more than a rough trend over the period: 1650–90, 16–18 years' purchase; 1709–14, 20 years' purchase; 1720, 45 years' purchase; 1723, 21 years' purchase; 1735–47, 23–5 years' purchase. For comparison with English areas, see C. Clay, 'The Price of Freehold Land in the Later Seventeenth and Eighteenth Centuries', EcHR, 2nd ser., XXVII, 2, 1974, pp. 173–89.

[59] NLW, Chirk Castle F.4,529; Margam and Penrice MS 5,971; Carmarthen RO, Cawdor/Campbell MS box 128 and Dynevor 162/5; NLW, Picton Castle papers; F. Jones, 'The Vaughans of Golden Grove, III: Torycoed, Shenfield, Golden Grove', Hon. Soc. Cymmrodorion, 1964, pt 2, p. 202.

[60] NLW, MS 1,352B, Stackpole letters, f. 231: letter of 10 Mar. 1744; UCNWL, Penrhos MSS 984, 1,054, 1,060, 1,076; E. Gwynne Jones, 'Correspondence of the Owens of Penrhos, 1712–42', Angl. Antiq. Soc., 1954, p. 66.

[61] NLW, Chirk Castle E.6,157, E.4,529; Mingay, op. cit., pp. 125–30; H. Owen, 'The Diary of William Bulkeley of Brynddu, Anglesey', Angl. Antiq. Soc., 1931: entry for 1 Oct. 1749.

[62] F. Jones, 'The Vaughans of Golden Grove, II: Anne, Duchess of Bolton', Hon. Soc. Cymmrodorion, 1963, pt 2, pp. 231, 236; NLW, Picton Castle MS 1,908; Carmarthen RO, Cawdor/Campbell MS box 128: letter of Mar. 1744.

By the mid eighteenth century the consequence of heedless extravagance and of too little attention being given to careful management was that the financial affairs of certain large estates were in a critical condition. These substantial properties nevertheless possessed certain advantages which enabled them to remain largely intact. Even so, indebtedness led to a limited amount of selling, as, for example, of parts of the Chirk Castle lands towards the middle of the eighteenth century and also of parts of the extensive Baron Hill estate, Anglesey, after 1738; in 1740 it was being claimed that its Bulkeley proprietors were "sinking under a load of debt".[63] Such sales meant that the large properties were vulnerable and did not always expand.

Welsh landowners of the rank of gentleman and above, like their English counterparts, let the greater part of their estates to tenant farmers and kept in their own hands merely a home farm. Landlords were therefore unimportant as agricultural producers. They were mainly concerned with estate management. This they placed in the hands of estate stewards and lesser officials, over whose activities they exercised varying degrees of control. The steward was the most important. He was not always solely concerned with one estate and could, if a lawyer, practise elsewhere.[64] A few of the very large estates (whose properties were usually scattered) were beyond the capacity of a single steward and were managed in various ways. On some estates like Chirk Castle and Wynnstay one chief steward had under agents to assist him. Stewards were sometimes appointed for separate manors or sub-estates, as on the Tredegar Park estate in the 1680s, and on the Golden Grove estate in the early eighteenth century, and they accounted individually with their employer. Again, two stewards could be appointed to manage an estate jointly, as happened in the early eighteenth century on the Derwydd estate and on the Margam and Penrice estate; in the case of the latter, one steward was responsible for letting the land, and the other for receiving and accounting. Separate stewards were sometimes appointed to manage the industrial development of large estates. Thus in 1680 Roger Williams was appointed to manage the Machen forge as well as furnaces intended to be built at Eglwyselan on the Tredegar Park estate, and in 1716 Lord Mansel of Margam was looking for a coal steward.[65] There was thus a strong element of divided responsibility, this partly stemming from the belief that fraudulency would be avoided by officials checking on one another, and partly from the prevailing idea that the estate was rather a unit of consumption than one of management. However, John Vaughan of Golden

[63] Mingay, op. cit., p. 126; Owen, op. cit.: entry for 27 Aug. 1740.
[64] Carmarthen RO, Cawdor/Vaughan MS 102/8,029: letter of 23 Nov. 1714; NLW, Margam and Penrice MS 6,007: instructions to a newly appointed steward, c. 1730.
[65] Wynnstay Rental 1736-9; Tredegar Park MS 871; Carmarthen RO, Cawdor/Vaughan MS 102/8,029: letters of 18 Mar. 1756 and 11 Nov. 1712; NLW, Margam and Penrice MS 7,212; Tredegar Park MS 871; Margam and Penrice MSS L.833 and L.834.

# LANDLORDS AND ESTATE MANAGEMENT IN WALES 393

Grove was advised in 1756 by the duke of Beaufort's agent that "things will never be properly carried on at the Courts in the three Commots unless one person be appointed, for here it is as it was formerly in the Duke of Beaufort's lordships, when many stewards, each was considering and contending for his own interest, and neglected the lord's".[66]

Many stewards of substantial Welsh estates were recruited from among the small local gentry (with a sprinkling of clergymen), who were often connected by family ties with their richer employers.[67] The qualifications of a steward included honesty and sobriety, the ability to account and write clearly, a knowledge of the law, and the ability to supervise lesser officials. (In only two instances have I found mention or hint of the advantage of appointing a Welshman rather than a 'stranger' as agent, the language being specifically an issue in one case).[68] Training was usually acquired through practical experience in junior positions, while occasionally sons followed fathers as stewards on the same estates. Sometimes lawyers were employed as stewards, as was, for example, John Hosier, gentleman, at Chirk Castle in the 1740s and early 1750s. While they were obviously suited to the legal work of large properties, they were seldom popular. Complaints were made about their pocketing the profits of estates through unnecessary lawsuits and their giving too much time to other legal business.[69]

The steward was expected to perform a wide range of duties. He was responsible for the letting of farms, the supervision of repairs to holdings, the collection of rents, the overseeing of the mines and of timber felling, the keeping of the lord's courts, the buying and selling of livestock connected with the home farm, the protection and promotion of his master's political interest, especially at election times, and the drawing up of regular accounts once a year. If properly executed the job was extremely demanding and on large estates stewards required the help of other officials. Rents were collected by part-time bailiffs on many parts of the outlying properties. Thus Thomas Cory, one of the two chief agents of the Margam and Penrice estate, in addition to his own collection, had about twenty bailiffs returning rents to him in 1712. Home farm bailiffs and park keepers were also employed. Significantly, when Thomas Price was appointed to look after the game at

[66] F. M. L. Thompson, *English Landed Society in the Nineteenth Century*, London, 1963, pp. 153–5; Carmarthen RO, Cawdor/Vaughan MS 102/8,029: letter of Mar. 1756 of J. Vaughan to R. Vaughan.

[67] E.g. John Lewis of Penywern, Caerns., was steward to his cousin, Morris Wynn of Gwydir, in the late 1670s – NLW, Wigfair MS 3: letter of 14 Mar. 1678 of J. Lewis to M. Wynn.

[68] NLW, Chirk Castle E.5,324: letter of 8 Apr. 1738; Smith, *Herbert Correspondence*, pp. 29–30, letter no. 21 of 1671; Roberts, *op. cit.*, p. 158.

[69] NLW, Powis Castle Correspondence, MS 1,113: letter of 29 Oct. 1745; Myddelton, *op. cit.*, p. 6 n. 21; John Williams followed his father at the turn of the eighteenth century as steward of the Edisbury family of Erthig – Clwyd RO, Erthig D/E/539; NLW, Chirk Castle E.4,478 and Myddelton, *op. cit.*, p. 504 n. 2,755; Carmarthen RO, Cawdor/Campbell MS box 128: letter of 17 Nov. 1764.

Chirk Castle around 1719 he was "to have recourse to his powers of justice of the peace".[70]

It is stressed that Welsh estates were generally small. Such properties were run either by a country attorney, who collected the rents and safeguarded the family interests, or by the owners themselves, sometimes with the help of their womenfolk. Attorneys were a sensible choice given the intermixture of many different properties at this time. This was explicitly emphasized in the mid-eighteenth-century appointment of Richard Knethell as "collector and steward" of the Nash estate, Pembrokeshire, which had a yearly rent of £500. Small estates of under £500 were frequently run by the owners themselves. The account book of one such estate in Carmarthenshire, worth £167 a year in 1685, and let out to thirty-six tenants, is happily extant, and from it we see that the owner himself managed the property. Similarly, William Bulkeley of Brynddu, Anglesey, was managing his own property in the first half of the eighteenth century.[71]

Most owners who employed stewards nevertheless took a keen interest in the running of their properties. In their absence from home, they were kept well informed by frequent correspondence. The degree of initiative allowed to stewards varied from landlord to landlord. The overall impression gained is that stewards were always careful about getting their employers' approval before undertaking any new venture, or even for the most routine tasks, although at the same time they were ready enough to convey their own inclinations over a particular matter. Some owners expressly encouraged their stewards to take decisions independently. They did so because they were often distant from the estate as a result of absenteeism; and too much dependence on landlords' decisions (as was pointed out by Richard Vaughan of Derwydd in 1712 and also by the London agent of Lord Powis in 1724) led inevitably to delay. Usually, however, landlords took the major decisions of estate policy and often issued instructions about the most trivial matters.[72]

Efficient management clearly depended a great deal upon the integrity and ability of stewards. They had a popular reputation for dishonesty, and, true enough, a number in Wales in this period abused their office for gain – men like George Higgins, gentleman, steward of the Llwydiarth estate (he was dismissed in 1699); Stephen Howard, agent at Margam (he was sacked in

---

[70] Edward Powell, ed., 'Pryce (Newtown Hall) Correspondence', *Mont. Colls.*, XXI, 1900, letter xxiii: of 20 Jan. 1640 of R. Amyas to Sir J. Pryce; NLW, Chirk Castle E.1,419: letter of 17 Feb. 1751; Glamorgan RO, D/DP/877/10: letter of 6 Mar. 1748; NLW, Margam and Penrice MSS 7,212, 1,451; Tredegar Park MS 871; Chirk Castle E.4,000.

[71] NLW, Eaton Evans and Williams MS 662; NLW, MS 4,275B: a Carmarthenshire landlord's account book, 1685–96; Owen, *op. cit.*; for the active supervision of the Cresselly estate, Pembs., by the daughter, Margaret Allen, see F.S.A., *Allens of Cresselly*, letter of 23 Nov. 1752.

[72] NLW, Margam and Penrice MSS 5,984, 2,544, 2,253; Clwyd RO, Erthig D/E/530: letter of 15 Apr. 1694; NLW, Chirk Castle E.730; Carmarthen RO, Cawdor/Vaughan MS 102/8,029: letter of 20 Dec. 1712; NLW, Powis Castle Correspondence, MS 1,029.

1711); John Parry, agent for the Owens of Porkington in the 1740s; and John Hosier, agent at Chirk Castle. Most, however, were no doubt reasonably honest and promoted with zeal and loyalty the interests of their employers, to whom they were often related by family ties.[73]

The appointment of full-time professional stewards led to a certain amount of improvement in estate management. Landowners in these years were becoming increasingly aware of the need for method and order in the running of their affairs. Sometimes stewards trained in the new techniques of management were appointed, but more often than not landowners, or their London accountants, endeavoured to encourage and instruct their country stewards in the stricter methods coming into vogue at this time. The traditional 'charge' and 'discharge' method of accounting was continued in use, but this period saw a greater regularity introduced whereby items of income and expenditure were arranged under systematic columns and careful attention was given to the striking and casting of balances. All this, as John Vaughan of Golden Grove urged, was in the interest of openness, clarity, and order. Examples of this striving towards method can be seen in the examination made in 1712 by a London accountant of the system of accounting in use at Margam, in the instructions given by Dr Wynne of Bodewryd to his Denbighshire agent at Plas Einon in 1725, and in the efforts of John Vaughan of Golden Grove in the early 1750s.[74] Although progress was being made (particularly in the second quarter of the eighteenth century) as a result of such efforts, it was slow and halting. Some agents like Lewis Lewis of the Golden Grove estate were simply not equal to the new standards of efficiency required. Only small advance was achieved in the case of Chirk Castle, where, despite efforts towards a more regular accounting in the early eighteenth century, the position in 1750 called for improvement. Accordingly, a steward well versed in the new techniques of management and in the law was appointed with the aim of bringing affairs "into an exact order and method both in accounts and economy".[75] As we shall see, a particular drawback to strict accounting was the high level of rent arrears on many Welsh estates, and this was partly a consequence of the stewards' failure to enforce punctuality.

[73] NLW, Wynnstay box 87, no. 68 and box 85, no. 25: concerning George Higgins; Margam and Penrice MS 7,212: concerning Stephen Howard; Brogyntyn MSS 1,831, 1,468, 1,469: concerning John Parry; Chirk Castle MSS E.4,478, E.4,479(ii), E.69 and Myddelton, *op. cit.*, p. 504 n. 2,755: concerning John Hosier; see also NLW, Eaton Evans and Williams MS 622 and A. L. Cust, *Chronicles of Erthig on the Dyke*, 2 vols., London, 1914, *I*, p. 130.

[74] NLW, Margam and Penrice MS 7,212; Bodewryd MS 531: letters of 29 Oct. and 20 Nov. 1725 of D. Roberts to Dr Wynne; Carmarthen RO, Cawdor/Vaughan MS 102/8,029: letter of 14 Nov. 1755 of J. Vaughan to Lewis Lewis.

[75] NLW, Chirk Castle E.5,957: letter of 20 Nov. 1726; E.6,298: letter of 18 Dec. 1734; E.6,234: letter of 22 Dec. 1750. Evidence of improvement in accounting can nevertheless be seen in Carmarthen RO, Cawdor/Vaughan MS 102/8,029: letters of 15 Sept. 1755, 21 Feb. 1756, 12 Mar. 1757 of J. Vaughan to L. Lewis.

Before examining the landowners' attitudes and policies towards the development of their estates it is necessary to consider their position as lords of the various manors or as tenants of those manors, and also the position of crown lordships. Freehold had always been the dominant form of tenure in the lordships and manors of the Welsh areas, but in the manors of the lowland anglicized areas, where freehold tenants were few, customary tenure was widespread in the 1640s and remained a significant element down to the late eighteenth century. From Tudor times, however, all forms of customary tenure were being gradually replaced by leasehold contracts, and the trend accelerated from the mid seventeenth century as manorial lords sought to swell their rent rolls. Freeholders of manors usually held by socage tenure in perpetuity, for which they were liable to pay relief, to render suit of court, and to pay heriots of the best beast and a small fixed rent. Freeholders ranged from cottagers to owners of huge estates. Customary tenants, holding their lands by 'the custom of the manor' and whose origin lay in villeinage, had by the seventeenth century been released from seignorial control through the commutation of the old agricultural services, but in addition to their fixed money rents they were still subject to certain obligations such as suit of court, payment of heriots, fines upon alienations, grinding at the lord's mill, labour services connected with mill repairs, and cleansing of mill leats. If the practical differences between freehold and customary tenure were of small significance outside politics from the mid seventeenth century, there remained on the Beaufort manors in Glamorgan a crucial difference between customary holders by inheritance, enjoying substantial protection from the custom of the manor, and copyholders at the will of the lord. The latter, as distinct from the former, did not enjoy the privilege of voting and, furthermore, were forbidden to work minerals under their lands. Landed estates of the gentry and large owners in these years might well comprise a number of types of tenure, therefore, for a gentleman could simultaneously be a lord of a manor and a freeholder, customary tenant, and leaseholder within other manors.[76]

Administration of private manors was carried out by means of the Courts Baron and Leet, run by a number of officers like the recorder, bailiffs,

---

[76] Carmarthen RO, Glasbrook coll., Foley of Abermarlais and Ridgeway: abstract of the estate of Francis Cornwallis, 1703; C. Baker and G. Grant Francis, *Lordship of Gower*, London, 1870, pp. 143–54: survey of the manor of Bishopston, 1673–5; Swansea Univ. Coll. Library, Gabriel Powell's survey of the seignories of Gower and Killay, 1764 (Mr David Bevan kindly placed his transcript at my disposal); G. H. Eaton, 'A Survey of the Manor in Seventeenth Century Gower', unpub. Univ. of Wales M.A. thesis, 1935, pp. 58–96, 206–9; Carmarthen RO, Cawdor, i, box 106: notes of inquiry to be made at the next Court Baron held for the manor of Castlemartin, c. 1708; F. Jones, 'The Vaughans of Golden Grove, III: Torycoed...', p. 193; Glanmor Williams, 'The Economic Life of Glamorgan, 1536–1642', in *Glamorgan County History*, IV, pp. 12–17; NLW, Badminton, ii, MSS 1,455, 1,457: concerning dispute between the duke of Beaufort and his Oystermouth tenants, 1749.

constables, and haywards, all responsible to the estate steward. Laxity and neglect were prevalent. Such was the case, for example, in Ruthin lordship in 1688 and 1704, in Llansadwrn lordship, Carmarthenshire, in 1703, in Lord Ashburnham's lordships in Brecknockshire in 1706, in a lordship belonging to the earl of Powis in 1725, in the Carmarthenshire lordships of the Vaughans of Golden Grove throughout the early eighteenth century, and in the manor of Cyfeiliog, Montgomeryshire (belonging to the Wynns of Wynnstay), in the same years.[77] Loss of traditional rights resulted, as payments simply fell into abeyance. Furthermore, such lax administration allowed tenants (sometimes, indeed, with the connivance of stewards) to encroach on manorial franchises like common rights. Thus in the late seventeenth century, freeholders of the lordship of Ruthin encroached on the commons there, enclosed them, and claimed them as their freehold estates. Similarly, many such encroachments and enclosures were made in the manors of Mechen Iscoed and Mochnant belonging to Powis Castle in the years before 1677, and sizeable enclosures were also made by tenants of the lordship of Gower in the early eighteenth century.[78] Not only freehold or customary tenants of the manor encroached; far more numerous were the small encroachments of squatters, comprising a cottage and a few acres. Although some of these were obliged to pay a rent, many through negligence went unchallenged.[79] The making of bricks upon the commons, the cutting of turves, and the burning of lime without the lord's permission were other encroachments.[80] Animosity arose sometimes when tighter administration was attempted to check the decay of manorial franchises and to recover lost rights. Such a situation occurred in Carmarthenshire in the 1750s when John Vaughan of Golden Grove, as lord of twenty-five manors there, was frantically searching out concealed and lost rights. Any attempt at collecting the fines and amerciaments in the manor of Cyfeiliog, it was claimed in 1763, "would be looked upon as bold and daring" by the inhabitants.[81]

[77] NLW, Ruthin MSS, 1,192, 1,321; Carmarthen RO, Glasbrook coll., Foley of Abermarlais and Ridgeway: abstract of estate of F. Cornwallis, 1703; NLW, Ashburnham MS 324: letter of 3 Jan. 1706; Powis Castle MS 1,006: letter of 13 Dec. 1725 of T. Budd to H. Parry; F. Jones, 'The Vaughans of Golden Grove, III: Torycoed...', pp. 189–95; NLW, Wynnstay deposit, 1952, vol. 1: survey of 1763.

[78] NLW, Ruthin MS 1,564; Powis Castle Manorial Records, group i, no. 74; Badminton, ii, MS 1,931.

[79] Carmarthen RO, Cawdor/Vaughan MS 103/8,061: rental of 1723–4 specifying 17 cottages on the common called the Black Mountain and 3 others on Bettus Mountain; NLW, Tredegar Park MS 344: survey (1690) of the Tredegar estate in Brecknockshire listing 12 small squatter encroachments in the parish of Devynock; Carmarthen RO, Cawdor/Vaughan MS 102/8,029: letter of May 1756 of J. Vaughan to L. Lewis claiming that there had been many "incroachments and concealments" on the Golden Grove Carmarthenshire property.

[80] NLW, Ruthin MS 728; Picton Castle, MS 1,678; Tredegar Park 124/66.

[81] Carmarthen RO, Cawdor/Vaughan MS 102/8,029: letter of Mar. 1756 of J, Vaughan to O. Rees; NLW, Wynnstay Deposit, 1952, vol. 1.

Income from manorial franchises was relatively insignificant until the growth of industrial enterprise in these years invested the mineral rights of the lords of the soil with a new value.[82] The clash of interest likely between the lord of a particular manor and the tenant over the right to work such minerals is well illustrated in the instance of the seignory of Gower belonging to the duke of Beaufort. Between the early 1740s and the late 1750s gentlemen in the seignory, like Thomas Price of Penllergaer, Robert Popkin of Forest, and Richard Dawkins of Kilvrough, disputed with the duke and his vigilant steward, Gabriel Powell, many of the rights and customs traditionally belonging to the lords of Gower. The duke's right to coal in the manor of Pennard and the fee of Trewyddva was denied, the gentleman-tenants claiming the right to work it for themselves and to dispose of it as they wished. The duke and Powell answered that the tenures of these two districts were copyhold and that tenants holding thereby, like Popkin and Price, were not entitled to work any mines. It was further claimed that the tenants in Gower Supraboscus (Welsh Gower) were entitled to dig coal under the duke's commons and wastes. Powell countered that coal could be worked under these commons only by virtue of leases from the duke. In 1759 he reminded the duchess of Beaufort of the great loss which would occur if the tenants' claims to the waste were allowed, for the coal was worth "several hundred thousand pounds". With this awareness of the great potential value of his coal the duke was reasserting his rights and preventing further encroachments by tenants whose settled rule, Powell alleged, was to "rob the lord as much as they can". Powell's strictly legalistic approach was reflected in his observation in 1748 that a "landlord may make the most of his lands without being guilty of any crime".[83] The Beaufort interest had been similarly involved in another celebrated enclosure dispute in the late seventeeth century. Conflicting views over timber rights on the common of Wentwood, Monmouthshire, resulted in a fierce clash between the duke of Beaufort, as lord of the manor, and his tenants, many of them esquires and gentlemen. The trouble began in the late 1670s when the duke enclosed the common and destroyed timber, stout resistance from the tenants being met with imprisonment.[84]

The crown was lord of the manor over wide areas of Wales, although we have seen that in order to raise money many lordships were alienated to private landowners in Wales during the seventeenth century, particularly in the reigns of Charles I and William III. The extensive manors which the crown retained were badly managed and crown rights were resented by the freehold and customary tenants. It was calculated in 1786 that the total annual

[82] Tredegar Castle received £33 5s. 6d. from 6 manors in 1680 – NLW, Tredegar Park MS 371. [83] NLW, Badminton, ii, MSS 1,936, 2,061, 1,930, 2,404, 2,334, 1,927.
[84] Nathan Rogers, *Memoirs of Monmouthshire*, London, 1708, app., pp. 87–110. Mr Frank Emery kindly directed me to this source.

amount of fee farm rents issuing to the crown from north and south Wales was £6,342 and that there were cumulative arrears of £38,771.[85] Neglect was especially evident in the north. In the crown lordship of Ruthin, for example, the arrears of the eight and a half years prior to 1668 amounted to £969, and, furthermore, no regular account was passed by any receiver of north Wales and Chester between 1711 and 1764.[86] Welsh landowners acting as stewards of crown lordships were in a particularly favourable position to make encroachments on the rights of the crown, but many tenants of the lordships, too, made encroachments on the wide tracts of open wastes within the crown manors and claimed them as their private freeholds. There was consequently much encroachment and concealment, and this led to confrontation towards the middle of the eighteenth century between the crown and private landowners when the mineral wealth of the commons offered rich rewards to the enterprising. One of the most notable instances of conflict occurred in the lead-mining districts of Cardiganshire where Lewis Morris, deputy steward of the crown lands within the county, made unpopular efforts to reassert the crown's right to ore found on the commons against the claims of owners like the squires of Nanteos, Gogerddan, and Crosswood.[87]

The remainder of this chapter will concentrate on the policies of the owners towards their estates. The demesnes of the large owners, containing pleasure grounds and gardens, a park, and a home farm, were quite extensive: Picton Castle demesne in Pembrokeshire in 1729 covered 767 acres, comprising 98 acres of meadow, 424 acres of arable, and 245 acres of woodland; Bodorgan demesne in Anglesey in 1705 comprised 303 acres; and Llangibby Castle demesne in 1709 totalled 963 acres out of the entire estate area of 3,860 acres.[88] Consequently, large number of menservants were required to work them, and the expense and nuisance of such people led a few owners to let part or even the whole of their demesnes to tenant farmers. Richard Vaughan of Derwydd declared his intention in 1714 of letting the greater part of the demesne of Derwydd to good, able tenants and of not keeping any tillage in his own hands (it was running at a loss), observing: "And in that case I need keep no men servants but Hugh and a boy under him."[89]

[85] NLW, MS 9,475E: "Second Report of the Commissioners to Inquire into the State of Land Revenues of the Crown, 11 December 1787".
[86] NLW, Wynn papers, MS 2,557 (the lordship was purchased by Chirk Castle in 1676); NLW, MS 9,475E: "Twelfth Report of the Commissioners...25 May 1792".
[87] O. Beynon, 'The Lead Mining Industry in Cardiganshire from 1700 to 1830', unpub. Univ. of Wales M.A. thesis, 1937, pp. 84–100 and app., pp. 18–20; S. R. Meyrick, *History and Antiquities of the County of Cardigan*, London, 1808, app., nos. 18, 19.
[88] NLW, Picton Castle, MS 1,694; UCNWL, Bodorgan MS 1,580; Gwent RO, D.43.4,634.
[89] Carmarthen RO, Cawdor/Vaughan MS 102/8,029: letter of 6 Nov. 1714 of R. Vaughan to W. Morgan, and see also letter of early 1757 of J. Vaughan to Richard Vaughan. For an example of servants' wages, see NLW, Wynnstay Rental 1745–7: Llangedwin servants' wages for one year due 1 May 1747.

Generally, however, the demesnes of the large estates were kept in hand in their entirety or at least in part. Although the home farms functioned mainly to supply domestic needs, it is likely that a limited amount of marketing was aimed at on some estates, the sales representing more than the mere disposal of surplus produce. Livestock were sold off the Tredegar Park estate in the fairs of Cardiff, Newport, and Caerleon, and in 1731 twenty fat oxen were sold for £149 9s. 6d., a bull and a fat cow for £5 8s., tallow for £8 16s., wool for £102 2s. 8d., and hides for £25 15s. Ten fat oxen were intended for sale off the Margam estate in Cardiff 'high market' in early 1712. The Bulkeleys of Baron Hill were selling livestock in Newborough and Borth fairs, disposing of eleven runts and nine cows in 1718 for £74 4s. 6d. Similarly, the Bodewryd estate marketed cattle, cheese, and butter, some 600 lb of butter and cheese being sold in Bangor in 1693. The Penrhos estate in Anglesey grew barley for the market and shipped it in the 1720s to Liverpool, Warrington, Chester, Mostyn, and Ireland.[90]

Although the stay-at-home owners of the small estates were rentiers, they were also in a very real sense practical farmers. They actively supervised the various farming tasks performed on their home farms and marketed produce at the local fairs, which they attended in person. The diary of William Bulkeley of Brynddu affords a rare insight into the farming activities of a Welsh gentleman in the first half of the eighteenth century. Typical entries were: for 28 June 1734, "sold 13 oxen at £4. 10s. each and one...for £3. 9s."; 29 August 1734, "finished barley harvest and wheat also"; 31 July 1735, "sold 9 oxen at Aberffraw fair for £5. 6s. 3d. per beast"; 28 April 1739, "shipped my oats today at Cemmaes for London, the rest to go to Warrington"; and 23 January 1748, "I am obliged to hire men for ploughing by the day instead of my servants that are affected [by colds]."[91]

Certain landowners were practising progressive farming techniques on their home farms from the late seventeenth century, although it is likely that they were a small minority. North-eastern Wales, in particular, was an area of improving landowners. Both Sir John Trevor of the Trevalun and Plas Têg estates near Wrexham (between 1668 and 1673) and Sir John Myddelton of Chirk Castle (before 1673) experimented, though with little success, in cultivating sainfoin. Sir Richard Myddelton was growing clover at Chirk in 1686 and sainfoin in 1703–4. Similarly, John Williams, steward of Joshua Edisbury of Erthig, was advocating clover cultivation with barley on the home farm in 1708 and 1709 and (revealingly) referred to a certain practice of sowing the crop which "is the common custom of this country". Clover

---

[90] NLW, Tredegar Park MS 344; Margam and Penrice MS L.728: letter of 28 Feb. 1712; UCNWL, Baron Hill MS 4,751; F. Jones, 'A Squire of Anglesey', *Angl. Antiq. Soc.*, 1940, p. 85; UCNWL, Penrhos, i. MS 1,387B; NLW, Bodewryd MS 353: letter of 1 Feb. 1723.

[91] UCNWL, Henblas MS A18: diary of William Bulkeley of Brynddu.

and barley were being regularly sown together on the estate from 1721.[92] Likewise, clover, ryegrass, and turnips were commonly sown on the demesnes at Mostyn (from the 1720s), Hawarden (from the 1730s), and Wynnstay (from the 1740s). In 1743 twenty wethers were brought to Wynnstay "for feeding on turnips". Much attention was paid to horse breeding at Chirk Castle in the early eighteenth century, while at Llanvorda (Oswestry) an attempt at an improvement in cattle breeds is made evident in a letter in 1728 in which George Shakerley, the cousin of Sir William Williams, second baronet, wrote informing him that he had bought him a bull calf and heifer; and "there are much larger to be had in the further part of Lancashire, and I have made such enquiry that whenever you have occasion, I can give you full directions where to be fitted with the finest and largest kinds, but it might be earlier in the year, the best fairs for such parts being about the beginning [of] May".[93]

Improvements were also in evidence elsewhere in north Wales. Robert Wynne of Bodysgallen and a neighbouring landowner of Degannwy, both in the parish of Llan-rhos, Caernarvonshire, were sowing grass seed (obtained from Banbury) in 1691, and in 1700 clover seed procured in Shrewsbury was being sown with barley on the Crogen demesne in Merioneth belonging to Sir Edward Roberts. These gentlemen (upon request) communicated their knowledge of the crops to Watkin Owen, the estate agent at Gwydir, Caernarvonshire.[94] Other such 'improving' gentry were Edward Williams of Ystumcolwyn, Montgomeryshire, who was sowing clover and ryegrass seeds from the late 1720s, and Hugh Lloyd of Berth, in the parish of Llanbedr Dyffryn Clwyd, Denbighshire, who was using marl and cultivating clover from the late 1730s.[95] By the 1740s progressive husbandry was also evident on the demesne at Lleweni, Denbighshire, and early in 1748 meadows were being watered there, as also at Plas y Ward, Denbighshire, and at Rhiwlas in Merioneth.[96] These were isolated examples of progressive practices, but in Anglesey a general spirit of improvement prevailed, matching that in the north-east. The progressive husbandry practised on the Bodewryd demesne from the second decade of the eighteenth century under the enlightened direction of the owner, Chancellor Edward Wynne, is well known. John Owen of Penrhos was writing to London in the 1680s and 90s enquiring about French furze seed, and in 1725 the mistress of Penrhos was even advising her brother, Chancellor Wynne, about the sowing of clover seed.

[92] Clwyd RO, D/G 3,277, 3,278 concerning Sir John Trevor and Sir Thomas Myddelton; Myddelton, *op. cit.*, pp. 214, 356; Clwyd RO, Erthig D/E/539, 547, 363, 373.

[93] UCNWL, Mostyn MSS 6,486, 5,508; NLW, Hawarden MS 78; Wynnstay Rentals; Chirk Castle E.1,106, E.3,637, E.917, E.3,615, E.4.151; Wynnstay 104, no. 105.

[94] NLW, MS 5,977D.

[95] UCNWL, General coll. MS 7,134; Merioneth RO, Rhagad DR30. Mr Gerallt Harries of Swansea Univ. Coll. kindly provided information about the Lloyds of Berth.

[96] UCNWL, Kinmel MS 1,675.

William Bulkeley of Brynddu was sowing turnips and clover seed mixed with local hayseed on his demesne in 1736–7, and was also watering his meadows and fertilizing his soil with sand. Shelly sand, which greatly improved the soil for corn crops, was widely used as a fertilizer in Anglesey from the Restoration by many of the great and small gentry alike, "and others". Trials with marling, too, were carried out from the 1650s on the island and quickly adopted by several small gentlemen like Pierce Lloyd of Llugwy, John Griffith of Llanddyfnan, and Hugh Lloyd of Marian. The Anglesey gentry were also experimenting with the use of lime from the late 1660s.[97]

A number of isolated examples of 'spirited improvers' were to be found also in various parts of south Wales. The large owners were growing clover from the closing decades of the seventeenth century, the crop allegedly having been introduced into Glamorgan in the 1680s by Sir Edward Stradling of St Donat's and Mr Seys of Boverton.[98] In the relatively accessible region of south-eastern Wales a significant (albeit small) number of lesser owners, many of them yeomen, were likewise beginning to cultivate clover in the last quarter of the seventeenth century.[99] It was also being grown at this time by a few large and small owners in south-west Wales.[100] Moreover, isolated instances occurred of owners practising other improvements. In the Picton Castle estate records lime is shown to have been used extensively on one occasion in 1703; on 29 September some "260 loads of lime [were] put in this 13 acres of ground [possibly on the Picton demesne] which, at 3s. per load, comes to £39". Further east, coal ashes were applied to wet parts of the Mackworth demesne at Gnoll, Neath, in 1739, and in the same year water meadows were a notable feature there. Cattle breeding was evidently making some progress at Margam, since an account of all stock on Henllys demesne (parish of Landewy, Glam.) in 1717 refers to "20 steers of Margam breed".[101]

It is clear that from the Restoration a small number of Welsh owners were taking an interest in improved techniques. The latest treatises on husbandry

[97] NLW, Bodewryd MSS 63, 64, 66; UCNWL, Penrhos, i, MSS 364, 365, 369–71, 524A, 847, 868, and v, MS 588; F. Jones, 'Squire of Anglesey', pp. 83–8; L. Owen, 'Letters of an Anglesey Parson', *Hon. Soc. Cymmrodorion*, 1961, pt 1; F. V. Emery, 'The Mechanics of Innovation: Clover Cultivation in Wales before 1750', *J. Hist. Geog.*, II, 1, 1976; UCNWL, Penrhos, v, MS 96, and i, 868; Henblas A18; H. Rowlands, *Idea Agriculturae*, Dublin, 1764, pp. xii–xvi, xxi–xxv.

[98] W. Davies, *A General View of the Agriculture and Domestic Economy of South Wales*, 2 vols., London, 1815, I, p. 575; see also NLW, Margam and Penrice MSS 2,256, 5,049 for growth of clover in the early eighteenth century at Margam.

[99] Emery, *op. cit.*, pp. 44–7.

[100] NLW, Picton Castle, MS 1457; NLW, MS 4,275B; Carmarthen RO, Cawdor/Vaughan MS 102/8,029: letter of 24 June 1755.

[101] NLW, Picton Castle, MS 1,709; Univ. Coll., Swansea, Mackworth MSS 426, 522, 552; NLW, Margam and Penrice MS 2,766.

housed in their libraries testify to their enthusiasm.[102] Their reference in their correspondence to various "trials" being undertaken on their properties is a cautionary reminder that their role as innovators in the earliest stages of the new agriculture should not be understated. Furthermore, there is some evidence that their example was followed by others. Henry Rowlands wrote in 1704 that "At Holyhead Mr. John Owen of Penrhos was the first, to speak of, that made improvement in this way [i.e. by using shelly sand for corn]; he showed his poorer neighbours the way of making the barrenest lands produce the richest crops of corn; they quickly took to it."[103] Yet the spread of improvements through emulation, particularly among the tenant farmers, remained very gradual.

The land outside the demesnes was let to tenants. Farms were generally small, the majority ranging from thirty to sixty acres.[104] Occupants of the many holdings below thirty acres or thereabouts could not make a living from farming and depended upon a by-employment; some were artisans, and others, colliers and carters, and it is likely that such jobs often provided the main income. Besides the paramount influence of the infertile terrain and distance from good markets, the small units were also partly a consequence of the old system of gavelkind, in operation in the Welsh hill and upland areas until Tudor times, whereby a unit of owned land was equally divided among the sons upon the death of the father. Such a system must have led to morcellation of holdings no less than of estates. Moreover, as far as north Wales was concerned, the custom under the leasehold system of subdivision of holdings among the sons and sometimes the grandsons, of a tenant in accordance with his will, a custom surviving down to the close of the eighteenth century, resulted in the division of holdings into 'shares' after the original lessee's death.[105] Contemporaries regarded a large farm as covering three hundred acres and over, and there were few of these in Wales. Farms

[102] E.g., NLW, MS 5,977D refers to the Gwydir estate agent consulting *The Mystery of Husbandry Discovered*, 1698, at the turn of the eighteenth century; Morgan Thomas, gent., of Old Castle-upon-Alun, in St Bride's Major, Glam., who made his will in 1667, possessed many "bookes on husbandry" – see M. I. Williams, thesis, p. 100.

[103] Rowlands, op. cit., p. xv.

[104] Gwent RO, D43.4,634: survey of Llangibby Castle estate, 1709/10 – 63 holdings averaged 41 acres; Clwyd RO, Erthig D/E 319: John Edisbury's lands in Denbighshire, 1657 – 34 holdings averaged 51 acres; NLW, MS 6,556E: Sir Thomas Stradling's St Donat's estate, 1732 – 79 farms averaged 34 acres; UCNWL, Bodorgan MS 1,580: survey of Bodorgan, 1725 – 146 holdings averaged 63 acres; Carmarthen RO, Cynghordy MS 1,070: survey of the Danyrallt estate, Carms., 1748 – 14 holdings averaged 60 acres; UCNWL, Mostyn MS 6,051: survey of Berth-lwyd, Mont., c. 1756 – 29 holdings averaged 63 acres; L. S. Andrews, 'Vaynor Lands during the Eighteenth Century', *Mont. Colls.*, XLVI, 2, 1940, early eighteenth-century survey – 7 holdings averaged 66 acres.

[105] *Report of the R. C. on Land in Wales and Monmouthshire*, PP, XXXIV, 1896, pp. 328, 345–6; R. O. Roberts, ed., *Farming in Caernarvonshire around 1800*, Caernarvon, 1973, p. 17.

of (or approaching) this category were usually located in the fertile 'English' areas, particularly in south Pembrokeshire, according to one contemporary. The general situation was thus one of family-run farms, which permitted men of small capital to take them. An estate owner of Almeley, Herefordshire, wrote to his steward in 1733: "I am sorry to find nothing but Welsh tenants offer for Upcot – they are the worst of tenants, generally poor and without stock."[106]

In 1750 Welsh farms were still frequently fragmented and intermixed with other holdings. This fragmentation was often a consequence of the intermixture of ownership of land, which had been greatly promoted under the operation of gavelkind. Their detached pieces meant that holdings were difficult to manage efficiently and tenants trespassed on one another. Intermixture of ownership could also mean that certain holdings were jointly owned in shares by two or perhaps more parties, the tenant of such a farm holding part from one owner and part from another, not necessarily under the same terms.[107] The situation was being gradually improved in these years as a result of the efforts of certain owners like Owen Meyrick of Bodorgan to consolidate their properties by making exchanges of land or purchases.[108] (Exchange of outlying lands distant from the estate nuclei was also aimed at, but this was principally a matter of administrative convenience and perhaps of aesthetic sensitivity.) Nevertheless, as mentioned, much consolidation of farms remained to be done after 1750, and until this was achieved land remained undervalued by a third or a quarter.[109]

Besides consolidating their fragmented holdings some owners, like, for example, Richard Vaughan of Derwydd between 1715 and 1721, were seeking to enlarge their farms by joining holdings. The process often took the form of merging small units, upon the expiration of their leases, with adjacent large ones.[110] Conversion into one holding would save repairs. Understandably, peasant tenants with strong emotional attachments to what were often 'family' holdings were opposed to such rationalization.[111] Nor

[106] G. E. Mingay, 'The Size of Farms in the Eighteenth Century', EcHR, 2nd ser., XIV, 3, 1962, p. 470; T. Dineley, *Official Progress of the First Duke of Beaufort through Wales in 1684*, ed. R. W. Banks, London, 1888, p. 276; Hereford RO, F/A iii/107.

[107] Carmarthen RO, Cawdor/Vaughan MS 102/8,029: letter of 7 Oct. 1718 of R. Vaughan to Morgan; Pembs. County Library, Haverfordwest, survey of Harcourt Powell's estate, 1778.

[108] F. A. Barnes, 'Estate Development and Agrarian Landscape in Anglesey, 1540–1780', unpub. paper for Soc. of British Historical Geographers, 1973, pp. 36–7; NLW, Lucas MSS 3,874, 3,244.

[109] NLW, Bute MSS, box 104, no. 9: valuation of Lord Windsor's estate in Glamorgan, 1774; R. O. Roberts, *Farming in Caernarvonshire*; Pembs. County Library, Haverfordwest, survey of Harcourt Powell's estate, 1778. For widespread intermixture of property in south-west Wales early in the next century, see my forthcoming *Patriarchs and Parasites*.

[110] Carmarthen RO, Cawdor/Vaughan MS 102/8,029: letters of 19 Apr. 1715 of R. Vaughan to Morgan and of 21 Sept. 1721 of J. Roberts to Morgan.

[111] *Ibid.*: letter of 9 Apr. 1713 of R. Vaughan to his agent.

was the policy always prudent from the landowners' point of view. It was desirable for social reasons to have a contented tenantry, and, again, men with capital were notoriously difficult to obtain. For whatever reasons, the amalgamation of farms had occurred only to a very limited extent by the mid century.

Farms were being enlarged and new ones created in these years by enclosure. The process of enclosure of the arable common fields of the lowland Englishries stretching across the coastal plain of south Wales had been almost completed by 1640. Piecemeal consolidation of strips in open arable fields in both Englishry and Welshry areas was nevertheless taking place in a few districts throughout this period, and open arable fields in areas like west Pembrokeshire, coastal Cardiganshire, and the eastern vales and plateaux of Montgomeryshire remained unenclosed at the end of the eighteenth century.[112] But by far the greatest amount of unenclosed land in the mid seventeenth century lay in the hill and moorland expanses, and this period saw a marked acceleration of the process of encroachment on, and enclosure of, these fringe tracts which had begun in earnest in late Tudor times. (Nevertheless, as late as 1800 around 25 per cent of the land surface was still common and waste.) We have seen that in addition to many piecemeal small encroachments by squatters, other encroachments and enclosures of the commons and wastes were being made by landowners who were freehold or customary tenants of the various manors. Sometimes landowners of a manor enclosed individually, by the consent of the neighbouring inhabitants who had rights of common, and also by consent of the lord of the manor, while, at others, a number would jointly agree, with the lord's consent, collectively to undertake an enclosure, but they often individually encroached without consent from any party.[113] In such instances they either claimed the property as theirs without paying any acknowledgement (as on the Beaufort seignory of Gower) or else they paid a fine in the manor court. Fences were sometimes broken down by the lord of the manor concerned or by enraged neighbouring landowners whose rights had been infringed.[114] We have also seen how private landowners were encroaching on crown wastes, claiming them as their freehold and doubtless fencing certain tracts. Such activity led Ellis Wynne in 1703 to denounce the "great man who steals

---

[112] F. Emery, 'The Farming Regions of Wales', in AHEW, IV, p. 153; D. Thomas, *Agriculture in Wales during the Napoleonic Wars*, Cardiff, 1963, p. 31; J. M. Powell, 'The Economic Geography of Montgomeryshire in the Nineteenth Century', unpub. Liverpool Univ. M.A. thesis, 1962, pp. 26–8.

[113] Glamorgan RO, D/DE 210: grant to T. Aubrey to enclose 9 acres of common in Cygorwen manor, 1713; NLW, Mayberry MS 5,184: concerning 25 commoners in 1677 enclosing 200 acres of Gilwern common in the lordship of Colwyn and sowing it with corn.

[114] NLW, Badminton, ii, MS 1,931' W. A. Griffiths, 'Some Notes on the Earlier Records of the Manor of Deythur', *Mont. Colls.*, LI, 1, 1949–50, pp. 43–8; NLW, Tredegar Park, box 124, no. 406; UCNWL, Garthewin MS 1,629.

from the mountain half a parish" and "robs the poor man of a living for his beast, and thereby a living for himself and his household".[115] Holdings were not only enlarged by landowners encroaching and adding to them, but by tenant farmers themselves making encroachments, as, for example, on Morva Havod y llyn in Beddgelert parish, Caernarvonshire, between 1723 and 1745. Doubtless, tenants in some instances were encouraged by their landlords to take parts of the mountain into their holdings. In legal theory the lord alone had the right to close the common, and one such lord (the owner of the Margam and Penrice estate) stipulated in a lease to a tenant farmer of his estate in 1672 that he "may enclose the waste land, if he thinks it fit".[116]

Many tenants of holdings had grazing rights on the wastes by virtue of their landlords being lords or tenants of the manor. Landowners were frequently squabbling and going to law over their respective rights of common.[117] Their tenants depastured their sheep, cattle, and horses and cut turf in a variety of ways which rested upon the customary arrangements entered into by the tenants and landowners of the manor concerned. In some instances the different parties could use any part of the commons, usually (though not always) without stint, which led to overstocking. In others, agreements were reached between different owners whereby individual tenements carried the exclusive right of depasturing a certain specified area of the common, usually that adjoining their boundaries, and the occupant could drive away stock straying onto his 'liberty'.[118] Such rights of common were vital to tenant farmers, and when squatters interfered with these rights their fences were pulled down by the landlords, who feared a loss of rents.[119]

The terms of leases granted to tenants varied even between different holdings on the same estate. In the late seventeenth century leases for twenty-one or thirty-one years, or (less frequently) for shorter periods like six, ten, and eleven years, were popular, few leases being granted for terms of lives. Terms of twenty-one years continued dominant on many estates down to the 1740s, as on the Edwinsford, Tredegar Park, and Crosswood estates, while on others, like Picton Castle, Slebech, Golden Grove, and Margam, leases for three lives, or for ninety-nine or ninety years, determinable upon three lives, were growing increasingly popular from the 1720s. Although in north Wales the

[115] Wynne, *Gweledigaetheu y Bardd Cwsc*, London, 1703, ed. J. Morris-Jones, Bangor, 1898, p. 21, cited in A. H. Dodd, *The Industrial Revolution in North Wales*, Cardiff, 1933, p. 55.

[116] NLW, Dolfriog MS 249; E. D. Evans, *A History of Wales 1660–1815*, Cardiff, 1976, p. 127; NLW, Margam and Penrice MS 6,349, no. 520.

[117] Merioneth RO, Tanybwlch Z/DV 343; NLW, Harrison and Sons, box 71, pcl i: Chancery suit, 1746, between Thomas Jones and Ann Owen.

[118] Dodd, *Industrial Revolution*, pp. 59–60; an example of stinting is seen in NLW, Margam and Penrice MS 1,466; Harrison and Sons, box 71, pcl i: Chancery suit, 1746; Beynon, thesis, app., p. 19. [119] NLW, Brogyntyn MSS 1,274, 904.

tendency in the late eighteenth century was increasingly towards granting tenancies-at-will and refusing leases on the grounds that tenants were indolent and inactive, a growing number of estates in the south were being leased for three lives from the mid century. The preference for three lives over terms of twenty-one years did not lie in the time element, for in this period leases for three lives were regarded as equivalent to a term of twenty-four years. Landlords considered that the crucial difference between these two forms of tenure lay in the respective mental attitudes that each encouraged in the tenants. Owners like John Campbell of Stackpole believed that tenants would be more likely to improve and keep their lands in good order under three-lives leases than under terms of years with a certain determination because under the latter the last three or four were likely to be employed to the great injury of the land.[120] John Vaughan of Golden Grove claimed in 1757 that the granting of leases for lives was the method "all the people chose and are well pleased with", but just how general such approval was among tenants is impossible to estimate. One possible objection from the tenants' standpoint was that by their very nature they contained an element of uncertainty. For whatever reason, in 1726 a number of Chirk Castle tenants met the agent "in a body" to declare that they would not take leases unless granted for the term of twenty-one years instead of the term of the natural life "as the leases are drawn".[121]

Very few tenancies-at-will were granted down to mid century, for leases were considered preferable to year-to-year lettings. Owners like Richard Vaughan of Derwydd felt that tenants holding from year to year would impoverish an estate, keeping the farm only while there was any heart in the ground and then throwing it up.[122] It is equally clear that substantial tenants at any rate were eager for leases of twenty-one years or for lives as security for laying out money in improvements. Thus Francis Meyrick wrote to the agent of the sixth Viscount Hereford in 1660 that he had no encouragement either to "manure, hedge or build" on the holding of Bowett farm near Hundleton, Pembrokeshire, "having no term", and requested a lease of three lives or twenty-one years.[123]

Leases were being drawn up in increasingly elaborate form over these years, and their growing number of penalties for default reflects the ever tightening

---

[120] *Reports to the Board of Agriculture*, 1794: *Denbighshire*, p. 17; *Lower Cardiganshire*, p. 17; Carmarthen RO, Cawdor/Campbell MS box 128: letter of 20 Nov. 1773 of John Campbell to his grandson.

[121] Carmarthen RO, Cawdor/Vaughan MS 102/8,029: letter of 25 Jan. 1757 to T. Price; NLW, Chirk Castle E.826.

[122] Carmarthen RO, Cawdor/Vaughan MS 102/8,029: letter of 12 July 1716 to Carmarthenshire agent; see also NLW, MS 17, 108D (NLW, Llangibby Castle C.527): letter of 7 Sept. 1728 of M. Roe to Mathew Powell.

[123] B. E. and K. A. Howells, eds., *Pembrokeshire Life: 1572–1843*, Pemb. Rec. Soc., 1972, pp. 42–3; see also NLW, Ruthin MS 1,531.

control of the landlord over his property.[124] While many leases were written, some (as on the Picton Castle estate) were oral, though in what proportion is unknown. In addition to the payment of money rent the tenant had to render certain duties, which included "cymorthas" (though by now rare), food payments, and labour services.[125] Such payments were a reflection of the essentially backward, uncommercial character of the region. Typical food renders were hens and eggs at Shrovetide, chickens at Whitsuntide, geese or fat capons at Christmas, and bushels of oats (the latter being sometimes specified as "marketable") at Shrovetide, while common labour services were a few days' reaping; a few days' service with a team for ploughing, harrowing, or mucking; and carriage of coal to the mansion. By the closing decades of the seventeenth century such duties were increasingly being rendered either in kind or in money, at the landlord's option, and at the turn of the next century the general rates of commutation were 6d. for a day's reaping, 8d. for a horse load of coal, 1s. for a couple of pullets, 1s. for a fat hen, and 4s. for a bushel of oats. Some estates were to continue exacting heavy labour services throughout these years. Thus on the Noyadd Trefawr estate in south Cardiganshire Jenkin James of Trevaes Fawr rendered in 1743/4 the following: 2 horse loads of coal, 6 reapers, 10 horse loads of sand, 2 horses to carry corn, 2 horses to lead hay, and 2 more "on occasion". A few tenants there had to provide a plough and harrow. A similar heavy exaction of labour services obtained on the Brynddu estate, where, besides reaping days, tenants were convenanted "to work by the day when called upon", for which they received payment. One lease of 7 April 1740 stipulated: "and he is to work with me all the time he can spare from his own farm". Probably small owners like these, farming their demesnes for the market, were anxious to gain as much labour from their tenants as possible.[126]

Tenants also covenanted to pay a heriot of the best beast. Once again, by the close of the seventeenth century it became increasingly common for it to be rendered in kind or in money, at the choice of the landlord. Heriots taken in kind were sometimes sold.[127] Tenants holding of more than one landlord were harshly treated, for each owner claimed payment.[128] Another

[124] 'Better' remedies against a bad tenant were introduced, for instance, on the Golden Grove estate shortly before 1715 and were soon copied on the Derwydd estate – Carmarthen RO, Cawdor/Vaughan MS 102/8,029: letter of 5 Mar. 1715 of R. Vaughan to Morgan.

[125] Cymorthas had been forbidden by the Tudor Act of Union. They had previously been contributions in money, kind, or labour to someone who had fallen on hard times. They were taken as late as the 1740s by the Morgans of Tredegar, as lords of the manor of Brecon – NLW, Tredegar Park 117/296 and 119/101; see also NLW, MS 4,275B.

[126] NLW, Noyadd Trefawr MS 742; G. N. Evans, 'The Artisan and Small Farmer in Mid-Eighteenth Century Anglesey', *Angl. Antiq. Soc.*, 1933, pp. 89–91.

[127] The Derwydd steward, for example, sold David Jones's heriot mare in 1712 for £4 – Carmarthen RO, Cawdor/Vaughan MS 102/8,029, f. 20.

[128] M. I. Williams, thesis, p. 59.

covenant enjoined tenants to grind at a particular mill, the tenants paying the accustomed tolls. Some leases covenanted tenants to keep a hound. Landlords reserved all the timber and mineral rights. Other clauses enjoined the lessees at their own expense to keep the premises in good repair, although owners of certain estates like Crosswood and Edwinsford granted timber free of charge.

Although jealously safeguarding holdings against the negligence of slothful tenants, very few leases before 1750 aimed at encouraging improved husbandry. There was thus an almost complete absence of such covenants as those requiring tenants to use the straw, fodder, and dung on their premises, to fold sheep and cattle in order to gain the benefit of the manure, to lime the land, to grow clover and not to plough fresh ground in the final year. Progressive husbandry clauses became more frequent (though not common) from the 1760s. One 'improving' lease will be cited to underline the potential of such instruments for agricultural progress. A lease by the Tredegar Park family in 1722 to Thomas Gamage of lands in Glasbury-on-Wye, Brecknockshire, for twenty-one years at a yearly rent of £147, covenanted him to leave as many acres of pasture as he first entered upon together with thirty acres of clover, to lime the fallow yearly, and to leave thirty-one acres of fallow limed and ten loads of lime upon each cover.[129]

The distribution between landlords' and tenants' capital was well defined in these years. Owners provided the land and the fixed capital and tenants the working capital. Landlords often neglected to let their holdings in good repair by replacing old, decaying buildings and other fixtures. What repairs they did undertake were often the basic minimum deemed necessary to attract takers or to prevent tenants from throwing up their holdings. Thus the landlord of Chirk Castle in 1721 paid John Lloyd £4 2s. 6d., "what he laid out in repairing the great house [i.e. dwelling house] at Llansannan he being a new tenant and had a promise to have him [sic] repaired when he came to it".[130] Complaints about dilapidated premises were frequently voiced by tenants. There was a "great solliciting for repairs" amongst the tenants of William Owen of Porkington (Brogyntyn) in 1729. In 1737 tenants of the Mackworth estate in the parish of St Mellon's, Cardiff, were uneasy about

[129] NLW, Tredegar Park 119/55; see also Margam and Penrice MS 1,760. Since this section was written others have demonstrated that three-lives leases were a handicap to husbandry improvements. Under them, landlords had little influence on the way their tenants farmed. But as Clay indicates, the change from customary tenure to leasehold gave the landlord power to enforce on his tenants beneficial practices – Martin, thesis, p. 76; A. W. Jones, 'Agriculture and the Rural Community of Glamorgan, circa 1830–1896', unpub. Univ. of Wales Ph.D. thesis, 1980, pp. 300, 302; C. Clay, 'Lifeleasehold in the Western Counties of England 1650–1750', AHR, XXIX, 2, 1981, p. 93.

[130] Myddelton, op. cit., p. 429; see also NLW, Wynnstay Rentals 1670–93, 1694–1705, 1706–13, 1714–23, 1718–24, 1725–9, 1730–5, 1736–9, 1739–42, 1743–4, 1745–7, 1748–9.

the repairs of their farms (particularly on account of ditching), and were ready to throw them up. By the early 1740s many farms on the Margam estate had fallen out of repair through "neglect of not doing what ought to have been done many years ago", and the owner was obliged to lay out large sums of money to repair them. Refusal to do so would have meant much land falling into hand. Several tenants of the Chirk Castle estate were complaining in 1754 that their buildings were badly out of repair. Many dwellings and outhouses on the Wynnstay estate in 1763 were old and built of timber, with clay walls and thatched roofs, and were often dilapidated.[131] Thus Dr Simmonds's later stricture on Welsh squires "who grudge to floor the house of a farmer that rents not more than £30 or £40 a year" was wholly applicable to these years also.[132] Tenants themselves, however, were partly responsible for the dilapidated state of many holdings. Although those holding under leases (as distinct from tenants-at-will) were obliged to keep up repairs, they frequently neglected to do so. Holdings that were let out in parcels (and there were a significant number) were especially run down, for each tenant put himself to as little expense as possible, and "never repairs hedge nor ditch".[133]

Landlords normally provided the durable capital (however inadequate) but sometimes they also helped their more progressive and enterprising tenants in finding the necessary working capital for financing improvements in husbandry. In 1728 Dr Wynne of Bodewryd leased Ty'nycae in the parish of Bodedern to Hugh Jones of Bodowyr (yeoman) for five years at £24 a year. Wynne promised to provide £21 worth of sand on condition that Jones carried it from the waterside and "spread it over the most convenient part of the premises". By careful sanding it was hoped eventually to raise the rent to £40.[134] A handful of Wynnstay tenants were granted yearly allowances from the late 1730s for liming and ditching. Doubtless there were other like instances, but such activity was exceptional. At the same time it is clear that landlords were anxious to assist their more enterprising tenants. In this context it is furthermore interesting to note that by the early eighteenth century outgoing tenants were to some extent already being granted allowances by their landlords or the incoming tenants for unexhausted improvements. Owen Lewis who left Rhyd Galed farm belonging to Wynnstay in 1710 was allowed 10s. "for muck he had left upon the land at his going of, and not allowed for, and delivered the present tenant". In

---

[131] NLW, Brogyntyn MS 1,427: letter of 21 May 1729 of G. Parry; Univ. Coll., Swansea, Mackworth MS 513; Glamorgan RO, D/DP 877/2, 877/9; NLW, Chirk Castle E.5,570; Wynnstay Survey and Valuation, 1763.
[132] BL, Add. MS 35,127, ff. 180–2: letter of 14 Sept. 1792 of Dr J. Simmonds to Arthur Young. I owe thanks to Professor G. E. Mingay for this reference.
[133] NLW, Margam and Penrice L.333, L.765; Brogyntyn MS 947.
[134] UCNWL, Penrhos MS 521.

1725 the Chirk Castle agent mentioned that allowances were "used now and then between tenant and tenant" for such items as compost in the ground. Later, in 1746, the Wynnstay agent compensated David Ffoulkes £4 10s. for "his share of corn, for clover seed sowed and for dung left on his late tenement in Llangedwin".[135]

The distinction between landowners' and tenants' capital was often blurred in times of agricultural depression. Certain individual years or runs of years were critical, namely, 1641, 1650–5 (1652–5 were favourable for English farmers), 1663, 1667–9, 1678–83, 1690–1, 1694–1703, 1708–9, 1722–3, 1731–8, 1740–2, 1747–8, and 1750–1.[136] At such times landowners came to their tenants' rescue by shouldering part of their losses. In the first place, arrears were permitted to mount to very high levels. For example, some of the best tenants of the Powis Castle estate were behind in their payments by two and even three years' rent in 1668. Again, in 1690 arrears amounted to £984 out of rental of £1,190 on part of the Wynnstay estate, while a portion of the Chirk Castle lands in the same year had arrears of £1,384 on a rental of £715.[137] Tenants were also allowed to pay in driblets at different times of the year so that optimum advantage could be taken of the periodic local fairs. Moreover, on some estates they were permitted to pay their rents partly, or even wholly, in kind. This happened, for instance, on the Powis Castle estate in 1668 and 1698, when the weakest tenants were allowed to pay with corn; or bacon, cheese, and butter; or an ox or a cow (the latter going as food for the workers in the estate's lead mines) and with work like ploughing and harvesting. Similarly, between 1699 and 1702 Chirk Castle was taking cattle instead of rents and sending them to England for sale. Yet again, in 1696 Stephen Morris instructed his brother, who was acting as rent collector for his estate in north-east Pembrokeshire, that if money was not available he should "let some of the drovers take cattle and take bills of them".[138] (It was seemingly customary in such instances for the landlord to buy the animal(s) from the tenants and to pocket from the purchase price the amount of rent owed. In this way tenants were shielded from the worst rigours of the open market.) Tenants on the Bodewryd estate, too, were allowed to clear their rents in 1732 by doing work for the landlord like carrying sand. Similarly, the Margam estate agent urged his employer in 1712 to undertake repairs through his own workmen rather than grant money allowances "especially since your Lordship has several tenants so far

[135] NLW, Wynnstay Rental 1714–23; Chirk Castle E.777; Wynnstay Rental 1745–7.

[136] A mass of evidence for such times of distress has been found in the correspondence between landowners and agents of a large number of Welsh estates.

[137] Smith, *Herbert Correspondence*, pt 2, letter no. 344; NLW, Wynnstay Rental 1670–93; Chirk Castle F.5,864.

[138] Smith, *Herbert Correspondence*, pt 2, letter no. 344; NLW, Powis Castle Correspondence, MS 463: letter of 12 Feb. 1698; Chirk Castle F.9,351, F.3,949, F.2,803, F.2,804, F.10,724; Owen and Colby MS 1,959.

in arrears that they will hardly ever be able to pay unless your Lordship will be pleased to employ them on such an occasion as this".[139]

In addition, allowances were made to tenants for building or repairing outhouses and for ditching and fencing. That landlords did this to ward off rent abatements and reductions or, worse, vacant holdings (the ultimate calamity in their eyes, involving "trouble, vexation and loss") emerges from a Wynnstay agent's remarks (those of John Jones) in the late-seventeenth-century rentals.[140] Thus he observed in 1680: "The two last particulars [allowances for buildings] I was forced to allow to encourage the tenants to stay being ready to part and for 2 or 3 years ago and very eager for abatements – which I have not yielded to as yet." Taxes were also allowed in unsettled times, as, for example, on the Crogen estate, Merioneth, in 1671, on the Wynnstay lands in 1689 and the 1690s, and on the Chirk Castle estate in the 1740s.[141] At Wynnstay as elsewhere, however, abatements and reductions were forced on the owner in critical years. As John Jones observed in the rental for Llanfrothen parish, Merioneth, in 1698, "Hugh David for his tenement in Croesor formerly £16, this year to keep him in having no tenant ready an abatement was made of 40s." The rent was reduced from £16 to £12 in 1701.

In 1700–1 the owner of Wynnstay assisted impoverished tenants by stocking their holdings. Ellis ap Richard and William David, for example, held separate moieties of Gweburnant farm in Penmachno parish, Caernarvonshire, at rents of £10 15s., and "in that these tenants grew poor and would have parted" the agent engaged to stock the ground with thirty young cattle, for the keeping of which over summer and winter they were allowed nearly 8s. a year for each beast. Similarly, in 1701 the tenant of the aforementioned holding of Croesor – "being poor and lest it should stand vacant being all mountains" – was not only allowed to keep the hundred sheep which the agent had already put there without charge in May 1700 but was also sent an extra fifty-two, he receiving 6d. apiece for keeping them.[142]

Despite these various rescue operations a few tenants collapsed.[143] Some such casualties on the Wynnstay estate were settled on lesser holdings on the estate, but no doubt most who failed here and elsewhere ceased to be farmers. It not infrequently happened that after the sale of tenants' distrained goods certain arrears were found to be 'desperate', in which instance owners either wrote them off or recovered them in work like guttering and repairing. A few Wynnstay tenants with irrecoverable arrears were referred to in the 1690s

[139] L. Owen, 'Letters of an Anglesey Parson', p. 93; NLW, Margam and Penrice MS 2,544.
[140] NLW, Wynnstay Rental 1670–93; for the nuisance of farms in hand, see Gwent RO, Medlycott D.760.135, and NLW, MS 17, 108D (NLW, Llangibby Castle C.527).
[141] NLW, Wynnstay Old Misc. Rental vol. IV and Wynnstay Rental 1670–93; Chirk Castle F.14,063.
[142] NLW, Wynnstay Rental 1694–1705.
[143] E.g. NLW, Clenennau MS 937 and Bodewryd MS 475.

as "beggars". Others of Wynnstay and Chirk Castle "fled the country". Predictably, when tenants were broken and threw up their farms, owners were sometimes unable to find suitable tenants to fill them. Detailed evidence is extant about what happened on the Wynnstay estate in such unwelcome circumstances. In the crisis years of the late seventeenth century either the grass of vacant holdings was let out to different parties, or cattle were bought from different tenants and turned onto the lands in hand, or individual farms were let to several tenants, each taking a separate parcel. Sometimes a mixture of these options was tried.[144]

Even outside the difficult years the small peasant tenants were slack in meeting their rents. This arose primarily from their want of reserves of money, although it owed something no doubt to inefficient estate management. Throughout, tenants were leniently treated when they fell behind with their payments. The London accountant of Lord Powis wrote to the Welsh agent in 1725 how his lordship "had as good be without tenants as have such as pay no rent; in fine I am resolved to bring these estates to the same custom as in Northampton and Middlesex to clear one half year before another is due; and not have whole volumes of arrears returned as has always been the custom of Mr. Hughes and your father".[145] Charles Parry of Bradley Green in Worcestershire was likewise frustrated over non-payment of rents on his Montgomeryshire estates in the mid 1740s. He harangued his agent in 1745: "I want to know what is the matter my tenants pay me no rents for at this rate I had as good sell or else give away my estates as to keep them."[146] Contemporary correspondence reveals that owners indulged their tenants because they had little alternative even in normal times.[147] The poverty of the Welsh farming community meant that a policy of changing backward tenants was merely wishful thinking and that the 'system of arrears' simply could not be avoided in a capital-starved society. Such a system meant, of course, that tenants frequently finished up utterly ruined and undone.

Sluggish payment was sometimes accentuated when tenants were charged rack rents.[148] This period saw a gradual conversion from the system of levying fines or charging premiums on the grant or renewal of leases, whether for lives or a term of years (together with a small annual reserved rent), to one of charging rack rents. It is emphasized that the replacement of the old fine system was slow and that rack leases became general only during the

---

[144] NLW, Wynnstay Rental 1694–1705; see also Edward Powell, 'Pryce (Newtown Hall) Correspondence', pp. 92–3: letter xxvii of 10 Apr. 1641.
[145] NLW, Powis Castle Correspondence, MS 1,021: letter of 12 July 1725.
[146] *Ibid.*, MS 1,907: letter of 12 October 1745; also MS 1,915: letter of 1 Feb. 1747.
[147] E.g. a letter of the steward of St Donat's Castle, Glam., in 1750, cited in A. H. John, *The Industrial Development of South Wales, 1750–1850*, Cardiff, 1950, p. 17.
[148] NLW, Margam and Penrice MS L.341: letter of 24 Mar. 1698 of C. Collins.

late eighteenth century.[149] (The fine system, moreover, survived on ecclesiastical property well into the nineteenth century.) Fines were widespread down to the second decade of the eighteenth century, but from the 1720s tenements were increasingly leased out at rack rents on estates like Margam, Tredegar Park, and Powis Castle.[150]

The reasons for this change were seldom explicitly stated. Rack rents certainly meant a more predictable annual income for owners, and tenants on merely nominal yearly payments (after initially 'purchasing' their holdings for a long period in advance) were inclined to let their farms fall into disrepair. John Clark, reporting in 1801–2 on the ruinous state of the lands of the see of St David's (leased under fines), contended that "the lower the rent is, the poorer will the tenant be, and worse will the land be cultivated".[151] Obviously owners calculated on the basis of self-interest, but it is likely that such a change was not unwelcome to peasant tenants acutely short of capital. (Indeed, under the old system many of the fines must have been paid in periodic driblets, and sometimes by borrowing.)[152]

Any attempted calculation of rent movements over these years is fraught with difficulties. There are only very few complete runs of rentals, and in addition the constantly changing sizes of estate units, as also of their separate holdings, the frequent switch from fines to rack rents, and the possibility of 'extraordinary' repairs (like the building of farmhouses) being undertaken by landlords all pose severe problems. Holdings under fines are especially difficult because without knowing the state of health and ages of the surviving lives concerned it is impossible to calculate the actual yearly payment for the holding, taking both rent and fine into consideration. The safest impressions are gained from contemporary statements and from a close study of individual tenements. In general terms, the low, stagnant prices of the late seventeenth and early eighteenth centuries (a consequence of the supply of farm produce outstripping demand) meant that rents did not move upwards to any significant extent. In Wales, as elsewhere in Britain, the noticeable rise came only from the 1760s, when prices turned upwards in response to increased demand which now for various reasons ran ahead of supply.[153]

---

[149] *Reports to the Board of Agriculture*, 1794: *Pembrokeshire*, p. 33; *Carmarthenshire*, p. 49. From 1756 rack rents only were to be charged, for example, on the Golden Grove estate – Carmarthen RO, Cawdor/Vaughan MS 102/8,029: letter of 21 Dec. 1756 of J. Vaughan to R. Vaughan.

[150] NLW, Margam and Penrice MS 5,971B; Powis Castle Correspondence, MS 1,027; Tredegar Park 108/32, 119/55; PP. *XXXIV*, 1896, pp. 382–5.

[151] Dr Martin drew my attention to the fact that rack rents meant a more predictable yearly income for owners. NLW, Church in Wales MS 14,229.

[152] Tenants of the Chirk Castle estate paid their fines in 1726 by borrowing – NLW, Chirk Castle E.5,956.

[153] Dr Martin advised me as to the difficulties of calculating the actual annual payment for holdings under fines. Mingay, *English Landed Society*, pp. 51–2; Carmarthen RO, Cawdor/Vaughan MS 102/8,029: letter of 28 Apr. 1757 of J. Vaughan to W. Thomas: NLW, Tredegar Park 124/97.

From the late 1660s rents fell as prices tumbled. Welsh farmers were primarily dependent on leanstock prices, and cattle prices sank in north-east Wales in 1668–9, the drop being partly blamed on "the carrying over of Irish cattle which brought the market so low".[154] (This is probably explained by the fact that the 1667 Irish Cattle Act was not yet being properly enforced. Once the act began to take effect, however, lean cattle "became dearer than they were before the prohibition".)[155] Depressed cattle prices were also prevalent in north and south-east Wales between 1677 and 1683, the crucial factor as always in this store-stock region being the level of demand from English graziers. Thus in June 1683 the fairs of north Wales were slack because of the very wet weather which deterred graziers from buying until "their ground be dryed up".[156] Cattle prices again ruled low in the 1690s, as, for example, in 1694 when lands were burned because of the dry summer, and again in 1702 when neither cattle nor woollen webs were selling in north Wales.[157] The fall in prices meant that down to about 1710 rents were reduced when leases fell in, albeit reluctantly. Thus Henry Baker requested a tenement in Monmouthshire in 1670 "at such reasonable terms as shall fit (farms being much fallen these late years by reason of the cheapness of corn and scarcity of money)". In north Wales rents of certain holdings on the Crogen estate, Merioneth, were reduced in 1671, while other farms on the same property remained unlet. The Chirk Castle agent noted in his 1677–8 rent roll of Cynllwyd parish, Merioneth: "David Thomas for Meini hirion late at £6 set by my master himself by reason of the late fall in lands to him for the year 1676 at £5."[158] It is impossible to calculate the general rate of reductions in these closing decades of the seventeenth century. A few isolated instances nevertheless provide some indication of what was happening: nine holdings in Denbighshire belonging to Robert Willoughby were reduced by 17 per cent in the 1670s and five holdings belonging to Chirk Castle in the townships of Coyd Tallog and Crane were reduced in the early nineties by 28 per cent.[159]

Leanstock prices picked up after 1710, but difficult times for Welsh stock breeders occurred again in 1722–3, 1731–8, 1740–2, 1747–8, and 1750–1.[160]

[154] Clwyd RO, D/G 3,274/4, D/G 3,278.    [155] T & C, p. 157.

[156] NLW, Chirk Castle E.3,670; see also Clwyd RO, D/KK 762; NLW, Kemeys-Tynte MSS 30, 46; Smith, *Herbert Correspondence*, pt 2, no. 457: letter of 29 Aug. 1681 of J. Read to Lord Herbert.

[157] NLW, Brogyntyn MS 934: letter of 11 Aug. 1694 of R. Wynn to Elizabeth Wynn; Powis Castle Correspondence, MS 803.

[158] NLW, Baker-Gabb MS 773; Wynnstay Old Misc. Rental, vol. IV; Chirk Castle F.12,788.

[159] NLW, Wynnstay Old Misc. Rental, vol. IV: 1680; Wynstay L/124.

[160] The Welsh situation is shown in the numerous letters between estate owners and agents contained in the various private estate collections at NLW, UCNWL, and other local ROs. For the general position of British stock breeders in the early eighteenth century, see A. H. John, 'The Course of Agricultural Change, 1660–1760', in L. S. Pressnell, ed., *Studies in the Industrial Revolution*, London, 1960, pp. 141–2.

Drought and consequent shortage of fodder were having a severe effect in Monmouthshire in the spring of 1723, shortage of grass in the vicinity of Cardiff was complained of in the summer of 1731, and cattle prices ruled low in Welsh fairs throughout the thirties. Typical was the complaint of David Roberts in 1736 about conditions in Denbighshire: "There is so much ground and lands unlet about here. Some years we may let and some may not and the fairs are very bad for selling beast in our country." Dry seasons and poor crops meant low demand for cattle also in 1740–1, barns being unroofed on one Anglesey estate to procure thatch for cattle. Cattle distemper was depressing prices in north-east Wales in 1750.[161]

Clearly, rents were unlikely to move up quickly in the first half of the eighteenth century. Yet there was an upward tendency. In one instance improved methods of husbandry were seen as the reason for increases in rents. Thomas Lewis, Esq., of Harpton Court, Radnorshire, wrote to his son around 1717 that "the estates in these parts are much improved of late years and are still rising by lime and water and also good husbandry".[162] There were other more general reasons for rent increases, however. Reference has been made to squatting on the common, and the growing incidence of this in the early eighteenth century suggests mounting population pressure on the limited supply of land under cultivation. Mounting pressure on the land was reflected, too, in the practice of many landlords letting their holdings to the best bidders from the early decades of the eighteenth century.[163] Peasant longing for a little plot of land was a powerful driving force, and men of little capital could offer for Welsh holdings because of their small acreage. In outbidding one another, tenants often overreached themselves. Certain of the large owners, however, increasingly had their holdings surveyed and valued in the early eighteenth century. This reflected a more business-like approach and, in fact, as happened on the Mansel lands in Gower in 1722, the new valuations could exceed what tenants were willing to go to even when in competition with one another.[164] Large owners were often keenly aware of the need to make 'improvements' in their rentals as a means of ridding their properties of embarrassing encumbrances. For example, the London accountant for the owner of Powis Castle instructed the Welsh agent

---

[161] Gwent RO, D 760.135: letter of 29 May 1723 of E. Riggs; Univ. Coll., Swansea, Mackworth MS 378: letter of 15 June 1731; NLW, Bodewryd MS 490: letter of 17 Oct. 1736 of D. Roberts. For other complaints about low cattle prices in the 1730s, see NLW, Chirk Castle E.1,098; Clwyd RO, Erthig D/E/547; NLW, Milborne MS 2,259, Margam and Penrice MS L.1,203; UCNWL, Henblas MS A18; Nannau MS 3,582; NLW, Bodewryd MS 704. For depressed cattle prices from the late 1740s, see UCNWL, Kinmel MS 1,675; Clwyd RO, D/E/550 and D/M/4,289; NLW, Powis Castle MS 1,959.   [162] NLW, Harpton Court C/14.
[163] Carmarthen RO, Cawdor/Vaughan MS 102/8,029: letter of 11 July 1717 of Vaughan to Morgan; NLW, Margam and Penrice MS L.989: letter of 25 Jan. 1722 of E. Hancorne to Lord Mansel, and MS L.1,128: letter of 12 Mar. 1725 of T. Craddock to T. Griffith.
[164] NLW, Margam and Penrice MS 989.

in 1724 to "use all your endeavour to make the best of everything for unless you do that the estate will never clear off the great incumbrances that are upon it".[165] Rising rents were noticeable to contemporaries by the second decade of the century. Richard Vaughan, for example, was stressing to his agent in 1715 how lands in Carmarthenshire were "much improved".[166] Rents of individual holdings belonging to a spread of Welsh estates moved upwards in the first half of the eighteenth century by amounts varying between 5 per cent (or even less) and 45 per cent, although in certain instances greater increases were being made.[167] The amount of rent advances varied between farms on the same estate; each holding was a peculiar entity with an individual history of rent movement.

Considerations of political and social advantage played a part in many aspects of estate management. Thus large owners with an eye on Westminster were conscious of the importance of being considered fair landlords. In 1718 Watkin Williams of Llanforda wrote to his father, Sir William Williams: "I never had and I hope I never shall deserve the character of imposing on my tenants", while, later, in 1739, John Campbell of Stackpole counselled his son: "I hope my dear neither you nor I shall ever enrich ourselves by oppression, but I am very glad to increase the estate when I can do it justly, without dealing harshly with the tenants."[168] Calculations of political gain also to some extent influenced the selection and retention of tenants, and this was so not only on the estates of the large owners but also on those of many lesser landlords who were committed to the support of one or other of the leading county families. Many Chirk Castle letters refer to the willingness of a prospective tenant to serve the landlord's interest when required.[169] Tenants were told for whom to vote, and non-compliance usually meant eviction from their holdings. Watkin Jenkins referred to election matters touching the Margam estate in his letter to Lord Mansel in 1740: "all persons that hold any lands under your lordship is safe and will obey your directions for they dare do no otherwise".[170] (One north Wales owner was exceptional in writing to John Myddelton in 1740 that he was ready enough to engage

---

[165] NLW, Powis Castle MS 1,030.

[166] Carmarthen RO, Cawdor/Vaughan MS 102/8,029: letters of 30 Apr. and 23 Aug. 1715.

[167] NLW, Picton Castle leases; Lucas MS 1,846: rental of the New Moat estate, Pembs., 1726; Chirk Castle MS 14,063: rental of 1743; Carmarthen RO, Cawdor/Vaughan MS 103/8,061: rental of 1723–4; NLW, Edwinsford MS 4,577: survey of leases (in Carms.) expiring in 1747; Tredegar Park 117/122 and 119/55.

[168] NLW, Wynnstay, box c, no. 69/62: letter of 13 Feb. 1718; Carmarthen RO, Cawdor/-Campbell MS box 128: letter of 1739.

[169] NLW, Chirk Castle E.663, E.1,510, E.865, E.4,356.

[170] NLW, Margam and Penrice MS L.1,199; see also Margam and Penrice MS L.1,104 and MS L.590. In one instance at least (in 1742) a Monmouthshire dissenter defied his landlord, the duke of Beaufort, at the poll out of principle. He was not evicted, however, because he owed the duke £700 which could not be recovered – NLW, Badminton, ii, MS 14,827.

his tenants in the Chirk interest, but he was unwilling "to give authority for any violence towards them".)[171] Actual evictions, however, were rare, tenants doubtless supporting their landlords as much out of affection, loyalty, and habit as out of fear. Political considerations may have led to rents being reduced on one occasion on the Chirk Castle estate. The owner was advised in 1739: "If you do abate to some of your tenants some 20s., some 30s., some 40s., a year to qualify them for a vote perhaps it will be above £200 a year out of your estate which will be easier spared than spend £2 or £3,000 treating and not certain then, and don't doubt your timber and coals will make that small gap up." The granting of three-lives leases was sometimes done for political reasons, as they were technically freehold leases conferring the right to vote. In this respect they were quite different from leases for years or chattel leases, which carried no such advantage. Certain tenants on the Chirk Castle estate were forced to take leases in early 1740 in order that they would be qualified to vote. The political behaviour of small freeholders was vital to large owners. Price of Penllergaer allegedly attempted to manipulate this in the 1740s in his dispute with the duke of Beaufort over mineral rights by encouraging the freeholders of the parishes of Llandilotalybont and Llangyfelach "not to promise their votes with the Duke's interest unless they should have their coal for nothing".[172]

Farm rents were by far the major source of income on estates in these years, but profits from timber and mineral exploitation often contributed a vital addition to estate revenues. It is, indeed, a noticeable feature that owners often relied upon this extra income to meet pressing financial needs. It was thus stated of the Powis Castle estate in 1728: "if the [lead] mines are rightly managed they will soon pay off the debts of the family", and, again, John Campbell of Stackpole rested his hopes in 1744 on "the mines" for rescuing the family finances. Timber sales, in particular, were a convenient means of clearing debts.[173]

Timber was sold off Welsh estates in these years to Liverpool, Bristol, and Swansea shipwrights, to local tanners, and to the Navy Board.[174] But the largest quantities went to iron forges and (increasingly as the eighteenth century advanced) to coal mines. To cite but one example, timber sales to local iron forges became a regular item of business on the Golden Grove estate, Carmarthenshire, in the early eighteenth century, the agent charging

[171] NLW, Chirk Castle E.4,356.

[172] *Ibid.*, MSS E.5,355, E.5,441, E.4,008; W. S. Holdsworth, *An Historical Introduction to the Land Law*, Oxford, 1927, p. 232; NLW, Badminton, ii, MS 2,120.

[173] NLW, Powis Castle Correspondence, MS 1,044; NLW, MS 1,352B, f. 231: letter of 10 Mar. 1744.

[174] NLW, MS 9,719E: Gwydir book of receipts, 1684; W. Linnard, 'A Glimpse of Gwydyr Forest and the Timber Trade in North Wales in the Late 17th Century', *Nat. Lib. Wales J.*, XVIII, 1974, pp. 397–404; NLW, Margam and Penrice L.190; Glamorgan RO, D/DP 877/6, 877/10.

himself with two years' rent in 1719 totalling £2,274 and with a further £238 received from timber sales in the same period. It was normal in these transactions for the landowner to allow the buyer to enter the premises to cut what timber had been sold. In 1705, for example, Richard Vaughan of Torycoed, Carmarthenshire, sold wood growing on specified holdings in the parish of Llanelli to Peter Chettle of Carmarthen for making charcoal; he was given a year for felling, cording, and carrying away the wood, and was bound to reimburse for any damage to crops.[175]

Coal deposits lying beneath estates in coastal areas (where costs of overland transport were low) were increasingly worked, particularly in the south along the shores of Carmarthen and Swansea bays, by large and small landowners alike. The area about Swansea and Neath was especially important; men like Sir Humphrey Mackworth of Neath and the successive heads of the families of Mansel of Margam, Popkin of Forest, and Price of Penllergaer were considerable coalmasters in the early eighteenth century. Thus Sir Humphrey's estate had an annual rental of £1,200, while his coal mines on average yielded an additional £700. The Mansel collieries at Swansea and Briton Ferry provided an average annual income of £800–900 in the first three decades of the century, the total annual value of the Margam estate in the 1720s being about £4,500. These and other owners worked their coal directly, but many avoided the risks and uncertainties involved by leasing works for terms like ten, twenty-one, and thirty-one years to capitalists, who were themselves generally local landowners, including yeoman farmers. Thus landowners controlled the coal industry in these years, English industrialists and their capital moving to south Wales only after 1750.[176] The normal arrangement in leases made in the south-west and the north was the primitive one of dividing the receipts of the mine between the landlord and the working capitalist, the landlord receiving proportions ranging from a third or a quarter (as in south-west Wales) to an eighth or a twelfth (as in Flintshire). On some estates like Picton Castle and Hawarden the landlord had the option of taking the part due to him either in coal and culm or in a cash equivalent. In the area between Llanelli and Neath, however, the more progressive form of payment by measure, usually 3s. or 3s. 6d. per way, was in general use by 1700.[177]

Lead mines were worked in Flintshire from the late seventeenth century

[175] Carmarthen RO, Cawdor/Vaughan MS 22/647; Cawdor/Vaughan MS 8/189.
[176] A. H. John, 'Iron and Coal on a Glamorgan Estate, 1700–40', EcHR, XIII, 1943, pp. 93–103; Univ. Coll., Swansea, Mackworth papers, MS 131A: letter of (probably) 1713 of Sir H. Mackworth to his brother; NLW, Margam and Penrice MS 2,219; Clwyd RO, Erthig D/E.1,574; A. H. Dodd, 'The North Wales Coal Industry during the Industrial Revolution', *Arch. Camb.*, LXXXIV, 2, 1929, pp. 201–2.
[177] NLW, Picton Castle papers: lease of 24 Mar. 1721 to W. Row and others, the landlord receiving a third; Hawarden MSS 1,214, 1,289, 1,314; H. Rees Rawson, 'The Coal-Mining Industry of the Hawarden District on the Eve of the Industrial Revolution', *Arch. Camb.*, XCVI, 2, 1941, pp. 117–20; John, *Industrial Development of South Wales*, pp. 183–4.

by families like the Grosvenors, Pennants, Mostyns, and Hanmers. The discovery by Sir George Wynn of Leeswood in that county of lead deposits on his property made him fabulously rich. The owners of Powis Castle and Chirk Castle similarly worked lead veins on their estates from the late seventeenth century, one Robert Evans being steward of the Chirk Llangynog works (Mont.) in 1734. The owner, Robert Myddelton, was advised in that year to sell his ore to a smelting concern in Flintshire, settling the price periodically according to the price of lead in the Bristol market. The breaking of the former monopoly of the Mines Royal Society in 1693 opened the way for the Cardiganshire gentry to develop lead mining on their properties by the granting of leases to speculators. The Vaughans of Crosswood took royalties ranging from a seventh to a ninth of all the ore mined. Their profits, as well as those of others, were uncertain, however, because of the intermittent nature of mining in these years.[178]

Iron ore was also mined. Sir Thomas Myddelton of Chirk erected a blast furnace on his estate in the 1630s and Charles Lloyd of Dolobran, Montgomeryshire, set up the Mathrafal forge on the estate some time before his death in 1698. The Chirk forge was probably reconstructed in 1710 and the forge at Mathrafal was rebuilt in 1719 by Charles Lloyd (the second) after his furnace at Bersham in Flintshire had failed.[179] In the south, the landowners were the chief ironmasters until the 1730s, when English capitalists increasingly leased forges from them. Iron ore was worked directly on the Margam estate from the second decade of the eighteenth century; in October 1713 the steward expected to have £1,300 worth of iron ready for sale by the following May, and referred to the whole business as being "of great consequence" to Lord Mansel, the owner. (At the same time, coal was of far greater importance on the estate.) Iron smelting was a vital element on the Tredegar Park estate: in 1688 it was estimated that the thousand acres of wood, together with the forges and furnaces, brought in £800 a year out of the total estate income of £6,026. As part of the trend mentioned, Thomas Pratt and Company took over the estate's Tredegar and Machen forges in 1732.[180]

Farm tenants were sometimes obliged to provide the necessary labour and carting in the running of their landlord's mines. Picton Castle tenants in St Issell's and Narberth parishes were in the early eighteenth century contracted to work in "the lessor's coalmines at the accustomed wages" and also to keep two carts to carry culm and coal to the point of shipment at Saundersfoot.

[178] Dodd, *Industrial Revolution in North Wales*, p. 21; NLW, Powis Castle Correspondence, MSS 985, 1,044, 3,566; Chirk Castle E.1,095; Myddelton, *Chirk Castle Accounts*, p. 496; J. M. Howells, 'The Crosswood Estate: Its Growth and Economic Development, 1683–1899', unpub. Univ. of Wales M.A. thesis, 1956, pp. 364–8; W. J. Lewis, 'The Cwmsymlog Lead Mine', *Ceredigion*, II, 1, 1952, p. 29.

[179] G. R. Thomas, thesis, pp. 361, 369–72; Dodd, *Industrial Revolution*, pp. 22–4.

[180] John, *Industrial Development*, p. 8; NLW, Margam and Penrice MS L.791, L.903; Tredegar Park MS 372.

Similarly, Margam tenants were to provide a number of "coal horses" on pain of being prosecuted. Further north, the Powis Castle lead mines were likewise dependent in the late 1720s upon tenants of that and neighbouring estates turning ore carriers. Such practices on the one hand may have resulted in the neglect of farming operations while, on the other, the supplementary income furnished a lifeline in adverse days.[181]

Welsh agriculture in the mid eighteenth century was strikingly backward, and tenants survived only by dint of a pinching frugality and with the help of extra income from the sale of the products of spare-time knitting and weaving. Allowing for the constraints imposed by physical factors and remoteness from good markets, agriculture was more inefficient than it need have been. Even 'improving' Anglesey was described in 1755 as "a naked unpleasant country without a tree or a hedge to be seen on it, and cultivated so ill from the obstinacy of the people in adhering to the ignorance of their forefathers that I am told it does not produce the tenth part of what the land would be capable of, if improved by the agriculture of England".[182] Landlords and agents found this stubborn attachment to the old ways a great hindrance. Thus a surveyor of the Ashburnham property in south Wales wrote in 1778 about the need for exchange of property to facilitate the growth of turnips and clover: "but I have seen such a total aversion to exchange and every sort of innovation in this country that I can by no means advise these alterations to be insisted upon".[183] Similarly, tenants believed that their rent should be kept at a level charged in the past. Thus the Margam agent observed in 1711 how applicants for farms had "no rule but such a one gave no more for it".[184]

Landlords were guilty on many counts of failing to develop their properties. They generally neglected to carry out improvements on their home farms. It was alleged in the 1790s that they tended to put any spare capital towards enlarging their estates rather than in practising improvements in husbandry.[185] At the same time, it is doubtful whether the progressive techniques of a few landlords achieved very much in the way of encouraging better farming among their tenants. They were regarded as too costly. It is significant in this context that the valuer of the Wynnstay Montgomeryshire property suggested in 1763 the settling on the estate of a few 'improving' English tenants as "the most likely expedient to bring the Welsh farmers out of that dull, slovenly method they have been for ages pursuing".[186] Nor

[181] NLW, Picton Castle papers: e.g. lease to W. Pendry, 15 Dec. 1737, of a tenement in Templeton, and lease to J. Thomas, 19 Oct. 1734, of Broadfield farm, near Saundersfoot; John, 'Iron and Coal on a Glamorgan Estate', p. 98; NLW, Powis Castle Correspondence, MS 3,566.
[182] NLW, MS 1,566B: letters of Lord Littleton to his brother, 1755.
[183] NLW, Ashburnham MS 328.
[184] NLW, Margam and Penrice MS 2,544: memo. concerning tenants, 1711.
[185] *Reports* (of the various Welsh counties) *to the Board of Agriculture*, 1794.
[186] NLW, Wynnstay Deposit, 1952, vol. I.

did owners do very much in the way of encouraging improved techniques through the insertion of progressive clauses in their leases. Some of the large and most of the lesser owners also neglected to sink sufficient capital in the development of their properties. Farms remained frequently fragmented, farm buildings were usually totally inadequate, and drainage was generally neglected. Tenants were here partly to blame through failing to keep up their holdings, a reflection of their extreme reluctance at laying out money. By the close of the eighteenth century a new and better arrangement was being advocated whereby tenants would be responsible for the haulage and rough construction work, and landowners for raw materials and any skilled labour required. Landowners adventured capital only on large holdings; their occupants were suitably enterprising and, furthermore, in a position to bargain for favourable terms.

But such tenants were the exception. To repeat, generally both landlords and tenants as partners in the business of agriculture failed to provide adequate capital. Owners were either too poor or plainly neglectful, and tenants were pitiably lacking in substance and wholly uncommercial in outlook. Rent arrears on large and small estates alike were a constant reminder of poverty and an obstacle to the striving for greater method and order in accounting. Adverse farming conditions plunged farmers into crisis and a number failed despite their landlords' forbearance. Owners had little option but to indulge their tenants' backwardness with rents and their lack of commercial attitudes. Again, large owners were generous because of political and social considerations. Nevertheless, it would be needlessly churlish not to recognize in their often lenient treatment a genuine element of altruism springing from an educated sense of paternalistic responsibility.

Appendix. *Yearly rentals of some of the (a) large owners and (b) substantial squires in mid- and late-seventeenth-century Wales*

| | Family & estate | Date | Rental (£) | Source |
|---|---|---|---|---|
| (a) | Large owners | | | |
| | Sir Henry Mansel, Margam, Glam. | 1645 | 4,000 | R. Symonds, *Diary*, ed. C. E. Long, Camden Soc., os LXXIV, 1859 |
| | William Thomas, Esq., Wenvoe, Glam. | 1645 | 2,500 | *Ibid.* |
| | Edward Lewis, Esq., Van & St Fagan's, Glam. | 1645 | 5,000 | *Ibid.* |
| | Sir Edward Stradling, St Donat's, Glam. | 1645 | 4,000 | *Ibid.* |

Appendix, *cont.*

| Family & estate | Date | Rental (£) | Source |
|---|---|---|---|
| Thomas Morgan, Tredegar, Mon. | 1688 | 6,026 | NLW, Tredegar Park MS 372 |
| Henry Lort, Esq., Stackpole Court, Pembs. | 1635 | 2,000 | Huntington Library, San Marino, Calif., EL 7,218 |
| Sir Thomas Myddelton, Chirk Castle, Denbs. | 1666 | 5,000 | G. R. Thomas, Univ. of Wales M.A. thesis, 1968, p. 306 |

(b) *Substantial squires*

| Family & estate | Date | Rental (£) | Source |
|---|---|---|---|
| David Evans, Esq., Neath, Glam. | 1645 | 1,000 | Symonds, *Diary* |
| Bussy Mansel, Esq., Briton Ferry, Glam. | 1645 | 1,100 | *Ibid.* |
| — Turberville, Esq., the Sker (Porthcawl), Glam. | 1645 | 600 | *Ibid.* |
| Edward Carne, Esq., Ewenny, Glam. | 1645 | 1,000 | *Ibid.* |
| — Winne, Esq., Llansannor, Glam. | 1645 | 600 | *Ibid.* |
| Sir Edward Thomas, Bettws, Glam. | 1645 | 1,600 | *Ibid.* |
| Sir Richard Bassett, Beaupré, Glam. | 1645 | 1,000 | *Ibid.* |
| John Van, Esq., Marcross, Glam. | 1645 | 500 | *Ibid.* |
| Sir John Awbrey, Llantrithyd, Glam. | 1645 | 1,000 | *Ibid.* |
| Judge David Jenkins, Hensol, Glam. | 1645 | 1,200 | *Ibid.* |
| Sir Thomas Lewis, Penmark, Glam. | 1645 | 800 | *Ibid.* |
| William Herbert, Esq., Cogan Pill, Glam. | 1645 | 1,000 | *Ibid.* |
| Humphrey Matthew, Esq., Castell y Mynach, Glam. | 1645 | 800 | *Ibid.* |
| — Matthew, Esq., Aberaman, Glam. | 1645 | 800 | *Ibid.* |
| Edward Prichard, Esq., Llancaiach, Glam. | 1645 | 800 | *Ibid.* |
| Thomas Lewis, Esq., Llanishen, Glam. | 1645 | 500 | *Ibid.* |
| William Herbert, Esq., Friars, Cardiff, Glam. | 1645 | 1,000 | *Ibid.* |

Appendix, *cont.*

| Family & estate | Date | Rental (£) | Source |
|---|---|---|---|
| David Matthew, Esq., Llandaff, Glam. | 1645 | 600 | *Ibid.* |
| Sir Nicholas Kemys, Cefn Mably, Glam. | 1645 | 1,800 | *Ibid.* |
| — Morgan, Esq., Ruperra, Glam. | 1645 | 1,000 | *Ibid.* |
| Walter Thomas, Esq., Swansea, Glam. | 1645 | 600 | *Ibid.* |
| William Bassett, Esq., Bromiskin, Glam. | 1645 | 600 | *Ibid.* |
| John Lewis, Prysaeddfed, Anglesey | Charles I's personal govt | 800 | Huntington Library, EL 7,155 |
| Owen Wood, Rhosmor, Anglesey | *Ibid.* | 700 | *Ibid.* |
| Hugh Owen, Bodeon, Anglesey | *Ibid.* | 700 | *Ibid.* |
| Pierce Lloyd, Llugwy, Anglesey | *Ibid.* | 500 | *Ibid.* |
| William Robinson, Monachdy, Anglesey | *Ibid.* | 500 | *Ibid.* |
| Sir Walter Mansell, Trimsaran, Carms. | 1635 | 1,000 | Huntington Library, EL 7,218 |
| John Vaughan, gent., Carms. | 1635 | 700 "at least" | *Ibid.* |
| Nicholas Williams, gent., Edwinsford, Carms. | 1635 | 600–700 | *Ibid.* |
| Sir Walter Vaughan, Pembrey, Carms. | 1635 | 600 | *Ibid.* |
| Col. Edward Thelwall, Plas y Ward, Denbs. | 1677 | 660 | NLW, Wynnstay General Rental, vol. 4 |
| Sir John Vaughan, Crosswood, Cards. | 1670 | 1,200 | J. M. Howells, Univ. of Wales M.A. thesis, 1956, p. 39 |
| Owen Salesbury, Rug, Mer. | 1694 | 734 | NLW, Wynnstay 85/26 |
| Sir Robert Owen, Glyn, Mer. | 1698 | 800 | P. R. Roberts, *NLW J.*, XIII, 1963–4 |
| John Lloyd, Rhiwaedog, Mer. | 1679 | 600 | *Id., J. Mer. Hist. Soc.*, V, I, 1965 |

# 7

# SELECT BIBLIOGRAPHY, 1640–1750

Addison, W. *English Fairs and Markets*. London, 1953.
Airs, M. *The Making of the English Country House, 1500–1640*. London, 1975.
Albert, W. A. *The Turnpike Road System in England and Wales, 1663–1840*. Cambridge, 1972.
Alcock, N. W. *Stoneleigh Houses*. Birmingham, 1973.
Allison, K. J. *The East Riding of Yorkshire Landscape*. London, 1976.
  'Flock Management in the Sixteenth and Seventeenth Centuries', EcHR, 2nd ser., XI, 1958.
  'The Norfolk Worsted Industry in the Sixteenth and Seventeenth Centuries', *Yorks. Bull. Ec. & Soc. Research*, XII–XIII, 1960–1.
  'The Sheep–Corn Husbandry of Norfolk in the Sixteenth and Seventeenth Centuries', AHR, V, 1, 1957.
Ambler, L. *Old Halls and Manor Houses of Yorkshire*. London, 1913.
Amery, C. *Period Houses and their Details*. London, 1974.
Andrews, J. H. 'The Port of Chichester and the Grain Trade, 1650–1750', *Sussex Arch. Coll.*, XCII, 1954.
Andrews, L. S. 'Vaynor Lands during the Eighteenth Century', *Mont. Coll.*, XLVI, 1940.
Appleby, A. B. 'Disease or Famine? Mortality in Cumberland and Westmorland, 1580–1640', EcHR, 2nd ser., XXVI, 1973.
Ashton, T. S. *Economic Fluctuations in England, 1700–1800*. Oxford, 1959.
  *An Economic History of England: The Eighteenth Century*. London, 1955.
Ashworth, G. J. 'A Note on the Decline of the Wealden Iron Industry', *Surrey Arch. Coll.*, LXVII, 1970.
Astbury, A. K. *The Black Fens*. Cambridge, 1957.
Atwell, G. *The Faithfull Surveyor*. Cambridge, 1662.
Aubrey, J. *The Natural History of Wiltshire*, ed. J. Britton. London, 1847.
Austen, R. *The Spiritual Use of an Orchard; or Garden of Fruit Trees*. Oxford, 1653.
Bailey, J. *A General View of the Agriculture of Durham*. London, 1810.
Bailey, J. and Culley, G. *General View of the Agriculture of Cumberland*. London, 1794.
  *General View of the Agriculture of the County of Northumberland*. 3rd edn. London, 1805.
Baker, A. H. R. and Butlin, R. A. (eds.). *Studies of Field Systems in the British Isles*. Cambridge, 1973.
Banister, J. *A Synopsis of Husbandry*. London, 1799.
Bankes, J. and Kerridge, E. *The Early Records of the Bankes Family at Winstanley*. Manchester, 1973.
Barley, M. W. 'The Double-Pile House', *Arch. J.*, CXXXVI, 1979.
  *The English Farmhouse and Cottage*. London, 1961.

'A Glossary of Names for Rooms in Houses of the Sixteenth and Seventeenth Centuries', in *Culture and Environment*, ed. I. Ll. Foster and L. Alcock. London, 1963.

*The House and Home.* London, 1963.

Barley, M. W. and Summers, N. 'Averham Park Lodge and its Paintings', *Thoroton Soc.*, LXV, 1961.

Barnes, D. G. *A History of the English Corn Laws from 1660–1846.* London, 1930. Repr. New York, 1965.

Barratt, D. M. (ed.). *Ecclesiastical Terriers of Warwickshire Parishes, II.* Dugdale Soc., 1971.

Batchelor, T. *General View of the Agriculture of the County of Bedford.* London, 1808.

Batey, Mavis. 'Oliver Goldsmith: An Indictment of Landscape Gardening', in P. Willis (ed.), *Furor Hortensis.* Edinburgh, 1974.

Baxter, R. *The Reverend Richard Baxter's Last Treatise*, ed. F. J. Powicke. Manchester, 1926.

Beale, J. *Herefordshire Orchards.* London, 1657.

Beale, J. and Lawrence, A. *Nurseries, Orchards, Profitable Gardens and Vineyards Encouraged...* London, 1677.

Beastall, T. W. *A North Country Estate.* London and Chichester, 1975.

Beavington, F. 'Early Market Gardening in Bedfordshire', *Inst. Brit. Geographers*, XXXVII, 1965.

Beckett, J. V. *Coal and Tobacco: The Lowthers and the Economic Development of West Cumberland, 1660–1760.* Cambridge, 1981.

'English Landownership in the Later Seventeenth and Eighteenth Centuries: The Debate and the Problems', *EcHR*, 2nd ser., XXX, 4, 1977.

'Regional Variation and the Agricultural Depression, 1730–50', *EcHR*, 2nd ser., XXXV, 1982.

Bell, V. *To Meet Mr. Ellis: Little Gaddesden in the Eighteenth Century.* London, 1956.

Bennett, M. K. 'British Wheat Yield per Acre for Seven Centuries', *Ec. Hist.*, III, 1935.

Beresford, M. W. 'The Common Informer, the Penal Statutes, and Economic Regulation', *EcHR*, 2nd ser., X, 1957.

'Glebe Terriers and Open Field Leicestershire', in *Studies in Leicestershire Agrarian History*, ed. W. G. Hoskins. Leicester, 1949.

'Glebe Terriers and Open-Field Yorkshire', *Yorks. Arch. J.*, XXXVII, 1951.

'Habitation versus Improvement', in *Essays in the Economic and Social History of Tudor and Stuart England*, ed. F. J. Fisher. Cambridge, 1961.

Best, Henry. *Rural Economy in Yorkshire in 1641, being the Farming and Account Books of Henry Best of Elmswell, East Riding of Yorkshire.* Surtees Soc., XXXIII. 1851.

Bettey, J. 'The Cultivation of Woad in the Salisbury Area during the Late Sixteenth and Early Seventeenth Centuries', *Textile Hist.*, IX, 1978.

Bigmore, P. *The Bedfordshire and Huntingdonshire Landscape.* London, 1979.

Billing, R. *An Account of the Culture of Carrots.* London, 1765.

Blake, S. *The Compleat Gardener's Practice.* London, 1664.

Blith, W. *The English Improver.* London, 1649. 2nd edn. 1649.

*The English Improver Improved.* 3rd edn. London, 1652. 4th edn. 1653.

Blome, R. *Britannia.* London, 1673.

Blomefield, F. *An Essay towards a Topographical History of Norfolk*. 5 vols. Norwich and King's Lynn, 1739–75. 2nd edn. 11 vols. 1805–20.
Blundell, N. *The Great Diurnall of Nicholas Blundell of Little Crosby*, ed. J. S. Bagley. 3 vols. Lancs. & Cheshire Rec. Soc. Manchester, 1968–72.
Bonfield, L. 'Marriage Settlements and the "Rise of Great Estates": The Demographic Aspect', EcHR, 2nd ser., XXXII, 1979.
Bonser, K. J. *The Drovers*. London, 1970.
Bouch, C. M. L. and Jones, G. P. *The Lake Counties, 1500–1830*. Manchester, 1961.
Bowden, P. J. *The Wool Trade in Tudor and Stuart England*. London, 1962.
Boys, J. *General View of the Agriculture of the County of Kent*. London, 1813.
Brace, H. W. *A History of Seed Crushing in Great Britain*. London, 1960.
[Braddon, L.]. *To Pay Old Debts without New Taxes by Charitably Relieving, Politically Reforming, and Judiciously Employing the Poor*. London, 1723.
Bradley, R. *A General Treatise of Husbandry and Gardening, II*. London, 1726.
Brigg, M. 'The Forest of Pendle in the Seventeenth Century', *Hist. Soc. Lancs. & Cheshire*, CXIII, 1961.
Broad, J. 'Alternative Husbandry and Permanent Pasture in the Midlands, 1650–1800', AHR, XXVIII, 2, 1980.
Brodrick, G. C. *English Land and English Landlords*. London, 1881.
Brooks, C. E. P. *Climate through the Ages*. 2nd edn. London, 1949.
Brown, E. H. Phelps and Hopkins, S. V. 'Builders' Wage-Rates, Prices and Population: Some Further Evidence', *Economica*, NS, XXVI, 1959.
'Seven Centuries of the Prices of Consumables, compared with Builders' Wage-Rates', *Economica*, NS, XXIII, 1956.
Brown, J. *General View of the Agriculture of the County of Derby*. London, 1794.
Brunskill, R. W. *Illustrated Handbook of Vernacular Architecture*. London, 1970.
Buchanan, K. M. 'Studies in the Localisation of Seventeenth-Century Worcestershire Industries, 1600–1650', *Worcs. Arch. Soc.*, XVII, 1940; XIX, 1943.
Bulkeley, W. 'The Diary of William Bulkeley of Brynddu, Anglesey', ed. H. Owen, *Anglesey Antiq. Soc.*, 1931.
Campbell, Colin. *Vitruvius Britannicus, or the British Architect*. 3 vols. London, 1715–25.
Campbell, M. *The English Yeoman*. New Haven, 1942.
Carter, E. *A History of Cambridgeshire*. London, 1819.
Carter, W. *The Proverb Crossed*. London, 1677.
Cartwright, J. J. (ed.). *The Travels through England of Dr. Richard Pococke*. 2 vols. Camden Soc., NS, XLII, XLIV, 1888–9.
Cathcart, Earl. 'Jethro Tull, his Life, Times and Teaching', *J. RASE*, 3rd ser., II, 1, 1891.
Chalklin, C. W. 'The Rural Economy of a Kentish Wealden Parish, 1650–1750', AHR, X, 1962.
*Seventeenth Century Kent: A Social and Economic History*. London, 1965.
Chalklin, C. W. and Havinden, M. A. (eds.). *Rural Change and Urban Growth, 1500–1800: Essays in English Regional History in Honour of W. G. Hoskins*. London, 1974.
Chambers, J. D. *Nottinghamshire in the Eighteenth Century*. London, 1932.
Chambers, J. D. and Mingay, G. E. *The Agricultural Revolution, 1750–1880*. London, 1966.
Chapman, S. D. 'The Genesis of the British Hosiery Industry, 1600–1750', *Textile Hist.*, III, 1972.

Chartres, J. A. *Internal Trade in England, 1500–1700*. London, 1977.
  'Road Carrying in England in the Seventeenth Century: Myths and Reality', EcHR, 2nd ser., xxx, 1977.
Chauncy, H. *Historical Antiquities of Hertfordshire* (1700). Bishop's Stortford, 1826.
Chesney, H. E. 'The Transference of Lands in England, 1640–60', *Trans. RHS*, 4th ser., xv, 1932.
Chibnall, A. C. *Sherington: The Fiefs and Fields of a Buckinghamshire Village*. Cambridge, 1965.
Child, Sir J. *Discourse about Trade*. London, 1690.
  *New Discourse of Trade*. London, 1694.
Clapham, Sir John. *A Concise Economic History of Britain from the Earliest Times to 1750*. Cambridge, 1949.
Clarke, P. and Slack, P. (eds.). *Crisis and Order in English Towns, 1500–1700*. London, 1972.
Clarkson, L. A. 'The Leather Crafts in Tudor and Stuart England', AHR, xiv, 1, 1966.
  *The Pre-Industrial Economy in England, 1500–1750*. London, 1971.
Clay, C. '"The Greed of Whig Bishops"? Church Landlords and their Lessees, 1660–1760', PP, no. 87. 1980.
  'Marriage, Inheritance, and the Rise of Large Estates in England, 1660–1815', EcHR, 2nd ser., xxi, 3, 1968.
  'The Misfortunes of William, Fourth Lord Petre', *Recusant Hist.*, xi, 2, 1971.
  'The Price of Freehold Land in the Later Seventeenth and Eighteenth Centuries', EcHR, 2nd ser., xxvii, 2, 1974.
  *Public Finance and Private Wealth*. Oxford, 1978.
Cliffe, J. T. *The Yorkshire Gentry from the Reformation to the Civil War*. London, 1969.
Clifton-Taylor, A. *The Pattern of English Building*. London, 1972.
Coate, M. *Cornwall in the Great Civil War and Interregnum*. 2nd edn. Truro, 1963.
Coleman, D. C. *The Economy of England, 1450–1750*. Oxford, 1977.
  'Growth and Decay during the Industrial Revolution: The Case of East Anglia', *Scand. Ec. Hist. Rev.*, x, 1962.
  'An Innovation and its Diffusion: The "New Draperies"', EcHR, 2nd ser., xxii, 1969.
  'Labour in the English Economy of the Seventeenth Century', EcHR, 2nd ser., viii, 1956.
  'Naval Dockyards under the Later Stuarts', EcHR, 2nd ser., vi, 1953.
  *Sir John Banks – Baronet and Businessman*. Oxford, 1963.
Coleman, D. C. and John, A. H. (eds.). *Trade, Government and Economy in Pre-Industrial England*. London, 1976.
Colville, James (ed.). *Letters of John Cockburn of Ormistoun to his Gardener, 1727–1744*. Scottish Hist. Soc., xlv. 1904.
Colvin, H. M. *Biographical Dictionary of British Architects*. London, 1978.
  *History of the King's Works*, V. London, 1976.
Colvin, H. M. and Harris, J. (eds.). *The Country Seat*. London, 1970.
Colvin, H. M. and Newman, J. (eds.). *Of Building – Roger North's Writings on Architecture*. Oxford, 1981.

Colyer, R. J. 'Cattle Drovers in the Nineteenth Century', *Nat. Lib. Wales J.*, XVIII, 1973–4.
  *The Welsh Cattle Drovers.* Cardiff, 1976.
Cooper, J. P. 'Patterns of Inheritance and Settlement by Great Landowners', in J. Goody *et al.* (eds.), *Family and Inheritance.* Cambridge, 1976.
  'The Social Distribution of Land and Men in England, 1436–1700', EcHR, 2nd ser., XX, 1967.
Cordingley, R. A. 'British Historical Roof-Types and their Members', *Ancient Monuments Soc.*, NS, IX, 1961.
Cornwall, J. C. K. 'Agricultural Improvement, 1560–1640', *Sussex Arch. Coll.*, XCVIII, 1960.
Court, W. H. B. *The Rise of the Midland Industries, 1600–1838.* Rev. edn. Oxford, 1953.
Cox, T. *Magna Britannia.* London, 1720.
Cracknell, B. E. *Canvey Island.* Leicester, 1959.
Cranfield, G. A. *The Development of the Provincial Newspaper, 1700–1760.* Oxford, 1962.
Crosweller, W. T. *The Gardeners' Company: A Short Chronological History, 1605–1907.* London, 1908.
Darby, H. C. *The Draining of the Fens.* Cambridge, 1940. 2nd edn. 1956.
Davies, Margaret G. 'Country Gentry and Falling Rents in the 1660s and 1670s', *Midland Hist.*, IV, 2, 1977.
Davies, Walter. *A General View of the Agriculture and Domestic Economy of South Wales.* 2 vols. London, 1815.
Davis, O. R. F. 'The Wealth and Influence of John Holles, Duke of Newcastle, 1694–1711', *Renaissance & Mod. Stud.*, IX, 1965.
Davis, R. *General View of the Agriculture of the County of Oxford.* London, 1794.
Davis, T. *General View of the Agriculture of the County of Wiltshire.* London, 1794.
Deane, P. and Cole, W. A. *British Economic Growth, 1688–1959.* Cambridge, 1962. 2nd edn. 1969.
Defoe, Daniel. *The Complete English Tradesman.* 2 vols. London, 1745.
  *A Tour through the Whole Island of Great Britain*, ed. G. D. H. Cole and D. C. Browning. 2 vols. London, 1962.
Dell, R. F. 'The Decline of the Clothing Industry in Berkshire', *Newbury & Dist. Field Club*, X, 1954.
Dexter, K. and Barber, D. *Farming for Profits.* London, 1961.
Dodd, A. H. 'Caernarvonshire in the Civil War', *Caerns. Hist. Soc.*, XIV, 1953.
  'The Civil War in East Denbighshire', *Denbs. Hist. Soc.*, III, 1954.
  'Flintshire Politics in the Seventeenth Century', *Flints. Hist. Soc.*, 1953–4.
  *The Industrial Revolution in North Wales.* Cardiff, 1933.
  *Life in Wales.* London, 1972.
  'The North Wales Coal Industry during the Industrial Revolution', *Arch. Cambrensis*, LXXXIV, 1929.
  'The Pattern of Politics in Stuart Wales', *Hon. Soc. Cymmrodorion*, 1948.
  *Studies in Stuart Wales.* 2nd edn. Cardiff, 1971.
Doddington, George Bubb. *The Political Journal of George Bubb Doddington*, ed. J. Carswell and L. A. Dralle. London, 1965.

Donnelly, T. 'Arthur Clephane, Edinburgh Merchant and Seedsman', AHR, XVIII, 2, 1970.
Dony, J. G. *A History of the Straw Hat Industry*. Luton, 1942.
Doughty, H. M. *Chronicles of Theberton*. London, 1910.
Douglas, J. 'The Culture of Saffron', *Philos. Trans. Roy. Soc.*, XXXV, 1728.
Downes, K. *English Baroque Architecture*. London, 1966.
Driver, A. and Driver, W. *General View of the Agriculture of the County of Hampshire*. London, 1794.
Drummond, J. C. and Wilbraham, A. *The Englishman's Food*, rev. D. Hollingsworth. London, 1957.
Dugdale, W. *The History of Imbanking and Drayning*. London, 1662.
Dyer, Alan. 'Growth and Decay in English Towns, 1500–1700', *Urban Hist. Yearbook*, 1979.
Eaton, Daniel. *The Letters of Daniel Eaton to the Third Earl of Cardigan, 1725–32*, ed. Joan Wake and Deborah Champion Webster. Northants. Rec. Soc., XXIV. 1971.
Edie, C. A. *The Irish Cattle Bills: A Study in Restoration Politics*. Amer. Philos. Soc., NS LX. 1970.
Edmunds, Henry. 'History of the Brecknockshire Agricultural Society, 1755–1955', *Brycheiniog*, III, 1957.
Edwards, J. K. 'The Gurneys and the Norwich Clothing Trade in the Eighteenth Century', *JFHS*, L, 1962–4.
Edwards, P. R. 'The Cattle Trade of Shropshire in the Late Sixteenth and Seventeenth Centuries', *Midland Hist.*, VI, 1981.
'The Development of Dairy Farming on the North Shropshire Plain in the Seventeenth Century', *Midland Hist.*, IV, 3–4, 1978.
'The Horse Trade of the Midlands in the Seventeenth Century', AHR, XXVII, 2, 1979.
Ellis, W. *Chiltern and Vale Farming Explained*. London, 1733.
*A Compleat System of Experienced Improvements*. London, 1749.
*The Compleat Planter and Cyderist*. London, 1756.
*The Practical Farmer, or The Hertfordshire Husbandman*. London, 1732. 2nd edn., 2 pts. 1732.
*The Modern Husbandman*. 8 vols. London, 1750.
Emery, Frank V. 'Early Cultivation of Clover in Gower', *J. Gower Soc.*, XXVI, 1975.
'The Mechanics of Innovation: Clover Cultivation in Wales before 1750', *J. Hist. Geog.*, II, 1, 1976.
'A New Account of Snowdonia, 1693, Written for Edward Lhuyd', *Nat. Lib. Wales J.*, XVIII, 1974.
Emery, Frank V. and Smith, C. G. 'A Weather Record from Snowdonia, 1697–98', *Weather*, XXXI, 1976.
Evans, E. J. *The Contentious Tithe*. London, 1976.
'Tithing Customs and Disputes: The Evidence of Glebe Terriers, 1698–1850', AHR, XVIII, 1, 1970.
Evans, G. N. 'The Artisan and Small Farmer in Mid-Eighteenth Century Anglesey', *Anglesey Antiq. Soc.*, 1933.
Evelyn, John. *Acetaria: A Discourse of Sallets*. London, 1699.
*Diary*, ed. E. S. de Beer. 6 vols. Oxford, 1955.
*Sylva...to which is annexed Pomona*. London, 1664.

Everitt, Alan M. 'The English Urban Inn, 1560–1760', in *Perspectives in English Urban History*, ed. Alan Everitt. London, 1973.
  'Social Mobility in Early Modern England', *PP*, no. 33, 1966.
Eversley, D. E. C. 'A Survey of Population in an Area of Worcestershire from 1660 to 1850 on the Basis of Parish Registers', in *Population in History*, ed. D. V. Glass and D. E. C. Eversley. London, 1965.
Ferris, J. P. and Oliver, R. C. B. 'An Agricultural Improvement of 1674 at Trewern, Llanfihangel-Nant-Melan', *Radnors. Soc.*, XLII, 1972.
Fieldhouse, R. T. 'Agriculture in Wensleydale from 1600 to the Present Day', *Northern Hist.*, XVI, 1980.
Fieldhouse, R. T. and Jennings, B. *A History of Richmond and Swaledale*. Chichester, 1978.
Fiennes, Celia. *The Journeys of Celia Fiennes*, ed. C. Morris. London, 1947.
Firth, C. H. and Rait, R. S. (eds.). *Acts and Ordinances of the Interregnum, 1642–60*. 3 vols. London, 1911.
Fisher, F. J. 'The Development of London as a Centre of Conspicuous Consumption in the Sixteenth and Seventeenth Centuries', in *Essays in Economic History, II*, ed. E. M. Carus-Wilson. London, 1962. (Repr. from RHS, 4th ser., XXX, 1948.)
  'The Development of the London Food Market, 1540–1640', in *Essays in Economic History, I*, ed. E. M. Carus-Wilson. London, 1954. (Repr. from EcHR, v, 1935.)
Fisher, F. J. (ed.). *Essays in the Economic and Social History of Tudor and Stuart England*. Cambridge, 1961.
Fisher, H. E. S. 'Anglo-Portuguese Trade, 1700–1770', EcHR, 2nd ser., XVI, 1963.
Fletcher, A. J. *A County Community in Peace and War: Sussex, 1600–1660*. London, 1975.
Flinn, M. W. 'The Growth of the English Iron Industry, 1660–1760', EcHR, 2nd ser., XI, 1958.
Fowler, J. and Cornforth, J. *English Decoration in the Eighteenth Century*. London, 1974.
Fox, Sir Cyril and Raglan, Lord. *Monmouthshire Houses*. 3 vols. Nat. Museum of Wales, 1953–4.
Fox, H. S. A. and Butlin, R. A. (eds.). *Change in the Countryside: Essays on Rural England, 1500–1900*. Inst. Brit. Geographers, Special Publ., no. 10. London, 1979.
Freeman, C. *Pillow Lace in the East Midlands*. Luton, 1958.
Fuller, T. *The Worthies of England*, ed. J. Freeman. London, 1952.
Fussell, G. E. *The English Dairy Farmer, 1500–1900*. London, 1966.
  'Four Centuries of Farming Systems in Hampshire, 1500–1900', *Hants. Field Club & Arch. Soc.*, XVII, 3, 1949.
  'Four Centuries of Leicestershire Farming', in *Studies in Leicestershire Agrarian History*, ed. W. G. Hoskins. Leicester, 1949.
  'History of Cole (*Brassica* sp.)', *Nature, London*, 9 July 1955.
  *The Old English Farming Books from Fitzherbert to Tull, 1523 to 1730*. London, 1947.
Fussell, G. E. and Goodman, Constance. 'Eighteenth-Century Traffic in Livestock', *Ec. Hist.*, III, 1936.
Garret[t], Daniel. *Designs and Estimates for Farm Houses*... 3rd edn. London, 1772.
Gazley, J. G. *The Life of Arthur Young, 1741–1820*. Philadelphia, 1973.

Gentles, I. 'The Sales of Bishops' Lands in the English Revolution, 1646–1660', EHR, xcv, 1980.
  'The Sales of Crown Lands during the English Revolution', EcHR, 2nd ser., xxvi, 4, 1973.
Gerarde, John. *The Herbal, or General Historie of Plantes*. London, 1636.
Gill, H. and Guilford, E. L. (eds.). *The Rector's Book of Clayworth, Notts*. Nottingham, 1910.
Girouard, M. *Robert Smythson*. London, 1966.
Girouard, Mark. *Life in the English Country House: A Social and Architectural History*. New Haven and London, 1978.
Godber, Joyce. *History of Bedfordshire, 1066–1888*. Bedford, 1969.
Godfrey, W. H. *The English Almshouse*. London, 1955.
Gooder, A. *Plague and Enclosure: A Warwickshire Village in the Seventeenth Century*. Coventry & N. War., Hist. Pamphlets, no. 2. 1965.
  'The Population Crisis of 1727–30 in Warwickshire', *Midland Hist.*, I, 4, 1972.
Gough, R. *Antiquityes and Memoyres of the Parish of Myddle*. London, 1875.
Grainger, J. *General View of the Agriculture of Co. Durham*. London, 1794.
Granger, C. W. J. and Elliott, C. M. 'A Fresh Look at Wheat Prices and Markets in the Eighteenth Century', EcHR, 2nd ser., xx, 1967.
Gras, N. S. B. *The Evolution of the English Corn Market from the Twelfth to the Eighteenth Century*. Harvard Ec. Stud., xiii. Cambridge, Mass., 1915.
Gray, H. L. *English Field Systems*. Cambridge, Mass., 1915.
  'Yeoman Farming in Oxfordshire from the Sixteenth Century to the Nineteenth Century', *Qtly J. Ec.*, xxiv, 1910.
Green, D. *Gardener to Queen Anne: Henry Wise and the Formal Garden*. Oxford, 1956.
Green, F. 'The Stepneys of Prendergast', *W. Wales Hist. Rec.*, vii, 1917–18.
Green, I. M. 'The Persecution of Parish Clergy during the English Civil War', EHR, xciv, 1979.
Gunther, R. T. *The Architecture of Sir Roger Pratt*. Oxford, 1928.
Habakkuk, H. J. 'Daniel Finch, 2nd Earl of Nottingham: His House and Estate', in *Studies in Social History*, ed. J. H. Plumb. London, 1955.
  'The English Land Market in the Eighteenth Century', in *Britain and the Netherlands*, ed. J. S. Bromley and E. H. Kossmann. London, 1960.
  'English Landownership, 1680–1740', EcHR, x, 1940.
  'The Land Settlement and the Restoration of Charles II', RHS, 5th ser., xxviii, 1978.
  'Landowners and the Civil War', EcHR, 2nd ser., xviii, 1965.
  'Marriage Settlements in the Eighteenth Century', RHS, 4th ser., xxxii, 1950.
  'Public Finance and the Sale of Confiscated Property during the Interregnum', EcHR, 2nd ser., xv, 1962–3.
  'The Rise and Fall of English Landed Families, 1600–1800', RHS, 5th ser., xxix–xxx, 1979–80.
Hadfield, Miles. *A History of British Gardening*. London, 1969.
Halfpenny, William. *Twelve Beautiful Designs for Farmhouses*. London, 1750.
Hammersley, G. 'The Charcoal Iron Industry and its Fuel, 1540–1750', EcHR, 2nd ser., xxvi, 1973.
  'The Crown Woods and their Exploitation in the Sixteenth and Seventeenth Centuries', *Bull. IHR*, xxx, 1957.

Harris, A. 'The Agriculture of the East Riding before the Parliamentary Enclosures', *Yorks. Arch. J.*, XL, 1962.
*The Open Fields of East Yorkshire*. York, 1959.
Hartley, M. and Ingilby, J. *The Old Hand-Knitters of the Dales*. Clapham, 1951.
Hartlib, S. *His Legacie, or An Enlargement of the Discours of Husbandrie Used in Brabant and Flanders*. London, 1651. 2nd edn. 1652.
[C. Dymock]. *A Discovery for Division or Setting Out of Land*. London, 1653.
Harvey, John H. *Early Gardening Catalogues*. London, 1972.
*Early Nurserymen*. London, 1974.
'The Family of Telford, Nurserymen of York', *Yorks. Arch. J.*, XLII, 167, 1969.
'Leonard Gurle's Nurseries and Some Others', *Garden Hist.*, III, 3, 1975.
'The Nurseries on Milne's Land-Use Map', *London & Middx Arch. Soc.*, XXIV, 1973.
'The Stocks Held by Early Nurseries', AHR, XXII, 1, 1974.
Havinden, M. A. 'Agricultural Progress in Open Field Oxfordshire', AHR, IX, 2, 1961.
Henrey, Blanche. *British Botanical and Horticultural Literature before 1800*. 3 vols. Oxford, 1975.
Henstock, A. 'Cheese Manufacture and Marketing in Derbyshire and North Staffordshire, 1670–1870', *Derbs. Arch. J.*, LXXXIX, 1969.
Hervey, Lord Francis (ed.). *Suffolk in the Seventeenth Century: A Breviary of Suffolk by Robert Reyce, 1618*. London, 1902.
Hey, D. *An English Rural Community: Myddle under the Tudors and Stuarts*. Leicester, 1974.
*Packmen, Carriers and Packhorse Roads*. Leicester, 1980.
*The Rural Metalworkers of the Sheffield Region*. Leicester, 1972.
Hill, M. C. 'The Wealdmoors, 1560–1660', *Shrops. Arch. J.*, LIV, 1951–3.
Hill, O. and Cornforth, J. *English Country Houses: Caroline*. London, 1966.
Holderness, B. A. 'The Agricultural Activities of the Massingberds of South Ormsby, Lincolnshire, 1638 – c. 1750', *Midland Hist.*, I, 3, 1972.
'Capital Formation in Agriculture', in *Aspects of Capital Investment in Great Britain, 1750–1850*, ed. J. P. P. Higgins and S. Pollard. London, 1971.
'Credit in English Rural Society before the Nineteenth Century', AHR, XXIV, 1976.
'The English Land Market in the Eighteenth Century: The Case of Lincolnshire', EcHR, 2nd ser., XXVII, 4, 1974.
Holiday, P. G. 'Land Sales and Repurchases in Yorkshire after the Civil Wars, 1650–1670', *Northern Hist.*, V, 1970.
Holland, H. *General View of the Agriculture of Cheshire*. London, 1808.
Hollingsworth, T. H. 'The Demography of the British Peerage', suppl. to *Pop. Stud.*, XVIII, 1964.
Holmes, G. S. 'Gregory King and the Social Structure of Pre-Industrial England', RHS, 5th ser., XXVII, 1977.
Holt, J. *General View of the Agriculture of the County of Lancaster*. London, 1795.
Hopkins, E. 'The Bridgewater Estates in North Shropshire during the Civil War', *Shrops. Arch. Soc.*, LVI, 2, 1960.
'The Re-Leasing of the Ellesmere Estates, 1637–42', AHR, X, 1, 1962.

Hoskins, W. G. 'Harvest Fluctuations and English Economic History, 1620–1759', AHR, XVI, 1, 1968.
Houghton, John. *A Collection for Improvement of Husbandry and Trade*. 9 vols. London, 1692–1703. Ed. R. Bradley. 4 vols. London, 1727–8.
*A Collection of Letters for the Improvement of Husbandry and Trade*. 2 vols. London, 1681–3.
Howard, C. 'The Culture of Saffron', *Philos. Trans. Roy. Soc.*, XII, 1678.
Howells, B. E. (ed.). *A Calendar of Letters relating to North Wales*. Cardiff, 1967.
Hughes, E. *North Country Life in the Eighteenth Century: The North-East, 1700–1750*. Oxford, 1952.
*North Country Life in the Eighteenth Century, II, Cumberland & Westmorland, 1700–1830*. Oxford, 1965.
Hull, F. 'The Tufton Sequestration Papers', *Kent Rec.*, XVII, 1960.
Hussey, C. *English Country Houses: Early Georgian*. London, 1965.
Innocent, C. F. *The Development of English Building Construction*. Cambridge, 1916. Newton Abbot, 1971.
Jacob, G. *The Country Gentleman's Vade Mecum*. London, 1717.
James, M. 'The Political Importance of the Tithes Controversy in the English Revolution, 1640–60', *Hist.*, XXVI, 1941.
James, W. and Malcolm, J. *General View of the Agriculture of the County of Buckingham*. London, 1794.
*General View of the Agriculture of the County of Surrey*. London, 1793.
Jancey, E. M. 'An Eighteenth-Century Steward and his Work', *Shrops. Arch. Soc.*, LVI, 1, 1957–8.
'The Hon. and Rev. Richard Hill of Hawkstone, 1655–1727', *ibid.*, LV, 1954–6.
Jenkins, J. G. *The Welsh Woollen Industry*. Cardiff, 1969.
*The English Farm Waggon: Origins and Structure*. Newton Abbot, 1972.
Jenkins, R. 'Suffolk Industries: An Historical Survey', *Newcomen Soc.*, XIX, 1940.
Jennings, B. (ed.). *A History of Harrogate and Knaresborough*. Huddersfield, 1970.
*A History of Nidderdale*. Huddersfield, 1976.
John, A. H. 'Agricultural Productivity and Economic Growth in England, 1700–1760', *J. Ec. Hist.*, XXV, 1965.
'The Course of Agricultural Change, 1660–1760', in *Studies in the Industrial Revolution*, ed. L. S. Pressnell. London, 1960. Repr. in W. E. Minchinton (ed.), *Essays in Agrarian History*, I. Newton Abbot, 1968.
'English Agricultural Improvement and Grain Exports, 1660–1765', in D. C. Coleman and A. H. John (eds.), *Trade, Government and Economy in Pre-Industrial England*. London, 1976.
*The Industrial Development of South Wales, 1750–1850*. Cardiff, 1950.
'Iron and Coal on a Glamorgan Estate, 1700–40', EcHR, XIII, 1943.
Johnson, George W. *A History of English Gardening*. London, 1829.
Jones, E. L. 'Agricultural Conditions and Changes in Herefordshire, 1600–1815', *Woolhope Naturalists' Field Club*, XXXVII, 1962.
'Agricultural Origins of Industry', PP, no. 40, 1968.
'Agricultural Productivity and Economic Growth, 1700–1760', in E. L. Jones (ed.), *Agriculture and Economic Growth in England, 1650–1815*. London, 1967.
'Agriculture and Economic Growth in England, 1660–1750: Agricultural Change', *J. Ec. Hist.*, XXV, 1965.

'Eighteenth-Century Changes in Hampshire Chalkland Farming', AHR, VIII, 1, 1960.
*Seasons and Prices: The Role of Weather in English Agricultural History.* London, 1964.
Jones, F. 'The Old Families of Wales', in *Wales in the Eighteenth Century*, ed. D. Moore. Swansea, 1976.
'A Squire of Anglesey', *Anglesey Antiq. Soc.*, 1940.
'The Vaughans of Golden Grove. I, The Earls of Carbery', *Hon. Soc. Cymmrodorion*, 1963, pt 1.
'The Vaughans of Golden Grove. II, Anne, Duchess of Bolton, 1690–1715', *ibid.*, 1963, pt 2.
'The Vaughans of Golden Grove. III, Torycoed, Shenfield, Golden Grove', *ibid.*, 1964, pt 2.
Jones, G. P. 'Sources of Loans and Credits in Cumbria before the Rise of Banks', *CW2*, LXXV, 1975.
Jones, Stanley and Smith, J. T. 'Breconshire Houses', *Brycheiniog*, IX, 1963.
Kalm, Pehr. *Kalm's Account of his Visit to England on his Way to America in 1748*, ed. J. Lucas. London, 1892.
Kelch, R. A. *Newcastle: A Duke without Money: Thomas Pelham-Holles 1693–1768.* London, 1974.
Kent, N. *General View of the Agriculture of Norfolk.* London, 1796.
*Hints to Gentlemen of Landed Property.* London, 1775.
Kenyon, G. H. 'Kirdford Inventories, 1611 to 1776, with Particular Reference to the Weald Clay Farming', *Sussex Arch. Coll.*, XCIII, 1955.
'Petworth Town and Trades, 1610–1760', *ibid.*, XCVI, 1958.
Kerridge, E. *The Agricultural Revolution.* London, 1967.
*Agrarian Problems in the Sixteenth Century and After.* London, 1969.
'The Sheepfold in Wiltshire and the Floating of the Water Meadows', EcHR, 2nd ser., VI, 1954.
'Turnip Husbandry in High Suffolk', EcHR, 2nd ser., VII, 1956.
Lambton, L. *Temples of Convenience.* London, 1978.
Lane, Carolina. 'The Development of Pastures and Meadows during the Sixteenth and Seventeenth Centuries', AHR, XXVIII, 1980.
Langley, Batty. *The City and Country Builder's and Workman's Treasury of Designs.* London, 1745. Repr. 1969.
La Quintinye, M. de. *The Complete Gard'ner*, tr. G. London and H. Wise. London, 1701.
Laurence, Edward. *The Duty of a Steward to his Lord.* London, 1727.
Laurence, John. *A New System of Agriculture.* London, 1726.
Law, C. M. and Hooson, D. J. M. 'The Straw Plait and Straw Hat Industries of the South Midlands', *E. Midlands Geographer*, IV, 6, 1968.
[Lee, J.]. *Considerations concerning Common Fields.* London, 1654.
Lees–Milne, J. *English Country Houses: Baroque, 1685–1715.* London, 1970.
Leigh, C. *The Natural History of Lancashire, Cheshire and the Peak of Derbyshire.* Oxford, 1700.
Lennard, R. V. 'English Agriculture under Charles II: The Evidence of the Royal Society's "Enquiries"', EcHR, IV, 1932.
L'Estrange, R. *A Treatise of Wool and Cattel.* London, 1677.

Lewis, W. J. 'The Cwmsymlog Lead Mine', *Ceredigion*, II, 1, 1952.
Lightoler, Thomas. *Gentleman and Farmer's Architect*. London, 1762.
Linnard, W. 'A Glimpse of Gwydyr Forest and the Timber Trade in North Wales in the Late 17th Century', *Nat. Lib. Wales J.*, XVIII, 1974.
Linnell, C. D. 'The Matmakers of Pavenham', *Beds. Mag.*, I, 1947.
Lisle, Edward. *Observations in Husbandry*. London, 1757. 2nd edn. 2 vols. London, 1757.
Lloyd, T. H. *The Movement of Wool Prices in Medieval England*. EcHR suppl., no. 6. Cambridge, 1973.
Lodge, E. C. (ed.). *The Account Book of a Kentish Estate, 1616–1704*. Oxford, 1927.
Long, W. H. 'Regional Farming in Seventeenth-Century Yorkshire', AHR, VIII, 2, 1960.
Loudon, J. C. *An Encyclopaedia of Gardening*. London, 1822.
Lowe, N. *The Lancashire Textile Industry in the Sixteenth Century*. Manchester, 1972.
Lowe, R. *General View of the Agriculture of Nottinghamshire*. London, 1798.
McCutcheon, K. L. *Yorkshire Fairs and Markets*, Thoresby Soc., XXXIX. 1940.
Machin, R. 'The Great Rebuilding: A Reassessment', *PP*, no. 77, 1977.
Machin, R. (ed.). *Probate Inventories and Memorial Excepts of Chetnole, Leigh and Yetminster*. Bristol, 1976.
Madge, S. J. *The Domesday of Crown Lands*. London, 1938.
Manley, G. *Climate and the British Scene*. London, 1952.
Manning, B. *The English People and the English Revolution*. London, 1976.
Markham, G. *The Inrichment of the Weald of Kent*. London, 1625.
Marshall, G. 'The "Rotherham" Plough', *Tools & Tillage*, III, 3, 1978.
Marshall, J. D. *Furness and the Industrial Revolution*. Barrow in Furness, 1958.
  *Kendal, 1661–1801: The Growth of a Modern Town*. Kendal, 1975.
  *Old Lakeland*. Newton Abbot, 1971.
Marshall, W. *Review and Abstract of the County Reports to the Board of Agriculture*. 5 vols. London and York, 1808–17. 5 vols. in 1. 1818.
  *The Rural Economy of Gloucestershire*. 2 vols. Gloucester, 1789.
  *The Rural Economy of the Midland Counties*. 2 vols. London, 1790. 2nd edn. 1796.
  *The Rural Economy of Norfolk*. 2 vols. London, 1787.
  *Rural Economy of the Southern Counties*. 2 vols. London, 1798.
  *The Rural Economy of Yorkshire*. 2 vols. London, 1788.
Mathias, P. *The Brewing Industry in England, 1700–1830*. Cambridge, 1959.
Mavor, W. *General View of the Agriculture of Berkshire*. London, 1809.
Meager, Leonard. *The English Gardener*. London, 1670.
Meek, M. 'Hempen Cloth Industry in Suffolk', *Suffolk Rev.*, II, 1961.
Mercer, Eric. *English Vernacular Houses: A Study of Traditional Farmhouses and Cottages*. RCHM (England). London, 1975.
Meredith, R. 'A Derbyshire Family in the Seventeenth Century: The Eyres of Hassop and their Forfeited Estates', *Recusant Hist.*, VIII, 1965.
Michell, A. R. 'Sir Richard Weston and the Spread of Clover Cultivation', AHR, XXII, 2, 1974.
Middleton, J. *General View of the Agriculture of Middlesex*. 2nd edn. London, 1807.
Millward, R. 'The Cumbrian Town between 1600 and 1800', in *Rural Change and Urban Growth, 1500–1800*, ed. C. W. Chalklin and M. A. Havinden. London, 1974.

## SELECT BIBLIOGRAPHY 437

Mingay, G. E. 'The Agricultural Depression, 1730–1750', EcHR, 2nd ser., VIII, 1956.
 'The Eighteenth Century Land Steward', in *Land, Labour and Population in the Industrial Revolution*, ed. E. L. Jones and G. E. Mingay. London, 1967.
 *English Landed Society in the Eighteenth Century*. London, 1963.
 'Estate Management in Eighteenth-Century Kent', AHR, IV, 1, 1956.
 'The Size of Farms in the Eighteenth Century', EcHR, 2nd ser., XIV, 3, 1962.
Mitchell, B. R. with Deane, P. *Abstract of British Historical Statistics*. Cambridge, 1962.
Moore, B. J. S. *Goods and Chattels of our Forefathers: Frampton Cotterell and District Probate Inventories, 1539–1790*. Chichester, 1976.
Morant, P. *A History of Essex*. London, 1768.
Mordant, J. *The Complete Steward*. 2 vols. London, 1761.
Mortimer, J. *The Whole Art of Husbandry*. London, 1707.
Mullett, C. F. 'The Cattle Distemper in Mid-Eighteenth Century England', *Agric. Hist.*, XX, 3, 1946.
Munby, L. N. (ed.). *East Anglian Studies*. Cambridge, 1968.
Myddelton, W. M. (ed.). *Chirk Castle Accounts, 1666–1753*. Manchester, 1931.
Neve, Richard. *City and Country Purchaser and Builder's Dictionary*. 3rd edn. London, 1736. Repr. Newton Abbot, 1969.
Nichols, J. *The History and Antiquities of the County of Leicester*...4 vols. London, 1795–1811.
Norden, J. *The Surveyor's Dialogue*. London, 1607.
North, Roger. *The Lives of the Norths*, ed. A. Jessopp. 3 vols. London, 1890.
Oliver, J. 'The Weather and Farming in the Mid-Eighteenth Century in Anglesey', *Nat. Lib. Wales J.*, X, 1958.
Ormrod, D. J. 'Dutch Commercial and Industrial Decline and British Growth in the Late Seventeenth and Early Eighteenth Centuries', in *Failed Transitions to Modern Industrial Society: Renaissance Italy and Seventeenth-Century Holland*, ed. F. Krantz and P. M. Hohenberg. Montreal, 1975.
Osborne, B. S. 'Glamorgan Agriculture in the Seventeenth and Eighteenth Centuries', *Nat. Lib. Wales J.*, XX, 1979.
Outhwaite, R. B. 'Dearth and Government Intervention in English Grain Markets, 1590–1700', EcHR, 2nd ser., XXXIII, 3, 1981.
Overton, M. 'Computer Analysis of an Inconsistent Data Source: The Case of Probate Inventories', *J. Hist. Geog.*, III, 4, 1977.
Owen, L. 'Letters of an Anglesey Parson', *Hon. Soc. Cymmrodorion*, 1961, pt 1.
Owen, W. *Owen's Book of Fairs*. London, 1756.
Parker, R. A. C. *Coke of Norfolk: A Financial and Agricultural Study 1707–1842*. Oxford, 1975.
Parkinson, John. *Paradisi in Sole*. London, 1629.
Parkinson, R. *General View of the Agriculture of Huntingdonshire*. London, 1813.
Patten, J. 'Patterns of Migration and Movement of Labour to Three Pre-Industrial East Anglian Towns', *J. Hist. Geog.*, II, 1976.
 'Population Distribution in Norfolk and Suffolk during the Sixteenth and Seventeenth Centuries', *Inst. Brit. Geographers*, LXV, 1975.
 'Village and Town: An Occupational Study', AHR, XX, 1972.
Peate, I. C. 'A Flintshire Barn at St. Fagan's', *Country Life*, July–Dec. 1952.
 *The Welsh House*. Liverpool, 1944.

Pelham, R. A. 'The Agricultural Revolution in Hampshire, with Special Reference to the Acreage Returns of 1801', *Hants. Field Club & Arch. Soc.*, XVIII, 1953.
Penney, N. (ed.). *The Household Account Book of Sarah Fell.* Cambridge, 1920.
Perkins, J. A. *Sheep Farming in Eighteenth- and Nineteenth-Century Lincolnshire.* Occ. Papers in Lincs. Hist. & Arch., no. 4, Soc. Lincs. Hist. & Arch. Sleaford, 1977.
Peters, J. E. C. *The Development of Farm Buildings in... Staffordshire.* Manchester, 1969.
Pettit, P. A. J. *The Royal Forests of Northamptonshire: A Study in their Economy, 1558–1714.* Northants. Rec. Soc., XXIII. 1968.
Petty, W. *Economic Writings...* ed. C. H. Hull, Vol. I. Cambridge, 1899.
Pilkington, J. *A View of the Present State of Derbyshire.* Derby, 1789.
Plot, Robert. *The Natural History of Oxfordshire.* Oxford, 1676/7. 2nd edn. 1705.
*The Natural History of Staffordshire.* Oxford, 1686.
Plumb, J. H. *Sir Robert Walpole.* 3 vols. London, 1956.
'Sir Robert Walpole and Norfolk Husbandry', EcHR, 2nd ser., V, 1952.
Plumb, J. H. (ed.). *Studies in Social History.* London, 1955.
Plymley, J. *General View of the Agriculture of Shropshire.* London, 1803.
Postgate, M. R. 'The Field Systems of Breckland', AHR, X, 1961.
Postlethwayt, Malachy. *Britain's Commercial Interest Explained and Improved... I.* London, 1757.
Poynter, F. N. L. *A Bibliography of Gervase Markham, 1568?–1637.* Oxford, 1962.
Prichard, M. F. Lloyd. 'The Decline of Norwich', EcHR, 2nd ser., III, 1951.
Priest, St John. *General View of the Agriculture of Buckinghamshire.* London, 1813.
Prince, H. *Parks in England.* Shalfleet Manor, I.O.W. 1967.
Pringle, A. *General View of the Agriculture of Westmorland.* Edinburgh, 1794.
Radley, J. 'Holly as a Winter Feed', AHR, IX, 2, 1961.
Raistrick, A. and Jennings, B. *A History of Lead Mining in the Pennines.* London, 1965.
Ramsay, G. D. *The Wiltshire Woollen Industry in the Sixteenth and Seventeenth Centuries.* Oxford, 1943.
Ravensdale, J. R. *Liable to Floods.* Cambridge, 1974.
Rawson, H. Rees. 'The Coal Mining Industry of the Hawarden District on the Eve of the Industrial Revolution', *Arch. Cambrensis*, XCVI, 1941.
Rees, Alwyn. *Life in a Welsh Countryside.* Cardiff, 1950.
Rennie, G. B., Brown, R., and Shirreff, S. *General View of the Agriculture of the West Riding.* London, 1794.
Reyce, R. *See* Hervey (ed.).
Riches, N. *The Agricultural Revolution in Norfolk.* Chapel Hill, 1937.
Roberts, P. 'The Decline of the Welsh Squires in the Eighteenth Century', *Nat. Lib. Wales J.*, XIII, 1963–4.
Roebuck, P. 'Absentee Landownership in the Late Seventeenth and Early Eighteenth Centuries: A Neglected Factor in English Agrarian History', AHR, XXI, 1, 1973.
'The Constables of Everingham: The Fortunes of a Catholic Royalist Family during the Civil War and Interregnum', *Recusant Hist.*, IX, 1967.
Roebuck, P. (ed.). *Constables of Everingham Estate Correspondence, 1726–43.* Yorks. Arch. Soc. Rec. Ser., CXXXVI. 1974.
Rogers, Benjamin. *The Diary of Benjamin Rogers, Rector of Carlton,* ed. C. D. Linnell. Beds. Rec. Soc., XXX. 1950.

Rogers, J. E. T. *A History of Agriculture and Prices in England from 1259 to 1793*. 7 vols. Oxford, 1866–1902.
Rogers, Nathan. *Memoirs of Monmouthshire*. London, 1708.
Rowlands, Henry. *Idea Agriculturae*. Dublin, 1764.
Rowlands, M. B. *Masters and Men in the West Midland Metalware Trades before the Industrial Revolution*. Manchester, 1975.
Salaman, R. N. *The History and Social Influence of the Potato*. Cambridge, 1949.
Salmon, N. *The History of Hertfordshire*. London, 1728.
Scarfe, N. *The Suffolk Landscape*. London, 1972.
Schumpeter, E. B. *English Overseas Trade Statistics, 1697–1808*. Oxford, 1960.
Seaborne, M. *The English School*. London, 1971.
Sharp, Lindsay. 'Timber, Science and Economic Reform in the Seventeenth Century', *Forestry*, XLVIII, 1, 1975.
Sharrock, Robert. *The History of the Propagation and Improvement of Vegetables*. Oxford, 1660.
 *An Improvement to the Art of Gardening*. London, 1694.
Sheail, J. 'Rabbits and Agriculture in Post-Medieval England', *J. Hist. Geog.*, IV, 4, 1978.
Sheppard, J. A. *The Draining of the Hull Valley*. York, 1958.
Sidwell, R. W. 'A Short History of Commercial Horticulture in the Vale of Evesham', *Vale of Evesham Hist. Soc., Research Papers*, II, 1969.
Simpson, A. 'The East Anglian Fold-Course: Some Queries', *AHR*, VI, 1958.
Skipp, V. *Crisis and Development: An Ecological Case Study of the Forest of Arden, 1570–1674*. Cambridge, 1978.
 'Economic and Social Change in the Forest of Arden, 1530–1649', in *Land, Church and People: Essays Presented to Professor H. P. R. Finberg*, ed. Joan Thirsk. Suppl. to *AHR*, XVIII, 1970.
Slicher van Bath, B. H. 'Yield Ratios, 810–1820', *A.A.G. Bijdragen*, X, 1963.
Smith, J. T. 'The Evolution of the English Peasant House in the Late Seventeenth Century: The Evidence of Buildings', *J. Brit. Arch. Assoc.*, XXXIII, 1970.
 'The Long-House in Monmouthshire, a Reappraisal', in *Culture and Environment*, ed. I. Ll. Foster and L. Alcock. London, 1963.
 'Medieval Roofs: A Classification', *Arch. J.*, CXII, 1958.
Smith, Peter. *Houses of the Welsh Countryside*. London, 1975.
Smith, W. J. (ed.). *Calendar of Salusbury Correspondence*. Cardiff, 1954.
 *Herbert Correspondence*. Cardiff, 1963.
Smout, T. C. *Scottish Trade on the Eve of Union, 1660–1707*. Edinburgh, 1963.
Speed, Adolphus [Adam]. *Adam Out of Eden*. London, 1659.
Spenceley, G. F. R. 'The Origins of the English Pillow Lace Industry', *AHR*, XXI, 1973.
Spufford, Margaret. *A Cambridgeshire Community: Chippenham*. Leicester, 1965.
 *Contrasting Communities: English Villagers in the Sixteenth and Seventeenth Centuries*. Cambridge, 1974.
Stanes, R. G. F. (ed.). 'A Georgicall Account of Devonshire and Cornwalle in Answer to Some Queries concerning Agriculture, by Samuel Colepresse, 1667', *Devonshire Assoc.*, XCVI, 1964.
Steer, F. W. (ed.). *Farm and Cottage Inventories of Mid-Essex, 1635–1749*. Chelmsford, 1950.

Steers, J. A. *The Coastline of England and Wales*. Cambridge, 1946.
Steers, J. A. (ed.). *Cambridge and its Region*. Cambridge, 1965.
Stern, W. M. 'Cheese Shipped Coastwise to London towards the Middle of the Eighteenth Century', *Guildhall Misc.*, IV, 1973.
Stone, L. *Crisis of the Aristocracy, 1538–1641*. Oxford, 1965.
   *Family and Fortune: Studies in Aristocratic Finance in the Sixteenth and Seventeenth Centuries*. Oxford, 1973.
   *The Family, Sex and Marriage in England, 1500–1800*. London, 1977.
Stone, Lawrence and Stone, Jeanne C. F. 'Country Houses and their Owners in Hertfordshire, 1540–1879', in *The Dimensions of Quantitative Research in History*, ed. W. O. Aydelotte et al. Princeton and Oxford, 1972.
Stout, William. *The Autobiography of William Stout of Lancaster, 1665–1752*, ed. J. D. Marshall. Manchester, 1967.
Straker, E. *Wealden Iron*. London, 1931.
Strickland, H. E. *General View of the Agriculture of the East Riding of Yorkshire*. London, 1812.
Summerson, J. *Architecture in Britain 1530 to 1830*. London, 1953.
   'The Classical Country House in 18th-Century England', *J. Roy. Soc. Arts*, CVII, 1959.
Switzer, Stephen. *A Compendious Method for the Raising of Italian Brocoli*. London, 1729.
Tate, W. E. 'Cambridgeshire Field Systems', *Proc. Cambridge Arch. Soc.*, XL, 1939–42.
   *A Domesday of English Enclosure Acts and Awards*, ed. M. Turner. Reading, 1978.
   'Inclosure Movements in Northamptonshire', *Northants. Past & Present*, I, 2, 1949.
Taylor, C. C. *The Cambridgeshire Landscape*. London, 1973.
Thirsk, Joan, 'Agrarian History, 1540–1950', in *VCH Leics.*, II. London, 1954.
   *Economic Policy and Projects: The Development of a Consumer Society in Early Modern England*. Oxford, 1978.
   *English Peasant Farming: The Agrarian History of Lincolnshire from Tudor to Recent Times*. London, 1957. Repr. London, 1981.
   'The Fantastical Folly of Fashion: The English Stocking Knitting Industry, 1500–1700', in *Textile History and Economic History*, ed. N. B. Harte and K. G. Ponting. Manchester, 1973.
   'Horn and Thorn in Staffordshire: The Economy of a Pastoral County', *N. Staffs. J. Field Stud.*, IX, 1969.
   *Horses in Early Modern England: For Service, for Pleasure, for Power*. Stenton Lecture, 1977. Reading, 1978.
   'Industries in the Countryside', in *Essays in the Economic and Social History of Tudor and Stuart England*, ed. F. J. Fisher. Cambridge, 1961.
   'New Crops and their Diffusion: Tobacco-Growing in Seventeenth Century England', in *Rural Change and Urban Growth, 1500–1800*, ed. C. W. Chalklin and M. A. Havinden. London, 1974.
   'Plough and Pen: Agricultural Writers in the Seventeenth Century', in T. H. Aston et al., *Social Relations and Ideas*. Cambridge, 1983.
   'Projects for Gentlemen, Jobs for the Poor: Mutual Aid in the Vale of Tewkesbury, 1600–1630', in *Essays in Bristol and Gloucestershire History*, ed. P. McGrath and J. Cannon. Bristol, 1976.

'The Restoration Land Settlement', *JMH*, XXVI, 4, 1954.
'The Sales of Royalist Land during the Interregnum', EcHR, 2nd ser., V, 1952–3.
'Seventeenth-Century Agriculture and Social Change', in *Land, Church and People: Essays Presented to Professor H. P. R. Finberg*, ed. Joan Thirsk. Suppl. to AHR, XVIII, 1970.
Thirsk, Joan (ed.). *The Agrarian History of England and Wales, IV, 1500–1640*. Cambridge, 1967.
Thirsk, Joan and Cooper, J. P. (eds.). *Seventeenth-Century Economic Documents*. Oxford, 1972.
Thomas, D. 'The Social Origins of the Marriage Partners of the British Peerage', *Pop. Stud.*, XXVI, 1972.
Thomas, H. *A History of Wales, 1485–1660*. Cardiff, 1972.
Thomas, K. R. 'The Enclosure of Open Fields and Commons in Staffordshire', *Staffs. Hist. Coll.*, 1931.
Thompson, E. P. 'The Moral Economy of the English Crowd in the Eighteenth Century', PP, no. 50, 1971.
*Whigs and Hunters: The Origins of the Black Act*. London, 1975.
Thompson, F. M. L. 'The Social Distribution of Landed Property in England since the Sixteenth Century', EcHR, 2nd ser., XIX, 1966.
'Landownership and Economic Growth in England in the Eighteenth Century', in *Agrarian Change and Economic Development*, ed. E. L. Jones and S. J. Woolf. London, 1969.
Thomson, G. Scott. *Family Background*. London, 1949.
*Life in a Noble Household, 1641–1700*. London, 1937.
Tibbutt, H. G. *Bedfordshire and the First Civil War*. 2nd edn. Elstow, 1973.
*Torrington Diaries*, ed. C. Brayn Andrews. London, 1954.
Trinder, B. S. *The Industrial Revolution in Shropshire*. Chichester, 1973.
Trinder, B. S. and Cox, J. *Yeomen and Colliers in Telford*. Chichester, 1980.
Trow-Smith, R. *A History of British Livestock Husbandry to 1700*. London, 1957.
*A History of British Livestock Husbandry, 1700–1900*. London, 1959.
Tubbs, C. R. 'The Development of the Smallholding and Cottage Stock-Keeping Economy of the New Forest', AHR, XIII, 1965.
Tucker, G. S. L. 'Population in History', EcHR, 2nd ser., XX, 1967.
Tuke, J. *General View of the Agriculture of the North Riding of Yorkshire*. London, 1800.
Tull, J. *A Supplement to the Essay on Horse-hoing Husbandry...* London, 1736.
Tupling, G. H. 'The Early Metal Trades and the Beginnings of Engineering in Lancashire', *Lancs. & Cheshire Arch. Soc.*, LXI, 1951.
Turner, J. 'Ralph Austen, an Oxford Horticulturist of the Seventeenth Century', *Garden Hist.*, VI, 2, 1978.
Turner, M. *English Parliamentary Enclosure: Its Historical Geography and Economic History*. Folkestone, 1980.
Underdown, D. 'A Case concerning Bishops' Lands', EHR, LXXVIII, 1963.
Unwin, R. W. 'The Aire and Calder Navigation, Part II: The Navigation in the Pre-Canal Age', *Bradford Antiq.*, NS XLIII, 1967.
Utterström, G. 'Climatic Fluctuations and Population Problems in Early Modern History', *Scand. Ec. Hist. Rev.*, III, 1955.
Vanbrugh, Sir John. *The Complete Works, IV, Letters*. London, 1928.

Vancouver, C. *General View of the Agriculture in the County of Cambridge.* London, 1794.
  *General View of the Agriculture of Essex.* London, 1795.
  *General View of the Agriculture of Hampshire.* London, 1813.
Verney, F. P. *Memoirs of the Verney Family during the Civil War.* 2 vols. London, 1892.
Verney, F. P. and Verney, M. M. *Memoirs of the Verney Family during the Seventeenth Century.* 2nd edn. 2 vols. London, 1904.
Veysey, A. G. 'Col. Philip Jones, 1618–74', *Hon. Soc. Cymmrodorion.* 1966, pt 2.
Warner, J. 'General View of the Agriculture of the Isle of Wight', in A. and W. Driver, *General View of the Agriculture of the County of Hampshire.* London, 1794.
Watts, S. J. 'Tenant-Right in Early Seventeenth-Century Northumberland', *Northern Hist.*, VI, 1971.
Weatherill, L. *The Pottery Trade and North Staffordshire, 1660–1760.* Manchester, 1971.
Webber, Ronald. *Covent Garden, Mud-Salad Market.* London, 1969.
  *Market Gardening.* Newton Abbot, 1972.
Webster, C. *The Great Instauration.* London, 1975.
Westerfield, R. B. *Middlemen in English Business, Particularly between 1660 and 1760.* Conn. Acad. Arts & Sci., XIX. New Haven, 1915. Repr. Newton Abbot, 1968.
Weston, R. *A Discours of Husbandrie Used in Brabant and Flanders.* London, 1605 [recte 1650].
Weston, Richard. *Tracts on Practical Agriculture and Gardening.* London, 1773.
Whetter, J. *Cornwall in the Seventeenth Century: An Economic Survey of Kernow.* Padstow, 1974.
Whistler, L. *The Imagination of Vanbrugh.* London, 1954.
White, Gilbert. *The Natural History of Selborne*, ed. G. Allen, London, 1908.
Wiliam, Eurwyn. 'Adeiladau Fferm Traddodiadol yng Nghymru' (with English summary), *Amgueddfa*, XV, 1973.
Willan, T. S. *The English Coasting Trade 1600–1750.* Manchester, 1938.
  *The Inland Trade.* Manchester, 1976.
  'The River Navigation and Trade of the Severn Valley, 1600–1750', EcHR, VIII, 1937–8.
  *River Navigation in England, 1600–1760.* Oxford, 1936. New impr. London, 1964.
[William, Richard]. *Wallography, or the Britton Described.* London, 1673.
Williams, Glanmor (ed.). *The Glamorgan County History, IV.* Cardiff, 1976.
Williams, J. E. 'Whitehaven in the Eighteenth Century', EcHR, 2nd ser., VIII, 1956.
Williams, L. A. *Road Transport in Cumbria in the Nineteenth Century.* London, 1975.
Williams, Michael. *The Draining of the Somerset Levels.* Cambridge, 1970.
Wilson, C. H. *England's Apprenticeship, 1603–1763.* London, 1965.
Wood-Jones, R. B. *Traditional Domestic Architecture of the Banbury Region.* Manchester, 1963.
Woodward, D. M. 'The Anglo-Irish Livestock Trade in the Seventeenth Century', *Irish Hist. Stud.*, XVIII, 72, 1973.
  'Cattle Droving in the Seventeenth Century: A Yorkshire Example', in *Trade and Transport: Essays in Economic History in Honour of T. S. Willan*, ed. W. H. Chaloner and B. M. Ratcliffe. Manchester, 1977.

'A Comparative Study of the Irish and Scottish Livestock Trades in the Seventeenth Century', in *Comparative Aspects of Scottish and Irish Economic and Social History, 1600–1900*, ed. L. M. Cullen and T. C. Smout. Edinburgh, 1977.

Wordie, J. R. 'Social Change on the Leveson-Gower Estates, 1714–1832', EcHR, 2nd ser., XXVII, 4, 1974.

Worlidge, J. *Systema Agriculturae*. London, 1669.

*Systema Horti-Culturae, or the Art of Gardening*. London, 1677.

Wrigley, E. A. 'A Simple Model of London's Importance in Changing English Society and Economy, 1650–1750', PP, no. 37, 1967.

Yarranton, Andrew. *England's Improvement by Sea and Land*. London, 1677.

*The Improvement Improved, by a Second Edition of the Great Improvement of Lands by Clover*. London, 1663.

Yates, E. M. 'Aspects of Staffordshire Farming in the Seventeenth and Eighteenth Centuries', *N. Staffs. J. Field Stud.*, XV, 1975.

'Enclosure and the Rise of Grassland Farming in Staffordshire', *ibid.*, XIV, 1974.

Yelling, J. A. 'Changes in Crop Production in East Worcestershire, 1540–1867', AHR, XXI, 1, 1973.

'The Combination and Rotation of Crops in East Worcestershire, 1540–1660', AHR, XVII, 1, 1969.

*Common Field and Enclosure in England, 1450–1850*. London, 1977.

Youd, G. 'The Common Fields of Lancashire', *Hist. Soc. Lancs. & Cheshire*, CXIII, 1961.

Young, A. *The Farmer's Tour in the East of England*. 4 vols. London, 1771.

*General View of the Agriculture of Hertfordshire*. London, 1804.

*General View of the Agriculture of the County of Lincoln*. London, 1799.

*General View of the Agriculture of the County of Norfolk*. London, 1804.

*General View of the Agriculture of Oxfordshire*. London, 1809.

*A Six Months Tour through the North of England*. 4 vols. London, 1770.

*A Six Weeks' Tour through the Southern Counties*. 3rd edn. London, 1772.

*Tours in England and Wales (Selected from 'The Annals of Agriculture')*. London, 1932.

Young, A. (ed.). *The Annals of Agriculture*. 46 vols. London, 1784–1815.

Young, the Rev. A. *General View of the Agriculture of the County of Sussex*. London, 1813.

# INDEX

Abbey Cwmhir, 110
Abbots Ripton (Hunts.), 73
Abbotsbury (Dorset), 261
Abbott, Archbishop, 173
Abel, William, 301
Abergavenny (Mon.), 147, 150
Abergavenny, Lady, 354
Abergavenny, Lord, 58
Abergavenny Priory, 149, 150
Abergwili, 147, 150, 154
Abermarlais estate (Carms.), 388
Abingdon, earl of, 313
accounting methods, 41–2, 79, 372–3, 395
Acton Beauchamp (Worcs.), 197
agriculture, see farming
Alberbury (Salop.), 168
Albury (Herts.), 214
Aldersey, Hugh, 95
Alderton (Glos.), 324
Almeley (Herefords.), 404
Almondsbury (Glos.), 80
Aloesbridge Hundred (Kent), 162–3
Alston Moor (Cumb.), 278
Altcar (Lancs.), 112
Althorp, 42, 55
Alvington (Glos.), 73
Amble (Northumb.), 170
Andertone, James, 196
Andrews, John, 195
Andrews, Richard, 115
Anglesey, 124, 387, 421; estate management, 401–2, 416; estates, 138, 140, 141–2, 381, 382, 424
Anne, John, 82
Anwyl, Robert, 385
Appleby (Westmor.), 42, 47
Appledore marsh, 80
arable husbandry, 75, 77, 90–1, 183, 344–9; new crops, 362–3, 365, 376, 400–2
Archer family, 320
Ardeley (Herts.), 188, 221
Arden, Forest of, 192
aristocracy, see nobility
army garrisons, private houses as, 260–2; see also quartering of troops
Arnold, Nicholas, 150

Arscott, John, 119, 120
Arundell, Lord, 260
Ash (Kent), 349
Ashburnham estate, 397, 421
Ashford (Kent), 163
Ashridge (Herts.), 256, 259
Ashton, Hillary, 332
Aston, Lord, 335
Audelet, Mr, of Abingdon, 77
Audley, Henry, 150
Audley End (Essex), 308
Augmentations, Court of, 27–9, 52, 98–100, 102–3, 106–7, 116
Austen, John, 195
Awbrey, Sir John, 423
Axholme, Isle of (Lincs.), 170, 172, 191n.

Backewell, John and Margaret, 82
Bacon, Dame Jane, 343
Bacon, Sir Nicholas, and family, 15, 52, 58–9, 64, 111–12
Baggrave (Leics.), 81
Baker, Henry, 415
Baker, Samuel, 324
Bangor, diocese of, 146, 155, 158, 159–60
Bank of England stock, 305
Bankes, James, 69, 206
Bankes, Sir John, 261
Barham (Kent), 226
Barham Court (Kent), 259
Barlow, John, 382
Barlow, Bishop William, 152–3
Barlow family, 151
Barnbow (Yorks.), 61
Baron Hill estate (Anglesey), 384, 390, 392, 400
Basildon (Essex), 60
Basing House (Hants.), 261
Baskerville, Thomas, 201
Bassett, Sir Richard, 423
Bassett, William, 424
Bath, earl of, 278
Bath, Robert, 93
Bath Abbey, 86, 99
Bath and Wells, bishops of, 7, 30, 120–1
Batley (Yorks.), 62

444

# INDEX 445

Baxter, Richard, 216, 218
Bayley, Bishop Lewis, 158
Beaufort, duke of, 393, 398, 418
Beaufort manors (Glam.), 396, 398, 405
Beaumaris, 138
Beaumont, Sir John, 30
Beckett, J. V., 17, 387
Beddgelert (Caerns.), 406
Bedford, earl of, 116, 118, 119, 318; estates, 344–5, 358, 362, 377; see also Russell
Bedfordshire: estates, 249, 266, 291, 311; patterns of tenure, 350, 352, 354
Bedingfield, Sir Edmund, 106n.
beer, 218
Belknap, Sir Edward, 25
Bellow, John, 115
Belvoir (Leics.), 366
Benson, Jane, 323
Berkeley, Bishop, 121
Berkeley, Lord, 62, 64
Berkeley, lordship of, 74
Berkshire, 195; estates in Civil War, 253, 270
Bernwood Forest (Bucks.), 193
Berry, Major General, 379
Bersham furnace (Flints.), 420
Berth (Denbs.), 401
Best, Henry, 199, 201n., 215
Best, Isabel, 103
Bettey, J. H., 252
Betws estate (Carms.), 389
Beverley, Robert, 95
Bidford (War.), 98
Billington (Lancs.), 224
Birch, Colonel, 288
Birdsall (Yorks.), 338
bishops, episcopal estates, 7–8, 30, 120–1, 284–9 passim; in Wales, 146–7, 152–60 passim
Bishopstrow (Wilts.), 93
Blackeshawe, Richard, 225
Blackwell, John, 287
Blagdon (Somerset), 254
Blenheim Palace (Oxon.), 310
Blundell, William, 273, 372
Boarstall (Bucks.), 171
Bodedern (Anglesey), 410
Bodeon estate (Anglesey), 381, 424
Bodewryd (Anglesey), 395, 400, 401, 410, 411
Bodorgan (Anglesey), 399, 404
Bodysgallen (Caerns.), 401
Bolingbroke, Lord, 374
Bolton, Anne, duchess of, 391
Bolton Priory, 42, 47
bondmen, 32, 165n., 190
Bonfield, L., 292
Bonham manor, 280
Booth, Sir George, 283

Bordesley Abbey, 78, 109
Bossenden Wood, Battle of, 228n.
Boughton Monchelsea (Kent), 204, 225
Boulton, Mathew, 300
Bourne, Bishop, 121
Bowett farm (Pembs.), 407
Boyle, Elizabeth, 321
Brabourne (Kent), 226
Bradbury (Durham), 33
Bradenstoke Priory, 82
Bradford manor (Devon), 119
Bradgate, Thomas, 66
Bradley Green (Worcs.), 413
Bradley Priory, 96
Bradshaw, John, 150, 151
Brampton Bryan (Salop.), 260
Bray, Sir Reginald, 24, 25
Breakspear's farm (Herts.), 344
Brecon (Brecknock), 135, 150
Brecon Priory, 149, 150
Breconshire, 387, 397
Breda, Declaration of, 271
Brembridge family, 61
Bridgewater, earl of, 54; estates, 250, 252, 256, 259
Bridlington Priory, 85
Bridport (Dorset), 362
Briggs, Myles, 58
Brigstock Park (Northants.), 254
Brill (Bucks.), 171
Brilley (Herefords.), 110
Brinkelow, Henry, 29
Brinklow (War.), 221
Bristol, 262, 418, 420; diocese of, 150; see also St Augustine's Abbey
Bristol, John Hervry, first earl of, 306
Briton Ferry (Glam.), 419, 423
Brockett Hall (Herts.), 324
Brokylsbye, Richard, 115
Brome (Suff.), 59
Brooksbank, Stamp, 361
Brough (Westmor.), 47
Brough, Margaret, 225
Brougham (Westmor.), 47
Broughton, Vale of Cleveland, 169
Brownlow family, 54
Broxholme, John, 115
Bruce, Lord, 352, 354
Brudenell, Thomas, Lord, 69, 120n.
Bruern Abbey, 78
Bruton (Somerset), 216
Bryan, Sir Francis, 111
Brydges, James, 315
Brymore (Somerset), 340
Brynddu (Anglesey), 394, 400, 402, 408
Brynkinallt, 141
Buckfast Abbey, 92, 93

Buckingham, dukes of, 32, 39
Buckinghamshire, 171, 190; estates, 248, 251, 253, 273, 311, 354, 361
Buckland Abbey, 84–5, 86
Budd, Richard, 13
Buildwas Abbey, 105
Bulkeley, Thomas, 384
Bulkeley, William, 394, 400, 402
Bulkeley family, 138, 390, 392, 400
Bunbury, Sir William, 309
Burghley, Lord (William Cecil), 30, 31–2, 33, 39, 40, 43, 52
Burnley (Lancs.), 169, 195–6
Burrington manor (Devon), 116
Burton, Francis, 225
Burton Agnes (Yorks.), 224
Burton Dassett (War.), 65
Burwell manor (Cambs.), 28
Bury St Edmunds, 216
Busby, John, 78
Butler, Lady Charlotte, 321
Buttes, Thomas, 42
by-employments, 14, 167–8, 175–6, 187, 190–4; *see also* industries

Caddie, James, 211
Caergai (Mer.), 385
Caernarvon, 383
Caernarvonshire, 390
Caesar, Sir Julius, 37, 38, 41
Calvert, George, 35
Cambridgeshire, 6
Campbell, John, 388, 389, 391, 407, 417, 418
Campbell, M., 70
Campden, Viscount, 261
Cannock Chase, 192
Canonbury (Glos.), 74
Canons Ashby (Northants.), 75, 78
Canonsleigh (Devon), 76
Canterbury, 15; Cathedral Priory, 76, 80, 86
Carbery, earl of, 382, 385
Cardigan, earl of, 339, 365
Cardigan Priory, 149
Cardiganshire, 139, 405; lead mining, 399, 420
Carew, Sir George, 114, 116
Carew, Lady Mary, 116
Carew, Richard, 208, 213
Carey, Sir Henry, 247
Carleton (Yorks.), 211
Carleton, Bishop, 158
Carlinghow (Yorks.), 62
Carlisle (Cumb.), 253
Carmarthen, 150
Carmarthenshire, 139; estate management, 394, 397, 417, 419
Carne, Sir Edward, 149, 150, 423
Carne family, 151

Carreg y Pennill (Denbs.), 385
Carter, Colonel John, 384
Carter, Thomas, 213
Cartmel (Lancs.), 169, 170, 202, 217
Casbeard, John, 287
Cassell Parks (Devon), 362
Castle Ashby (Northants.), 260
Catesby, nuns of, 75
Catesby, Simon, 94, 113
Catholic landowners, 60, 61, 151, 279; impact of Civil War on, 255, 256, 268, 269, 273, 275, 276
Catlin, Sir Robert, 56, 120n.
Caton, Robert, 202
Cattell Moor (Yorks.), 169
Catterton (Yorks.), 361
cattle: breeding, in Wales, 401, 402, 415–16; labourers', 178–9, 180 (table), 182; legislation (Irish Cattle Act), 415; plague, 357, 358, 372, 416; *see also* dairy farming
Cause Castle (Salop.), 266
Cavendish, William, 149
Cecil, Robert, earl of Salisbury, 33–40 *passim*, 50, 52–3
Cecil family, 4, 118; *see also* Burghley, Lord; Salisbury, earls of
Cefn Mably (Glam.), 383, 424
Cefn y Wern (Debns.), 385
'censuses', occupational (1608, 1638), 136
cereals, 183, 215–16
Chaddesley (Worcs.), 109
Chalfield House (Wilts.), 249
Chaloner, Sir Thomas, 58
Chamber administration, 23–7
Chamberlain, Leonard, 115
Chambers, J. D., 308
Champernon, Sir Arthur, 114, 116, 119
Champernon, Sir Philip, 93, 114
Chancery, 24, 220, 327
chantries, 8–9, 29; Welsh, 147, 148
Charborough (Dorset), 261
Charles I, King, 40, 46, 48, 159
Charles II, King, 222–3, 271
Charlett, John and Thomas, 100
Charlton Abbots (Glos.), 88
Chatsworth (Derbs.), 42, 366
cheese, 212, 213, 216
Chepstow Priory, 149
Chesham Magna (Bucks.), 252
Cheshire: estates in Civil War, 251, 259; patterns of tenure, 327, 332, 365
Chesney, H. E., 270
Chester, 31, 400
Chettle, Peter, 419
Childerditch estate (Essex), 314
Chillington (Somerset), 212
Chirk Castle (Denbs.), 324, 385, 390–3

*passim*, 395, 400, 401; minerals, 420; tenants, 407, 409–15 *passim*, 417, 418, 423
Chiswick (Middx.), 377
Chittern (Wilts.), 77, 93
Chopwell (Durham), 293
Chorley (Lancs.), 94
Church estates, non-monastic, 7–9, 120–1, 414; impact of Civil War on, 283–9, 383; in Wales, 146–7, 152–60, 383; *see also* monasteries
Churchstoke (Wales), 156
Churton, Robert, 69
Cirencester, 78
Cistercian order, 74, 147
Civil War and Interregnum, 15–16, 40, 41; and Church estates, 283–9, 383; and Crown lands, 281–3, 287–8; effect on rents, 250, 252–5; impact on private landowners, 246–81 *passim*; impact on social structure, 229–30, 275; long-term consequences for estates, 272–81; plunder and damage to property, 251–2, 259–62, 267; taxation, 247–50, 384; *see also* composition fines; confiscation of estates; sequestration
Clare, earls of, 55, 369
Clark, John, 414
Clavering, John, 293
Clavering, Mary, 295
Clay, C., 386, 387
Clay, T., 62
Claydon (Bucks.), 273, 368, 371
Cleator (Cumb.), 211
Cleeve (Glos.), 100
Clenennau, 141, 382
clergy, 120–1, 283–9; Welsh, 146–7, 152–60
Clerke, John, 83
Cleveland (Yorks.), 59, 169, 317
Cleveland, earl of, 271
Clifford family, 42, 47–8; *see also* Cumberland, earls of
Clinton and Saye, Lord, 119
Clopton, John, 196, 204
cloth industries, 190–1; *see also* spinning; weaving
Clynnog, 147
coal, 218; common rights in, 169, 398; landowners' profits from, 318–19, 419
Cobbett, William, 14, 189
Cochwillan (Caerns.), 141
Cockersand Abbey, 91, 94, 197
Cockfield (Durham), 173
Cockington (Devon), 247
Cocks, Charles, 295
Cocks, John, 77
Cocks, Sir Robert, 295
Coddrington family, 317
Coke, Sir Edward, 58, 66

Coke, Thomas, earl of Leicester, 324
Coke estates, 324, 345, 376
Colchester family, 309
Cole Green (Herts.), 366
Coleshill (Berks.), 293
Colle, Joan, 195
Collins, John, 94
Colt, Susannah, 312, 323
Colwinston, 150
commission of concealment, 154
Committee for Compounding, 43, 254, 260, 262–6 *passim*
Committee for Relief on Articles of War, 263
common rights, 168–71, 190, 897, 405–6
commons: cottage building on, 210–11; restrictions on, 169, 224; *see also* common rights; enclosure; encroachment
commotes, 124
composition fines, 246, 262–7
Compton family, 273
confiscation of estates, 268–72, 282, 284–5, 288–9; legislation, 268, 271, 382; in Wales, 382
Conisborough (Yorks.), 173
Conishead, 197
Conquest, Richard, 258
consolidation of holdings, 18, 306–10, 311, 313, 324, 325, 360–1; in Wales, 127, 391, 404–5
Constable, Sir Marmaduke, 277
Constable, Sir Philip, 276
Constable family, 172, 273, 276, 277
Conway, 138
Cook, Jane, 321
Cooke, Adam, 68
Cooper, J. P., 6, 289, 290
copyhold, 34–5, 58, 299, 326–35, 396; conversion to freehold, 334–5
Corfe Castle (Dorset), 261
Cork, countess of, 322
Cornwall, 190, 388; labourers, 181, 208, 212, 213, 222; royalists, 248, 255, 256, 259, 262, 264–5, 267
Cornwall, duchy of, 38
Cornwallis, Lord, 321
Cornwallis, Sir Thomas, 59–60
corrodies, 79
Cory, Thomas, 393
Costock (Notts.), 93
Cotham (Notts.), 62
Cothelstone (Somerset), 261
cottagers, *see* labourers
cottages, 207–14
Coughton (War.), 99
Courts: Baron and Leet, 396–7; *see also* Augmentations; Chancery; First Fruits and

Tenths; Requests; Star Chamber; Wards
Coventry Priory, 86
Cowper, earls 295, 308, 312, 323, 334, 366, 370; estates, 295, 323, 345n. 349, 354; *see also* Cowper, William
Cowper, William, Lord Chancellor, 295, 315, 324, 356, 371
Coyd Tallog (Denbs.), 415
Cranbourn House (Dorset), 262
Crane (Pembs.), 415
Cranfield, Lionel, *see* Middlesex, earl of
Cranmer, Archbishop, 229
Craven, Clifford estates at, 42, 47-8
Crayke (Yorks.), 172
credit dealings, 64-5, 272, 276-7, 298-9, 303, 305-6, 359
Croesor (Mer.), 412
Crogen estate (Mer.), 401, 412, 415
Cromwell, Thomas, 27, 28, 88; and Dissolution, 40, 72, 91, 92, 94-7 *passim*, 100, 106, 108
Crosland, Mrs Jane, 260
Crosswood estate (Cards.), 385, 399, 406, 409, 420
Crosthwaite (Cumb.), 58
Crouch, Gilbert, 277
Crowden, Gilbert, 225
Crown lands, 2-3, 21-41, 281-3, 287-8; administration of, 22-41; dispersal of, 3, 9, 28-9, 30, 33, 38, 281-2; extent of, 22, 26, 27, 281; lessees and grantees, 31-5, 37, 282-3; revenue from, 22, 25, 26, 28, 30-1, 36-40 *passim*, 281; in Wales, 383, 398-9
Croxton (Leics.), 81, 93
Cubert (Cornwall), 212
Cullompton (Devon), 86
Culmstock (Devon), 328
Cumberland: Crown lands, 37; estate management, 319, 366; estates in Civil War, 256, 271; labourers, 173, 210, 211, 214, 215; land tenure, 57-8, 167 (table), 168, 334, 388
Cumberland, earl of, 47-8, 113; *see also* Clifford family
Cumbria, 299, 303, 387-8
Curwen family, 319
customary tenure, 34, 58, 84, 111, 325-35, 396, 397
Cuthbertson, John, 211
Cutte, John, 24
Cwm-hir, 150
Cyfeiliog (Mont.), 397
Cynllwyd (Mer.), 415

Dacre, Lord, 247
dairy farming: cottage, 179; monastic, 78-80
Darkenall, Robert, 113
Dartmoor, 192
David, Hugh, 412
David, William, 412
Davie, Ellen, 225
Davies, Bishop Richard, 155, 156, 158
Dawkins, Richard, 398
De La Pré Abbey, 75, 100, 109
Dean, Forest of: Crown revenue from, 37; people of, 175, 176n., 177, 192, 218; riots, 172
Deene (Northants.), 69, 365
Deerfold Forest (Herefords.), 168
Degannwy (Caerns.), 401
Denbigh, 138
Denbighshire, 381, 384, 385, 415, 416
Denby Grange, 60
Dennis, Sir Thomas, 93, 113
Denny, Henry, 58, 59
Dentdale (Yorks.), 191
Denton (Yorks.), 60
Derby, 216, 250
Derby, earls of, 4, 22, 306
Derbyshire, 320; labourers, 194, 212, 216; land tenure, 57, 327
Derwentwater, earls of, 278-9
Derwydd estate (Carms.), 392, 394, 399, 404, 407
Des Bouverie, Sir Jacob, 351, 371
Devereux family, 151, 153
Devon, 8, 98n.; labourers, 176, 210, 216, 218; land tenure, 70, 291, 328, 331, 333n., 362-3; monastic lands, 9, 28, 72-3, 76, 85, 96, 108, 115-16, 118-20
Devonshire, earl of, 366
Dewes, Sir Henry, 107
Dewes, Paul, 202
Dietz, F. C., 103, 104
Dinefwr estate, 139-40
Dishley (Leics.), 88
Doddington (Glos.), 317
Doggett, John, 214
Dolman, Marmaduke, 202
Dolobran estate (Mont.), 420
Donne, Abbot Gabriel, 92
Dore (Herefords.), 150
Dorset, 369; estates in Civil War, 252, 261-2; gentry, 5; industries, 190, 192
Dorset, duke of, 366
Dorset, earl of, 33, 37
Dowe, Katherine, 78
Downe, John, 115
Downe, William, 116
Downhamford Hundred (Kent), 163
drink, labourers', 217-18
Dudley, Edmund, 25
Duke, Richard, 119-20
Dumbleton (Glos.), 295

## INDEX

Duncombe, Charles, 311
Dunkeswell Abbey, 85
Durham, County, 172, 319
Durham, diocese of, 57; estates, 203, 287, 289
Dutton, Richard, 385
Dyer, Dr Christopher, 6, 7
Dymock, Andrew, 24
Dyon, John, 115

Earle, Sir Walter, 261
Earsby Priory, 99
Easingwold (Yorks.), 172, 175
East Anglia, 5; estates in Civil War, 256, 260; labourers, 166–7, 181–2, 185, 187, 191, 215, 219; land tenure, 57, 59–60, 336; *see also individual counties*
East Budleigh (Devon), 76
East Claydon (Bucks.), 301
East Coker (Somerset), 317
East Sutton (Kent), 204
Eastington (Glos.), 340
Edgmond (Salop), 334
Edisbury, Joshua, 400
Edmondes, Sir Thomas, 39
Edward IV, King, 21–2
Edward VI, King, 29, 31, 40, 103, 105, 149
Edwinsford (Carms.), 406, 409, 424
Egerton family, *see* Bridgewater, earls of
Eglwysilan, 159, 392
Eland family, 62
Elizabeth I, Queen, 46, 121; Crown lands under, 30–3, 36; disposal of Church property, 103, 154
Ellerton Priory, 99
Ellis, Richard, 92
Elmswell (Yorks.), 199
Elton, Dr G. R., 27
Elwes, Mr, merchant, 345
Ely, bishop of, 30
Emley (Yorks.), 254
employers, relations between labourers and, 14–15, 203–7, 225–7
Empson, Richard, 25
enclosure, 171–4, 308–9, 377; monastic, 81–2; *see also* Wales
encroachment on commons, 18, 171, 174–7; *see also* Wales
Englebourne, 93
Epcombes estate (Herts.), 312
episcopal estates, *see* bishops
equipment, farm, 196–7, 222
Erthig (Denbs.), 400
Esclus (Wrexham), 382
Esholt Priory (Yorks.), 79, 103
Essex, 313; estates in Civil War, 247, 249, 253, 257, 270; monastic lands, 90–1; patterns of tenure, 341, 352–4 *passim*, 363

Essex, earl of, 259, 267
estate management, 15–17, 325–78; monastic, 76–97; surveys and maps, 307, 342–3; *see also* accounting methods; home farms; improvement; repairs; stewards; tenants; tenure, patterns of; Wales
estate records, 41–5
Evans, David, of Neath, 423
Evans, Robert, 420
Everingham (Yorks.), 273, 276, 277
Everitt, Alan, 13, 14, 15
Evesham, 78
Ewenni Priory, 148, 149, 150, 423
Exchequer, 22–3, 25–7, 37
Eyre, Rowland, 276, 279
Eyre family, 273, 279–80

Fairfax, Lord, 254, 263, 296
Fairfax, Sir Thomas, 60
Fairford (Glos.), 324
family studies, 4–5
Fanshawe family, 54
farm labour, 161, 195–200; hours, 195, 201n.; seasonality, 14, 164, 196, 199; specialized, 197–9, 201, 222; tools, 196–7; variety of, 195–6; *see also* migration
farm labourers, *see* labourers
farm servants, live-in, 13, 202, 214
farming, 195–9, 200–7; cottage husbandry, 177–84; landowners and, 18, 68, 302–4, 308, 332–3, 341, 344–51, 361–3, 376–7, 409; monastic, 75, 77–9, 91–1; in Wales, 421–2; *see also* arable husbandry; farm labour; improvement; livestock
Feckenham Forest (Worcs.), 168, 175
Feltnes, Henry, 189
Fenwick, Sir William, 278
Fermanagh, Lord, 301
Ferrar, Bishop, 152
Fessher, John, 215
feudal survivals, 23, 24, 31, 40, 105–6, 203–4, 225–6
Ffoulkes, David, 411
Field, Bishop, 159
Fillongley (War.), 188
Filmer, Sir Robert, 204
Finch, Daniel, earl of Nottingham, 363
fines, 58–60 *passim*, 69–70, 326–30 *passim*; Civil War, 262–7, 272–3, 348, 382–3; on Crown leases, 32, 34–5, 101; on monastic leases, 83, 92–4; in Wales, 151–2, 382–3, 413–14
Finn, Tom, 195
Firsby Moor, 173
First Fruits and Tenths, Court of, 27, 28
Fisher, H. A. L., 108, 117
fishing rights, 95, 170

# 450 INDEX

Fithlers manor (Essex), 314
Fitzford Barton farm (Devon), 377
Fitzharding, Lord, 371
Fitzwilliam, Lord, 338, 353, 357, 367, 371
Fitzwilliam family, 65
flax, 183, 191, 363
Flintshire, 384, 419–20
Foljambe, Sir Francis, 63
Folkestone (Kent), 351
food, 366; labourers', 170, 215–18; prices, 56–7
Forest (Gower), 398, 419
forests, woodland: communities, 14, 168, 174–8, 182, 185–90 passim, 199–200, 207, 210, 212–13, 218, 227–9 passim; industries, 184, 192, 193; monastic, 88, 107–8, 114; royal, 3, 36–7, 218, 281
Forrester, Lady Mary, 363
Fortescue, Sir John, 21, 22
Fothergill, S., 300
Foulness (Essex), 359
Fountains Abbey, 75, 82, 96–7
Fox, Henry, 315, 369
Fox, Sir Stephen, 294, 335, 338, 359, 377
fragmentation of estates, 125–8, 298, 403, 404
Framfield, 33
Frampton (Dorset), 88
Frankley (Worcs.), 261
Fraystrop rectory, 85
Freeman, John, 95
Frithelstock Priory, 113
fuel, 36, 218; see also turf
Fugglestone (Wilts.), 92
Fuller, Thomas, 66
Furness Abbey, 99, 113
furniture, cottage, 211–14, 219
Furse, Robert, 69, 70
Furse family, 61

Galtres Forest, 54, 175, 217
Gamage, Thomas, 409
Gardiner, John, 83
Garendon Abbey, 81, 82, 88
Gargrave, Sir Richard, 63
Garsdale (Yorks.), 168, 191
Gascoigne, John, 61
Gascoigne family, 55, 61
gavelkind (partible inheritance), 168, 174n. 194; in Wales, 125–7, 133, 139, 140, 403–4
Gell, Sir John, 250
Gelli Aur, 141
Gentles, I., 15, 287
gentry, 3–6 passim, 45–6, 50–1, 229, 422–4; households, 204, 366; impact of Civil War on, 246–81 passim; income from estates, 55–66; landownership patterns, 290–1, 297–325 passim, 334; as lessees of monastic lands, 93–4; relations with tenants, 173, 225–7, 342, 357–72 passim; in Wales, 10–12, 122–3, 135–46 passim, 151, 379–81, 386, 387–91, 422–4
Gery family, 249
Gestone, Annes, 220
Gibbon, Edward, 355, 370
Gillam family, 198
Gillingham Forest (Dorset), 192; riots, 172
Gilnot, Goodwife, 226
Gisbourne, Elizabeth, 252
Glamorgan, 17; estate management, 388, 402; landowners, 11, 293n., 381, 386, 387, 389, 390, 423–4; monastic lands, 149; tenure, 396
Glasbury-on-Wye (Brecons.), 409
Glastonbury Abbey, 88, 97, 100, 114
Glendŵr's revolt, 122, 125
Glentworth (Lincs.), 115
Gloucester, 78; diocese of, 150
Gloucester Abbey, 148, 150
Gloucestershire: Crown lands, 24; estates, 251, 254, 295; labourers, 163, 165, 192, 194, 212, 215; monastic lands, 73, 117–18; patterns of tenure, 335, 363
Glynne, John, 384
Gnathan farm (Devon), 85
Gnoll (Neath), 402
Godalming (Surrey), 191
Godington (Kent), 165, 195, 249
Gogerddan estate (Cards.), 399
Golden Grove (Carms.), 389, 391, 392–3, 395, 397, 406, 407, 418
Goldston, Thomas, 76
Goldwell, Bishop Thomas, 152, 153
Good, Robert, 95
Goodleigh (Devon), 115–16
Goodman, William, 95
Goodricke estate (Yorks.), 352
Goosy, John, 221
Gorhambury (Herts.), 310, 311, 321, 335, 343, 370, 375
Goring, George, 54
Gostwick, Sir John, 112
Gower, lordship of, 397, 398, 405
Gower, Sir Thomas, 278
Gower family estates (Staffs.), 319, 377
Gowran, Baroness, 350
Grace Dieu (Pembs.), 149
Grafton estates (Northants.), 344
granges, monastic, 74–5, 96, 104
Grantham, earl of, 295, 323
Granwine, Thomas, 214
Gras. N. S. B., 67
Gray, Dr Madeleine, 12
Great Amwell (Herts.), 221
Great Chart, 195

Great Contract, the, 38, 40
Great Driffield (Yorks.), 189
Great Easton (Essex), 84
Great Malvern, 102
Great Ribstone (Yorks.), 352
Great Wratting (Suff.), 196
Greenwich, 31
Grey, Sir Edward, 105
Grey, Lady Jane, 26
Griffin, Sir John, 308
Griffin family, 273
Griffith, John, 402
Griffith family, 139
Grimston, Sir Harbottle, 302, 311, 335, 343, 370
Grimston, Sir Samuel, 344, 354
Grimston, William, 321
Grimston estates, 297, 310, 341, 345–6, 348, 353, 356, 375
Grindal, Archbishop, 173
Griston (Norf.), 206n.
Grosvenor family, 420
Guevara, John, 61, 64
Gunter family, 13, 151
Gurleye, Richard, 179
Gweburnant farm (Caerns.), 412
Gwersyllt (Denbs.), 382
Gwersyllt Issa (Flints.), 385
Gwydir (Caerns.), 136, 141, 154, 385, 401
Gwynedd, 10
Gybbe, John, 214

Habakkuk, H. J., 19, 71n. 101, 115; and estates in Civil War, 249, 266, 382; and landownership patterns, 6, 291, 324, 379, 385–7
Hackings, John, 195
Hailes (Glos.), 78, 115
Hale, Sir Matthew, 324
Hales, Sir Thomas, 340
Hales estate (Somerset), 349
Hall, Bishop, 214
Hall, Thomas, 188
Hall, William, 170
Halston Hall (Salop.), 366
Hammersley, G., 36
Hampshire: estates in Civil War, 247, 251, 270; labourers, 167 (table), 192, 218; monastic lands, 95, 96, 104, 114–15, 118; patterns of tenure, 327, 355
Hampton Gay (Oxon.), 77
Hanmer, Sir Thomas, 309
Hanmer family, 420
Harborne, John, 100
Hardingstone (Northants.), 75
Hardwick (Glos.), 254
Hardwick family, 293

Hardwick Hall (Derbs.), 48
Hare family, 249
Harley, Sir Edward, 286
Harley, Sir Robert, 260
Harper, Richard, 23
Harper, Roger, 195
Harpton Court (Radnors.), 416
Harris, William, 82
Harrison, William, 59, 184, 213
Hartest (Suff.), 167
Hartland Abbey, 75, 85
Hartlib, Samuel, 164
harvest-home, 203, 222
Harvey, Dr Barbara, 9
Harwell (Berks.), 195
Haseley (War.), 80–1
Hassop (Derbs.), 273, 279
Hatfield (Herts.), 191, 334
Hatfield Chase (Yorks.), 170, 217
Hatherleigh manor (Devon), 119
Hatherop (Glos.), 93
Hatton, Sir Christopher, 54–5
Hatton family, 273
Haveray Park (Yorks.), 344
Hawarden estate (Wales), 382, 401, 419
Hawkesley (Worcs.), 261
Hawksworth (Yorks.), 103
Hawling (Glos.), 88
Haydon, George, 115–16
Hazlewood (Yorks.), 60
Heal, Dr Felicity, 7–8
Healaugh (Yorks.), 361
Healaugh Park Priory, 100
Heard, John, 85
Hearth Tax Returns, 162–3
Heath, Dr Peter, 8
Heathcote, Sir John, 365
hedges and ditches, upkeep of, 351
Hellier, Alice, 83
Hellier, Christopher and John, 83
Hellier, Thomas, 83
Helmsley (Yorks.), 260, 311
Helyar family, 317
Hembry, Dr Phyllis, 7
hemp-spinning, 191
Heneage, Sir Thomas, 150
Henley family, 54
Henllys (Glam.), 402
Henry VII, King, 21–5, 31, 47, 76, 139
Henry VIII, King, 32, 40, 72, 97, 108, 121, 150
Hepple (Northumb.), 348
Heptinstall, William, 211
Herbert, John, 99
Herbert, Lord, 385
Herbert, William, of Cogan Pill (Glam.), 423
Herbert, William, of Friars (Glam.), 423

## 452 INDEX

Herbert family, 151, 155; see also Pembroke, earls of
Hereford, diocesan estates, 286
Hereford, Viscount, 407
Herefordshire, 168, 194, 286
heriots, 34, 84, 326–7, 331, 396, 408
Herstmonceaux Castle (Sussex), 247
Hertfordshire: estates, 270, 302, 308, 323; labourers, 178n., 183–94 passim, 207–8, 213–15 passim, 218–19; patterns of tenure, 335, 345–6, 351, 356
Hertingfordbury (Herts.), 334, 335
Hervey, Lord John, 306
Hesilrige, Sir Arthur, 287
Hesketh, Sir Robert, 94
Hexham (Northumb.), 340
Hexter, J. H., 44
Heyman, Ralph, 226
Higgins, George, 394
High Ercall (Salop.), 261
Hill, Richard, 334, 339, 356, 360, 365, 367, 371
Hilton (Durham), 33
Hilton, R. H., 84
hiring fairs, 200
Hoare, Henry, the elder, 311, 323
Hoare, Henry, the younger, 309, 311, 312, 322, 323, 364–5, 370
Hoare, Richard, 323
Hoare family of Stourhead, 302n., 309, 311, 312, 322, 323, 364–5, 370
Hobson, William, 165
Holdenby (Northants.), 55
Holderness (Yorks.), 172
Holderness, B. A., 376, 387
Hole's tenement, Thorverton (Devon), 346
Holiday, P. G., 265, 269, 270, 271
Holkham (Norfolk), 324, 345, 376
Holland, Lord, see Fox, Henry
Holles, Gervase, 42
Holles, John, duke of Newcastle, 314
Holme upon Spalding Moor (Yorks.), 202
Holme Cultram (Cumb.), 93
Holmes, C., 249
Holmes, G. S., 315n.
Holmesdale (Kent), 169
Holyhead, 147
Holywell (Hunts.), 73
Home Counties: estates, 46, 302; gentry, 317
home farms, 18, 362, 392, 400, 421
Hooker, John, of Exeter, 8, 70
Horner, Thomas and John, 114
Horsefrith Park (Essex), 348
horses, labourers', 180 (table), 181, 182, 220
Hosier, John, 393, 395
Hoskins, Henry, 172
Hoskins, W. G., 61, 67, 68

Hotham, Sir Charles, 316
Hotham family, 376
Hothfield (Kent), 267
Houghton (Hunts.), 73
Houlbrooke, Dr Ralph, 8
Houlden, Robert, 195
houses, 66–7, 207–10
Howard, Stephen, 394
Howard family, 15, 53, 113
Howe, Robert, 86
Howell, Dr Cicely, 6
Huddersfield (Yorks.), 67
Hudson, John and Agnes, 79
Huet, Thomas, 158
Hughes, Admiral Sir Edward, 312
Hughes, Bishop, 158
Humphreys, T. M., 17, 18, 19
Hundleton (Pembs.), 407
Hungate, Lady, 339
Hungerford, Sir Giles, 296
Hungerford, Lady Margaret, 23
Huntingdon, earl of, 33
Huntingdonshire, 73, 84, 311
Hurdwick, 77, 97
Hurstfield, J., 31, 32
Hussey, John, 113–14
Hyende, John, 215

Ightenhill (Lancs.), 169
Ilchester, earls of, 294, 306, 315
Ilketshall (Suff.), 58
implements, see equipment, farm
improvement: 'improving' leases, 346, 350, 354, 409; monastic, 80–1; role of landowners, 18, 68, 273, 303–4, 308, 361–2, 376–8; see also Wales
industries, 14, 190–4; landowners' investment in, 318–20, 367, 398, 419; see also by-employments; iron industries; mining
Ingarsby (Leics.), 81
Ingilby, Sir John, 344, 348, 357
Ingram, Sir Arthur, 53–4
Ingram family, 60
inheritance: customs, 7, 221, 292–7, 298, 301, 323–5; failure of male heirs, 17, 292, 387; women and, 292–7 passim; younger sons, 6, 294–5, 297, 298; see also gavelkind; marriage settlements; Wales
interest rates, 64
Interregnum, see Civil War and Interregnum
inventories, probate, 43; labourers', 177–8, 184–9 passim, 207, 211–15 passim
Ireland, trade with, 400, 415
iron industries, 36, 192, 320, 392, 420
Irwin, Lord, 338
Isham, John, 63
Isham, Thomas, 63

# INDEX   453

Jacques, Thomas, 368
James I, King, 33–8, 40, 46, 58
James, Jenkin, 408
Jefferies, Richard, 199, 206
Jenkins, David, of Hensol (Glam.), 423
Jenkins, P., 17
Jenkins, Watkin, 417
Johnston, Dr Nathaniel, 63
Jones, Francis, 389
Jones, Hugh, 410
Jones, John, 412
Jones, Colonel John, 384
Jones, Sir Philip, 383
Jones, Colonel Philip, 384
Jones family of the Friary, Newport, 13
Jones family, of Usk, 13
Joyce, Henry, 181, 188

Kaye, John, 61
Kaye family, of Yorkshire, 60, 61
Keates, Alice, 195
Keele (Staffs.), 107
Kemys, Sir Nicholas, 383, 424
Kenilworth Priory, 98
Kennington (Kent), 169
Kent, 36, 175 (table), 193, 374; estates in Civil War, 247–9 passim, 256, 270, 275, 277–8, 286; gentry, 5, 57, 165, 226; labourers, 162–3, 169, 175–6, 199, 201–2, 203n., 217, 218, 223; patterns of tenure, 326, 343, 351, 354, 363; Weald, 163, 169, 175–6, 192, 194
Kent, Nathaniel, 308, 364, 374, 378
Kew, Dr John, 9
Kibworth Harcourt (Leics.), 6
Kilvrough (Gower), 398
King's Langley (Herts.), 224–5
Kingston estates, 341, 375
Kingswood Forest (Glos.), 174, 218
Kinver Forest, 168
Kirby Bellars (Leics.), 81, 96
Kirk, Richard, 95
Kirk Leavington (Yorks.), 254
Kirkby Moorside (Yorks.), 169
Kirklington Hall (Yorks.), 60
Kitchen, Bishop, 152
Kitching, Dr Christopher, 8–9
Kitson, Sir Thomas, 56
Klotz, E. L., 45
Knaresborough Forest, 177n.
Knebworth (Herts.), 179
Knethell, Richard, 394
Knightley family, 56
Knights of St John, Slebech (Pembs.), 148
Knipe, Anthony, 58
knitting, 190–1, 421
Knole (Kent), 217, 259, 366

Knowles, D., 71n., 83, 91
Knyvett, Sir Thomas, 250, 348
Kussmaul, A., 13

labour services, 408
labourers, 13–15, 91, 161–230, 363–6; attitudes and aspirations, 219–30; clothing, 214–15; cottage husbandry, 177–84; cottages, 107–14; differences between fielden and forest communities, 14, 168, 174–8, 182, 185–94 passim, 199–200, 207–10 passim, 212, 217–18, 227–9; domestic life, 207–19; effects of enclosure and encroachment on, 171–7; family ties, 220–1; food, 170, 215–18; holdings, 165–8; household goods and furniture, 186–7, 211–14, 219; inventories, and wealth of, 177–8, 184–90 passim, 207, 211–15 passim, 218–19; local loyalty, 223–4; and manorial custom and feudal authority, 170, 224–7, 229; numbers, 162–5; pleasures and pastimes, 222–3; relations with employers, 14–15, 203–7, 225–7; wages and perquisities, 200–3; see also by-employments; common rights; farm labour
Lacock Abbey, 77, 93
Laleham manor (Middx), 319
Lambarde, William, 57
Lambert estates (Surrey), 282, 287
Lancashire, 175; estates in Civil War, 256, 273; labourers, 166, 167 (table), 168, 193, 201, 211; gentry, 5, 318; monastic lands, 98n., 103n.; patterns of tenure, 326, 332, 357–8, 372, 377
Lancaster, duchy of, 21–8 passim, 30–1, 32, 37–8, 98, 103n., 113
land improvement, see improvement
land market, 67–8, 70; during Civil War and Interregnum, 268–72, 273–5, 278, 285–9; prices, 272, 299, 300 (table), 303, 310, 377–8; records, 42; after the Restoration, 297–325; see also Wales
land tax, 247–50 passim, 304–5, 351–2, 384, 388
Landewy (Glam.), 402
landowners, private: absentee, 19, 230, 301–2, 307, 333, 351, 357, 367, 370, 394; indebtedness, 64–5, 272–3, 276–7, 298–9; investment in their estates, 372–8; as improvers, 18, 68, 273, 303–4, 308, 361–2, 376–8, 400–3; non-agricultural income, 50–5, 305–6, 315–20, 388–9, 418–21; urban, 317–18; see also tenants
landownership patterns, 3–7, 16, 45–50, 289–325; demographic factors, 29–7; see also consolidation; fragmentation; inheritance customs; land market; marriage

454 INDEX

settlements; Wales
Langdale, Sir Marmaduke, 61
Langley Priory, 81
*Lark Rise to Candleford* (Flora Thompson), 229
Lasynys (Mer.), 389
Latimer, Bishop, 173
Latimer, Lord, 49
Latton Priory, 103
Laud, Archbishop, 121, 158–9, 173
Laugharne, Major-General Rowland, 385
Laughton (Sussex), 249, 253
Launceston Priory, 119
Launde Priory, 81
Laurence, Edward, 355, 363
Lavenham (Suff.), 167
Layfield, William, 213
Lea (War.), 251, 252
lead mining, 320, 419–20
leases, leasehold, 58–9, 331–5, 351–7; of Church lands, 7–8, 12, 76–7, 84–6, 92–8 *passim*, 105–6, 110–11, 147–8, 151–5 *passim*, 286–7; covenants and husbandry clauses, 18, 331, 332–3, 339–51, 408–9; of Crown lands, 2–3, 32, 35, 101; lengths, 69, 84–6, 339–41; life, 18, 85, 330–4, 406–7, 418; rack-rent, 341–351; sub-letting, 333–4, 336, 350; for terms of years, 336, 340–1, 355, 406–7; verbal, 339–40; *see also* fines; Wales
Lee, Sir Henry, 32
Lee, Sir Richard, 264
Leeds (Kent), 220
Leeswood (Flints.), 420
Leicester, 24
Leicester, earls of, 142–3, 145, 324, 345; *see also* Coke, Thomas
Leicester Abbey, 81
Leicestershire, 69, 320; labourers, 162, 170, 210, 218; monastic lands, 84, 94, 96, 104, 108, 114, 118–19
Leigh (Somerset), 94
Lenborough (Bucks.), 370
Lennox, duchess of, 39
Lenthall Stark (Herefords.), 102
Lenton Priory, 94, 113
Levens, George, 62
Leveson, Sir Richard, 267, 278, 280
Leveson-Gower, Sir William, 278
Leveson-Gower, estates, 17n., 337, 345n., 356, 377
Lewis, Edward, of Glamorgan, 422
Lewis, John, of Prysaeddfed (Anglesey), 424
Lewis, Lewis, 395
Lewis, Owen, 410
Lewis, Thomas, of Harpton Court (Radnors.), 416
Lewis, Thomas, of Llanishen (Glam.), 423

Lewis, Sir Thomas of Penmark (Glam.), 423
Lewknor, Alexander, 226
Lexington, Lord, 296
Lightwood Forest (Staffs.), 377
Lilleshall (Salop.), 267
Lincolnshire: estates, 68, 291, 365, 389; labourers, 162, 191; monastic lands, 95; patterns of tenure, 337, 339, 358; *see also* Axholme, Isle of
Lisle, Lord, 113, 114
Lister, Michael, 99
Little Boynton Hall (Essex), 344
Little Crosby (Lancs.), 225, 372
Littleham-and-Exmouth (Devon), 76
Liverpool, 400, 418
livestock: labourers', 178–83; monastic, 77–9, 90–1; *see also* cattle; sheep
Llan-rhos (Caerns.), 401
Llanarth estate (Mon.), 383
Llanbadarn Fawr, 150
Llanbedr Dyffryn Clwyd (Denbs.), 401
Llandaff, diocese of, 146, 149, 152–5 *passim*, 157, 158, 159
Llanddewibrefi (Cards.), 147, 154
Llanddyfnan (Anglesey), 402
Llandilotalybont (Glam.), 383, 418
Llanelli (Carms.), 419
Llanfrothen (Mer.), 412
Llanfyrnach (Brecon), 389
Llangibby Castle (Mon.), 399
Llangyfelach (Glam.), 418
Llansadwrn (Carms.), 397
Llanthony Priory, 73, 78, 150
Llanvorda (Denbs.), 385, 401
Lleweni (Denbs.), 141, 401
Lloyd, Bevis, 385
Lloyd, Charles, 420
Lloyd, Colonel Edward, 385
Lloyd, Hugh, 401, 402
Lloyd, John, of Llansannan, 409
Lloyd, John, of Rhiwaedog (Mer.), 424
Lloyd, Pierce, 402, 424
Lloyd, Sir Richard, 382
Llugwy estate (Anglesey), 381, 402, 424
Llwydiarth estate (Mont.), 394
Llŷn, 124, 142
Loddiswell (Devon), 83
Loder, Robert, 68, 195, 201–2, 203n., 205–6
Loder family, 61
Londesborough (Yorks.), 42, 47
London, 367; City and money market, 269, 270, 276–7, 287, 299, 305–6, 390, 391; estates, 317–18; Welsh connections, 395, 413, 416
Long Parliament, 282, 284
Longbridge Leaze (Kent), 210–11
Longford (Salop.), 340

# INDEX

455

Longney (Glos.), 102
Longstock (Hants.), 181
Lonsdale, Viscounts, 306, 335; see also Lowther family
Lord's Island, Derwentwater, 278
Lort, Henry, 423
Lowden, Robert, 225
Lowther, Sir James, 319
Lowther, Sir John, 319, 334, 366
Lowther, Robert, 317
Lowther family, 317, 319; see also Lonsdale, Viscounts
Luckyn, Sir Harbottle, 297
Ludlow, Edmund, 286
Luke, Sir Samuel, 251
Lyon, John, 70

Machen ironworks (Mon.), 392, 420
Mackworth, Sir Humphrey, 419
Mackworth estates, 402, 409
Maidstone, 163
Mainwaring, Humphrey, 365
Mallory, Sir John, 63
Malpas Priory, 148
Malton (Yorks.), 199
Malvern, 102
Manley, Thomas, 373, 375
manorial custom and usages, 170, 204, 224–7, 396–8
manorial surveys, 162, 163, 166, 167
manors, monastic, 72–4, 105
Mansel, Bussy, of Briton Ferry (Glam.), 423
Mansel, Sir Edward, 390
Mansel, Sir Henry, 422
Mansel, Rice, 150–1
Mansel, Thomas, 388, 392, 420
Mansel, Sir Walter, 424
Mansel family, 150–1, 359, 388, 390, 392, 416, 417, 419, 420
Manwaring, Bishop, 159
Manwood, John, 36
maps, estate, 307–8
Marden (Kent), 184
Margam Abbey, 150–1
Margam estates (Glam.), 150–1, 388, 390–5 passim, 400, 402, 406, 410, 411, 414, 417, 419, 421, 422
Marian (Anglesey), 402
Maristow manor, 114
marketing of produce: by labourers, 183–4; by landowners, 400
markets, labourers' dependence on, 215–16
Markham, Sir John, 62
Markham, Robert, 62
Markham family, 62
Marlborough, duke of, 310
marriage settlements, 5, 16, 63, 293–6, 320–3;

in Wales, 386–7, 389, 391
Marrick Priory, 113
Marston (Glos.), 248
Marston (War.), 251, 252
Martin, J. O., 17, 18, 19, 386, 389
Mary, Queen, 30, 119, 149, 153
Masham, Lord, 323
Massingberd, Burrell, 358, 362
Massingberd, Drayner, 362
Massingberd family, of Lincolnshire, 345
Mathafarn (Mont.), 141, 385
Mathew family, of Radyr, 152
Mathrafal forge (Mont.), 420
Matthew, David, of Llandaff (Glam.), 424
Matthew, Humphrey, 423
Mayfield (Sussex), 346
Maynard, John, 100
Mayowe, Joseph, 184
Medlar (Lancs.), 94
Meisey Hampton, 324
Melbourne (Derbs.), 250
Melbury (Dorset), 294
Melcombe farm (Somerset), 114
Mellish, Edward, 357
Mells and Leigh, manor of (Somerset), 114
Menabilly (Cornwall), 259, 260
Merevale Abbey, 88
Mereworth (Kent), 189
Merionethshire, 142, 381, 384, 387, 390
Methodism, 228
Methwold (Norfolk), 58
Mettingham College, 58
Meyrick, Francis, 407
Meyrick, Owen, 404
Middle Claydon (Bucks.), 254, 273, 279
Middlesex, Lionel Cranfield, earl of, 3, 4, 54
Middleton, Bishop Marmaduke, 155, 158
Middleton, Robert, 324
Midlands: labourers, 185–90 passim, 201, 207–9, 212, 215, 218–19; land-ownership, 273, 302, 303, 305, 312, 313, 318, 391; patterns of tenure, 326, 327, 336; see also individual counties
migration, 174–7; migrant labour, 15, 164–5, 199–200, 228
Milcote (War.), 15
Mildenhall (Suff.), 309
Milton (Northants.), 338
Mimardière, A. M., 305
Mines Royal Society, 420
Mingay, G. E., 308, 324, 375, 385, 387, 388
mining, minerals, 190n., 398; landowners' exploitation of, 318–20, 367, 388, 418–21
Mochnant manor, 397
Molyneux, Sir More, 377
Molyneux, Sir Robert, 112
Molyneux family, 357–8

Monachdy estate (Anglesey), 381, 382, 424
monasteries, 71–2; buildings, 104, 108; commercial activities, 77–80; dissolution, 26–9, 89–103, 106, 117, 118, 148–52; indebtedness, 92; lay employees, 88–9, 197–8; in Wales, 147–52; *see also* granges; monastic lands
monastic lands, 40, 72–6; Crown seizure of, 26–9, 97–103; disposal of, 9, 12–13, 103–20, 148–50; grantees, 103–5, 108–9, 117–20, 150–1; improvement, 80–2; management of, 76–97; profits from, 28, 110–17, 151; tenants, 82–8, 89, 92–5 *passim*; value of, 71–2, 90, 100–1, 107–8, 109–10; in Wales, 12–13, 147–52
Monck, General George, 283
Monmouth Priory, 12
Monmouthshire, 172, 382, 416; monastic lands, 12, 13, 149
Montague, Sir Edward, 44
Montgomery, 250, 385
Montgomeryshire, 17, 18, 142, 405
Moole, John and Joan, 220
Mordant, J., 368, 370
More, Sir Thomas, 81, 195, 205
Morgan, John, 382
Morgan, Thomas, of Tredegar (Mon.), 423
Morgan, Bishop William, 154
Morgan family, of Monmouthshire, 151, 155, 390
Morris, Lewis, 399
Morris, Richard, 389
Morris, Stephen, 411
mortgages, 64, 277–8, 299, 310, 314–15, 321–2; in Wales, 385
Morva Havod y llyn (Caerns.), 406
Morwell, 77
Mostyn (Flints.), 400, 401
Mostyn family, 420
Mousley, Miss J. E., 60
Moyle, Sir Thomas, 91
Myddelton, Sir John, 400
Myddelton, Sir Richard, 390, 400
Myddelton, Robert, 420
Myddelton, Sir Thomas, 385, 420, 423
Myddelton family, 385, 390, 391, 417–18, 420
Myddle (Salop.), 6
Mytton, John, 366

Nannau, 136, 141, 142
Nanteos (Cards.), 399
Narberth (Pembs.), 420
Naseby, battle of, 261, 262
Nash estate (Pembs.), 394
Nassington (Northants.), 166, 169
Navy, timber for, 418

Neath (Glam.), 148, 419, 423
Needwood Forest, 37
Netley Abbey, 99
Neville, Sir John, 119
Newcastle, dukes of, 255, 271, 314, 348, 369
Newcastle-under-Lyme, 193
Newenham Abbey, 93, 113
Newnham Priory (Beds.), 75
Newport (Pembs.), 150
nobility, 3–6, 16–17, 45–50; decline of, 62–6; demographic factors, 292–7; estate management, 48–50, 308, 326–63 *passim*; expansion and consolidation of estates, 47, 304–25 *passim*; households, 366; impact of Civil War on, 246–67 *passim*, 273–80 *passim*; income from estates, 55–6, 58–62; investment in estates, 375–7; non-agricultural income, 315–20, 367, 418–21; profits of office, profession and trade, 50–5, 315–16, 388–9; relations with tenants, 365, 367–72, 410–18 *passim*; in Wales, 10–11, 17, 122–46 *passim*, 379–422 *passim*; *see also* marriage settlements
Nonsuch Palace, 282
Norden, John, 67–8, 69, 164, 176, 204, 218
Norfolk, 30, 67; estates, 249, 251, 324, 372; labourers, 187, 192, 206, 212, 215, 229
North Aston (Oxon.), 82
North Dalton (Yorks.), 61
Northampton, earl of, 260, 266–7
Northamptonshire, 3, 173; estates, 44, 249, 251, 266, 291; gentry, 56n.; labourers, 163, 166–9 *passim*, 178, 189, 191, 212; monastic lands, 75, 117–18; patterns of tenure, 353, 357, 367
Northern Rebellion of 1536, *see* Pilgrimage of Grace
Northumberland, 57–8, 67, 210, 254, 257, 279
Northumberland, earls of, 41, 48–50, 57, 61, 254, 257; *see also* Percy family
Norton family, 172
Norwich, 8, 78
Norwich Cathedral Priory, 78
Nostell Priory, 63
Nottingham, earls of, 359, 363
Nottinghamshire, 175, 261, 319, 338, 341
*nouveaux riches*, 4, 16, 370, 310
Noyadd Trefawr estate (Cards.), 408
Nun Appleton, 113
Nuneaton (War.), 179, 188, 212

Oakley (Bucks.), 171
Oakley (Suff.), 59
O'Day, Dr Rosemary, 8
Oglander, Sir John, 61
Okeover, Sir Leeke, 372

INDEX 457

Old (Northants.), 221
Onley family, of Pulborough, 63
Osborne, Sir Thomas, 315
Osborne family, 54
Oseney Abbey, 77–8, 80
Oswestry, 142
Otterton (Devon), 76
Ouse fishery, 95
Outrawcliffe (Lancs.), 332
Overland farm (Kent), 349
Owen, George, 126–7, 199
Owen, Hugh, 424
Owen, John, of Penrhos, 401, 403
Owen, Sir John, 382
Owen, Sir Robert, 424
Owen, Watkin, 401
Owen, William, 391
Owen family of Porkington, 395, 409
Oxford, earls of, 62
Oxfordshire, 229, 327; estates in Civil War, 250, 251, 253, 255, 270
Oxinden, Henry, 226, 286

Packington estate (Leics.), 300
Pampheton, John, 84
Panshanger farm (Herts.), 345
Paramore, Alexander, 67
Park (Mer.), 385
Parker, Sir Henry, 103
Parliament: House of Commons, 268, 284, 286; House of Lords, 271; Long, 282, 284
parliamentarians, 255–6, 260; in Wales, 384
Parry, Bishop, 157
Parry, Charles, 413
Parry, J. G., 17
Parry, John, 395
Parson, Henry, 113
partible inheritance, *see* gavelkind
Paulet, Lord, 118
Paulet, Richard, 99
Paulet, Sir William, 27
Pearman, Robert, 188, 221
peasant labourers, *see* labourers
peasant risings, 26, 172–3
peat, *see* turf
Peatling Parva (Leics.), 66
Peck, John, 384
peerage, *see* nobility
Pelham, Sir Thomas, 249, 253
Pemberton (Lancs.), 303
Pembroke, 149
Pembroke, earls of, 11, 111; *see also* Herbert family
Pembrokeshire, 124; estates, 388, 390, 404, 405; gentry, 11, 379
Pendleburie, Nicholas, 195
Pendragon (Westmor.), 47

Penllergaer (Gower), 398, 418, 419
Penmachno (Caerns.), 412
Pennant, Thomas, 390
Pennant family, 420
Pennard manor (Gower), 398
Penny, Mr, tenant, 338
Penrhos estate (Anglesey), 391, 400, 401, 403
Penrhyn, 139
Penrice (Glam.), 391, 392, 393, 406
Penrose, Richard, 166
Peper Harow estate (Surrey), 338
Percy family, 42, 58, 172, 203; *see also* Northumberland, earls of
Perkins, Richard, 197
Perrot, Sir John, 11
Perry, John, 221
Pershore, 78
Petre, ninth Lord, 297, 313–14
Petre, William, fourth Lord, 247, 249, 253, 256–8 *passim*, 273, 274, 280; indebtedness, 276–7
Petre, Sir William, 32, 51–2, 113
Petre estates, 32, 51–2, 249, 275, 297, 313–14, 328, 353; rents, 253, 257; tenants, 247, 249, 333, 336n., 341, 344, 348, 352
Petworth (Glos.), 248
Petworth (Sussex), 257
Pewsey manor (Wilts.), 364
Philipps, Sir Erasmus, 391
Phillips, C. B., 271
Pickering, Vale of, 168
Pickering family, 93
Picton Castle (Pembs.), 385, 391, 399, 402, 406, 408, 419, 420
Pierce, T. Jones, 10–11
pigs, cottagers', 180 (table), 181, 182, 225
Pilgrimage of Grace, 26, 49, 173
Pilton Priory (Devon), 75, 115
Pipewell Abbey, 101
Pirton (Herts.), 213
planter families, 317
Plas Einon (Denbs.), 395
Plas y Ward (Denbs.), 385, 401, 424
Pleydell, Sir Mark, 294, 343
Pleydell, Thomas, 293
Plommer, Robert, 166
ploughteams, sharing of, 181
Plucknett, T. F. T., 31
poaching, 170, 217
Pollard, A. F., 46
Pollard, Richard, 91, 97, 100
Polsloe Priory (Devon), 116, 119
Ponsonby, John, 254
Pontefract (Yorks.), 35, 220
poor law, 224
poor rates, 351, 360, 363–4
poor relief, 204–5

Popkin, Robert, 398, 419
Porkington (Salop.), 395, 409
potatoes, 181, 217
Potter Newton estate (Yorks.), 293
Poulett, Sir John, 263
poultry, cottagers', 180 (table), 181–2, 217
Powell, Gabriel, 398
Power, John, 181
Powis, Lord, 105, 394, 397, 413
Powis Castle estate, 411, 414, 416–17, 418, 420, 421
Pratt, Sir George, 293–4
Pratt, Mary, 293
Pratt, Thomas, and Company, 420
Pray farm (St Alban's), 343
Prendergast (Pembs.), 383
Preston (Yorks.), 172
Price, John, 149, 150
Price, Thomas, 393–4
Price, Thomas, of Penllergaer, 398, 418, 419
prices: agricultural, 67, 415–16; food, 56–7; land, 272, 299, 300 (table), 303, 310, 377–8
Prichard, Edward, 423
Prittlewell Priory, 90–1
Prysaeddfed estate (Anglesey), 381
Punyer, Barnaby, 195
Punyer family, 198

quartering of troops, during Civil War, 252, 254, 352

rabbits, 60, 170, 217
Radcliffe, Sir Edward, 278
Radcliffe, Sir Francis, 278–9
Radcliffe family, 278–9
Radstock (Somerset), 326
Radyr (Glam.), 152
Raleigh, Sir Walter, 43
Ramsey Abbey, 73
Rashleigh, Jonathan, 259, 260, 267
Reade, Sir John, 324
Redbourn (Herts.), 335, 343
Reddaway family, 66
Redgrave (Suff.), 112
Redlingfield Priory (Suff.), 106n.
Reedness (Yorks.), 211
religion, rural, 223, 228
rents, 57, 59–60, 69–70, 326, 351–4, 363–4; abatements, 254, 357–9, 365, 411–12; during Civil War, 249–50, 252–5; on Crown lands, 32, 35, 37; in kind, 86–7, 99–100, 327, 351n., 408, 411; landlords' action to support, 359–63; monastic, 82, 86–7, 99–101; rack, 18, 326, 335–6, 341–51, 413–14; of tenants-at-will, 337–8; see also Wales
repairs: landowners', 261–2, 339, 340, 374–6;

409–12 *passim*; neglect during Civil War, 250, 259; tenants', 332, 349–50, 353–4, 359, 410
Requests, Court of, 103
Reyce, Robert, 70, 161, 206, 210
Rhiwlas (Mer.), 401
Rhosmor estate (Anglesey), 381
Rhyd Galed farm (Wynnstay), 410
Riborough (Norfolk), 42
Rice, Elizabeth, 225
Rice, Margaret, 225
Rich, Lord, 229
Richard, David ap, 110
Richard, Ellis ap, 412
Richard, Sir Richard, 106
Richardson, W. C., 23
Rickinghall, 112
Rickmansworth (Herts.), 214
'ring fence' estates, 307, 324, 335
Rishangles (Suff.), 341
Rivers, Countess, 259
Robartes, Lord, 255
Roberts, David, 416
Roberts, Sir Edward, 401
Robinson, John, 382
Robinson, Sir Tancred, 368
Robinson, William, of Monachdy (Anglesey), 424
Roborough, 82, 85
Roche Abbey, 99
Rockingham Forest, 169
Rolle, George, 115–16
Roman Catholics, *see* Catholic landowners
Romney Marsh, 162, 195
Rosedale Priory, 100
Rossendale (Lancs.), 175
Rowe, John, 58
Rowlands, Henry, 403
royalists, 43, 45, 255–8 *passim*, 262–78 *passim*; in Wales, 382, 385
Rudd, Bishop, 158
Rudstone family, 204
Ruin Clifford iron mill, 320
Rupert, Prince, 251
Russell, John, Lord, 105, 111
Russell, Francis, second earl of Bedford, 111
Russell family, 118; *see also* Bedford, earls of
Ruthin (Denbs.), 147, 390, 397, 399
Rutland, duke of, 296
Rutland, earls of, 4, 105, 118, 276, 320, 366

Sackville, Sir Richard, 116, 119
Sadleir, Ralph, 335
Sadler, Ralph, 114
St Albans (Herts.), 343, 356
St Andrew's Priory (Northants.), 100–1
St Asaph, diocese of, 146, 152, 153, 155, 157,

# INDEX 459

158, 159
St Augustine's Abbey, Bristol, 72, 74, 80, 82, 85, 87, 94, 150
St Bees (Cumb.), 58
St Bride's (Pembs.), 385
St David's, College of B. V. M., 147
St David's, diocese of, 146, 152–9 *passim*, 414
St Dogmael's, 150, 151
St Donat's (Glam.), 402, 422
St Issell's (Wales), 420
St John of Jerusalem, Order of, 107
St Mellon's (Mon.), 409
St Osyth's (Essex), 259
St Sexburga's Nunnery, 198
St Werburgh's Abbey, 95
Salesbury, Owen, 424
Salford Priors, 98
Salisbury, earls of, 318, 334, 369; estates, 248, 253; *see also* Cecil, Robert; Cecil family
Salusbury, Sir John, 153
Salusbury, Thomas, 384
Salusbury family, 138, 152
Sandridge (Herts.), 214
Sandys, Lord, 118
Saundersfoot (Pembs.), 420
Savine, A., 72, 99, 108, 117
Sawtry (Hunts.), 91
Scarborough, earls of, 319, 339
Scots' Hall (Kent), 173
Scott, Sir Thomas, 226
Scott family, of Kent, 173
Scottish troops, 251, 252
Screech, Robert, 93
Scrope, Lord, 99
Scudamore, Sir John, 150
Sedgeley (Staffs.), 220
Selborne (Hants.), 191n.
Selby Abbey, 95
Sellindge (Kent), 226
sequestration, 246, 255–9, 262, 266, 284
servants, 366–7, 373, 399; *see also* farm servants
Servington, John and Agnes, 85
Seys, Mr, of Boverton, 402
Shakerley, Sir George, 401
Shakerley, Sir Jeffrey, 385
Shakespeare, Richard, 81
Shapwick (Somerset), 97
Sharland, William, 99
Sharpe, Robert, 166
sheep farming: labourers' flocks, 179–81, 182, 218; landowners', 55–6, 350–1; monastic, 77–8, 80n., 96
Sheils, W. J., 15
Sheldon, William, 100
Shelford House (Notts.), 261
Shenley (Herts.), 213

Sheparde, John, 31
Sherborne (Glos.), 88
Sherborne Abbey (Dorset), 76
Sherford (Devon), 115
Sheriff Hutton (Yorks.), 54
Sherington (Bucks.), 6, 109, 247, 302
Ship Money, 247
Shireburn, Richard, 276
Shirley, Sir Thomas, 54
Shorwell, 93
Shrewsbury, 384, 401
Shrewsbury, sixth earl of, 48
Shrivenham, (Berks.), 293
Shropshire: estates, 261, 278, 319; labourers, 212; patterns of tenure, 356, 360, 363, 365, 367, 373
Shuttleworth family, 195
Sibton Abbey, 75, 78, 79
Simmonds, Dr J., 410
Simpson, A., 45, 71
Skawton (Yorks.), 253
Skelton, Steven, 93
Skipton (Yorks.), 47
Slebech (Pembs.), 148, 151, 382, 406
Slingsby, Sir Henry, 366
smallholders, 165–8, 179–84
Smith, A. Hassell, 15
Smith, Thomas, 221
Smyth, John, 62, 64
Smyth, William, 204
Snell, Dr K. D. M., 13–14
Sneyd, William, 107
Snowshill (Glos.), 88
social structure, 203–7, 223–9, 311–12; impact of Civil War on, 229–30, 275; *see also* feudal survivals
Somerset, 67; Crown lands, 30; estates, 287, 294; labourers, 185–91 *passim*, 193 (table), 212, 215, 216, 219; patterns of tenure, 338, 359
Somerset, duke of, 121
Somerset family, 151; *see also* Worcester, earls of
Sondes, Sir George, 205, 230, 267, 371
Sopwell (Herts.), 344
South Brent (Devon), 51
South Chaladon farm (Devon), 85
South Ormsby (Lincs.), 345, 362
Southampton, earls of, 56, 118, 119, 247, 318
Southowram (Yorks.), 220
Southwell, Robert, 100
Southwell family, 202
Sowerby (Yorks.), 191
Spaldwick (Hunts.), 34
Speldhurst (Kent), 189
Spencer, Sir John, 55–6

Spencer, Sir William, 56
Spencer, William, second Baron, 56
Spencer family, 55–6, 58, 63, 118, 120n.
spinning and spinning wheels, 190–1, 193 (table), 212, 213
Sprott, George, 215
Spufford, Dr Margaret, 6
squatters, 18, 174, 176, 210–11, 364, 397, 405, 406, 416
Squire, John and Joan, 82
squires, 225–7, 379; *see also* gentry
Stackpole Court (Pembs.), 388, 391, 407, 417, 418, 423
Stafford, Sir Henry, 24
Staffordshire: estates, 278, 319; labourers, 168, 192, 212; patterns of tenure, 337, 356
Standish, William, 94
Stanford Rivers (Essex), 297
Stanley, Sir William, 22
Star Chamber, Court of, 82, 103
Staunton Grange, 82
Stawell, Sir John, 261
Steadman family, 151
Stepney, Sir John, 383
Stevenson, Thomas, 225
stewards, 35, 307, 342, 370; in Wales, 392–5
stocking-knitting, 168, 190–1
Stoke Barton (Devon), 75
Stoke St Nectan (Devon), 75
Stondon (Herts.), 334
Stone, Lawrence, 3–4, 46, 52
Stonyhurst (Lancs.), 276
Stourbridge, 78
Stourhead (Wilts.), 311, 312, 323
Stourton (Wilts.), 311
Stourton, Lords, 280, 344, 352
Stourton Caundle (Dorset), 311
Stradling, Sir Edward, 402, 422
Strafford, Thomas Wentworth, earl of, 54, 55, 60–1, 205
Strangeways, Sir John, 261
Strangways family, 294
Strata Florida, 148, 151
Strowde, Thomas, 184
Stubbs, Philip, 44
Studley (Yorks.), 63
Studley estate (Oxon.), 250
Studley Priory (Oxon.), 90
Studley Priory (War.), 76, 83
subdivision of estates, *see* fragmentation of estates
subsidy assessments of 1524, 162
Suffolk, 30, 70, 161; estates in Civil War, 247, 256; labourers, 167, 188, 191, 194, 206, 210, 212, 224, 229
Surrey: estates, 270, 282, 287; labourers, 191, 192, 218; patterns of tenure, 326
Survey, Court of, 27, 28, 29
Survey of Crown lands, 23–5, 26, 29, 35, 37, 98
surveys, manorial, 162, 163, 166, 167
Sussex, 5, 36; estates in Civil War, 249, 253, 261, 270; of labourers, 166–8, 192; patterns of tenure, 326, 354, 355
Sutton (Cheshire), 95
Sutton, Bridget, 296
Sutton, Captain Ellis, 385
Sutton-on-Derwent (Yorks.), 169
Swansea, 418, 419
Swift, Thomas, 225
Syon Abbey (Middx), 74, 76, 83

Talbot, Philip and Joan, 85
Talbot, Richard, 85
Talbot, Thomas, 340
Talbot family, 42
Tanfield, Sir Lawrence, 35
Tarleton (Lancs.), 94
Tarrant Rushton (Dorset), 253
Tavistock Abbey, 77, 78, 79, 85, 87, 97, 111, 119
Tawney, R. H., 10, 44, 45–6, 50, 66, 117–18
tax, 351; assessments (Civil War), 247–50, 384; land, 247–50 *passim*, 304–5, 351–2, 384, 388; records, 43; in Wales, 304, 388
Taylor, John, 69, 214
Temmse, Christopher, 93
Temmse, Joan, 93
Temmse, Thomas, 93
Tempest family, 319
Temple, John, 65, 66
Temple, Nicholas, 115
Temple, Peter, 65
Temple, Sir Peter, 65–6
Temple, Sir Thomas, 65
Temple family of Stowe, 65–6
Temple Newsam (Yorks.), 54, 60
tenants, relations with landlord, 69–70, 112, 173, 342, 353–63 *passim*, 365, 368–72; *see also* tenure, patterns of; Wales
tenure, patterns of, 105–6; annual tenancies, 336, 341; socage, 31, 105, 137, 396; tenancies from year to year, 339–41; tenantright, 327n.; tenants-at-will, 18, 103, 111, 325, 335–9, 355–6, 407; *see also* copyhold; customary tenure; leases; Wales
'Terramania', 312
Tetcott (Devon), 119
Tewkesbury Abbey, 150
Thanet, earl of, 267, 321
Thelwall, Colonel Edward, 424
Thelwall, Simon, 385
Theobalds, 53

# INDEX 461

Thirlwall, Mrs, 340
Thirsk, Dr Joan, 6, 270, 271
Thomas, Colin, 122n., 144n.
Thomas, Sir Edward, of Bettws (Glam.), 423
Thomas, Leyson, 389
Thomas, Sir Rhys ap, 139–40
Thomas, Richard ap, 110
Thomas, Walter, of Swansea, 424
Thomas, William, of Wenvoe (Glam.), 422
Thomas, Sir William, 383
Thompson, F. M. L., 6, 289, 290
Thompson, Flora, 229n.
Thorney (Cambs.), 344, 345, 358, 362
Thoroton, Robert, 62
Thorverton (Devon), 346
Three Houses (Herts.), 204
Thremhall Priory (Essex), 90
Throckmorton, Sir George, 99–100
Throckmorton, Robert, 100
Throckmorton estates (War.), 99–100, 359
Thurloe, John, 379
Thurston, Richard, 78
Thynne, Sir Henry, 266
Thynne family, 118
Tilty Abbey, 84
timber: monastic sales, 88, 114; restriction on sale by tenants, 332, 350; rights, 398, 409; sales from Crown lands, 36–7; sales by private landowners, 59, 272, 418–19; values, 107–8, 373
Tintern Abbey, 150
tithes, 8; monastic, 74, 87, 102, 106; in Wales, 147, 154–6
Tivetshall (Norfolk), 60
Toke, Nicholas, 249; estates, 165, 195, 196, 198, 201–5 *passim*
Toke family, 165
Tom, John Nichols, 228
Tomlinson, Christopher, 189
tools, *see* equipment, farm
Torycoed (Carms.), 419
Touke, John, 23
Townshend family, 202
trade, 183–4, 215–16, 400
Trawsfynydd (Mer.), 382
Trawgoed, 141
Tredegar Park (Mon.), 390, 392, 400, 406, 409, 414, 420, 423
Tregellest, John, 212
Trelowarren (Cornwall), 267
Trentham (Staffs.), 278
Treowen estate (Mon.), 383
Tresham, Sir Thomas, 61, 65, 120n.
Trevaes Fawr (Cards.), 408
Trevalun estate (Denbs.), 384, 400
Trevor, Sir John, 400
Trevor-Roper, H. R., 44, 50

Trewyddva (Gower), 398
Tunstall, Brian, 85
Tunstall, Isabel, 85
turf (peat) and turf-coal, 169, 192, 218
Turkdean (Glos.), 77
Tutbury (Staffs.), 24
Twistleton, George, 384
Twysden, Sir Roger, 247
Ty'nycae (Anglesey), 410
Tywardreath Priory, 102

Ulverscroft Priory, 94
Umberslade (War.), 320
unemployment, 203
Upwood (Hunts.), 73
Usk, 12, 13
Uvedale, Sir John, 93, 113
Uxbridge, earl of, 338

*Valor Ecclesiasticus*, 9, 72, 89–90, 95, 96, 100, 107–8, 120, 146–8 *passim*, 157
Van, John, 423
Vaughan, John, of Carms., 424
Vaughan, John, of Golden Grove, 392–3, 395, 397, 407
Vaughan, John, of Grace Dieu, (Pembs.), 149
Vaughan, Sir John, of Crosswood, 424
Vaughan, Richard, of Derwydd, 394, 399, 404, 407, 417
Vaughan, Richard, of Gray's Inn, 389
Vaughan, Richard, of Torycoed, 419
Vaughan, Rowland, 194n.
Vaughan, Sir Walter, of Pembrey, 424
Vaughan family of Crosswood, 420, 424
Vaughan family of Golden Grove, 392–3, 395, 397, 407
Vaughan family of Nannau, 136, 142
Vavasour, William, 60
vegetables, 217
Veredy, Richard, 220
Verney, John, 279
Verney, Sir Ralph, 279, 368, 372; tenants, 265, 273, 341, 354, 357, 361, 371
Verney family, 253, 273, 275, 276, 279, 345n. 370, 371
Vernon, William, 335
Vesey, David, 345
villeinage, 68, 165n.; *see also* bondmen
Villiers, Edward, 93
Villiers, Sir Edward, 39
Vyvyan, Sir Richard, 267

wages, 56, 57, 200–3
Wakefield (Yorks.), 193
Waldegrave, Lord, 326
Wales, Welsh: agricultural improvement, 400–3, 409, 421–2; cattle farming, 401, 402,

## 462    INDEX

415–16; Church lands, 12–13, 146–60, 383; clanlands, 122–3, 128–30, 140–1; Crown lands, 383, 398–9; enclosure, 27, 142–6, 397, 405; encroachment on commons, 142–4, 397, 399, 405–6; English settlers and influence, 122, 136–7, 138–9, 404, 405; estate management, 17–19, 379–422 *passim*; evolution of landed society, 135–7; impact of Civil War, 255, 381–5; industries, 191, 419–21; inheritance customs, 17, 125–7, 133–4, 139, 140, 386–7, 403–4; land market, 123, 387–8, 389–92; landownership patterns, 122–3, 125–46, 379–92, 404–5; leases, 12, 18, 147–8, 151–5 *passim*, 406–9, 418; manorial structure, 396–9; mining, 388, 398, 418–21; nobility and gentry, 10–12, 17, 122–46 *passim*, 151, 379–424 *passim*; rents, 141, 142, 393, 395, 408, 411–18, 422–4; royalists, 382, 385; settlement patterns, 123–4; taxes, 384, 388; tenant–landlord relations, 410–18; tenure, patterns of, 122–8, 131–41, 396–9, 406–18 *passim*; tithes, 147, 154–6; types of freehold estate, 127–8, 137–41; Union with England, 126, 129, 133–4, 135, 137; *see also* fines; marriage settlements; mortgages; Welsh border counties
Walpole, Sir Robert, 315–16
Walsham (Suff.), 59
Walshe, Thomas, 82
Walter, John, of Griston, 206n.
Waltham, 93
Walthew, Robert, 303
Walton (Yorks.), 253
Walton Abbey, 77
Walwyn, William, 230
Wandesford, Christopher, 64–5
Wandesford family, 60
War of the Spanish Succession, 377
Warboys (Hunts.), 73
Warden Abbey, 112
Wardour Castle (Wilts.), 260
Wards, Court of, 27, 28, 30, 31, 38, 39–40, 43, 52, 54, 106
wardship, royal 24, 25, 39–40
Warley (Yorks.), 191
Warwick, earl of, 116, 276
Warwick Hall, 340
Warwickshire, 251–2; estates, 291; gentry, 305–6; labourers, 172, 189, 192–3, 212, 215; monastic lands, 117–18; patterns of tenure, 84, 327
Washfield (Devon), 74
Waterhouse, William, 211
Watt, James, 300
Watton (Yorks.), 197
weather conditions, 415

weaving, 190, 193 (table), 421
Weeks' Lodge (Essex), 353
Welbeck Abbey, 101
Welsh border counties, 304; estates in Civil War, 251, 255, 264, 272; labourers, 191, 207; patterns of tenure, 326, 333, 357
Wensleydale, 174
Wentwood (Mon.), 398
Wentworth, Thomas, *see* Strafford, earl of
Wentworth family, 60
Wentworth Woodhouse (Yorks.), 225
Werrington (Devon), 77, 87, 111
West Indies, 317
West Knoyle (Wilts.), 298, 309, 364, 370
Westbury (Glos.), 309
Westby, William, 93
Westcote, Thomas, 61
Westminster Abbey, 253
Westmorland, 57, 319; Crown lands, 37; estates in Civil War, 256, 271; labourers, 173, 211
Weston (Somerset), 86, 99
Weston, William, 195
Weston-under-Redcastle (Salop.), 360
Whalley, Richard, 30
Wharton, Sir Thomas, 58, 100
Whatborough, (Leics.), 81
Wheldrake (Yorks.), 165
Whitbread, Samuel, 300
Whitchurch (Salop.), 339
White, Gilbert, 191n.
Whitehaven (Cumb.), 319
Whitland (Carms.), 148, 149
Whitmore (Staffs.), 225
Whitmore family, 101
Widdrington, Lord, 367
Wight, Isle of, 118
Wigmore Abbey, 102
Wigston Magna (Leics.), 94, 113, 302
Wildman, John, 270
Wilkins, Philip, 212–13
Willesborough (Kent), 211
Williams, David, 389
Williams, Edward, 401
Williams, John, 393n., 400
Williams, Sir John, 111, 150
Williams, Roger, 392
Williams, Nicholas, of Edwinsford, 424
Williams, Watkin, 417
Williams, William, 390
Williams, Sir William, 385, 401, 417
Williams family, of Monmouth, 13
Willingdon, 24
Willoughby, Lord, 61, 64
Willoughby, Richard, 298
Willoughby, Robert, 415
Willoughby family, 319

## INDEX

wills, 42–3; labourers', 221; *see also* inventories, probate
Wilson, Thomas, 44–5, 67
Wilton (Yorks.), 59, 189, 308
Wilton Abbey, 78, 92, 106n., 111
Wiltshire: estates, 251, 291, 294, 311; labourers, 218; patterns of tenure, 57, 335, 344, 352, 374
Wimbledon manor, 282
Wincanton (Somerset), 216
Winch, Michael, 204n.
Winchcombe (Glos.), 101
Winchcombe Abbey, 78, 88
Winchelsea, countess of, 363
Winchelsea, earl of, 197
Winchester, bishops of, 30
Winchester, marquess of, 261
Windsor, dean and canons of, 118
Wingham Court Farm (Kent), 349
Winslade, John, 113–14
Winstanley, Gerrard, 230n.
Winterburn Grange, 113
Wintney (Hants.), 99
Winwick (Northants.), 181, 188
Wirral (Cheshire), 254
Wiston (Sussex), 267
Wiveliscombe (Somerset), 121
woad, 15, 193, 365
Woburn Abbey, 111
Wolfe, Morgan, 149
Wolffe, B. P., 2
women, and estates, 250, 293–5; *see also* marriage settlements
Wonersh (Surrey), 191
Wood, Owen, 424
Wood, Robert, 179, 188, 212
Wood, Thomas, 103
Woodham, Richard, 81
Woodhouse, Sir Henry, 64
woodland, *see* forests
woodworking, 184, 192, 193

wool, monastic sales of, 77–8
Woolnough family, 340
Worcester, diocese of, 6, 7–8, 100, 328
Worcester, earls of, 150, 151, 159, 382
Worcester Cathedral Priory, 86, 100
Worcestershire, 212, 261
Workington (Cumb.), 211, 219
Wotton, Sir Henry, 171
Wrightson, K., 7
Writtle (Essex), 32, 348
Wroxall Priory (War.), 81, 88
Wyatt's rebellion, 26
Wymondham (Norfolk), 192
Wyndham, Dr Katherine, 9
Wynn, Sir George, 420
Wynn, Sir John, 126, 154
Wynn family, 136, 390, 391, 397
Wynne, Edward, 395, 401, 410
Wynne, Ellis, 389, 405
Wynne, Robert, 401
Wynnstay estates, 390–3 *passim*, 397, 401, 410–13 *passim*, 421

Yarcombe (Devon), 83
yeomanry, 6–7, 66–71, 89, 181; landownership patterns, 298–304; as lessees of monastic lands, 94; in Wales, 381, 389
Ynysmaengwyn (Mer.), 385
York, archbishops of, 7
York, Vale of, 168, 183, 187
Yorkshire, 36–7; Crown lands, 37, 100; estates in Civil War, 254, 256, 263n., 265, 268–9, 270–1; gentry, 5, 60–1, 63, 68, 246n., 312, 318; labourers, 166–9 *passim*, 172, 191, 193, 211–12, 215, 218, 222; patterns of tenure, 344, 357, 361
Young, Arthur, 369
Ystumcolwyn (Mont.), 401

Zell, Dr Michael, 9

RECEIVED 08 MAR 1994